Wrongful Termination Claims

A Preventive Approach

Second Edition

Wrongful Termination Claims

A Preventive Approach

Second Edition

Wrongful Termination Claims

A Preventive Approach

Second Edition

Stuart H. Bompey
Max G. Brittain, Jr.
Paul I. Weiner

Date of Publication: February 1991

H1-3000
Practising Law Institute
New York City

Library of Congress Catalog Card Number: 90-63269

ISBN 0-87224-014-2

This work is dedicated to my mother, father, wife, and my three great children for their continued help, support, and understanding, without which I could not have reached this level in my professional career. I want to especially remember my mother, whose example of dedication and hard work is a constant inspiration to me.

STUART H. BOMPEY

I dedicate this book to my brother Bill.

MAX G. BRITTAIN, JR.

I dedicate this book to my wife Ellen, who has been my source of inspiration through the years.

PAUL I. WEINER

Table of Chapters

Table of Contents

Appendixes

Acknowledgments

The authors acknowledge the excellent and substantial contribution of Joseph M. Cohen, Marcia E. Goodman, and M. David Bieber toward the preparation of this book. These three individuals added substantially to the final manuscript. Mr. Cohen, a graduate of the University of Michigan Law School, is admitted to practice in the states of Michigan and New York, the United States District Courts for the Eastern and Southern Districts of New York, and the Eastern District of Michigan. Mr. Cohen has been an attorney at Baer Marks & Upham since 1988, specializing in a broad range of employment issues, including employment litigation. Ms. Goodman is a graduate of the Harvard Law School and is an attorney at Kovar Nelson Brittain Sledz & Morris, specializing in labor and employment-related law. Ms. Goodman is admitted to practice in the state of Illinois, the United States District Court for the Northern District of Illinois, and the United States Court of Appeals for the Seventh Circuit. Mr. Bieber is a graduate of The John Marshall Law School and is also an attorney at Kovar Nelson Brittain Sledz & Morris, specializing in labor and employment-related law. Mr. Bieber is admitted to practice in the state of Illinois, the United States District Court for the Northern District of Illinois, and the United States Court of Appeals for the Seventh Circuit.

Acknowledgments

In appreciation for his confidence in and encouragement of each edition, the authors wish to thank William C. Cubberley, Director of Hardcover Publishing, at the Practising Law Institute. They also thank Patricia L. Clancy, Managing Editor, for her editorial suggestions to this edition.

About the Authors

STUART H. BOMPEY is currently a senior partner and co-chair of the labor and employment law department of the New York City law firm of Baer Marks & Upham. Mr. Bompey, a 1965 *cum laude* graduate of Boston University School of Law, is a member of the bar in the states of Connecticut and New York, and is admitted to practice before the United States Supreme Court and the Second, Third, and Fifth Circuit Courts of Appeals and the various district courts within the jurisdiction of the Second Circuit Court of Appeals. Mr. Bompey is a member of the Equal Employment Opportunity Committee of the American Bar Association and currently serves as its Program Division Chair. In addition, Mr. Bompey is currently a member of the Individual Rights Committee of the New York State Bar Association and past Chair of the Personnel Relations, Tenure and Retirement Section of the National Association of College and University Attorneys. Mr. Bompey's practice is devoted exclusively to representing management in all areas of employee relations and employment-related litigation. Mr. Bompey is nationally recognized as a writer, speaker, and lecturer on labor relations, discrimination, and employment-related litigation issues.

MAX G. BRITTAIN, JR. is a named partner with the Chicago law firm of Kovar Nelson Brittain Sledz & Morris. The firm specializes in the representation of management in labor-related matters, including contract bargaining, arbitration cases, discrimination lawsuits, OSHA matters, pension plan administration, and unjust discharge cases. Mr. Brittain has extensive experience before the NLRB, EEOC, and state and federal courts. He was a *cum laude* graduate of Loyola Law School in 1976 and is a member of the ABA Labor Law Committee, serving on the EEO and Individual Rights Subcommittees. He is a frequent lecturer on labor and personnel law and has been an adjunct professor at Loyola Law School.

PAUL I. WEINER is the partner in charge of the employment and labor law department at the law firm of Weiner Lesniak in Roseland, New Jersey. He is admitted to the bar in New York, New Jersey, and Pennsylvania. Mr. Weiner is the author of numerous articles discussing employment law including "OSHA's Standard Setting Process," *CCH Labor Law Journal* and "Seniority Systems Under Teamsters and Bryant," *Employer Relations Law Journal.* Mr. Weiner has lectured extensively in the field of employment law at universities, including the New York University Labor Law Forum and Georgetown Law School, American Bar Association seminars, American Law Institute seminars, PLI-OSHA seminars, and various other PLI seminars. He is the Chairman of PLI's Annual Institute on Employment Law. Mr. Weiner is a member of the American Bar Association Equal Employment Opportunity Committee and Employment/Labor Law Committee. He is also a member of the New Jersey State Bar Association Labor Committee and an Arbitrator for the New Jersey State Board of Mediation. Mr. Weiner has practiced extensively in the fields of labor, OSHA, and employment law, working in both private and corporate practice.

Introduction

"Wrongful termination" and the protection of employee rights have been the source of continued litigation since this book was originally published in 1986. Employment litigation has become a significant part of both the federal and state court dockets, and of concern to every employer. In addition, state legislation involving employee rights has added significant statutory restrictions on the employment-at-will doctrine.

Due to the onslaught of state and federal court litigation, appellate courts have continued to recognize certain employee rights emanating from employee handbooks and implied employment contracts. The courts have also been interpreting and expanding tort concepts impacting on employee rights, including claims for infliction of emotional distress, negligence, defamation, and invasion of privacy.

It is with this changing background in mind that the authors have expanded the coverage of this book to face the expansion of employee rights and employer responsibilities in the 1990s. In addition to updating the topics previously covered, this second edition discusses numerous defenses to wrongful discharge litigations, issues in reductions in workforce, the use of waivers, the use of alternative dispute resolutions, the use of employment contracts, and human resource audits. This edition also includes expanded sections dealing with employee handbooks, employment-at-will disclaimers, steps to follow when terminating an employee, a practical approach to preparing employee performance appraisals, and additional sample forms.

The authors have tried to combine the detailed description of the substantive law in all states with a practical approach to many of the numerous problems facing employers in this changing environment. It is our goal to balance the rights of all parties involved and to help employers maintain their right to hire, evaluate, discipline, and terminate employees, when necessary. Faced with this knowledge and understanding, employers will be better able to deal with the competitive pressures of the marketplace with a workforce that is treated equitably and fairly, within the ever-growing legal constraints placed upon management.

Wrongful Termination Claims

A Preventive Approach

Second Edition

CHAPTER ONE

Historical Analysis

Judges, lawyers, and commentators have long debated when, and under what circumstances, an employer or employee may terminate an employment relationship that does not have a stated duration. By the late nineteenth century, American jurisprudence developed the "employment-at-will" doctrine, under which either party could end such a relationship at any time, and for any reason. The American rule was later narrowed by statutory and contractual protections for certain employee groups. In contrast, English common law, which had influenced early American law, presumed that such contracts had a duration of one year. The history of both English and American doctrines provide a background for current American legal principles governing this area of law.

English Law Governing Contracts Without Stated Duration

When employment contracts did not state their duration, English law established a rebuttable presumption that the employment relationship was created for one year. Thus, in 1765, Blackstone stated that:

> [t]he contract between them and their masters arises upon the hiring. If the hiring be general without any particular time

> limit, the law construes it to be a hiring for a year; upon a principle of natural equity, that the servant shall serve, and the master maintain him, throughout all the revolutions of the respective seasons; as well when there is work to be done, as when there is not; but the contract may be made for any larger or small term. . . .[1]

This presumption could be rebutted by evidence that the parties intended the contract to last for a different duration, especially when the contract encompassed a custom of the trade for a duration of less than one year.[2]

The English also discussed the amount of notice an employer was required to give to end an employment relationship of unstated duration. The general principle was that service contracts were terminable on reasonable notice. The common law developed different time periods for various groups of employees.[3] Many English employees currently receive statutory termination notice of up to three months.[4]

The American Approach

Early American law was greatly influenced by the English rules.[5] In the late nineteenth century, however, American law abandoned the English presumption in favor of the "employment-at-will" rule. The new doctrine was championed by H.G. Wood, an Albany, New York, lawyer and treatise writer. His

1. 1. W. BLACKSTONE, COMMENTARIES ON THE LAWS OF ENGLAND, 413 (1979 ed.).
2. CHARLES MANLEY SMITH, A TREATISE ON THE LAW OF MASTER AND SERVANT, 75–78 (1884). (Blackstone's rule was framed for domestic servants. Subsequent English cases extended it to other servants, such as clerks.)
3. *Id.* at 82–87; FEINMAN, THE DEVELOPMENT OF THE EMPLOYMENT AT WILL RULE, 20 A. J. of Legal Hist. 118, 121 (1976) [hereinafter FEINMAN].
4. Employment Protection (Consolidation) Act 1978, § 49, ch. 44, as amended by Employment Act 1980, § 20, ch. 2, ¶ 3.
5. FEINMAN, *supra* note 3, at 123.

1877 treatise on master and servant law was influential in coalescing American jurisprudence around the new rule. Wood stated the American doctrine as follows:

> With us the rule is inflexible, that a general or indefinite hiring is *prima facie* a hiring at will, and if the servant seeks to make it out a yearly hiring, the burden is upon him to establish it by proof. A hiring at so much a day, week, month or year, no time being specified, is an indefinite hiring, and no presumption attaches that it was for a day even, but only at the rate fixed for whatever time the party may serve. It is competent for either party to show what the mutual understanding of the parties was in reference to the matter; but unless their understanding was mutual that the service was to extend for a certain fixed and definite period, it is an indefinite hiring and is determinable at the will of either party, and in this respect there is no distinction between domestic and other servants.
>
> But a contract to pay one $800 a year for services is not a contract for a year, but a contract to pay at the rate of $800 a year for services actually rendered, and is determinable at will by either party. Thus it will be seen that the fact that the compensation is measured at so much a day, month, or year, does not necessarily make such hiring a hiring for a day, month, or year, but that in all such cases the contract may be put an end to by either party at any time, unless the time is fixed, and a recovery had at the rate fixed, for the services actually rendered.[6]

In 1895, the New York Court of Appeals adopted the new rule in *Martin v. New York Life Insurance Co.*[7] The plaintiff in *Martin* was employed for eleven years as the head of defendant's real estate department. His salary was calculated on a yearly basis with no agreed upon contract duration. The court rejected the plaintiff's contention that his "general hiring" meant employment from year to year. It then held that

6. Wood, A Treatise on the Law of Master and Servant, 272–273 (1891).
7. Martin v. New York Life Ins. Co., 148 N.Y. 117, 42 N.E. 416 (1895).

"the present condition of the law as to the legal effect of a general hiring is thus stated by Mr. Wood . . . ," and quoted from the section of Wood's treatise excerpted above. The court concluded that "it follows, therefore, that the hiring of the plaintiff was a hiring at will and the defendant was at liberty to terminate the same at any time."[8]

The American rule was consistent with other prevalent legal and social principles. The employment-at-will doctrine used the formalistic approach to contract interpretation that dominated the legal circles of that time. Under that doctrine, promises were only enforceable when "definite, express terms" evidenced the parties' assent to the disputed term.[9]

The employment-at-will rule was also supported by the contemporary importance placed on the freedom to contract. In 1908, the Supreme Court stated its view of the law in this area:

> In the absence, however, of a valid contract between the parties controlling their conduct towards each other and fixing a period of service, it cannot be, we repeat, that an employer is under any legal obligation, against his will, to retain an employe(e) in his personal service any more than an employe(e) can be compelled, against his will, to remain in the personal service of another. . . . The [employee] was at liberty to quit the service without assigning any reason for his leaving. And the [employer] was at liberty, in his discretion, to discharge [the employee] from service without giving any reason for so doing.[10]

The Court then declared unconstitutional a law that made it a criminal offense for a railroad engaged in interstate commerce to discharge an employee because of membership in a labor organization. The Court ruled that the law violated the employer's freedom of contract, which was protected by the

8. Martin v. New York Life Ins. Co., 148 N.Y. at 121.
9. Comment: *Protecting at Will Employees Against Wrongful Discharge: The Duty to Terminate Only in Good Faith,* 93 HARV. L. REV. 1816, 1825 (1980).
10. Adair v. United States, 208 U.S. 161, 175–176 (1908).

fifth amendment's prohibition against depriving an individual of liberty or property without due process.[11]

The employment-at-will doctrine is no longer constitutionally protected against all restraints. The Supreme Court subsequently reversed its decision in *Adair* and held that the National Labor Relations Act (NLRA) and the Railway Labor Act were constitutional, even though both imposed civil restrictions similar to those invalidated in *Adair.*[12]

The Supreme Court also limited the Constitution's protection to the "normal exercise of the right of the employer to select its employees or to discharge them." It then stated that the "employer may not, under cover of that right, intimidate or coerce its employees with respect to their self-organization and representation. . . ."[13]

As will be discussed, Congress and state legislatures added other restrictions that further narrowed the employer's exercise of its contractual rights. With the demise of *Adair* and absolute freedom of contract, employment at will was once again based on contractual grounds.

Exceptions to the Employment-At-Will Rule

Both statutes and contracts have narrowed the scope of the employment-at-will rule. Today, federal and state laws prohibit employers from discharging employees for numerous reasons. Further, many employers have contractually agreed that they will only discharge employees for just cause and, in some instances, that a neutral arbitrator will make a final and binding decision as to each case. In addition, some employers

11. *Id.* at 172.
12. Texas & New Orleans R.R. v. Railway Clerks, 281 U.S. 548, 570–571 (1930); Phelps Dodge Corp. v. NLRB, 313 U.S. 177, 187 (1941) (cases subsequent to *Adair* "completely sapped [*Adair* of its] authority").
13. NLRB v. Jones & Laughlin Steel Corp., 301 U.S. 1, 45–46 (1937).

have entered into binding employment agreements that regulate the employment relationship.[14]

Statutory Exceptions

A plethora of federal and state laws have restricted the employment-at-will rule by prohibiting specific types of discharges. Although these laws restrict employers' freedom with respect to certain groups of employees, they do not restrict the general application of the employment-at-will rule.

Federal Laws

Certain laws establish procedures for discharges, and require the employer to show "cause" in order to discharge an employee. The Civil Service Reform Act,[15] and the Veterans' Reemployment Rights Act,[16] follow this approach.

Many other federal statutes prohibit particular kinds of discharges, thus protecting specific groups of employees. These statutes, and their respective protections, include the follow-

---

14. Of course, in the college and university community, tenure and tenure rights substantially restrict the employment-at-will relationship.
15. 5 U.S.C. §§ 7511–7513. Competitive service employees can only be discharged for "such case as will promote the efficiency of the service." 5 U.S.C. § 7513(a); covered employees must normally receive thirty days advance written notice of the discharge and have seven days in which to respond to the notice; employees are entitled to be represented by an attorney, receive a written decision on their discharge, and appeal that decision to the Merit Systems Protection Board and the courts.
16. 38 U.S.C. §§ 2021–2026. Veterans returning from active duty are guaranteed the right to return to their former position or its equivalent. 38 U.S.C. § 2021(a); veterans returning from active duty cannot be discharged "from such position without cause within one year" after returning to work. 38 U.S.C. § 2021(b)(1); reservists returning from twelve or more consecutive weeks active duty are similarly protected and cannot be discharged without cause for six months after returning to their jobs. 38 U.S.C. § 2024(c).

ing: NLRA,[17] Federal Service Labor Management Relations Act,[18] Title VII of the 1964 Civil Rights Act,[19] Age Discrimination in Employment Act (ADEA),[20] Fair Labor Standards Act,[21] Railway Labor Act,[22] Occupational Safety and Health Act,[23] Urban Mass Transportation Act,[24] Consumer Credit

---

17. 29 U.S.C. §§ 157, 158(a) 1, 3, 4. Prohibits discharges that interfere, restrain, or coerce employees from engaging in protected concerted activities for collective bargaining; prohibits discharges that encourage or discourage union memberships; prohibits discharges in retaliation for employee filing charges or testifying under the Act.
18. 5 U.S.C. §§ 7101, 7116(a)(1), (2), (4), 7121(b)(3)C. Prohibited discharges include those that interfere with employees' rights to engage (or not engage) in concerted activity, discharges that discriminate against membership in a labor organization, and discharges that retaliate against employees filing charges or providing information as part of the act's enforcement proceedings; the act also mandates grievance procedures ending with binding arbitration.
19. 42 U.S.C. §§ 2000e–2(a), 3. Prohibits discharge because of an "individual's race, color, religion, sex or national origin," and as retaliation for activities authorized by the act, including filing charges, testifying, and opposing unfair practices. In 1980, Title VII was amended to include a prohibition regarding discrimination on account of "pregnancy" or "pregnancy-related" conditions.
20. 29 U.S.C. §§ 621, 623(a), (d). Under the ADEA, it is illegal to discharge any individual "because of such individual's age," currently between the ages of 40 and less than 70, or as retaliation for participating in investigations, proceedings, or litigation under the act, or for opposing unfair practices.
21. 29 U.S.C. §§ 201, 215(a)(3). Prohibits discharges that retaliate against an employee who initiates a proceeding under the act, who testifies in such proceeding, or who serves on an industry committee.
22. 45 U.S.C. §§ 151, 152. Employer cannot discharge an employee when the object is to interfere with employees' organizing efforts, or to induce employees to join or remain in a labor organization, or refrain from joining or remaining in such organization.
23. 29 U.S.C. §§ 651, 660(c). Prohibits discharges to retaliate against an employee who filed a complaint, instituted, or participated in a proceeding under the act, or exercised any statutory rights.
24. 49 U.S.C. §§ 1601, 1609(c)(3). Contracts granted under the act must contain certain "protective arrangements," one of which is the "protec-

Protection Act,[25] Migrant and Seasonal Agricultural Protection Act,[26] Rehabilitation Act of 1973,[27] Executive Order 11,478,[28] and Executive Order 11,246.[29]

State Laws

Numerous laws, similar to the federal statutes discussed above, have been enacted by state legislatures. A discussion of a sample of state laws in several key areas follows.

Several states extend protections against discharges similar to those in the NLRA. These laws thus prohibit discharges when one or more of the motives for the discharge is to: (1) interfere, restrain, or coerce employees who take part in concerted protected activity for collective bargaining, (2) encourage or discourage union membership, or (3) retaliate against an employee who initiates, or participates in registering a complaint under the statute, or testifies in a proceeding under the law.[30]

---

tion of individual employees against a worsening of their positions with respect to their employment."

25. 15 U.S.C. §§ 1601, 1674. Illegal to discharge an employee because his or her earnings have been subject to garnishment for an indebtedness.
26. 29 U.S.C. §§ 1801, 1855(a). Employers cannot discharge a migrant or seasonal agricultural employee who, with just cause, filed a complaint or instituted a proceeding under the act, testified in such proceeding, or exercised his or her statutory rights.
27. 29 U.S.C. §§ 701, 794. An otherwise qualified handicapped employee, who works in a program or activity receiving federal financial assistance, cannot be discharged solely because of his or her handicap.
28. (1969 as amended 1979.) Federal employees protected from discharge for race, color, religion, sex, national origin, handicap, and age.
29. 29 U.S.C. §§ 202, 301 (1967 as amended 1978). All covered contracts must contain contractor's pledge not to discriminate "because of race, color, religion, sex or national origin," to take affirmative action to implement this pledge, and to include these obligations in each subcontract or purchase order that is part of the contract.
30. *E.g.*, (public employees); *Arizona,* ARIZ. REV. STAT. ANN. §§ 23-1381–

Further, some states provide veterans' protection similar to that in the Federal Veterans' Reemployment Rights Act.[31]

Many states protect "whistle-blowing" employees who re-

23-1385 (1983) (agricultural employees); *California,* CAL. GOV'T CODE §§ 3560, 3571(a) (West 1980) (higher education employees), §§ 3512, 3519(a) (state employees), CAL. LAB. CODE §§ 1140, 1153(a) (West 1980), 1153(c), 1153(d) (West Supp. 1986) (agricultural employees); *Connecticut,* CONN. GEN. STAT. §§ 31-101, 31-105 (West 1985) (private sector non-agricultural employees), §§ 5-270, 5-272(a) (West Supp. 1986) (state employees), §§ 7-467, 7-470(a) (West Supp. 1986) (municipal employees), §§ 10-153a, 10-153e(b) (West Supp. 1986) (teachers); *Illinois,* ILL. REV. STAT. ch. 20, §§ 1–3 (1987) (employee may not be discharged for filing a health insurance claim); ch. 48, paras. 1601, 1610(a) (1986) (public employees except teachers), ch. 48, paras. 1701, 1714(a) (1986) (educational employees, including higher education); *Maine,* ME. REV. STAT. ANN. title 22, §§ 1580-A(1)–1580-A(7) (1986) (an employee may not be discharged for enforcing the smoking regulation); *Michigan,* MICH. COMP. LAWS §§ 423.1, 423.16 (1979) (private sector employees); §§ 423.201, 423.210 (1979) (state and local public employees); *Montana,* MONT. CODE ANN. §§ 39-32-101, 39-32-109 (1985) (nurses in health care facilities), §§ 39-31-101, 39-31-401 (1985) (public employees); *New York,* N.Y. CIV. SERV. LAW §§ 200, 209(a)(1) (McKinney 1983) (public employees), N.Y. LAB. LAW §§ 700, 704 (McKinney 1977 & Supp. 1986) (private sector employees); *Ohio,* OHIO REV. CODE ANN. §§ 4117.01, 4117.11(A) (Page 1980 & Supp. 1985) (public employees); *Pennsylvania,* PA. CONS. STAT. ANN. §§ 211.1, 211.6(1) (Purdon 1964) (private sector employees), §§ 1101.101, 1101.1201(a) (Purdon 1964) (public employees) (employers must prove "just cause consistent with existing legislation" for discharge); *Rhode Island,* R.I. GEN. LAWS §§ 28-7-1, 28-7-13 (1979 & Supp. 1985) (private sector employees); *Tennessee,* TENN. CODE ANN. §§ 49-5-601, 49-5-609(a)(1983) (educational professionals); *Vermont,* VT. STAT. ANN. title 18, §§ 1423–1428 (1987) (an employee may not be discharged for enforcing the smoking prohibition law), title 21, §§ 1501, 1621(a) (private sector) (1978), title 3, §§ 901, 961 (1985) (state employees), title 21, §§ 1721, 1726(a) (1978) (municipal employees; includes prohibition against discrimination for "race, color, religion, creed, sex, national origin, age or political affiliation").

31. *E.g., Illinois,* ILL. REV. STAT. ch. 126½, paras. 31–35 (1967 & Supp. 1986); *New York,* N.Y. MIL. LAW § 317 (McKinney 1953 & Supp. 1986); *Texas,* TEX. CODE ANN. § 5765 (Vernon Supp. 1985) (employment guarantee only, for state militia).

port misfeasance by their private or public employers.[32] Various states protect employees from politically motivated discharges.[33] A number of states have laws that provide protection similar to that in Title VII—prohibiting discharges based on race, color, religion, sex, or national origin, and those dis-

---

32. *E.g., Florida,* FLA. STAT. § 112.3187(1)–112.3187(10) (1986) (public employees); *Hawaii,* HAW. REV. STAT. § 9 (1987) (public employers and private employers with one or more employees); *Illinois,* PERSONNEL CODE, §§ 19c.1 (state employees); *Indiana,* IND. CODE §§ 4-15-10-1–4-15-10-6, 20-12-1-8(a)–20-12-1-8(d), 22-5-3-3(a)–22-5-3-3(d), 36-1-8-8(a)–36-1-8-8(d) (1987) (wide range of public and private employers); *Kentucky,* KY. REV. STAT. ANN. §§ 61.101–61.103, 61.990 (1986) (public employees only); *Louisiana,* LA. REV. STAT. ANN. § 30:1074.1 (West Supp. 1986) (reporting environmental violations) covers a wide range of public and private employers; *Maine,* ME. REV. STAT. ANN. title 26, §§ 833–834-A (1988) (includes reporting suspected abuse or neglect); *Minnesota,* MINN. STAT. §§ 181.931–181.935 (1987) (protects employee's identity); *Missouri,* MO. REV. STAT. 1(1)–1(6) (1987) (state employees); *Nebraska,* NEB. REV. STAT. § 48-1114 (1986) (matter of public policy); *New Hampshire,* N.H. REV. STAT. ANN. §§ 275-E:1–275-E:7 (1987) (applies to public and private employers); *New Jersey,* N.J. REV. STAT. §§ 34:19-1–34:19-8 (1986) ("Conscientious Employee Protection Act"); *New York,* N.Y. LAB. LAW § 740.1–740.7 (McKinney Supp. 1986) (all employers with one or more employees); *Ohio,* OHIO REV. CODE ANN. §§ 4113.51–4113.53 (1988) (public employers and private employer with one or more employees); *Pennsylvania,* 43 PA. CONS. STAT. §§ 1421–1428 (1986) (supervisor of one or more employees); *Rhode Island,* R.I. GEN. LAWS §§ 36-15-1–36-15-10 (Supp. 1985) (public employees and employees of firms subject to state toxic waste law); *South Carolina,* S.C. CODE ANN. §§ 8-27-10–8-27-50 (Law. Co-op. 1988) (public employees only); *Utah,* UTAH CODE ANN. §§ 67-21-1–67-21-9 (Supp. 1985) (public employees); *West Virginia,* W. VA. CODE §§ 6C-1-1–6C-1-8 (1988) (public employees only); *Wisconsin,* WIS. STAT. ANN. §§ 230.80–230.88 (West Supp. 1985) (public employees).
33. *E.g., Louisiana,* LA. REV. STAT. ANN. §§ 23:961, 962 (West 1985); *Massachusetts,* MASS. GEN. LAWS ANN. ch. 56, § 33 (West 1978); *Michigan,* MICH. STAT. ANN. § 6.1931 (Callaghan Supp. 1986); *Mississippi,* MISS. CODE ANN. §§ 23-3-29 (1972), 79-1-9 (1972), CONST. art. 7, § 191; *Missouri,* MO. ANN. STAT. § 115.637 (Vernon Supp. 1986); *Nebraska,* NEB. REV. STAT. § 32-1223 (1984); *Wisconsin,* WIS. STAT. ANN. § 103.18.

charges that retaliate against employees using their statutory rights. These statutes often add other protected categories as well.[34] Certain states protect employees who have filed state or federal workmens' compensation claims.[35]

---

34. *E.g., Alaska,* ALASKA STAT. §§ 18.80.010, 18.80.220 (1981) (adds age, physical handicap, sex, marital status, change in marital status, pregnancy, or parenthood, when the reasonable demands of the positions do not require distinctions on the basis of those specific factors); *California,* CAL. GOV'T CODE §§ 12900(a), 12940 (West Supp. 1986) (adds anccstry, physical handicap, medical condition, marital status), § 12941 (West Supp. 1986) (age); *Colorado,* COLO. REV. STAT. §§ 24-34-301, 402(1) (Supp. 1985) (adds ancestry and handicap), § 8-2-116 (age); *District of Columbia,* D.C. CODE ANN. §§ 1-2501, 1-2512, 1-2525 (Supp. VII 1980) (adds age, marital status, personal appearance, sexual orientation, family responsibilities, physical handicap, matriculation, or political affiliation); *Hawaii,* HAW. REV. STAT. §§ 378-1, 378-2 (Supp. 1984) (adds age, physical handicap, ancestry, marital status, or arrest and court record); *Kentucky,* KY. REV. STAT. ANN. §§ 344.010, 344.040 (1983) (adds age), §§ 207.130, 207.150 (Supp. 1984) (physical handicap), §§ 45.550c, 45.570c (1980) (government contractors and subcontractors must agree not to discriminate on the basis of race, color, religion, sex, age, or national origin); *Louisiana,* LA. REV. STAT. ANN. §§ 23:892, 972 (West 1985) (age), § 23:1006 (West 1985) (employment discrimination with Title VII factors), §§ 46:225, 2254 (West 1982) (handicap); *Maine,* ME. REV. STAT. ANN. title 26, §§ 843–849 (1988) (employer may not discharge employee for exercising his right to family medical leave); *Missouri,* MO. REV. STAT. § 296.010 (Supp. 1986), § 296.020 (adds ancestry, handicap, creed); *New Mexico,* N.M. STAT. ANN. §§ 28-1-1, 28-1-7 (1978) (adds age, ancestry, physical or mental handicap); *Rhode Island,* R.I. GEN. LAWS §§ 28-48-1–28-48-8 (1987) (employer may not discharge an employee for taking a parental leave); *Wisconsin,* WIS. STAT. §§ 111.31, 111.321 (West 1985) (adds age, handicap, marital status, ancestry, arrest record, or conviction record) § 893.96 (1988) (an employer may not discharge an employee for opposing a practice that is prohibited under the law protecting the right to family and/or medical leave).
35. *E.g., Illinois,* ILL. REV. STAT. ch. 48, para. 138.4(h); *Louisiana,* LA. REV. STAT. ANN. § 23:1361 (West 1985); N.C. GEN. STAT. §§ 96-15.1(a)–96-15.1(d) (1987), *Texas,* TEX. CODE ANN. § 8307c. (Vernon 1986).

Contractual Restrictions on the Employment-At-Will Rule

Through the collective bargaining process many employers have agreed to limit their freedom to discharge employees. Approximately 22 percent of the American workforce is covered by union contracts.[36] The vast majority of collective bargaining agreements require that the employer have specific grounds for discharge. Some contracts specify that discharges must be for "cause" or "just cause" while others specify the offenses for which an employee may be discharged. A survey of 400 contracts showed that 94 percent restricted discharge by one or both of those methods. "Cause" provisions were found in 83 percent of the sample contracts, and specific offenses were listed in 71 percent.[37]

Almost all of these contracts allow employees to challenge discharges through a contractual grievance procedure ending in binding arbitration.[38] Courts are empowered to enforce agreements to arbitrate and any resulting arbitration awards under section 301 of the Labor Management Relations Act.[39] State laws also provide judicial enforcement of arbitration awards and agreements to arbitrate.[40]

---

36. "Employment and Earnings," U.S. Dept. of Labor, Bureau of Labor Statistics, Vol. 35, No. 1 (January 1985), Table 52, p. 208. Data are average annual data for 1984. Total employed includes public and private sector wage and salaried workers, aged sixteen and over, and excludes self-employed workers with incorporated businesses.
37. 2 *Collective Bargaining Negotiations and Contracts* (BNA) at 40:1 (1983).
38. Of the 400 contracts in the BNA sample, 97 percent provided for binding arbitration of grievances. 2 *Collective Bargaining Negotiations and Contracts* (BNA) at 51:5.
39. 29 U.S.C. § 185. Textile Workers Union v. Lincoln Mills, 353 U.S. 448, 455–456 (1957).
40. *Minnesota,* MINN. STAT. §§ 572.08, 572.09, 572.18, 572.19 (Supp. 1986); *New York,* N.Y. CIV. PRAC. L. & R. §§ 7501, 7503, 7510, 7511 (McKinney Supp. 1985). State courts must apply federal substantive law when determining whether to compel arbitration or enforce the award. Textile Workers Union v. Lincoln Mills, 353 U.S. at 448.

Plant Closing

In 1988, Congress enacted the Workers Adjustment and Retraining Act (WARN).[41] The regulations under WARN became effective on May 22, 1989. Employers with at least 100 full-time employees who work a total of at least 4000 hours per week are covered by WARN. Part-time employees are not counted. WARN requires companies to give at least sixty days' written notice before a plant closing or a mass layoff. Notices must be given to the employees or the employees' representative, and to state and local officials.

A plant closing is defined as a permanent or temporary shutdown of a single site of employment that results in an employment loss during any thirty-day period for fifty or more employees. The employment losses may occur within one or more operating units within the single site.

A mass layoff is a reduction in work force during a thirty-day period that is not the result of a plant closing. The layoffs must involve fifty or more employees constituting at least 33 percent of non-part-time employees at a single site of employment, or at least 500 employees. In addition, the definition of a mass layoff or plant closing includes the employment of an aggregate of fifty or more employees from two or more different groups at a single site of employment within a ninety-day period.

There are several exceptions to the sixty-days' notice requirement.

1. If, at the time notice would have been required, the employer was actively seeking capital or business that would have prevented or postponed the shutdown;
2. The shutdown or layoff was caused by unforeseen business circumstances;

41. Pub. L. No. 100-379, 102 Stat. 890 (1988) (effective Feb. 4, 1989).

3. The shutdown or layoff was caused by an Act of God, such as a flooding or earthquake.[42]

WARN allows for civil remedies only and expressly prohibits the courts from enjoining any plant closing or mass layoff.[43] Returnable damages are limited to wage and benefit losses for each day of the violation, less any payments received from the employer.[44]

The statute raises a variety of unanswered questions, which no doubt will be the source of future litigation. For example, the statutory language leaves questions as to the meaning of "plant closing," "employment loss," "single site of employment," and "unforeseen circumstances."

Several states have also enacted plant closing statutes.[45] The regulations range from requiring two weeks' notice (South Carolina) to ninety-days' notice and severance pay (Virgin Islands).

Wrongful Discharge Legislation

In 1987, Montana became the first state to enact a broad wrongful termination statute.[46] The Montana statute covers termination not only for whistleblowing, but also for "good cause and violation of company policies."

Wrongful discharge is defined under the Montana act as discharge under the following circumstances:

1. Retaliation for employee's refusal to violate public policy;

---

42. *Id.* at § 3(b).
43. Id. at § 5(b).
44. *Id.* at § 5(a).
45. *Hawaii,* HAW. REV. STAT. § 3; *Maryland,* MD. CODE ANN. § 206H(B); *Massachusetts,* MASS. GEN. LAWS ANN. ch. 151A, §§ 71A–71D, ch. 149, § 179B; *Michigan,* MICH. COMP. LAWS § 450.736; *South Carolina,* S.C. CODE ANN. § 41-4-40; *Tennessee,* TENN. CODE ANN. § 4; *Virgin Islands,* V.I. CODE ANN. title 24, §§ 471–478.
46. MONT. CODE ANN. §§ 39-2-902 *et seq.* (1987).

2. Discharge not for good cause after completing a probationary period;

3. Violation of the express provisions of an employer written personnel policy.

Good cause is defined as "reasonable job related grounds for dismissal based on a failure to satisfactorily perform job duties, disruption of the employer's operation or other legitimate business reason."

Significantly, the Montana law provides for arbitration of termination disputes and limited damages. If a party who requests arbitration is turned down by the other party and eventually prevails, the prevailing party is entitled to attorneys' fees from the date of the offer to arbitrate. Other remedies include back pay for up to four years from the date of discharge and punitive damages if fraud or malice is established. Damages for pain and suffering, however, are not available.

The Montana Supreme Court, in a three-to-two decision, recently upheld the constitutionality of the section of the Act limiting damages to lost wages and fringe benefits for four years.[47] The Court held that the legislature has the right to define causes of action and the remedies, and that the Constitution merely guarantees "the equal right to be made whole again by what the law defines as a cause of action and its elements."[48]

In a strongly worded opinion, the dissent argued that the majority holding that "the legislature has the power to limit remedies,"[49] without judicial interference, in effect, freed the legislature from all constitutional restraint.[50] The dissent would hold that it is the court's function to ensure that the legislature remain within constitutional bounds, which in-

47. Meech v. Hillhaven W. Inc., 238 Mont. 21, 776 P.2d 488, 507 (1989).
48. *Id.* 776 P.2d at 498.
49. *Id.* 176 P.2d at 514–15.
50. *Id.*

cludes a fundamental right to full legal redress under common law.[51]

Since Montana enacted the Wrongful Discharge Prohibition Act in 1987, two other American jurisdictions, Puerto Rico and the Virgin Islands, have also enacted similar statutes. In Puerto Rico, an employer may not discharge an employee without good cause. If an employee is wrongfully discharged, he or she is entitled to receive one month's pay and another month's pay as indemnity.[52] The Virgin Islands' statute restricts violations to an "unlawful" discharge within the categories specified in the statute.[53] An employer found violating this statute will be required to reinstate the employee or to pay compensatory and punitive damages.[54]

Employment Termination Act

Recently, the National Conference of Commissioners on Uniform State Law met to draft an employment termination act (the Act) that prohibits a broad range of "wrongful termination" practices. It is expected that this proposal will be the source of a great deal of controversy in years to come and will be revised numerous times. However, it is a possible alternative to wrongful termination litigation.

The Act prohibits terminations based on grounds of discrimination as defined in both federal and state law. Prohibited discriminatory acts include termination because of sexual orientation, marital status, and "similar categorical grounds." Section 2(b)(1). The "similar categorical grounds" prohibition, on its face, seems to be a broad catch-all clause. However, the comment to this section states that "[t]here is no intent to

51. *Id.*
52. P.R. LAWS ANN. title 29, § 185A (1988).
53. V.I. CODE ANN. title 24, §§ 76–79 (1986).
54. *Id.*

enlarge the area of 'categorical discrimination' beyond that protected by existing federal or state law."

It also proscribes retaliatory terminations based on the fact that the employee filed legal charges or claims, or because of participation in investigations. Section 2(b)(2). The purpose of this section seems to be to provide efficient and expeditious resolution of wrongful discharge claims. "The purpose of subsection (b) is to enable an individual to avoid 'splitting' a cause of action by being forced into different forums to challenge a single termination." Section 2(b) comment.

This model act further provides that an employer may not terminate an at-will employee without just cause if the employee has been with the employer for at least one year (Section 3(c)), if the termination is against public policy, or if the termination is in retaliation for employee's whistleblowing activities (Section 3(b)).

The Act not only prohibits a broad range of employer actions, it also limits the types of causes of action that the employee may commence. "This Act preempts and extinguishes all state common law rights and claims . . . in tort, contract, or otherwise . . . on the basis of acts or facts arising out of the termination. . . ." Section 2(d). It does not, however, extinguish any claims that arise out of contract rights covered under either (1) a collective bargaining agreement or (2) an express written contract of employment.

Under the model Act, the employee may file a complaint with the appropriate agency within 180 days of termination. He must, however, prior to filing a claim, give the employer at least twenty days' written notice of his intent to file a claim and exhaust all existing internal procedures. Section 4(a).

The employer must file his answer within thirty days after a complaint is filed, and the agency must begin mediation proceedings immediately. Section 4(d). If the mediation fails to bring about a resolution, the employee may demand arbitration within thirty days of the mediation. Section 4(e).

Within thirty days after the arbitration hearing, or after the briefs are submitted, the arbitrator must issue an opinion and award. Section 6(a). The arbitration award is final and binding. Section 6(c). However, either party may appeal to a court of general jurisdiction to either review or enforce the award. Section 7(a).

The arbitrator may award: (1) reinstatement; (2) full or partial backpay; (3) liquidated damages; (4) severance pay if reinstatement is not granted; (5) reasonable attorney fees and costs to the prevailing party; and (6) punitive damages if "the termination of employment was a malicious violation of section 3(b)." Section 6(b). The arbitrator may not grant an award for "pain and suffering, emotional distress, defamation, fraud, or other injury under the common law. . . ." Section 6(d).

The model Act might well form the basis for wrongful termination claims in the future. Only time will tell.

CHAPTER TWO

*Contract Claims**

Implied Contract Claims

Many states have accepted wrongful discharge claims brought by discharged at-will employees against their former employers based on the "implied contract" theory. Unlike an express contract that may be written or oral, an implied contract arises from inferences drawn from particular circumstances. These inferences may operate as a matter of fact or law. For example, when the conduct and statements of the parties, or other relevant evidence, indicates that they intended to impose some limitation on an employer's traditional authority over its employees, such as the right to terminate for any reason or no reason whatsoever, the facts are said to imply that the parties contracted to the limitation. In addition, under specific circumstances, certain jurisdictions imply contractual limitations into an employment relationship as a matter of law, regardless of the parties' intent. Finally, the traditional doctrine of promissory estoppel is frequently invoked to enforce an employer's promises of job security, in lieu of, or in conjunction with, implied contract claims.

---

*This chapter discusses the substantive law. For further analysis of the practical issues involving employment manuals, i.e., disclaimers, see chapter 7 herein.

Implied in Fact

A significant number of states, including such influential jurisdictions as New York, New Jersey, and California, have recognized actions for wrongful discharge based upon an employer's breach of a contract implied in fact. This situation arises when an employee claims that the employer's representations, oral or otherwise, or the employer's personnel manual or other written policies imply that the parties intended to bestow certain contractual rights upon the employee, such as the right not to be discharged other than for good cause.

New York adopted an exception to the employment-at-will doctrine based on an implied-in-fact contract in *Weiner v. McGraw-Hill, Inc.*[1] In *Weiner,* the court found that a cause of action was stated on four factual grounds: (1) the plaintiff left other employment because of assurances in the defendant-employer's personnel manual that it would discharge employees only for just cause, (2) this assurance was incorporated into the employment application that the plaintiff signed, (3) the plaintiff rejected other offers of employment in reliance on this policy, and (4) the defendant generally enforced its just cause policy. To reach this result, the court rejected the claim by the employer that the employee's unrestricted ability to leave his employment at will necessarily defeated the condition of mutuality generally required by contract law. Instead, the court reasoned that the defendant was bound by its just cause policy because it was a promisor by virtue of its manual, application, and other assurances, and it received valid consideration under the law, defined as, either in the form of benefit to it (the plaintiff's initial and continued employment) or detriment to him (the plaintiff's passing up alternative offers of employment) or leaving a prior employer based upon representation.

1. Weiner v. McGraw-Hill, Inc., 57 N.Y.2d 458, 457 N.Y.S.2d 193 (1982).

The New York courts have construed the exception to the employment-at-will doctrine recognized in *Weiner* quite narrowly. In *Sabetay v. Sterling Drug, Inc.*,[2] the New York State Court of Appeals noted how difficult it is for a terminated employee to maintain a cause of action under the promise-reliance approach adopted in *Weiner.*[3] In *Sabetay,* New York's highest court affirmed a lower court's ruling that Sabetay had failed to state a cause of action under the principles espoused in *Weiner,* because he was unable to show either that the employer's personnel manual constituted an *express* agreement to terminate employment only for the reasons stated in the manual, or that he relied on the manual in accepting his position.[4]

However, most jurisdictions that recognize a cause of action under an implied contract theory based upon an employer's written policy statements do not impose an evidentiary burden on the employee as onerous as the requirements in New York. These jurisdictions have allowed employees to maintain claims that a personnel manual or other document distributed by the employer constitutes a contract between the employer

2. Sabetay v. Sterling Drug, Inc., 69 N.Y.2d 329, 514 N.Y.S.2d 209 (1987).
3. *Accord,* Brown v. General Elec. Co., 144 A.D.2d 746, 534 N.Y.S.2d 743 (N.Y. App. Div. 1988).
4. *See also,* DiCocco v. Capital Area Community Health Plan, Inc., 135 A.D.2d 308, 310, 525 N.Y.S.2d 417, 419 (N.Y. App. Div. 1988) (to be successful in alleging that a provision in an employer handbook expressed or implied a promise to terminate only for just cause, the employee must prove that the provision directly addresses the issue of job termination, that they were aware of the provision when they accepted employment, that they turned down other job offers in reliance on the provision, and that their dismissal was in violation of the provision.) Leathem v. Research Found. of the City Univ. of N.Y., 658 F. Supp. 651, 655 (S.D.N.Y. 1987) (where personnel guidelines published and distributed after employee started working were not known to the employee at the time he began his employment, the guidelines could not be relied upon by the employee and they will not be deemed express limitations on the employer's right to terminate his employment under *Weiner*).

and employee and that a termination not in accordance with the manual or other document constitutes a breach of that contract.

In *Wooley v. Hoffman-LaRoche, Inc.,*[5] the New Jersey Supreme Court applied a unilateral contract analysis to allow the discharged employee to pursue a wrongful discharge claim. The court stated that when an employer of a substantial number of employees circulates a manual that provides that certain benefits are an incident of the employment relationship, the judiciary should construe the manual in accordance with the reasonable expectations of the employees. The court held that the context of the manual's preparation and distribution supported the conclusion that an employee would almost inevitably regard it as a binding commitment concerning terms and conditions of employment. The employees' continued employment, when they had no obligation to remain, constituted consideration given to the employer that converted the manual into a unilateral contract, even without proof of actual reliance by the employee.[6] (See Chapter 7—Employment Manuals.)

Other jurisdictions have used the same unilateral contract analysis to allow a discharged employee to maintain a breach of contract claim.[7] The Minnesota Supreme Court, however,

---

5. Woolley v. Hoffman-LaRoche, Inc., 99 N.J. 284, 491 A.2d 1257 (1985), *modified,* 101 N.J. 10, 499 A.2d 515 (1985).
6. *Accord,* Preston v. Claridge Hotel & Casino, 231 N.J. Super. 81, 555 A.2d 12. (Super. Ct. App. Div. 1989).
7. Pine River State Bank v. Mettille, 333 N.W.2d 622 (Minn. 1983); Washington Welfare Ass'n Inc. v. Wheeler, 496 A.2d 613, 121 LRRM (BNA) 3361 (D.C. App. 1985) (a personnel manual is evidence of terms and conditions both the employer and employee accept as part of their agreement); Shannon v. Huntley's Jiffy Stores, Inc., 174 Ga. App. 125, 329 S.E.2d 208 (Ct. App. 1985) (policies in an employee handbook of which the employee is aware do form part of a contract of employment); Wyman v. Osteopathic Hosp., 493 A.2d 330 (Me. 1985) (employee handbook was held to be part of an employer's contract of employment); Stone v. Mission Bay Mortgage Co., 99 Nev. 802, 672 P.2d 629 (1983) (an employer is bound by limitations, procedures, and standards for termination contained in handbooks, manu-

stated that the provisions in the manual must be clear.[8] The court held that vague statements in a handbook concerning termination constitute nothing more than general statements of policy, which fall short of meeting contractual requirements of enforceable covenants.[9] In *Hoffman-LaRoche v. Campbell,*[10] the Alabama Supreme Court held that language contained in a handbook can constitute an offer to create a binding unilateral contract. Such a contract exists, according to the court, if the language in the handbook is specific enough to constitute an offer, if the offer was communicated to the employee through issuance of the handbook, and, lastly, if the employee accepted the offer by continuing to work after he became generally aware of the offer. Actual performance of the job supplies the necessary consideration.[11]

Similarly, in *Kinoshita v. Canadian Pacific Airlines,*[12] the Hawaii Supreme Court held that employees had contractual rights based on the publication of a personnel manual by their employer. However, an employer in Hawaii cannot be bound under an implied contract theory if the manual contains language affirming the at-will employment relationship or pre-

---

als, or written representations made to employees); Berube v. Fashion Centre Ltd., 771 P.2d 1033 (Utah Sup. Ct. 1989) (an employer's written disciplinary policy for at-will employees creates an implied contract that employees would be fired only for cause); Mobil Coal Producing, Inc. v. Parks, 704 P.2d 702 (Wyo. 1985); *accord* Allen v. Safeway Stores, Inc., 699 P.2d 277 (Wyo. 1985); Rompf v. John Q. Hammons Hotel, Inc., 685 P.2d 25 (Wyo. 1984) (court affirmed judgment for employee because employer failed to follow specific discharge procedures of its own manual).

8. *Id.*
9. Hunt v. IBM Mid-Am., 384 N.W.2d 853 (Minn. 1986).
10. Hoffman-LaRoche v. Campbell, 512 So. 2d 725 (Ala. 1987).
11. *See also,* Whitefield v. Finn, 731 F.2d 1506 (11th Cir. 1984) (under Alabama law, a notice to the plaintiff signed by him regarding termination during a probationary period may have limited the employer's freedom to discharge after such period).
12. Kinoshita v. Canadian Pac. Airlines, 68 Haw. 594, 724 P.2d 110, *remanded,* 803 F.2d 471 (9th Cir. 1986). *Accord* Pagdilao v. Maui Intercontinental Hotel, 1988 U.S. Dist. LEXIS 15327 (D. Haw. 1988).

serving for the employer the discretion to change policies.[13] (See disclaimer discussion in Chapter 7.)

In *Duldulao v. St. Mary of Nazareth Hospital Center,*[14] the Illinois Supreme Court set forth the standards for determining whether a cause of action arises under a unilateral contract analysis. The court held that an employee handbook or other policy statement creates rights enforceable in contract only if the traditional requirements for contracts formation are satisfied. The language of the policy statement must contain a promise of sufficient clarity to justify an employee's reasonable belief that an offer has been made. In addition, the statement must be communicated to the employee in such a way that the employee has knowledge of its contents and reasonably believes it to be an offer. Finally, the employee must accept the offer by beginning or continuing to work after learning of the statement. If these circumstances are present, the court commented, the employee's continued work then constitutes consideration for the promises contained in the statement, and a valid contract is established.[15] However, under no circumstances will a policy manual supersede or modify the clear and unambiguous terms of an express employment contract.[16] Fur-

13. Courtney v. Canyon TV Rentals, 3 IER Cas. (BNA) 619 (D. Haw. 1988).
14. Duldulao v. St. Mary of Nazareth Hosp. Center, 115 Ill. 2d 482, 505 N.E.2d 314 (1987).
15. *Accord* Hicks v. Clyde Fed. Sav. & Loan, 696 F. Supp. 387 (N.D. Ill. 1988). *See also* Anderson v. Hewlett-Packard Corp., 694 F. Supp. 1294 (N.D. Ohio 1988) (follows *Duldulao* provided that the handbooks are distributed to all employees, not just managers).
16. McWhorter v. Realty World-Star, Inc., 171 Ill. App. 588, 525 N.E.2d 1205 (App. Ct. 1988); *Accord* Johnston v. Panhandle Co-op. Ass'n, 225 Neb. 732, 408 N.W.2d 261 (1987) (handbook provisions become part of the employment contract where the handbook language constitutes an offer definite in form that is communicated to the employee, and the offer is accepted and consideration is provided for the enforceability of the offer); Simpson v. Western Graphics Corp., 53 Or. App. 205, 631 P.2d 805 (1981), *aff'd,* 293 Or. 96, 643 P.2d 1276 (1982); Frazier v. Minnesota Mining & Mfg. Co., 728 P.2d 87 (Or. Ct. App. 1986).

thermore, when there is a clear disclaimer in the personnel manual, the unilateral contract theory cannot be used as a basis for holding that a personnel manual creates contractual rights.[17]

In *Finley v. Aetna Life & Casualty Co.*,[18] the Connecticut Supreme Court also held that the unilateral contract theory can be applied to bind an employer to statements in a personnel manual. The court stated that an employer may be held to statements made in an employee handbook, if facts indicate a unilateral contract based upon offer (distribution) and acceptance (continued employment).

Similarly, the Arizona Supreme Court determined that an employer's representations in a personnel manual may become terms of the employment contract and can limit an employer's ability to discharge employees.[19] In order to establish a breach of contract based on such a violation of personnel rules, a plaintiff must prove that the personnel manual actually became part of the employment contract and that the terms of the manual were breached.[20] However, if the employer adds a clear and conspicuous disclaimer to the employee handbook and personnel policy manual after the policies are established, such a disclaimer constitutes an offer to modify the unilateral employment contract. An employee accepts that offer by continuing to work.[21]

Under Colorado law, an employee handbook or employment manual that sets forth specific procedures for termination of employment, when relied upon by the employee and supported by the consideration of continued service, may result in the employer being bound to comply with the hand-

---

17. Morgan v. Harris Trust Sav. Bank, 2 IER Cas. (BNA) 577 (N.D.Ill. 1987) *aff'd*, 868 F.2d 1023 (7th Cir. 1989).
18. Finley v. Aetna Life & Casualty Co., 202 Conn. 190, 520 A.2d 208 (1987).
19. Leikvold v. Valley View Hosp., 141 Ariz. 544, 688 P.2d 170 (1984).
20. Wagner v. City of Globe, 150 Ariz. 82, 722 P.2d 250 (1986).
21. Chambers v. Valley Nat'l Bank of Ariz., 721 F. Supp. 1128 (D. Ariz. 1988).

book termination procedures.[22] The Colorado Supreme Court recently reaffirmed this principle when it held that an employee states a claim for wrongful discharge based on a contract implied in fact when the employee establishes that the employer's promulgation of termination procedures was an offer and that the employee's initial or continued employment constitutes acceptance of that offer.[23]

In *Staggs v. Blue Cross & Blue Shield of Maryland,*[24] the Maryland Court of Appeals held that employer policy statements that limit the employer's discretion to terminate an employee hired for an indefinite term or that set forth required procedures for termination of employment may, if properly communicated and expressed to employees, become an enforceable contract. However, the insertion of a disclaimer in a manual stating that the manual does not constitute an express or implied contract effectively nullifies the existence of such a contract.[25]

In *Menard v. First Security Service Corp.,*[26] the court held that under Massachusetts law, the discharge of a manager did not violate the policies and procedures set forth in a personnel handbook when (1) the handbook was not intended to apply to managers and was not presented to the manager at the time he was hired, (2) his letter of hire did not mention the hand-

---

22. Salimi v. Farmers Ins. Group, 684 P.2d 264 (Colo. Ct. App. 1984). *Accord* Evans v. Geriatrics, Inc., 1 IER Cas. (BNA) 762 (D. Colo. 1986); Cronk v. Intermountain Rural Elec. Ass'n, 765 P.2d 619 (Colo. Ct. App. 1988), *cert. denied*, (11/28/88).
23. Continental Airlines, Inc. v. Keenan, 731 P.2d 708 (Colo. 1987). *Accord* Churchey v. Adolph Coors Co., 759 P.2d 1336, 3 IER Cas. (BNA) 1032 (Colo. 1988).
24. Staggs v. Blue Cross & Blue Shield of Md., 61 Md. App. 381, 486 A.2d 798, 2 IER Cas. (BNA) 1018 (Md.), *cert. denied,* 303 Md. 295, 493 A.2d 349 (1985).
25. Castiglione v. Johns Hopkins Hosp., 69 Md. App. 325, 517 A.2d 786 (1986), *cert. denied*, 309 Md. 325, 523 A.2d 1013 (1987).
26. Menard v. First Sec. Serv. Corp., 848 F.2d 281 (1st Cir. 1988).

book, and (3) he did not sign the handbook. Furthermore, when the employer retains the right to modify the terms of the manual unilaterally, the manual is not an implied contract even if the employer adheres to the grievance procedures set forth in the manual.[27]

Under Mississippi law, an express provision in an employee handbook may modify the at-will employment relationship. However, where the handbook specifically states that the employer has the right to discharge the employee at any time, the employee may not maintain a claim for breach of an oral promise of employment.[28]

In New Mexico, a handbook that characterizes disciplinary policy as established procedure creates an implied contract where the employer: (1) distributed it to all employees, (2) asked each to acknowledge receipt, (3) agreed to conform to stated policies, and (4) placed the acknowledgment signed by the employees in their personnel files.[29] However, nonpromissory handbook language that is merely a declaration of an employer's general approach to a subject matter is not a contract.[30]

The Ohio courts have held that handbooks, manuals, and other employer representations to employees may give rise to implied contracts modifying the at will relationship.[31] Furthermore in *Towns v. Emery Air Freight Inc.,* a federal court, applying Ohio law, held that a disclaimer, which stated that an employer's handbook is not a contract and that employment

---

27. Jackson v. Action for Boston Community Dev. Inc., 403 Mass. 8, 525 N.E.2d 411 (1988).
28. Perry v. Sears, Roebuck & Co., 508 So. 2d 1086 (Miss. 1987). *Accord* Samples v. Hall of Miss., Inc., 673 F. Supp. 1413, 2 IER Cas. (BNA) 799 (N.D. Miss. 1987).
29. Lukoski v. Sandia Indian Management Co., 106 N.M. 664, 748 P.2d 507 (1988). *Accord* Zaccardi v. Zale Corp., 856 F.2d 1473 (10th Cir. 1988); Boudar v. E.G. & G., 106 N.M. 279, 742 P.2d 491 (1987).
30. Sanchez v. The New Mexican, 106 N.M. 76, 738 P.2d 1321 (1987).
31. Helle v. Landmark Inc., 115 Ohio App. 3d 1, 472 N.E.2d 765 (1984).

may be terminated at any time, is void as to the rights created by the handbook, where the disclaimer was executed after the employee started work and he received no consideration for his waiver of rights contained in the handbook.[32]

In South Carolina, an employee manual may not create an implied contract in and of itself, but it is to be considered along with other evidence in deciding whether there were any limitations on the employee's at-will employment status.[33]

In *Ferrero v. Koelsch,*[34] the Wisconsin Supreme Court held that acceptance by an employee of a handbook that sets forth conditions of employment, including an employer's promise to discharge only for cause, binds an employer and alters the at-will contract. However, the Wisconsin Court of Appeals recently held that employment contracts require a mutual meeting of minds and an intention to contract. Accordingly, an implied contract claim will not stand where there is no evidence that the employee relied on the policies in question or was aware of them during employment.[35] Furthermore, the U.S. Court of Appeals for the Seventh Circuit, interpreting Wisconsin law, held that the use of nonmandatory guidelines in an employee handbook to govern workplace behavior and discipline does not create an implied contract.[36]

In *Troutman v. Travenol Laboratories, Inc.,*[37] the North Carolina Court of Appeals rejected a plaintiff's claim that policies regarding termination modified her employment agreement because she did not allege employment for a fixed term. Subsequently, the North Carolina Supreme Court held that in order

32. Towns v. Emery Air Freight Inc., 3 IER Cas. (BNA) 911 (S.D. Ohio 1988).
33. Small v. Springs Indus., Inc., 292 S.C. 481, 357 S.E.2d 452 (1987).
34. Ferrero v. Koelsch, 124 Wis. 2d 154, 368 N.W.2d 666 (1985).
35. Garvey v. Buhler, 146 Wis. 2d 281, 430 N.W.2d 616 (Ct. App. 1988).
36. Mursch v. Van Dorn Co., 851 F.2d. 990 (7th Cir. 1988).
37. Troutman v. Travenol Laboratories, Inc., 70 N.C. App. 497, 320 S.E.2d 441 (N.C. Ct. App. 1984).

for a procedure manual to create an implied contract, it must be directed at the employee. The court found that a management procedure manual could not reasonably be interpreted as a manual of rules of conduct to be followed by employees, and therefore could not rise to the level of a contractual obligation, where the entire content of the manual was directed toward managerial personnel.[38]

In South Dakota, detailed disciplinary procedures in a handbook, including provisions that require an employer not to discharge except for just cause, are enforceable as an implied contract.[39] However, a good cause requirement will not be implied from general employer policies.[40] More recently, the South Dakota Supreme Court held that employees are terminable at will unless an employee handbook contains a "for cause only" agreement.[41]

Under Washington law, when an employer issues an employee manual containing promises of specific treatment in certain situations, thereby creating an atmosphere of job security and fair treatment that induces employees to remain on the job and not seek other employment, the promises become an enforceable part of the employment relationship and the employer is obligated to act in accord with those promises.[42] However, where a provision in a manual stated that consideration will be given to performance, experience, and length of service when economically motivated layoffs occur, the Washington Supreme Court held that such a provision does not

38. Harris v. Duke Power Co., 319 N.C. 627, 356 S.E.2d 357 (1987).
39. Osterkamp v. Alkota Mfg. Inc., 332 N.W.2d 275 (S.D. 1983).
40. Cutter v. Lincoln Nat'l Life Ins. Co., 794 F.2d 352 (8th Cir. 1986). *Accord* Bauer v. American Freight Sys. Inc., 422 N.W.2d 435 (S.D. 1988) (statement in handbook about fair play and just and equitable dealings are too general).
41. Butterfield v. Citibank (S.D. Sup. Ct. 3-15-89).
42. Thompson v. St. Regis Paper Co., 102 Wash. 2d 219, 685 P.2d 1081 (1984).

promise specific treatment in a specific situation and the employer is not bound.[43]

In *Aiello v. United Air Lines, Inc.,*[44] the U.S. Court of Appeals for the Fifth Circuit held, following Texas law, that the issuance of detailed employee manuals containing a provision that required good cause for discharge and providing a procedure whereby terminated employees could grieve their discharge, gave rise to an express contract modifying the at-will relationship. The court stated that because the airline followed the procedures of the employee handbook in discharging the employee and notified her that she was entitled to them, and the fact that the supervisor who fired her treated the procedures as a contract obligation, the application of the Texas employment-at-will doctrine was obviated.

Michigan has long held that employers may be bound by representations made in their personnel manuals.[45] The enforceability of a manual arises not from the theory of unilateral contract, but from the fact that the employer derives a benefit by establishing such policies.[46] The Michigan Supreme Court recently settled an important issue when it held that an employer may, without expressly reserving the right to do so, unilaterally change its written policy from one of discharge for cause to one of termination at will, provided that the employer gives affected employees reasonable notice of the policy change.[47]

The most prominent case in California on this issue is

43. Stewart v. Chevron Chem. Co., 111 Wash. 2d 609, 762 P.2d 1143 (1988).
44. Aiello v. United Air Lines, Inc., 818 F.2d 1196 (5th Cir. 1987).
45. Toussaint v. Blue Cross & Blue Shield of Mich., 408 Mich. 579, 292 N.W.2d 880 (Mich. 1980) (personnel manual creates express agreement even though unilaterally amendable and even if employee has no knowledge of its contents).
46. Boynton v. TRW, Inc., 781 F.2d 555 (6th Cir. 1986).
47. Bankey v. Storer Broadcasting Co. (Mich. Sup. Ct., 6/6/89); *Accord In re* Certified Question, 882 F.2d 208 (Mich. 1989).

Foley v. Interactive Data Corp.[48] Here, the California Supreme Court held that even in the absence of an express promise not to terminate employment except for good cause, the totality of the circumstances surrounding the employment relationship, including oral representations and the parties' course of conduct, could create an implied-in-fact contract term bestowing job security upon an employee. Quoting from *Pugh v. See's Candies, Inc.*,[49] the court noted that "oblique language will not, standing alone, be sufficient to establish agreement." However, self-imposed limitations on the employer's power to discharge at will set forth in a manual may provide the basis for a cause of action for breach of an employment contract, because the trier of fact can infer an agreement to limit the grounds for termination based on the employee's reasonable reliance on the company's personnel manual or policies.

A Pennsylvania court has commented that in order for a handbook to be construed as a contract, it "must contain unequivocal provisions that the employer intended to be bound by it and, in fact, renunciated the principle of at-will employment."[50] A personnel manual that merely sets forth a general code of conduct or that contains promises that an employer will treat employees fairly does not create a requirement of just cause for discharge.[51]

Although many employers have taken to inserting disclaimers in their employee manuals in an attempt to defeat a judicial finding of an implied contract, the Supreme Court of Kansas,

48. Foley v. Interactive Data Corp., 47 Cal. 3d 654, 254 Cal. Rptr. 211, 765 P.2d 373 (1988).
49. Pugh v. See's Candies, Inc., 116 Cal. App. 3d 311, 171 Cal. Rptr. 917 (1981).
50. Reilly v. Stoemman Bros., 367 Pa. Super. 411, 532 A.2d 1212 (1987).
51. Gaiardo v. Ethyl Corp., 697 F. Supp. 1377 (M.D. Pa. 1986); Lofton v. Wyeth Laboratories, Inc., 643 F. Supp. 170 (E.D. Pa. 1986).

in *Morriss v. Coleman Co.,*[52] held that a disclaimer in the personnel manual, which stated that nothing in the manual should be construed as an employment contract, is not binding because it was not brought to the personal attention of employees and there was no evidence that it was intended by the employer to create an unqualified employment-at-will relationship.

On the other hand, the Kentucky Court of Appeals held that a clear disclaimer in a personnel manual or a job application will defeat an employee's breach of contract claim based on a manual's policy statements and procedural guidelines.[53] Furthermore, in *Eldridge v. Evangelical Lutheran,*[54] the North Dakota Supreme Court held that a disclaimer in an employee handbook prevented an employee from attempting to maintain a claim on the theory that the handbook entitled him to any contractual rights.

Although many states now permit a cause of action for breach of a provision in a personnel manual under an implied contract theory, such recognition is not universal; several jurisdictions steadfastly refuse to limit the employer's discretion to terminate employees on account of representations made in a handbook. In *Brumbaugh v. Ralston Purina Co.,*[55] a federal court held that, in its opinion, the Supreme Court of Iowa would treat an employer's personnel manual "as a gratuitous, unilateral expression of the employer's position, which is not

52. Morriss v. Coleman Co., 241 Kan. 501, 738 P.2d 841 (1987).
53. Nork v. Fetter Printing Co., 738 S.W.2d 824 (Ky. Ct. App. 1987).
54. Eldridge v. Evangelical Lutheran, 417 N.W.2d 797 (N.D. 1987).
55. Brumbaugh v. Ralston Purina Co., 656 F. Supp. 582 (S.D. Iowa 1987); *accord* Caster v. Hennessey, 727 F.2d 1075 (11th Cir. 1984) (under Florida law, a manual is only a unilateral expression of the employer's policies and procedures; its terms are not bargained for and do not become part of an employment contract); Spero v. Lockwood Inc., 721 P.2d 174 (Idaho 1986) (employees hired for an indefinite term are terminable at will despite employee manuals and procedures).

bargained for, lacks consideration, and does not become part of the employment contact."

In *Johnson v. McDonnell Douglas Corp.*,[56] the Missouri Supreme Court held that the unilateral contract or "handbook exception" to the employment-at-will doctrine was not available in Missouri. The court stated that the employer's unilateral act of publishing a handbook was not a contractual offer to its employees, and therefore, no power of acceptance was created in the aggrieved employee and no employment contract was formed.

Similarly, in *McQueenly v. Glenn*,[57] the Indiana Court of Appeals held that a handbook's discharge procedures do not create a binding mutual contract,[58] while the Tennessee Court of Appeals has noted that employee handbooks do not provide sufficient guarantees or binding commitments to constitute employment contracts for a definite term.[59]

Implied in Law

When certain facts are present, such as exceptionally long and satisfactory performance or an employer's attempt to frustrate the employment arrangement, the law imposes a quasi-contract on the employer, which limits its right to terminate an at-will employee.

56. Johnson v. McDonnell Douglas Corp., 745 S.W.2d 661 (Mo. 1988). *Accord* Enyeart v. Shelter Mut. Ins. Co., 4 IER Cas. (BNA) 491 (Mo. Cir. Ct. 1989); Hargis v. Affiliated Medical Transp. Inc., 764 S.W.2d 741 (Mo. Ct. App. 1989); Link v. K-Mart Corp., 689 F. Supp. 982 (W.D. Mo. 1989).
57. McQueenly v. Glenn, 400 N.E.2d 806 (Ind. App. 1980), *cert. denied,* 449 U.S. 1125 (1981).
58. *But see* Streckfus v. Gardenside Terrace Coop., 504 N.E.2d 273 (Ind. 1987) (the court implied that if a manual contains language from which specific limitations on discharge can be implied, it may be binding. The court stated that before the question of considerations arises, language must be present from which specific limitations on discharge can be inferred).
59. Graves v. Anchor Wire Corp., 692 S.W.2d 420 (Tenn. Ct. App. 1985).

California is the leading state in recognizing claims implied in law. In *Pugh v. See's Candies, Inc.*,[60] the court inferred an agreement requiring just cause for termination from the length of plaintiff's employment, his commendations and promotions, and employer assurances that as long as the plaintiff was loyal and did a good job, his position was secure. In *Newfield v. Insurance Co. of the West*,[61] the court regarded the doctrine as inapplicable to a vague oral reference to a "permanent" career but reiterated that factors such as longevity of service, established personnel policies and practices, industry practice, lack of criticism of an employee's performance, and oral representations, may give rise to an implied contract in law not to terminate at will.

In New Hampshire, an employee's longevity and the fact that he had moved his entire family to accommodate his employment have been found to be significant in implying the possible existence of a contract.[62] Furthermore, the New Jersey Supreme Court recently held that an employee stated a claim where he alleged that the employer specifically promised him that he would have a job for life or at least could not be fired without cause if he revoked his acceptance of a job offer with another firm and stayed with the employer.[63]

In New York the dissenting judge, in *Murphy v. American Home Products Corp.*,[64] would have recognized a claim for breach of a contract implied in law since the plaintiff alleged that he was discharged for following company procedures. The dissenting judge alternatively characterized the theory as one

---

60. Pugh v. See's Candies, Inc., 116 Cal. App. 3d 311, 171 Cal. Rptr. 917 (1981).
61. Newfield v. Insurance Co. of the W., 156 Cal. App. 3d 440, 203 Cal. Rptr. 9 (1984).
62. Foley v. Community Oil Co., 64 F.R.D. 561 (D.N.H. 1974).
63. Shebar v. Sanyo Business Sys., 111 N.J. 276, 544 A.2d 377 (1988).
64. Murphy v. American Home Prods. Corp., 58 N.Y.2d 293, 461 N.Y.S.2d 232, 448 N.E.2d 86 (1983).

"recognizing an implied in law obligation on the part of the employer not to discharge an employee for doing that which the employment contract obligated him to do," or "the covenant implied by the law that the parties 'will not frustrate the contracts into which they have entered.' "[65]

The concept of implying a contract limitation as a matter of law has not achieved the widespread judicial acceptance as limitations implied in fact.

The Minnesota Court of Appeals has held that a good cause requirement is not implied from years of service and positive performance reviews.[66] Similarly, the Missouri Supreme Court has consistently held that longevity of service is not considered in determining whether the discharge of an at-will employee is lawful.[67]

Furthermore, although the Washington Supreme Court recognizes that extra consideration resulting in a detriment to the employee and a benefit to the employer may form a basis for an exception to the at-will doctrine, length of service, foregoing other job opportunities, relocating, and deferring compensation do not constitute sufficient consideration to establish an implied contract.[68]

Promissory Estoppel

The elements of promissory estoppel are set forth in Section 90 of the Restatement of Contracts (1932): "A promise which the promisor should reasonably expect to induce action or forbearance . . . on the part of the promisee and which does

65. *Id.*
66. Bakker v. Metropolitan Pediatric P.A., 355 N.W.2d 330 (Minn. Ct. App. 1984).
67. Carr v. Montgomery Ward & Co., 363 S.W.2d 571 (Mo. 1963); Egloff v. Wilcox Elec. Co., 529 F. Supp. 190 (W.D. Mo. 1981), *aff'd*, 694 F.2d 1102 (8th Cir. 1982).
68. Roberts v. Atlantic Richfield Co., 88 Wash. 2d 887, 568 P.2d 764 (1977).

induce such action or forbearance is binding if injustice can be avoided only by enforcement of the promise."

Several courts have bound employers in otherwise at-will employment relationships based on the doctrine of promissory estoppel. The Ohio Supreme Court restated the rule set forth in the Restatement and enunciated the following test: whether the employer should reasonably have expected the representation to be relied upon and, if so, whether the expected action or forbearance actually resulted and was detrimental to the employee.[69] In *Grouse v. Group Health Plan, Inc.*,[70] the plaintiff was offered employment with the defendant and, in reliance on the offer, resigned his current employment and declined alternative opportunities. The court applied the principle of promissory estoppel and sustained plaintiff's complaint.

Other courts have applied the doctrine of promissory estoppel and held that good cause is required for terminating an employee when the employee, through action or forbearance, provides separate consideration for the promise, which either benefits the employer or acts to the employee's detriment. For example, the Alabama Supreme Court held that where there is a promise of permanent employment, the relinquishment of a prior position may constitute sufficient consideration to bind the employer.[71]

Other courts place more emphasis on the employer's actions. For example, in *Bower v. AT&T Technologies, Inc.*,[72] the Eighth Circuit Court of Appeals applied Missouri law and stated that if the plaintiff-employee could show that the em-

69. Mers v. Dispatch Printing Co., 19 Ohio St. 3d 100, 483 N.E.2d 150 (1985).
70. Grouse v. Group Health Plan, Inc., 306 N.W.2d 114 (Minn. 1981).
71. Scott v. Lane, 409 So. 2d 791 (Ala. 1982). *Accord* Spulak v. K-Mart Corp., 664 F. Supp. 1395 (D. Colo. 1985) (an employee who alleges that his employer made representations that induced him to continue employment rather than to look elsewhere states a claim under the theory of promissory estoppel).
72. Bower v. AT&T Technologies, Inc., 852 F.2d 361 (8th Cir. 1988) (applying Missouri law).

ployer's repeated specific promises of employment reasonably induced him to refrain from pursuing other job opportunities, then the employer would be liable for compensatory damages caused by its actions. Applying a similar analysis, the Indiana Supreme Court held that when an employee accepts a job offer because he received assurances that the position offered the same permanency of employment, advancement, and benefits as his former position, an employment contract requiring termination only for good cause is created.[73]

The Colorado Supreme Court has applied the promissory estoppel theory to enforce termination procedures contained in an employee manual. In *Continental Airlines v. Keenan,*[74] the court held that an employee may be able to enforce the termination procedures in an employee manual on the theory of promissory estoppel if the procedures constituted a promise on which the employee reasonably and detrimentally relied. However, it has been held under Colorado law that it is not reasonable for an employee to rely on the provisions in the handbook where the employee executes an agreement specifically reciting that the handbook was not a contract of employment.[75]

A few courts have explicitly refused to recognize the theory of promissory estoppel to bind employers to promises altering the at-will relationship. For example, the federal district court in Hawaii refused to apply the theory of detrimental reliance based on verbal representations made by an employer to a discharged employee,[76] while in Maryland, when the employee relinquished a job and benefits to assume a new position, the court found such actions were insufficient as a matter of law to provide consideration for a lifetime contract.[77] Similarly, the

73. Romack v. Public Serv. Co., 511 N.E.2d 1024 (Ind. 1987).
74. Continental Airlines v. Keenan, 731 P.2d 708 (Colo. 1987).
75. Evans v. Geriatrics Inc., 1 IER Cas. (BNA) 762 (D. Colo. 1986).
76. Stancil v. Mergenthaler Linotype Co., 589 F. Supp. 78 (D. Haw. 1984).
77. Page v. Carolina Coach Co., 667 F.2d 1156 (4th Cir. 1982).

Utah Supreme Court stated that the fact that the employee took a new job at a reduction in salary, incurred expenses in moving to the area of employment, and lost other benefits, furnishes no basis for invoking the estoppel doctrine.[78]

It is well established in Louisiana that employers are not required to show just cause for termination even when employees relied on promises made by the employer. The Louisiana Court of Appeals refused to require such a showing where an employee understood his employment to be permanent and moved to the state in reliance on the promise of permanent employment.[79] More recently, the Louisiana Supreme Court found that leaving one job to take a higher paying position did not provide consideration sufficient to enable the employee to be employed permanently.[80]

North Carolina remains unsettled as to whether an employee's detrimental reliance on the promises of the employer may modify the employment-at-will doctrine. In *Sides v. Duke Hospital,*[81] the North Carolina Court of Appeals held that a Michigan resident, who was induced to accept employment in North Carolina by the employer's assurance that she could only be discharged for incompetence, stated a cognizable claim for breach of an employment contract. The court found that the additional consideration of moving from Michigan was sufficient to remove the employment contract from the terminable at-will rule. However, the U.S. District Court for the Western District of Pennsylvania applied North Carolina law and held that a former employee's relocation and moving expenses did not provide the additional consideration needed to create an exception to the at-will doctrine.[82]

---

78. Bullock v. Deseret Dodge Truck Center, Inc., (2 Utah 2d, 354 P.2d 559 (1960).
79. Griffith v. Sollay Found. Drilling Inc., 373 So. 2d 979 (La. Ct. App. 1979).
80. Brannan v. Wyeth Laboratories, Inc., 526 So. 2d 1101 (La. 1988).
81. Sides v. Duke Hosp., 74 N.C. App. 331, 328 S.E.2d 818 (Ct. App. 1985).
82. Rupinsky v. Miller Brewing Co., 627 F. Supp. 1181 (W.D. Pa. 1986).

Finally, it should be noted that the doctrine of promissory estoppel does not result in a contract of employment. The significance of this distinction lies in the damages potentially recoverable under the estoppel theory as opposed to claims based on a contract of employment implied in fact or law. If the employee succeeds with a claim based on a promissory estoppel theory, relief may be limited to damages directly traceable to the promisee's reliance, i.e., not so much what a plaintiff would have earned from the employer as what he or she lost in declining alternative employment.

Implied Covenant of Good Faith and Fair Dealing

Most jurisdictions have refused to recognize an implied covenant of good faith and fair dealing as a limitation on an employer's right to terminate an at-will employee.[83] Where ac-

83. Scott v. Sears, Roebuck & Co., 798 F.2d 210 (7th Cir. 1986) (applying Illinois law); *accord* Cresswell v. Baush & Lomb, Inc., 2 IER Cas. (BNA) 1925 (N.D. Ill. 1986) (not even a contract's implied covenant of good faith and fair dealing can limit the circumstances under which an employer can discharge an at-will employee); Therrien v. United Air Lines, Inc., 670 F. Supp. 1517 (D. Colo. 1987); *accord* Farmer v. Central Bancorporation, 761 P.2d 220 (Colo. Ct. App. 1988) (Colorado does not recognize the implied covenant of good faith and fair dealing in the employment-at-will context); Boyd v. Doskocil Sausage Co., 686 F. Supp. (D. Kan. 1988); McCart v. Brown-Forman Corp., 713 F. Supp. 981 (W.D. Ky. 1988); Poirier v. Sears, Roebuck & Co., 116 LRRM (BNA) 2086 (Me. 1983); Chekey v. BTR Realty Inc., 575 F. Supp. 715 (D. Md. 1983); Perry v. Hartz Mountain Corp., 537 F. Supp. 1387 (S.D. Ind. 1982); *accord* Hamblen v. Danners, Inc., 478 N.E.2d 926 (Ind. Ct. App. 1985); Hunt v. IBM Mid-Am. Employees' Fed. Credit Union, 384 N.W.2d 853 (Minn. 1986); Giddings v. Shalom Geriatric Center Inc., 3 IER Cas. (BNA) 671 (W.D. Mo. 1988); Wakefield v. Northern Telecom, 769 F.2d 109 (2d Cir. 1985); *accord* Citizens State Bank of N.J. v. Libertelli, 215 N.J. Super. 190, 521 A.2d 867 (Super. Ct. App. Div. 1987); Melnick v. State Farm Mut. Auto. Ins. Co., 106 N.M. 726, *cert. denied,* 109 S. Ct. 67 (1988); Sabetay v. Sterling Drug Co., 69 N.Y.2d 329, 506 N.E.2d 919 (1987); Hillesland v. Federal Land Bank Ass'n, 2 IER Cas. (BNA) 150 (N.Y. 1987);

cepted, the implied covenant of good faith and fair dealing precludes discharges of at-will employees that are motivated by bad faith or that frustrate the purposes of the employment agreement itself. For example, Nebraska will find the implied covenant in termination cases only when the employee is deprived of constitutional or statutory rights or where contractual agreements guarantee that an employee will not be fired without just cause.[84]

There are a few jurisdictions that do recognize an implied covenant of good faith and fair dealing in an at-will employment relationship. In *Siles v. Travenol Laboratories, Inc.*,[85] the Massachusetts Court of Appeals held that the covenant is implicit in all contracts and bad faith terminations are actionable. However, the mere absence of good cause to discharge an employee does not give rise to a breach of the covenant unless the employee can show that the discharge involved an intent by the employer to benefit financially at the employee's expense or that the employer's reason behind the termination was contrary to public policy.

Similarly, the Arizona Supreme Court in *Wagenseller v. Scottsdale Memorial Hospital,* stated that an implied covenant of good faith and fair dealing will be recognized in employment at-will contracts but that such recognition does not establish a contractual right to continued employment. The court explained that the good faith covenant protects the right of the

---

Burk v. K-Mart Corp., 770 P.2d 24 (Okla. 1989); Thompson v. St. Regis Paper Co., 685 P.2d 1081 (Wash. 1984); Brockmeyer v. Dun & Bradstreet, 335 N.W.2d 834 (Wis. 1983); *accord* Banyard v. McDonald's Restaurants, 1 IER Cas. (BNA) 623 (E.D. Wis. 1986); Galbraith v. Philips Information Sys., 116 LRRM (BNA) 2819 (E.D. Pa. 1984); Cockels v. International Business Expositions, 159 Mich. App. 30, 406 N.W.2d 465 (Ct. App. 1987).

84. Jeffers v. Bishop Clarkson Mem. Hosp., 222 Neb. 829, 387 N.W.2d 692 (1986).

85. Siles v. Travenol Laboratories, Inc., 13 Mass. App. 354, 433 N.E.2d 103 (1982).

parties to an agreement to receive the benefits of the contract they have entered. When people enter into an at-will employment contract, the court noted, the employee agrees to do work required by the employer and the employer agrees to provide the necessary working conditions and pay the employee for work done. The covenant protects the employee only from discharge motivated by the employer's desire to avoid payment of benefits already earned by the employee. A guarantee of continued employment is not one of the agreed upon benefits nor does the covenant create a duty on the part of the employer to terminate its employees only for good cause. The Arizona court further held that there is no tort recovery for breach of the covenant.[86]

The California Supreme Court is in agreement that a claim of breach of the implied covenant of good faith and fair dealing sounds in contract rather than tort. The court justified such a characterization of the claim by stating that the implied covenant is read into contracts in order to protect the express covenants of the contract, not to protect some general public policy.[87]

---

86. Wagenseller v. Scottsdale Memorial Hosp., 147 Ariz. 370, 710 P.2d 1025 (1985); *accord* Vermillion v. AAA Pro-Moving & Storage, 146 Ariz. 215, 704 P.2d 1360 (Ct. App. 1985); *accord* Magnan v. Anaconda Indus., 193 Conn. 558, 479 A.2d 781 (1984); Mitford v. de Lasala, 666 P.2d 1000 (Alaska 1983); High v. Sperry Corp., 581 F. Supp. 1246 (S.D. Iowa 1984).
87. Foley v. Interactive Data Corp., 47 Cal. 3d 654, 254 Cal. Rptr. 211, 765 P.2d 373 (1988).

CHAPTER THREE

Wrongful or Abusive Discharge Claims

In addition to limiting an employer's right to terminate at-will employment on the basis of an implied contract right or considerations of promise and reliance, courts have further constrained an employer's right to discharge an employee when the discharge conflicts with some public policy. This public policy exception to the employment-at-will doctrine can be roughly divided into four categories: (1) exercising statutory rights, (2) unlawful employer purpose, (3) satisfying legal obligations, and (4) reasons deemed repugnant to public policy.

Exercising Statutory Rights

When a statute expressly confers a right upon an employee, many jurisdictions have held that the employee may not be discharged for exercising that right.

The most widely recognized cause of action in this area is an action for retaliatory discharge contrary to workers' compensation rights. In one early case, despite the absence of a provision in the state's workers' compensation statute expressly prohibiting retaliation, an Indiana court held that an at-will employee could not be discharged for filing a workers' compensation claim.[1] The court reasoned that the important pub-

1. Frampton v. Central Ind. Gas Co., 260 Ind. 249, 297 N.E.2d 425 (1973).

lic policy inherent in the adoption of a workers' compensation statute would be frustrated if employees were deterred from seeking benefits under the law for fear of employer reprisal.[2] At least thirteen states have followed Indiana's lead and found that an employer acts in contravention of public policy when it discharges an employee for exercising rights granted by the applicable workers' compensation law.[3]

In at least one jurisdiction, it is not even necessary for the employee to have actually filed a claim for benefits in order to state a cause of action. The Kansas Supreme Court has recently held that an employee who is discharged for *intending* to file a workers' compensation claim can maintain a retaliatory discharge action.[4] The court reasoned:

---

2. *Id.*
3. *California:* Meyer v. Byron Jackson, Inc., 120 Cal. App. 3d 59, 174 Cal. Rptr. 428 (1981); *Florida:* Smith v. Piezo Technology, 427 So. 2d 182 (Fla. 1983); *Illinois:* Kelsay v. Motorola, Inc., 74 Ill. 2d 172, 384 N.E.2d 353 (1978); Leach v. Lauhoff Grain Co., 51 Ill. App. 3d 1022, 366 N.E.2d 1145 (App. Ct. 1977); Midgett v. Sackett-Chicago, Inc., 105 Ill. 2d 143 (1984); *Indiana:* Vantine v. Elkart Brass Mfg. Co., 572 F. Supp. 636 (N.D. Ind. 1983); Frampton v. Central Ind. Gas Co., 260 Ind. 249, 297 N.E.2d 425 (1973); *Iowa:* Springer v. Weeks & Leo Co., 429 N.W.2d 558 (Iowa 1988); *Kansas:* Murphy v. City of Topeka-Shawnee County Dep't of Labor Serv., 6 Kan. App. 2d 488, 630 P.2d 186 (1981); Kistler v. Life Care Centers, 629 F. Supp. 1268, (D. Kan. 1985) (testifying at unemployment hearing); *Kentucky:* Firestone Textile Co. v. Meadows, 666 S.W.2d 730 (Ky. 1983); *Michigan:* Sventko v. Kroger Co., 69 Mich. App. 644, 245 N.W.2d 151 (Ct. App. 1976); *Missouri:* Henderson v. St. Louis Hous. Auth., 605 S.W.2d 800 (Mo. 1979); McKiness v. Western Union, 667 S.W.2d 738 (Mo. Ct. App. 1984); *Nevada:* Hansen v. Harrah's, 675 P.2d 394 (Nev. 1984); *New Jersey:* Lally v. Copygraphics, 85 N.J. 668, 428 A.2d 1317 (1981); *Oregon:* Brown v. Transcon Lines, 284 Or. 597, 588 P.2d 1087 (1978); *Tennessee:* Clanton v. CainSloan Co., 677 S.W.2d 441 (Tenn. 1984); *Texas:* Murray Corp. of Md. v. Brooks, 600 S.W.2d 897 (Tex. Civ. App. 1980); Texas Steel Co. v. Douglas, 533 S.W.2d 111 (Texas Civ. App. 1980); *West Virginia:* Shanholtz v. Monogahela Power Co., 270 S.E.2d 178 (W. Va. 1980); Messenger v. Volkswagen of Am., 585 F. Supp. 565 (S.D.W.Va. 1984); Thomas v. Kroger Co., 583 F. Supp. 1031 (S.D.W.Va. 1984).
4. Chrisman v. Phillips Indus., Inc., 242 Kan. 772, 751 P.2d 140 (1988). *But*

> [T]o hold otherwise would permit an employer to discharge an employee shortly after an industrial accident and before the employee has filed a workers' compensation claim. To fire an employee because he or she has been injured and intends to file a workers' compensation claim is no less subversive of the Workers' Compensation Act, and no less opposed to public policy than the firing of the employee in retaliation for the actual filing of a claim.[5]

Other statutory rights, the exercise of which may support a claim of wrongful or abusive discharge, include the right to refuse to submit to polygraph examinations,[6] the right to participate in union activities,[7] and the right to serve on a jury.[8] In *Perks v. Firestone Tire & Rubber Co.*,[9] for example, the Court of Appeals for the Third Circuit held that the discharge of an employee because he refused to submit to a polygraph examination violated public policy in Pennsylvania as evidenced by that state's antipolygraph statute. The court emphasized that

---

see Wilson v. Acacia Park Cemetery Ass'n, 3 IER Cas. (BNA) 1210 (Mich. 1987) (retaliatory discharge based on anticipation of workers' compensation claim is not a cause of action).

5. Chrisman v. Phillips Indus., Inc., 242 Kan. at 774, 751 P.2d at 142.
6. Ambroz v. Cornhusker Square Ltd., 229 Neb. 899, 416 N.W.2d 510 (1987); Heller v. Dover Warehouse Mkt. Inc., 515 A.2d 178 (Del. Super. Ct. 1986); Perks v. Firestone Tire & Rubber Co., 611 F.2d 1363 (3d Cir. 1979) (Pennsylvania law). *But see* Ballaron v. Equitable Shipyards, Inc., 3 IER Cas. (BNA) 520 (5th Cir. 1988) (Louisiana polygraph statute does not create an action in wrongful discharge, nor is discharge for refusal to take the test a violation of public policy).
7. Stepanishcen v. Merchants Dispatch Transp. Corp., 722 F.2d 922 (1st Cir. 1983) (Federal Railway Labor Act); Glenn v. Clearman's Golden Cock Inn, Inc., 192 Cal. App. 2d 793, 13 Cal. Rptr. 769 (1961); Sand v. Queen City Packing Co., 108 N.W.2d 448 (N.D. 1961). *But see* Anco Constr. Co. v. Freeman, 236 Kan. 626, 693 P.2d 1183 (1985) (federal law preempts state claim).
8. *See, e.g.,* Bender Ship Repair, Inc. v. Stevens, 379 So. 2d 594 (Ala. 1980); Nees v. Hocks, 272 Or. 320, 536 P.2d 512 (1975); *see also* United States v. Adamita, 3 IER Cas. (BNA) 1770 (1988) (employer liable for employee's salary during service on jury).
9. Perks v. Firestone Tire & Rubber Co., 611 F.2d at 1363.

there was a strong public policy prohibiting polygraph examinations and noted that the statute subjected employers to criminal penalties for requiring a polygraph examination as a condition of employment or continuation of employment.[10]

Although the current trend is toward increasing judicial acceptance of wrongful discharge claims based on public policy grounds, some jurisdictions continue to limit such claims to a statutory cause of action where one exists,[11] and refuse to presume a cause of action when the legislature has elected not to provide the aggrieved employee with a means to protect its statutory enactments. For example, in *Scott v. Otis Elevator Co.,*[12] the Florida Supreme Court pointed out that since Florida "does not recognize a common law cause of action for retaliatory discharge," an employee terminated for invoking rights granted by a workers' compensation statute is limited to the statutory cause of action and cannot bring a claim based in tort for lost wages.

Unlawful Employer Purpose

Employees also have succeeded in maintaining wrongful discharge claims either for refusing to commit illegal acts or for reporting or threatening to expose the illegal or suspected

---

10. *Id.* at 1366.
11. *See, e.g.,* Scott v. Otis Elevator Co., 3 IER Cas. (BNA) 457 (Fla. 1988); Cox v. Radiology Consulting Assocs., Inc., 658 P.2d 264 (W.D. Pa.), *aff'd,* 835 F.2d 282 (3d Cir. 1987) (reporting violations of nuclear regulatory statute); Grubba v. Bay State Abrasives, 803 F.2d 746 (1st Cir. 1986) (handicap laws); Mier v. Masonite Corp., 109 Ill. 2d 1, 485 N.E.2d 312 (1985) (age); Mead v. Goodyear Tire & Rubber Co., 121 LRRM (BNA) 2204 (C.D. Cal. 1985) (race); Gryzb v. Evans, 700 S.W.2d 399 (Ky. 1985) (sex); Self v. Bennett, 475 So. 2d 673 (Ala. 1984) (workers' compensation); Mr. B's Oil Co. v. Register, 181 Ga. App. 166, 351 S.E.2d 533 (1986) (polygraph).
12. Scott v. Otis Elevator Co., 3 IER at 458.

illegal activities of their employers, i.e., "whistle-blowers."[13] Similarly, courts have held that an employee can maintain an action in wrongful discharge for insisting on compliance with state or federal laws.

An employee may have a cognizable wrongful discharge claim if he is terminated for refusing to engage in an unlawful practice countenanced by the employer or for failing to comply with an employer's directive to commit an illegal act. California was the first state to protect an employee who refused to participate in illegal activity when, in *Petermann v. International Brotherhood of Teamsters,*[14] the court held that an employee could not be discharged for refusing to commit perjury. The discharged employee instituted an action for wrongful discharge after he was terminated for refusing to accede to his employer's request to commit perjury. The court held that it would be contrary to state interests, to public policy, and to accepted moral standards to allow employers to discharge employees on such grounds.[15] More recently, a California court permitted an action in tort by an employee terminated for refusing to engage in illegal price-fixing.[16]

---

13. Several states provide varying statutory protection for whistle-blowers and/or employees who refuse to participate in their employer's violations of the law. They include: Arizona, California, Connecticut, Delaware, Florida, Hawaii, Illinois, Indiana, Iowa, Kansas, Kentucky, Louisiana, Maine, Maryland, Michigan, Minnesota, Missouri, Montana, New Hampshire, New Jersey, New York, Ohio, Oklahoma, Oregon, Pennsylvania, Rhode Island, Texas, Utah, Washington, and Wisconsin.
14. Petermann v. International Bhd. of Teamsters, 174 Cal. App. 2d 184, 344 P.2d 25 (Ct. App. 1959). *See also* Sides v. Duke Hosp., 74 N.C. App. 331, 328 S.E.2d 818, *review denied,* 314 N.C. 331, 335 S.E.2d 13 (1985) (on perjury exception).
15. Petermann v. International Bhd. of Teamsters, 174 Cal. App. 2d at 188–89, 344 P.2d at 27.
16. Tameny v. Atlantic Richfield Co., 27 Cal. 3d 167, 610 P.2d 1330, 164 Cal. Rptr. 839 (1980). *See also* Winther v. DEC Int'l, Inc., 625 F. Supp.

Similarly, a Minnesota court upheld an employee's cause of action where the employee refused to violate a federal environmental statute and was consequently discharged.[17] The court stated:

> The [federal statute] is . . . a clearly mandated public policy to protect the lives of citizens and the environment, and we hold that an employee may bring an action for wrongful discharge if that employee is discharged for refusing to participate in an activity that the employee, in good faith, believes violates any state or federal law or rule or regulation adopted pursuant to law.[18]

The Indiana Supreme Court recently explained the deterrent effect of providing employees with a judicial remedy when discharged for refusing to violate the law:

> Depriving [the plaintiff] of any legal recourse . . . would encourage criminal conduct by both employee and the employer. Employees faced with the choice of losing their jobs or committing an illegal act for which they might not be caught would feel pressure to break the law simply out of financial necessity. Employers, knowing the employee's susceptibility to such threats and the absence of civil retribution, would be prompted to present such an ultimatum.[19]

The desire to prevent criminal activity has led other courts to recognize actions for wrongful discharge when an employee is discharged for refusing to violate state or federal laws,[20]

---

100 (D. Colo. 1985); Perry v. Hartz Mountain Corp., 537 F. Supp. 1387 (S.D. Ind. 1982); McNulty v. Borden, Inc., 474 F. Supp. 1111 (E.D. Pa. 1979).

17. Phipps v. Clark Oil & Ref. Corp., 408 N.W.2d 569, 2 IER Cas. (BNA) 341 (Minn. 1987); Sabine Pilot Servs., Inc. v. Hauck, 687 S.W.2d 733 (Tex. 1985); Sventko v. Kroger Co., 69 Mich. App. 644 (1976).
18. Phipps v. Clark Oil & Ref. Corp., 2 IER 343.
19. McClanahan v. Remington Freight Lines, Inc., 517 N.E.2d 390, 393 (Ind. 1988).
20. *See* Laws v. Aetna Fin. Co., 667 F. Supp. 342 (N.D. Miss. 1987) (Missis-

including truck safety laws[21] and laws prohibiting indecent exposure.[22]

In addition, many courts have held that an employee states a cause of action in wrongful discharge when he is discharged for reporting the illegal or suspected illegal activities of his employer to the proper authorities—whistle-blowing.[23]

While the Arizona Supreme Court recognized a cause of action in favor of an employee who refused to participate in illegal activities in 1985,[24] the next year it broadened the protection afforded at-will employees by adopting the whistle-blowing theory in *Wagner v. City of Globe.*[25] In *Wagner,* a police officer was discharged because he had informed a judge who was sentencing a prisoner that the prisoner had been unlawfully detained.[26] The court refused to allow the employer to terminate the police officer with impunity for disclosing the commission of unlawful acts.[27]

The Arizona Supreme Court explained the rationale for extending public policy protection to such informants, as follows:

---

sippi would recognize a cause of action in favor of an employee who alleges she was discharged for failing to "pack" insurance policies in violation of federal and state law). Beasley v. Affiliated Hosp. Prod., 713 S.W.2d 557 (Mo. Ct. App. 1986) (cause of action recognized for employee who alleges he was discharged for refusing to predetermine the winner of a raffle, in violation of federal and state law.); Boyle v. Vista Eyewear, Inc., 700 S.W.2d 859 (Mo. Ct. App. 1985) (cause of action recognized for employee who alleges she was discharged for threatening to report violations of federal law to the Food and Drug Administration (FDA)).

21. Coman v. Thomas Mfg. Co., 91 N.C. App. 327, 371 S.E.2d 731 (1988).
22. Wagenseller v. Scottsdale Memorial Hosp., 147 Ariz. 370, 710 P.2d 1025 (1985).
23. *See, e.g.,* Garcia v. Rockwell, 187 Cal. App. 3d 1556, 232 Cal. Rptr. 490 (1986).
24. Wagenseller v. Scottsdale Memorial Hosp., 147 Ariz. at 370, 710 P.2d at 1025.
25. Wagner v. City of Globe, 150 Ariz. 82, 722 P.2d 250 (1986).
26. *Id.* at 84, 722 P.2d at 252.
27. *Id.* at 89–90, 722 P.2d at 257–58.

> We believe that whistleblowing activity which serves a public purpose should be protected. So long as employee's actions are not merely private or proprietary, . . . the decision to expose illegal or unsafe practices should be encouraged. We recognize that there is a tension between the obvious societal benefits in having employees with access to information expose activities which may be illegal or which may jeopardize health and safety, and accepted concepts of employee loyalty, nevertheless we conclude that on balance actions which enhance the enforcement of our laws or expose unsafe conditions or otherwise serve some singularly public purpose, will inure to the benefit of the public. Indeed, our legislature has recognized that whistleblowing activity is worthy of protection.[28]

Closely akin to the whistle-blowing situation are those cases recognizing a cause of action in favor of an employee who is discharged for *threatening to expose* illegal employer activity or insisting on employer compliance with state or federal laws. For example, in *Palmer v. Brown,*[29] an employee was discharged after failing to assure one of her superiors that she would not report her discovery that another superior was fraudulently billing Medicaid for unperformed laboratory work. The Kansas court held that public policy favors the protection of citizens from retaliation for good-faith reporting of statutory and regulatory infractions.[30]

Similarly, a West Virginia court has held that a discharged employee states a cause of action in wrongful discharge where the discharge was precipitated by an attempt to report to banking authorities illegal overcharges on consumer credit accounts being made by the employer bank.[31]

In *Sheets v. Teddy's Frosted Foods, Inc.,*[32] the Connecticut

28. *Id. See also* Vermillion v. AAA Pro Moving & Storage, 146 Ariz. 215, 704 P.2d 1360 (Ct. App. 1985).
29. Palmer v. Brown, 242 Kan. 893, 752 P.2d 685 (1988).
30. *Id.* at 900, 752 P.2d at 689.
31. Harless v. First Nat'l Bank, 162 W. Va. 116, 246 S.E.2d 270 (W.Va. 1978).
32. Sheets v. Teddy's Frosted Foods, Inc., 179 Conn. 471, 427 A.2d 385 (1980).

court upheld an action in wrongful discharge brought by an employee who insisted that his employer comply with state drug labelling requirements. The court noted that it is impermissible to force an employee to choose between possible criminal sanctions and continued employment.[33] Similar actions have been upheld in Illinois,[34] Maryland,[35] and West Virginia.[36]

Even in those jurisdictions that protect the employee who exposes wrongdoing, the employee might have a difficult burden to overcome in presenting his or her case. In *Schriner v. Meggini's Food,*[37] the court granted summary judgment to the employer because the employee failed to establish that he had a reasonable, good-faith basis for reporting to the Attorney General his suspicion that his employer unlawfully altered the odometer mileage on a vehicle it sold him. The court found that while the employee had reasonable cause to believe someone had changed the mileage, he had no reason to believe it was his employer.[38] Similarly, the Kansas Supreme Court required the employee to establish that the whistle-blowing was motivated by good faith in order to hold the employer liable for attempting to coerce the employee to remain silent regarding the employer's illegal billing practices.[39]

In addition, the illegal activity reported must be sufficiently egregious to constitute a violation of public policy. In *Suchodolski v. Michigan Consolidated Gas Co.,*[40] a discharged employee could not maintain a cause of action in wrongful

---

33. *Id.*
34. Witt v. Forest Hosp., Inc., 115 Ill. App. 3d 481, 450 N.E.2d 811 (App. Ct. 1983).
35. Adler v. American Standard Corp., 538 F. Supp. 572 (D. Md. 1982) (employee threatened to expose antitrust law violations).
36. Stanley v. Sewell Coal Co., 285 S.E.2d 679 (W.Va. 1981).
37. Schriner v. Meggini's Food, 3 IER Cas. (BNA) 129 (Neb. 1988).
38. *Id.* at 132.
39. Palmer v. Brown, 242 Kan. at 900, 752 P.2d at 690.
40. Suchodolski v. Michigan Consol. Gas Co., 412 Mich. 692, 316 N.W.2d 710 (1982).

discharge where he claimed that his attempt to report and correct his employer's internal accounting practices caused his discharge. The accounting practices allegedly violated the code of ethics of the Institute of Internal Auditors. The court held that discharging an employee for reporting such a violation does not contravene public policy.[41]

Judicial acceptance of a public policy cause of action for wrongful discharge based on illegal acts is not universal. For example, in *Ivy v. Army Times Publishing Co.,*[42] the Court of Appeals for the District of Columbia declined to recognize a wrongful discharge cause of action where the employee was terminated in retaliation for refusing to commit perjury while testifying before a government agency. Similarly, in Louisiana, refusing to perform an illegal act does not create an exception to the employment-at-will doctrine.[43]

In *Sides v. Duke Hospital,*[44] the United States Court of Appeals for the Fourth Circuit, applying North Carolina law, appeared to recognize the illegal act exception to at-will employment when it found that a discharged employee who refused to testify falsely at a trial against her employer could maintain a wrongful discharge action. Subsequently, however, in *Guy v. Travenol Laboratories, Inc.,*[45] the same court affirmed the dismissal of an employee's complaint alleging he was discharged for refusing to violate FDA regulations, limiting the exception to the perjury situation. At least two

41. *Id.*
42. Ivy v. Army Times Publishing Co., 428 A.2d 831 (D.C. App. 1981).
43. Gil v. Metal Serv. Corp., 412 So. 2d 706 (La. App.), *cert. denied,* 414 So. 2d 379 (La. 1982).
44. Sides v. Duke Hosp., 74 N.C. App. 331, 328 S.E.2d 818, *review denied,* 314 N.C. 331, 335 S.E.2d 13 (1985).
45. Guy v. Travenol Laboratories, Inc., 812 F.2d 911 (4th Cir. 1987).

other federal courts, in Pennsylvania[46] and New Mexico,[47] have refused to recognize an exception to the at-will doctrine under state law for employees who are discharged for refusing to engage in and/or for reporting illegal activity.

Satisfying Legal Obligations

Some courts have held that an employee may not be discharged for complying with an obligation imposed by the law. These courts reason that an employee should not be forced to choose between continued employment and fulfilling legal obligations. This public policy exception to the at-will doctrine is best exemplified by those cases in which the court recognized that an employee's legal obligation to serve on a jury may not serve as the basis for termination.[48] These courts recognize that jury duty is an important obligation of every citizen in furtherance of one of America's fundamental institutions.

Similarly, complying with one's legal duty to obey a subpoena may support a wrongful discharge claim in some states.[49] When the Supreme Court of South Carolina was called upon to decide whether an employee discharged for obeying a subpoena had a valid claim in that state, it pointed out that an employee faced with the prospect of discharge for

46. O'Neill v. ARA Servs., Inc., 457 F. Supp. 182 (E.D. Pa. 1978) (only statutory causes of action recognized).
47. Odell v. Humble Oil & Ref. Co., 201 F.2d 123 (10th Cir.), *cert. denied,* 345 U.S. 941 (1953).
48. *See, e.g.,* Nees v. Hocks, 272 Or. 210, 536 P.2d 512 (1975); Reuther v. Fowler & Williams, Inc., 255 Pa. Super. 28, 386 A.2d 119 (1978); *see also* United States v. Adamita, 3 IER Cas. 1770 (D.C.N.Y. 1988) (employer may not withhold full salary from employee serving protracted jury duty). *But see* Bender Ship Repair, Inc. v. Stevens, 379 So. 2d 594 (Ala. 1980) (employee terminated for serving on a grand jury not protected).
49. Ludwick v. This Minute of Carolina, 287 S.C. 219, 337 S.E.2d 213 (1985).

complying with this legal obligation is "confronted with the dilemma of choosing between her livelihood, on the one hand, and obedience to the law of the State, on the other."[50] The court held that "the public policy exception is invoked when an employer requires an at-will employee, as a condition of retaining employment, to violate the law. To hold otherwise would sanction defiance of the legal process legislated by the General Assembly."[51]

One court has expanded this aspect of the public policy exception by imposing liability pursuant to a wrongful discharge theory where the employer discharged an employee for assisting in a criminal investigation.[52] To reach this result, the court credited a public policy in favor of citizen crime fighters even though no constitutional or statutory provision required the employee *qua* citizen to participate actively in such an investigation.[53]

Reasons Repugnant to Public Policy

In recent years the courts have expanded the scope of the public policy exception to the at-will employment doctrine by accepting wrongful discharge claims predicated on the notion that a discharge may be repugnant to public policy in a broad sense rather than a policy grounded in a specific statutory mandate or prohibition.[54] Typically, courts recognizing this

50. *Id.* at 225, 337 S.E.2d at 216.
51. *Id.*
52. Palmateer v. International Harvester Co., 85 Ill. 2d 124, 421 N.E.2d 876 (1981); *see also* Harless v. First Nat'l Bank in Fairmont, 246 S.E.2d 270 (W.Va. 1978) (employee may not be dismissed for insisting on employer's compliance with credit laws).
53. Palmateer v. International Harvester Co., 85 Ill. 2d at 132–33, 421 N.E.2d at 880.
54. This cause of action is also known as "discharge against the general public good."

exception do so on the theory that a discharge contrary to broad public policy thwarts community interests. Courts often discern public policy from legislative enactments, state constitutions, and decisional law.

Some jurisdictions have upheld a cause of action in wrongful discharge based on very broad policy considerations. For example, in *Payne v. Rozendaal,*[55] the Vermont Supreme Court held that in order to maintain a wrongful discharge action based on public policy, the employee need not find an expression of such public policy in legislative enactments or statutes. Thus, it was impermissible for an employer to terminate an employee on account of his age notwithstanding the absence of a Vermont statute prohibiting age discrimination. Similarly, in California, an employee who was discharged for refusing to continue to work in a hospital under conditions jeopardizing the health and safety of patients, could proceed with a wrongful discharge claim even though the California legislature and state judiciary had not made any pronouncements in favor of a policy supporting such conduct.[56]

Some jurisdictions have adopted a different approach to the public policy issue. To illustrate, the New Hampshire Supreme Court has held that the existence of a public policy limiting the employer's right to terminate is a jury question.[57] The court noted that the decision as to whether a public policy exists is appropriately left to a jury because it involves a balancing process requiring an assessment of several factors.[58] Allowing the jury to make this determination significantly broadens this exception because a jury may find that a discharged employee

55. Payne v. Rozendaal, 147 Vt. 488, 520 A.2d 586, 1 IER Cas. (BNA) 800 (1986).
56. Dabbs v. Cardiopulmonary Management, 188 Cal. App. 3d 143, 234 Cal. Rptr. 129 (1987).
57. Cilley v. New Hampshire Ball Bearings, 128 N.H. 491, 514 A.2d 818 (1986).
58. *Id.*

has a cause of action under the public policy exception even if there is no legislative or constitutional underpinning. For example, a jury could find, as recognized by the New Hampshire court, that a public policy in favor of honesty protects an employee who is discharged for refusing to lie on behalf of a senior company official.[59]

Other jurisdictions have adopted a narrower view. For example, the Oklahoma Supreme Court, while acknowledging that employment at will continues to be the general rule, aligned itself with those jurisdictions recognizing a public policy exception in those few instances where a "clear mandate" of public policy can be derived from specific sources of positive law:[60] "We follow the modern trend and adopt today the public exception to the at-will termination rule in a narrow class of cases in which the discharge is contrary to a clear mandate of public policy as articulated by constitutional, statutory, or decisional law."[61] Stressing that the exception is to be "tightly circumscribed,"[62] the court stated:

> In determining whether a clear mandate of public policy is violated, courts should inquire whether the employer's conduct contravenes the letter or purpose of constitutional, statutory, or regulatory provision or scheme. Prior judicial decisions may also establish the relevant public policy. However, courts should proceed cautiously if called on to declare public policy absent some prior legislative or judicial expression on the subject.[63]

---

59. *Id.*
60. Burk v. K-Mart Corp., 4 IER Cas. (BNA) 182 (Okla. 1989) (clarifying Hinson v. Cameron, 742 P.2d 549 (Okla. 1987) and Hall v. Framers Inc. Exch., 713 P.2d 1027, 4 IER Cas. (BNA) 189 (Okla. 1985)).
61. *Id.* at 185.
62. *Id.* (citing Parnar v. Americana Hotels, Inc., 65 Haw. 370, 377, 652 P.2d 625, 631 (1982)).
63. *Id.* at 380, 652 P.2d at 531.

The Alaska Supreme Court took a novel approach to the public policy issue when it applied a balancing test to determine that an employer lawfully discharged two employees who refused to submit to urinalysis screening.[64] The court found that "where the public policy supporting . . . privacy . . . conflicts with the public policy supporting the protection of the health and safety of other workers, the health and safety concerns are paramount."[65]

Among the states that have adopted a broad public policy exception are: Arkansas,[66] Hawaii,[67] Iowa,[68] Kansas,[69] Massachusetts,[70] New Hampshire,[71] New Jersey,[72] New Mexico,[73] Oregon,[74] Washington,[75] and Wisconsin.[76] In addition, federal courts interpreting the law of other state jurisdictions also have recognized a broad public policy exception.[77] However, courts

64. Luedtke v. Nabors Alaska Drilling Inc., 768 P.2d 1123 (Alaska 1989).
65. *Id.*
66. Scholtes v. Signal Delivery Serv., Inc., 548 F. Supp. 487 (W.D. Ark. 1982).
67. Parnar v. Americana Hotels, Inc., 65 Haw. at 370, 652 P.2d at 625.
68. Springer v. Weeks & Leo Co., 429 N.W.2d 558 (Iowa 1988).
69. Palmer v. Brown, 242 Kan. 893, 752 P.2d 685 (1988).
70. *See, e.g.,* DeRose v. Putnam Management Co., 398 Mass. 205, 496 N.E.2d 428 (1986); Gram v. Liberty Mut. Ins. Co., 429 N.E.2d 21 (Mass. 1981).
71. Howard v. Door Woolen Co., 414 A.2d 1273 (N.H. 1980) (combining public policy and implied covenant of good faith and fair dealing).
72. Pierce v. Ortho Pharmaceutical Corp., 84 N.J. 58, 417 A.2d 505 (1980); Worthen v. Toms River Hosp., 199 N.J. Super. 18, 488 A.2d 229 (Super. Ct. App. Div. 1985), *cert. denied,* 101 N.J. 255, 501 A.2d 926 (1985).
73. Vigil v. Arzola, 102 N.M. 682, 699 P.2d 613 (1983), *rev'd on other grounds,* 101 N.M. 687, 687 P.2d 1038 (1984).
74. Holien v. Sears Roebuck & Co., 677 P.2d 704 (Or. Ct. App. 1984); McQuary v. Bel Aire Convalescent House, Inc., 69 Or. App. 107, 684 P.2d 21, *review denied,* 298 Or. 37, 688 P.2d 845 (1984).
75. Thompson v. St. Regis Paper Co., 685 P.2d 1081 (Wash. 1984).
76. Bushko v. Miller Brewing Co., 134 Wis. 2d 136, 396 N.W.2d 167 (1986).
77. *See, e.g.,* Buethe v. Britt Airlines, Inc., 787 F.2d 1194 (7th Cir. 1986) (Indiana law); Fulford v. Burndy Corp., 623 F. Supp. 78 (D.N.H. 1985) (Alabama law); Novo Sel v. Nationwide Ins. Co., 721 F.2d 894 (3d. Cir. 1983) (Pennsylvania law).

in Georgia,[78] New Mexico,[79] Rhode Island,[80] and Texas[81] have declined to recognize a broad public policy exception.

Although most jurisdictions that recognize the broad public policy exception treat such an action as one in tort, some courts have recently concluded that the claim sounds in contract.[82] In *Sterling Drug Inc. v. Oxford,* the South Dakota Supreme Court recognized that it was taking the minority position; however, it found such a position to be "pragmatic and well reasoned."[83] The court stated:

> Since a public policy discharge action is essentially predicated on the breach of an implied provision that an employer will not discharge an employee for an act done in the public interest, a contract cause of action is most appropriate. The exclusive contract approach strikes a fair balance in that it provides employees with protection from employer retaliation, while at the same time limiting recovery to contract remedies.[84]

This distinction between contract and tort is significant since a greater variety of damages is recoverable in tort: Contract remedies exclude, among other things, recovery for mental distress and punitive damages.[85]

Although many jurisdictions now recognize the public policy exception, in at least one of the forms discussed in the preceding, others remain steadfast in rejecting such an excep-

---

78. Goodroe v. Georgia Power Co., 148 Ga. App. 193, 251 S.E.2d 51 (1978) (rejecting all nonstatutory exceptions).
79. Botijliso v. Hutchinson Fruit Co., 96 N.M. 789, 635 P.2d 992 (1981).
80. Brainard v. Imperial Mfg. Co., 571 F. Supp. 37 (D.R.I. 1983) (applying Rhode Island law).
81. Maus v. National Living Centers, 633 S.W.2d 674 (Tex. Ct. App. 1982).
82. Sterling Drug Inc. v. Oxford, 3 IER Cas. (BNA) 1967 (S.D. 1988); Brockmeyer v. Dun & Bradstreet, 113 Wis. 2d 561, 335 N.W.2d 834 (1983); Lopus v. L&L Shop-Rite Inc., 3 IER Cas. (BNA) 1690 (Mich. Ct. App. 1988).
83. Sterling Drug Inc. v. Oxford, 3 IER at 1064.
84. *Id.*
85. Lopus v. L&L Shop-Rite Inc., 3 IER at 1692.

tion to the at-will doctrine. These jurisdictions continue to require the express grant of a personal right of action by the legislature.

For example, in *Murphy v. American Home Products Corp.*,[86] the New York Court of Appeals held that exceptions to the at-will doctrine are created *solely* by the legislature, noting that "it is well settled that New York does not recognize a cause of action in tort for abusive or wrongful discharge."[87] Thus, an employee allegedly discharged because of his age and in retaliation for whistle-blowing activity did not state a cause of action in New York.[88] Similarly, the Nebraska Supreme Court recently stated that, "unless constitutionally, statutorily, or contractually prohibited, an employer may terminate an employee at any time with or without reason and not be liable for his actions."[89]

86. Murphy v. American Home Prods. Corp., 58 N.Y.2d 293, 461 N.Y.S.2d 232 (1983).
87. *Id. See also* O'Donnell v. NPS Corp., 133 A.D.2d 73, 75, 518 N.Y.S.2d 418, 420 (1987).
88. Murphy v. American Home Prods. Corp., 58 N.Y.2d at 293, 461 N.Y.S.2d at 233.
89. White v. Ardan Inc., 3 IER Cas. 1640, 1643 (1988).

CHAPTER FOUR

Related Tort Claims

Introduction

With increasing frequency, wrongful discharge suits are accompanied by claims alleging tortious conduct. Generally, a tort can be defined as that which causes injury to another, either through words or action. Inventive attorneys representing employees have begun to assert such additional claims because they provide the potential for certain procedures that would not be otherwise available to plaintiffs in employment cases, e.g., a jury and punitive damages. These causes of action pose a serious threat of increased liability; accordingly, employers need to be aware of the bases for such action and how to avoid them. The most common torts in the employment context are addressed in the following. Discussion of each tort will include: (1) what a plaintiff must prove to establish the tort; (2) the circumstances under which an employer can be sued, in addition to, or rather than, the employee causing the harm; (3) what defenses are available to employers; and (4) what damages are available to a prevailing plaintiff.

Intentional Infliction of Emotional Distress

Intentional infliction of emotional distress, or the tort of "outrage," is a relatively new cause of action, recognized by courts only in the last two decades. It is an "extension of the right to recover damages for emotional distress into areas involving nontraditional intentional torts."[1]

A plaintiff must prove the following elements to establish the tort: (1) that the defendant's conduct was extreme and outrageous; (2) that the defendant intentionally or recklessly caused harm; and (3) that distress resulted.[2]

Extreme and outrageous conduct, the essential component, is measured against the following standard:

> Liability has been found only where the conduct has been outrageous in character, and so extreme in degree, as to go beyond all possible bounds of decency, and to be regarded as atrocious, and utterly intolerable in a civilized community. Generally, the case is one in which the recitation of the facts to an average member of the community would arouse his resentment against the actor, and lead him to exclaim, "Outrageous!"[3]

Judges are often skeptical when reviewing these claims; accordingly, very few fact situations give rise to a viable suit for this tort. For example, a routine termination of an employee will never suffice, if handled in a nonabusive manner.[4] Similarly, where an employer merely insists that an employee perform his or her duties in a particular way, no matter how trivial or demeaning, this tort action cannot be maintained since an employer is merely asserting its legal right.[5]

---

1. Harless v. First National Bank in Fairmont, 169 W. Va. 673, 289 S.E.2d 692, 704 (1982).
2. Restatement (Second) of Torts, § 46(1) (1965) (hereinafter cited as Restatement).
3. *Id.*, comment d.
4. Batchelor v. Sears, Roebuck & Co., 574 F. Supp. 1480 (E.D. Mich. 1983); Novosel v. Sears, Roebuck & Co., 495 F. Supp. 344 (E.D. Mich. 1980).
5. Burgess v. Chicago Sun Times, 132 Ill. App. 3d 181, 476 N.E.2d 1284 (1st

These results can be explained, in part, by what our society views as outrageous conduct. "Until such a time as job security is recognized as some sort of national right, reasonable people can be expected to endure the pain of job loss as 'part of the price of living among people.' "[6]

Likewise, allegations of favoritism and unjust criticism have not given rise to an actionable level of outrageous conduct,[7] nor have allegations that the employer created a tense work environment.[8]

In a number of cases, however, employees have been able to frame personnel issues as torts and have survived motions to dismiss or motions for summary judgment. This can be crucial because, absent a favorable ruling on a motion to dismiss or a motion for summary judgment, the case will be presented to the jury as the ultimate trier-of-fact and employers generally have not fared well with juries. Accordingly, the plaintiff who can survive pretrial motions and reach the jury greatly increases his or her leverage to negotiate a settlement (or ultimately to prevail).

In emotional distress cases where plaintiffs were successful, courts have found that "the extreme and outrageous character of the conduct may arise from an abuse by the actor of a position, or a relation with the other, which gives him actual or apparent authority over the other, or power to affect his

---

Dist. 1985). *See also* Gibson v. Chemical Card Servs., Corp., 157 Ill. App. 3d 211, 510 N.E.2d 37 (1st Dist. 1987) (merely assisting in an investigation of theft is insufficiently outrageous because the employer has a legitimate interest to solve prior theft and prevent future theft).

6. Fletcher v. Wesley Medical Center, 585 F. Supp. 1260, 1262 (D. Kan. 1984) (quoting RESTATEMENT (SECOND) OF TORTS, §46, comment j); Lekich v. IBM Corp., 469 F. Supp. 485, 488 (E.D. Pa. 1979). *See also* Thomason v. Mitsubishi Elec. Sales of America, Inc., 701 F. Supp. 1563 (N.D. Ga. 1988).
7. Miller v. Aluminum Co. of Am., 679 F. Supp. 495 (W.D. Pa. 1988), *aff'd*, 856 F.2d 184 (3d Cir. 1988).
8. Britt v. Georgia Power Co., 677 F. Supp. 1169 (N.D. Ga. 1987).

interests."[9] For example, one court held that the plaintiff's allegations that the employer coerced the plaintiff to falsify work reports and retaliated against him for refusing to falsify the reports stated a cause of action. The court noted that this type of "extortion" was rendered extremely outrageous due to the relative imbalance of power: "It is the alleged abuse of power by a large corporation over one of its front line employees which aggravates the outrageousness of the conduct alleged in this case."[10]

Claims of sexual harassment, like situations of abuse of power, are often successful in surviving motions to dismiss or motions for summary judgment. For example, one court found that claims that a supervisor threatened to discharge his subordinate and otherwise made her job difficult after she refused his sexual advances could state a cause of action for intentional infliction of emotional distress.[11] In another case, the court held that an employee's claim against her supervisor for intentional infliction of emotional distress resulting from sexual harassment stated a claim since "acts of sexual harassment may rise to a level supporting a claim. . . ."[12] The employee also asserted a claim against her employer because it allegedly retaliated against her after she reported her sexual harassment. The employee alleged that her employer: (1) discharged

9. RESTATEMENT comment e; Lucas v. Brown and Root, Inc., 736 F.2d 1202, 1206, 1207 (8th Cir. 1984) (Kansas law).

10. Milton v. Illinois Bell Tel. Co., 101 Ill. App. 3d 75, 427 N.E.2d 829, 832 (1st Dist. 1981). *See also* MBM Co., Inc. v. Counce, 268 Ark. 269, 596 S.W.2d 681, 688 (1980).

11. Cummings v. Walsh Constr. Co., 561 F. Supp. 872, 882 (S.D. Ga. 1983). It should be noted that the expansion of the tort of outrage means that this remedy overlaps with other, established legal actions. For example, the sexual harassment alleged in *Cummings* would be actionable under Title VII of the Civil Rights Act of 1964, 42 U.S.C. §2000e *et seq.*, and perhaps under a comparable state or local statute.

12. Coleman v. American Broadcasting Co., 119 L.R.R.M. (BNA) 3324, 3330 (D.C. D.C. 1988).

her without notice, (2) ransacked her office to give an erroneous impression of her conduct, (3) spread untrue rumors about her, and (4) barred her from the employer's premises. The court held that these allegations stated a claim since an employer's response to an individual's claim of such harassment may by itself present a claim of intentional infliction of emotional distress.

Employers who use high-pressure tactics are also likely to have to defend themselves before a jury on a claim for intentional infliction of emotional distress. The following examples are illustrative of the kind of conduct that has been found to be sufficiently offensive.

> 1) The employer's investigators used intense, coercive tactics to interrogate an employee suspected of theft, such as sequestering her in a windowless room for three hours. The employer fired her after she signed a confession even though she was told she would most likely be able to keep her job.[13]
>
> 2) The plaintiff's supervisor organized an intensive attempt to force her to take disability leave rather than work through her pregnancy. The plaintiff alleged that a miscarriage she suffered the week after she was fired was the direct result of this campaign. The harassment included pressure on the plaintiff's husband and attacks on her work competence.[14]
>
> 3) An employer who suspected that waitresses were stealing, but who could not identify the alleged culprit, fired the plaintiff as part of a threat to fire all waitresses in alphabetical order until the identity of the alleged perpetrator was revealed. The court held that the plaintiff alleged conduct sufficiently outrageous to state a cause of action.[15]

Assuming that the alleged conduct is sufficiently outrageous, the second element a plaintiff must establish to prove the tort

---

13. Smithson v. Nordstrom, Inc., 63 Or. App. 423, 664 P.2d 1119, 1120, 1121 (1983), *review denied,* 295 Or. 840, 671 P.2d 1176 (1983).
14. Rice v. United Ins. of America, 465 So. 2d 1100 Ala. (1984).
15. Agis v. Howard Johnson Co., 371 Mass. 140, 355 N.E.2d 315, 318–19 (1976).

of outrage is that the defendant intended to cause the severe emotional distress suffered by the plaintiff or that the defendant engaged in reckless conduct.[16] In one case, intentional conduct was proven by a plaintiff where the defendant embarked upon a concerted course of conduct to induce the plaintiff to surrender his insurance policy or enter into a disadvantageous settlement of a nonexistent dispute. The defendant knew that no legitimate dispute existed, yet continued to harass the plaintiff in an effort to terminate its legal obligations to the plaintiff. The court held that the plaintiff had stated a cause of action for intentional infliction of emotional distress.[17]

The reckless nature of the type of conduct that will support a cause of action for this tort is conduct that, while not maliciously intended to cause such distress, is such that the actor knows or should know that severe emotional distress is certain or substantially certain to result. Liability extends to situations in which there is a high degree of probability that severe emotional distress will follow and the actor proceeds in conscious disregard of it.[18] For example, where the defendant knew that the plaintiff was recuperating from a heart attack and yet continued to harass the plaintiff, reckless behavior was established, because of the high probability that plaintiff would suffer severe emotional distress due to the seriousness of the plaintiff's condition.[19]

In addition to establishing outrageous conduct and intent by

---

16. Public Fin. Corp. v. Davis, 66 Ill. 2d 85, 360 N.E.2d 765 (1977); RESTATEMENT, § 46. *But see* Alsteen v. Gehl, 21 Wis. 2d 349, 124 N.W.2d 312 (1963) rejecting recklessness as a basis for liability. It should be noted that some courts recognize the tort of negligent infliction of emotional distress. Cases arising under this tort are discussed elsewhere in this chapter.
17. Fletcher v. Western Nat'l Life Ins. Co., 10 Cal. App. 3d 376, 89 Cal. Rptr. 78 (1970).
18. *Id.*
19. McGrath v. Fahey, 163 Ill. App. 3d 584, 520 N.E.2d 655, 659 (1st Dist. 1987), *aff'd*, 533 N.E.2d 806 (Ill. 1988).

the defendant, a plaintiff must also suffer severe emotional distress in order to recover. Sufficient distress has been defined as that which is: "so severe that no reasonable man could be expected to endure it. The intensity and the duration of the distress are factors to be considered in determining its severity."[20]

Finally, the defendant's conduct must have proximately caused the severe emotional distress suffered by the plaintiff. For example, a defendant defending such a claim might be able to demonstrate that the plaintiff's disabling emotional condition was the result of a preexisting condition of psychological stress rather than the defendant's intervening conduct. If this showing is successfully made, there is no liability despite the outrageousness of the defendant's conduct or the severity of the plaintiff's emotional distress.[21]

Once the elements of the cause of action are established, the focus will switch to whether the employer is liable and potential damages. Usually, the acts that support an action for mental distress are committed by a supervisory employee, yet the employer is sued. As with all intentional torts, the employer (as principal) will be liable for the acts of its employees (its agents) when the acts are done in the course of the employer's business or for the purpose of promoting its business, rather than for the employee's own enjoyment.[22] In addition, an employer can be liable for the acts of its employees if it is aware of the proscribed conduct and takes no steps to prevent it.[23] Unless it is a plain and indisputable case, the question of whether an employee was acting in the scope of his employment and in furtherance of the employer's business is a question for the jury.[24] For example, summary judgment was granted in the

20. RESTATEMENT, § 46.
21. Alsteen v. Gehl, 21 Wis. 2d at 349, 124 N.W. 2d at 312.
22. Cummings v. Walsh Constr. Co., 561 F. Supp. at 872.
23. *Id.*
24. Springer v. Seamen, 821 F.2d 871 (1st Cir. 1987) (applying Maine law).

employer's favor when the plaintiff admitted that her supervisor's sexually discriminatory behavior was outside the course of his employment.[25]

However, absent clear evidence of self enjoyment, an employer can be held liable for intentional infliction of emotional distress caused by its employees when an employee uses his position to abuse or sexually harass the plaintiff, such as assigning unfavorable job tasks or giving negative performance evaluations, even if the employer is unaware of the harassment.[26] Similarly, an employer can be liable for an employee's acts if his or her supervisors knew or should have known of the conduct.[27]

The lesson from these cases is that employers should develop policies that prohibit conduct that could form the bases of an intentional infliction claim and that encourage employees to complain of abusive behavior and provide adequate channels for doing so. Furthermore, employers should take prompt remedial steps once a problem is presented.

In addition to taking precautions to insulate themselves from liability, employers should also be aware of available defenses. Although defenses available to employers are addressed in more detail in subsequent chapters, it is important

---

However employers should also be aware of the resurgence in lawsuits including tort claims of negligent hiring or retention. This tort is discussed under Negligence elsewhere in this chapter.

25. Saulsberry v. Atlantic Richfield Co., 673 F. Supp. 811 (N.D. Miss. 1987). It should be noted, however, that even though an employer may not be liable for its supervisor's intentional torts when the behavior is outside the supervisor's scope of employment, the employer may nonetheless remain liable under the same facts for damages under Title VII of the Civil Rights Act for sexual discrimination because, depending upon the circumstances, an employer may be strictly liable for the acts of its supervisors.

26. Shrout v. Black Clawson Co., 689 F. Supp. 774, 781 (S.D. Ohio 1988); Cummings v. Walsh Constr. Co., 561 F. Supp. at 882.

27. Shrout v. Black Clawson Co., 689 F. Supp. at 781.

to note that defenses that have been particularly applicable to the tort of intentional infliction of emotional distress are preemption of the tort by a collective bargaining agreement and the exclusivity of workers' compensation acts. Whenever an employee's employment was or is governed by a collective bargaining agreement, the defense of preemption should be asserted. Similarly, courts have been divided on whether a state workers' compensation act provides an exclusive remedy for alleged mental injuries, so that employers are advised to consult local laws to determine the applicability of the defense.

Employers who fail to protect themselves and to whom no defenses are available face liability for compensatory and punitive damages. When determining a reasonable award to compensate the plaintiff for his or her mental suffering, the court will consider the duration and intensity of the harassment or abuse and the degree of emotional harm suffered by the plaintiff.[28] An employer may also be liable for punitive damages if a court finds that it authorized, ratified, participated, or acquiesced in the wrongdoing. One court held the employer liable for punitive damages when high-level management knew or should have known of the conduct that caused the emotional distress but took no action.[29]

Although the tort of outrage is one of the newest weapons in the plaintiff's arsenal, its usefulness has been somewhat limited by the heavy burden placed on plaintiffs to show that the employer's actions rose to the level of extreme and outrageous conduct. Nevertheless, employers should be cognizant of the fact that certain types of conduct, particularly sexual harassment and intimidating investigative tactics, pose a substantial risk of liability. Actions based on these types of conduct are especially difficult to dispose of at the motion to dismiss or

28. *Id.*
29. *Id.*

summary judgment stage because the distinction between conduct that is no more than unpleasant and that which is outrageous, as well as whether an employee has acted within the scope of his employment, present subjective and largely factual questions, which a court is likely to defer to a jury.

Defamation

Employers routinely provide information concerning employees or former employees (insiders) to outsiders such as government agencies or other employers. It is important to be aware that these disclosures may subject employers to claims for defamation when that information is false and derogatory.

The elements of the tort of defamation are: (1) defamatory language is used by the defendant; (2) the defamatory language must be "of or concerning" the plaintiff; (3) the defamatory language is publicized by the defendant to a third person; (4) there is fault on the part of the defendant; and (5) there is damage to the plaintiff's reputation.[30]

Defamatory language is that which tends to injure "reputation" in the popular sense; namely, that which diminishes the esteem, respect, goodwill, or confidence in which the plaintiff is held or that which excites adverse, derogatory, or unpleasant feelings or opinions against the plaintiff.[31] A statement may be defamatory on its face, such as: "Max is a thief." Defamation may also occur where the defamatory meaning of a statement becomes apparent by providing additional facts, such that a defamatory meaning exists by *innuendo.*[32] Where it is reason-

30. Whitby v. Associates Discount Corp., 59 Ill. App. 2d 337, 207 N.E.2d 482 (3d Dist. 1965).
31. W. PROSSER, LAW OF TORTS, ¶ 111 at 739. (4th ed. 1971). Newell v. Field Enters., Inc., 91 Ill. App. 3d 735, 415 N.E.2d 434 (1st Dist. 1980).
32. Talens v. Bernhard, 669 F. Supp. 251 (E.D. Wis. 1987); Harris Trust & Sav. Bank v. Phillips, 154 Ill. App. 3d 574, 506 N.E.2d 1370 (1st Dist. 1987), *appeal denied,* 116 Ill. 2d 554, 515 N.E.2d 108 (1987).

able to do so, however, statements must be innocently construed.[33]

The second element requires that a plaintiff establish that a reasonable listener, reader, or viewer could understand that the defamatory statement referred to the plaintiff.[34] For example, a cartoon drawn by an employer unflatteringly depicting striking workers could not form the basis for a defamation claim because no reasonable reader could think that the attributes of a crudely drawn cartoon were intended to be applied literally to striking workers.[35]

A statement must not only be defamatory and of or concerning the plaintiff but must also be "published" to be actionable. Thus, the plaintiff must prove that it was communicated by the defendant to a third party. Normally, a statement is not published when it is communicated between officers of a corporation or between different branches of the same corporation.[36] However, an increasing number of states now recognize that intracorporate communications can be sufficient legal publication.[37]

The majority of states recognize that there is no publication when the employee merely alleges that the employer communicated the statement to the employee himself.[38] For ex-

---

33. Chapski v. Copley Press, 92 Ill. 2d 344, 442 N.E.2d 195 (1982).
34. Cosgrove Studio & Camera Shop, Inc. v. Pane, 408 Pa. 314, 182 A.2d 751 (1962); Gnapinsky v. Goldyn, 23 N.J. 243, 128 A.2d 697 (1957); Davis v. Costa-Garvas, 619 F.Supp. 1372 (S.D.N.Y. 1985).
35. Cline v. McLeod, 180 Ga. App. 286, 349 S.E.2d 232 (1986).
36. Rouly v. Enserch Corp., 835 F.2d 1127 (5th Cir. 1988); Holsell v. Kimberly-Clark Corp., 683 F.2d 285, 289 (8th Cir. 1982), *cert. denied,* 459 U.S. 1205 (1983) (Wisconsin law); L. Cohen Co. v. Dun & Bradstreet, Inc., 629 F. Supp. 1425 (D. Conn. 1986); Jones v. Golden Spike Corp., 97 Nev. 24, 623 P.2d 970 (1981).
37. Jones v. Britt Airways, Inc., 622 F. Supp. 389 (N.D. Ill. 1984); Kelly v. General Tel. Co., 136 Cal. App. 3d 278, 186 Cal. Rptr. 184 (1982); Pirre v. Printing Developing, Inc., 468 F. Supp. 1028 (S.D.N.Y. 1978), *aff'd* 614 F.2d 1290 (2d Cir. 1979).
38. Crocker v. Chamber of Commerce, 115 LRRM (BNA) 4067, (D.C. 1983)

ample, where the reason for an employee's termination is communicated solely to the employee, the employer would not be liable because there was no publication to a third party. However, a few states have recognized the doctrine of "compelled self-publication," which allows employees to meet the publication requirement of defamation by alleging that they were forced to repeat the defamatory statement, e.g., where the reason for discharge (like theft) has to be communicated to a prospective employer.[39] These courts reason that publication is established under this doctrine because it should be foreseeable to an employer that, in the ordinary course of events, an ex-employee would have to repeat the reasons for discharge to a third party.

Publication may also be established when an employer adopts a statement made by one of its employees, such as where a supervisor's subordinate painted a defamatory sign on the plant walls, which management allowed to remain for eight months, even though the sign was visible to all on a daily basis.[40]

To prevail on a claim for defamation, a plaintiff must also demonstrate that the employer was at fault. At common law, a defendant was held strictly liable for publishing a false and defamatory remark. The defendant was liable despite exercising due care to determine the accuracy of his statements and his reasonable belief that the statements were true.[41] The United States Supreme Court, however, has altered this standard due to its interpretation of the first amendment guaran-

---

(applying District of Columbia law); Beauvoir v. Rush-Presbyterian St. Lukes Medical Center, 137 Ill. App. 3d 294, 484 N.E.2d 841, 845 (1st Dist. 1986).

39. Lewis v. Equitable Life Assurance Soc'y of the U.S., 389 N.W.2d 876 (Minn. 1986); McKinney v. County of Santa Clara, 110 Cal. App. 3d 787, 168 Cal. Rptr. 89 (1980).

40. Tacket v. General Motors Corp., 836 F.2d 1042, (7th Cir. 1987).

41. Restatement (Second) of Torts § 592A (1977).

tees of free speech and free press. Thus, generally the defendant must now be shown to have been at least negligent in ascertaining the truth of what was published.[42]

For example, negligence was established where an employer failed to investigate the truth of a statement, even though circumstances indicated that it might be false.[43] The company president had observed the plaintiff place a box in his trunk, assumed that the box contained the product produced by the employer, and thus concluded the plaintiff was stealing. Rather than approach the plaintiff, the president told the plaintiff's foreman that he saw the plaintiff stealing and told the foreman to "take care of the matter." The plaintiff was fired immediately without investigation by his foreman, even though the plaintiff invited the foreman to inspect his trunk and even his house. The court held that under these circumstances, the president's assumption that the box contained liquor could and should have been easily verified so that the employer negligently failed to ascertain the truth and thus was liable in defamation.

The final element to prevail is that the plaintiff suffered damage to his or her reputation as a result of an employer's statement. Damage to the plaintiff's reputation is presumed by statements that are facially defamatory, such as statements suggesting: (1) the commission of a crime; (2) the infection with a loathsome disease; (3) the unfitness or want of integrity in performing the duties of an office or employment; (4) words that adversely reflect on a particular party's ability to perform in his business, trade, or profession; or (5) imputation of unchastity to a woman.[44]

---

42. Gertz v. Robert Welch, Inc., 418 U.S. 323 (1974); Matafis v. Erie Ins. Exch., 775 F.2d 593 (4th Cir. 1985); Dun & Bradstreet, Inc. v. Greenmoss Builders, Inc., 472 U.S. 749, 780–85 (1985).
43. Mendez v. M.S. Walker, Inc., 26 Mass. App. Ct. 431, 528 N.E.2d 891 (1988).
44. Levinson v. Time, Inc., 89 Ill. App. 3d 338, 411 N.E.2d 1118 (1st Dist. 1980); PROSSER, TORTS, ¶ 112, at 754 (4th ed. 1971).

As long as the defamation does not fall within those specified categories, a plaintiff must specifically allege, and prove, the specific monetary damage that was incurred as a result of the statement.[45]

As far as damages are concerned, a plaintiff is always compensated for actual injury. Actual injury is not limited to out-of-pocket loss but can include a monetary amount that seeks to compensate for impairment of reputation and standing in the community, personal humiliation, and mental anguish.[46] In addition, punitive damages (i.e., damages to punish) may be awarded, sometimes even in the absence of malice.[47] However, many states refuse to allow private parties (e.g., employees) to recover punitive damages,[48] while others require malice before such damages will be imposed.[49]

In addition to establishing the foregoing elements, a plaintiff must also prove that the employer was responsible for the actions of its employees. An employer may be held responsible for the defamatory remarks of its employees only when the employee acted within the scope of his or her employment or in furtherance of the employer's business.[50] In many states, this means that the employer must expressly authorize or direct an employee to speak the words in question.[51] For example, a federal court found that a salesman's remarks to his contacts in the industry concerning a former employee's dis-

45. Whitby v. Associates Discount Corp., 59 Ill. App. 2d at 337.
46. Gertz v. Robert Welch, Inc., 418 U.S. at 323.
47. Dun & Bradstreet v. Greenmoss Builders, Inc., 472 U.S. at 749.
48. DeMeo v. Goodall, 640 F. Supp. 1115 (D.N.H. 1986) (applying New Hampshire law); Brandtley v. Zantop Int'l Airlines, 617 F. Supp. 1032 (E.D. Mich 1985).
49. Inker v. Joseph Markovits, Inc., 643 F. Supp. 1043 (S.D.N.Y. 1986); Babb v. Minder, 806 F.2d 749 (7th Cir. 1986) (applying Illinois law).
50. Tacket v. General Motors Corp., 836 F.2d at 1042.
51. Georgia Power Co. v. Busbin, 242 Ga. 612, 250 S.E.2d 642 (1978); Presnell v. Pell, 298 N.C. 715, 260 S.E.2d 611 (1979).

charge for alleged involvement in a theft-kickback scheme could not be the basis for the former employee's defamation claim against the employer, since the salesman's remarks were not authorized by the employer and an employer could be liable under Louisiana law only for employee actions within the course and scope of employment.[52]

If an employee was acting within the scope of his or her employment, in many states punitive damages may be assessed against an employer for the intentional wrongdoing of its employees *only* where management has authorized, participated in, consented to, or ratified the conduct giving rise to such damages, or deliberately retained an unfit servant.[53]

Even if an employee is able to establish each and every element of a defamation claim and demonstrate employer responsibility, several defenses are available to employers. Some defenses, like truth and consent, are true defenses that in reality undermine any claim of defamation because if these defenses exist there really is no damage to plaintiff's reputation. Other defenses, such as privileges, have been created by the courts, which have presumed that some conduct is so important to industrial relations that it will be privileged even if reputational damage resulted.

An employer can always defeat a defamation claim by demonstrating that the statement is true, or substantially true; truth is an absolute defense to defamation.[54] However, establishing the truth of the statement can be difficult in many cases, like where an employer has insufficient documentary evidence of an ex-employee's deficiencies. Similarly, a statement might be protected opinion. The line between fact and opinion un-

52. Rouly v. Enserch Corp., 835 F.2d at 1127.
53. Loughry v. Lincoln First Bank, 67 N.Y.2d 369, 494 N.E.2d 90 (N.Y. Sup. Ct. 1986), *cert. denied,* 479 U.S. 930 (1986).
54. RESTATEMENT OF TORTS, § 581A comment (1977); Hejmadi v. AMFAC, Inc., 202 Cal. App. 3d 525, 249 Cal. Rptr. 5 (1988).

fortunately is not always clear.[55] One court found that an employee failed to state sufficiently a claim for defamation by alleging that her coworkers stated that she had made sexually explicit comments and was flirtatious. The comments were opinion and absolutely protected under the first amendment, the court held.[56]

A plaintiff's consent to the publication is another defense.[57] For example, one court held that an employee consented to the statements where the statements related to her employment and they were made at a meeting she requested.[58] Similarly, an employee consented to a publication where he executed a release authorizing the communication of his work record.[59]

Privileges, unlike true defenses, protect conduct that might have resulted in reputational damage. Privileges may be absolute or conditional. An absolute privilege is never lost. There are, however, several ways to abuse a conditional privilege, and, if abused, the privilege is lost and the employer liable.

Statements made during judicial, quasi-judicial, administrative, legislative, and executive proceedings are absolutely privileged.[60] Likewise, statements made because compelled by a collective bargaining agreement have also been held to be absolutely privileged. For example, an absolute privilege has been accorded to an employer's defamatory remarks about its employees to the union when the employer was required by the express terms of a collective bargaining agreement to

---

55. MacFarlane v. Turner Broadcasting Sys. Inc., 120 LRRM 3203 (D.D.C. 1985).
56. Lee v. Metropolitan Airport Comm'n, 428 N.W.2d 815 (Minn. Ct. App. 1988).
57. Ernst v. Indiana Bell Tel. Co., 475 N.E.2d 351 (Ind. Ct. App. 1985).
58. Hollowell v. Career Decisions, Inc., 100 Mich. App. 561, 298 N.W.2d 915 (Mich. Ct. App. 1980).
59. Walsh v. Consolidated Freightways, 278 Or. 347, 563 P.2d 1205 (1977).
60. Lewis v. Elliot, 628 F. Supp. 512, 516 (D.D.C. 1986).

communicate the reasons for discharge to the union.[61] Statements made during grievance and arbitration proceedings involving an employee grievance have been protected by absolute privilege.[62] Similarly, in most jurisdictions, statements made in unemployment compensation proceedings are covered by an absolute privilege.[63]

There are also circumstances where employers are protected by a qualified privilege. This privilege applies to statements concerning an employee or former employee, when the statement is made "for a proper purpose and to one having a legitimate interest in the subject matter of the statements."[64] Thus, in one case, a qualified privilege existed when a statement by a security guard that an employee had taken property belonging to the employer was made in the presence of the store manager and the personnel manager, both of whom had a legitimate interest in the conduct of the employees.[65] Similarly, a privilege was found by the court when a negative evaluation of the employee was communicated to the department head by the employee's supervisor.[66] A qualified privilege could exist for statements made by a supervisor to the plaintiff's co-employees explaining the plaintiff's discharge because the co-employees have an interest in knowing why discipline was rendered.[67]

---

61. Merritt v. Detroit Memorial Hosp., 81 Mich. App. 279, 265 N.W.2d 124 (1978).
62. Hull v. Central Transp., Inc., 628 F. Supp. 784 (N.D. Ind. 1984).
63. Zuniga v. Sears, Roebuck & Co., 100 N.M. 414, 671 P.2d 662 (Ct. App. 1983), *cert. denied*, 671 P.2d 1150 (N.M. 1983). Magnan v. Anaconda Indus., Inc., 37 Conn. Supp. 38, 429 A.2d 492 (1980). See GA. CODE ANN. § 54-642.1 (Supp. 1985) (statutory privilege) ILL. REV. STAT. ch. 48 § 640.1 (West Supp. 1989) (statutory privilege). *But see* Sanders v. Stewart, 157 Ind. App. 74, 298 N.E.2d 509, 512 (1973) (limited to qualified privilege).
64. Zuniga v. Sears Roebuck & Co., 100 N.M. at 414.
65. *Id.*
66. McCone v. New England Tel. & Tel., 393 Mass. 231, 471 N.E.2d 47 (1984).
67. Mendez v. M.S. Walker, Inc., 26 Mass. App. Ct. at 431; Tacket v. General

Employers must be aware that qualified privileges are conditional and may be lost if the plaintiff proves that the employer has abused the privilege. Privileges can be abused in any of several ways, including unnecessary or excessive publication, the existence of malice by the employer when making the statement, and finally, if the statement was made when the employer knew or should have known that a statement was false.[68] For example, one employer forfeited its privilege to publish statements to those with a legitimate interest due to unnecessary, unreasonable, and excessive publication of the allegedly defamatory statements.[69] There, the defendant communicated the defamatory statements to the plaintiff in front of several bystanders despite the plaintiff's request that they move to a more private area. Similarly, a qualified privilege will be lost if the plaintiff proves that the employer made the statement with malice, ill will,[70] or with the knowledge that it was false or in reckless disregard for its truth or falsity.[71] For example, one employer lost its privilege when it discharged an employee for theft and told his foreman and union steward of the theft, without verifying the facts. The court held that the employee could recover for defamation because the theft allegations were false, and, thus, he was recklessly discharged because of unverified circumstantial evidence. That court noted "recklessness can . . . be shown by a failure to verify in circumstances where verification is practical and the matter is sufficiently weighty to call for safeguards against error."[72]

Motors Corp., 836 F.2d at 1042; Arnold v. Diet Center, Inc., 113 Idaho 581, 746 P.2d 1040 (Ct. App. 1987).

68. Prosser, Torts, §115 at 792–796.
69. Galvin v. New York, New Haven & Hartford, 341 Mass. 293, 168 N.E.2d 262 (1960).
70. Nowik v. Mazda Motors of Am. (kEast) Inc., 523 So. 2d 769 (Fla. Dist. Ct. App. 1st Dist. 1988); O'Brien v. Papa Gino's of Am., Inc., 780 F.2d 1067 (1st Cir. 1986).
71. Burger v. McGilley Memorial Chapels, Inc., 856 F.2d 1046 (8th Cir. 1988).
72. Mendez v. M.S. Walker, Inc., 26 Mass. App. Ct. at 431.

However, mere negligence is insufficient to destroy a qualified privilege. As one court has noted, the malice standard fosters freedom of communication since employees and employers frequently find themselves in emotionally charged situations where defamatory words are likely to be uttered negligently.[73]

Employment references to present or prospective employers present special problems for employers. The law clearly recognizes that a former employer has a qualified privilege to make "defamatory" communications about the character or conduct of its employees to present or prospective employers.[74] As with all qualified privileges, though, an employer's right to give references can be abused. For example, an employer lost its privilege when the plaintiff demonstrated that the employer made false statements maliciously and with knowledge of their falsity.[75]

Thus, whenever an employer communicates negative information about an employee or former employee, it should be cognizant of the possibility of a suit for defamation and be appropriately circumspect. The contents of an employee's evaluation and, indeed, any assessment of an employee's performance, conduct, or morals should be disclosed only to those who have a legitimate interest in the information and only when necessary to accomplish proper business objectives. If a former employee's new or prospective employer requests information about the former employee, employers should not respond to telephonic inquiries but should demand written requests on company letterhead. This is to protect employers from claims of publication to an individual without a legitimate interest and also to avoid claims of excessive publication. The

---

73. Banas v. Matthews Int'l Corp., 348 Pa. Super. 464, 502 A.2d 637 (Super. Ct. 1984).
74. Walsh v. Consolidated Freightways, 278 Or. 347, 563 P.2d 1205, (1977); Lewis v. Equitable Life Assurance Soc'y of the U.S., 389 N.W.2d at 876.
75. Burger v. McGilley Memorial Chapels, Inc., 856 F.2d at 1046.

information provided should be limited to strictly factual information, and a waiver and consent from the employee should be obtained prior to any disclosure. Some companies refuse to give new or prospective employers the reasons for a former employee's termination and limit the information they provide to verifying dates of employment and the last position the employee held before leaving the company. Although employers need not go to those lengths to protect themselves from defamation claims, they should be aware that giving more information could invite needless litigation from disgruntled employees who feel that they lost prospective employment due to a former employer's negative reference. At the very least, employers should not provide information without a waiver and consent form, and the information they do provide should be both neutral and factually unassailable.

Tortious Interference

The tort of tortious interference compensates an individual who has been improperly deprived of the benefit of a business or employment relationship by the conduct of someone who is not a party to that relationship. In the employment-at-will area, a claim for tortious interference with contract rights is becoming an increasingly popular ancillary claim. In the employment context, this tort occurs when the defendant improperly induces a breach or termination of a contract (or prospective contract) between the plaintiff and another party that usually results in plaintiff's loss of employment (or prospective employment).

The courts have generally recognized two related causes of action: (1) tortious interference with an existing business relationship (including both employment contracts (oral and written) and at-will relationships) and (2) tortious interference with a prospective business relationship or economic advantage.

When the cause of action arises in the employment context, most jurisdictions accord greater protection to an existing business relationship.[76]

Tortious Interference with an Existing Business Relationship

The tort of tortious interference requires that the plaintiff prove that the interference giving rise to the tort was carried out by a third party *not* a party to the employment relationship at issue. Such third parties can include officers and directors of the corporate employer, as well as supervisors and fellow employees.[78]

Tortious Interference with a Contractual Relationship

The Restatement of Torts explicitly recognizes the theory of tortious interference with contracts. It provides:

> One who intentionally and improperly interferes with the performance of a contract (except a contract to marry) between another and third person by inducing or otherwise causing the third person not to perform the contract, is subject to liability to the other for the pecuniary loss resulting to the other from the failure of the third person to perform the contract.[79]

In the employment context, a plaintiff who is alleging tortious interference with a contractual relationship must prove: (1) the existence of a valid contract (oral or written); (2) knowledge of the relationship on the part of the interfering third party; (3) intentional interference, which induced or caused a breach of the relationship; (4) the resultant damage to the party whose relationship was disrupted; and (5) improper ac-

76. Restatement (Second) of Torts § 766 comment b (1977).
77. Restatement (Second) of Torts § 766 (1977).
78. Trimble v. City & County of Denver, 697 P.2d 716 (Colo. 1985).
79. Restatement (Second) of Torts § 766 (1977).

tion by the interfering third party.[80] For example, a plaintiff who was a nurse was able to state a cause of action for tortious interference against several doctors affiliated with her hospital.[81] The plaintiff had testified against the doctors in a malpractice suit; she alleged that they then retaliated against her by causing the hospital to discharge her. Finding that the plaintiff had a contractual employment relationship with the hospital, the court held that she stated a claim for tortious interference. When plaintiffs have alleged a contractual relationship and have been unable to prove such a relationship, however, there can be no claim for tortious interference.[82]

The Restatement (Second) of Torts states that the factors to be considered in determining what is "improper conduct" by a third person are (1) the nature of the third party's conduct; (2) the third party's motive; (3) the interests of the plaintiff with which the third party's conduct interferes; (4) the interests sought to be advanced by the third party; (5) the social interests in protecting the freedom of action by the third party and the contractual interests of the plaintiff; (6) the proximity or remoteness of the third party's conduct to the interference; and (7) the relations between the parties.[83]

Such actions for interference with an existing employment contract by a third party generally fall into two categories: (1)

---

80. Wagenseller v. Scottsdale Memorial Hosp., 147 Ariz. 370, 710 P.2d 1025 (1985); Sagen v. Jewel Cos., 148 Ill. App. 3d 447, 499 N.E.2d 662 (2d Dist. 1986); Bernstein v. Aetna Life & Casualty, 843 F.2d 359 (9th Cir. 1988); Ingle v. Glamore Motor Sales, Inc., 528 N.Y.S. 2d 602 (1988), *order aff'd by* Ingle v. Glamore Motor Sales, Inc., 538 N.Y.S.2d 771, 535 N.E.2d 1311 (1989); Hicks v. Clyde Fed. Sav. & Loan, 696 F. Supp. 387 (N.D. Ill. 1988).
81. Sides v. Duke Hosp., 74 N.C. App. 331, 328 S.E. 2d 818 (1985), *rev. denied by* 314 N.C. 331, 335 S.E.2d 13 (1985).
82. Dickstein v. Del Laboratories, 535 N.Y.S.2d 92, *appeal denied*, Dickstein v. Del Laboratories, Inc., 540 N.Y.S.2d 1004, 538 N.E.2d 356 (1989); Bernstein v. Aetna Life & Casualty, 843 F.2d at 359; Borowski v. Vitro Corp., 634 F. Supp. 252 (Md. 1986).
83. Restatement (Second) of Torts § 766 (1977).

actions alleging that a former employer has communicated information to the plaintiff's current (or prospective) employer, which caused it to discharge (or fail to hire) the plaintiff[84] and (2) actions alleging that the employer itself, its officers and directors, or plaintiff's individual supervisor interfered with plaintiff's employment relationship.[85]

Actions in the first category are analyzed in the same manner as claims that a former employer's communications have prevented the plaintiff from obtaining other employment, and the same prerequisites and defenses apply. For example, one court found that the plaintiff had established a business relationship with a new employer and that said relationship was then terminated by the new employer when the defendant, her former employer, gave a bad reference. The plaintiff was therefore able to state a cause of action for tortious interference.[86]

Actions in the second category, however, require a different analysis. As noted in the Restatement, a fundamental principle of the tort of intentional interference is that the interference must be caused by someone not a party to the contract. While in most circumstances a corporate employer cannot be sued for interference with its own employment relationship with the plaintiff, many courts have held that this immunity is a qualified privilege that can be lost when an agent of the corporate employer acts outside of the scope of his employment.[87]

---

84. Potthoff v. Jefferson Lines, Inc., 363 N.W. 2d 771 (Minn. App. 1985); *see also* Nowik v. Mazda Motors of Am. (kEast) Inc., 523 So. 2d at 769.
85. Worrick v. Flora, 133 Ill. App. 2d 755, 272 N.E.2d 708 (3d Dist. 1971); Springer v. Weeks & Leo Co. 429 N.W.2d 558 (Iowa 1988); Roy v. Woonsocket Inst. for Sav., 525 A.2d 915 (R.I. 1987).
86. Nowik v. Mazda Motors of Am. (kEast) Inc., 523 So. 2d at 769.
87. Welch v. Kennedy Piggly Stores, Inc., 63 B.R. 888, 3 IER Cas. (BNA) 523 (W.D. Va. 1986); Becket v. Welton Becket & Assocs., 39 Cal. App. 3d 815, 114 Cal. Rptr. 531 (1974); *but see* Springer v. Weeks & Leo Co., 429 N.W. 2d at 558; Worrick v. Flora, 133 Ill. App. 2d at 755, 272 N.E.2d at 708; Roy v. Woonsocket Inst. for Sav., 525 A.2d at 915; King v. Schaeffer, 123 Ga. App. 735, 181 S.E.2d 700 (1971); Avins v. Moil, 610 F. Supp. 308

For example, a plaintiff was able to state a cause of action against his employer for tortious interference when the employer hired a polygraph examiner to falsify the results of plaintiff's polygraph in order to justify plaintiff's termination and cause the state to deny him unemployment benefits.[88] Similarly, a plaintiff who was discharged for filing workers' compensation claims against his employer stated a cause of action even though the employer was a party to the contract,[89] where the plaintiff's employer had induced a third-party polygrapher to falsify the results of plaintiff's polygraph in order to support its decision to terminate the plaintiff. In both instances, the courts found that the employers had tortiously interfered with the relationship between the plaintiffs and the polygraph company because the polygraphers had established relationships with the plaintiffs, owed a duty to plaintiffs to report truthful results of their polygraphs, breached their duty to the plaintiffs by falsifying results, and caused the plaintiffs to suffer damage as a result.[90]

(D.C. Pa. 1984), *aff'd,* 774 F.2d 1150 (3d Cir. 1985); Bradley v. Consolidated Edison Co. of N.Y., 657 F. Supp. 197 (S.D.N.Y. 1987); Morast v. Lance, 807 F.2d 926 (11th Cir. 1987).

88. Lewis v. Oregon Beauty Supply Co., 302 Or. 616, 733 P.2d 430 (1987); Elbe v. Wausau Hosp. Center, 606 F. Supp. 1491 (W.D.Wis. 1985); Wagenseller v. Scottsdale Memorial Hosp., 147 Ariz. at 370, 710 P.2d at 1025; Murray v. Bridgeport Hosp., 40 Conn. Supp. 56, 480 A.2d 610 (Conn. Super. 1984); *but see* Kinter v. Nidec-Torin Corp., 662 F. Supp. 112 (D. Conn. 1987).
89. Springer v. Weeks & Leo Co., 429 N.W.2d at 558.
90. Georgia has a minority rule whereby supervisors are privileged to discharge employees when they have absolute authority to do so, irrespective of the supervisors' motives. Other states, however, have rejected this absolute privilege as incorrect. Taylor v. Foremost-McKesson, Inc., 656 F.2d 1029 (5th Cir. 1981). Wagenseller v. Scottsdale Memorial Hosp., 147 Ariz. at 370, 710 P.2d at 1025; Trimble v. City & County of Denver, 697 P.2d at 716.

Tortious Interference with an At-Will Relationship

A plaintiff who is alleging tortious interference with an at-will relationship must prove that: (1) a reasonable expectation of continued employment existed; (2) the defendant had knowledge of the business relationship; (3) the defendant's conduct was intentional; and (4) the plaintiff suffered damage as a result of the defendant's interference.[91] The plaintiff must also prove that both parties to the at-will employment relationship were willing to, and desired to, continue the relationship.[92] For example, one plaintiff, the president of a savings and loan association, was unable to state a cause of action for tortious interference where he served at the will of the board of directors, and the board voted to terminate his services. In that event, the plaintiff was unable to show that both parties wished their business relationship to continue.[93]

The cause of action arises from a third party's interference with the business relationship itself; therefore no employment contract is required.[94] Courts adopting this theory have reasoned that there is a presumption of continuity in employment and that "but for" the third party's interference with the at-will relationship the employment agreement would have continued in effect. For example, a plaintiff was able to state a cause of action for tortious interference where his supervisor improperly recommended plaintiff's layoff in retaliation for plaintiff's complaints about the supervisor's improper relationship with a supplier.[95]

---

91. Cashman v. Shinn, 109 Ill. App. 3d 1112, 441 N.E.2d 940 (4th Dist. 1982).
92. Getschow v. Commonwealth Edison Co., 111 Ill. App. 3d 522, 444 N.E.2d 579 (1st Dist. 1982), *aff'd in part, rev'd in part,* 99 Ill. 2d 528, 459 N.E.2d 1332 (1984).
93. Cashman v. Shinn, 109 Ill. App. 3d at 1112, 441 N.E.2d at 940.
94. Haupt v. International Harvester Co., 582 F. Supp. 545 (N.D. Ill. 1984).
95. *Id.; see also* Zappa v. Seiver, 706 P.2d 440 (Colo. App. 1985).

Tortious Interference with a Prospective Economic Advantage

A plaintiff who is alleging tortious interference with a prospective economic advantage must prove: (1) a reasonable expectancy of entering into a valid business relationship with a specific third party or an identifiable class of third parties; (2) knowledge of the valid expectation on the part of the interfering third party; (3) intentional interference by the interfering third party, which prevented the plaintiff's expectation from developing into a business relationship; and (4) the resultant damages to the plaintiff on account of the interfering third party's improper actions.[96] In one case, for example, the plaintiff had accepted a position with a competitor but had not yet begun to work for the new employer. The defendant induced plaintiff to remain in its employ, while at the same time it was searching for a replacement for him. The court found that plaintiff had stated claims for both tortious interference and fraudulent misrepresentation.[97]

In the employment context, actions for tortious interference with a prospective economic advantage most often involve a situation in which the plaintiff's former employer has allegedly provided a prospective employer with information that prevented the plaintiff from obtaining a new position.[98] Because both causes of action arise from similar factual circumstances, claims for interference with a prospective employment relationship are often brought in conjunction with a claim for

96. Crinkley v. Dow Jones & Co., 67 Ill. App. 3d 869, 385 N.E.2d 714 (1st Dist. 1979), modified on other grounds, 119 Ill. App. 3d 142, 456 N.E.2d 138 (1st Dist. 1983); Nowik v. Mazda Motors of Am. (kEast) Inc., 523 So. 2d at 769.

97. Shebar v. Sanyo Business Sys., 526 A.2d 1144 (N.J. Sup. Ct. 1987), *aff'd*, 111 N.J. 276, 544 A.2d 377 (1988).

98. Potthoff v. Jefferson Lines, Inc., 363 N.W.2d 771 (Minn. App. 1985); Brown v. Chem Haulers, Inc., 402 So. 2d 887 (Ala. 1981); Nowik, v. Mazda Motors of Am. (kEast) Inc., 523 So. 2d at 769.

defamation based on the same misconduct.[99] Like the defendant's qualified privilege in defamation cases to make statements to those having a legitimate interest in the subject matter, defendant employers in interference cases may also claim a qualified privilege to take an action interfering with a plaintiff's expectancy, where they have given a third person "truthful information, or . . . honest advice within the scope of a request for advice."[100] However, if the information is not true, or goes beyond the scope of the third party's request, then the interference is not privileged.[101]

Conclusion

Because actions for defamation and for tortious interference tend to arise from similar factual circumstances, the same precautions that apply to actions for defamation apply with equal force to tortious interference claims, particularly those based on information provided in response to requests from present or prospective employers. The information provided should be kept to a minimum and should be strictly factual.

Although actions against employers based on the employer's own interference (or that of its agents) have become more prevalent in recent years, such actions rarely succeed. The plaintiff alleging that a supervisor interfered with his employment relationship faces a significant hurdle in overcoming the supervisor's privilege to act within the scope of his employment duties. Corporate employers are virtually immune from such actions and, as long as there is sufficient documentation to establish that the officer, director, supervisor, or other agent

99. Paros v. Hoemako Hosp., 681 P.2d 918, 140 Ariz. 335 (Ariz. App. 1984); Colucci v. Chicago Crime Comm'n, 31 Ill. App. 3d 802, 334 N.E.2d 461 (1st Dist. 1975).

100. Geyer v. Steinbronn, 351 Pa. Super. 536, 506 A.2d 901, 910 (Super. Ct., 1986); RESTATEMENT, § 772.

101. Geyer v. Steinbronn, 506 A.2d at 910–11, n.8

involved was acting within the scope of his authority, individual liability is equally unlikely.

Negligence

In order to maintain a cause of action for the tort of negligence in the employment setting, an employee must show that: (1) the employer had a duty to him; (2) that duty was breached; (3) the employee suffered an identifiable injury; and (4) the proximate cause of the injury to the employee was the employer's breach of its duty to the employee. The plaintiff in a negligence action does not have to prove intent on the part of the defendant and thus has a much higher probability of success on a tort claim in the employment arena. Plaintiffs have successfully maintained claims in the areas of negligent performance appraisal, negligent maintenance of employment records, negligent infliction of emotional distress, and negligent misrepresentation. Plaintiffs who were not employees of defendant employers have also maintained successful claims against employers for negligent hiring and retention.

Negligent Performance Appraisal

A private employer has no legal duty to appraise the performance of its employees during the course of their employment. However, if the employer chooses to conduct such appraisals, it should do so in a careful and consistent manner. A successful claim for negligent performance appraisal requires that the employee establish that: (1) the employer had a duty (usually contractual in nature by means of a written policy or consistent practice) to evaluate his performance; (2) that duty was breached by the employer's failure to warn the employee of his performance shortcomings; (3) the employee sustained an identifiable injury (usually discharge); and (4) the employer's failure to warn the employee regarding his performance shortcomings was the proximate cause of his injury.[102]

This theory to date, however, has found little support outside the state of Michigan.[103] For example, a federal district court in Massachusetts has rejected a claim for negligent performance appraisal based on an alleged underlying contractual obligation.[104] The plaintiff had alleged that his employer had undertaken a contractual duty to conduct his performance appraisals, had negligently conducted the appraisals, and had negligently failed to provide training. The plaintiff further alleged that as a result of his employer's negligence, he was forced to choose between early retirement and involuntary termination. The court dismissed his tort claim finding that under applicable state law, to the extent that a duty to conduct performance appraisals existed, it arose solely from the promises and intentions of the parties and thus was not actionable in tort. The court further stated that any cause of action that plaintiff might have would be for breach of contract.

Later decisions in the state of Michigan have rejected claims for negligent performance evaluation, reasoning that a negligence claim must be based on a duty created by law or statute rather than on a duty arising out of a contract.[105] Two recent

---

102. Chamberlain v. Bissell, Inc., 547 F. Supp. 1067 (W.D. Mich. 1982); Haslam v. Pepsi-Cola Co., 117 LRRM (BNA) 2950 (E.D. Mich. 1984).
103. Prost v. F.W. Woolworth Co., 647 F. Supp. 946 (D. Kan. 1985), *aff'd*, 1986 WL 32744 (10th Cir. 1986); Budd v. American Sav. & Loan Ass'n, 89 Or. App. 609, 750 P.2d 513 (Ct. App. 1988); Karren v. Far W. Fed. Sav., 79 Or. App. 131, 717 P.2d 1271 (1986), *rev. denied*, 301 Or. 666, 725 P.2d 1293 (1986).
104. Treadwell v. John Hancock Mut. Life Ins. Co., 666 F. Supp. 278 (D. Mass. 1987).
105. Gach v. National Educ. Corp., Civ. No. 84-1792 (E.D. Mich. 1985); Reid v. Sears Roebuck & Co., 588 F. Supp. 558 (E.D. Mich. 1984), *aff'd*, 790 F.2d 453 (6th Cir. 1986); Kay v. United Technologies Corp. 757 F.2d 100 (6th Cir. 1985); Dahlman v. Oakland Univ., 172 Mich. App. 502, 432 N.W.2d 304 (1988). The *Dahlman* court also rejected a cause of action for negligent termination stemming from the alleged breach of an employer's contractual duty to exercise reasonable care in evaluat-

cases, however, have indicated that a tort claim for negligent performance appraisal may stand on an underlying contract claim. The Michigan Court of Appeals recently found that a discharged employee who could state a claim for wrongful discharge could put forth an ancillary claim in tort for negligent performance appraisal.[106] Similarly, a federal district court in the same state found that a terminated employee had established an oral contract claim under state law. The court found further that under the oral contract the employer had a duty to conduct plaintiff's yearly performance appraisal in a fair and objective manner.[107]

Given the fact that a cause of action for negligent performance appraisal has been recognized in Michigan since 1982 but has failed to find support in other jurisdictions, it appears likely, at least for the foreseeable future,[108] that employers in other states are not at risk in this area. However, the prudent employer with a performance appraisal procedure in place would be well advised to follow its own rules.

Negligent Maintenance of Employment Records

Employees have maintained successful claims where their employers have a duty to maintain employment records but do so in a negligent manner. A successful claim for negligent maintenance of employment records requires the employee to establish that: (1) the employer had a statutory, regulatory, or contractual duty to maintain complete and accurate employment records; (2) the employer breached its duty by failing to

---

ing the plaintiff's performance because Michigan law requires that an action in tort be premised on a duty separate and distinct from a breach of contract and arising independently of the contract itself. *See also* Haas v. Montgomery Ward, 812 F.2d 1015 (6th Cir. 1987).

106. Loftis v. G.T. Prods., Inc., 167 Mich. App. 787, 423 N.W.2d 358 (1988).
107. Diggs v. Pepsi-Cola Metro. Bottling Co., 861 F.2d 914 (6th Cir. 1988).
108. *See* Gossage v. Little Caesar Enters., Inc., 698 F. Supp. 160 (S.D. Ind. 1988).

properly maintain said records; (3) the employee sustained an identifiable injury; and (4) the employer's failure to maintain accurate records was the proximate cause of his injury.[109]

For example, a plaintiff was able to state a cause of action for negligent maintenance of employment records where he was laid off in a reduction in force and given a letter of recommendation at the same time the employer was erroneously furnishing negative personnel information to an outside third party. The court determined that the negligent maintenance of employment records caused the employer to furnish the erroneous information, thus giving rise to a cause of action in tort. The court noted further that the wrongful recordkeeping itself, and not the publication thereof, was tortious. The court then went on to state that publication of the erroneous information could give rise to additional counts in libel or slander.

It should be noted that courts have sustained a cause of action on the basis of negligent maintenance of records in both the public and private sector.[110] However, where an employer had no specific duty to maintain employment records, the employee could not sustain a cause of action for negligent maintenance of records.[111]

While there has not been a great deal of litigation in this area, the tort has been recognized for a number of years and in several states. The employer who chooses to maintain, or is required by law to maintain, employment records must exercise due care in seeing to it that such records are maintained in an accurate and confidential manner. Employers should physically maintain such records in a secure place and limit access to personnel information contained therein to those with a need to know.

---

109. Bulkin v. Western Kraft East, Inc., 422 F. Supp. 437 (E.D. Pa. 1976).
110. *Id.;* Quinones v. United States, 492 F.2d 1269 (3d Cir. 1974); *but see* Doe v. Town of Blandford, 402 Mass. 831, 525 N.E.2d 403 (1988).
111. Prouty v. National R.R. Passenger Corp., 572 F. Supp. 200 (D.D.C. 1983).

Negligent Infliction of Emotional Distress

The tort of negligent infliction of emotional distress may subject one to liability for resulting illness or bodily harm if the actor "should have realized that his conduct involved an unreasonable risk of causing the distress otherwise than by knowledge of the harm or peril of a third person" and "from facts known to him should have realized that the distress, if it were caused, might result in illness or bodily harm."[112]

In the employment context, claims for negligent infliction of emotional distress generally involve an emotional injury to an employee based upon an alleged negligent or reckless act by his or her employer. Such claims are usually pled as alternative claims to intentional infliction of emotional distress claims. As is the case in all negligence actions, a claim for negligent or unintentional infliction of emotional distress does not require proof of intent. Courts have found that conduct that is not sufficiently "outrageous" to support a claim of intentional infliction of emotional distress may be sufficient to establish a claim for the negligent infliction of emotional distress.[113] For example, a federal district court found testimony by a plaintiff, who was terminated after eleven years of employment, that he felt "anger, depression, embarrassment, distress and shock" was sufficient to state a cause of action for negligent infliction of emotional distress because "outrageous conduct" is not a necessary element of the tort.[114] While some courts have found that employees must plead and prove either a physical injury or risk of bodily harm, at least two others have held that emotional distress without accompanying physical harm may support an actionable claim.[115]

---

112. RESTATEMENT (SECOND) OF TORTS § 306 (1977).
113. Abston v. Levi-Strauss & Co., 684 F. Supp. 152 (E.D. Tex. 1987).
114. *Id.* at 157.
115. Avallone v. Wilmington Medical Center Inc., 553 F. Supp. 931 (D. Del. 1982); Beidler v. W.R. Grace, Inc., 461 F. Supp. 1013 (E.D. Pa. 1978),

Several courts have simply refused to recognize a cause of action for negligent infliction of emotional distress holding that employers have no legal duty to refrain from negligence in discharging employees.[116] At least one court, however, has found that even where a plaintiff's wrongful discharge claim failed to state a cause of action, he could maintain a claim for negligent infliction of emotional distress based on the unreasonable nature of the employer's conduct during the termination process.[117] Although the court determined that an eleven-year employee who was dismissed for alleged misappropriation of funds could have maintained such a cause of action for negligent infliction of emotional distress based on the employer's unreasonable conduct during the termination process, the court nevertheless dismissed plaintiff's claim because he failed to allege that the employer's conduct exposed him to risk of bodily harm.

While this is an unsettled area of the law as the cases make abundantly clear, it is also a "growth" area. Employers can expect to see more and more plaintiffs incorporating a cause of action for negligent infliction of emotional distress into their complaints because of the fact that neither do they have to prove intent on the part of the employer, nor do they have to prove "outrageous" conduct, in order to recover damages.

---

aff'd mem. 609 F.2d 500 (3d Cir. 1979); Morris v. Hartford Courant Co., 200 Conn. 676, 513 A.2d 66 (1986); Jeffers v. Convoy Co., 636 F. Supp. 1337 (D. Minn. 1986) (require physical injury or risk of injury); *but see* Robards v. Gaylord Bros., 854 F.2d 1152 (9th Cir. 1988); Beasley v. Affiliated Hosp. Prods., 713 S.W.2d 557 (Mo. Ct. App. 1986) (physical harm not required).

116. Wilson v. Vlasic Foods, Inc., 116 LRRM (BNA) 2419 (C.D. Cal. 1984); Stoklosa v. Consolidated Rail Corp., 864 F.2d 425 (6th Cir. 1988).

117. Morris v. Hartford Courant Co., 200 Conn. at 676, 513 A.2d at 66.

Negligent Misrepresentation

A successful claim for negligent misrepresentation requires that an employee prove most of the essential elements of both negligence and misrepresentation. The employee, however, is not required to prove intent. The essential elements of this tort are set forth in the Restatement (Second) of Torts as follows:

> (1) One who, in the course of his business, profession or employment, or in any other transaction in which he has a pecuniary interest, supplies false information for the guidance of others in their business transactions, is subject to liability for pecuniary loss caused to them by their justifiable reliance upon the information, if he fails to exercise reasonable care or competence in obtaining or communicating the information.
>
> (2) except as stated in Subsection (3), the liability stated in Subsection (1) is limited to loss suffered:
>
> (a) by the person or one of a limited group of persons for whose benefit and guidance he intends to supply the information or knows that the recipient intends to supply it; and
>
> (b) through reliance upon it in a transaction that he intends the information to influence or knows that the recipient so intends or in a substantially similar transaction.
>
> (3) The liability of one who is under a public duty to give the information extends to loss suffered by any of the class of persons for whose benefit the duty is created, in any of the transactions in which it is intended to protect them.[118]

Requirements for stating a cause of action for negligent misrepresentation vary widely from jurisdiction to jurisdiction. Promissory statements have been held to sustain a cause of action in some states, but not in others.[119] For example, a

---

118. RESTATEMENT (SECOND) OF TORTS § 552 (1977).
119. See Price v. Mercury Supply Co., 682 S.W.2d 924 (Tenn. Ct. App. 1984) (no claim); Doody v. John Sexton & Co., 411 F.2d 1119 (1st Cir. 1969) (actionable claim); Wildes v. Pens Unlimited Co., 389 A.2d 837 (Me.

plaintiff was able to state a cause of action against the employer defendant for statements made by its president and vice president. Although the officers did not have actual authority to do so, they promised the employee lifetime employment, and the corporation was potentially liable. While many jurisdictions have held that a claim for negligent misrepresentation does not require intent, other courts have required some showing of an intent to deceive.[120] Even a representation made with the belief in its truth can constitute negligent misrepresentation if, because of a lack of reasonable care in ascertaining the facts, the representation is untrue.[121] For instance, a plaintiff was able to state a cause of action for negligent misrepresentation when he relocated to Florida to accept a new job with the employer defendant only to find that the individual who had offered him the position was no longer employed and the position was not available.

Employers can expect to see this cause of action pled in more and more complaints. The tort of negligent misrepresentation can provide a theory of recovery for employees who are unable to state a cause of action under a contractual theory, an equitable theory, or a fraud theory.[122] Once again, it is easier for a plaintiff to meet the negligence standard because he or she is not required to prove intent, which is often an insur-

---

1978); McWhorter v. First Interstate Bank of Or., N.A., 67 Or. App. 435, 678 P.2d 766 (1984) (actionable claim).

120. McAfee v. Rockford Coca-Cola Bottling Co., 40 Ill. App. 3d 521, 352 N.E.2d 50 (2d Dist. 1976) (no intent required); Rohde v. First Deposit Nat'l Bank, 127 N.H. 107, 497 A.2d 1214 (1985) (no intent required); Bubbel v. Wien Air Alaska, Inc., 682 P.2d 374 (Alaska 1984), *appeal after remand*, 723 P.2d 627 (Alaska 1986); Hudson v. Venture Indus., Inc., 243 Ga. 116, 252 S.E.2d 606 (1979) (intent required).

121. Eby v. York Div., Borg-Warner, 455 N.E.2d 623 (Ind. Ct. App. 1983).

122. D'Ulisse-Cupo v. Board of Directors of Notre Dame High School, 6 Conn. App. 153, 503 A.2d 1192 (1986), *aff'd in part, rev'd in part*, 202 Conn. 206, 520 A.2d 217 (1987).

mountable hurdle for a plaintiff in an employment case. This tort also has the potential to significantly expand the class of potential plaintiffs to include all those who were foreseeably injured by the negligent misrepresentation.[123]

Negligent Hiring and Retention

Inventive plaintiffs have breathed new life into the tort of negligent hiring and retention. While plaintiffs have always been able to recover damages from employers for the actions of their employees committed within the scope of their employment under the theory of "respondeat superior," the tort of negligent hiring and retention holds the employer liable for acts committed by his employee *outside* the scope of the employee's duties.

The elements of the tort are as follows: (1) The employer either had knowledge of the employee's lack of fitness or would have had such knowledge through reasonable investigation; (2) a person to whom the employer owes a duty suffered an injury; and (3) the employment of the unfit person was the proximate cause of the injury.[124] In a recent case, the defendant employer was found liable for the negligent hiring of a convicted sex offender with a history of assaults on young girls.[125] The defendant had given him duties that brought him in constant contact with children, which culminated in the employee repeatedly raping a ten-year-old girl. The court found that the employer knew or should have known of the employee's criminal record and was therefore liable to the victim for damages.

---

123. RESTATEMENT (SECOND) OF TORTS § 552 (1977); *see discussion in* Eby v. York Div., Borg-Warner, 455 N.E.2d at 623.
124. DiCosala v. Kay, 91 N.J. 159, 450 A.2d 508 (1982).
125. J.V. v. Victory Tabernacle Baptist Church, 236 Va. 206, 372 S.E.2d 391 (1988).

Most courts agree that an employer has a duty to use due care in the selection and retention of employees, and that the duty is owed to those third parties for whom it is foreseeable that the employees will come in contact as a result of their employment.[126]

Furthermore, when an employer is in the business of providing personal services or providing for the safety of others, that employer will be held to a higher standard of care.[127] For example, employers who provide security services, messenger services, or home maintenance services should conduct a more thorough pre-hire investigation of potential employees.

With heightened interest in the tort of negligent hiring and retention, all employers would be well advised to adopt more thorough pre-hire screening procedures to protect themselves in the event of such lawsuits. At the very least, employers should ask job applicants all questions permitted by state and federal law, verify all information received from the applicant, investigate all gaps in schooling and employment, and verify all licenses held.

Invasion of Privacy

A common law tort challenge for invasion of privacy in the employment setting can take the form of any one of four separate causes of action: (1) unreasonable intrusion upon the seclusion of another, (2) appropriation of another's name or likeness, (3) unreasonable publicity given to the other's private life, or

126. *See* Chesterman v. Barmon, 82 Or. App. 1, 727 P.2d 130 (1986), *rev granted,* 302 Or. 614, 733 P.2d 449 (1987), *aff'd en banc,* 305 Or. 439, 753 P.2d 404 (1988); Garcia v. Duffy, 492 So. 2d 435 (Fla. Dist. Ct. App. 1986); Malorney v. B & L Motor Freight, Inc., 146 Ill. App. 3d 265, 496 N.E.2d 1086 (1st Dist. 1986).

127. *See* Easley v. Apollo Detective Agency, Inc., 69 Ill. App. 3d 920, 387 N.E.2d 1241 (1st Dist. 1979).

(4) publicity that unreasonably places the other in a false light before the public.[128]

Intrusion upon Seclusion

Unreasonable intrusion upon seclusion is the invasion of privacy cause of action that is pled most frequently in employment cases. The Restatement of Torts defines actionable "intrusion upon seclusion" as: "One who intentionally intrudes, physically or otherwise, upon the solitude or seclusion of another or his private affairs or concerns, is subject to liability to the other for invasion of his privacy if the intrusion would be highly offensive to a reasonable person."[129] Private sector employers have greater latitude in this area than do public sector employers because they do not operate under the constraints on permissible searches imposed by the fourth amendment to the U.S. Constitution.

For many years, courts were reluctant to apply this tort in the employment setting. They reasoned that the action required intrusion into a private physical place, such as a home or a hotel room, and the workplace was not such a private place.

However, recent decisions have expanded the tort in workplace settings. For example, the Court of Appeals for the Eleventh Circuit recently affirmed a damage award for intrusion of an employee's psychological privacy in her workplace.[130] The plaintiff was allowed to recover damages for the employer's intrusive sexual demands and threats including inquiries into the nature of the sexual practices between the plaintiff and her spouse. In affirming the trial court's determination that the plaintiff met all requirements to prove a cause of action for

128. Restatement (Second) of Torts 262A (1977).
129. Restatement (Second) of Torts 262B (1977).
130. Philips v. Smalley Maintenance Servs., Inc., 711 F.2d 1524 (11th Cir. 1983).

invasion into privacy under state law, the court of appeals noted that it was not necessary that any information actually be acquired from the plaintiff or that any information be communicated to a third party.[131]

Courts have also held that specific areas in the workplace are protected by the tort of intrusion upon seclusion. These cases have generally involved workplace searches, and the decisions have turned on whether the plaintiff had a reasonable expectation of privacy. For example, one court affirmed a jury verdict for a private sector plaintiff whose locker and purse were searched during an investigation for missing company property.[132] On the facts of that case, the court ruled that the plaintiff had a reasonable and legitimate expectation of privacy because she had provided her own lock for the company's locker and had not been required to give the employer a duplicate key. However, the court did note that when an employee uses a company-provided lock, or the locker is unlocked, an expectation of privacy has not been created and the lockers are subject to reasonable searches.

Courts have routinely dismissed other intrusion upon seclusion claims.[133] Many of these claims, particularly in the past few years, have involved testing employees for drug use. In a recent case, the Alaska Supreme Court held that the right to privacy guaranteed in the state constitution did not prohibit a

---

131. *Id.*

132. K-Mart Corp. v. Trotti, 677 S.W.2d 632 (Tex. Ct. App. 1984), *writ of error to Tex. Sup. Ct. denied*, 686 S.W.2d 593 (1985); *See also* Bratt v. International Business Mach. Corp., 785 F.2d 352 (1st Cir. 1986); *but see* O'Conner v. Ortega, 480 U.S. 709, 107 S. Ct. 1492 (1987) (public sector desk search prohibited by the fourth amendment).

133. *See* Spencer v. General Tel. Co. of Pa., 551 F. Supp. 896 (M.D. Pa. 1982) (no cause of action where employer requested information to conduct employment-related investigation) and Gretencord v. Ford Motor Co., 538 F. Supp. 331 (D. Kan. 1982) (no cause of action based on periodic, random vehicle searches conducted on employer's property).

private sector employer from testing for off-duty drug use by oil rig drilling employees.[134] The court reasoned that the protection of the health and safety of the employees stationed on the oil rig was the paramount public policy when balanced against the individual right to privacy. In another private sector drug testing case, a Texas Court of Appeals determined that there had been no violation of the plaintiff's common law right of privacy where he had consented to the employer's drug testing program by continuing his employment relationship with the employer after the testing program was implemented.[135] Like the Alaska court, the court in Texas noted the strong state interest in eliminating drug users from the private sector workplace.[136]

In a case involving public sector employees, the Supreme Court recently ruled that no warrant was needed for drug testing of Treasury Department employees.[137] The Court balanced the government interest in maintaining a drug-free workplace against the individual right to privacy and determined that the testing program was not an unreasonable search and seizure prohibited by the fourth amendment to the U.S. Constitution. In another fourth amendment case, a federal district court ruled that a statute requiring the fingerprinting of employees who had unescorted access to nuclear power facilities was not an unreasonable search

---

134. Luedtke v. Nabors Alaska Drilling Co., 768 P.2d 1123 (Alaska 1989).
135. Texas Employment Comm'n v. Hughes Drilling Fluids, 746 S.W. 2d 796 (Tex. Ct. App. 1988).
136. *See also* Monroe v. Consolidated Freightways, 654 F. Supp. 671 (E.D. Mo. 1987) and Greco v. Halliburton Co., 674 F. Supp. 1447 (D. Wyo. 1987) (no cause of action for violation of common law right to privacy for plaintiffs' refusal to take drug tests). It remains to be seen what effect, if any, the implementation of the Drug-Free Workplace Act of 1988 (which requires private sector federal contractors to maintain a drug-free workplace) will have. *See* Pub. L. No. 100-160, Title V, Subtitle D, § 5151 *et seq.* 102 Stat. 4186 (1988).
137. National Treasury Employees Union v. Von Raab, 489 U.S. 656 (1989).

and seizure.[138] The court found that the purpose of fingerprinting employees was to verify their identities and uncover any criminal records; as such, the intrusion was minimal, reasonable, and bore a rational relationship to a legitimate government objective.

Employers can expect to see intrusion upon seclusion tort claims pled with increasing frequency in the future. However, in the case of private sector employees who, unlike workers in the public sector are not protected by the fourth amendment in the workplace, private sector employers have great latitude in this area. Private sector employers can take steps to legitimately limit their employees' reasonable expectations of privacy and avoid liability on intrusion upon seclusion tort claims. For example, employers can post signs warning employees that packages, purses, lockers, and desks are subject to periodic random searches; employers can also supply the locks and keys for these lockers and desks. Employers who institute drug testing programs can also take steps to reduce their exposure to invasion of privacy claims. Such steps should include advance notice of the testing policy, implementation of confidentiality directives, and steps to safeguard the test results.

Appropriation of Another's Name or Likeness

The Restatement defines "appropriation of another's name or likeness" as follows: "One who appropriates to his own use or benefit the name or likeness of another is subject to liability to the other for invasion of his privacy."[139]

An invasion of privacy action based on this tort is relatively rare and usually arises in connection with an employer's use of an employee's picture in company advertisements or publications.

---

138. Utility Workers v. Nuclear Regulatory Comm'n, 664 F. Supp. 136 (S.D.N.Y. 1987).
139. Restatement (Second) of Torts § 652C (1977).

In one case, the plaintiff alleged that his employer had invaded his privacy by publishing his photograph in a company magazine without his express consent.[140] The court determined, however, that the plaintiff had no cause of action for the employer's use of his photograph when the plaintiff had impliedly consented to publication of the picture and had in fact received compensation for its use.

Employers can protect themselves from lawsuits premised on this tort by obtaining releases from their employees for use of their likenesses in company publications.[141]

Unreasonable Publicity Given to Another's Private Life

The Restatement defines this tort as:

> One who gives publicity to a matter concerning the private life of another is subject to liability to the other for invasion of his privacy if the matter publicized is of a kind that (a) would be highly offensive to a reasonable person and (b) is not a legitimate concern to the public.[142]

A successful cause of action based on this tort requires that such publicity be communicated "to the public at large, or to so many persons that the matter must be regarded as substantially certain to become one of public knowledge."[143] Where employers have been able to show legitimate business reasons for dissemination of private information, plaintiffs have been unable to state a cause of action. For example, where a tape of a personal telephone conversation was disseminated to five management employees, all of whom had a job-related reason

---

140. Johnson v. Boeing Airplane Co., 175 Kan. 275, 262 P.2d 808 (1953).
141. Several states have regulated the appropriation of another's name, face or likeness by statute. *See, e.g.,* N.Y. CIV. RIGHTS LAW §50 (McKinney 1988); R.I. GEN. LAWS §9-1-28.1 (1985); VA. CODE §8.01-40 (West 1977); FLA. STAT. §540.08 (1989); CAL. CIV. CODE §3344 (West 1984).
142. RESTATEMENT (SECOND) OF TORTS § 652D (1977).
143. RESTATEMENT (SECOND) OF TORTS § 652D comment a.

to know its contents, the discharged plaintiff-employee was unable to state a cause of action.[144] In another recent case, the plaintiff admitted during a polygraph test to taking merchandise and money from her employer, as well as to using drugs and alcohol on the job.[145] When the plaintiff was terminated from her position, she filed an action for wrongful discharge and invasion of privacy. The plaintiff alleged that her employer had acted unlawfully when it communicated the reason for her termination to her spouse, to her fellow employees, and to the state employment security commission. The court, however, found that the employer had a qualified privilege to communicate the reasons for the plaintiff's termination to these parties, and thus, the communication was not actionable. In reaching this decision, the court took note that the state recognized a qualified privilege when a communication is made in good faith, and on a subject matter in which the person making it has an interest (if made to a person or persons having a corresponding interest or duty), as well as a privilege when communicating with the state employment security commission unless the communication is false in fact and maliciously made for the purpose of denying benefits.

In another case, where an employee had been terminated after violating a company policy prohibiting the discussion of confidential company business with noncompany personnel, the court also found that the employer had a qualified privilege to communicate this information to remaining employ-

---

144. Beard v. Akzona Inc., 517 F. Supp. 128 (E.D. Tenn. 1981).

145. Gordon v. Tenneco Retail Serv. Co., 666 F. Supp. 908 (N.D. Miss. 1987); *See also* Garziano v. Dupont de Nemours & Co., 818 F.2d 380 (5th Cir. 1987) (employer had qualified privilege to communicate to other employees that plaintiff had been terminated for violation of its sexual harassment policy); Trought v. Richardson, et al., 78 N.C. App. 758, 338 S.E.2d 617 (1986), *rev. denied* Trought v. Richardson, 316 N.C. 557, 344 S.E.2d 18 (1986) (employer had qualified privilege to communicate to other employees that plaintiff had been terminated for her "lack of credibility").

ees.[146] In granting summary judgment to the employer on all claims, the court reasoned that the employer had a legitimate interest in stressing to employees the importance of complying with their agreement to maintain confidentiality and found that the employer had not acted in bad faith so as to lose its qualified privilege.

Employers have the same qualified privilege in cases based on this tort as they do in defamation cases. Thus, an employer who acts in good faith, communicates the truth, and limits the communication to those with a legitimate reason to know, should be able to successfully defend against this tort action.

Publicity Unreasonably Placing Another in a False Light Before the Public

The Restatement of Torts defines this tort as:

> One who gives publicity to a matter concerning another that places the other before the public in a false light is subject to liability to the other for invasion of his privacy, if (a) the false light in which the other was placed would be highly offensive to a reasonable person, and (b) the actor had knowledge of or acted in reckless disregard as to the falsity of the publicized matter and the false light in which the other would be placed.[147]

In cases where plaintiff-employees allege a cause of action based on this tort, employers again can raise the qualified privilege defense. In one recent case, the plaintiff alleged that the employer's action in suspending him for possible violation of the company conflict-of-interest policy on the same day and under the same circumstances as several other employees who were later indicted for criminal activity involving kickback schemes unreasonably placed him in a false light.[148] However,

146. Arnold v. Diet Center, Inc., 113 Idaho at 581, 746 P.2d at 1040.
147. Restatement (Second) of Torts § 652E (1977).
148. Rouly v. Enserch Corp., 835 F.2d at 1127.

the court determined that it was not unreasonable for the employer to have acted as it did; since the employer was protecting important interests by terminating all of these employees, there were practical considerations for terminating all of the employees on the same day, and the employer could present a strong posture to the remaining employees. The court granted summary judgment for the defendant.

In another recent case, a state court of appeals reversed summary judgment by the trial court on several claims including an invasion of privacy claim.[149] The plaintiff had been terminated based on facts uncovered by a private investigator who was investigating the validity of the plaintiff's workers' compensation claim. Although the plaintiff had been reinstated by an arbitrator, he was subsequently convicted of perjury when the employer turned over the investigator's films of the plaintiff to the district attorney's office. The plaintiff then instituted a civil suit alleging, among other causes of action, invasion of privacy by being unreasonably placed in a false light by his employer. In reversing the lower court, the appellate court found that the editing of the film by the investigator could have inaccurately portrayed the plaintiff's physical condition and, thus, unreasonably have placed him in a false light. The case was remanded to the lower court for trial. It remains to be seen whether the plaintiff can actually prove his case.

As noted, employers also have a qualified privilege in cases based on this tort. Thus, as in tort cases alleging "unreasonable publicity given to another's private life," employers can protect this qualified privilege by asserting a legitimate business reason for the communication, by acting in good faith, by communicating the truth, and by limiting the communication to those with a legitimate reason to know.

149. Allen v. Bethlehem Steel Corp., 76 Md. App. 642, 547 A.2d 1105 (1988), *cert. denied*, 314 Md. 458, 550 A.2d 1168 (1988).

Fraudulent Misrepresentation

In today's competitive business environment, employers often paint a rosy picture of corporate life at their companies in order to attract the best employees. When corporate fortunes take a turn for the worse, however, the old rule of "caveat emptor"[150] often gives way to a new rule: a tort claim for fraudulent misrepresentation.

Fraudulent misrepresentation (also known as deceit) is defined in the Restatement (Second) of Torts as:

> One who fraudulently makes a misrepresentation of fact, opinion, intention or law for the purpose of inducing another to act or to refrain from action in reliance upon it, is subject to liability to the other in deceit for pecuniary loss caused to him by his justifiable reliance upon the misrepresentation.[151]

The elements of proof for fraudulent misrepresentation include: (1) a material misrepresentation of an existing fact; (2) falsity; (3) knowledge of the falsity; (4) deception; and (5) an identifiable injury.[152] An action for fraudulent misrepresentation is a cause of action that may be pled in addition to, or as an alternative to, an action for breach of contract.[153] However, this claim does not depend upon a contractual agreement between the parties; rather, it consists of deliberate intentional misrepresentations of facts that are relied upon by the plaintiff to his or her detriment.

For example, the plaintiff in a recent case was induced to change his mind (after accepting a position with a competitor)

---

150. "Let the buyer beware."
151. RESTATEMENT (SECOND) OF TORTS § 525 (1977).
152. Channel Master Corp. v. Aluminum Ltd. Sales, Inc., 76 N.Y.S.2d 259, 151 N.E.2d 833 (1958).
153. *See* Shaitelman v. Phoenix Mut. Life Ins. Co., 517 F. Supp. 21 (S.D.N.Y. 1980); DuSesoi v. United Ref. Co., 540 F. Supp. 1260 (W.D. Pa. 1982); Brudnicki v. General Elec. Co., 535 F. Supp. 84 (N.D. Ill. 1982). *But see* Dalton v. Union Bank of Switz., 520 N.Y.S.2d 764 (1987).

and remain with the defendant employer.[154] At the time the employer convinced him to stay, it was already conducting a search for his replacement and actually wanted him on board only until a replacement could be hired. The court had little difficulty in determining that the plaintiff stated a cause of action for fraudulent misrepresentation.

In another recent action, the court found that a plaintiff who had relocated upon receiving assurances that the defendant employer was profitable (when in fact the company had lost money for two straight years), stated a cause of action for fraudulent misrepresentation when he was laid off seven months later.[155] The court stated that Ohio law imposed a duty on the defendant employer to make full disclosure of all the facts when such disclosure was necessary to correct the misleading impression that might have been created by the defendant's partial revelation of facts, i.e., that the company was profitable during the accounting period that the plaintiff was actually interviewed.

Whether the underlying agreement itself is enforceable, one who fraudulently represents himself as intending to perform the agreement may be liable for damages in tort for fraudulent misrepresentation.[156] For instance, the plaintiff in a recent case was able to state a cause of action for fraudulent misrepresentation under applicable law when the defendant employer agreed to pay his relocation expenses, including purchasing his home in the event he failed to sell it himself, and then terminated him when he asked the defendant to purchase the unsold home two months later.[157]

However, under traditional fraud principles, a plaintiff usually cannot recover based on a defendant's misrepresentations

---

154. Shebar v. Sanyo Business Sys., 526 A.2d at 1144.
155. Harlan v. Intergy, Inc., 721 F. Supp. 148 (N.D. Ohio 1989).
156. *See* Shaitelman v. Phoenix Mut. Life Ins. Co., 517 F. Supp. at 21; Doody v. John Sexton & Co., 411 F.2d 1119 (1st Cir. 1969).
157. Palmer v. Beverly Enters. 823 F.2d 1105 (7th Cir. 1987).

of future conditions. Accordingly, the tort of fraudulent misrepresentation has had limited application in the employment setting.[158] Courts have dismissed claims in which the employee alleges that an employer promised employment on a permanent basis, guaranteed a position for a specific period of time, promised specific promotions and salary levels in the future, or failed to disclose the upcoming sale of the company.[159] Courts have similarly rejected claims of fraudulent misrepresentation in the face of an unambiguous disclaimer preserving the employment-at-will relationship.[160]

At the same time, other courts have allowed such claims to stand by focusing not on the future nature of the promises made, but rather on the actual intent of the defendant at the time the promises were made.[161] For example, courts have

---

158. However, see discussion of the tort of negligent misrepresentation elsewhere in this chapter.

159. Silver v. N.L. Indus., 118 LRRM (BNA) 2695, 1985 WL 241 (S.D.N.Y. 1985); Anselmo v. Manufacturers Life Ins. Co., 595 F. Supp. 541 (W.D. Mo. 1984), *aff'd,* 771 F.2d 417 (8th Cir. 1985); Payne v. AHFI/Neth. B.V., 522 F. Supp. 18 (N.D. Ill. 1980); Pfeifer v. U.S. Shoe Corp., 676 F. Supp. 969 (C.D. Cal. 1987); Stowman v. Carlson Cos., 430 N.W.2d 490 (Minn. Ct. App. 1988).

160. For example, Sears Roebuck & Company has used an employment application which provides:

> [M]y employment and compensation can be terminated with or without cause, and with or without notice, at any time, at the option of either the company or myself. I understand that no store manager or representative of Sears, Roebuck & Co., other than the President or Vice President of the company, has any authority to enter into any agreement for employment for any specified period of time, or make any agreement contrary to the foregoing.

See Batchelor v. Sears, Roebuck & Co., 495 F. Supp. at 344; Eliel v. Sears, Roebuck & Co., 150 Mich. App. 137, 387 N.W.2d 842 (1985); Reid v. Sears, Roebuck & Co. 790 F.2d 453 (6th Cir. 1986); MacDougal v. Sears Roebuck & Co., 624 F. Supp. 756 (E.D. Tenn. 1985). *See also* Deschler v. Brown & Williamson Tobacco Co., 797 F.2d 695 (8th Cir. 1986).

161. Forstmann v. Culp, 648 F. Supp. 1379 (M.D.N.C. 1986).

found allegations sufficient to state a cause of action in the following circumstances: (1) where an employee closed his business in reliance on the defendant's promise of future employment and the defendant had no present intention to employ the employee and (2) where a defendant promised to employ an employee for a minimum of three years even though the defendant had actual present knowledge that the position would be eliminated in less than three years.[162]

As the foregoing demonstrates, employers must become cognizant of the fact that written and oral statements made to their employees, or prospective employees, may come back to haunt them. Prudent employers will limit the number of corporate officials who may speak for the company, scrutinize and revise all written communications to employees and prospective employees, incorporate a written disclaimer signed by all applicants into their employment application, and avoid making promises they cannot keep.[163]

---

162. Bondi v. Jewels by Edward, Ltd., 267 Cal. App. 2d 672, 73 Cal. Rptr. 494 (2d Dist. 1968); DuScsoi v. United Ref. Co., 540 F. Supp. at 1260. *See also* Sea-Land Serv., Inc. v. O'Neal; 224 Va. 343, 297 S.E.2d 647 (1982); Shaitelman v. Phoenix Mut. Life Ins. Co., 517 F. Supp. at 21. Brudnicki v. General Elec. Co., 535 F. Supp. 84 (N.D. Ill. 1982); Brooks v. Trans World Airlines, 574 F. Supp. 805 (D. Colo. 1983). In instances where employees are unable to show intent on the part of the defendant, they may still be able to establish a cause of action for negligent misrepresentation as discussed elsewhere in this chapter. See *supra* notes 120, 121 and accompanying text.

163. An example of a written disclaimer in an employment application would be as follows:

> I understand that my employment with ABC Company is at-will and can be terminated at anytime at the option of either the Company or myself. I have not received any oral promises or assurances regarding the terms and conditions of my employment with ABC Company and understand that no one, other than the President or Vice President of ABC Company has the authority to change my status from that of an at-will-employee.

False Imprisonment, Assault and Battery

Routine security checks and performance reviews have recently fueled an accelerating number of false imprisonment and assault and battery claims against employers.

To establish false imprisonment, a plaintiff must show that: (1) the defendant intended to confine him; (2) the plaintiff was conscious of the confinement; (3) the plaintiff did not consent to the confinement; and (4) the confinement was not otherwise privileged.[164] Confinement may be effected by words alone, by acts alone, or by both.[165] There is no imprisonment if there is a known, safe means of escape involving only a slight inconvenience.[166] Thus, one court rejected the plaintiff's claim where the only confinement was a threat to remove him from the premises and plaintiff could have escaped by simply leaving the building.[167]

The fear of discharge or other adverse employment action is insufficient to constitute the detaining force necessary to establish false imprisonment.[168] Thus, an employer was entitled to detain an employee to investigate allegations of sexual assault made by another employee against that employee.[169] Also, "moral pressure, as where the plaintiff remains to clear himself of suspicion of theft, . . ., is not enough. . . ."[170] Nonethe-

164. Broughton v. State, 37 N.Y.2d 451, 456, 335 N.E.2d 310, 314, *cert. denied,* 423 U.S. 929 (1975).

165. Marcus v. Liebman, 59 Ill. App. 3d 337, 375 N.E.2d 486 (1st Dist. 1978); Munsell v. Ideal Food Stores, 208 Kan. 909, 494 P.2d 1063 (1972).

166. Chicarelli v. Plymouth Garden Apartments, 551 F. Supp. 532 (E.D. Pa. 1982).

167. Krochalis v. Insurance Co. of N. Am., 629 F. Supp. 1360 (E.D. Pa. 1985).

168. Malanga v. Sears, Roebuck & Co., 487 N.Y.S.2d 194, 109 A.2d 1054 (N.Y. App. Div. 1985); Foley v. Polaroid Corp., 400 Mass. 82, 508 N.E.2d 72 (1987).

169. Malanga v. Sears, Roebuck & Co., 487 N.Y.S.2d at 194, 109 A.2d at 1054, and Foley v. Polaroid Corp. 400 Mass. at 82, N.E.2d at 72.

170. Lopez v. Winchell's Donut House, 126 Ill. App. 3d 46, 466 N.E.2d 1309,

less, threats of discharge, together with other conduct that creates an atmosphere conducive to a threat of physical confrontation could satisfy the confinement requirement.[171] An employer should never attempt to physically force an employee to remain on the premises. Appropriate disciplinary action may always be taken if an employee refuses a request to stay (e.g., termination for insubordination or refusal to cooperate with an investigation).

Employers should note that even if a plaintiff was sufficiently confined so as to constitute a false imprisonment, a corporate employer can be liable for the acts of its employees only if those acts were within the scope of the employee's employment. A plaintiff may sue the imprisoning employee or, because of the employee's relative insolvency, the plaintiff may sue the employer. When sued for false imprisonment, as with any intentional tort, an employer might be able to claim that the employee acted outside the scope of his employment or to further his or her own interests. However, an employer is more likely to be held responsible for false imprisonment than other torts because the acting employee is more apt to be within the scope of his employment or to be furthering the employer's interest when imprisoning the plaintiff, whether it be during an investigatory interview[172] or while apprehending a shoplifter.[173]

Even if an acting employee is within the scope of his or her employment and furthering the employer's interests when falsely imprisoning the plaintiff, the employer may still assert any applicable defenses. Consent is one defense available to

---

1311 (1st Dist. 1984) (*quoting* W. PROSSER, THE LAW OF TORTS ¶ 11, at 45 (4th ed. 1971)).

171. Foley v. Polaroid Corp. 400 Mass. at 82, N.E.2d at 72.

172. *Id.*

173. Adams v. Zayre Corp., 148 Ill. App. 3d 704, 499 N.E.2d 678 (1st Dist. 1986).

employers. A plaintiff's consent to confinement vitiates any false imprisonment claim.[174] Similarly, many states authorize any merchant who has reasonable grounds to believe that a person has committed retail theft to detain such person in a reasonable manner and for a reasonable length of time.[175] Even absent such a statute, some states recognize an employer's right to confine an employee in a reasonable manner and for a reasonable time to investigate allegations of wrongdoing.[176]

If an employee establishes the elements necessary for a false imprisonment claim and no defenses are available to the employer, the employee is entitled to damages. Recoverable damages for false imprisonment include compensation for interruption of business, humiliation, harm to one's reputation or credit, loss of the company of one's family, and the expense of securing release from confinement, in addition to damages for physical and mental suffering.[177] Punitive damages may be awarded when the arrest is effected recklessly, oppressively, insultingly, or willfully and maliciously with a design to oppress and injure.[178] One court awarded punitive damages under this standard when the security guard grabbed the plaintiff tightly by the upper arm and continued to hold her tightly after he had been shown a sales receipt and a sales clerk verified that the plaintiff purchased the merchandise in ques-

174. Lopez v. Winchell's Donut House, 126 Ill. App. 3d at 46.

175. *See e.g.,* ILL. REV. STAT., ch. 38 ¶ 16 A.5 (1988 West Supp.); MASS. GEN. LAWS ANN. ch. 231 § 94B (West 1984) as amended by St. 1985, C.347 §2; N.M. STAT. ANN. § 30-16-23 (1988).

176. Proulx v. Pinkerton's Nat'l Detective Agency, 343 Mass. 390, 178 N.E.2d 575 (1961).

177. Karfunkel v. Compagnie Nationale Air France, 427 F. Supp. 971 (S.D.N.Y. 1977); Shelton v. Barry, 328 Ill. App. 497, 66 N.E.2d 697 (1st Dist. 1946).

178. Kajtazi v. Kajtazi, 488 F. Supp. 15 (S.D.N.Y. 1978); Robinson v. Wieboldt Stores, Inc., 104 Ill. App. 3d 1021, 433 N.E.2d 1005 (1st Dist. 1982).

tion.[179] This court rejected the employer's argument that punitive damages should not be awarded against a corporate defendant for acts committed by its employees. The court noted that punitive damages may be awarded against an employer for its employee's acts when it ratifies or approves the acts of its agents and, in that case, the employer had defended the guard throughout the course of the litigation and had made no attempt to alter its procedures with respect to situations such as the one encountered by the plaintiff.[180]

Considering the possible liability the employer might have in an action based upon the tort of the false imprisonment, employers would be well advised to instruct their supervisory personnel to avoid obstructing the movements of employees. They should allow an employee to exit the premises and then take appropriate personnel action against the individual. If an employee is detained for investigation, ensure that the detention is performed civilly, for a reasonable period of time, and that the suspected individual is released promptly upon completion of the investigation.

Assault and Battery

Claims for assault and battery can arise in connection with many different kinds of incidents in the employment relationship, such as sexual harassment, an internal investigation, or a confrontation between an employee and a supervisor. A plaintiff may maintain an action for assault where there is a serious threat to his or her person that places one in apprehension of immediate harm.[181] A claim for battery is established when

179. Kajtazi v. Kajtazi, 488 F. Supp. at 15, and Robinson v. Wieboldt Stores, Inc., 104 Ill. App. 3d at 1021, 433 N.E.2d at 1005.

180. *Id.*

181. Di Gilio v. William J. Burns Detective Agency, 359 N.Y.S.2d 688, 46 A.2d 650 (N.Y. App. Div. 1974); Cucinotti v. Ortmann, 399 Pa. 26, 159 A.2d 216 (1960).

the employer intentionally subjects the plaintiff to harmful or offensive touching that actually and proximately causes the plaintiff injury.[182]

For example, an assault claim was established where an employee was placed in apprehension of immediate harm because an investigator revealed a firearm during a security investigation.[183] However, when a supervisor threatened over the telephone to have security guards bring the plaintiff to his office, but was in no position to immediately enforce the threat and took no action to do so, the plaintiff's assault action was dismissed.[184]

Several courts have awarded an employee damages for battery after the employee was victimized by unwanted, sexually offensive touching.[185] These courts have noted, however, that an employer may be held liable for an employee's intentional torts only when such acts are committed in the course of, and in furtherance of, the employer's business.[186] In one case, an employee's sexual indiscretions were held to have been committed for his own enjoyment and not in furtherance of his employer's business, so that the plaintiff's claim against the employer failed.[187] The court noted that force was not a requirement of the employee's job, nor did the employer authorize its employee to sexually assault another. As noted earlier, however, an employer could be liable for its employees' acts if it ratifies or approves of the acts.[188]

---

182. People v. Martinez, 3 Cal. App. 3d 886, 83 Cal. Rptr. 914 (1970).
183. Leahy v. Federal Express Corp., 609 F. Supp. 668 (E.D.N.Y. 1985).
184. Krochalis v. Insurance Co. of N. Am., 629 F. Supp. at 1360.
185. Priest v. Rotary, 634 F. Supp. at 571 (N.D. Cal. 1986).
186. *Id;* Tierra Drilling Corp. v. Detmar, 666 S.W.2d 661 (Tex. App. 1984). An employer's liability may also be predicated on a negligent failure to supervise if that failure results in injury. Rubin v. Yellow Cab Co., 154 Ill. App. 3d 336, 507 N.E.2d 114 (1st Dist. 1987).
187. Valdez v. Church's Fried Chicken, Inc., 683 F. Supp. 596 (W.D. Tex. 1988).
188. *Id.*

Self-defense is a defense available to an employer defending an assault and/or battery claim.[189] If the alleged perpetrator reasonably perceived that he was in danger of immediate bodily harm and used reasonable force to resist the attack, the defense may apply.[190]

If successful on an assault and/or battery claim, an employee may receive compensatory and punitive damages. Compensatory damages include lost earnings, pain, suffering, sleeplessness, and mental anguish.[191] Punitive damages are awardable only when the assault or battery was willful, malicious, and in wanton disregard of the plaintiff's rights.[192] Thus, a Texas court awarded punitive damages where the plaintiff's supervisor exercised his position of authority to solicit sex from an employee, and in wanton disregard of the employee's legal rights, including attempted rape.[193]

Finally, the same conduct could give rise to a false imprisonment and an assault claim. For example, if an employee prematurely attempts to terminate a disciplinary meeting by leaving the supervisor's office but is prevented from leaving either because the supervisor physically blocks the employee's only reasonable exit or verbally threatens to physically assault the employee if he leaves, an action may lie for both false imprisonment and assault. It should also be noted that if the employee in the above scenario physically removes the supervisor from his path, the supervisor may have a counterclaim for battery against the employee.

---

189. W. PROSSER, THE LAW OF TORTS ¶19 at 108 (4th ed. 1971).
190. *Id.*
191. *Id.;* Kren v. Payne, 81 Ill. App. 3d 283, 401 N.E.2d 19 (4th Dist. 1980).
192. Lancy v. Rosenberg, 316 Ill. App. 452, 45 N.E.2d 187 (1st Dist. 1942); Bennett v. Howard, 141 Tex. 101, 170 S.W.2d 709 (1943).
193. Valdez v. Church's Fried Chicken, Inc., 683 F. Supp. at 596.

Loss of Consortium

Loss of consortium is a common law cause of action based on an injury to the spousal relationship. It is a derivative, or collateral, claim that requires liability on another underlying cause of action. In other words, it is generally added to other torts by the spouse of the allegedly injured person as a means of obtaining additional damages.[194]

The elements of the tort are: (1) the allegedly injured person must be entitled to recovery before the deprived spouse can recover for injury to his or her consortium and (2) the deprived spouse must establish a legal marriage to the impaired spouse at the time the alleged injury occurred.[195] Consortium is generally defined to include more than material services; it also includes elements of guidance, companionship, felicity, love, affection, and sexual relations.[196]

Generally, an action for loss of consortium requires some underlying *physical* injury to the impaired spouse.[197] However, as wrongful discharge tort claims against employers become more frequent, claims by spouses for loss of consortium caused by the claimed injuries to these terminated employees also increase. In several jurisdictions, courts have allowed such actions premised on the spouse's wrongful discharge tort claims.[198] For example, the U.S. Court of Appeals for the Sixth Circuit recently affirmed a damage award

---

194. Jarvis v. Stone, 517 F. Supp. 1173 (N.D. Ill. 1981); Agis v. Howard Johnson Co., 371 Mass. at 140, 355 N.E.2d at 315.
195. Sostock v. Reiss, 92 Ill. App. 3d 200, 415 N.E.2d 1094 (1st Dist. 1980).
196. Shreve v. Faris, 144 W. Va. 819, 111 S.E.2d 169 (1959); Agis v. Howard Johnson Co., 371 Mass. at 140, 355 N.E.2d at 315; Johanek v. Ringsby Truck Lines, Inc., 157 Ill. App. 3d 140, 509 N.E.2d 1295 (1st Dist. 1987).
197. Slovensky v. Birmingham News Co., 358 So. 2d 474 (Ala. App. 1978); *but see* Bowersox v. P.H. Glatfelter Co., 677 F. Supp. 307 (M.D. Pa. 1988).
198. Agis v. Howard Johnson Co., 371 Mass. at 140, 355 N.E.2d at 315; Hoke v. Paul, 65 Haw. 478, 653 P.2d 1155 (1982).

for loss of consortium premised on a successful claim for the intentional infliction of emotional distress.[199] The plaintiff had been employed by the defendant for several years when his wife began to receive obscene telephone calls at home. The couple was unable to discover the identity of the caller until the plaintiff's wife recognized the voice of another employee of the defendant as the obscene caller. When the plaintiff brought this information to the attention of the defendant's president, the president terminated the plaintiff's employment. A short time later, the defendant's president admitted to plaintiff that the accused employee was indeed responsible for the obscene calls and offered plaintiff reemployment on the condition that he apologize to the accused, work directly under the accused's supervision, and attend church services with the accused. Under these circumstances, the plaintiff recovered a substantial award on his claim for intentional infliction of emotional distress, and his wife was awarded ancillary damages on her claim for loss of consortium.

In some cases, where the employees' tort claims have been dismissed, courts have refused to allow a loss of consortium claim by the employee's spouse to stand.[200] In addition, courts have not allowed this cause of action to be premised on employment claims based on a contractual breach. Furthermore, the courts have generally refused to allow claims for loss of consortium in contract claims alleging violations of federal and state civil rights statutes.[201] One federal court, however, did allow a pendent state claim for loss of consortium in a Title VII case.[202] In that case, the court determined that the plaintiff's

199. Platt v. Brown Mach. Co., 855 F.2d 1225 (6th Cir. 1988).
200. Covert v. Allen Group, Inc., 597 F. Supp. 1268 (Colo. 1984); Slovensky v. Birmingham News Co., 358 S. 2d at 474.
201. Fritts v. Niehouse, 604 F. Supp. 823 (W.D. Mo. 1984), *aff'd*, 774 F.2d 1170 (8th Cir. 1985); Tauriac v. Polaroid Corp., 716 F. Supp. 672 (D. Mass. 1989).
202. Bowersox v. P.H. Glatfelter Co., 677 F. Supp. at 307.

supervisor's actions following the plaintiff's rejection of the supervisor's advances were sufficient to support her claims. The supervisor had forbidden the plaintiff to answer the telephone or to talk with anyone in the office, and had threatened her with suspension if she reported his conduct to anyone. The court rejected the premise the plaintiff must suffer a disabling physical injury to support her spouse's claim for loss of consortium and allowed the claim as ancillary to the plaintiff's claim for intentional infliction of emotional distress. It is noted that at least one state court has recently allowed damages for the loss of consortium in a sexual harassment claim under state civil rights act.[203] There the Michigan Supreme Court found that the state civil rights act, which provides for relief over and above actual damages, did not preclude a claim for loss of consortium, and affirmed the lower court's damages award.

Employers can expect to see more and more complaints that allege a cause of action for loss of consortium in addition to other tort and contract claims in the employment arena in view of the fact that such a claim derives from the same facts and circumstances that give rise to the underlying causes of action and the claim, if successful, provides for damages to the injured spouse separate and apart from damages recoverable by the plaintiff.

Conclusion

By understanding the circumstances under which certain tort claims are likely to arise in the employment context, employers can avoid the pitfalls that have caused others needless expense and inconvenience. An awareness of the essential elements of such claims and the available defenses will only become more important as the prevalence of related tort claims in wrongful discharge cases increases.

203. Eide v. Kelsey-Hayes Co., 431 Mich. 26, 427 N.W.2d 488. (1988).

CHAPTER FIVE

Defenses

Federal Preemption

The area of employment and labor relations has long been the subject of extensive federal legislation.[1] Because of pervasive federal legislation in the area, a plaintiff's wrongful or retaliatory discharge claims, or related state law tort claims, will occasionally involve issues that implicate applicable federal legislation. In such cases, the defendant may want to consider asserting the doctrine of federal preemption.

Arguing that the plaintiff's claim is preempted offers several advantages. The employer may remove the claim to federal court and might be able to assert additional procedural or statutory defenses not available at common law.

The doctrine of federal preemption essentially provides that when the federal government has acted within its constitutional authority, federal law will preempt, or take precedence over, state law governing the same subject matter.[2] Almost any

1. *See* Allis-Chalmers Corp. v. Lueck, 471 U.S. 202, 208 (1985).
2. New York v. F.C.C., 486 U.S. 57, 108 S. Ct. 449, 100 L. Ed. 2d 48, 56–57 (1988). *See also* U.S. CONST. art. VI, § 2. In general, federal law preempts state law under three circumstances. First, federal law preempts state law where Congress expressly stated its intent, and/or the extent to which it intends, to preempt state law. Second, even in the absence of express language regarding preemption, federal law will nonetheless preempt

federal statute that indicates Congress's intent to occupy an entire field of law, or that restricts state court jurisdiction with respect to a certain subject, may be used to invoke a preemption defense.[3] However, the issue of preemption in the employment litigation context arises with sufficient frequency in connection with three particular statutes to warrant more detailed consideration: (1) the National Labor Relations Act (NLRA); (2) Section 301 of the Labor Management Relations Act (Section 301); and (3) the Employee Retirement and Income Security Act of 1974 (ERISA).

NLRA Preemption

The issue of NLRA preemption will generally arise in two situations: (1) where the plaintiff alleges that he has been discharged in retaliation for activity that is protected by Section 7 of the NLRA and (2) where the defendant's alleged misconduct arises in the course of collective bargaining negotiations

state law, where Congress has indicated its intent to occupy an entire field by enacting such a comprehensive legislative and regulatory scheme that there is no room for the state to supplement federal law. Finally, federal law preempts state law to the extent that it actually conflicts with federal law. Such a conflict arises when compliance with both federal and state law is impossible or when state law stands as an obstacle to the accomplishment and execution of the full purposes or objectives of the federal legislation. Michigan Canners & Freezers Ass'n v. Agriculture Mktg. & Bargaining Bd. 467 U.S. 461, 469 (1984); Capital Cities Cable, Inc. v. Crisp, 467 U.S. 691, 698–99 (1984). In most cases, issue of whether there is an actual conflict arises because the state law allegedly stands as an obstacle to the execution of federal legislative objectives. *See, e.g.,* Allis-Chalmers Corp. v. Lueck, 471 U.S. at 209–11.

3. *See, e.g.,* French v. Pan Am Express, Inc., 869 F.2d 1 (1st Cir. 1989) (pilot's state law for wrongful discharge, based upon refusal to take urinalysis test which did not comply with state statute, preempted where pervasive legislative and regulatory scheme set forth in Federal Aviation Act indicates Congressional intent to occupy the field of air safety).

and runs afoul of the prohibition in Section 8 against bargaining in bad faith.

When a plaintiff bases his claim on conduct that is arguably prohibited or arguably protected by the NLRA, his state law claim is preempted under the principles set forth by the Supreme Court in *San Diego Building Trades v. Garmon.*[4] In *Garmon,* the Supreme Court declared that, if the plaintiff's state law claim is based on conduct that "arguably amounts" to an unfair labor practice, the court must defer to the National Labor Relations Board's (the Board) exclusive jurisdiction to resolve unfair labor practice claims in order to avoid a possible conflict between state law and national labor policy.[5]

In the proper case, the threshold showing required to assert the defense of NLRA preemption is comparatively slight. A defendant need only demonstrate that the plaintiff's state law claim alleges misconduct that arguably amounts to an unfair labor practice "under an interpretation of the [NLRA] that has not been authoritatively rejected by the courts or the Board."[6] Thus, it is not necessary that the Board or the courts have actually held that the alleged misconduct is an unfair labor practice. Rather, the key inquiry is whether the "controversy raised by the state law claim is identical to that which *could have been* presented to the [Board]."[7]

Applying these principles to the first situation—reprisals for activities arguably protected by Section 7—the courts have consistently held that state law retaliatory discharge and related tort claims brought by an employee alleging discharge in reprisal for organizing or other union activities fall within the

4. San Diego Bldg. Trades v. Garmon, 359 U.S. 236, 245 (1959).
5. *Id.;* Int'l Longshoreman's Ass'n v. Davis, 476 U.S. 380, 391–92 (1986).
6. Int'l Longshoreman's Ass'n v. Davis, 476 U.S. at 395; Marine Eng'rs v. Interlake S.S. Co., 370 U.S. 173, 184 (1962).
7. Kolentus v. Avco Indus. Inc., 798 F.2d 949, 961 (7th Cir. 1986) (emphasis supplied), *cert. denied,* 479 U.S. 1032 (1987).

exclusive jurisdiction of the Board and are therefore preempted.[8] However, organizing and collective bargaining activities are not the only activities protected by Section 7 of the NLRA.

Section 7 also protects "other concerted activities for the purpose of . . . mutual aid and protection" from employer interference or reprisal.[9] Although the use of NLRA preemption as a defense to claims based on concerted activities for mutual aid and protection—other than organizing and bargaining activity—has not been tested in the courts, there is no reason why, under the proper factual circumstances, an NLRA preemption defense would not prevail in such a case. In theory at least, a state law claim that an employee or employees were discharged for conduct that "arguably" amounted to concerted activity for mutual aid and protection—such as complaints regarding unsafe working conditions or unlawful employment practices—would be preempted by Section 7.

The success or failure of an NLRA preemption defense in such a case would depend on the employer's ability to establish that the employee's conduct meets, at least arguably, the definition of concerted activity established by the Board in *Meyers Industries, Inc.*[10] In *Meyers,* the Board established a much narrower definition of what constitutes concerted activity

8. *See, e.g.,* Viestenz v. Fleming Cos., 681 F.2d 699 (10th Cir.), *cert. denied,* 459 U.S. 972 (1982); Morris v. Chemlawn Corp., 541 F. Supp. 479 (E.D. Mich. 1982).

9. 29 U.S.C. §§ 157, 158(a)(1). Moreover, employees need not be represented by a union or covered by a collective bargaining agreement to have their activity protected by Section 7. See NLRB v. Washington Aluminum Co., 370 U.S. 9 (1962) (walk-out by unrepresented employees to protest working conditions is protected under Section 7).

10. Meyers Indus., Inc. v. NLRB, 268 NLRB 493 (1984), *aff'd after remand,* 835 F.2d 1481 (1987), *cert. denied,* 487 U.S. 2847, 108 S. Ct. 2847, 101 L. Ed. 2d 884 (1988). *See* International Longshoremen's Ass'n v. Davis, 476 U.S. 380, 395 (1986).

within Section 7 than it had used previously.[11] Under *Meyers*, an employee's activity will only be considered "concerted" if it was "engaged in with or on behalf of other employees, and not solely on behalf of the employee himself."[12]

The second situation in which the issue of NLRA preemption typically arises is in cases alleging employer misconduct in the course of collective bargaining negotiations. The courts have routinely held that NLRA preemption applies in such cases because they are based on conduct that is arguably prohibited by Section 8(d) of the NLRA, which requires the employer to bargain in good faith and Section 8(a)(5), which makes it an unfair labor practice for an employer to refuse to do so.[13]

---

11. *Compare* Meyers Indus., Inc. v. NLRB, 268 NLRB at 497 *with* Alleluia Cushion Co. v. NLRB, 221 NLRB 999, 1000 (1975) (single employee's activity is concerted if actions are a matter of concern to employees generally or would be likely to benefit other employees).
12. Meyers Indus., Inc. v. NLRB, 268 NLRB at 497. Pursuant to the Board's *Interboro* doctrine, a single employee's activity may also be considered "concerted" if he is seeking to enforce a right guaranteed, or an obligation imposed, by the applicable collective bargaining agreement—e.g., the right to refuse an unsafe or illegal work assignment. In such a case, the employee's individual activity takes place "within the framework of the contract and thus constitute[s] concerted activity which is protected by Section 7 of the Act." Interboro Contractors, Inc. v. NLRB, 157 NLRB 1295, 1298 (1968), *enf'd*, 388 F.2d 495 (2d Cir. 1967). The Board expressly distinguished *Interboro*, in *Meyers*, and the Supreme Court subsequently upheld the Board's application of the *Interboro* doctrine in NLRB v. City Disposal Sys., Inc., 465 U.S. 822 (1984). Of course, a case involving NLRA preemption under the *Interboro* doctrine would almost certainly be preempted under Section 301 of the LMRA as requiring interpretation of the applicable collective bargaining agreement. See pp. 107–12 *infra*.
13. 29 U.S.C. §§ 158 (a)(5), 158(d). *See, e.g.*, Kolentus v. Avco Indus., Inc., 798 F.2d at 961 (fraud claim alleging misrepresentations and material nondisclosures during contract negotiations); Lumber Prod. Indus. Workers, Local 1054 v. West Coast Indus. Relations Ass'n, 775 F.2d 1042 (9th Cir. 1985) (claim of tortious interference with prospective contractual rela-

For example, in *Serrano v. Jones & Laughlin Steel Co.,*[14] a group of laid-off employees brought an action for fraud against the defendant employer alleging that the employer had made misleading statements and had failed to disclose relevant information in connection with its decision to close down the plant where plaintiffs worked. The court dismissed the plaintiffs' claim, stating: "No matter how it is stated, the gravamen of the . . . fraud charges is that [the defendant] did not bargain in good faith."[15] According to the court, the plaintiffs' fraud claim therefore concerned conduct that was arguably prohibited by Sections 8(d) and 8(a)(5) of the NLRA and was preempted.[16]

The doctrine of NLRA preemption, however, is not without exceptions. The courts, including the Supreme Court, have refused to apply the NLRA preemption doctrine to state law claims alleging misconduct that is only of "peripheral concern" to the NLRA or that "touches interests deeply rooted in local feeling and responsibility."[17] The balancing of national labor interests and local concerns that the courts employ in analyzing these exceptions is extremely complex, and practitioners would be well advised to review carefully the major cases in the area if an exception argument is raised. Generally, however, exceptions to NLRA preemption have generally been limited to certain types of misconduct, such as violence, threats and intimidation, and malicious libel, which Congress plainly did not intend to come within the Board's exclusive jurisdiction.[18]

---

tions against labor consultants preempted where court would have to examine employer's bargaining strategy and activities to resolve claim).

14. Serrano v. Jones & Laughlin Steel Co., 790 F.2d 1279 (6th Cir. 1986).
15. *Id.* at 1283.
16. *Id.* at 1286.
17. Farmer v. United Bhd. of Carpenters, Local 25, 430 U.S. 290, 298–99 (1977); Linn v. Plant Guard Workers, 383 U.S. 53, 61 (1966); United Auto. Workers v. Russell, 356 U.S. 634, 640 (1958).
18. *Farmer,* 430 U.S. at 299–305. *See, e.g.* Linn v. Plant Guard Workers, 383 U.S. 53 (1966) (malicious libel); United Auto. Workers v. Russell, 365 U.S.

Section 301 Preemption

Whenever an employee who is covered by the terms of a collective bargaining agreement brings a state law wrongful discharge claim or related tort claim, the employer should consider asserting a Section 301 preemption defense.

Section 301 of the Labor Management Relations Act[19] gives employees who are covered by a collective bargaining agreement the right to sue their employer for breach of that agreement in either state or federal court.[20] However, regardless of whether such suits are brought in state or federal court, they must be brought under Section 301 and must be decided by reference to a specialized body of federal common law developed in accordance with national labor policy.[21]

The determination of whether a plaintiff's claim requires interpretation of a collective bargaining agreement involves a two-step analysis.[22] First, the court must determine the essential elements of the plaintiff's state law claim and the defenses available to the employer.[23] The court must then analyze the elements of the plaintiff's claim and the employer's affirmative defenses and determine whether either requires the court to interpret the provisions of the applicable collective bargaining agreement.[24]

The Seventh Circuit's recent decision in *Douglas v. Ameri-*

---

634 (1958) (mass picketing and violence). In addition, to escape preemption, a state law claim based on a libelous statement it must meet the standards for actual malice established by the Supreme Court in New York Times Co. v. Sullivan, 376 U.S. 254 (1964). Linn v. Plant Guard Workers, 383 U.S. at 65–66.

19. 29 U.S.C. § 185(a)(1983).
20. *Id.* Charles Dowd Box Co. v. Courtney, 368 U.S. 502 (1962); Smith v. Evening News Ass'n, 371 U.S. 195 (1962).
21. Textile Workers v. Lincoln Mills, 353 U.S. 448, 456 (1957).
22. Lingle v. Norge Div. of Magic Chef, 486 U.S. 399 (1988).
23. *Id.* at 406–07.
24. *Id.*

can Information Technologies Corp.,[25] provides a good example of the application of this two-step analysis. In *Douglas,* the court was called upon to determine whether the plaintiff's claim against her employer for intentional infliction of emotional distress was preempted under Section 301. The plaintiff alleged a series of wrongs committed by the employer, which had caused her "severe and extreme" emotional distress.[26] The wrongs alleged included arbitrarily denying the plaintiff excused work days, denying the plaintiff's request to carry over excused days with pay as she claimed to be entitled to "under the contract," giving her an "unjustified final warning," and subjecting her work to "unwarranted and excessive scrutiny."[27]

The court began its analysis by setting forth the elements of a prima facie case for intentional infliction of emotional distress under the applicable state law.[28] It focused its analysis on the first element: whether the employer's conduct was truly extreme and outrageous.[29] In analyzing that element, the court noted that under state law, a defendant could not be held liable for intentional infliction of emotional distress "where he has done no more than to insist upon his legal rights in a permissible way, even though he is well aware that such insistence is certain to cause emotional distress."[30]

The question of whether the defendant's conduct in *Douglas* was extreme and outrageous thus required the court to determine whether the defendant had done no more than insist on its rights in a permissible way.[31] Much of the conduct

25. Douglas v. American Information Technologies Corp., 877 F.2d 565 (7th Cir. 1989).
26. *Id.* at 567–68.
27. *Id.*
28. *Id.* at 570.
29. *Id.* at 570–71.
30. *Id.* at 571.
31. *Id.* at 571–72.

that the plaintiff alleged to be extreme and outrageous—i.e., the denial of excused work days, the refusal to carry over days off, the unjustified final warning—related to plaintiff's terms and conditions of employment. Those terms and conditions in turn were governed by the collective bargaining agreement between the employer and the union.[32] Accordingly, the court concluded that the resolution of whether the defendant's conduct was extreme and outrageous required interpretation of the collective bargaining agreement and affirmed the lower court's dismissal of the plaintiff's claim as preempted.[33]

The key to successfully establishing a Section 301 preemption defense under the two-step analysis outlined in the preceding is to establish a connection between the elements of the plaintiff's state law claim, on one hand, and the parties' rights and obligations under the collective bargaining agreement, on the other. Establishing this connection is especially crucial in tort cases because the Supreme Court has specifically held that where the duties imposed and the rights established by the state law tort derive from, or are defined by, the rights and obligations established in the contract, the state law claim is preempted.[34]

If the plaintiff specifically relies on the substantive provisions of the collective bargaining agreement in asserting his or her claim, or if the conduct of the employer that is alleged to be wrongful—such as a layoff or plant shutdown—is governed by the express terms of the agreement, establishing the connection will present few difficulties.[35] However, where the plaintiff's complaint has been studiously drafted to avoid all reference to the collective bargaining agreement, and the

---

32. *Id.* at 572.
33. *Id.*
34. Allis-Chalmers Corp. v. Lueck, 471 U.S. at 220–21.
35. *See, e.g.,* Newberry v. Pacific Racing Ass'n, 854 F.2d 1142, 1147 (9th Cir. 1988); Brown v. Keystone Consol. Indus., 680 F. Supp. 1212, 1217 (N.D. Ill. 1988).

agreement does not expressly govern the employer's conduct, establishing that a contractual interpretation is required to resolve the case might be more problematic.

Nonetheless, there are two principles that are useful in demonstrating that a contractual interpretation is necessary to resolve tort claims that, on their face, rely solely on state law. First, the Section 301 preemption issue must be analyzed, not only by reference to essential elements of the plaintiff's claim, but by reference to the affirmative defenses available to the employer.[36]

Thus, if an employer can plead or establish an affirmative defense that depends upon an interpretation of the collective bargaining agreement, the plaintiff's claim will be preempted. For example, in *Hanks v. General Motors Corp.,*[37] the plaintiff brought suit against her former employer alleging, among other things, infliction of emotional distress.[38] The allegations of her claim centered around an incident that occurred at her work place in which her supervisor sexually molested her daughter in full view of other employees.[39] Nonetheless, following hospital treatment for severe depression, her employer refused to allow her to return to work unless she returned to her normally scheduled work assignment, subject to the same supervisor.[40] The employer's refusal to assign her to another work assignment formed the basis for her emotional distress claim against her employer.[41]

As in *Douglas v. American Information Technologies,* the applicable state law provided that a defendant could not be held liable for intentional infliction of emotional distress where

36. Hanks v. General Motors Corp., 859 F.2d 67, 70 (8th Cir. 1988). *But see* Nelson v. Central Ill. Light Co., 878 F.2d 198, 201–02 (7th Cir. 1989).
37. *Id.*
38. Hanks v. General Motors Corp., 859 F.2d at 68.
39. *Id.* at 68.
40. *Id.* at 68.
41. *Id.*

he was merely doing what he was legally permitted to do.[42] Unlike *Douglas,* however, whether the employer was relieved from liability based upon its legal right to engage in the conduct in question was based on an affirmative defense of privilege, rather than whether its conduct was sufficiently outrageous to establish an essential element of the plaintiff's claim.[43]

The court concluded that to determine whether the employer's conduct was privileged, it would be necessary to interpret the provisions of the collective bargaining agreement that governed the conditions that the employer could place upon the plaintiff's return to work.[44] Because those conditions were governed by the collective bargaining agreement, the court concluded that the plaintiff's claim was preempted under Section 301.[45]

The second principle that may prove useful in establishing a Section 301 preemption defense is that the language of the collective bargaining agreement need not expressly govern the wrongfulness of the alleged misconduct for the plaintiff's claim to be preempted.[46] Rather, in determining whether a plaintiff's state law claim is preempted, the court must also take into account whether the express language of the collective bargaining agreement creates implied rights or obligations that might govern the alleged misconduct upon which

42. Hanks v. General Motors Corp., No. 87-0254-CV-W-5, (W.D. Mo. March 13, 1989) (LEXIS, Genfed. library, Dist file), *on remand from,* 859 F.2d 67 (8th Cir. 1988), *rev'd*, No. 89-1557 (8th Cir., June 18, 1990) (LEXIS, Genfed library, Dist file).
43. *Id.* at pp. 4–5. Although the Eighth Circuit reversed, it did not quarrel with the general proposition that if the defendant's affirmative defense of privilege required the court to interpret the collective bargaining agreement, the plaintiff's claim was preempted. It merely concluded that analysis of the employer's defense did not require interpretation of the collective bargaining agreement.
44. *Id.*
45. *Id.*
46. Douglas v. American Information Technologies Corp., 877 F.2d at 572–73.

the plaintiff bases his claim or upon which the employer bases its defense.[47] Thus, one way in which an employer can establish Section 301 preemption is to establish that resolution of the plaintiff's claim requires interpretation of the collective bargaining agreement in the sense that the court must resort to past practice, industry custom, or plant work rules, to resolve the plaintiff's claim.[48]

If the court determines that a plaintiff's state law tort claim is preempted under Section 301, it must either dismiss the claim as preempted, or treat it as a claim under Section 301.[49] A decision to treat the plaintiff's claim as a Section 301 claim may make available additional defenses peculiar to claims under Section 301, such as the plaintiff's failure to exhaust his contractual remedies or his failure to file his claim within the relative short statute of limitations period generally applied to Section 301 claims.[50]

ERISA Preemption

The third major area of federal preemption to be considered is preemption under ERISA.[51] Section 514(a) of ERISA specifically provides that its provisions "shall supersede any and all state laws insofar as they may now or hereafter relate to any employer benefit plan."[52]

The preemptive effect of ERISA is not limited to state statutes. ERISA defines the term "state law" to include "all laws, decisions, rules, regulations or other State action having the effect of law in any State.[53] Thus, by definition, ERISA also

47. *Id.* at 573.
48. *Id.*
49. Allis-Chalmers Corp. v. Lueck, 471 U.S. at 220–21.
50. *See, e.g.*, Douglas v. American Information Technologies Corp., 877 F.2d at 574; Johnson v. Anheuser, Inc., 4 IER Cas. (BNA) 709, 710, 714 (8th Cir. 1989).
51. 29 U.S.C. §§ 1001–1461 (1983).
52. 29 U.S.C. § 1144(c)(1).
53. 29 U.S.C. § 1144(a).

preempts state law wrongful discharge or related tort claims to the extent they relate to employee benefit plans.

As the language of ERISA's preemption provision suggests, the scope of claims preempted by ERISA is extremely broad. Indeed, one court has described the breadth of ERISA's preemption provision as "unparalled."[54]

Determining whether ERISA preempts a state law claim is essentially a two-step process. First, the court must determine whether the plan in question is an employee benefit plan.[55] The criteria to establish an employee benefit plan that is covered by ERISA is minimal. The plan need not even be in writing.[56] ERISA covers plans providing for nearly all categories of employee benefits, including medical, hospital, liability, group life insurance, vacation, severance, pension, apprenticeship and training, and prepaid legal services.[57]

Essentially, any administrative scheme from which a reasonable person can ascertain benefits, intended beneficiaries, source of financing, and a procedure for receiving benefits is an employee benefit plan for purposes of ERISA.[58] For example, in *Petrella v. NL Industries,*[59] the court concluded that an internal unpublished policy statement that provided for varying severance allowances based upon length of service and that established standards for granting such allowances was an employee benefit plan for purposes of ERISA.[60]

Of course, what constitutes an employee benefit plan for ERISA preemption is not without limits. For example,

---

54. Holland v. Burlington Indus., Inc., 772 F.2d 1140, 1147 (4th Cir. 1985), *cert. denied,* 477 U.S. 903 (1986). *See generally* Ingersoll Rand Co. v. McClendon, 59 U.S.L.W. 4033 (Dec. 3, 1990).
55. *See* Pane v. RCA Corp., 868 F.2d 631, 635 (3d Cir. 1989).
56. Donovan v. Dillingham, 688 F.2d 1367, 1372 (11th Cir. 1982).
57. 29 U.S.C. § 1002(1)(2)(3).
58. *Id.* at 1373. *See also* Pane v. RCA Corp., 868 F.2d at 635. Note, however, that state laws which regulate insurance are not preempted. 29 U.S.C. § 1144(b)(2)(A).
59. Petrella v. NL Indus., 529 F. Supp. 1357 (D.N.J. 1982).
60. *Id.* at 1362.

the Supreme Court has held that the lump sum severance payment, triggered by operation of state law, to employees who lose their jobs as the result of a plant closing, was not an employee benefit plan for purposes of preempting the state's plant closing law.[61] In *Fort Halifax Packing Co. v. Coyne,*[62] the employer challenged the severance pay provisions of Maine's plant closing law, arguing preemption under ERISA.[63] The Supreme Court rejected the employer's argument first because it ran contrary to the plain language of ERISA's preemption provision.[64] By its express terms, ERISA's preemption provision does not refer to state laws relating to employee "benefits," but to state laws relating to "benefit plans."[65] Thus, according to the Court, under the plain language of ERISA, a state statute could not be preempted merely because it related to benefits; the statute had to relate to a benefit plan.[66]

The Court went on to point out that preempting the Maine statute would serve neither the purpose of the preemption provision nor the regulatory concerns of ERISA as a whole.[67] The purpose of the preemption provision was to eliminate the threat of conflicting, or inconsistent, state and local regulation of employee benefit plans.[68] In enacting ERISA, Congress recognized that eliminating potential conflicts with state and local laws was essential to minimize state and local interference with the uniform procedural administration of employee benefit plans that formed the foundation for the enactment of ERISA in the first place.[69]

---

61. Fort Halifax Packing Co. v. Coyne, 482 U.S. 1, 14, 23 (1987).
62. *Id.* at 1.
63. *Id.* at 6–7.
64. *Id.* at 7–8.
65. *Id.* at 8.
66. *Id.*
67. *Id.* at 8–9, 15.
68. *Id.* at 9.
69. *Id.* at 9–11.

According to the Court, the Maine statute posed no such threat.[70] The statute did not establish, or require employers to establish, the ongoing administrative procedures characteristic of a plan; it merely required the employer to pay a one-time benefit upon the occurrence of a discrete event.[71] Because the statute required no administrative procedures, it posed no threat to the uniform administrative procedures mandated by ERISA.[72]

The same was true with respect to the overall purpose of ERISA. As the Court noted, the focus of ERISA was to protect employees by ensuring the administrative integrity of benefit plans.[73] If nothing is being "administered" under the state statute—in the sense of ongoing operations and procedures—there were no administrative procedures established by the statute that might be subject to employer abuse.[74]

Similarly, in *Massachusetts v. Morash,* the Supreme Court held that a state statute requiring a lump-sum payment for unused vacation was not preempted by ERISA.[75] The Court's decision in *Morash* turned on the distinction between payroll practices and benefit plans.[76] Payroll practices are specifically excluded from the definition of employee benefit plans by regulation.[77] The relevant regulations expressly define payments to employees while on vacation out of the employer's general assets as a payroll practice.[78]

Nonetheless, the employer argued that because the vacation

70. *Id.* at 12–14.
71. *Id.*
72. *Id.* at 14.
73. *Id.* at 15–16, 18.
74. *Id.* at 16–18.
75. Massachusetts v. Morash, — U.S. —, 109 S. Ct. 1668, 104 L. Ed. 2d 98, 108 (1989).
76. Massachusetts v. Morash, 104 L. Ed. 2d at 111, 112.
77. 29 C.F.R. § 2510.3-1(b)(3)(i) (1988).
78. *Id.*

payments were paid only at termination, they amounted to severance payments.[79] According to the employer, because accrued vacation pay amounted to a severance benefit, the state statute purported to regulate a severance benefit plan and should be preempted.[80]

The Court concluded that the payroll practice regulations were intended to exclude not only payments to an employee while he was on vacation, but also payments of accrued vacation pay when an employee terminated his employment.[81] The payments required by the Massachusetts statute were therefore a payroll practice and excluded from ERISA.[82]

According to the Court, it was unlikely that Congress intended to subject vacation benefits—which, by their nature, are payable on a regular basis out of the employer's general assets and accumulated only at the option of the employee—to the stringent procedural requirements of ERISA.[83] The Court found it further unlikely that ERISA was intended to effectively force the employer to choose between complying with its detailed procedural requirements or discontinue compensating their employees for unused vacation time at termination.[84]

Notwithstanding the Supreme Court's decisions in *Fort Halifax Packing* and *Morash,* the fact that those cases were brought at all, much less taken to the Supreme Court, illustrates the breadth of the definition of an employee benefit plan for purposes of ERISA preemption. So long as the alleged plan provides for the payment of benefits to an identifiable class of participants and requires some sort of minimal administrative scheme, with rare exceptions, state laws, including judicial

79. Massachusetts v. Morash, 104 L. Ed. 2d at 106.
80. *Id.*
81. *Id.* at 112.
82. *Id.*
83. *Id.* at 110.
84. *Id.* at 111.

decisions establishing common law tort claims, are preempted.[85]

The second requirement for ERISA preemption is that the state law must "relate to" an employee benefit plan. Like the term employee benefit plan, the term "relate to" has also been given a broad construction by the courts. According to the Supreme Court, "a law 'relates to' an employee benefit plan in the normal sense of the phrase if it has a connection with or reference to such a plan."[86]

Under this broad construction, the courts have consistently held that ERISA preempts state law claims for intentional infliction of emotional distress caused by the refusal to pay plan benefits.[87] In addition, ERISA has also been held to preempt state law tort and contract claims that directly impact on the administration of plan benefits, such as claims that a plaintiff's pension fund service date was calculated improperly[88] or actions alleging that benefit claims were improperly processed.[89] Finally, state law fraud claims that depend upon analysis of the fiduciary duties imposed by ERISA have been similarly preempted.[90]

Although whether a state law "relates to" an employee benefit plan for ERISA preemption purposes has been given an extremely broad interpretation by the courts, its application is not without limits. For example, in certain cases the plaintiff's state law tort claim might be too tenuously related to the

85. Pane v. RCA Corp. 868 F.2d at 635.
86. Shaw v. Delta Airlines, Inc., 463 U.S. 85, 96–97 (1983).
87. *See, e.g.,* Howard v. Parisian, Inc. 807 F.2d 1560, 1564 (11th Cir. 1987). *But see* Clark v. Coats & Clark, Inc., 865 F.2d 1237, 1243–44 (11th Cir. 1989) (common factual setting alone insufficient to establish preemption of plaintiff's emotional distress claim).
88. Jackson v. Martin Marietta Corp., 805 F.2d 1498, 1500 (11th Cir. 1986).
89. Pilot Life Ins. Co. v. Dedeaux, 481 U.S. 41, 57 (1987).
90. Philips v. Amoco Oil Co., 799 F.2d 1464, 1470 (11th Cir. 1986), *cert. denied,* 481 U.S. 1016 (1987). *But see* Lee v. E.I. DuPont de Nemours & Co., 894 F.2d 755 (5th Cir. 1990).

administration of an applicable employee benefit plan to warrant preempting the plaintiff's state law claim.[91] However, given the expansive scope of ERISA's preemption provision, both as enacted by Congress and interpreted by the courts, such cases are plainly the exception and not the rule.

Employees planning to use an unpublished or unwritten "plan" to assert an ERISA preemption defense should be aware that there are some risks involved. In relying on such a plan to preempt state law claims, the employer may assume the role of plan administrator for purposes of ERISA.[92]

ERISA imposes stringent reporting, disclosure, and procedural requirements upon plan administrators.[93] It also imposes fiduciary obligations on plan administrators with respect to decisions made in administering plan assets.[94] Thus, an employer asserting an ERISA preemption defense based upon a plan that does not comply with ERISA's procedural requirements may find the plaintiff's state law claims preempted, only to face liability based upon a violation of ERISA's procedural requirements or a violation of their fiduciary obligations under ERISA.[95]

For example, in the leading case on the issue, *Blau v. Del Monte,*[96] the plaintiffs brought an action against their former employer alleging that the employer's decision to deny them severance benefits violated ERISA.[97] The plaintiffs also brought seven pendent state law claims under various common law theories.[98] The employer moved to dismiss the state

---

91. Clark v. Coats & Clark, 865 F.2d at 1243–44. *See also* Howard v. Parisian, 807 F.2d at 1564 (and cases cited therein).
92. *See* Blau v. Del Monte Corp., 748 F.2d 1348, 1352 (9th Cir. 1984), *cert. denied,* 474 U.S. 865 (1985).
93. *Id.*
94. *Id.*
95. *Id.* at 1352–53.
96. Blau v. Del Monte Corp., 748 F.2d 1348 (9th Cir. 1984).
97. *Id.* at 1350.
98. *Id.* at 1351.

law claims based on ERISA preemption. The court of appeals affirmed the lower court's grant of summary judgment as to the plaintiffs' state law claims on those grounds.[99]

The employer based its preemption argument on a confidential "Separation Allowance Policy," which it had distributed only to corporate officers and corporate human resource staff managers, and not to the plaintiffs. The stated purpose of the policy was to provide a flexible and general guide for management in determining appropriate separation allowances for employees whose positions were eliminated as a result of reorganization, consolidation, or elimination of operations to which they have been assigned.[100] In order to be eligible under the policy, there had to be appropriate alternative employment opportunities available for the employees whose positions had been eliminated *within the corporation.*[101] The policy also provided certain eligibility standards that employees had to meet to receive severance benefits.[102]

The *Blau* case arose when the defendant sold the subsidiary at which the plaintiffs worked.[103] The plaintiffs continued their employment under the new ownership, with similar responsibilities and similar rates of pay, but with somewhat different benefits.[104]

Several months later, the plaintiffs demanded severance benefits.[105] The defendant refused.[106] Although it did not disclose its reasons to the plaintiffs at the time, in the district court and on appeal, the employer argued that the plaintiffs' jobs had

99. *Id.* at 1356–57.
100. *Id.* at 1350.
101. *Id.* at 1354.
102. *Id.* at 1351.
103. *Id.*
104. *Id.*
105. *Id.*
106. *Id.*

not been eliminated and that their continued employment with the new owner amounted to alternative employment within the corporation.[107]

Although the court concluded that the plaintiff's state law claims were preempted, the court also found that in asserting that the separation allowance policy was a plan under ERISA, the employer had assumed the role of a plan administrator.[108] The court further found that despite assuming that role, the employer had made no attempt to comply with any of the duties imposed by ERISA.[109] To the contrary, the *Blau* court concluded that the employer had actively concealed the separation allowance policy in violation of ERISA's reporting and disclosure requirements and had made no provision in the policy for internal review of adverse determinations.[110]

Ordinarily, an employer's failure to comply with ERISA's procedural requirements would not, in and of itself, entitle a plaintiff to relief.[111] Generally, a claimant who suffers because of a fiduciary's failure to comply with ERISA's procedural requirements is entitled to a procedural, not a substantive remedy.[112]

Nonetheless, the court concluded that the defendant in *Blau* had "flouted [ERISA's procedural requirements] in such a wholesale flagrant manner" that its procedural shortcomings had "infected" its decision to deny the plaintiffs benefits.[113] The employer's continuing procedural violations—in particular its concealment of the plan and the policy's lack of an internal dispute resolution procedure—were therefore highly

107. *See id.* at 1354–56.
108. *Id.* at 1352.
109. *Id.* at 1353.
110. *Id.* at 1353–54.
111. JC Penney Co. v. Wolfe, 710 F.2d 388, 393 (7th Cir. 1983); Grossmuller v. U.A.W. Int'l, 511 F. Supp. 709, 710–11 (E.D. Pa. 1981).
112. *Id.*
113. Blau v. Del Monte Corp., 748 F.2d at 1354.

probative that the employer's decision to deny benefits was made "in conformity with an objectionable scheme" and has worked a substantive harm on the plaintiffs.[114]

Accordingly, the court concluded that the employer's interpretation of the plan and its resulting decision could not be said, as a matter of law, not to be arbitrary and capricious—the appropriate standard for judicial review of an administrator's discretionary decisions when the case was decided.[115] Further, the court found that the employee's decision was so rcplctc with procedural error, that it may have worked a substantive harm on the plaintiffs.[116] Accordingly, the court remanded the decision to the lower court for further proceedings.

Although, in *Blau,* the court remanded the plaintiffs' claim for a determination of whether the employer's decision should be reversed and whether the plaintiffs were entitled to substantive relief for the employee's procedural violations, it did so only because the employer's violations were so egregious that they amounted to evidence of the type of arbitrary and capricious conduct necessary to raise an inference of substantive harm.[117] Subsequent cases have distinguished *Blau* in situations where, although the employer's plan did not strictly comply with ERISA's procedural requirements, the employer's violations did not rise to the level of those in *Blau,* and therefore caused no substantive harm to the plaintiffs.[118] Under those circumstances, the employer's noncompliance has been held not to amount to arbitrary and capricious behavior and the administrator's determinations have been upheld.[119]

---

114. *Id.*
115. *Id.* at 1353.
116. *Id.* at 1354–1356.
117. *Id.* at 1354.
118. *See, e.g.,* Simmons v. Diamond Shamrock Corp., 844 F.2d 517 (8th Cir. 1984); Brown v. Babcock & Wilcox Co., 589 F. Supp. 64 (S.D. Ga. 1984).
119. Simmons v. Diamond Shamrock Corp., 844 F.2d at 523–25, Brown v. Babcock & Wilcox Co., 589 F. Supp. at 71.

Since *Blau* was decided, the standard of review for a plan administrator's discretionary actions has changed. An administrator's discretionary determination is no longer entitled to the deference embodied in the arbitrary and capricious standard used in *Blau.* Courts may now conduct a de novo review of an administrator's decisions to determine if the administrator's interpretation of the plan is reasonable.[120]

It remains to be seen what effect this less deferential standard of review will have on the impact of *Blau.* It can, however, be expected that the level of procedural noncompliance from which the court may infer substantive harm will be much lower. This more stringent standard of review counsels even greater caution in asserting a preemption defense based on a plan that does not comply with ERISA.

Perhaps the best way to avoid the risks associated with relying on plans that do not comply with ERISA is to bring those plans into at least substantial compliance—in particular, to disclose the plan and its eligibility requirements to the employees. If, however, there are legitimate business reasons for maintaining the confidentiality of such plans, and it is hard to imagine what those reasons might be, employers can reduce their risk by ensuring that those plans provide an internal remedy for adverse determinations that is communicated to the employee at the time the decision is made, and that standards for determining eligibility for benefits are consistently applied.

Whenever an employee brings a wrongful discharge claim or related tort claim that touches upon an area regulated by the federal government, employers and practitioners should be alert to the possibility that such claims may be preempted by federal law. Particular attention should be paid to claims that implicate union activities, the substantive provisions of an

---

120. Firestone Tire & Rubber Co. v. Bruch, — U.S. —, 109 S. Ct. 948, 103 L. Ed. 2d 80, 95 (1989).

applicable collective bargaining agreement, or the denial of employee benefits. By being alert to the possibility of preemption, the employer might not only be able to dispose of the employee's claims at an early stage of the litigation, it may also avail itself of procedural and statutory defenses and substantive arguments that might not be available at common law.

Internal Remedies

If an employee is subject to a collective bargaining agreement, many, if not all of the employee's wrongful discharge claims may be barred because of the existence of a grievance and arbitration procedure in the agreement. Such procedures are less common in the nonunionized setting; however, counsel should nevertheless consider whether the availability of internal procedures or remedies may be raised as to preclude a nonunion employee's wrongful discharge claim. For example, the argument may be raised where an employee handbook contains a grievance and arbitration procedure,[121] or where an employee is subject to an employment contract containing a clause requiring that disputes arising out of the employment relationship be submitted to arbitration or to an internal dispute resolution procedure.[122]

---

121. As the Michigan Supreme Court stated in Toussaint v. Blue Cross & Blue Shield, 408 Mich. 579, 292 N.W.2d 880, 892 (1980), "the employer can avoid the perils of any assessment by providing for an alternative method of dispute resolution. A written agreement for a definite or indefinite term to discharge only for cause could, for example, provide for binding arbitration on the issues of cause and damages."

122. Until recently, these cases generally involved the procedures set forth in individual form agreements signed by stockbrokers under the rules of the New York Stock Exchange or form agreements provided to promoters by the American Federation of Musicians. The theory as applied to run of the mill handbook or employment policy situations is a new one.

Union Setting

Employees who are represented by a union typically are subject to a collective bargaining agreement that provides for a grievance and arbitration procedure to resolve all disputes or, at a minimum, those disputes involving the interpretation or application of the agreement between the parties. In many cases, Section 301 of the Labor Management Relations Act precludes an employee covered by a collective bargaining agreement from bringing a state law tort or contract claim for disputes arising out of the employment relationship, including a claim relating to his or her discharge from employment. As noted, the Supreme Court has held that if the resolution of a state law claim depends upon a substantive analysis of the terms of the applicable collective bargaining agreement, the claim will be preempted by federal law.[123] As a result, an initial inquiry should always be made as to whether the plaintiff was covered by a collective bargaining agreement.[124]

Nonunion Setting

Michigan courts have pioneered in cases precluding wrongful discharge claims based on just cause provisions in employee handbooks that also contain a dispute resolution mechanism. In *Khalifa v. Henry Ford Hospital,*[125] a Michigan appellate court stated that if an employee consents at the outset of his employment to resolve disputes with his employer according to a dispute resolution procedure established by the employer in an employee handbook, the decision rendered in the internal procedure is final unless the procedures used were patently

---

123. Allis-Chalmers Corp. v. Lueck, 471 U.S. 202 (1985).
124. This topic is discussed more extensively in the section on "Preemption."
125. Khalifa v. Henry Ford Hosp., 156 Mich. App. 485, 401 N.W.2d 884 (1986), *appeal denied,* 428 Mich. 902 (1987).

unfair.[126] The court stated a hearing is fair if the parties are given adequate notice of the time and place and an opportunity to prepare, and are given an opportunity at the hearing to present evidence and argument. As the plaintiff had been able to present his case to a committee comprised of an impartial body of fellow employees, the court in *Khalifa* concluded that the employee's subsequent wrongful discharge claim was barred.

On the other hand, in *Renny v. Port Huron Hospital,*[127] the Michigan Supreme Court held that an employee's resort to a grievance procedure set forth in a company handbook did not bar her subsequent wrongful discharge claim because the grievance procedure did not comport with elementary standards of fairness. The court identified several factors that must be present for an internal grievance mechanism's decision to be final and binding, including adequate notice, the right to present evidence and argument and to rebut an opposing party's evidence and argument, and a rule specifying a point in the proceeding where a final decision is rendered.[128] In *Renny,* the court determined that the plaintiff did not have adequate prior notice of the witnesses who were testifying against her, nor was she allowed to read the complaint against her. Moreover, the plaintiff was not allowed to present certain evidence, nor was she permitted to attend portions of the hearing. Thus, the court concluded that the determination reached in the grievance procedure was not binding and did not preclude her subsequent wrongful discharge action.[129]

---

126. *Id.*
127. Renny v. Port Huron Hosp., 427 Mich. 415, 398 N.W.2d 327 (1986), *reh'g denied,* (Feb. 1987).
128. The court cited RESTATEMENT (SECOND) OF JUDGMENTS, §§ 83(2), 84(3)(b).
129. *See also* VanderToorn v. City of Grand Rapids, 132 Mich. App. 590, 348 N.W.2d 697 (1984), *appeal denied,* (Feb. 25, 1986) (court refused to

Additionally, an internal dispute resolution procedure generally will not be considered final and binding if the procedure is considered optional for one or both of the parties. For example, in *Cannon v. National By-Products, Inc.,*[130] the Iowa Supreme Court held that the stated procedure did not bar an employee's wrongful discharge claim, where a handbook did not mandate that employees follow the internal grievance procedure as a condition for the receipt of employment benefits.[131]

It is noted that some courts hold that if an employer provides for an internal dispute resolution procedure, the employer generally must follow that procedure in order to retain the right to subsequently rebut an employee's claim that he or she was terminated without cause. For example, in *Woolley v. Hoffman-LaRoche,*[132] the New Jersey Supreme Court held that a defendant must prove it complied with contractual termination procedures in order to have the court reach the issue of whether the employer had good cause for its decision.

Moreover, in *Cassel v. Ancilla Development Group,*[133] a federal district court in Illinois held that an employee stated a claim for breach of contract based upon the employer's refusal to process the plaintiff's grievance under the procedures

---

give a museum commission's decision concerning plaintiff's discharge preclusive effect because the grievance procedures did not meet minimal standards of fairness. The principal concern was that the dispute had not been resolved by an impartial arbitrator).

130. Cannon v. National By-Prods., Inc., 422 N.W.2d 638 (Iowa 1988).

131. *But see* Sablosky v. Edward S. Gordon, Inc., 139 App. Div. 2d 416, 526 N.Y.S.2d 820, *appeal granted,* 72 N.Y.2d 810, 534 N.Y.S.2d 938, 531 N.E.2d 658 (1988), *rev'd,* 73 N.Y.2d 133, 538 N.Y.S.2d 513, 535 N.E.2d 643 (1989) (clause in employment contract that compels one party to submit all disputes to arbitration but allows other party choice of pursuing arbitration or litigation is not invalid for lack of mutuality where consideration exists for entire agreement).

132. Woolley v. Hoffman-LaRoche, 101 N.J. 10, 499 A.2d 515 (1985).

133. Cassel v. Ancilla Dev. Group, 704 F. Supp. 865 (N.D. Ill. 1989).

set forth in an employee handbook, where the handbook specifically defined grievances to include complaints regarding termination. Notably, however, the court stated that it remained to be seen whether the plaintiff could show any damages for breach of the grievance procedure. Thus, counsel should be aware that internal grievance mechanisms may constitute a basis for some causes of action, not a defense.

Securities Industry

In the securities industry, stockbroker employees are generally required, as a condition of their employment, to agree to submit to the arbitration provisions of New York Stock Exchange Rule 347.[134] In essence, Rule 347 provides that any controversy arising out of the broker's employment, or the termination of his or her employment, will be submitted to arbitration.[135] As in other industries, wrongful discharge suits brought by brokers in the security industries have commonly included related tort claims such as defamation, invasion of privacy, and intentional infliction of emotional distress.[136] In response, brokerage employers have sought to compel arbitration of such claims under Rule 347.[137] The question raised in such cases is whether the related tort claims are arbitrable on the ground that, like the broker's wrongful discharge claim, they arise out of the broker's employment.[138]

In answering that question, despite some initial reluctance, courts have generally upheld the employer's right to arbitrate

134. *See* Morgan v. Smith Barney, Harris Upham & Co., 729 F.2d 1163, 1164–65 (8th Cir. 1984).
135. *Id.* at 1164 (quoting Rule 347).
136. *See, e.g.,* Coudert v. Paine Webber Jackson & Curtis, 705 F.2d 78, 79–80 (2d Cir. 1983).
137. *Id.* at 80.
138. *Id.* at 81–82. *See also* Drayer v. Krasner, 572 F.2d 348 (2d Cir.), *cert. denied,* 436 U.S. 948 (1978).

the broker's tort claims. In one of the first cases to address the issue, *Coudert v. Paine Webber,*[139] however, the court refused to enforce the arbitration provision.[140]

In *Coudert,* the plaintiff brought an action against her former employer for defamation, invasion of privacy, and intentional infliction of emotional distress, based on statements that her employer had made after she resigned, but that concerned her performance while she was still employed.[141] Nonetheless, the court concluded that the plaintiff's tort claims were not arbitrable.[142]

According to the court, the plaintiff's claims could not have arisen out of her employment because her employment had terminated before the employer had made the statements at issue.[143] Similarly, in the court's view, the statements had only a minimal connection to the plaintiff's resignation, did not involve the denial of termination benefits, and her claims did not arise from the termination of her employment.[144]

Less than a year later, the Eighth Circuit addressed the same issue but with different results, in *Morgan v. Smith Barney.*[145] Similarly to the plaintiff in *Coudert,* the plaintiff in *Morgan* sued his employer for slander and prima facie tort.[146] However, instead of emphasizing the timing of the employer's conduct as in *Coudert,* the *Morgan* court focused on whether the plaintiff's claims involved significant aspects of the employment relationship.[147]

Accordingly, the court concluded that the plaintiff's allega-

139. Coudert v. Paine Webber Jackson & Curtis, 705 F.2d at 78.
140. *Id.* at 82.
141. *Id.* at 79–80.
142. *Id.* at 82.
143. *Id.*
144. *Id.*
145. Morgan v. Smith Barney, Harris Upham & Co., 729 F.2d at 1163.
146. *Id.* at 1166–67.
147. *Id.* at 1167–68.

tions that the employer had deliberately misinformed customers that the plaintiff's broker's license had been suspended bore a significant relationship to plaintiff's employment.[148] That particular claim therefore arose out of the plaintiff's employment and was arbitrable under Rule 347.[149]

On the other hand, the court found the plaintiff's allegations that the employer had told co-employees that plaintiff was guilty of stealing from their desks at night, bore only a tenuous connection to the plaintiff's employment responsibilities.[150] Therefore, those particular claims were not arbitrable.[151]

Cases arising after *Morgan* and *Coudert* have generally adopted the *Morgan* court's emphasis on whether the plaintiff's tort claims involved significant aspects of his or her employment: either because they threatened the plaintiff's relationships with present or prospective customers or because they threatened the plaintiff's standing with various state and federal agencies regulating the securities agencies.[152]

Although these cases arise in the specific context of the securities industry, they hold a valuable lesson for employers and practitioners in other industries as well. In each case, the question of whether the plaintiff's tort claims were arbitrable arose because the scope of the arbitration provision was limited to claims arising out of the plaintiff's employment or the termina-

148. *Id.* at 1168.
149. *Id.*
150. *Id.*
151. *Id.*
152. Aspero v. Shearson Am. Express, Inc., 768 F.2d 106 (6th Cir.), *cert. denied,* 474 U.S. 1026 (1985) (following *Morgan* and rejecting *Coudert* under similar factual circumstances); Zolezzi v. Dean Witter Reynolds, 789 F.2d 1447 (9th Cir. 1986) (following *Morgan* and rejecting *Coudert* under similar factual circumstances); McMahon v. RMS Elecs., Inc., 618 F. Supp. 189 (S.D.N.Y. 1985) (adopting variation of *Morgan* test: tort claim based in substantial part on parties' contractual rights and responsibilities is arbitrable).

tion thereof.[153] Although such arbitration language plainly provides for arbitration of wrongful discharge claims, it leaves the employer open to a challenge that related tort claims are not subject to arbitration.[154]

To avoid similar problems regarding the arbitrability of tort claims in other settings, employers who choose to adopt internal dispute resolution procedures should be encouraged to use language that brings as many claims as possible within the scope of those procedures. For example, by providing that the employer and its employees agree to submit "all disputes between them" to arbitration, employers can greatly reduce the likelihood that related tort claims will be excluded from the scope of their internal remedies procedures.

Statutory Claims

In *Alexander v. Gardner-Denver,*[155] the Supreme Court established the principle that claims based on a plaintiff's rights under federal employment statutes—i.e., Title VII, are not subject to arbitration pursuant to the provisions of a collective bargaining agreement.[156] Until very recently, the courts have uniformly extended the rationale of *Gardner-Denver* to claims under other federal employment statutes and to arbitration agreements outside of the collective bargaining context.[157]

Notwithstanding the courts' consistent refusal to compel the arbitration of federal employment discrimination claims, the Fourth Circuit has recently held, in *Gilmer v. Interstate/John-*

---

153. See Morgan v. Smith Barney, Harris Upham & Co., 729 F.2d at 1167; Coudert v. Paine Webber Jackson & Curtis, 705 F.2d at 82.
154. *Compare* Coudert v. Paine Webber Jackson & Curtis, 705 F.2d at 83–84 *with* Drayer v. Krasner, 572 F.2d at 350, 359–60.
155. Alexander v. Gardner-Denver, 415 U.S. 36 (1974).
156. *Id.* at 58–60.
157. See, *e.g.,* Nicholson v. CPC Int'l, Inc., 877 F.2d 221, 230–231 (3d Cir. 1989); Steck v. Smith Barney, Harris Upham & Co., 661 F. Supp. 543, 546–47 (D.N.J. 1987).

son Lane Corp.,[158] that claims arising under the Age Discrimination in Employment Act (ADEA) must be submitted to arbitration pursuant to the provisions of an individual arbitration agreement.[159] In so holding, the court relied on a trilogy of recent Supreme Court cases endorsing arbitration under the Federal Arbitration Act (FAA)[160] as an effective and efficient means of resolving disputes and declaring a federal policy favoring arbitration.[161]

In those three cases, the Supreme Court found that under the FAA, the enforcement of an arbitration agreement is equally appropriate whether parties have agreed to arbitrate rights created by contract or statute.[162] According to the Court, "by agreeing to arbitrate, a party does not forego the substantive rights afforded by the statute, it only submits to their resolution in arbitral, rather than a judicial forum."[163]

In one of the three Supreme Court cases upon which the *Gilmer* court relied, *Shearson/American Express, Inc. v. McMahon,*[164] the Court established an analytical framework to determine whether individual arbitration agreements may be enforced with respect to federal statutory claims. The Court held that the FAA mandates the enforcement of arbitration agreements absent a showing of congressional intent to preclude arbitration of the statutory claim at issue.[165] Congressional intent is to be determined from the statute's text, its legislative history, or from an inherent conflict between arbi-

158. Gilmer v. Interstate/Johnson Lane Corp., 895 F.2d. 195 (4th Cir. 1990).
159. *Id.* at 10. (The pagination used is that of a text printed from a LEXIS terminal onto an attached printer).
160. 9 U.S.C. §§ 1 *et seq.*
161. Rodriguez de Quijas v. Shearson/Am. Express, Inc., 109 S. Ct. 1917 (1989); Shearson/Am. Express, Inc. v. McMahon, 482 U.S. 220 (1987); Mitsubishi Motors Corp. v. Soler, 473 U.S. 614 (1985).
162. Gilmer v. Interstate/Johnson Lane Corp., 895 F.2d. at 195.
163. Mitsubishi Motors Corp. v. Soler, 473 U.S. at 628.
164. Shearson/Am. Express, Inc. v. McMahon, 482 U.S. 220 (1987).
165. *Id.* at 226–27.

tration and the statute's underlying purpose.[166] The burden of proving contrary congressional intent is on the party opposing arbitration.[167]

Applying this framework to the ADEA claim before it, the Fourth Circuit noted that arbitration is nowhere mentioned in the ADEA, and "this silence in the text is matched by silence in the statute's legislative history."[168] Further, the court saw no inherent conflict between arbitration and the underlying purposes of the ADEA.[169]

In that regard, the *Gilmer* court specifically rejected the plaintiff's argument that arbitration would intrude upon the Equal Employment Opportunity Commission's (EEOC) role in conciliating employment discrimination disputes and enforcing discrimination claims.[170] According to the court, the EEOC's continued effectiveness did not depend on its participation in resolving all ADEA claims.[171] Rather, the court analogized individual arbitration agreements to unsupervised waivers of ADEA claims.[172] The court reasoned that arbitration of ADEA claims would serve the same purpose as unsupervised waivers of relieving crowded agency dockets.[173]

The court also rejected the plaintiff's argument that ADEA claims are inherently ill-suited to arbitration, quoting the Supreme Court's declaration that "the streamlined procedures of arbitration do not entail any consequential restriction on substantive rights" and that "suspicion of arbitration . . . had fallen far out of step with [the Supreme Court's] current strong en-

166. *Id.* at 227.
167. *Id.*
168. Gilmer v. Interstate/Johnson Lane Corp., 895 F.2d. at 197. (quoting Shearson/Am. Express, Inc. v. McMahon, 482 U.S. at 238).
169. *Id.* at 199–200.
170. *Id.* at 197–98.
171. *Id.* at 197–98.
172. *Id.* at 198.
173. *Id.*

dorsement of the federal statutes favoring [arbitration]."[174]

In the same vein, the *Gilmer* court was not convinced that ADEA claims were too subtle or complex for arbitral resolution. As the court pointed out, ADEA claims are no more complex than those under the Securities Act of 1933 (Securities Act) or the Racketeering Influenced and Corrupt Organizations Act (RICO), and the Supreme Court had held that Securities Act and RICO claims were arbitrable under the FAA.[175]

Finally, the court distinguished *Gardner-Denver* and its progeny on the grounds that they were decided in the collective bargaining context.[176] The potential conflicts between the union's interest and the claimant's, and the restrictions on the arbitrator's authority to invoke statutory authority—present in the collective bargaining context—were simply not present in the case of an individual arbitration agreement such as the one in *Gilmer.*[177]

The *Gilmer* court acknowledged that in that regard and others, its decision is in direct conflict with the Third Circuit's decision in *Nicholson v. CPC International, Inc.*,[178] which considered the same issue under virtually identical circumstances.[179] Each of the cases on which the *Gilmer* court relied arose in the business, not the employment, context.[180] Unlike the *Nicholson* court, the *Gilmer* court did not find the distinction significant.[181] The Supreme Court has not yet addressed

174. *Id.* at 201–02.
175. *Id.* at 201.
176. *Id.* at 201–02.
177. *Id.*
178. Nicholson v. CPC Int'l, Inc., 877 F.2d at 221; Gilmer v. Interstate/Johnson Lane Corp., 895 F.2d. at 202.
179. Nicholson v. CPC Int'l, Inc., 877 F.2d at 222–231.
180. Gilmer v. Interstate/Johnson Lane Corp., 895 F.2d. at 203.
181. *Compare* Gilmer v. Interstate/Johnson Lane Corp., 895 F.2d. at 202–03. *with* Nicholson v. CPC Int'l, Inc., 877 F.2d at 224.

the arbitration of discrimination claims under individual arbitration agreements in the employment context.

The conflict between *Gilmer* and *Nicholson* sets the stage for a possible Supreme Court ruling on the issue. If and when the Supreme Court faces the issue, its decision will have far-reaching implications on the resolution of discrimination claims no matter how it rules.

As can be seen from the preceding, the availability and use of internal remedies and procedures can provide the employer with a useful weapon for preventing and defending against a wide variety of claims in a wide variety of contexts. Moreover, as internal dispute resolution becomes more common and as the case law develops, the value of adopting internal dispute resolution procedures is likely to increase. In that regard, employers should consider the possibility of adopting such procedures and take care in carefully developing those procedures to ensure that they are fair and that they are broad enough to encompass as many types of claims as possible.

Administrative Remedies

Where a legal action contains claims that are properly the subject of an administrative action, a number of defenses might be available. In some instances, the employer can allege that the administrative forum constituted the employee's exclusive remedy. In other situations, an administrative remedy must have been pursued before initiating a court suit. Thus, if administrative remedies were not exhausted, a plaintiff's suit may be barred on this basis. Finally, in situations where there is a choice of forums, a plaintiff may be barred by his original choice from subsequently pursuing the same claim in the second forum.

Preclusion by Federal or State Employment Discrimination Statutes

If a plaintiff brings a wrongful discharge action alleging that his discharge was based on a characteristic protected by state or federal antidiscrimination statutes, a commonly recognized defense is that the wrongful discharge action is precluded by state or federal antidiscrimination laws.[182]

For example, in *Parlato v. Abbott Laboratories,*[183] the Fourth Circuit considered a former at-will employee's claim that his discharge violated Maryland public policy against age and race discrimination as embodied in Maryland's Fair Employment Practices Act.[184] The court conceded that plaintiff's claims, if taken as true, violated the public policy of Maryland as embodied in the state's civil rights law. However, the court concluded that a common law tort action for wrongful discharge founded on a claim of discrimination is precluded where, as here, the state statute does not create a private cause of action, but does contain an administrative procedure and provides for various forms of relief for discriminatory conduct.

Similarly, a federal district court in Indiana considered an employee's claim that he was terminated in retaliation for his efforts to oppose his employer's unlawful campaign of firing or refusing to hire older workers, constituting a violation of Indiana public policy.[185] The court dismissed the employee's complaint, stating that although Indiana's Age Discrimination

---

182. Note that where an employee is covered by a collective bargaining agreement, a claim that he or she was wrongfully discharged because of age, sex, etc., may be preempted by Section 301 of the Labor Management Relations Act. *E.g.,* Rodriguez v. Valley Planning Mill, 2 IER Cas. (BNA) 723 (C.D. Cal. 1987).
183. Parlato v. Abbott Laboratories, 850 F.2d 203 (4th Cir. 1988).
184. Some of plaintiff's allegations also were premised under federal discrimination laws. For several reasons, the court did not consider these allegations. The court noted, however, that the public policies expressed in the Maryland statute and the federal statutes are the same.
185. Helman v. AMF, Inc., 675 F. Supp. 1163 (S.D. Ind. 1987).

in Employment Act makes it an "unfair employment practice and against public policy" to refuse to hire or to fire someone solely on the basis of age, the statute did not provide remedies for violations.[186] Moreover, the court refused to fashion any common law remedies. The court concluded that the legislature's intent was to make the federal ADEA the employee's exclusive remedy. Thus, the court held that the plaintiff's claim was precluded by the federal ADEA.[187]

On the other hand, where a statute implicitly or explicitly provides for a private right of action, some courts have found that wrongful discharge actions premised on discrimination claims are not precluded by state or federal antidiscrimination laws. For example, in *Erickson v. Marsh & McLennan Co.*,[188] a New Jersey Superior Court held that a plaintiff's claim of wrongful discharge based upon the state's public policy against sex discrimination was not preempted by New Jersey's antidiscrimination statute, as the act authorized private complaints and did not "foreclose judicial enforcement of independent rights of redress."[189] The court treated plaintiff's wrongful discharge and statutory discrimination claims as a single claim

186. The court observed that the state legislature may have intended the federal ADEA to provide adequate remedies in these circumstances.
187. Other jurisdictions similarly have held that a plaintiff's claim of wrongful discharge in violation of a public policy against discrimination is preempted by state antidiscrimination laws. *E.g.*, Gamble v. Levitz Furniture Co., 759 P.2d 761 (Colo. App. 1988), *cert. dismissed,* 782 P.2d 1197 (1988) (wrongful discharge in violation of public policy claim based upon statutory right to participate in handicap training programs not available where state statutory remedy for handicapped workers exists); *see also* Makovi v. Sherwin-Williams Co., 316 Md. 603, 561 A.2d 179 (Ct. App. 1989) (existence of state and federal remedies for sex discrimination in employment preclude common law tort action for abusive discharge based upon pregnancy discrimination claim).
188. Erickson v. Marsh & McLennan Co., 227 N.J. Super. 78, 545 A.2d 812 (N.J. Super. App. Div.), *rev'd in part on other grounds,* 117 N.J. 539, 569 A.2d 793 (1988).
189. The plaintiff also had a statutory discrimination claim.

and applied the standard of proof applicable to sex discrimination claims under New Jersey's antidiscrimination statute. Based upon this criteria, the court held that the plaintiff failed to meet his burden of proving intentional discrimination. Other courts similarly have interpreted some state civil rights statutes as not precluding wrongful discharge actions premised upon a claim of discrimination.[190]

In *Clay v. Advanced Computer Applications,*[191] a Pennsylvania Superior Court considered several claims from two former employees, husband and wife, including the allegation that their termination had occurred because the wife had rebuffed the sexual advances of a manager. The trial court held that state and federal discrimination statutes provided the exclusive remedy. The superior court disagreed, stating that the Pennsylvania Human Relations Act (PHRA) did not foreclose plaintiffs' right to choose at the outset between the courts or the Human Relations Commission. However, the court noted that the PHRA prevented the plaintiffs from pursuing both an administrative and judicial remedy.

Nevertheless, you should be aware that in some cases, the same facts that support a plaintiff's claim of discrimination may be found to support a claim for an intentional tort. This often arises in suits alleging sexual harassment. A few courts have held that a plaintiff may sue for both sexual harassment under Title VII or state discrimination laws and for tortious conduct under state law based on the same set of facts.[192]

---

190. *E.g.,* Bernstein v. Aetna Life & Casualty, 843 F.2d 359 (9th Cir. 1988), *reh'g denied,* 859 F.2d 1395 (9th Cir. 1988); Abston v. Levi Strauss & Co., 684 F. Supp. 152 (E.D. Tex. 1987).

191. Clay v. Advanced Computer Applications, 370 Pa. Super. 497, 536 A.2d 1375 (Super. Ct. 1988), *rev'd in part on other grounds,* 559 A.2d 917 (1989).

192. *E.g.,* Helmick v. Cincinnati Word Processing, Inc., 4 IER Cas. (BNA) 472 (Ohio Ct. App. 1988), *aff'd,* 45 Ohio St. 3d 131, 543 N.E.2d 1212 (1989) (Ohio antidiscrimination law for sexual harassment is not the exclusive remedy with respect to plaintiff's assault and invasion of pri-

Other Administrative Remedies

A plaintiff might also make allegations that are properly the subject of administrative remedies,[193] other than the antidiscrimination laws. Depending upon the statute at issue, a plaintiff may be limited to an administrative forum or must have first pursued his claim in that forum prior to bringing a court action.

For example, in *Cockels v. International Business Expositions, Inc.,* a Michigan Appeals Court considered a plaintiff's allegations that she was discharged for demanding certain commissions in violation of public policy as embodied in Michigan's wages and fringe benefits act. This statute contained an administrative procedure for resolving such claims. As the court observed, "administrative remedies provided by the Legislature must be pursued before a grievant may seek legal redress in the courts."[194] The court held that since plaintiff failed to pursue the administrative remedies provided by this statute, the plaintiff's court action properly was barred. Similarly, some state whistle-blower protection statutes provide that a court action alleging a violation of the statute may be pursued only after other steps, such as the exhaustion of administrative or contractual remedies, have been exhausted.[195]

Moreover, in certain circumstances, the existence of an administrative remedy is considered to preempt an employee's

---

vacy claims, where Ohio legislature limited preemption to inconsistent laws); Martin v. Merriday, 706 F. Supp. 42 (N.D. Ga. 1989) (plaintiff may sue for both sexual harassment under Title VII and tortious conduct under state law) (citing cases).

193. See also the sections on Exclusivity of Workers' Compensation Acts and Preemption elsewhere in this chapter.

194. Cockels v. International Business Expositions, Inc., 159 Mich. App. 30, 406 N.W.2d 465 (1987).

195. *E.g.,* McGregor v. Board of Comm'rs, 674 F. Supp. 858 (S.D. Fla. 1987) (failure to exhaust administrative remedies bars former employee's claim under Florida Whistle-Blower's Act for discharge in retaliation for audits critical to county's handling of public funds).

court claim entirely. For example, the Fourth Circuit has held that the "whistle-blower provisions" of the Federal Railroad Safety Act have been held to constitute an employee's exclusive remedy for retaliatory discharge.[196]

On the other hand, where the administrative remedies afforded by a statute are considered inadequate, a court may conclude that such remedies need not be exhausted prior to instituting a suit for wrongful discharge based upon a violation of the statute.[197] For example, the Oregon Court of Appeals held that an Oregon statute that makes it unlawful for an employer to retaliate against an employee for reporting in good faith an employer's possible violation of regulations for patient care did not bar an employee's common law action for wrongful discharge where the statutory remedy would not make the employee whole.[198] Additionally, a court may conclude that the existence of an administrative remedy does not preclude a court action based upon the same facts if the statute at issue authorizes alternative methods for pursuing a remedy, including a private cause of action.[199]

---

196. *But see* Norris v. Lumberman's Mut. Casualty Co., 881 F.2d 1144 (1st Cir. 1989) ("whistle-blower provision of Energy Reorganization Act does not preclude a state law action for wrongful discharge"). *See also* Rayner v. Smirl, 873 F.2d 60, *cert. denied,* 110 S. Ct. 213 (1989) (4th Cir. 1989).

197. *See, e.g.* Collins v. Elkay Mining Co., 371 S.E.2d 46 (W. Va. 1988) (because administrative remedies are not adequate, former employee may institute retaliatory discharge action under West Virginia Mine Safety Act without exhausting administrative remedies).

198. McCool v. Hillharan Corp., 97 Or. App. 536, 777 P.2d 1013 (Ct. App.), *rev. denied,* 308 Or. 593, 784, P.2d. 1100 (1989).

199. Brevik v. Kite Planning, Inc., 416 N.W.2d 714 (Minn. 1987) (Minnesota Occupational Safety and Health Act authorizes both administrative and private causes of action; administrative remedy need not be exhausted where, as here, statute gives plaintiff alternative methods to pursue remedies). *See also* "Internal Remedies" *supra* pp. 141–52.

Challenging the Existence of an Implied Contract Based on Written Policies

A plaintiff who asserts a wrongful discharge claim based on alleged implied contract must first be prepared to prove the existence of that implied contract. Some implied contract claims are premised upon oral or written employer representations, while others are based upon changes in an employee's position, or certain types of employee conduct. Generally, the jurisdictions that have recognized an implied contract exception to the employment-at-will doctrine have set forth specific criteria that must be present to establish such a claim. For example, in *Duldulao v. St. Mary of Nazareth Hospital,*[200] the Supreme Court of Illinois, drawing on the traditional elements of contract formation, stated that an employee handbook or other policy statement creates enforceable contract rights only if the following factors are present:

> First, the language of the policy statement must contain a promise clear enough that an employee would reasonably believe that an offer has been made. Second, the statement must be disseminated to the employee in such a manner that the employee is aware of its contents and reasonably believes it to be an offer. Third, the employees must accept the offer by commencing or continuing to work after learning of the policy statement. When these conditions are present, then the employee's continued work constitutes consideration for the promises contained in the statement, and under traditional principles a valid contract is formed.[201]

A number of other states have relied on similar factors to establish an implied contract.[202] Some courts, however, have

200. Duldulao v. St. Mary of Nazareth Hosp., 115 Ill. 2d 482, 106 Ill. Dec. 8, 505 N.E.2d 314 (Ill. 1987).

201. *Id.*

202. *E.g.,* Hoffman-LaRoche v. Campbell, 512 So. 2d 725 (Ala. 1987); Pine

varied from the above formulation in one significant respect, requiring that the employee must have known and relied upon express policies or statements at the time he or she accepted employment in order to establish an implied contract limiting the employer's right to discharge at will.[203] Whatever the formulation, a defense that should always be considered is the argument that the statement of the policy at issue does not satisfy the requisites of an implied contract. Thus, counsel should review case law in the relevant jurisdiction to determine whether the facts or allegations are sufficient to prove the plaintiff's claim of an implied contract.

Collateral Estoppel/Res Judicata

If a plaintiff was party to an administrative or other proceeding involving issues potentially the same as the plaintiff's subsequent litigation, the defendant should consider whether the doctrines of collateral estoppel or res judicata bar the plaintiff's lawsuit. Collateral estoppel bars the relitigation of issues actually adjudicated and necessarily decided in an earlier proceeding, irrespective of whether the causes of action in the two proceedings are the same.[204] The doctrine of res judicata gives

River State Bank v. Mettille, 333 N.W.2d 622 (Minn. 1983); Johnston v. Panhandle Co-Op. Ass'n, 225 Neb. 732, 408 N.W.2d 261 (1987); Panto v. Moore Business Forms, Inc., 130 N.H. 730, 547 A.2d 260 (1988); Cook v. Heck's Inc., 288 S.C. 466, 342 S.E.2d 453 (1986).

203. *E.g.,* Darlington v. General Elec., 350 Pa. Super. 183, 504 A.2d 306 (Super. Ct. 1986) (employment manual published unilaterally by employer did not amount to a "meeting of the minds" sufficient to establish a contract); DiCocco v. Capital Area Community Health Plan, Inc., 135 N.Y. App. Div. 2d 308, 525 N.Y.S.2d 417 (App. Div. 1988) (plaintiff must have been aware of the written policy providing for termination only for cause at the time employment commenced and must have relied upon the policy in accepting employment).

204. Collateral estoppel as opposed to res judicata is usually applied to ad-

preclusive effect to all issues relevant to the claims subject to a prior judgment, whether or not actually raised.[205]

Administrative Agency Proceedings

For collateral estoppel to apply to administrative agency decisions, courts have generally held that the following factors must be present. The agency must have been acting in a judicial capacity and must have afforded the parties the opportunity to fully and fairly litigate their claims. Moreover, a method of appeal must have been available, the agency must have resolved the factual issues before it, and the decision in the absence of an appeal must be considered final.[206] If these criteria are met, collateral estoppel may be applied if the issues presented in the two proceedings were the same (and the issue was essential to the administrative agency's decision) and the party against whom collateral estoppel is applied was a party to the administrative proceeding.[207]

Perhaps the most common administrative decisions at issue in wrongful discharge suits are from state unemployment compensation boards.[208] Employers usually seek to raise the issue

---

ministrative decisions. *See* Kremer v. Chemical Constr. Co., 456 U.S. 461, *reh'g denied,* 458 U.S. 1133 (1982). It also may apply to arbitrations. *E.g.,* Jeffers v. Convoy Co., 636 F. Supp. 1337 (D. Minn. 1986).

205. *E.g.,* Cemer v. Marathon Oil Co., 583 F.2d 830 (6th Cir. 1978) (plaintiff should have brought breach of employment claim in prior age discrimination suit; contract claim barred by res judicata).

206. *See* Storey v. Meijer, Inc., 431 Mich. 368, 429 N.W.2d 169 (1988); McClanahan V. Remington Freight Lines Inc., 517 N.E.2d 390 (Ind. 1988).

207. *E.g.,* Ryan v. New York Tel. Co., 62 N.Y.2d 494, 478 N.Y.S.2d 823, 467 N.E.2d 487 (1984).

208. Note that collateral estoppel may arise in the context of other administrative proceedings as well, such as workers compensation board determinations. *See, e.g.* Jordan v. Washington Metro. Area Transit Auth., 548 A.2d 792 (D.C. 1988) (collateral estoppel bars employee's claim of

of estoppel where an unemployment compensation board has determined that the employee engaged in willful misconduct;[209] employees often claim collateral estoppel when the board's determination is that the employee did not.[210] Whether unemployment compensation board determinations should have preclusive effect in wrongful discharge suits is hotly debated; courts are split on the issue,[211] where the issue has not been decided by statute.[212] A principal argument against applying collateral estoppel to unemployment compensation decisions is that it runs counter to the system's goal of getting "money into the pocket of the unemployed worker" as quickly as possible,[213] as parties will be forced to prepare for

---

retaliatory discharge for filing a worker's compensation claim based upon administrative decision on his worker's compensation claim); McCarthy v. State of Wash., 110 Wash. 2d 812, 759 P.2d 351 (1988) (if workers compensation appeals board determined that employee's illness was not occupational disease within scope of state's Industrial Insurance Act, collateral estoppel bars relitigation of determination in common law negligence suit alleging injury resulting from office tobacco smoke).

209. *E.g.,* Frederick v. American Hardware Supply Co., 384 Pa. Super. 72, 557 A.2d 779, *appeal denied,* 523 Pa. 636, 565 A.2d 445 (1989).

210. *See, e.g.,* Zlotnicki v. Harsco Corp., 672 F. Supp. 161 (M.D. Pa. 1987); Caras v. Family First Credit Union, 688 F. Supp. 586 (D. Utah 1988).

211. Several states have conflicting decisions in their jurisdictions, including New York and Ohio. *Compare* Ryan v. New York Tel. Co., 62 N.Y.2d 494, 478 N.Y.S.2d 823, 467 N.E.2d 487 (N.Y. 1984) *with* Dusovic v. New Jersey Transit Bus Operations, Inc., 124 A.D.2d 634, 508 N.Y.S.2d 26 (App. Div. 1986), *appeal dismissed,* 124 A.D.2d 621, 508 N.Y.S.2d 26 (1987); *compare* Pullar v. Upjohn Health Care Serv., 21 Ohio App. 3d 288, 488 N.E.2d 486 (Ct. App. 1984) *with* Distelzweig v. Hawkes Hosp. of Mt. Carmel, 34 Ohio App. 3d 277, 518 N.E.2d 43 (Ct. App. 1986).

212. States are beginning to enact legislation to prevent unemployment decisions from having preclusive effect. *See* COLO. REV. STAT. § 8-74-108 (1986); CAL. UNEMP. INS. CODE § 1960 (West Supp. 1987). Note that such legislation is currently the subject of debate at the federal level as well.

213. Storey v. Meijer, Inc., 431 Mich. App. 368, 429 N.W.2d 169 (1988),

hearings to cover all issues and claims that otherwise would have been asserted in a civil action.[214]

Several state supreme courts have held that an administrative adjudication of disqualification or qualification for unemployment benefits does not collaterally estop litigation of the same or similar issues in a subsequent wrongful discharge action.[215] Their reasons for doing so have included a lack of identity of issues, the lack of an opportunity to have the issues fully litigated and the parties heard, or the unemployment compensation board's lack of statutory jurisdiction to adjudicate such issues. Notwithstanding these arguments, on the other hand, many courts have given preclusive effect to unemployment compensation decisions in subsequent wrongful discharge actions.[216] Notably, these decisions generally involve estoppel against an employee, not an employer.

The issue of collateral estoppel also occasionally arises where the claim has previously been subject to arbitration proceedings.[217] For example, in *Jeffers v. Convoy Co.,*[218] the court

---

quoting California Dept. of Human Resources Dev. v. Java, 402 U.S. 121, 135 (1971).

214. *See supra* ns.210 and 212.

215. *See* Storey v. Meijer, Inc., 431 Mich. App. 368, 429 N.W.2d 169 (Mich. 1988); McClanahan v. Remington Freight Lines Inc., 517 N.E.2d 390 (Ind. 1988); White v. Ardan, Inc., 230 Neb. 11, 430 N.W.2d 27 (1988); Luedtke v. Nabors Alaska Drilling Inc., 768 P.2d 1123 (Alaska 1989).

216. *E.g.,* Puckett v. Cook, 864 F.2d 619 (8th Cir. 1989) (wrongful discharge claims precluded by state court affirmance of unemployment compensation board's decision that employee had voluntarily quit without just cause); Frederick v. American Hardware Supply Co., 557 A.2d 779 (Pa. Super. Ct. 1989) (collateral estoppel of wrongful discharge in breach of implied contract claim); Ryan v. New York Tel. Co., 62 N.Y.2d 494, 478 N.Y.S.2d 823, 457 N.E.2d 487 (Ct. App. 1984) (unemployment compensation board determination collaterally estops plaintiff's claims of false arrest, slander, wrongful discharge, and malicious prosecution).

217. Note that when considering a prior arbitration award (or the effect of the fact that the plaintiff had the opportunity to pursue arbitration) the issue more frequently is whether the suit is preempted, whether the plaintiff failed to exhaust administrative remedies, or whether arbitra-

refused to give collateral estoppel effect to the determination of the Wisconsin Joint Auto Transportation Committee (a grievance committee) that the employer had just cause to discharge plaintiff in plaintiff's subsequent discharge action. As the court noted, the plaintiff did not appear at the hearing, nor was he represented by counsel, making collateral estoppel inappropriate.

Res Judicata

If an employee could have bought a claim in a prior action,[219] or if an earlier court action involving the claim has been decided on the merits, the principle of res judicata may bar the employee's subsequent litigation.[220] For example, in *Shaver v. F.W. Woolworth Co.,*[221] a former employee brought a discrimination action in federal court, including pendent state claims. The district court granted the employer's motion for summary judgment on the discrimination claims and declined to exercise pendent jurisdiction over the remaining state causes of action. The plaintiff did not attempt to allege an alternative jurisdictional basis for his state law claims (i.e., di-

---

tion was the plaintiff's exclusive remedy. These issues are discussed elsewhere in this chapter.

218. Jeffers v. Convoy Co., 636 F. Supp. 1337 (D. Minn. 1986).

219. This sometimes is referred to as the "entire controversy doctrine." *See, e.g.,* Giudice v. Drew Chem. Corp., 210 N.J. Super. 32, 509 A.2d 200, *cert. granted in part, denied in part,* 104 N.J. 465, 517 A.2d 448 (1986). In *Guidice,* the plaintiff first filed suit for defamation in New York, which was dismissed for failure to state a cause of action. He subsequently brought suit in New Jersey for wrongful discharge against two of the same defendants. The court held that even if the events arose from distinct transactions, they were "closely related and are constituent components of the entire controversy."

220. *E.g.,* Thibodeau v. Foremost Ins. Co., 605 F. Supp. 653 (N.D. Ind. 1985) (breach of contract and abusive discharge claims duplicated a contract claim resolved in a previous state court suit).

221. Shaver v. F.W. Woolworth Co., 840 F.2d 1361 (7th Cir.), *cert. denied,* 109 S. Ct. 145 (1988).

versity) nor did he appeal the court's judgment. The plaintiff subsequently filed a second suit in Wisconsin state court, including claims for breach of contract and negligent termination. Defendant removed on the basis of diversity. The Seventh Circuit held that under the doctrine of res judicata, plaintiff's failure to pursue his state law claims in his earlier action prevented him from attempting to do so in the second suit. The court noted that in contrast to collateral estoppel, which requires issues to have been actually litigated and decided, "res judicata bars not only those issues which were actually decided in the prior action but also any issues which could have been raised."[222]

Res judicata also may apply to bar suit for retaliatory discharge. In *Martinez v. Admiral Maintenance Service,*[223] an Illinois Appellate Court held that an unemployment compensation hearing review board's determination that the plaintiff had been fired for misconduct precluded plaintiff's action for retailiatory discharge. In the court's view, the plaintiff had the opportunity to raise her retaliatory discharge claim at the hearing to show that the reason stated by her employer for her termination was pretextual.

222. *Id.,* (quoting Lee v. City of Peoria, 685 F.2d 196 (7th Cir. 1982)). *See also* Carter v. Southeastern Mich. Transp. Auth., 135 Mich. App. 261, 351 N.W.2d 920 (Ct. App. 1984) (res judicata bars employee whose federal discrimination lawsuit had been dismissed for failing to obey the district court's orders from relitigating claim pending in state court alleging discharge in violation of an implied contract of employment on one basis that the state cause of action arose out of the same facts or transaction and thus should have been joined in one action; dismissed with prejudice in federal court constituted an adjudication on the merits).

223. Martinez v. Admiral Maintenance Serv., 157 Ill. App. 3d 682, 510 N.E.2d 1122 (App. Ct. 1987), *appeal denied,* Martinez v. Admiral Maintenance Serv., 116 Ill. 2d 561, 113 Ill. Dec. 302, 515 N.E.2d 111 (1987).

Disclaimers

In Chapter 7, we recommend the inclusion of disclaimers in employment applications, company manuals, and benefit plan documents as a way to avoid claims that the employer has undertaken a limitation of its right to discharge. Disclaimers frequently constitute a successful defense to actions alleging the breach of an implied contract to discharge for cause.[224] While requirements can vary depending upon the jurisdiction and the facts of a particular case, generally a disclaimer typically constitutes an effective defense to "just cause" contract claims where the disclaimer is clear and unequivocal,[225] is conspicuously placed,[226] and was made known to or acknowl-

224. *See, e.g.,* Morgan v. Harris Trust Sav. Bank, 2 IER Cas. (BNA) 577 (N.D. Ill. 1987), *aff'd,* 867 F.2d 1023 (7th Cir. 1989) (clear and unequivocal disclaimer in employee manual bars claim that manual created contract rights); Nork v. Fetter Printing Co., 738 S.W.2d 824 (Ky. Ct. App. 1987) (clear disclaimers in employee handbook or job application defeat breach of contract claim based upon a handbook's policy statements and procedural guidelines); Pratt v. Brown Mach. Co., 855 F.2d 1225 (6th Cir. 1988) (disclaimer in manual operates to defeat employee's claim that he could only be discharged for cause based upon written statements in manual and oral statements from supervisors). However, many courts do not view the issue as a matter of law for which summary judgment is appropriate. *E.g.,* Morriss v. Coleman Co., 241 Kan. 501, 738 P.2d 841 (1987); Zaccardi v. Zale Corp., 856 F.2d 1473 (10th Cir. 1988); *but see* Goos v. National Ass'n of Realtors, 715 F. Supp. 2 (D.D.C. 1989) (employer entitled to a summary judgment because the disclaimers are conspicuous as a matter of law).

225. *E.g.,* Perry v. Sears, Roebuck & Co., 508 So. 2d 1086 (Miss. 1987) (personnel handbook's explicit statement that employment is at-will sufficient to defeat breach of implied contract claim); *but see* Preston v. Claridge Hotel & Casino, 231 N.J. Super. 81, 555 A.2d 12, 493 (1989) (disclaimer that fails to explain impact on "maximum job security" provisions of earlier handbook is ineffective).

226. *E.g.,* Audette v. Northeast State Bank of Minneapolis, 436 N.W.2d 125 (Minn. Ct. App. 1989), the court noted that while the better practice is "to call attention to purported disclaimers . . . by bold print or other emphasis," an inconspicuous disclaimer in an employee manual barred

edged by the employee.[227] Thus, counsel should thoroughly explore written personnel documents and application forms to determine whether a disclaimer might be raised as a defense to an employee's claim.

In this section we focus on two issues that commonly arise with respect to the effectiveness of a disclaimer to bar an employee's claim: (1) the effect of disclaimers that did not come into existence until after an employee's hire, particularly where contrary language was in effect prior to the disclaimer and (2) the effect of contemporaneous or subsequent statements in manuals that allegedly contradict the statements made in an earlier disclaimer.[228]

Effect of Disclaimers Made Subsequent to Hire

The practice of including disclaimers in employee manuals or other company documents is a relatively recent phenomenon—the result of case law developed in the last decade that interprets many written personnel policies to form the basis of enforceable contracts. Thus, it is not surprising that a frequent issue is whether disclaimer language added during an employee's employment can supersede prior statements.

Some courts have refused to give effect to a disclaimer put into effect well after an employee was hired. For example, in *Towns v. Emery Air Freight, Inc.,*[229] the court held that a

---

plaintiff's claim where she did not claim that she lacked notice of the disclaimer.

227. *See, e.g.,* Therrien v. United Air Lines, 670 F. Supp. 1517 (D. Colo. 1987) (disclaimer signed by probationary employee precludes breach of implied contract and promissory estoppel claims). Although a written acknowledgment is helpful in defending such a claim, usually it is not required. *See* Pratt v. Brown Mach. Co., 855 F.2d 1225 (6th Cir. 1988) (even though employees were not required to sign page and return it to employer, disclaimer held effective).

228. Note that these two issues frequently arise together.

229. Towns v. Emery Air Freight, Inc., 3 IER Cas. (BNA) 911 (S.D. Ohio 1988).

disclaimer signed by the plaintiff seven months after he began work was "null and void" because there was no consideration for the plaintiff's waiver of implied contract rights.[230] However, courts increasingly have characterized a disclaimer arising months or even years after an employee's hire as constituting an offer to modify a unilateral contract of employment that the plaintiff accepts by continuing to work. Such was the case in *Chambers v. Valley National Bank.*[231] In *Chambers,* the employer asserted that a disclaimer that first appeared in the company's employee handbook fourteen years after the plaintiff's hire constituted a defense to her breach of implied contract claim. The court agreed, noting that employment contracts, like any other contracts, can be modified by the parties at any time.[232]

A 1989 Michigan Supreme Court opinion also lends strong support to the position that an employer can effectively alter an employee's status during the course of his or her employment from that of a "just cause" employee to an "at-will" employee. In response to a certified question from the Sixth Circuit Court of Appeals, the Michigan Supreme Court recently held that "an employer may, without an express reservation of the right to do so, unilaterally change its written policy from one to discharge for cause to one of termination at will, provided that the employer gives affected employees reasonable notice of the policy change."[233] As the court noted,

230. As the court further noted, "at the time of the execution of the waiver, Plaintiff already possessed those rights, if any, created by the implied contract between the parties." Towns v. Emery Air Freight, Inc. 3 IER at 914, n.3.

231. Chambers v. Valley Nat'l Bank of Ariz., 721 F. Supp. 1128 (D. Ariz. 1988).

232. *But see* Thompson v. Kings Entertainment, Inc., 653 F. Supp. 871 (E.D. Va. 1987) (mere fact that employee continues to work not sufficient to constitute acceptance).

233. *In re* Certified Question (Bankey v. Storer Broadcasting Co.), 432 Mich. 438, 443 N.W.2d 112 (Mich. 1989).

a contrary result would result in many employers being "tied to anachronistic policies in perpetuity merely because they did not have the foresight to anticipate the Court's *Toussaint* decision by expressly reserving at the outset the right to make policy changes." This rationale likely will be accepted by other courts faced with similar situations.

Finally, an employer should consider whether an employee was actually aware of statements or policies in existence prior to the company's addition of disclaimer language during the term of an employee's employment.[234] If the employee was not, there is even a stronger argument favoring the position that the disclaimer is effective to bar an employee's claim that he had a contract to be discharged only for cause.

Effect of Subsequent Statements That Contradict a Disclaimer

The flipside of the preceding issue is the effect of subsequent statements that allegedly are inconsistent with statements made in a prior disclaimer. This issue often arises when an employment application contains a disclaimer and an employee alleges that statements set forth in manuals or policies given to him after his hire create contractual obligations that are in conflict with, and supersede, the application's disclaimer. In *Reid v. Sears, Roebuck & Co.*,[235] the Sixth Circuit, applying Michigan law, noted that *Toussaint* explicitly provides that an employer can defeat just cause claims by "requiring prospective employees to acknowledge" that their em-

234. For example, in Sullivan v. Snap-On Tools Corp., 708 F. Supp. 750 (E.D. Va. 1989), *aff'd,* 896 F.2d 547 (4th Cir. 1990), the court held that the most recent version of an employee handbook (which contained a disclaimer for the first time) was controlling where the employee was not aware of earlier versions of the handbook prior to his discharge and where he received, relied upon, and signed the most recent manual.

235. Reid v. Sears, Roebuck & Co., 790 F.2d 453 (6th Cir. 1986).

ployment is at will.[236] The court held that unequivocal disclaimer language in the plaintiffs' employment application created contracts for employment at will. Thus, the court noted, the plaintiffs could not allege an implied contract for employment to terminate only for cause, as "there can not be an implied contract covering the same subject as an express one."[237]

Exclusivity of Workers' Compensation Remedy

As discussed in Chapter 4, plaintiffs bringing employment actions have, with increasing frequency, appended related tort claims seeking relief for emotional or mental distress allegedly suffered as the result of the employer's misconduct.[238] Even where a related tort claim is not filed, if the plaintiff's common law wrongful discharge claim sounds in tort, he may try to obtain compensatory damages for emotional or mental distress as part of his prayer for relief.[239] In either case, the plaintiff may also be eligible for relief under the applicable workers' compensation act.

State workers' compensation statutes typically provide that an employee's remedies under the workers' compensation act

---

236. *Id.*, quoting Toussaint v. Blue Cross & Blue Shield of Mich., 408 Mich. 579, 292 N.W.2d 880 (1980).

237. *Id. But see* McLain v. Great Am. Ins., 208 Cal. App. 3d, 1476, 256 Cal. Rptr. 863 (Ct. App. 1989) (at-will disclaimer on job application form was not an integrated contract precluding introduction of parol evidence to prove a just cause contract).

238. *See supra,* pp. 61–118. Such claims may include, *inter alia,* claims for intentional infliction of emotional distress, civil assault, or civil battery. *See, e.g.,* Bailey v. Unocal Corp., 700 F. Supp. 396 (N.D. Ill. 1988) (intentional infliction of emotional distress) (Illinois law); Lui v. Intercontinental Hotels Corp., 634 F. Supp. 684 (D. Haw. 1986) (assault and battery) (Hawaii law).

239. *See, e.g.,* Cagle v. Burns & Roe, 106 Wash. 2d 911, 726 P.2d 434 (1986).

for a covered injury are exclusive of all other remedies that the employee might have against his employer for the same injury.[240] Thus, if the plaintiff's common law tort claim alleges a physical, emotional, or mental injury resulting from the employer's alleged misconduct, the employer might want to defend on the ground that the plaintiff is eligible for relief under workers' compensation, and his claim is therefore barred, or that his prayer for relief for such injuries should be stricken.

Compensable Injury

The threshold issue in establishing that a plaintiff's claim is barred by his exclusive remedies under the workers' compensation act is to establish that the injury alleged in the plaintiffs' common law claim is compensable under the applicable workers' compensation act.[241] Litigation regarding whether a plaintiff's injury is compensable for purposes of workers' compensation exclusivity has centered around two lines of inquiry: (1) whether the plaintiff's injury meets the statutory requirements to entitle him to recovery under the workers' compensation statute and (2) whether the plaintiff's alleged injury is primarily mental or emotional, as opposed to physical.

Statutory Requirements

Most workers' compensation acts provide that an employee's injury is compensable if it occurs "by accident arising out of and in the course of his employment."[242] To understand

---

240. 2A A. LARSON, WORKERS' COMPENSATION LAW, § 65.00 at 12-1–12-9 (1987) (hereinafter LARSON).

241. Busse v. Gelco Express Corp., 678 F. Supp. 1398, 1400 (E.D. Wis. 1988) (Wisconsin law).

242. *See* Rogers v. State Accident Ins. Fund, 239 Or. 633, 616 P.2d 485, 488 (1986). *See, e.g.,* Cremen v. Harrah's Marina Hotel Casino, 680 F. Supp.

how the courts have applied the exclusivity of remedy defense in the employment context, it is necessary to have a general understanding of the various standards used to determine whether an injury is at least arguably compensable under the applicable workers' compensation act. In applying these standards, the courts have broken down the statutory provisions defining compensable injuries into three factors:

1. Whether the plaintiff's injury was accidental as that term is used for purposes of coverage under the workers' compensation act;
2. Whether the plaintiff's injury arose out of his or her employment; and
3. Whether the plaintiff's injury arose in the course of his or her employment.[243]

The first requirement for an injury to be compensable is that it must have occurred "by accident." However, an employer is not necessarily foreclosed from asserting an exclusivity defense simply because the employee's injury resulted from an intentional act.[244]

The term "accident" has been defined for workers' compensation purposes to include any unforeseen or unexpected event that causes an injury.[245] Whether the event was unforeseen or unexpected for workers' compensation purposes

150, 152 (D.N.J. 1988) (New Jersey law). Some statutes omit the phrase "by accident" and simply provide compensation for personal injuries arising out of and in the course of employment. *See, e.g.,* Lui v. Intercontinental Hotels Corp., 634 F. Supp. at 686.

243. *See, generally,* Cremen v. Harrah's Marina Hotel Casino, 680 F. Supp. at 150.

244. *See* Zabkowicz v. West Bend Co., 789 F.2d 540, 545 (7th Cir. 1986) (Wisconsin law); Cremen v. Harrah's Marina Hotel Casino, 680 F. Supp. at 153.

245. Zabkowicz v. West Bend Co., 789 F.2d at 545; Cremen v. Harrah's Marina Hotel Casino, 680 F. Supp. at 153.

must be determined from the plaintiff's viewpoint.[246] Thus, even injuries that are intentionally inflicted may be considered accidents for workers' compensation purposes if they are unexpected or unforeseen as to the plaintiff.[247]

With respect to the second requirement—that the plaintiff's injuries must have arisen out of his or her employment—the courts have developed a number of tests to determine whether an employee's injury is compensable.[248] The prevailing test for whether an alleged injury arises out of employment is the "increased risk" test.[249] Under the increased risk test, a plaintiff's injury "arises out of" his employment if his employment responsibilities place him at a greater risk of the injury incurred than the risk of such an injury faced by the general public.[250]

An increasing number of courts, however, employ a slightly broader test: the "positional risk" test.[251] Under the positional risk test, an injury arises out of employment if the injury would not have occurred but for the fact that the conditions and obligations of the plaintiffs' employment placed him in the "position" where he was injured.[252] As its name suggests, the "positional risk" test essentially provides that a plaintiff's injury arises out of employment whenever the plaintiff's employment puts him or her in a particular place where the injury occurred at the time it occurred.[253]

---

246. Zabkowicz v. West Bend Co., 789 F.2d at 545.
247. *Id.*
248. 1 LARSON, *supra* note 240, § 6.3, at 3-4–3-6.
249. *See, e.g.,* City of Chicago v. Illinois Ind. Comm'n, 45 Ill. 2d 350, 352–53, 259 N.E.2d 5, 7 (1970); 1 LARSON, *supra* note 240, § 6.1, at 3-4, 3-5.
250. Kirk v. Smith, 674 F. Supp. 803, 807 (D. Colo. 1987) (Colorado law); City of Chicago v. Illinois Ind. Comm'n, 45 Ill. 2d at 352–53, 259 N.E.2d at 7; 1 LARSON, *supra* note 240, § 6.30 at 3-4.
251. 1 LARSON, *supra* note 240, § 6.5 at 3-6.
252. Kirk v. Smith, 674 F. Supp. at 807–08; 1 LARSON, *supra* note 240, § 6.5 at 3-6.
253. 1 LARSON, *supra* note 240, § 6.5 at 3-6.

The final requirement for an injury to be compensable is that the plaintiff's injury must have arisen in the course of his employment. In theory, whether an injury "arises out of" employment and whether it occurs "in the course of employment" are separate requirements."[254]

The "arising out of" requirement is said to refer to the cause of the injury, and the "in the course of" requirement refers to time, place, and activity at the time of injury.[255] Generally, an employee is said to have been injured in the course of his employment if the injury takes place within the period of his or her employment, while the employee is fulfilling his or her duties, or doing something incidental to those duties, at a place where the employee could reasonably be expected to be performing his employment responsibilities.[256]

In practice, however, the distinction between "arising out of" and "in the course of" is of little significance.[257] Whether an injury occurs in the course of employment is seldom the decisive requirement. An injury not incurred in the course of employment generally does not arise out of it.[258] The decisive requirement is nearly always causation.[259]

Recognizing this breakdown in the distinction between the two requirements, a number of courts have combined the two requirements into a single test of causation: the unitary or work-connected test.[260] Under the unitary test, an injury is compensable if there is some causal connection between the

254. Kirk v. Smith, 674 F. Supp. at 807; Rogers v. State Accident Ins. Fund, 616 P.2d at 488.
255. Kirk v. Smith, 674 F. Supp. at 807.
256. Cremen v. Harrah's Marina Hotel Casino, 680 F. Supp. at 150; 1 LARSON, *supra* note 240, § 14 at 4-1.
257. Rogers v. State Accident Ins. Fund, 616 P.2d at 488–89.
258. *Id.*
259. *Id.* This is particularly true when causation is determined by the positional risk test with its emphasis on time and place.
260. *See, e.g.,* Rogers v. State Accident Ins. Fund, 616 P.2d at 490–91; Lui v. Intercontinental Hotels Corp., 634 F. Supp. at 687–88.

injury incurred and the incidents and conditions of employment.[261] The requisite connection needed to satisfy the unitary test is minimal. Even a tenuous connection between the plaintiff's injury and his or her employment will generally suffice to establish that the injury is compensable.[262]

Regardless of which test is used, the courts have traditionally interpreted the statutory requirements broadly to bring as many job-related claims within the coverage of the statute as possible.[263] This broad interpretation, although decried by employers, actually enhances the value of the exclusivity defense by bringing numerous common law tort claims within the statutory exclusivity provision.

Nonetheless, employers planning to assert an exclusivity defense should be aware that the courts have not been entirely consistent in their interpretation of what constitutes a compensable injury for purposes of recovering benefits under workers' compensation and what constitutes a compensable injury for purposes of exclusivity. These inconsistencies are particularly prevalent where the courts are called upon to determine whether the plaintiff has brought an intentional infliction of emotional distress claim in connection with a claim of sexual harassment. The issue of whether such claims are barred by the exclusivity provisions of the applicable workers' compensation act is by far the most frequently litigated issue in cases concerning the use of the exclusivity defense in the employment context.

Regardless of whether they conclude that emotional distress claims resulting from sexual harassment are barred, the courts that have considered the issue have generally analogized such

---

261. Courtney v. Canyon Television & Appliance Rental, Inc., 3 IER Cas. (BNA) 619, 622–23 (D. Haw. 1988) (Hawaii law); Phil H. Livesley Co. v. Russ, 296 Or. 25, 672 P.2d 337, 339 (1983).

262. Lui v. Intercontinental Hotels Corp., 634 F. Supp. at 687–88.

263. *See, e.g., id.* at 687–88.

claims to workers' compensation claims for injuries resulting from assaults in the workplace.[264] For purposes of recovering statutory benefits, the courts have generally held that assaults in the workplace, particularly those by co-employees or supervisors, are "accidents" for workers' compensation purposes because the resulting injuries are "unforeseen and unexpected" by the employee.[265]

Similarly, most courts have held that injuries resulting from assaults by co-employees or supervisors arise out of employment, even if the underlying dispute is not work-related, as long as the work of the participants brought them together and created relations or conditions that resulted in the assault.[266] The only generally recognized exception is where the employee has actually authorized or facilitated the assault in some way.[267]

In applying these principles in the sexual harassment context, some courts have had little trouble holding that related emotional distress claims are barred by exclusivity—particularly where the plaintiff had no relationship with the harasser outside of work or where the harasser was the plaintiff's supervisor and used his position to facilitate the harassment.[268] On the other hand, other courts have refused to bar such claims on the ground that they did not "arise out of an in the course of" employment—even where the plaintiff's work was the only

264. *See, e.g.*, Cremen v. Harrah's Marina Hotel Casino, 680 F. Supp. at 153, Brown v. Winn-Dixie, 469 So. 2d 155, 157 (Fla. Dist. Ct. App. 1985).
265. *See, e.g.*, Cremen v. Harrah's Marina Hotel Casino, 680 F. Supp. at 153. See also, *supra* notes 233–36, and accompanying text.
266. Cremen v. Harrah's Marina Hotel Casino, 680 F. Supp at 153. However, when it is clear that the origin of the assault is purely private and personal, and that employment contributed nothing to the episode, injuries from such an assault are generally noncompensable. Brown v. Winn-Dixie, 469 So. 2d at 159.
267. *Id.* at 157.
268. *Id.* at 158; Lui v. Intercontinental Hotels Corp., 634 F. Supp. at 688.

thing that brought her in contact with her harasser and was the only basis for any relationship between them.[269]

Much of the reluctance to bar such claims stems from the fact that regardless of analogous precedent in the workers' compensation arena, the courts are simply not prepared to accept sexual harassment as a "fact of life" or an "inherent risk" in the employment setting.[270] As a result, the courts have strained to find some way to distinguish prior authority holding similar injuries compensable and to allow sexual harassment plaintiffs to proceed with related emotional distress claims.[271]

Other courts have recognized that despite the apparently harsh results, consistency between what constitutes a compensable claim for purposes of recovering statutory benefits and for purposes of exclusivity is necessary to accomplish the beneficial purpose of the workers' compensation laws—to eliminate the need for the claimant to prove fault on the part of the employer, while providing claimant with an economical and efficient remedy for his or her injuries.[272]

---

269. *See generally* Cremen v. Harrah's Marina Hotel Casino, 680 F. Supp. 150; Kirk v. Smith, 674 F. Supp. at 803.
270. Cremen v. Harrah's Marina Hotel Casino, 680 F. Supp. at 158–59; Pryor v. United States Gypsum Co., 585 F. Supp. 311, 316 (W.D. Mo. 1984) (Missouri law).
271. *Cf., e.g.,* Kirk v. Smith, 674 F. Supp. at 808–09. (Common law claims of employee assaulted and knocked to floor in supervisor's office, by supervisor, during employment-related interview not barred. Claims did arise out of employment because supervisor did not use weapon provided by employer; claims did not arise in course of employment because incident that prompted assault was employee's attempt to tape-record interview; tape-recording such interviews was not part of employee's duties).
272. *See e.g.,* Lui v. Intercontinental Hotels Corp., 634 F. Supp. at 688.

Physical vs. Emotional or Mental Harm

The second line of cases regarding the issue of whether the plaintiff has incurred a compensable injury for exclusivity purposes focuses less on the connection between the plaintiff's injuries and his or her employment, and more on the nature of the employee's injury itself, particularly the extent of physical, as opposed to purely emotional, harm the plaintiff has suffered.

The courts have split widely as to the extent of physical harm that a plaintiff must allege in order for his or her claim to be barred by the exclusivity provision of a workers' compensation statute. Many have followed the leading commentator on the subject, taking the position that:

> If the essence of the tort, in law, is non-physical, and if the injuries are of the usual non-physical sort, with physical injury being at most added to the list of injuries as a makeweight, the suit should not be barred. But if the essence of the action is recovery for physical injury or death, the action should be barred even if it can be cast in the form of a normally non-physical tort.[273]

Courts adopting this "essence of the tort" analysis have generally held that intentional infliction of emotional distress or other common law tort claims are not barred if the plaintiff has suffered no substantial physical injury as a result of the employer's conduct.[274]

Other courts have looked to the common law and statutory language of the jurisdiction to determine whether employees have been afforded relief under workers' compensation for

---

273. 2A Larson, *supra* note 239, § 68.34(a) at 13-117.
274. *See, e.g.,* Hogan v. Forsyth Country Club Co., 79 N.C. App. 483, 340 S.E.2d 116, *rev. denied,* 317 N.C. 334, 346 S.E.2d 141 (1986); Vigil v. Safeway Stores, Inc., 555 F. Supp. 1049, 1050–51 (D. Colo. 1983)(Colorado law).

primarily, or purely, mental or emotional injuries.[275] If so, the courts have followed the general rule that because the plaintiff is entitled to relief under the workers' compensation act, his statutory remedy is exclusive.[276]

Finally, some courts have taken a middle ground. For example, the Florida courts have barred claims for mental or emotional harm where that harm resulted from "not insubstantial physical contacts," such as the unpermitted—but physically harmless—touching associated with sexual harassment.[277] The Wisconsin courts, on the other hand, have barred emotional distress claims where the emotional or mental harm results from a "situation of greater dimension than the day to day mental stresses to which all employees are subject," such as a continuing pattern of sexual harassment.[278]

Intentional Tort Exception

Even if the employer can demonstrate that the injury alleged in the plaintiff's common law tort claim is compensable under the applicable workers' compensation act, the inquiry does not end there. Most states have adopted an exception to workers' compensation exclusivity for injuries resulting from an employer's intentionally tortious conduct.[279]

Some states have done so by statute, some by judicial fiat.[280] In either case, the rationale is the same. Workers' compensa-

---

275. Haigh v. Matsushita Elec. Corp., 676 F. Supp. 1332, 1353 (E.D. Va. 1987) (Virginia law).
276. *Id.*
277. Brown v. Winn-Dixie, 469 So. 2d at 155, 158–59.
278. Zabkowicz v. West Bend Co., 789 F.2d at 540, 544.
279. Beauchamp v. Dow Chem. Co., 427 Mich. 1, 17 n.42, 398 N.W.2d 882, 884, n.42.
280. Haigh v. Matsushita Elec. Co., 676 F. Supp. at 1353; Bowen v. Aetna Life & Casualty Co., 512 So. 2d 248, 249 (Fla. Dist. Ct. App. 1987). In fact, the court's decision in *Beauchamp v. Dow Chem. Co.* has since been superceded by statute. *See* Temple v. H. J. Heinz Co., 180 Mich. App. 138, 446 N.W.2d. 869 (1989).

tion is designed to compensate accidental, not intentional, injuries.[281] Thus, the employer who inflicts an injury through its own intentional tortious conduct cannot argue that the injury is accidental for exclusivity purposes.[282]

Nevertheless, a plaintiff does not necessarily qualify for the exception simply because he or she has brought an intentional tort claim against his or her employer.[283] A more specific showing of intent is required.[284]

The courts have adopted two tests to determine whether there has been a sufficient showing of intent to bring the plaintiff's intentional tort claim within the exception: The "deliberate intent" test[285] and the "substantial certainty" test.[286] The deliberate intent test permits a common law action only when the employer is shown to have acted with an actual, specific, and deliberate intent to injure the employee.[287] To satisfy the deliberate intent test, the employer must have intended both the act and the injury.[288]

The substantial certainty test also requires that the employer intended the act that caused the injury, however, it does not require a showing that the employer intended to injure the employee.[289] A showing that the employer knew that its actions were "substantially certain" to cause the resulting harm will suffice.[290]

For the most part, the distinction between the two tests has had little effect on whether an employer's alleged misconduct

---

281. Beauchamp v. Dow Chem. Co., 427 Mich. at 17–18, 398 N.W.2d at 887.
282. *Id.* at 18–19, 398 N.W.2d at 889; Cooper v. Queen, 586 S.W.2d 830, 831 (Tenn. Ct. App. 1979).
283. Tribbet v. Tay Mor Indus., 471 N.E.2d 332, 333 (Ind. App. 1984).
284. *Id.* at 333–34.
285. Beauchamp v. Dow Chem. Co., 427 Mich. at 20, 398 N.W.2d at 891.
286. *Id.* at 20–22, 398 N.W.2d at 892.
287. *Id.* at 20–22, 398 N.W.2d at 891.
288. *Id.*
289. *See id.* at 21–22, 398 N.W.2d at 892.
290. *Id.*

falls within the intentional tort exception. However, one court has used the less stringent showing required by the substantial certainty test to bring an intentional infliction of emotional distress claim within the intentional tort exception.

In *Cremen v. Harrah's Marina Hotel Casino,*[291] the plaintiff brought, *inter alia,* an intentional infliction of emotional distress claim and a civil battery claim in connection with her Title VII sexual harassment claim against her employer.[292] The plaintiff alleged that, despite previous complaints to the company's affirmative action officer, her immediate supervisor had continued to sexually harass her.[293] The company moved for summary judgment as to the plaintiff's intentional tort claims on the ground that plaintiff's exclusive remedy for those claims was the applicable workers' compensation act.[294]

In analyzing the plaintiff's state law claims, the court first concluded that the plaintiff's injuries were compensable under the applicable workers' compensation act.[295] It accordingly granted summary judgment as to the plaintiff's negligent hiring and retention claim because it did not allege the requisite level of intent to escape the exclusivity bar.[296]

However, the court refused to bar the plaintiff's intentional tort claims because, according to the court, the plaintiff had made a sufficient showing of intent under the substantial certainty test to bring her emotional distress and civil battery claims within the intentional tort exception.[297] According to the court, by returning the plaintiff to a position where her supervisor continued to exert direct authority over her, without an adequate investigation, the employer had engaged in

291. Cremen v. Harrah's Marina Hotel Casino, 680 F. Supp. at 150.
292. *Id.* at 151.
293. *Id.* at 151–52.
294. *Id.*
295. *Id.* at 154.
296. *Id.* at 155–56.
297. *Id.* at 158–59.

intentional conduct that was substantially certain to cause the injury alleged.[298]

Notwithstanding the *Cremen* court's decision, the courts have not generally imputed the intentional acts of co-employees—including sexual harassment by supervisors—to a corporate employer without a showing that the employer actually authorized the assault or that the person who committed the act was an alter ego of the corporation.[299] Instead, the courts have held that the plaintiffs' injury—although intentional with respect to the co-employee—is accidental with respect to the employer, and workers' compensation provides the exclusive remedy.[300]

The exclusivity of remedies defense provides a valuable tool for the employer faced with claims for emotional distress, or other intentional tort claims, in the employment context. However, because the scope of the defense varies considerably from jurisdiction to jurisdiction, the practitioner should pay particular attention to the applicable state case law and statutory language before employing the defense.

Just Cause

When an employee alleges that he had an express or implied contract to be discharged only for cause and that he was discharged without cause, the employer might be able to assert the defense that the employee was terminated for cause. This raises the issue of what constitutes "good" or "just" cause. In some instances, courts have held that reasons constituting just

298. *See, e.g.,* Bailey v. Unocal Corp., 700 F. Supp. at 396, 400 (Illinois law); Brown v. Winn-Dixie, 469 So. 2d at 157.
299. Bailey v. Unocal Corp., 700 F. Supp. at 400. *But see* Oedewaldt v. JC Penney Co., 687 F. Supp. at 519 (D. Mont. 1988) (extending exception to intentionally tortious conduct of corporate employer's agent).
300. Bailey v. Unocal Corp., 700 F. Supp. at 400.

cause are limited to those reasons explicitly set forth in an employee manual or other document. For example, the Fifth Circuit held that an airline lacked good cause to discharge an employee for allegedly falsifying an expense report for car mileage in part because the applicable handbook did not contain a provision barring employees from claiming expenses before they were incurred.[301] On the other hand, if the employer has not specified any reasons in writing or has reserved the right to discharge for reasons other than those explicitly identified, courts are presented with the question of whether the reason constitutes just cause in the particular circumstances.[302]

In the union setting, the right to be disciplined or discharged for cause has long been a cornerstone of most collective bargaining contracts. Thus, there is a substantial body of arbitral authority discussing and defining what constitutes just cause in that setting.[303] On the other hand, in the nonunionized setting, there is much less guidance. While a few jurisdictions have enacted wrongful discharge statutes that define what constitutes good or just cause,[304] in most jurisdictions the subject of just cause is just beginning to be explored by the courts.

Especially if an employer has not bound itself to a specific list of reasons constituting just cause, there presumably are many

---

301. Aiello v. United Airlines, Inc., 818 F.2d 1196 (5th Cir. 1987), *reh'g denied,* 826 F.2d 12 (1987).

302. *E.g.,* Williams v. Maremont Corp., 875 F.2d 1476 (10th Cir. 1989)(where handbook stated that its contents were intended merely as summary of company's policies and stated at end of list of work rules that "violations not specifically described" will be handled as warranted, the reasons set forth in the work rules section of the handbook could not be considered "all inclusive" as reasons for discharge).

303. *See* F. Elkouri & E. Elkouri, How Arbitration Works (4th ed. 1985).

304. For example, Montana defines good cause as "reasonable job-related grounds for dismissal based upon failure to satisfactorily perform job duties, disruption of the employer's operation, or other legitimate business reason."

reasons that would constitute "just cause" for discharge. One reason that already has been considered by courts in several jurisdictions is an employer's institution of a reduction in force. While courts generally hold that this reason constitutes good cause,[305] they have refused to adopt a *per se* rule.[306] Rather, courts consider whether the reason is credible based upon the circumstances presented in each case. Thus, where conflicting reasons allegedly were given for an employee's termination, several courts have held that the issue is for the trier of fact to decide.[307]

For example, in *Coelho v. Posi-Seal International,* the Connecticut Supreme Court upheld a jury's finding of breach of an implied contract despite the employer's contention that plaintiff was terminated because of a reduction in force. As the court observed, the plaintiff introduced evidence that he was terminated because of a conflict among management and not because of the reduction in force. The implied contract between the plaintiff and the employer was that the employee would not be terminated as a result of management conflicts.[308] On the other hand, where evidence of a contradictory

---

305. *E.g.,* Malmstrom v. Kaiser Aluminum & Chem. Corp., 187 Cal. App. 3d 299, 231 Cal. Rptr. 820 (Ct. App. 1986); Linn v. Beneficial Commercial Corp., 226 N.J. Super. 74, 543 A.2d 954 (Super. App. Div. 1988); Rompf v. John Q. Hammons Hotels, Inc., 685 P.2d 25 (Wyo. 1984).
306. *E.g.,* Harlan v. Sohio Petroleum Co., 677 F. Supp. 1021 (N.D. Cal. 1988) (court concludes that California cases support holding that whether reduction in force constitutes good cause is to be decided on a case-by-case basis).
307. Coelho v. Posi-Seal Int'l, 208 Conn. 106, 544 A.2d 170 (Conn. 1988).
308. *See also* Boynton v. TRW, Inc., 781 F.2d 555 (6th Cir. 1986), *reh'g granted and opinion vacated,* (Apr. 10, 1986) (issue of whether employee was terminated due to reduction in force is for jury to decide); Flanigan v. Prudential Fed. Sav. & Loan Ass'n, 221 Mont. 419, 720 P.2d 257 (1986), *appeal dismissed,* Prudential Fed. Sav. & Loan Ass'n v. Flannigan, 476 U.S. 980 (1986) (where poor performance and reduction in force constituted contrary reasons for discharge, employer found to have isolated covenant of good faith and fair dealing); Ewers v. Stroh Brewery Co., 178 Mich. 371, 443 N.W.2d 504 (Ct. App. 1989) (em-

reason is lacking, courts generally will not infer contractual limitations on an employer's right to reduce its workforce and will hold that an employee's termination due to a reduction in force constitutes just cause for termination.[309]

Not surprisingly, many forms of employee misconduct constitute good cause for discharge. However, where the employer previously has condoned a practice (e.g., by not terminating other employees for engaging in similar conduct), some courts have held that the employer's decision does not constitute just cause. Thus, in *Kestenbaum v. Pennzoil,*[310] New Mexico's Supreme Court held that an employee who was terminated for engaging in illegal conduct (service of liquor to minors) was not discharged for good cause where other employees similarly had served minors but were not discharged.[311]

An inquiry into past practice and the treatment of similarly situated employees such as occurred in *Kestenbaum* frequently occurs in the collective bargaining context. Arguably, such an inquiry is appropriate because the comparison is between individuals who are subject to the same contract. It can be argued, however, that this inquiry is not appropriate in the nonunion setting because at issue is a contract between one individual and the employer.

Finally, employers should argue that the scope of a court's inquiry properly is limited to whether the employer's action

---

ployee has right to have jury decide whether employer's explanation that he was discharged due to reduction in force was pretextual, where there was no advanced study showing need for reduction and employer had operated at substantial profit and increased size of workforce).

309. Wilde v. Houlton Regional Hosp., 537 A.2d 1137 (Me. 1988).

310. Kestenbaum v. Pennzoil, 180 N.M. 20, 766 P.2d 280 (1988), *cert. denied,* Pennzoil Co. v. Kestenbaum, 109 S. Ct. 3163 (1989).

311. *Id. See also* Frazier v. Minnesota Mining & Mfg. Co., 82 Or. App. 328, 728 P.2d 87 (Ct. App. 1986), *review denied,* 303 Or. 74, 734 P.2d 354 (1987) (insubordination and use of abusive language does not constitute good cause where similar conduct by others was condoned).

was arbitrary and capricious, and not whether the court would have made the same decision. The Supreme Court of Washington adopted such a standard for reviewing whether an employee was discharged for just cause. The court stated:

> We hold "just cause" is a fair and honest cause or reason, regulated by good faith on the part of the party exercising the power. We further hold a discharge for "just cause" is one based on facts (1) supported by substantial evidence, (2) reasonably believed by the employer to be true, and (3) which are not for any arbitrary, capricious, or illegal reason.[312]

As the law in this area is developing rapidly, counsel should consult case law in the relevant jurisdiction to determine whether courts have articulated this or a similar standard and should formulate defenses accordingly.

Limitations on Damages

Even if an employer does not prevail on a wrongful discharge claim, there are means to limit the damages that may be claimed. First, as in other contract and employment matters, the complaining employee has an obligation to mitigate his damages.[313] In addition, certain moneys received by the employee subsequent to discharge may be used to offset damages assessed against the employer.

Duty to Mitigate

In order to mitigate damages, an employee who has been discharged is generally required to make a good faith effort to

312. Baldwin v. Sisters of Providence, 112 Wash. 2d 127, 769 P.2d 298 (1989).
313. *E.g.*, Zayre Corp. v. Creech, 497 So. 2d 706 (Fla. Dist. Ct. App. 1986); Bernoudy v. Dura-Bond Concrete Restoration Inc., 828 F.2d 1316 (8th Cir. 1987).

obtain similar employment. Obviously, this means that defense counsel must conduct discovery as to the extent of the plaintiff's efforts and the type of employment sought. (See discussion infra.) For example, in *Dawson v. Billings Gazette,*[314] the Montana Supreme Court held that although the employer had breached the covenant of good faith and fair dealing, it was not liable for any damages because the employee had failed to mitigate his damages by pursuing comparable employment.

The duty to mitigate may also place restrictions on employees who claim they have been constructively discharged. If a plaintiff asserts that he or she was constructively discharged,[315] an employer should consider whether the plaintiff failed to mitigate by not attempting to resolve the alleged wrong while still on the job. In this context, the duty to mitigate defense has been compared to the doctrine of avoidable consequences.[316] For example, if an employee could have sought redress through an established internal grievance procedure or through administrative or statutory remedies while remaining employed, he arguably failed to mitigate his damages by leaving his employment without doing so.[317]

---

314. Dawson v. Billings Gazette, 223 Mont. 415, 726 P.2d 826 (1986).

315. *E.g.,* Twilley v. Daubert Coated Prods., Inc., 536 So. 2d 1364 (Ala. 1988) (alleging constructive discharge in a retaliatory discharge claim); Anchor Packing Co. v. Pro Seal, Inc., 688 F. Supp. 1215 (E.D. Mich. 1988) (alleging constructive discharge in a breach of contract action).

316. Alicia Rosado v. Garcia Santiago, 562 F.2d 114 (1st Cir. 1977) (doctrine of avoidable consequences, which provides that "damages are not recoverable for harm that a wrongfully discharged employee could have foreseen and avoided by reasonable effort," applies to determine whether employee was constructively discharged).

317. *See, e.g.,* Dornhecker v. Malibu Grand Prix Corp., 828 F.2d 307 (5th Cir. 1987)(employee fails to establish constructive discharge as a result of sexual harassment because she failed to allow time for the employer's grievance procedure to work).

Offsets

In breach of contract actions, if the plaintiff obtains subsequent employment, his subsequent earnings usually are deducted from the amount of damages he can recover.[318] The same generally is true in retaliatory discharge actions based upon the violation of a public policy. Where, however, a state statute provides for a civil penalty (e.g., a year's wages) for the violation of a particular public policy, cases to date suggest that the employer will be liable for a minimum of the statutory penalty, with no offset for earnings during that time period.[319]

The majority of courts hold that backpay awards in wrongful discharge actions should not be reduced by amounts received in unemployment compensation benefits or social security benefits.[320] The rationale for not treating the amounts as an

---

318. *E.g.,* Perri v. Byrd, 436 So. 2d 359 (Fla. Dist. Ct. App. 1983) (musicians' breach of contract damages reduced by amounts received); Reese v. Dow Chem. Co., 728 P.2d 1118 (Wyo. 1986)(where earnings from subsequent employment exceeded wages employee could have earned from defendant, plaintiff is not entitled to damages despite jury's finding that employer breached covenant of implied good faith and fair dealing).

319. *See* Turner v. Winn Dixie La., Inc., 474 So. 2d 966 (La. Ct. App. 1985), *writ denied,* 478 So. 2d 147 (1985) (award of one year's salary upheld in employee's claim of discharge in retaliation for filing a worker's compensation claim even though employee found new job two months after termination where statute allows recovery for up to one year's wages); Moore v. McDermott, Inc., 504 So. 2d 982 (La. Ct. App. 1987) (damages owed employee in suit alleging retaliatory discharge for filing a worker's compensation claim is not reduced because of statute entitling employee to a year's salary).

320. *E.g.,* Washington Welfare Ass'n, Inc. v. Poindexter, 479 A.2d 313 (D.C. 1984) (damages in employee's breach of contract action should not be reduced by amounts received in unemployment compensation benefits, although certain sick and disability benefits are subject to offset); Hall v. Hotel L'Europe, 69 N.C. App. 664, 318 S.E.2d 99 (Ct. App. 1984)(unemployment benefits will not be subject to offset in employee's breach of employment contract claim); *but see* Mers v. Dispatch Printing Co., 39 Ohio App. 3d 99, 529 N.E.2d 958 (Ct. App. 1988) (in wrongful discharge based upon promissory estoppel, amount of

offset has been that the employer should not benefit from its wrongful conduct.[321] However, it might be argued that the employer's contributions help to pay for unemployment and social security benefits as well, so that an offset is appropriate.

Although there is little case authority on this subject, employers should also consider arguing that an offset should be given for workers' compensation benefits paid as salary substitution.

Reinstatement

Several courts have held that an employer's unconditional offer of reinstatement acts to limit (or, occasionally, relieve) an employer's liability for back pay.[322] As in discrimination cases, an offer of reinstatement generally must be clearly communicated and must be for substantially similar employment.[323] Courts reject offers of reinstatement as constituting

---

unemployment compensation benefits should be deducted from plaintiff's back pay award).

321. *E.g.,* Seibel v. Liberty Homes, Inc., 305 Or. 362, 752 P.2d 291 (1988) (court refuses to reduce damages in employee's breach of employment contract claim by amounts received in social security benefits, noting that if such amounts were offset in wrongful discharge actions, an employer might find it profitable to wrongfully discharge an employee and displace the costs to the provider of benefits); Hayes v. Trulock, 51 Wash. App. 795, 755 P.2d 830 (Ct. App. 1988), *review denied,* (Oct. 4, 1988) (court holds that trial court erred in reducing back pay award by amounts received in unemployment compensation benefits in plaintiffs' retaliatory discharge action, noting that to do so would award the employer for its wrongful conduct).

322. In at least one breach of contract case, an offer of reemployment constituted a complete bar to recovery for breach of contract. *See* Schisler v. Perfection Miller, Inc., 193 Minn. 160, 258 N.W. 17 (1934) (offer constituted complete bar to recovery where plaintiff was offered reemployment in the same position and salary as set forth in his original contract).

323. Flannigan v. Prudential Fed. Sav. & Loan Ass'n, 221 Mont. 419, 720 P.2d 257 (1986), *appeal dismissed,* Prudential Fed. Sav. & Loan v.

mitigation of damages, however, where the offer requires the employee accept fewer contractual rights than he had prior to discharge, or requires the employee to return to a hostile environment.[324] Moreover, if the employer's offer of reinstatement is for a lesser salary or substantially different employment, it will not serve to reduce the damages assessed against the employer.[325]

Parol Evidence Rule

The parol evidence rule prohibits the admission of extrinsic evidence, whether written or oral, that contradicts or alters the terms of an integrated written instrument.[326] The purpose of the rule is to protect the integrity of written agreements as constituting the agreement between the parties. In wrongful discharge actions, it is usually the employee who attempts to introduce parol evidence to contradict terms in a written

---

Flannigan, 479 U.S. 980 (1986) (plaintiff's damage award for employer's breach of implied covenant of good faith and fair dealing will not be reduced due to the employer's offer of reinstatement, where the offer was for an inferior part-time position).

324. *E.g.,* Billetter v. Posell, 94 Cal. App. 2d 858, 211 P.2d 621 (Ct. App. 1949)(plaintiff was not required to accept job at lower salary because to do so would modify plaintiff's employment contract); Pichignau v. City of Paris, 70 Cal. Rptr. 147, 264 Cal. App. 2d 138 (Ct. App. 1968) (offer of new position was for employment at will and as opposed to former contract, which was for five years); Ortiz v. Bank of Am. Nat'l Trust & Sav. Ass'n, 852 F.2d 383 (9th Cir. 1987) (in breach of covenant of good faith and fair dealing, action for employee's poor mental condition warrants finding that reinstatement was not a reasonable alternative).

325. *E.g.,* Smith v. Beloit Corp., 40 Wis. 2d 550, 162 N.W.2d 585 (1968) (employee not required to accept position with reduced pay in order to mitigate damages).

326. Gerdlund v. Electronic Dispensers Int'l, 190 Cal. App. 3d 263, 235 Cal. Rptr. 279 (Ct. App. 1987), *review denied,* (June 18, 1987).

agreement between the employee and employer. The parol evidence rule can be a defense for an employer in such a situation.[327]

To determine whether the parol evidence rule will bar the admission of certain evidence will depend on several factors, such as whether the agreement was intended by the parties to be "final," and whether "the agreement is susceptible of the meaning contended for by the party offering the evidence."[328] If a document originally was intended to be final and complete, the parol evidence rule would preclude consideration of any evidence of a prior oral agreement. If it was intended to be final but "partial" or incomplete, however, the written terms may be supplemented by consistent additional terms.[329] Similarly, when the terms of an agreement are ambiguous, or the agreement was procured by fraud[330] or was the result of a mutual mistake,[331] the parol evidence rule does not apply and extrinsic evidence will be allowed.

Because the rule has so many exceptions, many times the parol evidence rule will be found to be inapplicable, and the extrinsic evidence is admitted. For example, in *Stancil v. Mergenthaler Linotype Co.*,[332] the court ruled that a written employment agreement was ambiguous because it implicated facts outside of the four corners of the agreement. Thus, the court allowed the admission of plaintiff's extrinsic evidence that he stated at his interview that he had "twenty years to give somebody" and that the interviewer responded "you got it."[333] In another case, evidence of an oral agreement was

327. *Id.*

328. *Id.*

329. *E.g.*, Land Reclamation, Inc. v. Riverside Corp., 261 Or. 180, 492 P.2d 263 (1972).

330. *E.g.*, Hall v. Integan Life Ins. Co., 454 So. 2d 1338 (Ala. 1982).

331. *E.g.*, Dishman v. Crain Bros., 415 F. Supp. 277 (W.D. Pa. 1976).

332. Stancil v. Mergenthaler Linotype Co., 589 F. Supp. 78 (D. Haw. 1984).

333. Nevertheless, the court held that the verbal representations did not constitute sufficient evidence of an intent to formulate an employment

found not to be barred by the parol evidence rule because the court concluded that the document relied upon by the employer failed to constitute a contract.[334]

Nevertheless, the parol evidence rule does sometimes act to bar an employee's attempt to establish an oral agreement or evidence of oral terms when such evidence competes with a written agreement. This is particularly true when a written agreement contains an integration clause. For example, in *Malmstrom v. Kaiser Aluminum*,[335] a California appellate court held that an agreement that provided that it superseded all prior agreements precluded a former employee from introducing evidence of an implied contract for employment until age sixty-five.[336] Regardless of whether an agreement contains an integration clause, however, an employer should assert that the parol evidence rule bars evi-

---

agreement for a definite period. *See also* Stanley v. H.J. Justin & Sons, Inc., 672 S.W.2d 327 (Tex. Ct. App. 1984) (parol evidence was admissible to determine duration), Hansrote v. Amer Indus. Technologies, 586 F. Supp. 113 (W.D. Pa. 1984), *aff'd*, 770 F.2d 1070 (3d Cir. 1985) (where written contract was silent as to duration, evidence of parties' intent and surrounding circumstances was permitted as to whether parties intended reasonable period of employment). *But see* Joseph Comacho Assocs. v. Millard, 169 Ga. App. 937, 315 S.E.2d 478 (Ct. App. 1984)(where written contract contained conflicting salary figures, trial court erred in admitting parol evidence to resolve which figures controlled).

334. Ohanion v. Avis Rent a Car Sys., Inc., 779 F.2d 101 (2d Cir. 1985).

335. Malmstrom v. Kaiser Aluminum, 231 Cal. Rptr. 820, 187 Cal. App. 3d 299 (Ct. App. 1986).

336. *Id. See also* Gerdlund v. Electronic Dispensers Int'l, 235 Cal. Rptr. 279, 190 Cal. App. 3d 263 (Ct. App. 1987), *review denied* (June 18, 1987) (integration clause bars evidence of understanding as to grounds for discharge); Moore v. Georgeson, 679 P.2d 1099 (Colo. Ct. App. 1983)(where an employment contract is unambiguous and contains an integration clause stating that the writing constitutes the entire agreement between the parties, parol evidence rule bars evidence to establish that another agreement should be considered along with the employment contract as constituting a single agreement).

dence of alleged prior oral agreements[337] when they conflict with an unambiguous and fully integrated written document.

Releases and Waiver

In Chapter 13, we discuss the use of termination agreements as a way to minimize the potential for lawsuits arising from an employee's termination, focusing on the language and terms commonly included in such documents. Typically, a termination agreement includes an explicit waiver or release of claims arising from employment. However, the waiver of certain claims or releases also can arise in other contexts, as in connection with the settlement of a worker's compensation claim or, occasionally, the acceptance of certain benefits. It should be noted that special considerations may obtain when a party seeks to waive an ADEA or other statutory claims.[338]

Simply put, waiver typically is defined as the intentional relinquishment of a known right. As discussed in Chapter 13, the validity of a written waiver or release in a particular case will depend on several factors, including:

- Whether valuable consideration was given in exchange for the release;
- Whether the release was made knowingly and voluntarily and in the absence of fraud or mutual mistake;

337. *E.g.*, Whitehead v. Telesphere Int'l, Inc., 611 F. Supp. 961 (N.D. Ill. 1985) (applying Texas law, letter confirming employment and "Employment Agreement" stating that employment was at will constituted single unambiguous and complete employment contract; parol evidence of oral agreement for one year employment contract inadmissible); Montgomery v. American Hoist Derrick Co., 350 N.W.2d 405 (Minn. Ct. App. 1984) (where employment terms are evidenced by letter confirming employment, parol evidence rule bars proof of prior oral agreement of permanent employment).

338. *E.g.*, Isaacs v. Caterpillar, Inc., 702 F. Supp. 711 (C.D. Ill. 1988). See also Internal Remedies, Statutory Claims, *supra* pp. 148–52.

- Whether the asserted claim is subject to waiver; and
- Whether the asserted claim is the subject of the waiver or release.

In this section, we focus on two issues of particular importance with respect to asserting waiver or release as a defense: First, the issue of whether and under what circumstances the acceptance of post-termination benefits constitutes a waiver of the opportunity to pursue certain claims; and second, whether a waiver or release will be construed to have waived a particular claim.

In some instances, an employee's acceptance of post-termination benefits will constitute waiver of an employee's claims. This also is referred to as estoppel. The most obvious example is where the employee has accepted benefits pursuant to a termination agreement in exchange for release of liability. For example, in *Anselmo v. Manufacturers Life Insurance Co.,*[339] the Eighth Circuit considered an employee's claim that he assented to a termination agreement under duress and thus the agreement did not bar his fraudulent misrepresentation and breach of contract claims. The court held that the release was not given under duress, noting that even if it had been, the employee's acceptance of the benefits of the agreement ratified the agreement and waived any claim to duress he might have had.

A more difficult question is whether the acceptance of benefits unaccompanied by an express release constitutes waiver or estoppel of the employee's claim. Courts generally will not give preclusive effect to an employee's mere acceptance of benefits on the rationale that the employee cannot be said to have knowingly relinquished his rights. In *Shebar v. Sanyo Business Systems,*[340] the New Jersey Supreme Court held that the plaintiff's acceptance of four checks given to him at his

---

339. Anselmo v. Manufacturers Life Ins. Co., 771 F.2d 417 (8th Cir. 1985).
340. Shebar v. Sanyo Business Sys., 111 N.J. 276, 544 A.2d 377 (N.J. 1988).

termination meeting along with a note stating that the checks were offered as "termination pay," did not waive his ability to bring an action for wrongful discharge. The court concluded that the plaintiff could not have knowingly waived his rights in those circumstances.[341] Similarly, an employee's receipt of retirement benefits has been found not to bar an employee's subsequent wrongful discharge claims.[342] However, the Sixth Circuit, applying Illinois law, held that by accepting a pension rather than suing immediately for restoration of his job, the employee was barred from subsequently bringing an action for wrongful discharge.[343]

Another common issue associated with the use of a waiver as a defense to a particular wrongful discharge claim is whether the waiver contemplated the cause of action at issue. For example, in *Ortiz v. Bank of America,*[344] the plaintiff entered into a release in settlement of three worker's compensation claims. The release provided that the employer agreed to pay the plaintiff $12,500, in return for the plaintiff's agreement to "release and forever discharge [the employer] from all claims and causes of action, whether now known or ascertained, or which may hereafter arise or develop as a result of said injury." When the plaintiff later brought an action for breach of the implied covenant of good faith and fair dealing, the employer asserted that the release operated to bar such a claim.

---

341. *See also* Kitzmiller v. Washington Post, Inc., 115 LRRM (BNA) 3015 (D.D.C. 1984) (receipt of workers compensation benefits no bar to breach of implied contract claim, although amounts conceivably might be offset against any recovery).
342. *See* Morgart v. Union Mut. Life Ins. Co., 644 F. Supp. 934 (D.N.J. 1986) (court rejects employer's argument that by definition, if plaintiff retired, he was not terminated; if choice was between retiring or being fired or the retirement was a constructive discharge, acceptance of benefits did not bar contract action).
343. Diron v. City of Eastlake, 718 F.2d 1098 (6th Cir. 1983), *cert. denied,* 464 U.S. 1042 (1984).
344. Ortiz v. Bank of Am., 852 F.2d 383 (9th Cir. 1988).

The Ninth Circuit disagreed with the employer, however, on the basis that the release of claims under the state's workers' compensation act (which the court characterized as relating to injuries from, and risks of, employment) does not operate to bar claims based upon other rights or interests. The court characterized the right protected by the covenant of good faith and fair dealing as the right not to be unfairly deprived of the benefits of employment. In the court's view, plaintiff's suit alleged injuries flowing from unemployment, not employment. Thus, the court held that the plaintiff's release of claims associated with her work injuries did not bar her breach of an implied covenant claim.

Similarly, in *Beauvoid v. Rush-Presbyterian-St. Luke's Medical Center,*[345] an Illinois Appellate Court refused to award summary judgment on an employer's claim that a settlement agreement concerning the plaintiff's workers' compensation claims precluded her action for retaliatory discharge for filing such claims where the release did not specifically mention a claim for retaliatory discharge. As the Court emphasized, the release was general, covering "all claims of any kind."[346] The court stated that the general language raised the issue of the parties' intent, which required resolution by the trier of fact.

Thus, defense counsel should inquire not only into whether a plaintiff signed a termination agreement, but also whether the employee accepted certain benefits (e.g., pension benefits) or signed a written agreement with respect to the settlement of any claims, such as for a workers' compensation matter, as these might also be construed as constituting a waiver of the employee's right to bring a particular claim. Thereafter, the law in the particular jurisdiction should be consulted for guidance.

---

345. Beauvoid v. Rush-Presbyterian-St. Luke's Medical Center, 137 Ill. App. 3d 294, 484 N.E.2d 841 (App. Ct. 1985).

346. *Id.* at 298, 484 N.E.2d at 847.

Statute of Frauds

Frequently an employee alleges that he had an oral contract of employment entitling him to a fixed duration of employment, to permanent employment, or the right to be terminated only for cause. Where an employee's allegations include such oral representations, defense counsel should consider whether the statute of frauds bars the employee's claim.

In each state, the prohibition set forth in the statute of frauds is generally the same: an agreement, which by its terms, cannot be performed in one year is void unless it is in writing.[347] Although at first it would appear that the statute of frauds could operate to bar most oral contract of employment claims, in fact just the opposite is true, particularly where the employee alleges an oral contract of permanent employment or a contract to be terminated for just cause.[348] Since such contracts could be performed in one year, the statute of frauds would not bar enforcement. On the other hand, where an employee has alleged an oral contract to be employed until a particular date, the statute of frauds is more likely to constitute a defense to such a claim.[349]

---

347. For example, the New York statute of frauds, Section 5-701 of the General Obligations Law, provides in relevant part:

> Every agreement, promise or undertaking is void, unless it or some note or memorandum thereof be in writing, and subscribed by the party to be charged therewith, or by his lawful agent, if such agreement, promise or undertaking . . . [b]y its terms is not to be performed within one year from the making thereof or the performance of which is not to be completed before the end of a lifetime.

348. See discussion *infra* at notes 349–55. *But see* Rodriguez v. Benson Properties, Inc., 716 F. Supp. 275 (W.D. Texas 1989) (plaintiff's allegations of a contract to be employed so long as she performed satisfactorily and to be discharged only for cause is barred by the statute of frauds).

349. Harris v. Arkansas Book Co., 287 Ark. 353, 700 S.W.2d 41 (1985) (al-

In *Ohanian v. Avis Rent a Car System, Inc.*,[350] an employee claimed that he had oral assurances that he would be employed until he retired unless he was terminated for just cause. The employer raised the statute of frauds as a defense. The Second Circuit held that the oral contract was not barred by New York's statute. According to the court, there is a distinction "between an oral contract that provides for its own termination on the one hand, and an oral contract that is terminable within one year only upon its breach on the other. The former may be proved by a plaintiff and the latter is barred by the statute."[351] The court held that because it was possible that the employer could have terminated the plaintiff for good cause within a year without any breach by the plaintiff, the agreement was not barred by the statute of frauds.[352]

Some courts have stated that because an employee could die within a year, an alleged oral contract for permanent employment is not barred by the statute of frauds.[353] Other courts have viewed an employee's ability to leave at any time as satisfying the requirement that a contract be capable of being performed in one year.[354]

---

leged oral contract made between twenty or thirty years before for employment until plaintiff reached age 70 is barred by the statute of frauds); Nixon v. Celotex Corp., 693 F. Supp. 547 (W.D. Mich. 1988).

350. Ohanion v. Avis Rent a Car Sys., Inc., 779 F.2d 101 (2d Cir. 1985). *See also* Burke v. Bevona, 866 F.2d 532 (2d Cir. 1989) (interpreting and limiting *Ohanian*).

351. Ohanion v. Avis Rent a Car Sys. Inc., 779 F.2d at 106.

352. *Id. But see* Windsor v. Aegis Servs., Ltd., 691 F. Supp. 956, 960 (E.D. Va. 1988), *aff'd,* 869 F. Supp. 796 (1989) (because oral just cause employment contract is capable of being breached, but not performed, within one year statute of frauds bars plaintiff's claim).

353. Hodge v. Evans Fin. Corp., 823 F.2d 559, 262 U.S. App. D.C. 151 (D.C. Cir. 1987).

354. *E.g.,* Cresswell v. Bausch & Lomb, Inc., 2 IER Cas. (BNA) 1925 (N.D. Ill. 1986) (alleged oral contract for permanent employment not barred by statute of frauds because employee could leave employment at any time); Foley v. Interactive Data Corp., 47 Cal. 3d 654, 254 Cal. Rptr. 211, 765 P.2d 373 (Cal. 1988)(because plaintiff could quit or employer

A thorough discussion in support of the position that oral contracts for permanent employment or to terminate only for cause are not barred by the statute of frauds is found in the California Supreme Court's 1988 decision in *Foley v. Interactive Data Corp.*[355] As the *Foley* court explained, such contracts are akin to contracts for an unspecified period. Contracts for an unspecified duration usually are not barred by the statute of frauds; rather, they are barred only if their terms foreclose the possibility of completion by the employee within one year.[356] The California Supreme Court held that because an employee can quit, or the employer can discharge for cause within a year, oral contracts for permanent employment or for just cause are not barred by the statute of frauds. Citing cases from other jurisdictions, the *Foley* court also noted the possibility of the employee's retirement or the employer's cessation of business altogether as satisfying the requirement of being capable of completion within one year and barring application of the statute.

In sum, while counsel should review the case law in a particular jurisdiction, the statute of frauds likely will not bar an employee's allegations of an oral contract of permanent employment or a contract to discharge only for cause. However, the statute of frauds might be an effective defense if the contract alleged involves employment to a specified date more than one year from the commencement of the contract.[357]

---

could terminate employee for cause within one year, oral contract of permanent employment subject only to discharge for cause is not barred by statute of frauds).

355. Foley v. Interactive Data Corp., 47 Cal. 3d 654, 254 Cal. Rptr. 211, 765 P.2d 373 (1988).

356. *Id.*, quoting White Lighting Co. v. Wolfson, 68 Cal. 2d 336, 66 Cal. Rptr. 697, 438 P.2d 345 (1968).

357. *Supra* note 349.

Statutes of Limitations

The statute of limitations is obviously a defense to be considered in every wrongful discharge case.[358] However, it is not always clear which statute of limitations should apply. Most states have general statutes of limitations applying to contracts and torts. There are often more specific limitation periods that can be relied upon in a particular case.

Most states specify a statute of limitations period for intentional torts such as invasion of privacy or defamation.[359] Several states also specify a limitations period for bringing statutory causes of action and have applied this limitations period to statutorily based retaliatory discharge claims.[360] In addition, a few jurisdictions have wrongful discharge statutes that specify the limitations period for bringing a court action for violations of the statute.[361]

However, many wrongful discharge actions arise from common law, and no limitations period expressly governs the claims. When this is so, courts seek to apply "the most appropriate" statute of limitations period. In cases alleging retaliatory discharge arising from common law rather than an ex press statute, courts initially were split on whether the claim

---

358. Not only do limitations periods for the same cause of action vary by state, but courts applying "the most appropriate" limitations period often choose different limitations periods for the same cause of action. Therefore, counsel are advised to review case law from the relevant jurisdiction for each claim.

359. *E.g.*, ILL. REV. STAT. ch. 110, § 13-201 (one year for defamation and invasion of privacy); TEX. CIV. PRAC. & REM. § 16.002 (one year for defamation); Stockley v. AT&T Information Sys., 687 F. Supp. 764 (E.D.N.Y. 1988) (one-year statute of limitations for intentional torts applied to defamation claim).

360. *E.g.* Ingram v. Oneok, Inc., 775 P.2d 810 (Okla. 1989) (three-year statute of limitations period for actions upon liability created by statutes other than forfeiture or penalty applies to suit filed pursuant to state's Retaliatory Discharge Act).

361. *E.g.*, MONT. CODE ANN. § 39-2-911(1)(one year).

was best characterized as a tort or a contract action; however, most courts now view retaliatory discharge claims as "civil torts" and apply the limitations period applicable to tort actions for such claims.[362]

In breach of contract actions, many courts simply have adopted the limitations period governing written or oral contracts, as the case may be.[363] However, several jurisdictions have characterized such actions as essentially suits for wages and have applied the limitations period applicable to wage claims. The Minnesota Supreme Court adopted this view in *Portlance v. Golden Valley State Bank.*[364] A largely unspoken reason for looking to other statutes of limitations for contract actions in the employment context appears to be a desire to apply the shortest possible limitations period to such claims.

In *Portlance,* the plaintiff filed suit alleging breach of an employment contract based upon statements in an employee manual. In considering what statute of limitations should apply, the court admitted that to the extent a discharge is actionable at all, it is because there has been a breach of a contract of employment. The court noted, however, that the measure of damages in such cases is the compensation (i.e.,

---

362. *E.g.,* Scott v. Union Tank Car Co., 402 N.E.2d 992 (Ind. Ct. App. 1980) (allegations of discharge for filing workers' compensation claims sound in contract, not tort); Malquist v. Foley, 220 Mont. 176, 714 P.2d 995, *cert. denied,* 479 U.S. 994 (1986) (three-year statute of limitations period for tort actions governs plaintiffs' claims that they were blacklisted by construction firm in violation of state statute in absence of a specified limitations period in the state's blacklisting statute).

363. *E.g.,* Prouty v. National R.R. Passenger Corp., 572 F. Supp. 200 (D.D.C. 1983) (three-year statute of limitations period applicable to contract action bars employee's breach of contract claim based upon the employer's alleged failure to promote); Morris v. Great Lakes Steel Co., 702 F. Supp. 1332 (E.D. Mich. 1988) (six-year statute of limitations period for contract actions applies to claims alleging that defendant breached its implied agreement not to discharge plaintiff except for good cause).

364. Portlance v. Golden Valley State Bank, 405 N.W. 2d 240 (Minn. 1987).

wages) the employee would have received had he not been wrongfully discharged. As the *Portlance* court stated, "it makes little difference whether the wage claim is based on the failure to pay wages for services which have been rejected by termination of employment. Nice distinctions between wages and lost income do not change the nature of the claim."[365] Thus, the Minnesota Supreme Court held that an action for breach of an alleged employment contract is subject to the state's two-year limitations period applicable to suits for wages as opposed to the four-year limitations period applicable to contract claims.

Moreover, where an employee has alleged retaliatory discharge in a jurisdiction that has a "whistle-blower protection" statute, counsel should consider whether it was necessary for the employee to comply with the statute prior to initiating suit. Moreover, some whistle-blower protection statutes specify a particularly short limitations period for pursuing court action.[366]

An interesting issue is whether an employee can agree to a shorter limitations period than is provided by statute for employment related claims. Applying Michigan law, the Sixth Circuit considered whether such an agreement violated public policy. In *Myers v. Western Southern Life Insurance Co.*,[367] the court held that a written employment contract requiring that all actions against an employer be brought within six months after termination and waiving any statutes of limitations did not violate public policy. In the court's view, there was nothing inherently unreasonable about a six-month limitations period for such claims. Moreover, the court noted that

365. *Id.*

366. *E.g.*, CONN. GEN. STAT. § 31-51 (m) *et seq.;* (within ninety days after date of final administrative determination); MICH. COMP. LAWS § 15.361 *et seq.* (civil action may be brought within ninety days of alleged violation).

367. Myers v. Western-S. Life Ins. Co., 849 F.2d 259 (6th Cir. 1988).

there was evidence that the employee's waiver of other limitations periods was knowing and intelligent.

Finally, if a wrongful discharge claim is preempted under Section 301 as may be the case where the employee is subject to a collective bargaining agreement, pursuant to the Supreme Court's decision in *Del Costello v. International Brotherhood of Teamsters,*[368] the six-month statute of limitations period set forth in Section 10(b) of the Labor Management Reporting Act may apply.

Note

As this book was going to press, the Supreme Court issued its decision in *Ingersoll Rand Co. v. McClendon* (59 U.S.L.W. 4033 (Dec. 3, 1990)). In *Ingersoll Rand,* the Court reaffirmed ERISA's breadth in preempting common-law tort claims relating to employee benefit plans, subject only to very limited common-law and statutory exceptions. (See section on ERISA Preemption at page 130.)

---

368. Del Costello v. International Bhd. of Teamsters, 462 U.S. 151, (1983). *E.g.,* Kirby v. Allegheny Beverage Corp., 811 F.2d 253 (4th Cir. 1987) (claims arising under Section 301 such as claim for invasion of privacy must be brought within six months of when the cause of action occurred pursuant to *Del Costello*).

CHAPTER SIX

The Hiring Process

Introduction

The hiring process marks the commencement of potential liability with the prospective employee. During this process the employee should become aware of the nature of the employment relationship as well as the practices that will govern this relationship in the future. In this regard, it is important to keep in mind that from the first contact with the prospective employee, the information this individual receives will establish the standards by which potential future wrongful discharge litigation will be judged.

The entire application process introduces the employee to the company and its policies regarding the terms and conditions of his or her future employment. Therefore, it is imperative that this process be scrutinized to avoid creating restrictions on the employer's right to terminate the employee should such action become necessary at some later date.

Employees have a tendency to remember in great detail what is stated to them at the time of hiring. Employers, on the other hand, have a tendency to make many promises in order to induce individuals to accept employment. Such inducements are contained in oral statements as well as written documents. Any written document that is used during the hiring process should be carefully evaluated and reviewed. These documents include employment applications, applicant evaluation forms, company brochures, and any other documents presented to prospective employees. In addition, all company personnel involved in the hiring process must be trained to avoid unnecessary and potentially dangerous statutes and commands. Finally, the pre-employment investigations, including criminal searches, credit checks, and reference checks have the potential for legal liability. These and other subjects will be discussed in this chapter.

Techniques for Interviewing and Selection of Employees

Prior to conducting interviews, the employer should have in place a procedure to review and approve all job openings. Such a procedure will ensure that before the interviewing process commences, the requirements and duties for the open position as well as the qualifications for the position are clearly spelled out. In this regard, the employer must make sure that the qualifications sought are specifically related to the functions, responsibilities, and duties for the position.

In those situations where the position is an addition to staff or a newly created job, the employer should maintain a record setting forth the type of job, its title, its salary range and, of course, its proposed duties, functions, responsibilities, and qualifications. Further, job additions should be justified on the basis of valid business reasons.

After the job requirements or job specifications are established, the interviewing and selection process can take place. All interviewers should be advised and given documents setting forth the duties, responsibilities, and qualifications for the job in question. This will enable the interviewers to ask the appropriate job-related questions. As a basic principle it is important to emphasize to the interviewer that he or she conduct the interview based on the requirements and qualifications for the position in question.

After reviewing the requirements and qualifications for the position, the interviewer should compare these requirements with the applications and resumés of the individuals to be interviewed. The interviewer should prepare specific questions relating to the position in question and the individual's background as set forth in the job application and resumé.

After appropriately scrutinizing applications, individuals, who based upon their applications or resumé have the minimum qualifications for the position, should be invited for interviews, which should be conducted in a private place free from interruption. One must keep in mind that certain questions and answers that are given during the interview may contain elements of privacy, and therefore the physical surroundings of the interviews are important.

The questions asked during the interview process, orally and in writing, should be job related and nondiscriminatory. For example, if the interviewer is not going to ask the same question of both men and women or minorities and nonminorities that question should not be asked. In other words, the questions should be asked of all applicants regardless of their race, sex, age, etc. It is very important that the interviewer be familiar with the applicable state fair employment practice rules listing permissible and nonpermissible pre-employment inquiries.

At the outset of the interview, the interviewer should establish an agenda for the interview by outlining what he or she intends to accomplish. Next, the interviewer should describe the position in question and give a brief overview on the structure of the organization and where the position fits in. In asking questions, the interviewer should give the applicant as much time as reasonably necessary and let the applicant do the talking. The interviewer should be looking for a clear indication of the applicant's competence to do the job. Questions should require more than a yes or no answer and should allow the applicant an opportunity to explain why he or she is qualified for this position. The applicant, whenever possible, should be challenged. The applicant should also be advised at the end of the interview of the next steps in the process. The interviewer should be on guard against making future promises that would create unnecessary expectations and potential legal liabilities.

It is important to note that any comments made during the interview that need to be written down should not be made on the application. Employment applications generally have space for comments, but it is not recommended that these be utilized. A separate piece of paper or document with some notes should be sufficient. More importantly if there is any evaluation, it should be done on a separate document from the applicant's employment application. This document is generally discarded after the individual is hired, since these first impressions have little relationship to future employment.[1] This is especially true since employment applications are probably one of the few documents that remain in the personnel file for the entire employment of the individual. The employment application will be discussed further herein.

Interviewers have a tendency to make promises they later wished they had never made. Such statements are usually based on the interviewer's concern about selling the company, and the specific desire to hire the individual applicant. However, statements such as "term employment," "permanent employment," "just cause termination," "we will be 'fair,'"

---

1. However, at the conclusion of the interview process a document should be prepared stating which job the individuals interviewed for, who interviewed each, the reasons why the successful applicant was selected, and why the other applicants were not selected. This document should be retained by the human resources department, for reference, separate from the personnel file, should the selection be subsequently challenged.

"we do not fire unless 'you screw up'" (See *Ohanion v. Avis* case, *supra* p. 286.).

The courts on the other hand don't always find these promises to be "puffing." In a New York case, *Sivel v. Readers Digest, Inc.*,[2] the court found that the statement made at an interview "that I would not be fired except for serious cause" may be sufficient evidence of the express limitation to rebut the "at-will" employment presumption. Other courts have found otherwise.[3] In a recent decision, the Ohio Supreme Court held that remarks by an interviewer who promised advancement and job security if the plaintiff stopped her job search could be contractual in nature.[4]

It is due to these legal risks that interviewers should be carefully trained. They should be informed of the company's policy or practice regarding the termination of employees.

---

2. Sivel v. Readers Digest, Inc., 2 IER Cas. (BNA) 1880 (S.D.N.Y. 1988).
3. See, *e.g.*, Sullivan v. Snap-On Tools Corp., 708 F. Supp. 750 (E.D. Va. 1989), *aff'd*, 896 F.2d 547 (4th Cir. 1990). The plaintiff "testified during a deposition that his superior promised that as long as he performed his duties to Snap-On's satisfaction, he would be afforded job security." *Id.* at 751. Held: "oral just cause representation is [not] enforceable" because it is within the statute of frauds. *Id. See also* Hanlin v. Pitman-Moore, Inc., 1 IER Cas. (BNA) 1068 (D. Minn. 1986). "According to the plaintiff, Mr. Ruggieri promised him a salary increase if Hanlin would transfer to the Des Moines branch." 1 IER at 1070. Held: oral promise of a salary increase if the employee transferred to another branch does not constitute a contract because the terms are too vague. 1 IER at 1070–71. *See also* Nixon v. Celotex Corp., 693 F. Supp. 547 (W.D. Mich. 1988). "[A]t the time *Nixon* was recruited . . . [he was] assured . . . a lot of job security and that . . . the policy of Celotex was to never let an employee go because of economic circumstances." Held: oral contract not enforceable because it constitutes a unilateral policy that was changed and uniformly applied." 693 F. Supp. at 557.
4. Helmick v. Cincinnati Word Processing, Inc., 4 IER Cas. (BNA) 1249 (Ohio 1989).

These would include "at-will" employment, termination for "cause," or other specific reasons for termination. On the positive side, they should know what information they may tell the applicant about the company and its programs. As a general rule, only that information that will enable the company to hire qualified employees should be imparted to the employee.

DO

- Tell prospective employees that the company is a good place to work, treats employees fairly, is a progressive company, and is concerned about employee welfare. "We would like to have you as part of the team," etc.
- Tell prospective employees what the past history of the company has been on its fair treatment of employees.
- Tell prospective employees what procedure supervisors usually follow for informing them of unsatisfactory performance on the job.
- Tell prospective employees about the company's wage and benefit program.
- Tell prospective employees who in management has the authority to review any employment termination decision.

DON'T

- Give assurances of a job, job security, or continued employment, such as:
  - "As long as you do a good job," or "As long as you do your job."
  - "As long as you want to work here."
  - "As long as your reviews are good, satisfactory, or above average," etc.
  - "As long as I'm here."
  - "Your position is permanent."
  - "Until you're ready to retire."

- Do not try to induce individuals away from other employment with assurances or promises, such as:
  - "You'll have a permanent job here," or "you'll have all the job security you had with your prior employer plus . . . ,"
- After hiring an individual, with current employees, avoid any of the above promises or assurances.
- Do not promise or imply that employment will not be terminated:
  a. Except for "just cause," "reasonable cause," "cause," or "good reason."
  b. Unless a given individual "says so," "reviews it," "passes on it," or "approves it," etc.
- After hiring an individual, or with current employees, avoid any of the above promises or assurances.
- On promotion or transfers to other jobs within the company, avoid any additional assurances of job security as described above.

When the interview is conducted in the above fashion, a prospective employee can be given full information about the company in an appropriate manner. It is important to note that the right first impression can be very important in developing the employment relationship. The interview is an excellent vehicle to establish that impression. On the other hand, a poorly conducted interview can lead to a host of implied contractual commitments that can prove especially burdensome in the long run.

The Employment Application

Several samples of an employment application are set forth in Appendix A. However, it is important to remember a few points regarding applications. There is no doubt that the employment application is probably one of the most important forms an employer utilizes. Its contents can be both a defense and weapon in wrongful discharge cases. It is a document that stays with employees throughout their careers with the company.

The application is effective as an employer defense from many points of view. It gives the employer information regarding the employee that can later be the source of validating the truthfulness and honesty of an employee, i.e., if they misrepresented their previous employment.[5] It can be utilized in a future wrongful termination case as well and set forth some of the employer's policies regarding employment and termination. It can also be the source of an agreement since employees generally sign the application form.

The application should set forth instructions on how it should be completed. The employer should identify the areas it wishes to be filled out. There should be little question that

5. In wrongful discharge cases, a number of courts have ruled that misrepresentations as to prior work history and/or one's qualifications can bar a plaintiff's subsequent claim that he was discharged without just cuase. Robitzek v. Reliance Intercontinental Corp., 183 N.Y.S.2d 870, 7 A.2d 407 (App. Div. 1959), *aff'd,* 7 N.Y.2d 1041, 200 N.Y.2d 424, 167 N.E.2d 74 (1960); Forbes v. Hotel Intercontinental Maui, 2 IER Cas. (BNA) 833, 839–840 (D. Haw. 1987); Setzer v. South Columbia Basin Irrigation Dist., 19 Wash. App. 502, 576 P.2d 82 (Ct. App. 1978). Moreover, apart from facing dismissal of his claim due to prehire misrepresentations and lies, a plaintiff also runs the risk of being assessed costs and sanctions if he files a suit and then is subsequently found to have falsified or misrepresented his job history and background for employment. See Bynum v. Michigan State Univ., Case No. G 84-70 CA5, (W.D. Mich. June 22, 1987) (sanctions imposed against plaintiff pursuant to Fed. R. Civ. P. 11). In *Bynum,* plaintiff lied on his employment application about his prior work history and the reasons for leaving earlier jobs. In his Complaint, he swore that he was qualified for the job he applied for and was hired into. The Court, however, held that "by virtue of having falsified his application, he was not [qualified]" even though he had actually worked a number of years for the university. *Id.* at p.12. See also Mathis v. Boeing Military Airplane Co., 719 F. Supp. 991 (D. Kan. 1989).

the employee understood what to do and how to fill out the form.

The following is a sample:

INSTRUCTIONS TO ALL APPLICANTS:
The careful and thoughtful completion of this application is an important step in our consideration of individuals for employment. Therefore, *you must complete the entire application.* If you do not, you will not be considered for employment. Your application must also specify the position you are applying for; stating that you will do "anything" is too indefinite and will result in your application not being accepted by the company.

Please be further advised that your application will go into our inactive file 90 business days from the date of application. In order for you to keep your application current it will be necessary for you to inform our personnel office in writing, prior to the expiration of the 90-day period, that you wish to remain on the company's active applicant list. If, at the end of the 90-day period, we have not received written notice from you, your name will be taken off the active applicant list and you will not be considered for employment when a vacancy occurs. Should you contact the company after the 90-day period has expired, you will be treated as a new applicant.

The application provides information that enables us to determine whether an applicant has the interests, background, and experience to be given additional consideration for employment. In most cases, circumstances will prevent a preliminary interview; therefore, the conscientious completion of this form is necessary inasmuch as it will supply much of the information normally covered in such a session. At the appropriate time you will be required to establish your citizenship or, if not a citizen, your eligibility for employment. Please print in ink and use your own handwriting. Use the space on the last page to clarify any responses or, if desired, tell us anything else about yourself you believe relevant.

After you have read these instructions and prior to leaving the company's personnel office, please ask the personnel person any questions that you may have. He/she will be happy to answer them for you.

The listing of former employers is most important. Most applications generally list three or four previous employers. Some applications set forth *all* of the prior employers of the individual involved. This is a good practice for many reasons and will especially help the employer evaluate the individual's background and make certain there are no unexplainable gaps in employment as well as make certain that the individual set forth all of their prior work experiences.

In addition, the prospective employee should explain any gaps in employment and why the individual was unemployed for a period in excess of a month or so and should explain why they left their prior position.

Depending on the type of position involved, applications may also include specific questions regarding the use of office equipment, the utilization and operation of other kinds of equipment, and any education and/or special technical education that the individual might have.

Another important area that should be covered is the area of potential physical or medical problems. The application may have a question regarding the person's physical and medical problems that they believe would interfere with their ability to perform the job. One should check state law regarding what is permissible in this regard. Also, federal government contractors are required to ask individuals to indicate if they are handicapped or a veteran.

In regard to questions of prior criminal convictions, individual state laws need to be checked further. In summary, the following is an outline of an employment application:

I. Instructions
II. Name and Vital Statistics (Excluding Age)
III. Education
IV. Employment History (All Prior Jobs)

V. Specific and Relevant Job Skills (i.e., Driver's License)
VI. Specific Questions Regarding Medical Problems That Affect Ability to Do the Job, Criminal Convictions
VII. Disclaimers and Notices

Employment Application Disclaimers and Notices

At the end of the application there should be a place set forth where a clear employment at-will disclaimer should be written. This disclaimer should also be in all employment manuals and handbooks (see Chapter 7). The disclaimer should indicate that any individual who gives false information will be terminated and more importantly that their employment is at will and subject to termination at any time.

In addition to the information gathered, most employment applications should contain statements concerning a variety of topics, which applicants acknowledge and sign. These statements vary and can include the following:

1. An agreement that employment is subject to a physical examination.[6]
2. An agreement not to reveal trade secrets or confidential information.
3. An agreement that employment is subject to the company's ability to conduct a pre-employment investigation.
4. A statement that any fraudulent or false information contained in the application will be grounds for termination of employment.

---

6. Regulations of the Department of Labor applicable to programs receiving federal financial assistance and federal contractors require that pre-employment inquiries and physicals must be clearly job related. *See, e.g.,* 29 C.F.R. § 32.15; 41 C.F.R. § 60-741.6(c). Similar laws apply to private employers generally in many states. *See, e.g.,* MASS. GEN. L. ch. 151B, § 4(16) (1989).

5. An understanding that an employment relationship is terminable at will and there is no employment contract.

A typical at-will disclaimer for an employment application is:

> In consideration of my employment, I agree to conform to the rules and regulations of the company, and my employment is at-will and can be terminated with or without cause and with or without notice at any time at the absolute option of either the company or myself. I understand that no manager or representative other than the ______ of the company has authority to enter into any agreement for employment for any specified period of time, or to make any agreement contrary to the foregoing.

Courts have ruled upon the impact of job application disclaimers. In *Carpenter v. American Excelsior Co.,*[7] the issue was whether a job application disclaimer is binding if the plaintiff did not read or discuss the provision with the interviewer.

The plaintiff, a 62-year-old floor covering specialist, claims that he was terminated contrary to an implied oral contract that he could be terminated only for just cause.[8] The promise was supposedly made during the employment interview.

The employment application contained the following clause: "Further, I understand and agree that my employment is for no definite period and may regardless of the date of payment of my wages and salary be terminated at any time without any previous notice."[9] The plaintiff claims he never read the "fine print" containing this language, and that he and the interviewer never discussed this clause. Notwithstanding these arguments, the court granted summary judgment.

---

7. Carpenter v. American Excelsior Co., 650 F. Supp. 933, 1 IER Cas. (BNA) 1370 (E.D. Mich. 1987).
8. *Id.* at 934.
9. *Id.* at 935.

The court ruled that according to the Michigan Supreme Court, "failure to read or understand an agreement is not cause for avoiding the same."[10] The purpose of the employment application was to notify the plaintiff that his employment was terminable at will. "Therefore, he should be bound by the concession. . . ."[11] (Furthermore, the plaintiff did not establish "any basis for a specific durational contract.")[12]

It is important to note that there are cases that found some employment disclaimers to be invalid under certain circumstances. Notwithstanding such the employers should continue to use them in the contents of their particular state law.[13]

Other Application Statements

Another important statement that should be placed on the application is required by the federal Fair Credit and Report-

---

10. *Id.* at 937.
11. *Id.*
12. *Id.*
13. McLain v. Great Am. Ins. Co., 208 Cal. App. 3d 1476, 256 Cal. Rptr. 863 (1989) the court held the disclaimer was not integrated and found the following to be an invalid disclaimer:

> I agree that my employment and compensation can be terminated with or without cause, and with or without notice, at any time, at the option of either the Great American Insurance Company or myself. I also understand and agree that the terms and conditions of my employment may be changed, with or without cause, and with or without notice, at any time by the Great American Insurance Company. I understand that no representative of the Great American Insurance Company has any authority to enter into an agreement contrary to the foregoing." *Id.* at 1478, 256 Cal. Rptr. at 265.

see also Pagdilao v. Maui Intercontinental Hotel, 703 F. Supp. 863 (D. Haw. 1988). Held: the federal district court declined "to pronounce rule that employment-at-will disclaimers categorically preclude an argument based on implied-in-fact contract or contract modification," because Hawaii's highest court had not yet pronounced the rule. *Id.* at 866. "It is understood that if engaged, my employment may be terminated *at any time,* either by myself or the hotel." *Id.*

ing Act. If an employer is conducting an investigation of an employee that involves their general reputation in the community, their finances, and community standing, the Fair Credit and Reporting Act requires that the individual be notified that this investigation will take place and that they have a right to request the disclosure regarding the nature and scope of the information requested.

The Fair Credit and Reporting Act was written to protect mainly consumers who were involved in obtaining their credit standing. However, it does apply to employment situations. This purpose goes even further and covers situations involving individuals who are being evaluated for employment, promotions, reassignment, or retention as an employee. Therefore, it is important that the following type of written statement be placed on the application if this type of investigation is being conducted:

> We intend to request a background investigation regarding your general reputation, education, work experiences, finances, and community standing. In accordance with the Fair Credit and Reporting Act, you have a right to request in writing a disclosure of the nature and scope of the information requested.

or in the alternative:

> An investigative consumer report may be requested by the company in connection with my employment. I further understand that upon reasonable written request, I will be informed whether a consumer report was requested, and if requested, the name and address of the consumer reporting agency that furnished the report.

Special Situations

Pre-employment Physical Exams

Pre-employment physical exams are being utilized more and more. Some employers feel that due to the high cost of benefits it is important that they be able to hire employees when they know more about their physical condition. The utilization of the physical exam for this purpose can have many legal ramifications.

Firstly, the physical exam should be utilized only in accordance with and upon reviewing the specific job in question. In other words, the physical exam and the medical factors to be tested are to be job related. This is required by most state and federal laws regarding handicap discrimination. In addition, the information provided by a physical exam should be kept confidential. It is the issue of privacy that might eventually lead to litigation especially if an employee is later terminated for issues related to their physical condition and/or handicap.

Government contractors under the federal "Rehabilitation Act" as well as employers in certain states (i.e., New Jersey) are prohibited from conducting a physical exam until an offer of employment is made. However, federal contractors may condition offers of employment on the results of a pre-employment physical provided that all employees are subject to the same exam, the exam is job related, and the results are confidential.

Since wrongful discharge claims might arise under different causes of action including causes of action for privacy and slander, physical exam results and the ensuing records are potentially dangerous documents. Employers should make certain such records are kept confidential and the information therein not disseminated or made available to those who do not need to know the information.

Reference Checks and Slander

As discussed in Chapter 3, the cause of action for slander has become a popular cause of action in wrongful discharge litigation. It is not uncommon for an employer to hire an individual and thereafter find out that certain information regarding the individual's prior employment background is not correct. This usually occurs when the results of reference checks are received. At that point the individuals are generally terminated. These situations need to be carefully handled, and certain preventive policies need to be implemented.

For example, such litigation has occurred when an employer found out that an employee who had allegedly resigned had been "terminated." In such circumstances, the courts have held that the information that the employee was "terminated" can be defamatory, if untrue, and could create a false impression that the employee was fired.[14] Employers should attempt to avoid these situations in light of their potential for wrongful discharge litigation.

The right to obtain proper reference checks is of paramount importance to employers. In this regard, one method of avoiding the preceding situation, which might result in potential slander and privacy issues, is to have the former employees sign releases permitting their former employer to release truthful information to their future employer without the risk of litigation. Normally such statements will release the employer from any responsibility for obtaining these references and will release the prior employer from any potential liability. For example:

> I understand the company may contact my prior employers to verify the information supplied herein and obtain a reference. I, therefore, agree that these inquiries may be made and I will not hold the company responsible or liable for its conducting

14. See Denny v. Mertz, 106 Wis. 2d 636, 318 N.W.2d 141 (1982) and Patton v. Royal Indus., Inc., 263 Cal. 760, 70 Cal. Rptr. 44 (1968).

such inquiries and obtaining and utilizing this information. I also agree not to hold my prior employer responsible or liable for the information supplied and its contents.

This statement can help in preventing the employee from later claiming they were improperly slandered and at the very least will give their new employer a defense against this type of litigation. Where practical, when an employer obtains information from a reference check that shows the employee has given false information or shows the employee was a poor employee in prior positions, the company should attempt to verify this information. If the employee has already been hired, they should be given the opportunity to respond to this information and provide additional information in their defense. If other information is available to verify it should also be sought.

Questions That Should Not Be Asked

During the pre-employment process, there are a number of questions that have become basic "no-no's." These questions involve issues relating to the laws of discrimination and civil rights. Beyond the questions an employer should not ask regarding age and race, etc., there are a number of subtle areas that come into play during the recruiting and selection process.

A number of state agencies who are involved with the enforcement of civil rights laws as well as the Equal Employment Opportunity Commission have issued rulings on those questions that can and cannot be answered. However, employers should review their individual state agency's rules on pre-employment questions. The following general guidelines should apply.

The Offer of Employment

When worded improperly, employment offer letters can create unwanted contractual commitments. Employers should, therefore, avoid statements promising "permanent" or "lifetime" employment and should be aware of any language that potentially limits the at-will employment relationship. At the same time, an employer has an interest in presenting the offer in an optimistic manner to ensure that the employment relationship starts on a positive note. The employer is, thus, confronted with a delicate balancing act coupled with an awareness of the potential liability that careless language can create.

It is true that courts often require a fair degree of specificity in the offering letter before imposing "durational" or "just cause" restrictions on the employer. For example, in *Hillsman v. Sutter Community Hospitals,*[15] the employer wrote a "letter of understanding" to the plaintiff that stated, in part: "We look forward to a long, pleasant, and mutually satisfactory relationship with you. . . ." The court found that these words did not constitute a specific promise sufficient to impose a just-cause standard for termination, but rather that the language in the letter expressed a mere hope or expectation.

Other cases, however, have found that a just-cause limitation on an employer's right to terminate an employee may exist based on language promising "permanent" employment. Thus, in *Hodge v. Evans Financial Corp.,*[16] the employer promised the plaintiff that his employment with the company would be "permanent." The trial court, however, granted summary judgment for the employer, and noted that the plaintiff freely conceded that no company official had ever promised that he could work for a specific period of time. The

15. Hillsman v. Sutter Community Hosp., 153 Cal. App. 3d 743, 200 Cal. Rptr. 605 (Ct. App. 1984).
16. Hodge v. Evans Fin. Corp., 707 F.2d 1566 (D.C. Cir. 1983) (District of Columbia law).

appellate court nonetheless reversed, and held that the plaintiff was entitled to a trial to determine whether the parties interpreted "permanent" as constituting a limitation of the at-will employment relationship. On remand, the trial court awarded damages for breach of a "permanent" contract. The appellate court, however, then found the contract unenforceable under the Statute of Frauds.[17]

Since the employment at-will doctrine is in a state of erosion, a disgruntled employee's ability to subject an employer to a protracted legal battle is greatly enhanced. Even when a court ultimately determines that the words "permanent" or "for life" do not constitute a limitation on the at-will employment, employers have still paid a high cost to have ambiguous language construed in their favor.

Employers can reduce these risks by drafting restrained offer letters that do not engage in "puffery" or use unclear terms. Disclaimers can also be included, but employers should be aware of the potential chilling effect this may have on the employment relationship. Such disclaimers may be more appropriately placed in an employment application, formal contract, or employee manual.[18] Ideally, then, as the following form letter demonstrates, an offering letter should be positive but succinct:

> Dear [ ],
> It is our pleasure to extend to you an offer of employment at our company, in the position of [ ] at $ [ ] per [week]

---

17. Hodge v. Evans Fin. Corp., 778 F.2d 794, 797 (D.C. Cir. 1985) (District of Columbia law).
18. Moreover, courts typically hold that employment contracts that are silent as to duration are presumptively terminable at will. See, e.g., McNulty v. Borden, Inc., 474 F. Supp. 1111 (1979), *reh'g denied,* 542 F. Supp. 655 (E.D. Pa. 1982), *cert. denied,* 460 U.S. 1016 (1983) (employment contract under state law containing no specific provision respecting duration or termination is presumed to be terminable at will); Gordon v. Matthew Bender Co., 562 F. Supp. 1286 (N.D. Ill. 1983) (contract with no definite term is terminable at will).

> [month]. We hope that you will give this offer favorable consideration, and begin working with us shortly.
>
> Although this offer does not create a contract of employment or a specific term of employment it is our hope and desire that your acceptance of our offer will be the beginning of a long and successful relationship.
>
> If you have any questions regarding your position or [name of company], please do not hesitate to contact us.
>
> Again, we are pleased to make this offer to you, and look forward to having you start with us soon.
>
> Sincerely,

Such an offering letter creates no express limitation on the at-will relationship. More importantly, a letter of this type contains no language that can easily lead an employee to conclude that rights have been created in his or her favor. See the forms in Source Material Section C for additional sample offer letters.

Probationary Period

It is not uncommon for companies to institute probationary periods as a precondition to "full time" employment. Employers often establish such periods as a way of acclimating a new employee to the company, and to give both sides a chance to look each other over. Moreover, the employers may be reluctant to grant full job security to an untested employee before the applicant has had a chance to establish his or her credentials.

Many employers, however, labor under a misunderstanding of the legal implications of a probationary period. Indeed, some courts have held that probationary periods do not necessarily grant an employer greater rights vis-à-vis its employees. For example, in *Crenshaw v. Bozeman Deaconess Hospital,*[19] the court held that the doctrine of the implied covenant of

19. Crenshaw v. Bozeman Deaconess Hosp., 693 P.2d 487 (Mont. 1984).

good faith and fair dealing (which the court had previously determined exists in all employment relationships) applied equally to probationary employees. Although the employee manual in *Crenshaw* stated that "any employee may be discharged without notice during the probationary period," the court found that other evidence may have reasonably led the plaintiff to conclude that she had job security equivalent to that of regular full-time employees. This evidence included the fact that plaintiff was led to believe that she would start employment at "permanent full-time status," the employer considered plaintiff qualified for a health insurance program that only permanent employees could join, and the employer did not follow the company personnel policy requiring an evaluation meeting between the probationary employee and that employee's supervisor at the end of the probationary period.

Similarly, in *Stone v. Mission Bay Mortgage Co.,*[20] the employer argued that since the plaintiff was a probationary employee, she could be terminated at any time without cause during the probationary period regardless of the existence of a one-year contract. Reversing the summary judgment in favor of the employer, the court stated:

> The phrase "probationary employee" does not necessarily mean that the employee may be terminated without cause at any time during the probationary period. The conditions of a probationary period, like any other part of an employment contract, may be set out by agreement between parties . . . [Plaintiff] should be allowed to prove at trial the existence and terms of the agreement regarding her probationary period, since these facts are in dispute.[21]

Employers should, thus, understand that the words "probationary period" do not automatically reduce an employees's rights. Indeed, as *Crenshaw* and *Stone* demonstrate, courts

---

20. Stone v. Mission Bay Mortgage Co., 99 Nev. 802, 672 P.2d 629 (1983).
21. *Id.,* 672 P.2d at 630.

look closely at the express language of a company's policy regarding the terms of a probationary period and evaluate the surrounding circumstances to determine when such express language conflicts with the company's practices or procedures. Employers, therefore, must not only use specific language indicating the higher level of scrutiny under which a probationary employee is judged, but must also adopt procedures consistent with such language.

Employers must also guard against conveying the impression that once an employee completes the probationary period, he or she can only be terminated for just cause. Employees may inadvertently receive this message when companies promise "permanent" employment upon successful completion of the probationary period. Employers should, therefore, make it clear that employees who complete the probationary period become "regular, full-time employees," but that the employment relationship remains terminable at will by either party. Thus, completing the probationary period does not alter the at-will relationship.

CHAPTER SEVEN

Employment Manuals & Handbooks

Exploring the Needs for an Employee Manual

In 1991, it has become common practice for companies to prepare some form of handbook or manual for employees. Such manuals generally outline the company's practices and policies dealing with personnel benefits and human resources issues. It is generally felt that the handbook can be an effective communication tool to properly communicate to all employees the company's practices and policies in this area.

However, it is not always necessary for a company to prepare such a document. It should not be an automatic reaction that every company needs a manual or a handbook. Instead, the company should review its individual situation in order to ascertain whether it should have some form of employee personnel policy handbook, or some other method of officially informing employees about company employment practices and policies.

In determining whether a manual or a handbook is necessary, factors that should be considered include size and type of the work force, diversity of operations, need for control, types of facilities, prior experience with employment-related problems, history of actual and/or threatened employment litigation, union contacts, union organizational efforts, management organization, personnel department structure, and management needs and desires.

The first aspect of a needs analysis would logically include the size and type of work force and the type and diversity of operations. It is generally true that most small employers with less than twenty-five employees at one location might not need an employee handbook. Of course, this can also depend upon other factors. A small work force working over a large area might necessitate a manual. A manual might also be needed if there are plans to expand the work force, or if there is need for more communication.

Generally, if an employer has more than one location there will be a greater need for formal and uniform communication. In this case handbooks generally are preferable. However, where the workforce includes unskilled labor, who might not wish to read or understand a manual, a manual might be a waste of time.

When reviewing the company's needs for a manual, the employer should review prior employment-related problems to determine if better written communication would have alleviated some or all of the issues. Most importantly prior employment litigation dealing with termination, re-assignment, layoffs, and related issues would have a significant bearing on the need for a manual.

For example, the authors have had many experiences where an employee is terminated without any prior documentation. If there were some policy available it would have made the case more defensible. In addition, litigation has arisen where the employer had an outdated written procedure covering termination, which it did not follow but never abolished. In such cases it is necessary to explain why these procedures were not used in the case in question. Further, discrimination claims are in many instances based on an inconsistent application of "company policy." It is therefore very important that if an employer has had these or similar experiences, they consider developing a uniform and consistent manual, *which is followed.*

The use of employee handbooks or manuals also can be the heart of an employer's union prevention program. During an employer's needs analysis, any prior contact with unions or attempts to organize nonunion facilities should weigh heavily in favor of establishing an employee handbook. These handbooks act as a "substitute" for a labor contract and set forth the employer's areas of practices and policies. Therefore, any prior union contact, or attempt at organizing, no matter how insignificant, would point to a company that should seriously consider a handbook or manual.

In determining whether to develop a handbook or a manual, one cannot overlook the present organization and structure of the company. For example, if there is no personnel function established it might be unwise to develop a handbook since there would be no one to administer it. Thus, handbooks and manuals must be consistently applied and interpreted. Without a designated individual to administer the policies contained in the manual and to ensure consistent application of such policies, it makes little sense to write one. Finally, management style also dictates the needs of the company. Some management may prefer more informal methods of communication.

It is important to note that handbooks are not the only way to communicate company personnel policies and manuals. Information can be dispersed by individual memoranda, bulletin boards, employee meetings, and practice and management procedures. However, weighing all of the factors to be considered, it is generally felt that one document that sets out the company's employment-related policies and practices is desirable.

In summary, the following points and approximate weighting could be given to your analysis:

1. Size and type of work force (25%)
2. Diversity and plant location (15%)
3. History of employment problems and litigation (20%)
4. History of union organizational attempts (25%)
5. Personnel organization and departments (10%)
6. Management style and organization (5%)

Types of Employment Manuals

Employment manuals come in different forms, shapes, and sizes. They cover different needs and are not always written for the entire work force, but a particular plant or segment of the work force it manages. An employer should be aware of the varied formats that can be drafted as well as their legal significance and impact of each.

Different types of manuals will obviously not fit every employer's needs and requirements. The following hierarchy and relationship among the many different manuals is summarized in pictorial form.

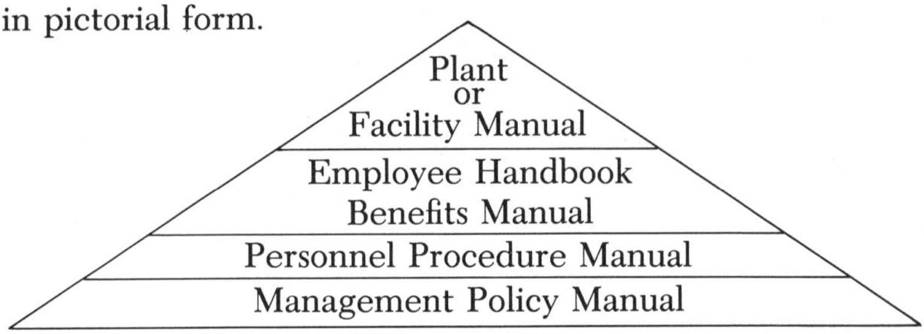

As depicted in the preceding triangle, each type of manual builds on the next. Personnel policies and practices must emanate from "above." It is the policies that management feel are important that establish the basic parameters for the company. To use a legal analogy, the policies are the constitution; the procedures that will follow are the regulations. The management policy manual is generally designed for dissemination to only department heads and officials of the company.

Management Policy Manual

The management policy manual generally deals with the basic rules and policies of the company, including:

- Accounting policy and financial reporting
- Benefit practices
- Business ethics
- Capital appropriations and lease commitments
- Compliance with antitrust laws
- Conflict of interest
- Contracts and contractual relationships
- Corporate development
- Corporate policies
- Credit and collections
- Employee health and safety
- Energy conservation and use
- Environmental protection
- Equality of opportunity in employment
- Financing
- General communications, internal and external
- Government relations
- Information services
- Internal auditing
- Investor relations
- Legal counsel
- Management guides and unit procedures
- New products approval
- Payroll practices
- Product quality and quality assurance
- Protection of proprietary technology trademarks
- Real estate
- Risk management
- Security
- Sensitive information

- Taxation
- Unsolicited ideas and suggestions

Policy manuals are generally prepared by very large corporations. In addition, it is common to establish a procedures manual. Such a manual generally is a compilation of different procedures that "implement" and interpret the general policies of the company.

The procedure or policy manual can be an effective way to communicate the company's procedures with less legal risk of it being enforced to the same extent as an employee handbook.[1] For example, in *Anderson v. Hewlett-Packard Corp.*,[2] the plaintiff, a personnel supervisor, was terminated for sexually harassing female employees. In his employment interview, the interviewer told plaintiff about the company's discipline and termination policy. He was also told about the "deadly sins," commission of one of which constituted grounds for immediate dismissal. The supervisor's manual combined policies concerning involuntary termination. That section gave managers and supervisors the discretion to summarily terminate an employee for gross misconduct. Harassment was included in the category of gross misconduct.[3]

In view of the fact that the manual "explicitly state[d] that '[s]uch conduct [that] has the purpose or effect of interfering with an individual's work performance or creating an unfriendly or offensive work environment' is a violation of H-P policy,"[4] the court held that the plaintiff's actions violated H-P's guidelines and that he was lawfully terminated.[5]

---

1. Numerous court decisions have ruled that procedures manuals may not constitute "contracts" since they are not generally disseminated to all employees but to a limited number of managers. This is discussed further when discussing termination policies herein at page 275.
2. Anderson v. Hewlett-Packard Corp., 694 F. Supp. 1294 (N.D. Ohio 1988).
3. *Id.* at 1297.
4. *Id.* at 1303.
5. *Id.* at 1304.

In *Stevenson v. Potlatch Corp.*,[6] the issue was whether a probation memo constituted an implied promise to terminate only for just cause. The plaintiff, a plant manager for the defendant, was given a memo dated September 27, 1984, placing him on probation until February 1985.[7] He was placed on probation for failing to correct a substance abuse problem that was prevalent at the plant.[8] Among his causes of action, the plaintiff alleges that he was not an employee at will because of an implied contractual right found in the Potlatch Salary Administration Manual.[9]

The court ruled in favor of the defendant and held that "the Salary Administration Manual was never intended by the defendant to be used as an employment manual. It was intended to be nothing more than a guide to be used by supervisors and managers to implement salary policy. Moreover, plaintiff never relied upon the manual as a source of continued employment."[10]

Personnel Procedures

Generally an employment-related procedures manual for management includes:

6. Stevenson v. Potlatch Corp., 674 F. Supp. 1410 (D. Idaho 1987), *aff'd*, 874 F.2d 816 (9th Cir. 1989).
7. *Id.* Stevenson v. Potlatch Corp., 674 F. Supp. at 1413.
8. *Id.*
9. *Id.* at 1417.
10. *Id.*

PERSONNEL PROCEDURES MANUAL

1. Introduction

    Foreword
    History of the Company Disclaimer
    Equal Employment Opportunity

2. Recruiting, Interviewing, and Selecting

    Nondiscrimination Policy
    Recruiting
    Interviewing
    Selection Criteria
    Screening Profile
    Reference Checks
    Hiring of Relatives
    Employing Minors
    Probationary Period

3. Work Hours

    Exempt/Nonexempt Employees
    Basic Hours
    Overtime
    Holidays
    Vacation
    Eligibility for Vacation Pay
    Jury Duty
    Sick Pay
    Leaves of Absence
    Adverse Weather Conditions
    Bereavement Leave
    Maternity Leave of Absence
    Time Cards
    Time Card Procedures
    Time Sheets

Immigration Reform and Control Act
Name Badges
Name Badge Request (Sample)
Privileged Information Agreement
Request for Addition to Staff (Sample)
Request for Temporary Help (Sample)

5. Employee Benefit Programs/Plans

Benefit
Benefit Summary
Continuation of Health Care Benefits (Federal Law COBRA)
Dental Plan
Disability Benefits
Disability/Leaves of Absence—Payment of Health Care Benefits
Eligibility
Employee Benefit Program
Group Enrollment Card (Sample)
Health Care Benefits
Health Maintenance Organizations Health Options
Life Insurance Plans
Pension Plan
Savings and Investment Retirement Plan
Worker's Compensation

6. Orientation and Training

Employee Orientation—Corporate
Employee Orientation—Sales Offices
Sales Office Operations Procedures
Training
Career Development

7. Conduct and Disciplinary Action

   Conduct—Guidelines
   Absenteeism
   Tardiness
   Personal Image
   Personal Phone Calls
   Disciplinary Action
   Disciplinary Procedures Causes for Immediate Termination
   Smoking Policy
   Smoking Policy—Sales Office
   Harassment
   Assisting Employees with Life Threatening Illnesses
   Solicitation
   Trade Secrets and Confidentiality Policy
   Noncomputation Policy
   Conflict of Interest Policy
   Drug and Alcohol Abuse
   Nondiscrimination Policy

8. Supervisors' Responsibility to the Company

   Working Through People
   Cost Control
   Other Supervisors on the Same Management Level
   Immediate Supervisor/Manager

9. Performance Appraisals

   Description
   Guidelines
   Procedure
   Performance Appraisal (Sample)

10. Job Descriptions/Organizational Charts

    Job Descriptions (Samples)
    Organizational Charts (Samples)

11. General

    Employee Communication Policies
    Personnel Files
    Employee Assistance Programs
    Travel and Expenses
    Company Vehicles
    Referral Fees
    Amendments to Policies

Supervisor's Handbook

The supervisor's handbook, given to all levels of management includes, when appropriate, the following:

ADMINISTRATIVE PRACTICES

- Recruitment and hiring, policies and procedures
- Employment opportunity, policies, and procedures
- Sexual harassment, policy and procedures
- Progressive discipline, policies and procedures*
- Salary and benefit policies continuation
- Termination, policies and procedures
- Leaves of absence and other time off
- Part-time employees
- Personnel records
- Contribution and solicitation policy
- Communication, policies and procedures

---

*Even though these procedures are written solely for management and supervisor policies, dealing with discipline should be carefully monitored. See discussion on Termination on page 275.

COMPENSATION

- Salary administration program
- Nonexempt compensation program guide
- Performance appraisal
- Annual incentive award program
- Commendation award program
- Exempt compensation program guide

EMPLOYEE BENEFITS
EMPLOYEE PROGRAMS

- Employee assistance program
- Employee communications
- Employee grievance procedures
- Employee community involvement program
- Program of matching gifts to education
- Service award program
- Suggestion system
- Exit interviews

INDUSTRIAL RELATIONS

- Facility closings
- Handling employee performance problems
- Discipline and termination, policies and procedures

PERSONNEL DEVELOPMENT

- Organization review process
- Tuition refund program
- Training
- Upward mobility

STAFFING

- Internal placements
- Recruiting, search, selection, and employment

- Reference checks
- Staffing authorizations

TRAVEL AND ENTERTAINMENT

- Travel and entertainment guidelines

YOU AND YOUR COMPANY

- Opportunity with (Company)
- (Company) wage policy
- Classification of employees
- Communications—complaint procedures
- Opportunity to express yourself
- Training and development

EMPLOYEE INFORMATION

- Absence and tardiness
- Disciplinary procedures
- Employee benefits
- Employee hours
- Overtime procedures
- Time off procedures
- Leave of absence policies
- Employee rules
- Hiring, promotion, and advancement
- Pay
- Performance reviews
- Personal purchases
- Salary increases
- Safety rules
- Telephone procedures
- Termination—procedures

The Employee Handbook

The employee handbook is probably the most common form of employer-employee communication vehicle. This handbook is generally given to all employees upon hire or subsequently. However, the employee handbook can create the greatest risks to the company.

The handbook generally covers all employment related issues, such as:

Alcohol and Drugs Policy
Attendance
Breaks/Rest Periods
Communications
Company History or Statement of Company Business
Company Philosophy
Company Property and Inspections
Company Work Rules
Confidentiality
Confidentiality of Work-Related Information
Customer Relations
Discipline Policy
Dress Code
Earned Compensable Time
EEO/Affirmative Action Statement
Employee Assistance Program
Employee Relations Policy
Employment At-Will Disclaimer
Employment of Relatives
Get Acquainted Period (Probation)
Holiday Pay
Holidays
Inclement Weather
Insurance Benefits
Job Classifications/Grading
Leaves of Absence

1. Medical Leave (Including Maternity)
2. Jury Duty
3. Military Leave/Reserve Duty
4. Bereavement Leave

Meal Money
Merit Increases
On-the-Job Training
Outside Employment
Overtime
Paid Rest Period
Pay Schedule
Performance Appraisal
Personal Appearance
Personal Use of Company Property
Personnel Records
Physical Examination
Premium Pay
Promotions
Retirement Program
Safety Rules
Sexual Harassment Policy Statement
Shift Differentials
Short-Term Paid Sick Leave
Smoking Policy
Solicitation/Distribution of Literature on Working Time/On Break Time
Tardiness
Telephone Use
Time Cards/Time Sheets
Transfers
Uniforms and Protective Devices
Vacations
Workers' Compensation Act and Insurance

Working Hours
Working Schedule
In specific areas, such documents normally include:

FRINGE BENEFITS

1. Health Insurance
   Contributory
   Noncontributory
2. Life Insurance
3. Short-Term Disability
4. Long-Term Disability
5. Pension Plan
6. Dental Plan
7. Opthamological Plan
8. Workers' Compensation Insurance
9. Others

PART-TIME EMPLOYMENT

1. Compensation
2. Overtime
3. Eligibility for Insurance Coverage
4. Pension Plan
5. Vacations
6. Holidays
7. Leaves of Absence

DISCIPLINE/DISCHARGE

Termination for Misconduct
Causes-
Verbal Warnings
Written Warnings

Layoffs
Grievance and Arbitration

Exit Interview
Conversion of Group Insurance (COBRA)
Retirement
Re-Employment

Plant or Facility Manual

The individual plant or facility manual includes numerous topics dealing with the particular facility. Companies with numerous facilities might need different manuals for each facility. Topics covered can include location of certain offices, availability of lunch and meal facilities, local rules and procedures, and local statutes. The following are some sample areas generally covered:

- Access between floors
- Access to company
- Cafeterias, company stores
- Car and van pooling
- Cashier services
- Company identification cards
- Company location and statistics
- Courier service
- Credit union
- Emergency telephone numbers
- Employee communications
- Facilities for the disabled
- Fire drills
- Local job bidding
- Meal allowance and commutation expense
- Medical department/health services
- Personal appearance
- Public telephones
- Recreational activities
- Security and fire safety
- Solicitation and distribution

- Speaker system
- Sprinkler system
- Telephone use
- Training and development programs
- Transfer policy
- Transportation information
- Visitors

The Legal Significance of Employment-Related Handbooks

Employee handbooks have continued to be a significant weapon for plaintiff's attorneys. Since the first edition of this book, additional courts have determined the legal impact of manuals on employee rights. For example, in *Aiello v. United Air Lines, Inc.*,[11] and *Zaccardi v. Zale Corp.*,[12] similar results were obtained in both cases. Both courts indicated that the personnel manual creates an implied contract. In *Aiello*, the employee operated under a manual that stated that the airline needed good cause for discharge. The court found the manual created binding disciplinary standards and procedures that apparently were not overcome by an effective disclaimer and reaffirmation of at-will employment. In *Zaccardi*, the employee prevailed upon the issue of whether the manual created an implied contract to defeat the motion for summary judgment.

The Importance of a Disclaimer

In light of the possible enforceability of handbooks and manuals as contracts, one of the important legal questions,

11. Aiello v. United Air Lines, Inc., 818 F.2d 1196 (5th Cir. 1987).
12. Zaccardi v. Zale Corp., 856 F.2d 1473 (10th Cir. 1988).

when preparing such documents, involves the use of disclaimers. A disclaimer is a statement that attempts to negate the legal impact of the manual as a contract. It also states the nature of the employment relationship is employment at will. In other words, the disclaimer states in effect that the manual is not a contract and that employment is terminable at will. Even in those states that have not ruled that handbooks or manuals create enforceable contractual obligations, it is recommended that disclaimers be used to avoid unwarranted employee expectations. The following general guidelines should be followed when drafting a disclaimer:

1. It should be in a prominent location in the manual, preferably on the first printed page.
2. It should be conspicuous and/or in capital letters. It should be in bold print, be easy to read, have a border, and it should be set off in a way that would attract attention.
3. Its language should be clear and unmistakable.
4. It should be reprinted and located wherever termination and discipline is discussed.
5. It should cover contract issues, employment at will, benefit policies, and the right to change or amend the policies contained in the document.
6. Whenever possible employees should sign and acknowledge it.
7. It should be written with applicable court decisions in mind.
8. The existence and meaning of the disclaimer should be discussed at employee meetings.
9. It should be repeated in some form in various portions of the document, where appropriate.
10. It should be reprinted in other documents, such as the employment application.

Court Analysis of Disclaimers

The courts have discussed disclaimers at great length in determining the enforceability of handbooks and manuals. For example, in *Chambers v. Valley National Bank of Arizona,*[13] the court noted that the "handbook . . . contained disclaimers prominently displayed in their introductory paragraphs . . . [and thus] [D]efendant complied with the dictates of the Arizona Supreme Court and added a clear and conspicuous disclaimer to prevent its personnel manual and handbook from becoming part of its employment contracts."[14] The particular handbook provided:

> The contents of this Employee Handbook . . . are intended as guidelines only. . . . As such, the contents of this handbook DO NOT CONSTITUTE THE TERMS OF A CONTRACT OF EMPLOYMENT. Nothing contained in this handbook should be construed as a guarantee of continued employment, but rather, employment with the Bank is on an 'at will' basis.[15]

In *Nettles v. Tech Plan Corp.,*[16] the court held that although the type was the same size and color as the rest of the text, the disclaimer was contained in a separate paragraph on the first page, and was therefore conspicuous and enforceable.[17]

In *Greely v. Clairol,*[18] the court stated that "Defendant reserved its common law right to terminate its employees at will in a clear and conspicuous manner in its employment manual."[19] The first sentence of the section entitled "Termination

---

13. Chambers v. Valley Nat'l Bank of Ariz., 721 F. Supp. 1128 (D. Ariz. 1988).
14. *Id.* at 1131.
15. *Id.*
16. Nettles v. Tech Plan Corp., 704 F. Supp. 95 (D. S.C. 1988).
17. *Id.* at 97–98.
18. Greely v. Clairol, 687 F. Supp. 1002 (D. Md. 1988), *aff'd*, 883 F.2d 68 (4th Cir. 1989).
19. *Id.* at 1003.

of Employment" stated, "employment at Clairol may be terminated by either party at any time or without cause."[20]

In *Eldridge v. Evangelical Lutheran,*[21] the court held that "we believe that the disclaimer contained in the Closing Statement of the Personnel Policy Handbook of the Society operated to preserve the presumption of at-will employment and therefore the Society was not bound to follow the Progressive Discipline Procedures set forth in its employee handbook."[22] The disclaimer in question stated:

> The contents of this handbook are presented for your information. While we fully intend to continue offering the benefits and policies as written, the Lutheran Good Samaritan Society reserves the right to change or revoke them, permanently or temporarily, if it is in the best interest of the Society to do so. *No policy, benefit, or procedure implies or may be construed to imply this Handbook to be an employment contract for any period of time.* [Emphasis added]. [sic].[23]

In the leading *Woolley v. Hoffman-LaRoche, Inc.*[24] decision, the New Jersey Supreme Court held that "absent a clear and prominent disclaimer, an implied promise contained in an employment manual that an employee will be fired only for cause may be enforceable against an employer even when the employment is for an indefinite term and would otherwise be terminable at will."[25] The court then noted:

> Our opinion need not make employers reluctant to prepare and distribute company policy manuals. Such manuals can be very helpful tools in labor relations, helpful both to employer and employees, and we would regret it if the consequence of this decision were that the constructive aspects of these manu-

20. *Id.*
21. Eldridge v. Evangelical Lutheran, 417 N.W.2d 797 (N.D. 1987).
22. *Id.* at 798.
23. *Id.* at 800.
24. Woolley v. Hoffman-LaRoche, Inc., 99 N.J. 284, 491 A.2d 1257 (1985).
25. *Id.*

als were in any way diminished. We do not believe that they will, or at least we certainly do not believe that the construction aspect should be diminished as a result of this opinion.

All that this opinion requires of an employer is that it be fair. It would be unfair to allow an employer to distribute a policy manual that makes the workforce believe that certain promises have been made and then to allow the employer to renege on those promises. What is sought here is basic honesty: if the employer, for whatever reason, does not want the manual to be capable of being construed by the court as a binding contract, there are simple ways to attain the goal. All that need be done is the inclusion in a very prominent position an appropriate statement that there is no promise of any kind by the employer contained in the manual; that regardless of what the manual says or provides, the employer promises nothing and remains free to change wages and all other working conditions without having to consult anyone and without anyone's agreement; and that the employer continues to have the absolute power to fire anyone with or without good cause.

In *Morris v. Coleman, Inc.*,[26] a married supervisor and an unmarried company secretary were discharged for taking the same flight together, although neither of them were scheduled to work at that time. Both claimed that the termination was without cause and relied upon the company's employee handbook and the supervisor's manual, which stated that the purpose of the document was to ensure "fair and uniform treatment of all employees," that all employees would be discharged "only for good cause," and that disciplinary procedures are progressive. Both employees sued claiming a breach of implied contract. The court found the disclaimers contained in both the handbook and manual were ineffective to rebut a finding of implied contract since it was not established that the disclaimer was brought to the attention of the employees or that the employer sought to establish an unqualified employment-at-will relationship.

---

26. Morriss v. Coleman, Inc., 241 Kan. 501, 738 P.2d 841 (1987).

In *Jiminez v. Colorado Interstate Gas Co.,*[27] Jiminez and others were issued standard operating procedures (SOPs), which were posted in the employees' coffee room; they contained language regarding termination, as well as a disclaimer. The court disallowed the disclaimer and stated that the disclaimer must be conspicuous, the type size must vary from the balance of the document, and effectively, they must be capitalized and/or set off by a border to draw the employees' attention to them. Lacking this, it was held that the SOPs created enforceable implied contract rights.

In *Preston v. Claridge Hotel & Casino,*[28] the New Jersey courts again followed the holding in *Woolley* that the handbook/policy manual may be construed as an implied contractual offer. The issue was: Did the handbook lead employees to reasonably believe that the company's policies would be honored as terms and conditions of employment? Although the handbook in question contained a disclaimer, the disclaimer was found not to be effective to remove the case from the area of implied contracts absent an indication in straightforward terms that the employee is subject to discharge at will. The court also suggested that the disclaimer should be coupled with training of employees regarding the company's policy of at-will employment.

A recent California court decision, *McLain v. Great American Insurance,*[29] shows the importance of the use of appropriate language in written disclaimers. In *McLain* some language in the disclaimer was found to be problematic. The language in question was: "I also understand and agree that the terms and conditions of my employment may be changed with or without cause, and with or without notice at any time by the

27. Jiminez v. Colorado Interstate Gas Co., 690 F. Supp. 977 (D. Wyo. 1988).
28. Preston v. Claridge Hotel & Casino, 231 N.J. Super. 81, 555 A.2d 12 (1989).
29. McLain v. Great Am. Ins., 208 Cal. App. 3d 1476, 256 Cal. Rptr. 863 (Ct. App. 1989).

company." Curiously, the court concluded that the statement "with or without cause" could imply that the plaintiff could only be terminated for cause.

Finally, the Supreme Court of Alaska, in ruling that manuals may modify at-will contracts in that state,[30] commented that a single sentence noting the manual was informational only and not an employment contract was *not* sufficient to disclaim the import of the manual.

Absent a clear disclaimer, courts are free to interpret the document and may imply standards not intended by the company. For example, in *Leong v. Hilton Hotels Corp.*,[31] the court held that the employee handbook did not make any promises at all and found that the plaintiff could not prove that Hilton issued the handbook in order to induce its employees to remain. Thus, the court held: "[N]owhere in the handbook does it promise termination for cause or provide any rules or procedures for the determination of cause."[32]

In *Towns v. Emery Air Freight, Inc.*,[33] the court held that "while the employment manual in this case does not explicitly state that an employee may only be terminated for cause, an employee could reasonably infer from the sections of the manual dealing with [the company's] corrective action policy that employees may only be terminated for cause."[34] The "Corrective Action Policy" in question provided that:

> To help maintain standards of conduct, ensure equitable treatment of all employees, and bring attention to inappropriate behavior, Emery has instituted the Corrective Action Policy. This policy provides a defined program of progressive corrective action designed to discourage recurrence of infractions and encourage responsible behavior. The Corrective Action Policy

30. Jones v. Central Peninsula Gen. Hosp., 779 P.2d 783, (Alaska 1989).
31. Leong v. Hilton Hotels Corp., 689 F. Supp. 1565 (D. Haw. 1988).
32. *Id.* at 1570.
33. Towns v. Emery Air Freight, Inc., 3 IER Cas. (BNA) 911 (Ohio 1988).
34. *Id.* at 913.

reflects the three-component nature of the Code of Conduct, and defines specific actions to be taken for major infractions, and attendance warnings.[35]

In *Sullivan v. Snap-On Tools*,[36] the Virginia Supreme Court held that

> The mere availability of suggested disciplinary procedures, when no limit is placed on an employer's discretion in their application, does not imply that an employer may discharge only for just cause. . . . Glaringly absent is any enumeration of the grounds for dismissal with cause and there is no mention of termination with cause.[37] Here the company manual stated "It is the policy of the Company that all jobs remain terminable at-will of the Company."[38] This statement is found at the conclusion of a list of actions that are grounds for immediate dismissal.

These cases are instructive in drafting appropriate disclaimer language. The following is a suggested sample disclaimer to be inserted in the preamble to the employer's handbook or manual.

Sample Disclaimers[39]

THE BASIS OF EMPLOYMENT WITH ABC IS, EMPLOYMENT AT WILL. THEREFORE, BOTH PARTIES HAVE THE ABSOLUTE RIGHT TO TERMINATE THE RELATIONSHIP AT ANY TIME, WITH OR WITHOUT GOOD CAUSE AND NOTICE. THE EMPLOYEE HANDBOOK IS BEING PROVIDED TO YOU FOR INFORMATIONAL PURPOSES ONLY. WHILE ABC EXPECTS TO ABIDE BY THE POLICIES AND PROCEDURES DESCRIBED IN THIS

35. *Id.* at 914.
36. Sullivan v. Snap-On Tools, 708 F. Supp. 750 (Va. 1989), *aff'd*, 896 F.2d 547 (4th Cir. 1990).
37. *Id.* at 753.
38. *Id.*
39. Local state laws should be reviewed before drafting a disclaimer.

HANDBOOK, THE HANDBOOK IS NOT, AND SHOULD NOT BE IMPLIED OR CONSTRUED, TO CONSTITUTE A CONTRACT OR CONTAIN A CONTRACTUAL COMMITMENT NOR DOES THIS HANDBOOK CONTAIN ANY ENFORCEABLE PROMISES OF ANY KIND. ABC RESERVES THE RIGHT AT ANY TIME TO SUBSTITUTE, MODIFY, REVOKE, SUSPEND, TERMINATE OR CHANGE ANY OR ALL TERMS OF THIS HANDBOOK, PLANS, POLICIES, OR PROCEDURES, IN WHOLE OR IN PART, WITHOUT HAVING TO CONSULT OR REACH AGREEMENT WITH ANYONE, AT ANY TIME WITH OR WITHOUT NOTICE. THIS HANDBOOK SUPERSEDES ALL PRIOR POLICIES AND PROCEDURES OF ABC, WHETHER ORAL OR WRITTEN, AND MAY ONLY BE AMENDED BY A WRITTEN DOCUMENT SIGNED BY THE CHIEF EXECUTIVE OFFICER OF ABC. ORAL STATEMENTS THAT ARE CONTRARY TO THIS STATEMENT BY ANY EMPLOYEE, REPRESENTATIVE, OR OFFICER OF ABC SHALL HAVE NO FORCE AND EFFECT. FINALLY, WHERE THE PROVISIONS OF THE HANDBOOK CONFLICT WITH SPECIFIC WRITTEN PLAN DOCUMENTS, SUCH AS EMPLOYEE BENEFIT PLANS, THE LANGUAGE OF THE SPECIFIC PLAN DOCUMENT WILL PREVAIL.

Other Disclaimers

Examples of other disclaimer language, include:

1. The statements contained in this booklet are not to be considered binding upon (Company), but may be revised from time to time as management deems appropriate. Because of the need to change policies to accommodate changes in (Company), the following rules are subject to change without prior notice. Only written documents signed by the chief executive officer of (company) may change, amend, or alter the provi-

sions of this booklet. Any suggestions you might have for changes in the policies set forth in this manual are welcome. This manual does not constitute a contract.

2. This section of the employee handbook summarizes many of the human resource policies and practices that can affect you as an employee of the Research Division. This handbook summarizes information in more detailed sources, such as the human resource manual, and it is not intended, therefore, to answer all of your questions about these policies or about your employment or to create any contractual rights in favor of you or of (Company). The human resource staff is always available to respond to any questions you might have and to clarify the information found in this handbook, the human resource manual, and other reference materials.

3. This guidebook has been prepared to give you a general outline of (Company's) personnel policies and how they are applied. The policies and procedures described here may change from time to time, and you should check with your supervisor or with the Department of Human Resources to make sure you are up-to-date on policies and regulations that affect you. This guidebook is not a binding contract, and the Company may modify any of its provisions at any time.

4. This personnel manual contains an outline of the personnel policies and procedures to be followed by all Company units. This manual is a reference book. It is suggested, however, that each manual holder study this manual sufficiently to become familiar with its general layout and use. Also, the revised pages that are issued from time to time should be read carefully. It is not possible to answer in these pages every question that might arise regarding the Company's personnel policies and practices. Therefore, when questions arise that

cannot be answered by consulting this manual, they should be referred to (Office). The policies and procedures described herein are subject to change from time to time, without notice to employees, and at (Company's) discretion. This manual, in common with other (Company) employee manuals, handbooks, etc., is not intended to, and indeed does not, bestow any rights to employment or employment benefits to (Company) employees.

More specific disclaimers may include:

1. The manual is subject to change at the employer's sole discretion.
2. Any decision to discharge remains within the absolute discretion of the employer.
3. Employee understandings and agreements must be reduced to writing and executed by an authorized officer of the company; purported oral understandings and agreements are deemed a nullity.
4. In the event of any contradiction between the contents of the manual and company practice, the manual governs.
5. In the event that statements by supervisors are inconsistent with the manual, the manual governs.
6. None of the policies or benefits contained in this manual are intended by reason of their publication to confer any rights or privileges upon specific employees or to entitle any person to be or remain employed by the employer.
7. Interpretations of this manual are to be restricted to specific persons. Other management personnel should be carefully instructed to refrain from interpreting this manual.
8. The statements contained in this manual are not to be considered binding upon the Company, but may be revised from time to time as management deems appropriate.
9. Because of the need to change policies to accommodate changes in the company, the following rules are subject to

change without prior notice. Any suggestions you might have for changes in the policies set forth in this manual are welcome. This manual does not constitute a contract.

10. When there is a conflict between the provisions of this manual and a specific plan or policy (e.g., pension plan) the provisions of the specific plan will prevail.

It is important to note that these disclaimers only limit liability for express or implied contracts and, in most jurisdictions that allow it, for the breach of the implied covenant of good faith and fair dealing.[40] They cannot limit employment rights based on public policy or tort liability.

A separate disclaimer might be appropriate for benefit manuals. This disclaimer should refer to the original benefit plans that govern all benefits and should include a clear statement about the right of the company to terminate or modify these plans.

The following is an example of one such disclaimer:

Benefit Disclaimer
(The Employee Benefits Booklet)

This booklet is intended as an explanation and description of the Company's employee benefit plans. Although we believe these descriptive materials are accurate, they are only summaries, and any discrepancies between these summaries and the terms of the actual plans, as well as any questions, must be governed by the actual terms of the underlying more detailed plans. Copies of these documents are available at the (Company) Corporate Personnel Office.

(Company) reserves the right at any time to modify, revoke, suspend, terminate, or change any or all terms of this booklet, plans, policies, or procedures, in whole or in part, without having to consult or reach agreement with anyone, at any time, with or without notice. Such changes, alterations, or

40. Chamberlain v. Bissell, Inc., 547 F. Supp. 1067 (W.D. Mich. 1982).

amendments must be in writing signed by the client executive officer of the company.

Employer Acknowledgment

Whenever manuals are given directly to employees, there should be an acknowledgment that they have received a copy of the manual and that they recognize the right of the company to make changes when necessary. A signature should be obtained when the employee first receives the manual. For example:

Example 1:

Dear Employee:

I am pleased to have you working for me and will do all that I can to make our association pleasant and interesting. To better acquaint you with company policies and procedures affecting your employment, the Company has prepared this employment manual. The policies explained in this manual are currently in effect, and no other policies will be given effect unless they are in writing and signed by me. The sole purpose of this manual is to let you know what we expect from you and what you can expect from the Company. While I believe wholeheartedly in these policies and intend to observe them when they apply, the Company reserves the right to modify, amend, and terminate these policies at any time for any reason. You will be notified of any such changes. This manual is not intended to create, nor is it to be construed as, a contract that is legally binding either on you or the Company. Nor is it intended or to be construed as a judicially enforceable assurance of job security since employment is at will. It is simply meant to provide a guide for you and me in the future. Please sign below, which will indicate your agreement to abide by this statement, and your acknowledgment that you understand its contents.

____________________ ____________________________

[Date] [Employee Signature]

Example 2:

> Nothing in these Company rules and regulations shall be construed to limit the Company in any way in the exercise of its regular and customary functions of management. These rules and regulations are for the guidance of both the Company and the employees but are not intended to create, nor are they to be construed as, a contract or an assurance of job security and benefits.
>
> While the Company believes wholeheartedly in these rules and intends to abide by them, it reserves the right to modify, amend, or terminate them at any time for any reason. All such changes will be effective when they are posted on the plant bulletin board.
>
> I, the undersigned, have read the above rules and regulations and agree to comply with them.

____________________ ____________________________

[Date] [Employee's Signature]

Termination Policies

When drafting an employment manual an employer should consider whether to include a termination policy. An appropriate termination policy should include specific areas of conduct that necessitate discipline and/or termination. Most policies incorporate some form of progressive discipline requiring employees to be warned either verbally or in writing and in some cases suspended before final termination.

The utilization of a termination policy in an employment manual that is disseminated to the work force can have many legal risks. For example, where an employer for some reason fails to follow the stated termination procedure, a terminated employee has the opportunity to attempt to have the policy enforced as a contract, notwithstanding the previously mentioned disclaimers.

Additionally, a termination policy can create certain expectations. It also can limit an employer's option when dealing with employee misconduct or poor performance. It is, therefore, important that these policies, especially if they are incorporated in an employment manual, be very carefully drafted and include an employment-at-will disclaimer similar to the disclaimers discussed in this chapter.[41]

It is generally recommended that detailed termination policies be included in a management/supervisor procedures manual and not in an employee handbook. Summaries of such policies should be included in an employee handbook. As noted, the supervisors manual is generally addressed to managers and supervisors who have a need to know what procedures they should follow when there are conduct and performance problems that necessitate discipline and termination. Supervisor manuals, because they are not disseminated to employees, do not generally establish contractual arguments for potential litigants. Thus, some courts have found that supervisor manuals are not contractual in nature since there is no contract made between the employee and the company.

For example, in *Skramstad v. Otter Tail County,*[42] the plaintiff was employed by the county as a deputy assessor. The county had a Personnel Committee that administered the Personnel Policy Manual, which was distributed only to department heads.[43] The court held "Skramstad's access to the Policy [did not] constitute[] communication of an offer by the County."[44]

---

41. *See* Goos v. National Ass'n of Realtors, 715 F. Supp. 2, (D.D.C. 1989), which upheld such a disclaimer. The disclaimer in *Goos* stated "as an employee of the National Association of Realtors, you are considered to be an employee at will. Under this consideration, either you or the Association has the option of terminating your employment and compensation at any time, with or without cause and/or notice."
42. Skramstad v. Otter Tail County, 417 N.W.2d 124 (Minn. 1987).
43. *Id.* at 126.
44. *Id.*

As previously noted in *Stevenson v. Potlatch Corp.*,[45] the issue was whether a probation memo constitutes an implied promise to terminate only for just cause. The plaintiff, a plant manager for the defendant, was given a memo dated September 27, 1984, placing him on probation until February 1985.[46] He was placed on probation for failing to correct a substance abuse problem that was prevalent at the plant.[47] Subsequently, he was terminated. Among his causes of action, the plaintiff alleges that he was not an employee at will because of an implied contractual right found in the Potlatch Salary Administration Manual.[48]

The court ruled in favor of the defendant and held that

> the Salary Administration Manual was never intended by the defendant to be used as an employment manual. It was intended to be nothing more than a guide to be used by supervisors and managers to implement salary policy. Moreover, plaintiff never relied upon the manual as a source of continued employment.[49]

It is also recommended that when discussing termination of employment in a procedures manual that general guidelines be written, but not so specific as to tie the hands of the supervisors who are following them. If an employer feels that there is need to discuss termination of employment in an employee handbook, the termination policy should start with the following statement:

> Even though employment is at will and the parties may terminate the relationship at any time with or without cause, the

---

45. Stevenson v. Potlatch Corp., 674 F. Supp. 1410, (D. Idaho 1987), *aff'd*, 874 F.2d 816 (9th Cir. 1989).
46. *Id.* at 1413.
47. *Id.*
48. *Id.* at 1417.
49. *Id. See also* Ware v. Prudential Ins. Co., 220 N.J. Super. 135 (1987), *cert. denied*, 113 N.J. 335 (1988), when the court ruled a policy manual did not have a contractual effect, since it had limited distribution.

> company would like to set forth certain basic guidelines that would cover employee conduct and performance. This policy is not to be considered all inclusive and is a general review for employees' information only; it should not be considered a contract and may be changed or revoked at any time. Finally, although this policy sets forth specific reasons for discipline, up to and including termination, there may be other reasons for such action or there may be circumstances that warrant a deviation from these procedures.

This type of statement should appropriately respond to any claims that there is some contractual element to the termination policy.

When dealing with corrective action or progressive discipline that includes warnings and suspension, the courts have on occasion found this type of policy implies that the employer maintained a just cause termination criteria. For example, in *Towns v. Emery Air Freight, Inc.*,[50] the court found that the company had a corrective action and progressive discipline program that was "designed to discourage the occurrence of infractions and encourage responsible behavior." The court held that while the employment manual did not explicitly state the employee may only be terminated for good cause, an employee could reasonably infer from sections of the manual dealing with corrective action policy that employees may only be terminated for cause.[51]

It is important to note from a practical point of view that even with the appropriate disclaimers in a termination policy, a court may be reluctant to dismiss a case of wrongful termination without a trial. Indeed, the termination policy might give the plaintiff a vehicle that will allow an individual to withstand

---

50. Towns v. Emery Air Freight, Inc. 3 IER Cas. (BNA) 911 (Ohio 1988).
51. *Id.* at 913. *See* Aiello v. United Air Lines, 818 F.2d 1196 (5th Cir. 1987); Morriss v. Coleman Co., 241 Kan. 501, 738 P.2d 841 (1987); Zaccardi v. Zale Corp., 856 F.2d 1473 (10th Cir. 1988). Other statements are found in the manual employing discharge for cause.

summary judgment and proceed to trial, at great cost and expense to the employer. Therefore, where termination policies are incorporated in employee handbooks they should contain appropriately phrased disclaimers, clearly in both the front of the manual and at the location of the termination policy itself. Further, the policy should be written in plain English so that managers and supervisors will be able to follow it and be easily trained in its implementation.

Pointers When Drafting a Personnel Handbook

Every employer will have different areas to stress in their employee handbook. However, there are some basic provisions that should be emphasized and included in most employee handbooks.

1. It is important that the employer provide a statement dealing with discrimination regarding employment. Discrimination provisions should meet the requirements of both the federal law dealing with race, sex, age, handicap, etc., as well as meet the requirements at the individual state level that apply to the company. Some states have laws that prohibit discrimination beyond the basic requirements of the federal law, such as marital status, and these areas should be covered in a discrimination clause.

2. The employer should also include in the personnel handbook a statement on sexual harassment. These types of cases are difficult, and a harassment policy should be clearly stated. The policy should also include a complaint procedure, whereby the individual has the right to complain about the harassment to their supervisor or personnel department.

3. The manual should also contain a grievance procedure. Grievance or complaint procedures may be as vague as an "open door" policy or may be detailed procedural statements giving an employee the right to escalate their grievance to

different levels of the company. This will be discussed at greater length in the chapter dealing with alternative dispute resolution.

4. The manual should contain an acknowledgment that the employee received and read the manual and understands its contents. This will provide the employer with evidence that the employee had notice of a particular policy and was aware of the contents of the personnel handbook. Suggested employee acknowledgments are discussed previously in this chapter.

5. When drafting the manual the company should use clear language that is easy to understand. Avoid words or phrases that would imply that there is a just cause standard for termination, avoid words such as "promise," "guaranty," "permanent employee," "promise of salary increases on an annual basis," etc. Wherever needed, terms or phrases should be defined so that there is little question of the meaning and intent of such statements.

6. The manual should always include appropriate disclaimer and amendment language, as discussed herein.

A sample manual is included in the appendix. However, there is no one final form that is applicable to all companies and for all situations, and the specific state law should always be checked before disseminating the manual. Counsel should also review it. However, at a minimum, the manual or handbook should communicate to employees the company's specific policies and philosophies.

After the manual is completed and disseminated to employees, the employer should discuss and review its impact with affected employees and monitor the manual's ability to cover situations. Generally an introductory meeting with employees would be helpful. It is recommended that a manual be put together in a looseleaf form so that pages can be added and subtracted without reprinting the entire book. All pages or sections of the manual should be dated. The manual should also be reviewed periodically, at least every two years, or whenever necessary to make certain that the provisions are up-to-date regarding company policies and the ever-changing law of employment.

Keeping these suggestions in mind, employment manuals of all types should contribute to good employee relations and an efficient operation.

CHAPTER EIGHT

Performance Evaluations

Performance evaluation systems allow an employer to review its employees' performance on a regular basis. In years past evaluation systems were as informal as paying an annual increase in salary with a verbal evaluation by the individual supervisor to no specific evaluation given except for the payment of an increase in salary. In recent times these systems have usually become more formalized.

As employers started to realize that the formal monitoring of performance of the employees contributed to the success of their businesses, these periodic evaluations became more routine. In the 1970s and 1980s employers structured their systems to include a specific written format that supervisors were required to utilize when reviewing the employees working for them.

In addition to obtaining the best performance from their employees, these systems also may play an integral part in a wrongful termination lawsuit. Performance evaluation can and will be an important aspect of the employer's case when defending wrongful terminations and/or layoffs. It is the evaluation that will show a continual trend of poor performance or behavior. For example, in the normal wrongful discharge case when the employer terminates an employee for performance, the evaluation system will probably be one of the most important parts of the employer's defense. When employees are laid off in a reduction in work force situation, performance evaluation might be the only employer defense to establish why certain employees were laid off.

In addition to utilizing evaluations to manage the work force and defend the company in wrongful discharge litigation, the evaluations are also very useful for employers when developing new programs. Such a system will be helpful in the monitoring of the work force and/or certain jobs to see if functions are being carried out in the prescribed manner. Employers can also monitor the supervision of their companies and make certain that supervisors are carrying out their duties and supervising and managing the employees in the most efficient manner.

Developing a Performance Evaluation System That Suits the Particular Employer's Needs

There are no specific formats or performance evaluation systems required by law. The courts have commented upon the systems in reduction in work force cases and in other specific wrongful termination cases under the legal theories of negligence and the Civil Rights Laws. Employers therefore should act in a reasonable manner and use good business judgment to develop systems that fit their particular needs, keeping in mind certain legal guidelines, which will be discussed herein.

Before establishing a specific performance evaluation system and procedure, an employer should evaluate its work force. Such an evaluation should include the analysis of the types of jobs and positions that the employer utilizes, the seniority of its employees, how long each employee has been in his or her particular position, and the nature of the employer's operation. The employer should also consider whether a personnel department or another individual is going to monitor the process, if bonuses will be given for production and/or performance, and any other factors that dictate the need to evaluate employee performance.

This analysis enables the employer to define its needs. For example, a work force that works in a highly mechanized operation and carries out routine and repetitive job duties and functions would require a more systematic performance evaluation process. On the other hand, an employer who has a service business where employees use their own discretion would need a system that evaluates particular positions on a more individualized basis. In the latter case an open-ended format comparing the specific job duties and goals and the employee's performance would be appropriate. Further, the employer might want to have one particular system for exempt employees who carry out more routine functions and a different system for nonexempt employees who exercise discretion. Lastly, an employer should evaluate its personnel function, that is, do they employ a full-time or part-time personnel manager?

Different Performance Appraisal Formats

There is no particular format for performance appraisal that is required by law. However, after conducting an analysis and determining the needs of a particular employer, it might become clear that one performance appraisal system could be utilized for similar positions. For example, many companies establish specific performance appraisal systems for their sales operations. Since sale representatives have similar jobs, the company can utilize a performance appraisal system that will deal specifically with the individual's sales responsibilities. Such a system can incorporate the company's desires, needs, and sales objectives.

Depending upon the employer's objectives, a more open-ended appraisal system can be utilized. Such a format generally sets forth the general job duties in one section and the performance of the individual with respect to these specific job duties is then analyzed. Such a format generally is better suited for positions that carry managerial and/or other professional responsibilities as well as those utilizing a great deal of discretion. Such a form could be as simple as the following:

JOB FUNCTIONS AND GOALS	ACTUAL RESULTS AND COMMENTS ON PERFORMANCE

Many companies prefer to have one format to fit all employees and their positions. Such a format is generally appropriate in smaller companies with a limited number of employees. (See Appendix C.)

Evaluation systems tend to differ substantially company by company. The evaluation procedure can be as basic as a blank sheet of paper to be filled in based upon an individual's duties, or it can be as complex as a system that includes numerous specifically worded questions and comments that leaves little room for creative appraisals. As discussed, the type of system or program used is usually based upon the needs of the individual business. However, there are some important aspects that every system should include:

1. An analysis of the job;
2. Performance measured against specific job elements;
3. Evaluation of the employee's strength and weaknesses;

4. Goals and objectives for the employee;
5. An opportunity for the employee to correct, comment, or appeal;
6. Reasonable guidelines and training for the evaluator and several levels of review and approval; and
7. A monitoring system for the program.

Analysis of the Job

An evaluation system must be based upon the employee's ability to perform the function of the position in question. The primary guidepost for this analysis is the function of the job performed by the employee. An analysis of the job's functions includes an examination of the actual job duties, the tasks the individual employee is expected to perform, and the goals established for the individual or the position.

In many cases companies already have a job description, which should be the first reference when analyzing the position. In addition, some systems provide a method for the employee and his or her supervisor to agree upon goals for a specific period of time. Progress toward these goals should be incorporated into the analysis.

Another commonly used method requires the employee to fill out his or her major job functions on a performance evaluation form. The form is then given to the supervisor who reviews and approves the key performance elements and comments on each element.

Performance Measured Against Job Elements

Once the key job elements are established, the actual performance of the employee should be measured against these elements. The evaluation form can easily be designed with the levels of performance noted for each key job element. In some instances, the employer might want to give varying weights to each job element.

When determining levels of performance, it is recommended that the supervisor utilize, whenever possible, objective reasons and measurements in support of his or her conclusions. This analysis should involve reference to certain specific incidents or performance, especially when the employee is given a low rating.

It is important to note that an employee cannot always be evaluated on objective criteria. Although subjectivity cannot be totally removed, especially when evaluating the employee's personal characteristics, emphasis should be on objectivity when dealing with the performance of job duties and functions.

Opportunity for Employee Review and Appeal

The evaluation system must provide adequate opportunity for the employee to review and comment on the evaluation. The employee should be given an opportunity to question the job analysis. In addition, the employee should have an opportunity to study the evaluation and prepare for the review. In this regard, it is recommended that the employee be given a copy of the evaluation at least twenty-four to forty-eight hours prior to the review meeting. After the meeting, the employee should also be asked to sign the evaluation. At that time the employee should be permitted to note his or her objections or comments on the evaluation form.

The evaluation systems should allow an employee to appeal the evaluation to either a higher level of management or to the human resources department. The natural flow of an appeal is normally up through the ranks of the individual's department. For example, in a very large company, the appeal might need to be only one level over the supervisor. In a smaller company, the appeal might go as high as the president of the company.

The appeal process is an important safeguard and escape valve. It supports the contention that the system is equitable and permits due process. In addition, it can be an effective defense in future litigation when an employee claims he or she received an improper review. Thus, the failure of an employee to appeal an adverse evaluation, despite an effective appeal process, may be evidence that the employee agreed to the evaluation or, at least, conceded the appropriateness of the conclusion contained in the evaluation. Finally, it should be noted that contrary to some fears, as a practical matter the right of appeal does not generally slow down the evaluation process.

Training Evaluators and Levels of Review

The performance evaluation system is not effective unless the evaluator knows how to use it. It is, therefore, necessary that training and written instructions be given to the evaluator. Of course, the larger the company, the more difficult this process becomes. In some cases, it might be necessary to train only a select group of evaluators who are utilized throughout the company. In other circumstances, each supervisor from each individual department might have to be trained.

Written instructions should clearly define performance levels. There are generally three to five performance levels. The most common are:

1. Below standard
2. Meets most expectations
3. Meets all expectations
4. Exceeds most expectations
5. Outstanding

Regardless of the number of standards applied, the definitions need to be as clear as possible and should be communicated to all evaluators.

It must be impressed upon the evaluator that the evaluation has to be honest, and the evaluator should not be reluctant to give employees negative evaluations. Although the natural tendency is to praise an employee, evaluation systems should identify the employee's weaknesses as well as strengths to help the employee grow and develop in his or her career.

As noted, the evaluation should also be reviewed by a higher level of management. Two levels of review are typical. Multiple levels of review help protect against any bias that might consciously or unconsciously affect the supervisor's rating.

Monitoring the System

Another important safeguard is a method of centralized monitoring of the system. Monitoring can determine the effectiveness of the system as well as prevent bias, discrimination, or unequal treatment.

The evaluation program should produce a natural statistical curve. Evaluators have a tendency to rate employees higher than they should be, thus, an effective evaluation system should produce rankings with at least some part of the workforce at the lower end of the performance spectrum and some portion at the higher end. Evaluators should be retrained when this does not occur.

Periodic monitoring is also important to determine whether protected groups are intentionally or unintentionally evaluated lower than nonprotected groups. For example, if females are consistently rated lower than males, a further analysis should be performed to ensure that sex is not a determining factor in the evaluation. This same analysis should be undertaken for each protected group—e.g., minorities, elderly, handicapped, etc. It is advisable to have this analysis be done by the company's legal department or outside counsel to protect the findings from discovery in case of litigation. Finally, monitoring of the program should determine if standards are being applied in a consistent and equal manner.

Performance Evaluation Is a Year-Long Process

In addition to the regular annual evaluation, it is recommended that managers continually evaluate their employees on a regular basis. This makes the final evaluation process more legally defensible. It is most important that the evaluator plan for the year-end evaluation. This plan would commence at the beginning of the performance year and would carry through that year until the actual appraisal.

At the beginning of each performance year the manager would review the particular jobs of his or her subordinates and define their responsibilities and expectations. This is especially true for management, professional, and other positions that involve the use of discretion. In addition to the job description the manager should define specific goals for the employee's performance during the upcoming year. These goals could include (1) results to be accomplished, with targeted dates, numerical measures, and other quantifiers that are appropriate, (2) corrective measures, if the responsibilities involve preventing problems or containing exposures, (3) how the manager will evaluate performance, especially in areas without clear measurements, and (4) growth or improvement of activities and goals for employees.

The development of future expectations or goals for the reviewing year can also be determined by answering What, When, and How Well. "What" is a goal and/or result to be achieved; "When" can be a simple completion date; and "How Well" can be expressed in numeric terms or with specific project goals.

After determining the above goals and expectations, the manager should discuss them with the employee to determine if the employee agrees with the goals and expectations. Such a process will ensure that the employee feels a sense of ownership regarding these expectations. The managers should in every way encourage the employee's participation in creating the goals and expectations through a complete discussion with the employee. After this meeting, it is recommended that the goals for the upcoming year should be put in writing. After the written document is prepared, a copy should be given to the employee to make certain he or she agrees with the goals.

During the appraisal year the manager should meet with the employee periodically to obtain feedback on how the employee is performing towards the stated objectives. Such discussions will also identify individual development needs and provide a plan for improvement. By utilizing this procedure, the manager will be completely involved with the employee's performance throughout the year and make his/her evaluation a more realistic and reasonable one at the end of the year. Further, if the manager is involved and has specific examples of good and poor performance when evaluating the employee at the year-end formal process, it is more likely that the evaluation will be accepted by a court or jury in a wrongful termination or layoff case. In addition, the above performance planning program makes good sense from a management point of view and establishes a framework to accomplish the employee's individual goals as well as the company's objectives. Lastly, an ongoing performance appraisal system can become an effective communication vehicle between the manager and the employee.

Legal Aspects of Evaluations

Most of the contractual theories of implied-in-fact and implied-in-law covenants discussed are equally applicable to performance evaluations systems. Additionally, an employer must be mindful of the dangers in negligently administering performance evaluation systems. As noted in *Chamberlain v. Bissell, Inc.,* the court found that an employer negligently administered its evaluation system when it failed to inform an employee during the evaluation that the company was considering his discharge and, in fact, later discharged him. The court required some advance notice of the discharge, notwithstanding the lack of such required notice in the company's evaluation policy. The court stated that the company negligently performed its contractual duty to conduct annual evaluations when it did not notify the plaintiff that it was considering discharge if he did not correct his problems, and when, without prior warning or notice, it discharged him.

The court's decision in *Chamberlain* has had less impact than expected. Tort-based liability for negligent evaluation is an isolated phenomenon. Subsequent cases have rejected the legal doctrine on which *Chamberlain* is based—that a contract can create the duty to use reasonable care—and have found that a duty of care must be created by law or statute, and not by contract.

In most cases, therefore, contract law governs claims that an employer did not properly administer an evaluation system. These cases stress that job security is created by contractual promises, not by tort-based duties of care. Thus, a number of decisions have held that evaluation procedures do not create a reasonable expectation that the employment contract would only be ended by just cause. Of course, courts have ordered a trial when the particular facts of the case indicate that the evaluation process did create a legitimate expectation of job security.

For example in *Quinones v. United States,* the Third Circuit reviewed on employee's performance and work record under the Federal Tort Claims Act where the employee maintained that the employer did not accurately evaluate his performance and work record. The plaintiff also claimed that the government did not follow its manual when dealing with personnel records and that his work records were inaccurate and caused adverse reaction by prospective employers. The court ruled that the Federal Tort Claims Act creates a duty to use reasonable care in maintaining the accuracy of records. In addition, under the Pennsylvania common law, the court noted that the employer "assumes to render a service obligates himself to care." For breach of that duty, the court held that the plaintiff may have a cause of action if he is injured thereby and if the defendant's breach is the proximate cause of his injury.

A lesson to learn from this decision is that if a performance appraisal system is established, the performance appraisals must be administered with due care and with an absence of negligence.

In sum, as a preventive measure an employer must ensure that its evaluation system: (1) is based on objectively stated criteria, (2) is being administered fairly and consistently, and (3) provides adequate notice and due process for affected employees. An employer must also be confident that the system is applied as it is written.

CHAPTER NINE

Termination of Employment

Introduction

The actual process of termination and its prior review is the critical point in the preventive process. An employer that is preparing to terminate an employee should proceed with care and engage in a number of preventive actions that should include the investigation of the surrounding circumstances, discussion of the important aspects of the situation with relevant management and the employee in question, and the final review process. When it comes time to terminate, an employer should be well aware of the employee's situation, his or her emotions, and carry it out in the most humane way possible.

This chapter discusses the preventive safeguards an employer should follow before terminating an employee. It is important to note that a review of the process and adherence to the suggested preventive measures can do a great deal to avoid and prevent future litigation.

Discipline Policies and Procedures

The handling of discipline and termination can generally be guided by company policies and procedures. These procedures can cover a variety of topics ranging from a very brief summary of the area to a lengthy procedure that includes recommended forms.

Regardless of which type of procedure is published, the procedure should clearly state that although it is generally applied, it may be disregarded for appropriate reasons or at management's discretion. Flexibility must be maintained since it is not possible to write a procedure that pertains to every conceivable situation.

The procedures can include the following topics: (1) problem identification, (2) follow-up and evaluation, (3) development of a plan of action, (4) review and monitoring of the problem, and (5) final actions. In addition, the employer may want to adopt a policy that defines at great length the reasons for termination and sets out the procedure for approval of the termination action.

Several concepts should be considered when drafting a termination policy to limit possible termination problems. A clear disclaimer should be incorporated into the policy, indicating that the policy is not a contract and that it merely indicates a general statement of intent for supervisors concerning termination. The following language might be appropriate:

> This section on employee terminations has been drafted for distribution to supervisory employees only. It is not intended that it shall form a contract between the Company and its employees. Rather, it describes for supervisory employees the Company's general philosophy concerning termination decisions. The Company recognizes, however, that each termination situation presents a unique set of circumstances. Fairness and common sense dictate that these unique situations be reviewed and decided on their individual facts and in the context of surrounding circumstances.

Set forth in Appendix E are sample termination procedures. (See also the forms contained in Appendix F.)

Progressive Discipline

Progressive discipline is a procedure that provides notice to an employee of his or her shortcomings and gives the employee an opportunity to correct them. The word *progressive* indicates that each step of this procedure becomes more severe if the employee's conduct is not rectified or improved. The normal progressive discipline system includes several warnings to the employee regarding his or her performance. In some cases the next step of discipline includes suspension from work. Generally, however, suspension is not applicable to middle management and upper management positions, and should be utilized only when the suspension is helpful and serves a purpose.

There has been a great deal of discussion by the courts and commentators regarding the use of progressive discipline in wrongful termination matters. Several courts have held that a progressive discipline policy contained in a manual or handbook is an enforceable contractual obligation. These decisions have enabled an employee to proceed in a litigation based on the alleged violations of the policy.[1] In *Pine River State Bank v. Mettille,*[2] the court upheld a jury verdict and damage award for the plaintiff and endorsed the philosophy of progressive discipline: "Had the procedural disciplinary steps been honored, Mettille might have corrected his deficiencies to the bank's satisfaction and have kept his job." In *Osterkamp v. Alkota Manufacturing, Inc.,*[3] the court upheld a jury verdict

1. Duldulao v. St. Mary of Nazareth Hosp. Center, 136 Ill. App. 3d 763, 483 N.E.2d 956, 957, 958 (1st Dist. 1985); Pudil v. Smart Buy Inc., 607 F. Supp. 440, 442, 443 (N.D. Ill. 1985); Damrow v. Thumb Coop. Terminal, Inc., 126 Mich. App. 354, 337 N.W.2d 338, 343 (1983) (court remands with finding of "substantial and material" noncompliance with policy in manual).
2. Pine River State Bank v. Mettille, 333 N.W.2d 622, 631–32 (Minn. 1983).
3. Osterkamp v. Alkota Mfg., Inc., 332 N.W.2d 275, 276–77 (S.D. 1983).

for the plaintiff, noting that none of the procedures were followed in this case. In *Wagenseller v. Scottsdale Memorial Hospital,*[4] the court had to determine the factual issue of whether the policy was part of a contractual relationship.

Other courts have declined to enforce progressive discipline policies, so that violations of such procedures do not result in contractual liability for the employer. The rationales of these decisions vary, and are quite instructive. In *Prost v. F. W. Woolworth Co.,*[5] the manual was confidential to management, and was not followed in 50 percent of the discharges. In *Bouzianis v. U.S. Air, Inc.,*[6] the policy was not distributed to the employees, and was essentially a disciplinary guideline for supervisors.[7]

Unlike *Bouzianis* and *Prost,* a court has enforced a progressive discipline policy even though the policy listed thirty-two exceptions and stated that it was not all inclusive, but was only a guideline.[8]

Some employers have fashioned policies that maximize their discretion to manage progressive discipline, and also exclude specific incidents from that program. In *Bouzianis,*[9] the manual allowed the employer to select the step at which it would begin the disciplinary process. The court upheld a decision to begin with the termination step for an airline employee who violated policy on block-booking seats for personal use. In *Reid*

4. Wagenseller v. Scottsdale Memorial Hosp., 119 LRRM (BNA) 3166, 3175 (Ariz. 1985).
5. Prost v. F.W. Woolworth Co., 120 LRRM (BNA) 2867, 2868 (D. Kan. 1985).
6. Bouzianis v. U.S. Air, Inc., 120 LRRM (BNA) 2927, 2930 (D. Mass. 1985).
7. *See also* Ring v. R.J. Reynolds Indus., Inc., 597 F. Supp. 1277, 1280 (N.D. Ill. 1984) (policy not bargained for); Williams v. Delta Haven, Inc., 416 So. 2d 637 (La. Ct. App. 1982) (plaintiff did not allege hiring for a fixed period of time); Shaw v. S. S. Kresge Co., 167 Ind. App. 1, 328 N.E.2d 775 (1975) (policy from handbook not enforceable).
8. Wagenseller v. Scottsdale Memorial Hosp., 119 LRRM (BNA) at 3175.
9. Bouzianis v. U.S. Air, Inc., 120 LRRM (BNA) at 2930.

v. Sears, Roebuck & Co.,[10] the court held that a discharge was not improper when a "corrective interview" policy was not applied because it excluded terminations due to willful misconduct, such as in the case in question.

Economically based discharges have elicited different rulings from courts under stated termination policies. The Sixth Circuit Court of Appeals allowed a jury to determine whether the specific economic adversity that caused an employee's termination was just cause for discharge.[11] Another court has held that an economically based termination was not covered by progressive discipline, because the employer "faced a financial, not a disciplinary, problem."[12]

In addition to the legal requirements, there are valid personnel reasons for implementing some form of progressive discipline. Initially, a progressive disciplinary procedure may result in the improvement of an unsatisfactory employee, thereby avoiding termination. Further, if the employee is ultimately terminated, the progressive discipline procedure provides significant evidence that the stated reason for the termination was not pretextual. Finally, progressive discipline establishes a record of fairness in the treatment of the terminated employee. As a court indicated in *Pugh v. Sees Candies, Inc.*,[13] good cause generally makes "a fair and honest reason regulated by good faith." Clearly, a progressive discipline system can therefore be evidence of an employer's good faith.

On the other hand, the development of a progressive discipline system is not always appropriate or applicable. For exam-

---

10. Reid v. Sears, Roebuck & Co., 588 F. Supp. 558, 561 (E.D. Mich. 1984), *aff'd*, 790 F.2d 453 (6th Cir. 1986).
11. Boynton v. TRW, Inc., 781 F.2d 555 (6th Cir. 1986) *reh'g granted en banc*, 121 LRRM (BNA) 3544 (1986) (jury verdict for plaintiff reversed on other grounds) (Michigan law).
12. Rompf v. John Q. Hammons Hotel, Inc., 685 P.2d 25 (Wyo. 1984).
13. Pugh v. Sees Candies, Inc., 171 Cal. Reptr. 917, 116 Cal.3d 311 (1981).

ple, there are cases of certain types of misconduct such as theft, assault, and insubordination that should not be treated under a progressive discipline system. Therefore, when a progressive discipline system is put into effect, a carefully worded disclaimer should be provided. For example:

> Not all performance or conduct issues lend themselves to a step-by-step approach such as that outlined above. There are times when immediate disciplinary action, including termination, is warranted on the first occurrence of a performance or conduct problem. Further, it is the Company's position that employees have the right to terminate their employment at any time and the Company reserves the same right at any time to terminate employment with or without good cause.

Progressive discipline may include placing an employee on probationary status. This alternative should be carefully monitored and limited to performance problems. Probationary status should not be specifically mandated in every case. It is generally advisable to incorporate language that provides that probationary status is optional, so that a terminated employee cannot demand to be placed on probation before he or she is terminated.

Another alternative to termination is the demotion of an employee to a less responsible position. Since demotions by their nature are demoralizing, they should be: (1) optional, (2) limited to situations in which the employee has substantial years of service, and (3) used only when a real need exists to fill a vacancy at a lower level.

For examples of progressive discipline procedures and policies, see the forms in Appendix F.

Termination Checklist and Problem Areas

Appendix D, sets forth an expanded termination checklist that an employer should review before actually terminating an employee. There are certain critical points in this checklist that deserve further discussion and amplification.

Rules and Documentation

If the employer has a stated rule or procedure, which the employee has allegedly violated, it is very important that the rule be reviewed to see if it is reasonable and based upon valid business reasons. An employer should not assume that since the rule has been in place for many years it has a reasonable business basis. In order to meet this test the rule must have some relationship with the business and its operation.

Assuming that the rule is valid, it is critical that the rule be communicated to employers. It is important for an employer to find out and make certain that the employee was aware that the rule existed.[14] Further, it is important to verify that the rule has been applied in a consistent manner.

In many cases termination is not the first act of discipline. Many employers have previously warned the employee about his or her conduct. Warnings will be discussed further in this chapter. However, it is vital that the employer make certain that the warnings are documented and, wherever possible, that the employee has been given copies of the warning.

The New Supervisor

When an employer is reviewing a termination situation, there are occasions when the recommendation for termination has been made by a new supervisor. It is not uncommon that an employee will work many years with one supervisor without any problems. When a new supervisor is assigned that

14. It is obvious in certain circumstances that the communication of rules is not always necessary. These occur in serious violations such as insubordination, theft, and fighting on the job. However, in cases that are less obvious it is helpful if the rule is published and communicated to employees so that they are aware of the conduct that is expected of them.

individual either finds fault with the employee's performance or has a different style of management.

When reviewing a termination situation involving a new supervisor, an employer should make certain that the employee has been given adequate time to improve and that the new supervisor has an objective, reasonable basis for his or her opinion of the employee's performance. This is most important, since in a wrongful discharge litigation the new supervisor's opinion can be suspect especially if he or she has only been supervising the employee for a brief period of time. It is, therefore, recommended that the employee be given a reasonable amount of time to prove that he or she can perform within the new supervisor's expectations. This time period depends on the circumstances but should be at least three to six months.

Prior Performance

When considering the termination of an employee for performance-related reasons, the employee's prior performance is extremely relevant. Initially, there should be an analysis done of all prior performance reviews. Employees who have had a long history of excellent performance and then suffer a decrease in their performance should be given the opportunity to improve their performance to prior levels. There might be circumstances beyond the work place that are affecting the employee's performance. The circumstances affecting the employee's performance should be thoroughly reviewed with the employee in an effort to improve performance and return to normal levels. Employees with substantial length of service should also be given greater opportunity to improve their performance and/or behavior. Long service has substantial weight with juries and judges in determining "fairness" and should be given similar recognition by the employer.

Losing Benefits or Vesting

The employer should also be very careful in situations when the termination of an employee prevents vesting of a benefit, which would normally occur within the near future, e.g., in cases of a pension where the employee is close to either retirement or vesting. There are also instances when a bonus will be earned in a short period of time after the termination date, as well as other benefits, such as stock options that will not vest until immediately after termination. An employer in these cases should be careful not to terminate the employee when they are close to receiving these benefits. Wherever possible, there should be some bridging made so that the employee will be vested in the benefit in question. Alternatively, the date of termination can be postponed until after the vesting date for these benefits.

Reviewing and Investigating the Termination Situation

The investigation or review of a termination situation includes many factors, starting with the hiring process.

The employer should be made aware of any representations that were made at the time of hire or shortly after the hire date. As discussed in previous chapters there are a number of promises that could have been made at hiring, which could be enforceable.

When considering the termination situation, the employer should also make certain that the personnel policy manual has been followed. The procedures stated in the termination policy therein should be carefully reviewed to ensure that they were followed. In many instances, such manuals, as stated in prior chapters, have and can be enforceable contracts.

During any investigation involving the termination of an employee, an employee should be given an opportunity to explain their feelings and position. The employer should give the employee ample opportunity to respond to the allegations regarding their performance and/or behavior and present any evidence in support of his or her position. The employee's position should be reviewed to make certain that the employer is giving the employee every reasonable opportunity to present his or her say. The employer should consider all evidence and not be surprised in court at a later date. Such a discussion should take place prior to making the final decision to terminate.

When dealing with performance-related issues, many subjective opinions are made about employees. Even though the courts recognize subjectivity, an employer should, wherever possible, make the decision to terminate based upon objective factors. Most juries and judges will find it easier to comprehend and understand factors that have specific basis. Moreover, as a practical matter it is more difficult to prove one's case if the termination is based upon subjective reasons alone. Therefore, the employer should attempt to ascertain the specific reasons behind the opinions that have been made about the employee's performance and/or behavior.

Implied Employment Contracts and What You Say May Be Used Against You

In a recent decision, *Shebar v. Sanyo Business Systems Corp.,*[15] the New Jersey Supreme Court found that under certain circumstances verbal or oral promises by an employer may be enforceable as implied contracts. This decision is in the forefront of this area and deserves careful review and scrutiny, since it can and may be followed in other states.

In *Sanyo,* the plaintiff was hired as a national sales manager for Sanyo's computer division. His employment was outlined in a memo to him stating that his annual salary was to be

15. Shebar v. Sanyo Business Sys. Corp., 111 N.J. 276 (1988).

$35,000 with an additional bonus. Plaintiff continued to work for Sanyo for several years. During that time he alleged that his performance was good, he received regular salary increases, and he was commended for his efforts and accomplishments.

In 1984, the plaintiff decided he needed to find other employment. He visited a placement agency, who sent him for an interview to Sony Corporation. Sony offered the plaintiff employment. He then tendered his written resignation to Sanyo. Upon receipt of the resignation, the president of Sanyo called the plaintiff into his office and stated that he was insulted by his resignation and that his performance was exceptionally good. The president stated that he did not want the plaintiff to resign but wanted him to eliminate any problems that existed. He indicated his concern by tearing up the resignation letter and told the plaintiff that he would not accept the resignation and that "we will solve our problems."

During this meeting, the plaintiff alleged that the Sanyo president stated that Sanyo doesn't fire its managers, stated further that he had a job for the rest of his life, and that he never intended to fire him or a corporate employee whose rank was manager or above.

As a result of the meeting, the plaintiff revoked his acceptance of Sony's offer. Interestingly, when the plaintiff notified the placement agency that he was going to stay with his present employer, they said that his company was presently seeking to replace him. The plaintiff thereupon confronted the president of Sanyo about this and was specifically told that he was not seeking to replace him. However, four months later, without notice, the plaintiff was called into the president's office and was told that he was terminated and that he should clean out his desk and leave immediately.

Based upon these facts, the lower court found it necessary to dismiss the case, stating that the assertions by the Sanyo president were friendly assurances and not contractual. Upon appeal to the appellate division in New Jersey, the court found otherwise. The Supreme Court of New Jersey in reviewing the case reiterated that employment was at will for cause or no cause. However, the Court stated there are certain exceptions to this principle. It stated that the promise in the *Shebar* case was one that he would be discharged *only for cause,* which created an implied contract.

The Supreme Court further discussed the need for consideration to support the contractual common alternant. In this regard, the court noted that the plaintiff's act of relying upon the promise of the Sanyo president and not proceeding further to secure other employment was sufficient consideration under contractual law. Consideration need not be only money but can be the forbearance from another act. In this case, the forbearance was the plaintiff not seeking other employment and bargained for exchange was ample consideration for an enforceable contract. The Supreme Court concluded that the promises made were contractual and were specific enough to be enforceable in court and returned the matter for trial.

The *Shebar* decision is not the only decision that deals with oral promises of employment. In another important case, the U.S. Court of Appeals for the Second Circuit in *Ohanion v. Avis Rent a Car Systems Inc.*[16] held that the oral promises therein were also enforceable. The court in *Ohanion* found that promises from Avis's general manager, "Unless he screwed up badly, there's no way he's going to get fired. You would never get hurt here in the Company" were sufficient to create a trial issue. The trial judge submitted Ohanion's claim to a jury, which found that he had proven that Avis agreed to employ him until he retired, unless he was terminated for cause, and that Avis had not proven the plaintiff was terminated for just cause. On appeal to the Second Circuit, the

---

16. Ohanion v. Avis Rent a Car Sys. Inc., 779 F.2d 101 (2d Cir. 1985).

court held the oral contract was not barred by the statute of frauds, and was enforceable.

Preventive Approaches to Avoid Implied Employment Contracts

How does this impact an employer and what should the employer do to avoid these kinds of issues?

These issues arise in a variety of different employment situations. For example, an employee is transferred to a new position out of state. The manager tries to convince him to accept the position and says "take the job, it is a secure one." Based upon this representation the employee accepts the job and later is terminated. He then claims in court he took the job and moved his family when promised a "secure" job.

Another fact pattern could include a prospective employee who is lured away from an excellent job based on a number of representations made by a new employer. One such representation is "don't worry, if you take this job you will not be terminated unless the Company goes out of business." Again, if this employee is terminated, an implied contract can be alleged.

It is therefore clear that employers should be very careful when making positive statements to employees about job security especially when the statements affect employee's decisions involving job opportunities inside or outside the company.

There is no doubt that verbal statements made in the employment context, especially when an employee is about to leave, transfer, be demoted, be promoted, or be hired, could be sufficient to establish a contractual obligation. On the other hand, employers and personnel managers are aware that many times it is necessary to promise employees some reasonable security in order that the employee either stays with the company or moves to a new location in the company, or be promoted, demoted, etc. It is when such "employee movement" occurs that employers must be careful, since there may be consideration and a contract.

In order to prevent establishing an implied contract:

1. All employment documents, especially employment applications, should state that no contracts of employment may be made without the express written permission of the chief executive officer at the company and all such contracts must be in writing.
2. Managers, personnel managers, and other supervisors should be instructed to avoid making broad statements as to someone's employment security.
3. Managers, supervisors, and others should be trained in the dos and don'ts of what can and cannot be stated in the hiring process or in transferring employees.
4. Written procedures and personnel manuals that deal with termination should be very carefully worded not to include promises of employment, i.e., "termination only for cause."
5. All other written documents dealing with termination should contain appropriate disclaimers that employees may be terminated at will, with or without cause, at any time.
6. Managers and supervisors should be informed that when dealing with transfers, terminations, promotions, or demotions, that no promises or assurances of further employment should be made without careful consideration, and all meetings with employees dealing in these situations should be documented for further reference. If possible, memos should be written to the employee confirming the discussions.

The preceding recommendations are just a few possible ways to avoid these difficult situations. There is no doubt that the employment setting from a legal standpoint is changing dramatically in this country, and employers should be aware of these issues. Basically, employers must keep in mind that statements made to employees about their job security must be made in a responsible manner. This is not only a good legal preventive practice but a good personnel practice. Remember "what you say may be held against you."

Documentation

A great deal has been said and written about the importance of documentation when dealing with employee termination or discipline. There is no doubt that the written word has been given great weight in the judicial process. Additionally, documentation at the time of discipline or termination is extremely helpful before a judge or jury.

In prior chapters we have discussed the importance of written termination procedures. Notwithstanding these procedures, an employer should, wherever possible, document employee performance and behavior problems or misconduct. The documentation can take the form of a verbal warning, which is later memorialized in writing, or an official written warning to an employee, or merely a memorandum to the file.

The best and most appropriate method of written documentation is to prepare a written memo that describes the employee's problems. This memorandum should be discussed with the employee and the employee should be given a copy of the written document.

There are some basic guidelines employers should follow when preparing performance memos, documents, or written warnings. The employer should define as clearly as possible the deficiencies or problems the employee is having and refer to a specific situation or conduct.

The performance memo should be constructive. It should

deal with the positive aspects of the employee's behavior and attempt to build upon them. The written warning that is composed to "put down" an employee can be misconstrued by a court or jury. The employer should make every effort to establish that it is trying to help the employee to improve.

The performance memo should invite the employee to seek assistance in solving the employee's problems and should explain to the employee the importance of inadequate performance to the company. It is also important that the employer summarize past discussions and problems and note if there is employee agreement. The memo should state that the manager has received the approval and concurrence of higher levels of management regarding this employee's conduct. It may also state the consequences if the employee fails to improve.

The memo should also offer, wherever possible, assistance but clearly place the responsibility for improvement on the employee. It should express serious concern and, if appropriate, even disappointment. The memorandum should set forth specific objections and time limits. Lastly, and most importantly, the employer should make it clear that it is hoped that the employee will succeed and that the supervisor will work closely with the employee to accomplish this result.

When an employee responds in writing to the warning memo, one must be careful not to prolong the writing back and forth between the employee and the company. As a general rule, if the answering memo includes new issues or facts and not just a denial, the employer should respond promptly to these new facts.

The following is a sample of a closing paragraph in a written performance memo:

> As noted above, there are many areas requiring your immediate attention. We in the company want to assist you and want you to succeed, but the primary responsibility for your success

or failure is in your hands. I hope the remarks and criticism contained in this memo is taken in the constructive manner in which it is given. I look forward to working with you and I am, of course, more than willing to discuss any of these problem areas with you in an effort to help you improve your performance. However, it is important to note that we expect a substantial improvement within the next sixty days or we will consider more serious disciplinary measures.

Understanding the Emotions Involved in Terminating an Employee

The termination of an employee is a very traumatic experience for the employee. The trauma includes a wide variety of specific emotions. It is important that the terminating manager be aware of this emotional process in order to handle all aspects of the termination in a humane and proper manner.

The entire process can be broken into several important stages. The first stage can be called "shock." The second stage generally includes "depression," and the last stage, "recovery." It is important to note that not everyone will react the same, but within normal degrees of emotional reactions all will fall into these categories. One must remember that "being fired" is one of the most stressful periods in an individual's lifetime and at the same level as the death of a loved one or a divorce.

The first stage occurs immediately upon telling the employee about the termination. The shock is generally related to being unaware that this would occur. Even employees who have been warned will not be prepared. The shock reaction will include disbelief. Some will not want to listen to what they are being told.

A manager carrying out this first stage needs to be as gentle as possible, but make the message of termination clear and unequivocal. If the employee senses any hesitation, he or she will immediately start to think there is hope that they can keep the job. This type of "wishful thinking" will only slow the process and not help the employee to start thinking about the future.

Another emotion that can occur immediately or soon after being notified of termination is anger. The expression of anger is an individual phenomenon. Some will express it verbally. However, most in these situations will hold it in and let it out in other ways, i.e., being uncooperative, bringing a law suit against the company, etc. The managers should be aware of this emotion and attempt to communicate the reasons for the decision and not make it a personal attack upon the individual.

The second stage can include different degrees of depression. The terminated employee will immediately lose self-esteem. Some, of course, will lose more self-confidence than necessary. Others will hold up better. There is no doubt that in many cases the employee at the time of termination will fall into one degree of depression.

In addition, the individual will at this point become aware that he or she will have to look for a new position. This can cause extreme concern or fear of what will happen in the future. The terminating manager can help here where possible by not attacking the person but only stating the reasons for termination. Again, avoid any personal attack.

Terminating the relationship with the company will in and of itself be similar to a marital divorce. The longer the service with the company, the stronger these feelings. In many cases, the company has become a paternal figure that has provided benefits, pay, support groups, and friends. The individual being terminated will actually grieve for this loss.

Many of these emotions in this stage will occur after the employee leaves the company. What can the company do?

Many organizations today provide out-placement services in many different forms. Out-placement services focus the employee on the future and can aid the employee's job search. If the service is not possible, a company might wish to provide counseling and at least help the employee during the job search with references and leads.

The use of out-placement counseling can also add significant relevance to the termination process. If an employer gives an employee the opportunity of utilizing out-placement services and the employee does not accept the offer, the employer could argue in a future litigation that the employee did not make a good-faith effort to mitigate their damages and find a new position. If the employee accepts the out-placement services there is less likelihood that the employee will commence a lawsuit since they will be working to recover from the termination and seek a new job or business.

The depression/high-emotion period varies for each individual. However, at some point the individual will commence the last stage called "recovery." It is during this time that they commence a productive effort to find a job. Their ego begins to repair and they become resolved and look toward the future. If the termination is handled with care, diligence, and gives the employee an opportunity to leave with dignity, this process of recovery will start sooner.

It is therefore very important that the employer be aware of these practical emotional realities when terminating an employee and institute practices to ensure that the termination process is humane and conducted with dignity and respect.

Carrying Out the Termination

There comes a time when the employer has no choice but to terminate the employee. However, the termination process should take into account the emotions associated with the process as well as the potential legal risk involved.

In addition to the employee's emotions, the employer should also be aware that generally the terminating manager also has emotions in dealing with the termination. Most individuals no matter how right they are will feel some guilt or concern about the employee. This is especially true if the employee has been employed by the company for many years and has previously been a good employee. Notwithstanding this, the manager who is terminating the employee should be aware that their emotions of guilt, concern, and plain fear must be controlled and understood in an effort to give the employee every opportunity to be terminated with dignity. The termination process and the actual communication of the discharge should be made in such a way as to avoid as much as possible the anger that the employee might feel after being terminated.

One must keep in mind that no matter how many times the employee has been warned, counseled, and evaluated, the termination is generally a surprise to the employee. The employee will in many cases be shocked and might not believe that this is occurring to them. Keeping these prominent emotions in mind, the employer should handle the termination as humanely as possible.

Generally, the terminating manager should have an additional person in the room to monitor the situation and act as a witness and give the manager additional support. The communication regarding the actual termination should be very direct and humane. The employer should state the reasons for the termination but avoid unnecessary detail, especially in cases where these matters had been previously discussed with the employee.

The terminating manager should make it clear that the decision to terminate has been made, other managers have concurred, and it is a final decision. The manager should not send the message that the company might change its decision. The manager should not apologize for the company's action.

During the termination interview, the manager should be alert to the employee's emotions. If the employee becomes too emotional the meeting should be cut short to give the employee a chance to "catch their breath."

A great deal has been said and written about how and when an employer should let an employee be permitted to remain in the workplace after he or she has been told of the terminating decision. This will depend on the level of the employee's position as well as level of maturity. In situations involving termination for misconduct or other serious behavior, it is generally felt that the employee should be removed from the premises immediately. In situations dealing with poor performance, if the employee has long service, there is no reason why he or she cannot remain at the workplace for a specific period of time before actually physically leaving the employer's premises. It is important that employees not be "thrown out" wherever possible. It is these situations that can lead to litigation because the employee feels that he or she has been treated in a poor and inhumane manner. The employer, of course, must make these decisions based on the individual circumstances of each case.

Encouraging Voluntary Terminations

Many employers have had occasion to encourage certain employees to voluntarily resign, in lieu of termination. It is a common misbelief that if an employee voluntarily resigns they will not have any recourse against their prior employer. However, a voluntary resignation can be in the employee's best interest.

In situations that warrant a resignation or voluntary retirement the employer should be aware of a number of important safeguards. In order for a voluntary resignation to have any impact on the legal rights of the employee and/or the company, the resignation must be truly "knowingly and voluntary." The voluntariness of the resignation will depend upon the circumstances.

It is important to note that if an employee is not carrying out job duties properly and the company is concerned about the employee's performance it is recommended that a voluntary resignation not be utilized. In such cases, the employer should deal directly with the termination situation and performance issue.

However, in certain situations where a voluntary resignation may be mutually beneficial, the employer should consider the following:

1. Whenever possible, the employee should be given viable options. These alternatives could include choices within the company, i.e., reassignment to another position within the company.
2. The employer should not pressure or coerce the employee into resigning. Thus, the employer should give the employee every opportunity to make his or her own decision, the employee should be given a reasonable period of time to make a decision, and the employee should not be pressured into making a decision.
3. In situations where there is a long-service employee or an employee is considering retirement, the company should also review the possibility of paying severance pay to the employee. The greater amount of severance pay the greater the opportunity for the company to argue that the employee's choice was voluntary and was based upon many factors including a reasonable severance package. The acceptance of this package should be voluntary, and the employee should be made aware that he or she can remain in the same position if the package is not accepted.[17]

17. See Ackerman v. Diamond Shamrock Corp., 670 F.2d 66 (6th Cir. 1982), in which the court ruled that the severence payment and compensation

4. When the decision is made by the employee it should be memorialized in writing and signed by the employee. This statement should include both the resignation as well as a statement verifying that the employee had alternatives, was given a reasonable amount of time to make a decision, voluntarily accepted the offer, and left the company voluntarily.

Voluntary resignation is not free from risks. In many instances, employees argue that they were constructively terminated, i.e., forced out or their resignation was not truly voluntary. If the previous suggestions are followed there is a better chance that the trier of fact will determine that the employee has voluntarily resigned. (See discussion herein dealing with constructive termination).

In addition to voluntary terminations there have been cases dealing with actual resignations. For example, in *Molinaar v. Western Electric Co.,*[18] the Court held that an employee, who was involuntarily terminated but voluntarily signed a resignation letter based upon the promise of a good job reference, cannot maintain a cause of action for wrongful discharge. But in *Yates v. Life of Montana Insurance Co.,*[19] the court upheld the jury award of punitive damages where the jury found fraud, malice, and oppression "in obtaining a resignation."

Constructive Termination

In many instances, the employer's strategy may be to make the employee's work life so miserable that the employee will have no choice but to quit the job. In such cases, the law has

---

was large enough to convince the court that the choice was sufficiently attractive to be voluntary.

18. Molinaar v. Western Elec. Co., 520 F.2d 521 (1st Cir. 1975), *cert. denied,* 424 U.S. 78, 96 S. Ct. 1485 (1976).
19. Yates v. Life of Mont. Ins. Co., 668 F.2d 213 (1983).

recognized that resignations under such circumstances are, in fact, a constructive termination. The standard in such cases is whether the employer created such intolerable conditions that would force a reasonable person to resign. Normally, in order to establish an intolerable condition, the situation would have to continue over a long period of time with continued "harassment" of the employee. Employers should be careful in following this type of approach since it is fraught with danger.

More importantly, the employer should realize that the best way to manage a work force is to deal directly with employees and their problems. No matter what the employee's rights may be, if they are treated in an equitable and proper manner most courts would sustain the employer's actions.

Constructive termination is not easy to prove, and the employee has the burden of proof. There have been many cases in which it has been alleged and argued, and the court has found that it has not occurred. A few examples of constructive termination follow.

In *Bailey v. Binyon,*[20] the plaintiff, Bailey, was employed as a cook at the defendant's restaurant. The restaurant owner complained about the soups and sauces. When the plaintiff said he was not in charge of the soups and sauces, the manager replied "all you niggers are alike." He made further disparaging comments about the plaintiff's race. The plaintiff then quit and promptly reported the incident to the Illinois Department of Human Rights. After exhausting all administrative remedies, the plaintiff filed a Title VII suit in federal district court.

The court held that the defendant's use of racial epithets went beyond "mere insults" or "ordinary discrimination" because such epithets "generate [ ] a feeling of inferiority as to [Black people's] status in the community that may affect their hearts and minds in a way unlikely ever to be undone" (quot-

20. Bailey v. Binyon, 36 E.P.D. § 34, 997 (N.D. Ill. 1984).

ing *Brown v. Board of Education*).[21] The court cannot say, as a matter of law, that the "Plaintiff . . . acted unreasonably when he allegedly walked out of the Defendant's restaurant. . . ." Whether the "Plaintiff was constructively discharged by Defendants in violation of Title VII . . . must be left to the trier of fact."

The court noted that to establish a constructive discharge test the "trier of fact must be satisfied that the . . . working conditions would have been so difficult or unpleasant that a reasonable person in the employee's shoes would have felt compelled to resign."[22] Some circuits have the additional requirement "that the employer's intent to force the employee to resign be shown."[23] The question of what a reasonable person would do is a question of fact for the trier to decide.

In general, "an employee who resigns solely on the basis of his or her employer's isolated violation of a employment discrimination statute . . . acts unreasonably."[24]

The *Bailey* court stated that this case was distinguishable from the prior cases because, despite the fact that it was an isolated incident, the defendant's racial slurs were not "harmless" or "casual."

---

21. Brown v. Board of Educ., 347 U.S. 483, 494 (1954).
22. Quoting Bourque v. Powell Elec. Mfg., Co., 617 F.2d 61 (5th Cir. 1980).
23. Johnson v. Bunny Bread Co., 646 F.2d 1250, 1256 (8th Cir. 1981); Muller v. United States Steel Corp., 509 F.2d 923, 929 (10th Cir.), *cert. denied,* 423 U.S. 825 (1975).
24. See Bourque v. Powell Elec. Mfg. Co., 617 F.2d at 66 (unequal pay for equal work because of employee's sex is not an "aggravated situation"); Muller v. United States Steel Corp., 509 F.2d at 929 (discriminatory failure to promote coupled with unfavorable job assignment is not sufficient); Johnson v. Bunny Bread Co., 646 F.2d at 1256–57 ("[t]he use, if any, of racial terms was infrequent, was limited to casual conversation among employees, and with possible rare exceptions was not directed toward [the plaintiffs]"); Irving v. Dubuque Packing Co., 689 F.2d 170, 172 (10th Cir. 1982) ("casual and intermittent racial slurs do not always give rise to constructive discharge").

In *Levendos v. Stern Entertainment,*[25] the plaintiff, who first began her employment with the defendant as a waitress, was later promoted to maître d' and pastry chef. She was the only female holding a management position. Her claims involved the following incidents:

1. In the past, the male maître d' had been included in management meetings, but she was not included.
2. The general manager had said that she "would not be there long."
3. [M]anagement . . . told other employees that she did not fit the "mold" for maître d' because [she] was a woman. . . ."
4. The "chef was asked . . . by the owner to find a male to replace [her]. . . ."
5. [M]anagement falsely accusing her of stealing, drinking and fraternizing with employees. . . ."
6. [O]ne evening she discovered wine bottles placed in [her] locker . . . to make it appear as if [she] were stealing."[26]

An affidavit filed by a co-worker stated that she was a good worker who was well-liked by the customers and by the community at large. It also stated that the management preferred a male staff, and there was a conspiracy to "get rid of her." The plaintiff finally resigned from her job and filed suit claiming sex discrimination.

The lower court granted the defendants' motion for summary judgment because the plaintiff did not establish that she had been constructively discharged. The appellate court held that there was "a genuine issue of material fact regarding whether she was constructively discharged from her job" and remanded the case to the lower court.[27] The court noted that

25. Levendos v. Stern Entertainment, 48 F.E.P. 443 (3d Cir. 1988).
26. *Id.* at 443–44.
27. *Id.*

"[A]cts of discrimination in violation of Title VII can make working conditions so intolerable that a reasonable employee would be forced to resign."[28] Constructive discharge under these circumstances would entitle an employee "to damages for wrongful termination in addition to damages for the pre-termination discrimination."[29]

The court found that the lower court erred in finding that the evidence was insufficient to legally prove constructive discharge. Instead, the court held that the plaintiff's evidence, if true, was sufficient to meet even the stringent test that the employer deliberately acted to force the employee to resign. This test was not required by the Third Circuit. All that is required is that the situation be so intolerable as to compel a reasonable person to resign.

The court recognizes that "[i]t is of course plausible that a jury could decide ultimately that a reasonable person would tolerate some or even all of these occurrences without being forced to quit. It is equally plausible, however, that a jury would come to the opposite conclusion."[30] Therefore, summary judgment was inappropriate, and the constructive discharge claim involves a question of material fact that should go to the jury.[31]

In conclusion, whether an employee is actually terminated or forced to resign, such situations should be dealt with care and due process. No matter how unfortunate it is to terminate an employee, if the employer follows appropriate procedures and deals in this situation with respect and dignity for the rights of the employee, the chances of employment-related litigation will be minimized.

---

28. *Id.* at 445.
29. *Id.*
30. *Id.* at 446.
31. *Id.* at 447.

CHAPTER TEN

Reductions in Work Force

During the 1980s, an unprecedented number of reductions in force (RIFs) in the corporate offices and factories have occurred throughout the country. These reductions started during the 1980–1982 recession and have continued in to 1990s, even though economic times have now improved. The trend in reductions was accelerated by specific instances, such as the impact of the October 1987 stock market crash, which resulted in extensive layoffs in the financial industry. In general, however, reductions in force will continue as American business adjusts to the changing world economy. Employers must adapt to this reality and understand the applicable legal framework.

Litigation arising out of reductions in force have been based in claims of age, race, or sex discrimination, violations of implied employment agreements, and other legal theories. Some of these claims have become class actions involving hundreds of terminated employees, and in some cases have resulted in judgments amounting to millions of dollars. Such confrontations can be avoided with proper planning and actions.

For instance, where a company finds it necessary to reduce positions and employees, it should consider the following: voluntary termination or open window programs; appropriate criteria for identifying affected employees; and general preventive measures with careful planning. Considering these issues will insure that it is more likely that a reduction will be carried out in an equitable, fair and humane manner, resulting in less risk of legal problems.

Open Windows

The so-called "open window program" is a voluntary termination program, which is offered to all or an identified group of employees. The program offers eligible employees the opportunity to accept certain additional benefits and voluntarily leave the employ of the company. These added benefits can include increased severance pay and improved pensions. Such programs generally are offered for a specific period of time, at the end of which the "window" is closed.

The legal enforceability of such programs is based on whether they are voluntary. Employees should have viable options when offered such programs. Courts will examine each aspect of the program and related communications when dealing with the question of the voluntariness of the plan.

For example, where an employee was given no alternatives, i.e., be terminated or accept the "voluntary" program, courts are likely to find that the program was involuntary and the termination unlawful.

It is this type of pressure, or lack of a true alternative, that taints a voluntary program. It is important that the company ensure that any type of pressure to accept the program be avoided and that eligible employees be given true options. If employees' working conditions are made so intolerable that they are forced to accept the program, they may make claims of "constructive" discharge.

Eligible employees should be reassured that their refusal to participate in the program will not affect their future job prospects in the company, either positively or negatively. Also, supervisors should be instructed not to pressure employees to accept or reject the program or offer them advice. If possible, only designated, trained human resources specialists should be involved.

Lastly, the courts will examine the amount of time eligible employees were given to make a decision and the amount of information provided to them. Normally, two weeks to thirty days allows eligible employees to obtain all of the necessary information and make an informed choice.*

Voluntary plans can incur high cost resulting in the loss of employees that the employer wishes to retain. However, such programs are more humane, help employees who can and want to leave to make that decision, and allow companies to reduce work forces with minimum adverse impact.

If an employer decides not to use a voluntary reduction program, or carries it out and finds that further cuts are necessary, the next step would be an involuntary reduction in work force. It is at this point that an employer should plan the use of certain legal and objective criteria to identify jobs and personnel affected.

Criteria and Alternatives

Probably the safest method of reducing a work force is to utilize seniority or company service criteria to decide which individuals are to be terminated. The use of seniority or service is a valid objective criteria that can withstand legal attack. Moreover, the application of a bona fide seniority system is exempt from the age discrimination and civil rights laws. One should keep in mind, however, that straight seniority or years of service can have an adverse impact on newly hired females and minorities and should be carefully monitored. Of course, such a system might eliminate good, productive employees while at the same time protecting less productive workers.

---

*One should review relevant state and federal court decisions regarding the amount of time to make a decision.

Another possible criteria often used in reductions is the identification and elimination of jobs, resulting in the termination of the incumbents. Such circumstances can be defended on the basis that the particular positions are no longer needed. However, the question remains why a particular employee was selected for termination rather than transfer. The main fact that only the incumbents are selected might not be sufficient to withstand attack.

Some employers have identified employees for layoff by lottery, i.e., random selection by a drawing. This method, of course, eliminates management's ability to choose and develop an efficient work force. On the other hand, it is legally neutral, if conducted properly. A lottery can be considered when most jobs or skills are interchangeable, and employee performance is difficult to differentiate.

Employers also have used productivity as a guideline in selecting employees for layoff. In such cases, sales goals and production quotas can be used, and the least productive employees are terminated. However, one should be careful in applying this criteria: Make certain it is applied even-handedly and that there are no possible business reasons, unrelated to the individual's performance, for a particular individual not meeting the goal.

Probably the most common method of identifying persons subject to layoff is the application of a performance evaluation system already in place. This type of system uses some form of documented periodic review of an employee's performance. If an employer has maintained a performance evaluation system it is a good basis for deciding who is to be selected. In this case, the poorest performers would be identified.

An effective evaluation system should include: (1) an analysis of the job; (2) performance measured against specific job elements; (3) reasonable and objective factors used in the evaluation; (4) opportunity for the employee to correct problems; (5) opportunity for employee comment and appeal; (6) reasonable guidelines and training for the evaluator; (7) several levels of review and approval; and (8) periodic monitoring of the system.

If the current evaluation system is inadequate or no evaluation system exists, managers and supervisors can be utilized to identify poor performing employees. In such instances it may be helpful to have department managers rank their employees on the basis of their current performance. Supervisors should base their decisions on as many objective factors as possible, such as prior job history, performance, and discipline record. The evaluators should be given specific criteria to make their judgments, and the evaluations should be in writing.

Written procedures regarding the reduction in force should include the selection criteria that will apply, e.g., seniority, performance appraisal, supervisor evaluation. These procedures should also address other issues, such as employee reassignment to other positions, severance pay, seniority, job combination, job elimination, leave of absence alternatives, and employee termination interviews.

A review committee should be formed to monitor the entire reduction-in-force process. This committee should include representatives from all levels of management (excluding senior management) and the human resources department. This committee should determine whether the evaluations of employees are based upon selected criteria, avoiding subjective judgments as much as possible.

The committee should determine if the reduction will have an adverse impact on "protected groups" and should ensure that factors, such as age, sex, race, or national origin, had no influence on the selection process. The review committee should also deal with issues such as job eliminations, the reassignment of duties to other positions, and consolidation of position or operations and the reassignments of employees.

Communication to the affected employees is critical. Care should be taken to ensure that the communicators are sensitive to the feelings and emotions of the affected employees. Interviews should therefore be conducted by a trained supervisor and a personnel professional. The reasons for the RIF and the selection criteria should be communicated to the affected employees. Communication with the employees who will remain employed is equally important. This group of employees should be given a sense of security.

Lastly, it is recommended that severance pay, as well as out-placement services, be considered for the affected employee. Out-placement severance may include resume preparation, interview guidelines, and job searches. Severance pay will enable the employee to have some sense of financial security while he or she is looking for another position and the out-placement service will provide guidance.

RIF Planning and Implementation

The following is a step-by-step procedure. Obviously, not all of the following considerations apply in every RIF plan. Thus, while a general checklist can be prepared, each plan has its own unique facts and circumstances that will affect the ultimate outcome.

STEP 1. *Freeze hiring to the extent possible.*

STEP 2. *Assess the situation carefully.* This means reviewing the prima facie case and burden of proof requirements in RIF cases. Thus, an employer must review the economic justification for the RIF if it is based on economic considerations. The RIF must be based on sound business reasons that can be substantiated and articulated at a later date by cogent and believable witnesses. Identify business units in need of a RIF. Documented communications should be sent to those units describing the need for the reduction. The employer should assess any contractual and tort-related obligations it might have, e.g., written employment contracts, labor agreements, employee handbooks, past practice, unwritten promises, tort claims, conciliation agreements, affirmative action plan commitments, and court orders. An assessment should be made of key statistics involving all business units, with special emphasis on those that are potentially affected. The assessment should focus on the protected equal employment opportunity classifications, seniority, and documentation of job performance. Review and consider possible alternatives to a RIF, e.g., wage freeze/reduction, work-sharing, and other cost controls. All business needs and goals should be documented. Avoid creating harmful documents.

STEP 3. *Implement alternatives to the RIF and modify your hiring freeze if appropriate.*

STEP 4. *Make a determination as to the appropriate organizational structure post RIF.* Ascertain the types and number of job functions. Undertake a skill assessment for those job functions. Create organizational charts and, at this stage, make no consideration of individual employees.

STEP 5. *Make a determination as to the selection criteria.* First, return to the original assessment regarding contractual and tort-related obligations, if any, that the company has. Evaluate potential problems associated with modifying existing policies or practices. Identify any potential problems in following existing policies or practices. Look at potential problems associated with relying on existing documentation of performance. To the extent possible, try to use job-related selection criteria. This will be extremely helpful should litigation arise. For example, in one case, the company did not rely upon annual written performance evaluations because they had been made by "inadequate" management personnel. Instead, the court accepted subsequent assessment, which was uniformly made, based upon: ability to perform present functions;

ability to adjust to necessary changes in the company's operations; effectiveness on the job, with particular focus on supervisory competence and past achievement in the context of the company's present problems; versatility, considering whether the individual had the ability to move into another area of operations; uniqueness, considering whether the individual had some special skills that were necessary to a particular function; and availability of replacements. The court was also impressed by the fact that the company had cut overhead costs severely, restricted pay raises, eliminated recruitment, dropped its membership in several trade associations, cancelled subscriptions to trade publications, frozen fringe benefits, and carefully reexamined all departmental budgets.[1]

There are dangers associated with using subjective criteria; it is not bad in and of itself but can cause problems. The vague criteria of "choosing the person you will miss the least" has been held not "in and of itself" to violate the ADEA absent discriminatory impact. Still, it is best to stick with objective criteria to the extent possible. Avoid age-related designations and criteria such as training, costs, retirement eligibility, or favored treatment for students.

STEP 6. *Make sure everything is documented.* The RIF criteria should be reduced to writing. Amend inconsistent written documents and communicate to decision makers and employees.

STEP 7. *Implement the RIF in a manner consistent with the company's articulated goals and rationale.* This will involve deciding which job functions must be retained, which can be consolidated, and which can be cut back or eliminated. Sometimes it is wise to conduct a job analysis to review the proposed changes to see if they are consistent with your goals. A well-defined criteria to select employees to be laid off must be

1. *See* Marshall v. Hills Bros., 423 F. Supp. 1320 (N.D. Cal. 1977).

established and followed. Evaluate each employee you determine will be retained and, as noted in the preceding, have uniform, job-related criteria for evaluating proficiency for the functions that will exist after the RIF. Many companies have engaged in ranking all employees in accordance with their relative value to the reconstituted department's remaining work function.

At this stage, decision makers should be directed to make their selections. All initial decisions should be reviewed by an independent committee of good witnesses of different gender, race, and age. Decisions should conform to policy, not have an adverse impact on any group (protect this inquiry under an attorney-client privilege) and should make sure that, if possible, no pension or bonus vesting entitlement has been adversely affected. Initial decisions should be revised as required and then reviewed by the legal department or outside counsel. The decisions should be finalized and then communicated at individual meetings that should be planned and documented both in advance and contemporaneously. If possible, advance notice should be provided. Consider your public relations. You don't want inconsistencies; it will make managers look bad and can be used against the company at a later date. At this stage you are, of course, reviewing the employee rankings and everything else that has been done in order to screen out questionable and/or unfair employment practices and decisions before it is too late. Set up an "800" number to field questions and complaints.

STEP 8. *Don't overlook the post-reduction stage.* Here, we're talking about out-placement and other positive actions. Maintain, if possible, your hiring freeze. Consider creating recall rights, if any, and limit them to one year at most. Also, consider establishing an appeals procedure, and settle charges and lawsuits while obtaining the necessary releases.

We have highlighted some of the important legal considerations an employer should take into account when planning to reduce its work force. This is not a substitute for specific legal advice and counsel at all stages of planning and implementation.

The bottom line, however, in RIFs is the equitable, fair, and justifiable choices that are made in these very difficult situations. The courts will generally recognize these considerations. If an employer makes all reasonable efforts, the final work force will be more productive and also serve the business needs of the company; at the same time, everyone will be treated with dignity, respect, and humanity.

CHAPTER ELEVEN

Can Employees Waive Age Discrimination Act and Other Rights?

As the country faces the new decade of the 1990s so does industry face numerous changes in both competition and changing markets. There are already signs that numerous industries including retail, computers, defense, and others are changing strategies for new markets.

One such strategy has been the restructuring of the workforce and in some cases downsizing. Even in the second half of the 1980s restructuring took place in an expanding economy. As stated in the prior chapter the 1990s will be more difficult to predict except to say downsizing or reduction-in-force should continue in one form or another especially in a weakened economy.

Employers, realizing both the personal and practical difficulties presented with these reorganizations, have attempted to soften the impact on employees by offering severance packages above and beyond the normal severance pay the company had usually offered. With the advent of the reorganization and the additional severance packages, employers started to utilize, on a more regular basis, the release of claims format for employees.

Employers felt that the payment of extensive severance pay should give them the right to request that the employee release the company from all claims. This release or waiver of claims has therefore become a part of the employment termination process.

Waivers are also used when an individual employee is involuntarily terminated, and the employee waives his or her right to bring legal action against the employer in exchange for enhanced severance pay or other valuable consideration. Obviously, the employer views the use of waivers as one way to resolve early claims of discrimination or other "wrongful discharge" lawsuits by former employees. However, waivers can also benefit employees since the employees can receive larger amounts of remuneration at the time they most need it. Recently, a number of employees who have signed releases have filed charges of age discrimination against their former employers, arguing that these releases cannot operate as valid waivers of their rights under the Age Discrimination in Employment Act (ADEA).

The question of the validity of private releases under ADEA arises because Congress did not explicitly address the issue when it enacted the ADEA. Congress did provide, however, that the enforcement provisions of the Fair Labor Standards Act (FLSA)[1] would be incorporated into the enforcement provisions of the ADEA.[2] Case law dealing with contractual waivers of FLSA rights do not permit waivers without government supervision, at least when there is a bona fide dispute between the parties over legal issues.[3] One must keep in mind that the FLSA is a specific defined benefit law, i.e., minimum wages, overtime pay, etc.

At the same time, however, it is well established that under Title VII of the Civil Rights Act of 1964, which is not a defined benefit law but rather prohibits discrimination by an employer on the basis of race, color, religion, sex, or national origin,[4]

1. 29 U.S.C. §§ 216–217.
2. 29 U.S.C. § 626(b).
3. P.A. Schulte, Inc. v. Gangi, 328 U.S. 108 (1946).
4. 42 U.S.C. §§ 2000 *et seq.*

employers and employees may privately settle disputes as long as any waiver of rights or release of potential liability is voluntary and knowing.[5] The common purposes of Title VII and the ADEA, to eliminate discrimination in employment and the preference to have disputes voluntarily settled,[6] suggest that private waivers and releases should be valid under the ADEA.

Relying on the similar purposes and structure of the ADEA and Title VII, the Equal Employment Opportunity Commission (EEOC) approved a regulation authorizing non-EEOC supervised waivers and releases of private rights under the ADEA.[7] However, Congress stayed the implementation of these regulations. In any event, the EEOC regulations are instructive to employers in the use of waivers.

Recognizing that such unsupervised waivers encourage employers and employees to reach voluntary settlements while maintaining flexibility for other workers, the EEOC has ruled that such waivers or releases are valid provided they (1) are knowing and voluntary, (2) do not provide for the release of prospective rights or claims, and (3) are not in exchange for consideration, including employment benefits, to which the employee is already entitled. The EEOC emphasizes that a determination of whether a release is "knowing and voluntary" must be made on a case-by-case basis. However, the EEOC recognizes the following factors as indicative of a knowing and voluntary waiver:

1. The agreement is in writing, in understandable language, and clearly waives the employee's rights or claims under the ADEA;
2. A reasonable period of time was provided for review and deliberation; and

---

5. Alexander v. Gardner-Denver Co., 415 U.S. 36 (1974); Carson v. American Brands, Inc., 450 U.S. 79 (1981).
6. *See* 29 U.S.C. § 626(d).
7. 52 Fed. Reg. 32,293 (1987) (codified at 20 C.F.R. pt. 1627).

3. The employee was encouraged to consult an attorney with regard to the waiver.

The EEOC regulations approving the private release of claims contain one important qualification: "No such waivers or releases shall affect the Commission's rights and responsibilities to enforce the Act. Nor shall such a waiver be used to justify interfering with an employee's protected right to file a charge or participate in a Commission Investigation."

This qualification is consistent with a 1987 age discrimination decision of the Fifth Circuit Court of Appeals in *Equal Employment Opportunity Commission v. Cosmair, Inc., L'Oreal Hair Care Division.*[8] In *Cosmair,* the Fifth Circuit ruled that a terminated employee did not waive his right to file an age discrimination charge with the EEOC by signing a release form in which he agreed not to take legal action against the employer in exchange for severance benefits.[9] The plaintiff in *Cosmair* signed the release and then filed an age bias charge with the EEOC. The employer ceased making severance payments after it received the EEOC charge and the plaintiff filed an additional charge for retaliation. The U.S. District Court for Northern Texas granted the EEOC's request for a preliminary injunction requiring the employer to pay severance benefits to the plaintiff notwithstanding the filing of the ADEA charges. The employer then appealed.

The Fifth Circuit found that a private waiver of the right to file an age discrimination charge with the EEOC violates public policy and that the release cannot be used to prevent the terminated employee from filing a charge. As the court stated:

---

8. Equal Employment Opportunity Comm'n v. Cosmair, Inc., L'Oreal Hair Care Div., 821 F.2d 1085 (5th Cir. 1987).
9. The waiver released Cosmair, the employer, "from all actions, causes of action, claims and demands . . . such as those under any federal, state, or local law dealing with discrimination in employment." *Id.* at 1087.

> Allowing the filing of charges to be obstructed by enforcing a waiver of the right to file a charge could impede EEOC enforcement of the civil rights laws. . . . A charge not only informs the EEOC of discrimination against the employee who files the charge . . . but also may identify other unlawful company actions. . . . We hold that an employer and an employee cannot agree to deny to the EEOC the information it needs to advance the public interest.[10]

The court, however, added a clarifying note to its decision. Even though an employee cannot waive the right to file a charge with the EEOC, the employee can waive the right to recover damages in his or her own lawsuit and can also waive the right to recover damages in a suit brought by the EEOC on the employee's behalf.[11] Thus, the court held that the employer can rely on the release as a defense to the employee's ADEA cause of action, but it cannot be used as a retaliatory shield to prevent the enforcement of the ADEA laws by the EEOC.

Consistent with the EEOC's position on private releases, several courts have found unsupervised releases of ADEA rights to be valid.[12] In *Runyan v. National Cash Register Corp.,*[13] the Sixth Circuit Court of Appeals, sitting *en banc,* held that an unsupervised release of an ADEA claim in a bona fide factual dispute could be valid. In that case, the plaintiff, Runyan, was terminated from his position as the company's assistant general counsel because of unsatisfactory job performance. At the time of his termination, the fifty-nine-year-

10. *Id.* at 1090.
11. *Id.* at 1091.
12. Runyan v. National Cash Register Corp., 787 F.2d 1039 (6th Cir.) (en banc), *cert. denied,* 479 U.S. 850 (1986); Moore v. McGraw Edison Co., 804 F.2d 1026 (8th Cir. 1986); Lancaster v. Buerkle Buick Honda Co., 809 F.2d 539 (8th Cir.), *cert. denied,* 482 U.S. 928 (1987).
13. Runyan v. National Cash Register Corp., 787 F.2d 1039 (6th Cir.) (en banc), *cert. denied,* 479 U.S. 850 (1986).

old Runyan told the general counsel that he believed his firing was based upon his age. Runyan and his employer agreed to a temporary consulting arrangement. Several months later, the parties negotiated an increase in Runyan's salary conditioned on Runyan's signing a termination agreement and a release of any and all claims he might have against the company arising out of the course of his employment. Runyan signed the release and received the additional compensation. When the consulting agreement expired, he filed an age discrimination suit against his employer.

The Sixth Circuit held that a private release under the circumstances of this case may waive ADEA rights. The court recognized that in the case at bar a bona fide factual dispute existed over whether the employer discharged Runyan in violation of the ADEA. Also, it noted that Runyan was not among the "lowest paid segment" of workers with little understanding of his legal rights, but rather, was a "well-paid, well-educated, labor lawyer with many years of experience in the area."[14] Thus, the court concluded that even though the language of the release was general and did not specifically mention a waiver of ADEA rights, the release was "knowingly and deliberately" signed by an attorney knowledgeable in employment discrimination and labor law matters.[15] The court was careful to note that in determining whether a particular ADEA settlement and release is valid under ordinary contract principles, a court should be certain that there exists an "amicable settlement of honest differences" without any "overreaching or exploitation."[16]

Relying in part on the Sixth Circuit's decision in *Runyan,* the Eighth Circuit Court of Appeals held that an employee who signed a form releasing the employer from any legal

14. Runyan v. National Cash Register Corp., 787 F.2d at 1044, *cert. denied,* 479 U.S. 850 (1986).
15. *Id.*
16. *Id.*

claims stemming from his discharge effectively waived his right to sue under the ADEA.[17] The plaintiff contended, among other things, that the termination agreement did not bar his suit because he did not knowingly and willingly release his employment-related claims. The court stated that the waiver was effective because the plaintiff had several days to look over the agreement before signing it, had the opportunity to consult an attorney, and the agreement was written in "clear and simple language" that covered only two typewritten pages.[18] The court added that the plaintiff was a well-paid management employee with experience in business who had signed numerous contracts in his lifetime.

The releases that gave rise to the lawsuits in *Runyan* and *Lancaster* were signed in the context of an involuntary termination. However, releases signed in exchange for the receipt of voluntary early retirement incentives have also been challenged. In *Bodnar v. Synpol,* for example, the court held that a release signed by an employee as part of an early retirement plan is valid and enforceable so as to preclude an employee from bringing suit under the ADEA.[19] In *Bodnar,* twenty-one employees who accepted a voluntary early retirement plan were required to sign an agreement releasing the employer from any and all claims arising under Title VII of the Civil Rights Act of 1964, as amended, and the ADEA. After they signed the agreement, the twenty-one employees brought suit under the ADEA alleging that they were involuntarily retired/constructively discharged. The court held that the release was voluntarily and knowingly executed. It found that the (1) language of the agreement was clear and unambiguous, (2) employees had sufficient time to obtain legal advice and

17. Lancaster v. Buerkle Buick Honda Co., 809 F.2d 539, 541 (8th Cir.), *cert. denied,* 482 U.S. 928 (1987).
18. *Id.* at 541.
19. Bodnar v. Synpol, Inc., 633 F. Supp. 13 (E.D. Tex. 1986), *aff'd,* 843 F.2d 190 (5th Cir. 1988).

consider the plan, and (3) employees were not unduly influenced or defrauded.[20]

It is interesting to note the language of the release in *Bodnar:*

"SPECIAL EARLY RETIREMENT INCENTIVE PROGRAM AGREEMENT"

This Agreement is entered into this ____ day of __________, 1983, between SYNPOL, INC., the "Employer" and __________________ the "Employee." The Employer and Employee mutually desire to enter into this Agreement whereby the Employee voluntarily elects early retirement under the Employer's retirement plan in consideration of an additional sum of money, specified in Paragraph 2, below.

1. The employee's retirement will become effective on ______________, 1983. The employee will thereafter receive his or her monthly retirement allowance as provided in the Pension Program for Non-Union Employees.

2. In addition to the monthly retirement allowance described in Paragraph 1, above, the Employee will receive $__________ in one lump sum payment.

3. The employee releases and discharges SYNPOL, INC., its officers, agents, and successors from any and all claims arising under Title VII of the Civil Rights Act of 1964, and amended, 43 U.S.C. 2000e et seq. The Age Discrimination in Employment Act, 29 U.S.C. 621 et seq.

In contrast to *Bodnar,* the releases used in connection with the voluntary separation program in *Anderson v. Montgomery Ward*[21] were not voluntary and knowing. The court found a material issue of fact with respect to whether the plaintiffs left Montgomery Ward "voluntarily" under its voluntary separation program. The court also found that a material issue of fact existed as to whether the plaintiffs voluntarily and knowingly signed the acceptance form. Each form contained a waiver of

20. Bodnar v. Synpol, Inc., 633 F. Supp. at 15.
21. Anderson v. Montgomery Ward, 650 F. Supp. 1480 (N.D. Ill. 1987), *vacated in part on other grounds,* 704 F. Supp. 162 (N.D. Ill. 1989).

"all provisions of any compensation practices, either express or implied" between the plaintiff and the company and declared each plaintiff's separation from the company "voluntary for all purposes under applicable state and federal law."[22]

The court initially noted that the language of the purported waiver, which referred only to "compensation practices" and not to federal employment discrimination laws, thus was not a waiver of ADEA rights. "Ambiguous or meaningless words are insufficient to waive rights under the ADEA," stated the court.[23] Further, the court held that a material issue of fact existed with respect to whether they "voluntarily and knowingly" signed the acceptance forms. With respect to this issue, the court found *Runyan* inopposite,[24] as the plaintiffs in the case at bar were not as sophisticated as the plaintiff in *Runyan* and never negotiated with the company for their separate package. Moreover, the court noted that there was no evidence that they attempted to take advantage of the employer by entering into an agreement they never intended to keep as had occurred in *Runyan.*[25] For these reasons the court ruled that the release form signed by the plaintiffs was an ineffective waiver of their ADEA rights.

As the court's decision in *Montgomery Ward* suggests, whether an employee knowingly and voluntarily signs a release of ADEA rights in exchange for early retirement incentives is closely related to the question of whether the incentives are voluntarily accepted. In addition, whether a release will be voluntarily and knowingly executed in cases involving both voluntary retirements and involuntary terminations will depend on a variety of factors including the language of the

22. *Id.* at 1486.
23. *Id.*
24. Runyan v. National Cash Register Corp., 787 F.2d 1039 (6th Cir.) (en banc), *cert. denied,* 479 U.S. 850 (1986).
25. Anderson v. Montgomery Ward, 650 F. Supp. at 1480, *vacated in part on other grounds,* 704 F. Supp. 162 (N.D. Ill. 1989).

release, whether the release was signed under fraud or duress, the employees' experience and sophistication, their knowledge of their ADEA rights, whether they had a reasonable amount of time to make a decision, and whether they could or did consult attorneys or other advisors in deciding whether to sign the release and accept the benefits offered to them. Other courts have ruled that certain aspects of release agreements are not enforceable. For example, an agreement that allows an employer to cease severance payments if the employee or the EEOC initiates litigation, will not be enforceable.[26] Similarly, employees who signed a release who agreed not to "counsel or assist" other age claims is not enforceable.[27]

In *Equal Employment Opportunity Commission v. American Express Publishing Corp.,*[28] the court specified six factors to determine whether a release of statutory claims is "knowing and voluntary":

> 1) the plaintiff's education and business experience, 2) the amount of time the plaintiff had possession of or access to the agreement before signing it, 3) the role of plaintiff in deciding the terms of the agreement, 4) the clarity of the agreement, 5) whether the plaintiff was represented by or consulted with an attorney, and 6) whether consideration given in exchange for the waiver exceeds employee benefits to which the employee was already entitled by contract or law.

In this regard, the unpublished Third Circuit Court opinion *Sullivan v. Boron Oil Co.,*[29] is instructive. Thus, the court stated:

---

26. Equal Employment Opportunity Comm'n v. Cosmair, Inc., 821 F.2d 1085 (1986).
27. Equal Employment Opportunity Comm'n v. U.S. Steel Corp., 671 F. Supp. 351 (W.D. Pa. 1987), *opinion supplemented by* 728 F. Supp. 1167 (W.D. Pa. 1989).
28. Equal Employment Opportunity Comm'n v. American Express Publishing Corp., 681 F. Supp. 216 (S.D.N.Y. 1988).
29. Sullivan v. Boron Oil Co., No. 87-3238 (3d Cir. Sept. 30, 1987) (LEXIS, Genfed library, U.S. App. file).

A knowing and voluntary release of rights confirmed by Federal employment discrimination Statutes will be enforced, if:
(1) The clarity and specificity of the release.
(2) Plaintiff's knowledge of his rights upon execution of the release.
(3) Whether the plaintiff had the benefit of counsel.
(4) Opportunity for negotiation.
(5) Acceptance of consideration.

In *Cirillo v. Arco Chemical Co.,*[30] the Third Circuit was again asked to address the issue. In *Cirillo,* the plaintiff was terminated as part of a company-wide workforce reduction program. He was sixty-nine-years-old and had worked for the company for forty-three years. Arco offered him a choice of two benefits packages, "each with differing tax consequences, . . ." that included a special, one-time substantial payment.[31] The plaintiff attended a small group meeting that explained the details of the packages. He met with the employee relations consultant privately two weeks later to inform the consultant of his choice of package. The consultant gave him a release form at that time and told him to review it at home.

The release explained the state and federal antidiscrimination laws and the functions of the EEOC. It also encouraged the employee to review the release with an attorney. It asked the employee to review and think about the release at least five days before signing it. The release stated that in return for the special one-time payment, the employee would release the company from "any claims, liabilities, demands and causes of action" arising from the termination.[32] The plaintiff signed it without consulting an attorney.

In entering the release, the court stated that the issue is "whether consultation with a lawyer was encouraged . . . rather than whether the plaintiff in fact received the benefit

30. Cirillo v. Arco Chem. Co., 862 F.2d 448 (3d Cir. 1988).
31. *Id.* at 449.
32. *Id.* at 450.

of counsel."[33] "Where it has been encouraged by the employer, the employee cannot be required to hire a lawyer before signing a waiver and it should normally suffice for the employer to suggest that the employee may wish to consult an attorney."[34] The one-time special payment was sufficient consideration in support of the release.[35] His normal retirement benefits would not be affected by a refusal to sign the release.[36] Therefore the release was signed voluntarily and knowingly.[37]

The Third Circuit again ruled on releases in *Coventry v. U.S. Steel Corp.*[38] Therein the plaintiff was an employee who was originally laid off as part of a workforce reduction program. He was subsequently terminated. Upon termination, the plaintiff filed an ADEA claim with the EEOC. He was then given the option to participate in the 70/80 retirement plan if he signed a release form or of being laid off indefinitely and not receiving any severance or medical benefits. He filed an amended complaint with the EEOC questioning the legality of the release. He then signed the release. Benefits were never paid out to him because of the ADEA claim.

The court held that the release was not a willing and voluntary release because the plaintiff did not have any "real options" or the advice of counsel.[39]

The court named six factors as "indicia of voluntariness":

1. Plaintiff's education;
2. Amount of time the plaintiff had possession of or access to the agreement before signing it;
3. Role of plaintiff in deciding the terms of the agreement;
4. Clarity of the agreement;

33. *Id.* at 454.
34. *Id.*
35. *Id.*
36. *Id.* at 454–455.
37. *Id.* at 455.
38. Coventry v. U.S. Steel Corp., 856 F.2d 514 (3d Cir. 1988).
39. *Id.* at 525.

5. Whether the plaintiff was represented by or consulted with an attorney;
6. Whether the consideration given in exchange for the waiver exceeds employee benefits to which the employee was already entitled by contract or law.[40]

While it appears from the EEOC's recent regulations on waivers and the various court decisions discussed herein that a private release of ADEA rights is enforceable so long as it is knowing and voluntary, a recent decision of the Ninth Circuit Court of Appeals has added further questions. In *Cassino v. Reichhold Chemicals, Inc.*,[41] the Ninth Circuit held that a "Settlement Agreement and Release" offered to the employee, Cassino, by his employer, Reichhold, at his termination meeting was not inadmissible under Section 408 of the Federal Rules of Evidence[42] in Cassino's ADEA lawsuit for discriminatory discharge. In *Cassino,* the plaintiff was offered a "Settlement Agreement and General Release," while simultaneously being informed of his termination, that provided for a payment of $18,000 to him in exchange for his release of all claims against Reichhold, "including, but not limited to, rights under federal, state or local laws prohibiting age or other forms of discrimination."[43] Cassino refused to sign the document, and shortly after he left the company he instituted a suit in federal court alleging that his termination violated the ADEA and state antidiscrimination laws.

The Ninth Circuit upheld the district court's ruling that the "Settlement Agreement and General Release" was admissible

40. *Id.* at 523 (quoting Equal Employment Opportunity Comm'n v. American Express Publishing Corp., 681 F. Supp. 216, 219 (S.D.N.Y. 1988)).
41. Cassino v. Reichhold Chems., Inc., 817 F.2d 1338 (9th Cir. 1987), *cert. denied,* 484 U.S. 1047 (1988).
42. This rule provides that evidence of offers "to compromise a claim which was disputed as to either validity or amount is not admissible to prove liability for or invalidity of the claim or its amount."
43. Cassino v. Reichhold Chems., Inc., 817 F.2d at 1342.

at trial, on the grounds that Cassino had not asserted any claim at the time Reichhold asked for the release. The Ninth Circuit distinguished the settlement of disputes arising *after* termination from the situation at bar in which an employee is terminated and the employer offers a contemporaneous severance pay package in exchange for a release of all potential claims. Under the former situation the employee is relinquishing the right to a judicial determination of an age claim in return for valuable consideration after having asserted a claim of discrimination.[44] The court finds settlement offers in the latter situation are generally made a part of the record in the case and are considered relevant to the circumstances surrounding the alleged discriminatory discharge.[45]

The court's opinion in *Cassino* therefore requires that there be an expressly asserted claim of discrimination by an employee before a settlement agreement and release can be considered inadmissible under Rule 408 in any later action. While the court does not specifically hold that a signed waiver of ADEA rights, absent any prior asserted claim of discrimination, would be unenforceable, the court's conclusion undermines the public policy favoring informal resolutions of claims or potential claims. The effect of the court's ruling is that employers will be adverse to using private waivers where there is no prior asserted claim of discrimination, because if the employee refuses to sign the release, the release will be admissible as evidence of discrimination. By discouraging employers from using private releases when there is no prior asserted claim of discrimination, the *Cassino* decision also undermines the EEOC's regulations on private waivers, which provide that *either* a clear understanding of the nature of the rights being waived *or* the presence of an asserted claim may satisfy an

44. This scenario was presented in Runyan v. National Cash Register Corp., 787 F.2d 1039 (6th Cir.) (en banc), *cert. denied,* 479 U.S. 850 (1986), on which the Ninth Circuit relied in its decision.
45. Cassino v. Reichhold Chems., Inc., 817 F.2d at 1342.

initial element of whether a release is knowing and voluntary and thus enforceable.[46]

Therefore, at the present time the Circuit Court of Appeals and a number of district courts have upheld the use of waivers in certain very defined situations. A knowing and voluntary waiver is not coercive and should be upheld by the courts. If individual resolution of matters is not encouraged, it will only enhance and increase the amount of employment-related litigation.

The Older Workers Benefit Protection Act

On October 16, 1990, President Bush signed the Older Workers Benefit Protection Act (OWBPA)[47] This legislation, in addition to dealing with age discrimination issues under employee benefit plans and authorizing voluntary early retirement plans, amends ADEA by adding a waiver provision to section 7 of the ADEA.

Section 7(f)(i) as amended by OWBPA now provides that an individual may waiver age claims if such waiver is knowing and voluntary. Such waiver may not be considered voluntary and knowing, unless at a minimum:

1. The waiver is part of a written agreement between the employee and the employer and is written in a manner so as to be understood by such individual or by the average individual eligible to participate;
2. The waiver specifically refers to rights or claims under the ADEA;
3. The individual does not waive rights or claims that may arise after the waiver is executed;
4. The individual waives rights or claims only in exchange

46. 52 Fed. Reg. 32,296 (1987) (to be codified at 29 C.F.R. § 1627).
47. 29 U.S.C. § 621(f)(i).

for consideration in addition to anything of value to which the employee is already entitled;

5. The individual is advised in writing to consult with an attorney prior to executing the waiver;
6. The individual is given *at least twenty-one days* to consider the waiver agreement; and
7. The waiver agreement provides that the individual will have *at least seven days* after signing the waiver to revoke the waiver agreement and the agreement will not become effective until the revocation period has expired.

Where a waiver is requested in connection with an exit incentive or other employment termination program (which would include a voluntary early retirement incentive plan as well as an enhanced severance program in connection with a reduction-in-force) offered to a group or class of employees, two additional conditions apply:

1. The employee must be given *forty-five days,* rather than twenty-one, within which to consider the waiver agreement; and
2. The employer must inform the individual in writing as to:
   - The group of employees covered by the program, any eligibility factors and any time limits applicable to the program; and
   - The job titles and ages of all employees eligible or selected for the program and of the individuals in the same job classification or organizational unit who are not so eligible or selected.[48]

These additional requirements can be problematic for many employers. In particular, employers may be hesitant to set forth their work force and layoff plans, as this data may be viewed as confidential business information. The burdens and litigation

48. *Id.*

risks created by these disclosure requirements may deter employers from using waivers in connection with early retirement incentive plans or from offering additional separation pay in exchange for a release in connection with a reduction-in-force.

OWBPA also authorizes the use of releases in connection with the settlement of an EEOC charge or court action. Under these circumstances, the waiver must meet the first set of requirements enumerated above, with the exception that rather than the twenty-one or forty-five-day period, the individual must be given "a reasonable period of time" within which to consider the settlement agreement. Also, the individual is not entitled to the seven-day revocation period, nor is the special information regarding group exit incentive or termination programs required.[49]

OWBPA contains a specific exception to the permissibility of private waivers of ADEA rights, that is, a waiver may not be used to prevent an employee from filing a charge with the EEOC or participating in an investigation or proceeding conducted by the EEOC.[50] As one court stated in a pre-OWBPA decision:

> Allowing the filing of charges to be obstructed by enforcing a waiver of the right to file a charge could impede EEOC enforcement of the civil rights laws. . . . A charge not only informs the EEOC of discrimination against the employee who files the charge . . . but also may identify other unlawful company actions. . . . We hold that an employer and an employee cannot agree to deny to the EEOC the information it needs to advance the public interest.[51]

However, by executing a release, an employee *can* waive the right to recover damages in his own *lawsuit* or in a suit brought by EEOC on his behalf.[52] Thus, an employer can rely

49. 29 U.S.C. § 626(f)(2).
50. 29 U.S.C. § 626(f)(4).
51. Equal Employment Opportunity Comm'n v. Cosmair, Inc., L'Oreal Hair Care Div., 821 F.2d 1085, 1090 (5th Cir. 1987).
52. *Id.* at 1091.

on the release as a defense to an employee's ADEA cause of action, but it cannot use the release as a retaliatory shield to prevent the enforcement of the civil rights laws by the EEOC.

The waiver section of OWBPA has a separate effective date. Thus, waivers entered into on or after October 16, 1990 will be subject to the new rules.

As noted earlier, OWBPA merely sets forth minimum standards that must be satisfied in order for a release to be knowing and voluntary. The legislation leaves intact preexisting case law that permits an employee to raise certain defenses such as fraud, duress, or mutual mistake in order to vitiate a release. OWBPA provides that where a dispute arises over whether the minimum requirements have been met, the *employer* will have the burden of proving that each of the specific requirements has been satisfied.[53] The House Statement of Managers indicates that beyond a showing that the statutory requirements have been satisfied, the burden of proving that the waiver was knowing or voluntary will be allocated according to preexisting law.[54] Presumably, an employee would have the opportunity to prove either through an examination of the totality of the circumstances or presentation of evidence of duress, coercion, or fraud that the release was not knowingly and voluntarily given.

In this regard, pre-OWBPA cases in which courts evaluated and weighed other factors in assessing the validity of a release will remain of some importance. For example, in finding that a release was knowingly executed, several courts have pointed to the education and business experience of the employee, especially where the employee was an attorney[55] or a management employee with experience signing contracts.[56] Other

53. 29 U.S.C. § 626(f)(3).
54. 136 *Cong. Rec.* at H 8620.
55. *See* Runyan v. National Cash Register Corp., 787 F.2d 1039, 1044 (6th Cir. 1986).
56. *See* Lancaster v. Buerkle Buick Honda Co., 809 F.2d 539, 541 (8th Cir. 1987).

courts have found additional support for the validity of a release where the employee not only was advised to, but in fact consulted an attorney in connection with execution of the release.[57] However, the cases, as well as OWBPA, suggest that an employer must merely advise the employee to seek counsel.[58] Additionally, although negotiation of terms of the release is not specifically required under the new law, negotiation over the waiver's terms, such as the amount of separation pay to be received by the employee, may be strong evidence of voluntariness.

Preventive Measures

As the discussion herein has indicated, there are many unanswered legal questions regarding the use of early retirement incentive plans and private releases of ADEA rights. Nevertheless, employers can take certain measures to minimize the risk of legal challenges to an early retirement incentive program or a private waiver of ADEA rights.

Employers, however, should not only follow the strict requirements of the October 16, 1990 amendments to the ADEA, but they should also attempt to follow some practical concerns when utilizing waivers under the ADEA. These concerns include the following:

1. The waiver should be based upon sufficient consideration that generally would include enhanced benefits and/or severance pay. This severance pay and benefits should be in addition to any "regular benefits or pay that are allowed to employees." Do not rely on preexisting obligations or considerations.

---

57. *See* O'Hare v. Global Natural Resources, 898 F.2d 1015 (5th Cir. 1990); Shaheen v. Goodrich Co., 873 F.2d 105 (6th Cir. 1989); Fay v. Petersen Publishing Co., 52 FEP Cases 1531 (S.D.N.Y. 1990).
58. *See* Cirillo v. Arco Chem. Co., 862 F.2d 448 (3d Cir. 1988) (plaintiff's failure to consult counsel did not invalidate release where employer had encouraged such consultation).

2. All efforts should be made to maintain the voluntariness of the use of the waiver by the employee. One should, of course, avoid misrepresentation or fraud and avoid putting any pressure upon the employee to sign.
3. An employee must be given as a minimum the statutory amount of time to decide if they wish to sign the release agreement and must be advised to consult an attorney prior to executing the release. The time should be used to discuss the agreement with the employee's family, attorney, financial advisors, and others, and if necessary, to negotiate the terms of the waiver.
4. The release should be as comprehensive as possible and clearly state the laws the employee is waiving his rights under, especially the ADEA.
5. The language of the release should be as comprehensive and as clear and nonlegalistic as possible.
6. The release should mention and acknowledge the consideration received for the release, that the consideration is more than what the employee would normally receive under such circumstances, and that the release is entered into voluntarily. (See Appendix H herein.)

The employer may also consider including other provisions in the separation agreement including:

• *Competition and other employee conduct.* During the period that the employee is receiving severance or some form of extended salary payment, the employer may require that the employee comply with reasonable standards of conduct. Such provisions can include a reasonable noncompetition clause, a restriction on contacting customers, lenders, and creditors, and a prohibition from engaging in activities that would be in conflict with the employer's interests. In some states, such as California, postemployment noncompetition clauses are not enforceable. For enforceability, it might be advisable to require that the employees, particularly in states that limit postemployment restrictive covenants, to be available to perform some services if requested. In any case, an employer should seek counsel before preparing this type of provision.

• *Confidentiality of terms of settlement.* Provisions prohibiting the employee from publicizing the financial arrangements are often used. If payment or severance pay is paid over a long period of time and the employee breaches the confidentiality clause, the payment may stop. Realistically, once payment has been made, it might be difficult to enforce these provisions.

• *General confidentiality provisions.* There should, of course, be general provisions reaffirming the employee's recognition that confidential information about the employer's business should not be disclosed. The employee should also agree to return all company documents and all documents that contain proprietary or confidential information relating to the company.

• *Attorneys.* If an attorney represents the employee, some agreements provide for the return of confidential information made available to the attorney and have a commitment from the attorney that the attorney will keep confidential such information as well as the terms of the separation agreement. Although it might raise ethical issues, in some cases the attorney might also be limited in representing other employees from the same company in future proceedings.

• *Other provisions to be considered.*

—Acknowledgment that the termination of employment was voluntary;

—Recitals relating to the circumstances giving rise to the release, including any special provisions relating to the date of termination of employment;

—Covenants not to sue;

—Specific recitals relating to the employee's opportunities to review and consider the release, including opportunities for review by the employee's attorney;

—Withdrawal of any administrative proceedings (e.g., EEOC or state human rights claims);

INCLUDE ALL PARTIES

In addition to releasing claims against the employer, the release should include a release of subsidiaries and divisions, their officers, directors, and employees. If appropriate, the release may also include the pension plan trustees or administrator.

SPECIFY REGARDING TERMINATION

• *Include amounts and operative dates for salary and severance.* Specify the amounts of salary for any continuing active employment and dates fixed for termination of salary, along with the amounts and dates for ending of severance pay.

• *Specify bonus, commissions, and vacation pay.* If determined, the amounts of any bonus, commission, and vacation payments should be specified. Normally, the employee will not accrue additional vacation time during severance. This might have to be specified if not stated in the employer's vacation policy.

• *Specify benefits not applicable during severance.* The employee should have available summary plan descriptions or be advised, perhaps in a separate document, when various employee benefits cease. Some employee benefit plans require that an employee be actively employed in order to continue coverage. This is particularly likely with disability plans (see below). The employee should be made clearly aware of his or her status. An area often overlooked is the availability of payments for courses started, both before and after termination of active employment, under a tuition reimbursement plan.

• *Consider disability during severance.* Potentially difficult areas, if not covered, are those where the employee becomes sick or disabled during a period of payment of severance or salary continuation. Normally, the severance or salary continuation payments would not be extended since the employee is not performing any duties. Short-term and long-term disability plan coverage may also terminate at the end of active employment since the employee will not be actively at work.

• *Include resignation as officer and director.* If the individual involved is an officer or director of the employer or any of its subsidiaries, resignations as an officer and director should be obtained. It is often convenient for the purposes of corporate minute books to have this as a separate letter.

• *Consider termination dates for use of office, telephone, and clerical support.* If appropriate, include dates for ending the use of an office, clerical or secretarial services, and telephone.

• *Employee outplacement fees and legal fees.* If the employer is assuming any employee outplacement costs or legal fees (or the release of any claims for legal fees), these should be discussed and specifically provided.

• *Future services.* If appropriate, be sure to provide for future consulting services or for other future assistance, e.g., as a witness in litigation.

• *Reemployment.* The agreement should provide for a clear waiver of reemployment by the employer or by a subsidiary, affiliate, or related company. This provision may include a termination of employment if the individual is subsequently employed.

• *No other compensation or perquisites.* If the release or termination agreement is intended to be comprehensive, include a "catchall" provision stating that there will be no compensation, benefits, or perquisites other than those specified in the release or agreement. The agreement should also contain a "zipper clause" voiding all prior oral or written agreement between the parties.

STRUCTURE PAYMENTS TO ACHIEVE MUTUALLY DESIRABLE RESULTS

• *Review salary or severance payment dates for effect on*

employee benefits. The timing of the commencement of severance or the duration of severance payments can have a significant impact on an employee's benefits:

—Check vesting dates under pension/profit sharing plans. Where an employee will miss a key vesting date by a relatively short time period, it may be possible to extend active employment (this might avoid a claim that the employee was terminated in order to prevent vesting).[59]

—Check medical/life insurance coverage to determine if the employee is covered during the initial period when the employee is not employed elsewhere.

• *Consider taxes.* Decisions as to the timing of termination of salary and severance payments and the characterization of other payments can significantly affect various taxes:

—*Income tax.* Salary and severance payments, as well as amounts in lieu of back pay, are normally taxable as wages for federal income tax and social security (FICA) tax purposes.[60]

—*Stretchout or deferral of payments—constructive receipt.* Stretching severance payments will normally have a corresponding effect on the applicable income taxes. Caution: If the employee elects the stretchout after he or she has a right to receive payment or retains the right to request an immediate lump sum payment and if the payments extend into a new tax year, under certain circumstances the employee may be subject to the tax rules involving "constructive receipt" of income. This could result in a possible acceleration of tax liability.

—*Damages received "on account of personal injury or*

59. ERISA 510, 29 U.S.C. 1140, provides: "It shall be unlawful to discharge . . . a participant . . . for the purpose of interfering with the attainment of any right to which such participant may become entitled under the plan. . . ." *See also* Dister v. Continental Group, Inc., 859 F.2d 1108 (2d Cir. 1988) (involuntary termination of employee about four months prior to being eligible for enhanced retirement benefit).

60. Generally, see Rev. Rul. 78-176, 1978-1 C.B. 303; Priv. Ltr. Rul. 7742028 (July 20, 1978).

sickness." Some settlements involve claims for mental distress, defamation, and other tort actions. Damages "on account of personal injury or sickness," not being wages, are not included in a taxpayer's gross income under IRC Section 104(a)(2). Recently, there have been several decisions quite favorable to former employees under this Section.[61]

If an employer follows these practical suggestions while being aware of the evolving and changing case law and legislation, there is no reason why an employee cannot sign a waiver and the employer can rely upon that action. One must keep in mind that the use of a release helps the employee by giving him or her additional compensation at the time of the termination and gives the employer the insurance that they will not be sued at a later date after the employee accepts this additional compensation.

In conclusion, it is the author's opinion that waivers and releases under the ADEA are appropriate vehicles under the law. Based on the present status of court decisions and law, it is expected that the courts will continue to recognize this as an equitable method to resolve issues arising under the ADEA and other laws.

---

61. Thompson v. Commissioner, 866 F.2d 709 (4th Cir. 1987) (liquidated damages received in connection with Equal Pay Act claim was in the nature of damages for personal injury); Rickel v. Commissioner, 92 T.C. 32 (Mar. 23, 1989) (liquidated damages under ADEA no income because they are intended to compensate for difficult to measure personal injuries resulting from age discrimination; despite failure of parties to allocate, court allowed 50 percent to be excluded); Byrne v. Commissioner, 90 T.C. 1000 (1988) (despite failure of parties to allocate damages, court upheld 50 percent allocation to "personal injury" where release included all types of claims arising out of termination of employment and state law permitted tort actions); and Bent v. Commissioner, 87 T.C. 236 (1986).

CHAPTER TWELVE

Human Resource Audits

It should now be evident from the discussion in the preceding chapters that the recent past is marked by a dramatic rise in the amount of employment-related litigation as a consequence of the heightened sensitivity of the American judiciary to the rights of employees. It is likely that the future will bring a continuation of the erosion of the employment-at-will doctrine through judicial acceptance of traditional contract and tort theories to restrict management's control over the employment relationship. Moreover, there is little doubt that an increasingly sophisticated American labor force will continue to resort to the judicial system to enforce individual employment rights as a growing number of jurisdictions carve out exceptions to an employer's authority to terminate the employment relationship. In light of this significant expansion of employee rights, and the constant changes in the law that define the parameters of permissible employer action, an employer must be ever mindful of implementing preventive measures to avoid or limit its exposure to potential liability in employment litigation.

To this end, although there is no sure-fire method of human resource management that an employer can institute to ensure that it will never be involved in wrongful discharge litigation, it is recommended that an employer periodically engage in a comprehensive internal audit of its employment policies and procedures to insulate such practices from attack should litigation occur. By reviewing its personnel practices on a regular basis, an employer will be able to determine whether such practices are appropriate under the current state of the law. Ideally, a properly conducted internal audit will result in the consistent application of an employer's practices and the creation of fair and objective procedures should the existing practices be found to be deficient or obsolete.

Establishing the Audit

Preliminary Steps

There are two threshold issues that must be addressed by every employer considering the implementation of an internal labor relations audit: (1) when should the audit take place and (2) by whom should it be conducted? The former is easily resolved. Since every organization regardless of size already utilizes a variety of employment-related practices and procedures, if the organization has never conducted an audit of such procedures, the audit should be conducted as soon as possible. Once the initial audit has occurred, all subsequent employment-related audits should be scheduled in conjunction with other audits of the company's internal procedures. Inasmuch as most organizations will normally conduct financial reviews or audits toward the end of the operating fiscal year as a planning tool for the next fiscal year, the employment-related audits should similarly be scheduled at that time in the event that the audit suggests changes in the employer's compensation system, employee benefits package, or in other policies or procedures requiring additional financial resources.

As to the second consideration at the outset, it is strongly urged that the audit be conducted by either in-house counsel or outside labor counsel in conjunction with the company's human resource department. The purpose behind assigning this responsibility to legal counsel is to preserve the confidentiality of the information obtained during the audit as well as any plans formulated as a result of the audit.

If certain procedures are followed at the initial stage of the audit and in connection with the preparation of documentation related to the audit, documents generated by the audit will arguably constitute attorney work product or fall within the scope of the attorney/client privilege, and thereby be immune from discovery by the opposing party in the event of litigation. Specifically, the audit should be initiated by written communication from the chief operating officer of the company to all appropriate parties authorizing a confidential internal audit of all personnel policies and procedures. This notification should specify that information related to the audit will be provided to counsel for review and for legal advice to ensure that the employer is in compliance with existing employment laws. Furthermore, the recipient should be instructed that all information must be kept confidential with access restricted to those individuals who "have a legitimate right to know."

During the pendency of the audit, great care must be taken to prevent public dissemination of any information in order to guard against forfeiture of the attorney-client privilege. Moreover, confidentiality concerns mandate that all communications and analyses related to the audit be prepared by counsel, labeled "attorney/client privileged communication," and be maintained in a separate, restricted file entitled "Attorney/Client Confidential Information." Another precautionary measure, if litigation is pending or anticipated, is to indicate on all documents that they are being prepared in anticipation of or in connection with such litigation. Finally, since the company's employees must eventually be told about the audit when the relevant documents are gathered from them during the audit, it is recommended that an initial communication be sent to all employees advising them that the internal audit is being conducted and that the results of the audit and any subsequent policy changes will be communicated upon the completion of the audit.

Documents to Be Reviewed

The internal audit necessarily involves a review of all procedures and policies relating to the four distinct stages of the employment relationship: (1) hiring; (2) employee evaluation or retention; (3) employee discipline or termination; and (4) postemployment. To accomplish this task, all existing written documents that incorporate personnel practices and procedures, such as handbooks, policy statements, orientation materials, recruitment material, and related documents, must be gathered by the employer and forwarded to counsel. It is recommended that the employer send a general memorandum to all employees requesting that all such documents in their possession be copied and forwarded to the human resource department in connection with the internal audit.

In addition, in order to ascertain whether unwritten or "outdated" policies exist, supervisory personnel should be interviewed by counsel. Individuals involved in the hiring process also should be contacted to discuss the substance of communications made to prospective employees, orally or in writing, regarding the organization or employment matters. Furthermore, documents used by the company to record data with respect to employees, e.g., "applicant logs," should be obtained for review.

Goals of the Audit

Once the employer has ascertained all written and unwritten employment-related policies, the review process should provide answers to several important questions regarding the application of these policies. The internal audit should be able to determine whether the policies are being applied in a consistent manner. Inconsistent application of existing policies or practices could make an employer susceptible to discrimination claims based on disparate treatment or serve as evidence of "unfair treatment" in an abusive discharge litigation. From a practical standpoint, inconsistent application of policies and practices can have a harmful effect upon employee morale. While an organization is by no means required to have the same policy for all groups of employees, e.g., a more lenient attendance policy for management-level employees as opposed to clerical employees, the audit should establish whether the policies are being applied uniformly to all employees intended to be covered by them.

In addition, the audit should enable an employer to determine whether the employment-related policies are equitable. To make such a determination, the internal auditor should obtain similar policies used by competitors or organizations located in the same geographic area. In this way, the employer can determine whether a particular policy is the norm both within the industry and within the community in which the organization operates.

Furthermore, the audit should reveal the method and means of communication of employment-related policies. Here, too, the important factor is whether there is consistency of communication of the policies utilized by an employer. For example, if the established mode of communication is an employment handbook or personnel policy manual, all policies should be included in the manual, and communication of such policies should be limited solely to this written medium. Oral communication of policies should be strictly avoided.

The internal audit procedure should also provide insight as to which individual(s) within the organization are responsible for the implementation and enforcement of employment-related policies. It is essential that every organization, including those organizations without a human resources department, have at least one individual whose job responsibilities specifically include the implementation, interpretation, and enforcement of employment-related policies.

Finally, the internal audit should distinguish between policies that are applicable to nonunion employees and the terms and conditions of employment for any employees who are represented for the purposes of collective bargaining by a labor organization. All collective bargaining agreements governing the latter should be reviewed as part of the audit to determine how, if at all, changes in the negotiated provisions relate to nonunion employees. Moreover, the employer must be aware that policy changes that purport to affect all employees may have to be the subject of negotiations with the appropriate collective bargaining agent. As such, those practices that on their faces appear to be applicable to both organized and unorganized employees must be examined to determine whether a specific exclusion exists for unionized employees.

Review of Specific Employment-Related Practices and Policies

Handbooks or Personnel Policy Manuals

Many employers have adopted personnel practices manuals as an effective means of communicating to all employees the employment-related practices and policies of the organization. If an employer has codified its employment-related practices and procedures in the form of an employee handbook or personnel policy manual, the internal audit will typically begin with a review of these documents. The purpose of reviewing the employee handbook or manual is to ensure that the manual reflects and protects the type of employment relationship intended by the employer. This is a legitimate concern of any employer in light of the substantial number of jurisdictions that now recognize that an employee handbook or policy manual may give rise to rights enforceable in contract with respect to the policies contained therein. As such, if it is the employer's intention not to establish any contractual rights through the issuance of the manual, a properly conducted audit will reveal whether the manual contains language best suited to achieve this result.

The audit will reveal whether an appropriate disclaimer of contractual rights is included in the manual and whether the employer has reserved the right to modify or eliminate any existing policies or practices. Furthermore, whereas a manual, if not carefully drafted, may create an employment relationship never intended by the employer or bind the employer to procedures relating to termination or other changes in employment status, the audit should enable an employer to determine whether appropriate disclaimers of any intent to establish contractual rights have been inserted wherever the manual addresses job security and reasons for discipline and termination. (See Chapter 7 herein.)

If the employer has previously implemented a progressive discipline policy and/or a probationary period for new employees, the manual should be reviewed to ensure that the language used does not suggest the creation of limitations on the employer's right to terminate employees at will. In this regard, the provision for a progressive discipline scheme should make clear that the employer is not bound to the policy in all instances, that employees may be terminated without the use of such procedures, and that the reasons listed for termination are not all-inclusive. In a similar vein, language indicating that a probationary employee may be terminated without notice or cause should be eliminated so as not to suggest that cause is required once the employee completes the probationary period.

In addition, the audit will indicate whether the manual contains a "zipper clause," a provision specifying that all employment-related policies in effect prior to the issuance of the manual, whether written or oral, are null and void. The inclusion of such a clause is intended to avoid disputes over whether a policy that existed prior to the adoption of the manual continues to exist even after the issuance of the manual.

The Hiring Process

With respect to the hiring process of any organization, the internal audit will be concerned initially with the nature of the employment relationship. The audit should focus upon whether the employer wishes to employ its employees at will, pursuant to employment contracts, or a combination of these two relationships. Once the employer has decided what type of employment relationship is desired, it is important that the relationship be stated clearly in all written materials used in the hiring process, such as employment applications and written offers of employment. (See Chapter 6 herein.)

In addition, the audit should entail an examination of the type of training provided any employee who has authority for recruitment and hiring. It may be necessary to establish a formal procedure involving legal counsel or a personnel department employee to educate these employees on any changes in employment law that affect the way they perform their functions.

Interview

It is imperative that the internal audit ascertain the substance of the communications made by the organization's interviewers to prospective employees. There should be an established procedure followed by all interviewers to ensure a consistent approach. A checklist of items to be discussed with the interviewee should be created and include the following topics:

1. Elements of the job in question;
2. Description of the salary and fringe benefits policy of the company;
3. List of the other individuals who will interview the applicant; and
4. A written summary of the interview.

Furthermore, the interviewer should be specifically instructed as to what statements should not be communicated to prospective employees. For example, interviewers should be told to avoid statements concerning job security, for example, "you have a job for life as long as you do a good job"; or statements that "puff" the job security aspects of the organization, for example, "we've never terminated an employee." Representations that might influence a potential employee to change his or her current position in reliance upon the representation should also be avoided. The best example of such a statement is a promise of employment causing the applicant to leave his or her present position. An employer may be bound to such representations under theories of detrimental reliance or promissory estoppel. It is essential that the same instructions provided company interviewers be given to any outside recruitment sources. (See Chapter 6 herein.)

Offers of Employment

The internal audit also focuses on how an offer is communicated once a decision to hire the applicant is made. Again, a consistent method of communication should be adopted. It is advisable to make all offers in writing so as to avoid a subsequent dispute between the parties as to the terms and conditions of that offer. With respect to the substance of the offer, the offer should state that the employee must serve a probationary period if such a requirement exists; that the offer is contingent upon the availability of the position at the time employment is scheduled to commence; and that such employment will be subject to the procedures contained in the company's personnel practices manual. (See Chapter 7 herein.)

Employment Application

Here, again, a properly drafted employment application can substantially reduce the company's vulnerability to wrongful discharge claims. To be effective, the application should clearly set forth the nature of the employment relationship and expressly provide that the relationship will be governed by the personnel practices manual. In any event, all comprehensive statements contained in the employment application should be in bold type and the phrase "read carefully" should both precede any such statements and appear immediately before the applicant's signature.

Managing Existing Employees

Probationary Period

Many employers require that the first sixty days, ninety days, or up to six months of initial employment be considered a "probationary period," a period in which the employer will monitor the progress of a newly hired employee. Since the use of a probationary period may suggest that an employee successfully completing the probationary period obtains the right to be discharged only for cause, the organization should clearly communicate to the employee that no greater job security attaches upon completion of the probationary period and that completion of the period is significant for purposes entirely separate from job security, such as employee fringe benefit programs. To this end, the organization should not refer to an employee who completes the probationary period as a "permanent" employee because of that term's connotation of an expected long-term duration of employment.

Performance Evaluation

An important part of the internal audit is the review of an organization's policies governing the performance evaluation of incumbent employees. An employer should have established a periodic performance appraisal system to provide the organization with a basis for deciding upon promotions, demotions, pay increases, transfers, and terminations. Ideally, the performance evaluation process should be a two-way communication device pursuant to which the organization not only indicates to employees their strengths and weaknesses in their current positions, but learns from the employees the strengths and weaknesses of the organization.

The achievement of a proper performance evaluation system requires constant monitoring as to its effectiveness and as to whether the criteria used to assess performance is being applied in a consistent manner. An internal review of the organization's appraisal system should include an examination of the following issues:

- How often are formal evaluations done?
- Are there instructions for filling out the evaluation forms?
- Are the evaluators trained on how to prepare an evaluation?
- Are the evaluators familiar with the employee's performance?
- Is the evaluation based upon job-related objective criteria?
- Does the evaluation list both the strengths and weaknesses of the employee?
- Is the evaluation reviewed by someone senior to the initial evaluator?
- Does the employee have the opportunity to comment on the evaluation?
- Is there an employee appeal process?

- How is the evaluation communicated?
- Is there central evaluation of the appraisal system?
- Is there adverse impact on any "protected" group?
- Are there mutually negotiated timetables and action plans to correct poor performance?
- Are there informal evaluations?

Supervisory personnel who are responsible for conducting performance appraisals of employees must be trained as to how to conduct an evaluation, and instructions must be prepared to ensure that terms and criteria are consistently applied. Furthermore, the appraisal must be conducted by a supervisor who knows the duties of the position and the employee's performance during the relevant time period. If there is a change in supervisors during the time period covered by the review, both supervisors should participate in the evaluation process.

In addition, it is essential that evaluations be based upon job-related objective criteria. Subjective criteria that require the evaluator to assess whether the employee exhibited certain character traits should be avoided. This means that employees should be evaluated on their performance as it relates to the accomplishment of the particular duties they are asked to perform. Employees should not be evaluated on non-job-related factors. Moreover, it is not uncommon for a well-intentioned evaluator to overinflate evaluations of employee performance. However, this tendency could cause problems for the company in justifying its subsequent decision to terminate the employee, should the former employee later bring a wrongful discharge action. Accordingly, in order to reflect an accurate portrayal of an employee's work performance, it is important that the performance evaluation system also incorporate an assessment of the employee's weaknesses, problems, and skills in need of improvement.

It is also recommended, as an internal control device to ensure consistency, accuracy, and the absence of any sympathy or bias, that someone superior to the initial evaluator in the organizational hierarchy review the evaluation before it is discussed with the employee. Furthermore, the evaluation should be presented personally to the employee by the same individual who prepared the evaluation. To prevent an employee from claiming that he or she was not privy to the contents of the appraisal, there should be a place for the employee's signature on the evaluation form. The employee should be given the opportunity to submit written comments in response to the appraisal and some mechanism should be available to an employee for appealing the evaluation if the employee is dissatisfied with the result. If the employee's performance is found to be deficient in any area, corrective action, short of disciplinary action, should be mutually agreed upon as a product of the evaluation process. This involves establishing timetables for accomplishing certain objectives agreed upon by the evaluator and the employee.

A tendency on the part of supervisors to base an appraisal on events immediately preceding the designated periodic formal evaluation may militate against a reliable evaluation. To assure that supervisors consider performance-related events occurring throughout the appraisal period, they should be instructed to thoroughly document any evaluation of the employee's performance during that time period, including any informal performance appraisal or the occurrence of any noteworthy event.

In assessing the effectiveness of an evaluation system, the internal audit should determine how frequently evaluations are given. Normally, evaluations should be done on an annual basis. In addition, more frequent evaluations should be scheduled for newly hired or recently promoted employees and employers experiencing performance-related problems. The failure of a company to conduct evaluations on at least an annual basis will weaken their effectiveness and their value in employment-related litigation.

Finally, the internal audit should focus on which performance appraisals are used for which employment decisions, e.g., salary increases, promotions, etc. The same performance appraisal used as the basis for an increase in compensation may not be valid in connection with a promotion decision. (See Chapter 8 herein.)

Termination

The initial question to be addressed in evaluating a company's termination policy is whether it has or wants a specific procedure for termination. Although a comprehensive disciplinary procedure makes the employer more susceptible to claims for noncompliance with said procedure, it is generally recommended that a termination procedure be established with sufficient disclaimers to permit variance under appropriate circumstances. The procedure should provide for a form of progressive discipline for certain transgressions and immediate termination in more severe cases. Again, however, in designing such a procedure, an organization should allow for maximum flexibility by inserting disclaimer language indicating that graduated discipline may not be used in all instances and will be completely disregarded under certain circumstances. Moreover, any listing of reasons for immediate termination should not be made all-inclusive. It should be noted, however, that in order to be successful and defensible if challenged by a terminated employee, the procedure must be objective, have the appearance of objectivity, and such objectivity must be capable of being verified.

Other considerations when assessing the termination procedure are whether a second opinion should be obtained and whether legal advice should be sought prior to the termination. It is suggested that a company establish a mechanism for an independent review of all termination decisions before the decision becomes final. The termination should be reviewed by an experienced person(s) superior to the immediate supervisor who has the authority to reverse the decision if necessary. A thorough investigation of the circumstances surrounding the termination should be conducted to determine whether the termination action is fair, consistent with company policy, and appropriate under the circumstances. The investigation should involve obtaining the underlying facts from both the supervisor and the employee, as well as conducting interviews with witnesses to the events leading to the termination decision.

Since the touchstone of any termination is its "fairness," certain questions should be asked and answered by an employer prior to finalizing the termination decision to determine whether this standard has been met. These questions include:

1. Was the employee aware of the performance standard or work rules leading to termination?
2. Was the termination decision consistent with prior similar situations?
3. Was there compliance with any progressive disciplinary requirements?
4. Were there mitigating circumstances that suggest a less drastic action?
5. What is the employee's side of the story?
6. Were stated practices and procedures of the company followed?
7. What was the employee's prior record?
8. Can the decision be supported if challenged?

   In essence, the ultimate consideration in assessing the propriety of the termination is whether the punishment fits the crime. If termination appears to be objectively excessive, further consideration of the decision might be warranted. (See Chapter 9 herein.)

Postemployment

Employment References

The issue of whether an employer should give an employment reference on behalf of a terminated employee, and the content of said reference, has become increasingly important as the courts show a willingness to find an employer liable for the tort of defamation on account of statements made to a prospective employer about a former employee.

As a preventive measure, the company should obtain a signed statement from the employee prior to departure indicating exactly what he or she would like the company to inform prospective employers. The employee should be informed that in the absence of a signed statement the employer will merely give dates of employment and job functions. An organization might wish to consider establishing a policy whereby only objective data is provided, i.e., dates of employment, wages earned, and the date of termination, with no mention made of the employee's performance or the reasons for termination.

In any event, the organization should give employment references only in response to a written request. Moreover, the reference should be prepared by the human resources or personnel department, and should not be given by the immediate supervisor of the former employee at the time of termination. Any statements made by the employer in an employment-related reference must be truthful and based upon facts, not speculation.

Retention of Records

Finally, the internal audit should focus on the employer's policy regarding the retention of employment records. Since federal, state and/or local statutes may impose requirements on an employer with respect to the type of records that must be retained and the period of retention, all relevant statutes, regulations, and ordinances must be reviewed to determine whether the employer's policies comply with applicable record-keeping requirements. For example, Title VII currently imposes a six-month retention period for certain specific personnel records made or kept by an employer; however, as of this writing, the Equal Employment Opportunity Commission has proposed revisions to the record-keeping regulations that would extend the retention period to one year. Such a change would make the Title VII regulations consistent with regulations promulgated under the federal age discrimination statute (the ADEA), which now require that individual employment records be kept for a period of one year from the date of the personnel action to which the record relates.

In addition, to protect the privacy rights of employees, disclosure of employment records should be limited to persons with an actual business-related reason to review the records or who are granted a right of access by statute. Even if the organization's policy provides for the destruction of records after a specified period of time has elapsed, certain cumulative data, such as a demographic analysis of hirings, terminations, or promotions, should be retained for an extended period of time for possible use in defending the company's actions in employment-related litigation.

With the potential for employer liability enhanced due to the growing number of jurisdictions embracing exceptions to the employment-at-will doctrine under various contract and tort theories, human resource audits have become a necessary tool for any employer seeking to reduce substantially the risk of a successful challenge to its employment decisions. By formally reviewing all personnel policies and procedures on an annual basis, an employer will be able to ensure that its practices conform to current legal requirements and that they are being consistently and uniformly applied in an objective fashion to all covered employees. Moreover, an internal audit of all policies and procedures should enable an employer to eliminate any representations made to employees regarding job security that could arguably form the basis of an employee's claim of an enforceable contract right. As such, the employment-related audit offers an employer a most effective way to insulate its employment practices from attack as the trend continues toward protecting the rights of the individual employee.

CHAPTER THIRTEEN

An Alternative—Employment Agreements

An employer that is interested in limiting its potential exposure to legal liability for wrongful discharge claims must be willing to consider new techniques to counteract increasing judicial acceptance of theories that erode the traditional employment-at-will relationship. Perhaps the single most effective way for an employer to minimize the risk of wrongful discharge claims is to enter into written employment agreements with some or all of its employees.

The use of an individual employment agreement allows the employer to avoid court-imposed terms and conditions of employment. When the employer and employee have specified the terms and conditions of employment in a contractual agreement, a court will generally enforce those terms as written and refrain from implying any terms of employment not expressed within the four corners of the written instrument. An employer thus gains the advantage of being able to set forth in detail specific terms and conditions of employment that would be applicable to a given situation and to predict, with reasonable certainty, liability for breach of the employment agreement. For example, the inclusion of an express contractual provision giving the employer the unfettered right to terminate the employment relationship at any time, for any reason or no reason, would arguably prevent a court from fashioning some form of job security from other indicia of the employment relationship. In addition, reducing the terms of the employment relationship to writing should substantially diminish the likelihood of any misunderstanding as to the respective rights of the employer and the employee.

In general, the employer and employee have wide discretion in setting the terms of an employment relationship and committing them to writing. The language of the specific terms set forth in the employment agreement should be clear as to their meaning. Thus, courts will construe an ambiguous contract term against the interpretation advanced by the drafter of the provision, which will usually be the employer. The type of provisions that are suitable for inclusion in a written employment contract are quite varied since the parties could address any aspect of the employment relationship in the agreement. Nevertheless, every written employment agreement should at least set forth all of the material terms of the employment relationship. It is recommended that the following provisions be included in all written contracts of employment:

- Nature of the relationship
- Services to be performed
- Term
- Compensation and benefits
- Probationary period
- Noncompetition and confidentiality provisions
- Invention provisions
- Termination
- Notice provisions
- Resolution of disputes
- Arbitration
- Integration and zipper clauses
- Statute of limitations
- Choice of law

- Severability clause
- Waiver

Nature of the Relationship

The mere existence of a written contract of employment does not necessarily mean that the employee enjoys some form of job security. The written employment agreement should specify whether the employment relationship is to be regarded as terminable at will or whether cause is required to terminate the relationship. In the absence of express language to the contrary, the employment relationship is considered to be at will, and no reason or any reason may be the basis for the employer's decision to end the employment relationship at any time. Nevertheless, if the employer wishes to preserve an at-will relationship, the contract should specifically state that the employee may be terminated at any time with or without cause. It should be noted that a written employment agreement establishing a fixed term of employment, e.g., three years, limits the employer's freedom to terminate the relationship. Where an employment agreement specifies a fixed term of employment, an employer may not discharge an employee without just cause even if the agreement does not expressly state such a requirement.

Services to Be Performed

Every written employment agreement should set forth the particular duties and responsibilities to be performed by the employee. This is especially important where the employment involves a complex or unorthodox work relationship, e.g., multiple employers. However, the type of responsibilities the employee will be expected to perform should not be defined as an all-inclusive listing, since a subsequent unilateral decision by the employer to change those duties may be regarded as a breach of contract. Thus, the employment agreement should specify that the employer has the discretion to change the nature of the employee's responsibilities, and the agreement should state that such responsibilities include, but are not limited to, the specific duties set forth in the contract.

Term

The standard employment agreement should set forth a specific term of employment. As previously noted, an employment contract for a fixed term is regarded under the law as imposing a just cause standard for termination. Accordingly, an employer may prefer, under appropriate circumstances (i.e., an employment contract for a nonexecutive position), a provision giving the employer the discretion to determine the duration of the employment. Such a provision would be tied to additional at-will language giving either party the right to terminate the relationship at any time upon appropriate notice.

If a fixed term of employment is intended by the parties, the language should be carefully drafted to avoid any ambiguity. For example, where the written contract provided that the term of employment was "not to exceed" three years, a court held that an at-will relationship was created because the three-year period indicated a maximum, and not a minimum, period of employment.[1] On the other hand, if an at-will relationship is to be established, language in the agreement indicating that the contract is for "lifetime" or "permanent" employment should be avoided to preclude a claim that greater job security was contemplated by the parties.

In addition, if the employment period is for a fixed term, the written contract should state whether the agreement is auto-

1. Terrebonne v. Louisiana Ass'n of Educators, 444 So. 2d 206 (La. Ct. App. 1983).

matically renewable upon the expiration of the initial period of employment. Typically, a contract will provide that it is renewed automatically on a year-to-year basis or for a period equal to the initial period of employment if notice of termination is not given by either party prior to the expiration date.

Compensation and Benefits

A written employment agreement should indicate the compensation to be paid to the employee, how increases in compensation are to be determined, the method of payment, and the applicable fringe benefits.

Probationary Period

Under certain circumstances an employer might want to evaluate whether the employee is capable of performing the responsibilities of the position before the employee becomes eligible for certain benefits or receives some form of job security. If so, the employment agreement should set forth a specific probationary period during which the employee may be terminated for any reason by the employer.

Noncompetition and Confidentiality Provisions

Where applicable, an employment agreement should incorporate various types of noncompetition covenants that extend beyond the termination of the employment relationship. The typical type of restraint set forth in an employment contract would be a provision prohibiting an employee who voluntarily resigns or is discharged from accepting employment with a competitor or entering into a competing business for a specified period of time. Although the enforcement of such restrictions after the termination of employment is questionable, it appears that postemployment restrictions, which continue during a severance payment period, are enforceable. Other types of restrictive covenants used to protect an employer's business interests include promises not to hire any employees of the former employer nor solicit customers and accounts of the former employer. Furthermore, if the employee has access to confidential information or trade secrets[2] of the employer, the employment agreement should include a provision prohibiting the unauthorized disclosure of such information both during the course of the employment relationship and post-employment.

Whether any particular type of noncompetition covenant will be enforceable in a given situation will necessarily depend on the law that has developed in that area in the applicable state jurisdiction. However, since noncompetition provisions are disfavored as a restraint on trade, such covenants are generally not enforceable unless they are limited to a geographical area and time period reasonably necessary to protect the employer's legitimate interests.

In addition, where the employee's responsibilities include the development of new products or processes, the employment agreement should include a provision assigning to the employer all ownership rights in any inventions developed by the employee during the employment relationship. In certain states (e.g., California, Minnesota, Washington, North Carolina, and Illinois), statutes have been enacted that limit the employer's ability to contract for an assignment of invention rights. These statutes render such an assignment unenforceable if the employer's resources were not used and the inventions were developed on the employee's own time.

---

2. Trade secrets should be limited to what truly amount to trade secrets for the particular business in question.

Termination

In addition, the employment agreement should specifically set forth under what conditions the employee may be terminated during the term of the agreement. For example, where the agreement is for a fixed period of employment, the agreement could provide that termination may result if the employee engages in willful misconduct or gross negligence in the performance of his duties, or knowingly and willfully engages in some act that reflects negatively on the general reputation of the employer. To preserve the at-will relationship, the agreement should state that the employee may be terminated at any time with or without cause.

Notice Provisions

The employment agreement should provide for a set number of days' notice for termination by either the employee or the employer. Even if such a provision is included in the agreement, it is a basic principle of contract law that where a contract of ordinary employment requires a certain period of notice prior to termination, the employment may be terminated on shorter notice or without any notice if the employee is paid his salary for the notice period. As such, in *Larson v. SYSCO Corp.,*[3] the court held that the employer did not breach the notice provision in the employment agreement by paying the employee two weeks' severance benefits in lieu of giving two weeks' notice as required by the terms of the contract.

Resolution of Disputes

The employment agreement should set forth whether disputes between the employer and the employee arising under

3. Larson v. SYSCO Corp., 4 IER Cas. (BNA) 98 (Utah 1989).

the terms of the contract are to be resolved through arbitration or in court. If the agreement provides for arbitration, both the employer and the employee should be granted the right to invoke the arbitral process. In *Sablosky v. Edward S. Gordon, Inc.*,[4] an arbitration clause contained in an employment agreement was deemed to be unenforceable because only the employer had the contractual right to compel arbitration. While the employer had the right to proceed directly to arbitration with its own claim or invoke arbitration if the employee initiated a lawsuit to resolve the dispute, the employee could not require that the employer submit to arbitration, and the absence of this right rendered the provision invalid.

Arbitration offers an employer an attractive alternative to the judicial process as the preferred method for resolving disputes with the employee concerning the proper application of the employment agreement. In general, arbitration is relatively less expensive, time consuming, and burdensome than a court action. Whereas a protracted discovery period and the sheer volume of cases awaiting decision by the judge may cause a substantial period of time to elapse before a final adjudication is rendered in a court action, the arbitration process ordinarily allows the parties to proceed expeditiously to a hearing on the merits and obtain a decision from the arbitration tribunal without undue delay. Furthermore, the monetary cost associated with arbitration is much lower than the expense of pursuing a contract claim through the judicial system. An additional benefit provided by arbitration is that the arbitrator selected to settle the dispute is more likely than a judge in a court of general jurisdiction to be knowledgeable about labor-related issues. Absent, however, an express provision in the employment agreement requiring the submission of the

4. Sablosky v. Edward S. Gordon, Inc., 3 IER Cas. (BNA) 1021 (N.Y. App. Div. 1988).

dispute to arbitration, the parties must resort to the courts to enforce their respective rights under the contract.

Integration and Zipper Clauses

It is important that the employment agreement contain an "integration clause" stating that the written contract contains the entire agreement between the parties. Where a written contract exists, a party to the agreement cannot rely on oral statements made during the contract negotiations to prove contract terms inconsistent with the written terms of the agreement. However, inclusion of an integration clause also will prevent the employee from using such "parol" evidence to establish additional contract terms that are not inconsistent with the written terms or that fill gaps in the agreement where the written terms are incomplete. In *Melnick v. State Farm Mutual Automobile Insurance Co.*,[5] the New Mexico Supreme Court refused to recognize an implied term of good faith and fair dealing where the employment agreement contained an integration clause reciting that the written contract was the sole and entire agreement between the parties.

In addition, the written employment agreement should contain a provision, referred to as a "zipper clause," indicating that oral statements cannot amend or modify the written agreement, and that the written agreement may only be modified by written amendment signed by the parties to the employment agreement.

5. Melnick v. State Farm Mut. Auto. Ins. Co., 3 IER Cas. (BNA) 730 (N.M. 1988).

Statute of Limitations

The employment agreement should specify the time period, i.e., statute of limitations, within which the employee must begin a lawsuit or commence an arbitration against the employer if he or she is aggrieved with respect to any matter pertaining to the employment relationship. Recent court decisions indicate that if a specific statute of limitations is contained in an employment agreement, such a limitations period may be enforceable even if it is shorter in time than the applicable statute of limitations for contract actions or other employment-related litigation.

In *Myers v. Western-Southern Life Insurance Co.,*[6] the U.S. Court of Appeals for the Sixth Circuit applying Michigan law enforced a six-month limitations period contained in an employment agreement for any claims relating to the employment relationship. As a result, the employee's claims of age and handicap discrimination under the applicable Michigan civil rights statutes could not be maintained even though they were timely under the statute of limitations ordinarily applied to such claims. The Sixth Circuit found that a six-month period for asserting rights under the contract was not unreasonable, and that the employee had voluntarily agreed to the shorter limitations period.

Choice of Law

The employment agreement should indicate the particular state law that will apply in interpreting or enforcing the agreement.

---

6. Myers v. Western-S. Life Ins. Co., 3 IER Cas. (BNA) 723 (6th Cir. 1988).

Severability Clause

A written employment agreement should state that if any provision of the employment agreement is declared illegal or unenforceable, the remainder of the agreement is enforceable.

Waiver

The agreement may contain a provision indicating that all disputes regarding the employee's employment, including potential discrimination disputes, must be resolved in accordance with the terms of the employment agreement.

An employer might ordinarily be adverse to the use of a written employment agreement because it creates a definite structure defining the employment relationship. However, it is clear that in some situations, this structure is preferable over having a court define the terms and conditions of the employment relationship. Accordingly, specifically tailored written employment agreements should be viewed by employers as an essential part of their litigation preventive strategy.

EMPLOYMENT AGREEMENT

AGREEMENT dated as of December 1, 1987, between ____________ a Delaware corporation (the "Company"), and ____________ (the "Employee").

WHEREAS, the Company desires to employ the Employee and the Employee desires to be employed by the Company;

NOW, THEREFORE, in consideration of the promises and the mutual agreements hereinafter contained, the parties hereto intending to be legally bound agree as follows:

1. *Employment.* The Company hereby agrees to employ the Employee to perform the services described in Section 2 hereof, and the Employee hereby agrees to perform such services upon the terms and conditions set forth herein.

2. *Service to Be Performed.* During the term of Employee's employment under this Agreement, the Employee will be employed as a senior executive for the Company and agrees to perform such duties as reasonably shall be assigned to the Employee by the Board of Directors of the Company. The Employee shall devote her entire business time and energy during normal business hours to the day-to-day business and affairs of the Company.

3. *Term.* Subject to Section 9 hereof, the term of the Employee's employment hereunder shall commence as of the date hereof and shall continue thereafter for an initial term of five (5) years and shall thereafter be renewed automatically on a year-to-year basis, unless terminated at any time thereafter upon ninety (90) days' written notice, by either party to the other, prior to the applicable anniversary date.

4. *Compensation.* During the term of the Employee's employment under this Agreement, the Employee shall be paid for all services rendered hereunder total cash compensation of $250,000 per year payable semimonthly. Such compensation shall be increased to the same extent and at the same time that compensation is increased for other senior executives of the Company, so that Employee's compensation will be the same as such other senior executives of the Company. In ad-

dition, on January 31, 1988, or sooner if this Agreement is terminated prior to January 31, 1988, the Employee shall receive from the Company an additional lump sum payment of $250,000.

5. *Additional Benefits.* The Employee shall be entitled to receive such benefits as are generally provided to senior executives of the Company.

6. *Vacation.* The Employee shall be entitled to reasonable vacation during each calendar year in addition to customary holidays, consistent with the past practice of the Company and generally applicable to all senior executives of the Company. The Employee shall receive full salary during vacation and holiday time.

7. *Expenses.* The Company shall reimburse the Employee for reasonable expenses, including travel and entertainment, incurred by the Employee in connection with the business of the Company.

8. *Noncompetition; Secrecy; Inventions, etc.*

(a) The Employee agrees that during the term of this Agreement, she shall not, without the prior written consent of the Company, engage, directly or indirectly, in the operations of or have any interest in any person, firm, corporation, or business (whether as employee, officer, director, agent, security holder, partner, creditor, consultant, or otherwise) that is primarily engaged in the manufacture of ____________ products, except as hereinafter provided. Notwithstanding the foregoing, the Employee may at any time own less than three (3) percent of a publicly held corporation.

(b) The Employee further agrees not to divulge, communicate, use to the detriment of the Company or for the benefit of any other person or persons, or misuse in any way, without the prior written consent of the Company, any confidential information or trade secrets of this Company, including, without limitation, personnel information, secret processes, know-how, customer lists, sales data, formulas, or other technical data.

(c) It is understood that the Employee may, during her employment by the Company, conceive or develop designs, inventions, manufacturing techniques, innovations, or discoveries relating to the business or operations of the Company, and which are confidential and proprietary with respect to the Company, either solely or jointly with others. In connection therewith, the Employee agrees to disclose promptly to the Company all such designs, inventions, innovations, or discoveries, to assign (and hereby does assign) to the Company all of the Employee's right, title, and interest in and to such designs, inventions, innovations, or discoveries, and agrees to do all things and sign all documents deemed by the Company to be necessary or appropriate to vest in it, its successors, and assigns, all of the Employee's right, title, and interest in and to such designs, inventions, innovations, or discoveries, and to file registrations, at the Company's expense, for patents, copyrights and/or trademarks covering such designs, inventions, innovations, or discoveries in the United States and its possessions and in foreign countries, all at the discretion and under the direction of the Company. In the event the Company is unable to secure the Employee's signature on such documents, the Employee hereby irrevocably appoints the Company and its duly authorized officers and agents as her agent and attorney-in-fact to execute such documents and to do such things with the same legal force and effect as if executed or done by her. In the event the Company is unable to secure the Employee's signature on such documents, the Company will give the Employee ten (10) calendar days written notice that it is invoking Employee's appointment herein to execute such documents. In the event the Employee's employment shall be terminated for any reason, any designs, inventions, innovations, or discoveries conceived or developed by her during such employment and disclosed to the Company pursuant to this Section 8(c) shall revert to the Employee unless the Company shall, within thirty (30) days following such termination, seek to register or take other action to obtain a patent, trademark and/or copyright for such invention, innovation, or discovery in its own name.

(d) For the purpose of this Section 8, it is agreed that the ______________ name, label, and trademark is the sole and exclusive property of the Employee and that notwithstanding anything contained in this Agreement all products and designs developed under the ______________ name shall be the exclusive property of the Employee.

(e) For purposes of this Section 8, the term "Company" shall include the subsidiaries, affiliates of the Company, and their successors and assigns.

(f) With respect to the covenants contained in this Section 8, the Employee agrees that money damages for any breach thereof will be an inadequate remedy and that, therefore, the Company shall be entitled to specific performance, injunctive and/or any other mode of equitable relief to enforce its rights hereunder.

9. *Earlier Termination; Compensation.*

(a) The employment of the Employee hereunder shall terminate as provided elsewhere herein or upon the Employee's earlier death and may terminate at the option of the Company upon:

(i) The disability of the Employee, which term shall mean the inability of the Employee to discharge properly her duties hereunder in a manner consistent with prior practice due to physical or mental illness, or bodily injury, for a period of 360 consecutive days (for purposes of this Agreement, the Employee shall be deemed to have become disabled upon the expiration of such 360-day period); a determination of disability, where appropriate, shall be made by a physician mutually satisfactory to the Board of Directors of the Company and to the Employee, and neither the Board nor the Employee shall act unreasonably in connection with the timely selection of such physician; or

(ii) Upon ninety (90) days' written notice, the Company may terminate the Employee's employment hereunder for willful misconduct by the Employee in connection with her activities on behalf of or in connection with her employment by the Company.

(b) In the event the Employee shall die or become disabled while employed hereunder or Employee's employment shall terminate hereunder for any reason, other than willful misconduct, the Employee or the Employee's estate (as the case may be) shall thereafter continue to receive all compensation, as provided in Section 4 hereof, and all Company fringe benefits, including coverage for the Employee's family, for the balance of such original term or any extension of the original term. The annual compensation payable hereunder shall be reduced by the amount provided by the Company, of

(i) The disability benefit payments, determined as if subject to income taxes, received by the Employee from Company liability income plans and

(ii) Life insurance proceeds for amounts in excess of $50,000 that are payable to the Employer's estate.

10. *Principal Place of Business.* The Company agrees that it will not move or transfer its principal place of business out of New York City, or more than twenty (20) miles from Manhattan if such transfer would necessitate the Employee's moving her principal residence, and that the Employee shall be assigned to such principal place of business during the entire term of this Agreement.

11. *Miscellaneous.*

(a) Except as expressly set forth herein to the contrary, the Employee shall be subject to the Company's rules, practices, and policies applicable to senior executives of the Company.

(b) Any notices required or permitted to be given hereunder by either party to the other shall be sufficient if in writing and if delivered personally or by mail, registered or certified, postage prepaid, and return receipt requested. Mailed notices shall be addressed to the parties at the following addresses:

If to the Company:

Attention: Chairman of the Board

If to the Employee:

Copy to:

subject to change by written notice in accordance with this paragraph. Notices delivered personally shall be deemed communicated as of actual receipt; mailed notices will be sent by registered or certified mail, return receipt requested, and deemed communicated as of five (5) days after mailing.

(c) This Agreement supersedes any other agreement between the parties hereto with respect to the employment of the Employee by the Company and contains all of the covenants and agreements between the parties with respect to such employment. No representations, inducements, promises, or agreements, oral or otherwise, have been made by any party, or anyone acting on behalf of any party, which are not embodied herein, and no other agreement, statement, or promise not contained in this Agreement will be effective only if it is in writing and signed by the party to be charged.

(d) This Agreement shall be governed by, construed, and endorsed in accordance with the laws of the State of New York.

(e) This Agreement shall inure to the benefit of the Company, its successors, and assign and any purchaser of all or a substantial part of the business or assets of the Company. The Employee shall be given at least thirty (30) calendar days written notice in the event of a sale of all or a substantial part of the business or assets of the Company.

IN WITNESS WHEREOF, the parties have executed this Agreement as of the day and year first written above.

By: ______________________________

____

EMPLOYMENT AGREEMENT

AGREEMENT made as of this ___ day of _____ 19___ between ____________________ of ______________, hereinafter called the "Employee," and ____________________, a New York corporation, having its principal office and place of business at 805 Third Avenue, New York, New York, hereinafter called the "Employer."

The Employee acknowledges that the services to be rendered by h___ hereunder are of a special, unique, unusual, extraordinary, and intellectual character, which give this Agreement a peculiar value to the Employer, the loss of which cannot be reasonably or adequately compensated for in damages in an action at law; and a material breach by the Employee of any of the provisions contained in this Agreement will cause the Employer irreparable injury.

Employee further recognizes, acknowledges, and agrees with Employer that the work for which _he is employed, and upon which _he will be engaged, is and will be of a secret, confidential, and proprietary nature. Employee warrants and agrees to receive in strict confidence all information of a confidential and proprietary nature belonging to Employer or customers of the Employer, and to maintain and assist Employer to maintain the secrecy of same, and covenants not to make use thereof except for or on behalf of or with the knowledge and consent of Employer.

Employee is aware and acknowledges that, in connection with the performance of h___ services on behalf of the Employer, the Employer will make available to h___ information of a confidential nature concerning its products, trading strategies, methods, operations, and clients. Employee warrants and represents that _he will not disclose any such information to any person or firm, directly or indirectly, except when necessary in the normal course and in the best interests of the Employer's business.

Employee recognizes and acknowledges that the relationship between the Employer and its customers and potential customers involves exchange of confidential information by both the customer or potential customer and the Employer. Employee acknowledges that information including but not limited to the identity of the Employer's customers or potential customers, the identity of the Employer's customers' representatives with whom the Employer has dealt, the identity of the services being performed for such by the Employer, the trading strategies being employed on behalf of that customer, and the needs of each customer are all trade secrets of the Employer and constitute confidential information disclosed to Employee in connection with h____ employment. Therefore, Employee agrees that disclosure of such information or the solicitation or business dealings with such customers or potential customers for a period of one year subsequent to Employee's termination of employment with Employer would thus constitute improper use of such information and trade secrets. The term "customer" as used herein shall refer to any entity to which the Employer has rendered services during any part of the year prior to termination of Employee's employment. The term "potential customer" as used herein shall refer to any entity who has been solicited, approached, or who has contacted Employer concerning the possible rendering of services during any part of the year prior to termination of Employee's employment.

Employee also covenants and agrees that, during a period of one year following the termination (for any cause) of Employee's employment, Employee will not (1) solicit or render services, for h____ own account or for the account of others, from any account of the Employer for which Employee has performed any services during any part of the year immediately preceding the termination of h____ employment agreement; (2) utilize any trading strategy that constitutes a trade secret of Employer, or variation thereof, that Employer utilized during the period of Employee's employment with Employer; and/or (3) hire any Employer personnel in any capacity whatsoever, or attempt to induce any Employer personnel to leave the employ of the Employer to work for Employee or any other person, firm, or corporation within the areas where the Employer now or hereafter does business.

During the term of h____ employment with Employer, Employee shall not, without the written consent of the Employer, alone or with others, directly or indirectly, participate, engage, or become interested in (as an owner, stockholder, partner, lender or other investor, director, officer, employee, consultant, or otherwise) any business activity that is competitive with, or otherwise relates to or arises from, the current or contemplated business of the Employer, as reasonably known to the Employee. Notwithstanding anything in this paragraph to the contrary, Employee may acquire an interest through the purchase of publicly traded securities in one percent or less of any business that competes with the business of the Employer.

Upon termination of the Employee's employment or at any other time as the Employer may request, the Employee shall promptly deliver to the Employer or its subsidiaries or affiliates all confidential data and materials in the possession of the Employee including, but not limited to, sales-presentation materials, customer-service agreement forms, other internal and external business forms, manuals, correspondence, notes, customer lists, account statements, confirmations of trades, and documents relating to trading strategies, together with all copies thereof, and the Employee shall not make or retain any copy or extract of any of the foregoing. At the request of the Employer, the Employee shall certify to the Employer that __he has returned to the Employer all such documents.

In the event of a breach or threatened breach by Employee of the provisions of this Agreement, the Employer shall be entitled, in addition to all other remedies available, to an injunction restraining the Employee from disclosing any confidential information or knowledge, from utilizing any proprietary product or trading strategy, or variation thereof, that Employer utilized during the period of Employee's employment with Employer, from soliciting or servicing any accounts for which __he performed services for a year preceding the termination of h____ employment, from disclosing any confidential information, and/or from hiring any Employer personnel or attempting to induce any Employer personnel to leave Employer's employ.

Upon two (2) weeks' notice or pay in lieu thereof, Employee's employment by Employer may be terminated by Employer for any reason whatsoever, or for no reason, at any time. Upon two (2) weeks' notice, Employee may terminate h____ employment by Employer for any reason whatsoever, or for no reason, at any time.

This instrument contains the entire agreement of the parties, and it may not be changed orally but only by an agreement in writing signed by the party against whom any waiver, change, modification, extension, or cancellation is asserted.

This Agreement shall be construed and interpreted under the laws of the State of New York.

Employee represents and warrants that __he heretofore has not entered into any other agreement that in any way will prevent full compliance by h____ with the terms of this Agreement.

IN WITNESS WHEREOF, the parties have caused this Agreement to be executed as of the date written above.

XYZ Company

By: ____________________________

(Seal)
ATTEST:

____

____
Employee

____
Witness

CHAPTER FOURTEEN

*Alternative Dispute Resolution of Employment Disputes: A Pro-Active Alternative to the Armorplate/Litigation Approach to Employment Disputes**

Preliminary Observations

A long time ago Willy Loman, when informed of his discharge, cried out:

> There were promises made across this desk! You mustn't tell me you've got people to see—I put thirty-four years into this firm . . . and now I can't pay my insurance! You can't eat the orange and throw the peel away—a man is not a piece of fruit!**

Given what has transpired in the last eight or so years, it appears that Willy's anguished appeal has found a willing ear. Indeed, the single most important development in the field of labor and employment law during the past decade has been the gradual modification of the employment-at-will doctrine through evolution of the applicable common law.

---

*By **Charles S. Mishkind**, Miller, Canfield, Paddock and Stone, Grand Rapids, Michigan and **Thomas J. Barnes** and **Joseph J. Vogan**, Varnum, Riddering, Schmidt & Howlett, Grand Rapids, Michigan.
Mr. Mishkind gratefully acknowledges the assistance of Gary E. Mitchell, also with Miller, Canfield.
**Arthur Miller, *Death of a Salesman,* Act II.

Prior to this evolution, the traditional American common law rule had been that a general hiring was to be construed as a hiring at will under which either party might at any time terminate. The Michigan Supreme Court in the landmark case of *Toussaint v. Blue Cross & Blue Shield of Michigan,*[1] rejected that principal and made it clear that "an employer's express agreement to terminate only for cause, or statements of company policy and procedure to that effect, can give rise to rights enforceable in contract."[2]

Toussaint recognized that this approach, coupled with its sweeping language, created a significant risk that courts and juries would in effect become the ultimate authority in employment decisions; however, the majority, not having to personally face the problem, decided to accept that risk. As a result, it appears that all the Willy Lomans of this world now have a cause of action to enforce employer promises and assurances. Since then the "wrongful discharge" doctrine has been extended to implied assurances of regular wage increases,[3] to corporate reorganizations,[4] and claims for severance pay.[5]

Because *Toussaint's* approach virtually makes the jury every employer's personnel manager and subjects the employer to self-serving, *post hoc* statements by disgruntled former employees that they were provided with assurances of job security, the *Toussaint* court, perhaps out of guilt, extended to employers, who were prepared to commit themselves to discharging employees only for cause, a way to avoid the highly

1. Toussaint v. Blue Cross & Blue Shield of Mich., 408 Mich. 579, 292 N.W.2d 880 (1980).
2. *Id.* at 610.
3. Enquist v. Livingston County, 139 Mich. App. 280, 361 N.W.2d 794 (1984).
4. Katch v. Speidel, Div. of Textron, 746 F.2d 1136, 1138 (6th Cir. 1984).
5. Ariganello v. Scott Paper Co., 588 F. Supp. 484 (E.D. Mich. 1984). In that case, the court concluded that the *Toussaint* doctrine could virtually extend to almost every type of employment selection decision, be they intermediate or final.

disturbing prospect of jury review: "[T]he employer can avoid the perils of jury assessment by providing for an alternative method of dispute resolution. A written agreement for a definite or indefinite term to discharge only for cause could, for example, provide for binding arbitration on the issues of cause and damages."[6] Since then not too many employers have adopted the "velvet glove" suggestion made in *Toussaint.* The obvious reason is a traditional reluctance on the part of management to voluntarily place itself in a situation where its decisions can be reversed or modified by others. Now, however, more and more employers are providing their employees with a formal internal complaint or grievance procedure. These systems come in many forms. Some cover virtually every employment selection decision and others are limited just to the issue of discharge (see Sample Forms).

These written materials raise and, hopefully, answer some of the questions that inevitably arise when an employer is contemplating establishing a "good-cause" standard and providing an internal grievance procedure as an option to the "armor plate"/litigation approach. The latter approach is designed to clearly shatter any expectations of job security by telling applicants and employees the company is an at-will employer. This approach requires adopting at-will provisions into all hiring and post-hire documents; purging "job security" type provisions from handbooks, etc.; and similar measures. Most courts enforce at-will disclaimers, but some disregard them for a variety of reasons.[7] In addition, states are considering good-cause legislation, and one, Montana, has already passed such a statute. Finally, similar proposed federal legislation is in the works.

---

6. Toussaint v. Blue Cross & Blue Shield of Mich., 408 Mich. at 624, 292 N.W.2d at 897.
7. *See, e.g.,* Helle v. Landmark, Inc., 15 Ohio App. 3d 1, 472 N.E.2d 765 (1985) (supervisor's statement modified at-will relationship); Aiello v. United Airlines, Inc., 818 F.2d 1196 (5th Cir. 1987) (court found "good cause" requirement in handbook overrode at-will disavowal).

Faced with these numbers and the erosion of the at-will doctrine, employers should reevaluate their relationship with their employees and, where appropriate and consistent with corporate philosophy, perhaps accept the challenge of the *Toussaint* court by adopting an in-house grievance arbitration procedure.

Introduction

These materials consider the pros and cons of adopting an alternative dispute resolution (ADR) process and address a myriad of issues that arise and must be considered when considering ADR in the workplace. Michigan cases are often cited because that state has led the erosion of the at-will doctrine and the 1980 seminal opinion encouraged ADR as an alternative to the perils of jury assessment. Cases are cited based on their significance, legal reasoning, uniqueness, and utility.

Essential Elements of Nonunion Grievance/Arbitration Procedure—A Checklist

A. Definitions

1. Define coverage—who and what.
   a. If limited to discharges only, include forced resignation, constructive discharges.
   b. Consider whether procedure should cover economically motivated layoffs, reductions in force, removal, and closure. If so, consider whether any special limitations should apply.
   c. Consider coverage of all employees up to Board of Directors.
   d. Cover "all claims arising out of termination of employment, including any claims based on federal, state or local law."

   e. Consider a termination appeal form that contains a checklist an employee can use to assert any and all claims.
2. Define the discharge standard, e.g., just or good cause, fair reason, reasonable cause, satisfaction of the employer.
   a. Consider a heightened just-cause standard for management level employees (e.g., leadership skills, role model, initiative, team builder).
   b. Consider also a list of offenses that constitute just cause so arbitrator cannot second guess and consider "no modification of penalty" provision.
3. Define the limits of arbitrator's authority.
   a. Interpret, apply, and be bound by the employer's handbooks, policies, rules, and procedures.
   b. Consider amount of weight to be given to employer's decision.
   c. Applicable federal, state, and local laws.
   d. Consider award of any damages allowable under federal, state, or local law (e.g., back pay, front pay, emotional distress, attorney fees).

B. Procedure

1. Simple grievance or complaint form and checklist for employee to initiate (personnel serves as ombudsman).
2. Provide for time limits to file grievance or complaints.
3. Provide for at least one meeting with employee to discuss and attempt to resolve.
4. Consider mediation and/or "employee committee."
5. Final step—arbitration by outside third party neutral or "impartial committee."
6. Reasonable time limits at each step, but provide for mutual extension to ensure use of procedure vs. court suit.

7. Discovery.
   a. Provide reasons for discharge.
   b. Lists of witnesses (before hearing) and expected testimony.
   c. Personnel file of terminated employee.
   d. Limited requests for relevant information.
8. Hearing (arbitration or impartial committee).
   a. Notice of hearing.
      1. As to time and place.
      2. As to purpose.
      3. As to rights.
   b. Right to counsel.
   c. Right to be confronted by charges and witnesses.
   d. Right to cross examine and present arguments.
   e. Formulation of issues of law and fact.
   f. Rules of conduct (e.g., AAA, FMCS, federal rules).
   g. Transcript.
   h. Written option specifying elements and basis for any monetary award.
9. Costs.
   a. Arbitrator—consider employer paying.
   b. Employee (modest) deposit might defer frivolous claims.
   c. Transcript—employer or party requesting pays.
   d. Witnesses—each party bears its cost.
   e. Paid release time for other employee witnesses.
   f. Attorney fees—each party bears, but arbitrator can award.
10. Representation.
    a. Prior to hearing consider assisting terminated employee with Personnel or other ombudsman (co-employee).
    b. Provide for right of employee to have counsel.
11. Arbitrator selection.
    a. E.g., AAA, FMCS.

b. Permanent panel (employee picks or strikes names).
c. Only attorneys (preferably with civil rights expertise).

C. Exclusive Remedy

1. Recite that procedure is exclusive, final, and binding on all claims arising from termination of employment.
2. Recite that arbitrator's award is enforceable in circuit court.
3. Provide that procedure is adopted in accordance with and governed by Federal Arbitration Act and/or corresponding state statute (i.e., Uniform Arbitration Act).
4. Have employee sign acknowledgment to above effect, but first ensure the "employment contract" obligates the employee to arbitrate.

Finality of Arbitration Award as Applied to Contract-Type Claims for Wrongful Discharge

An initial question is whether the proposed ADR procedure would have preclusive effect on *Toussaint* claims for wrongful discharge (i.e., claims based on an express or implied promise to discharge only for just cause). Case law indicates that if such claims are actually submitted to arbitration and are ruled on by the arbitrator, that award would have preclusive effect on such claims and would be subject to only narrow judicial review, provided that the arbitrator is "impartial."

General Rules Regarding Finality of Arbitration Awards

Generally speaking, when two parties have submitted a claim to arbitration and that claim has been ruled on by the arbitrator, the award "has the effect of a verdict, settles the differences and disputes between the parties and, so long as it remains standing, precludes the party against whom it was rendered from resorting to an action at law to enforce his claim."[8] Such an award is enforceable in court and is subject to limited judicial review.[9] Moreover, even when the parties have not expressly agreed that the arbitration award should be final and binding, it may be interpreted as having that effect.[10]

Finality of Arbitration as to Contract Claims

Applying these general concepts to the *Toussaint* situation, the Michigan Supreme Court has specifically held that an "employer can avoid the perils of jury assessment [of such claims] by providing for an alternative method of dispute resolu-

8. 8 Callaghan's Michigan Pleading & Practice, *Arbitration & Award* 61.47 at 367 (2d ed. 1982).

9. *Id.*, 61.47–61.49, at 369–397. In Michigan, there are generally two types of arbitration enforcement procedures: (1) common law enforcement procedures and (2) statutory enforcement procedures. *See id.*, 61.02–61.03, at 302–303.

> Under present statute and court rules, a statutory arbitration is effected (1) where competent persons have submitted an existing controversy to the decision of one or more arbitrators and agreed that judgment shall be rendered upon the award to be made, (2) where the submission is in writing, (3) where the selected arbitrators have appointed a time and place for a hearing, have been sworn, and have met together and heard the proofs and allegations of the parties, (4) where an award in writing has been made pursuant to the submission, and has been filed and confirmed, as made or modified, and (5) where the judgment has been rendered upon the award for recovery of the amount specified or for performance of an act ordered to be done by either party.

Id., 61.03, at 303 (footnotes omitted). Where the submission and proceedings do not comply with the statutory prerequisites, however, the award may still be enforced at common law, E.E. Tripp Excavating Contractor, Inc. v. Jackson County, 60 Mich. App. 221, 235, 230 N.W.2d 556, 563, 569–70 (1975).

10. *E.g.*, F.J. Siller & Co. v. City of Hart, 400 Mich. 578, 255 N.W.2d 347 (1977).

tion."[11] As an example, the court went on to state that "a written agreement for a definite or indefinite term to discharge only for cause could . . . provide for binding arbitration on the issues of cause and damages."[12]

Since *Toussaint* was decided, there have been five notable decisions involving internal resolution of *Toussaint* claims.[13] In each case, the court recognized that a private method of dispute resolution can have binding effect on a *Toussaint* claim, but limited the doctrine by requiring resolution by an "impartial arbiter" in a procedure that provided "elementary fairness."[14]

In *Renny v. Port Huron Hospital,* a sharply divided Michigan Supreme Court refused to set aside a jury decision in favor

---

11. Toussaint v. Blue Cross & Blue Shield of Mich., 408 Mich. at 624, 292 N.W.2d at 897.
12. *Id. See generally* Matter of Comac Co., 402 F. Supp. 43, 45 (E.D. Mich. 1975) (even dictum is entitled to serious consideration by lower federal courts when it appears in opinion by Supreme Court); People v. Bonoite, 112 Mich. App. 167, 171, 315 N.W.2d 884, 886 (1982) (even dicta by Michigan Supreme Court is entitled to considerable deference by lower courts).
13. These cases are Renny v. Port Huron Hosp., 427 Mich. 415, 398 N.W.2d 327 (1986); Khalifa v. Henry Ford Hosp., 156 Mich. App. 485, 401 N.W.2d 884 (1986), *appeal denied,* 428 Mich. 902 (1987); Levin v. City of Ann Arbor, No. 82-1211, slip op. (6th Cir. July 22, 1983) (LEXIS, Genfed library, Cir. file) (Note: Sixth Circuit Rule 24 limits citation of *Levin* to certain situations. Practitioners should check Rule 24 before citing *Levin* in proceedings in the Sixth Circuit.), Vander Toorn v. City of Grand Rapids, 132 Mich. App. 590, 348 N.W.2d 697 (1984); and Dahlman v. Oakland Univ., 172 Mich. App. 502, 432 N.W.2d 304 (1988).
14. The court did not indicate, however, whether the traditional common law rules or statutory rules regarding arbitration would apply. In this regard, it should be noted that the arbitration statute does not apply "to collective contracts between employers and employees or associations of employees in respect to terms and conditions of employment." Revised Judicature Act, MICH. COMP. LAWS ANN. § 600.5001(3) (West 1968). It is not clear whether this preclusion would apply to *Toussaint*-type "contracts" for job security.

of a dischargee, even though it conflicted with the decision of the grievance board established by an ADR unilaterally implemented by an employer. There, the hospital had established a just-cause standard of employment in its handbook. The same handbook contained a grievance procedure that required determination of employee disputes by six employees sitting as a grievance board. The six employees consisted of three supervisors and three nonsupervisors, selected by the grievant from a panel of ten employees. These ten employees, five supervisors and five nonsupervisors, were selected by the employer's Director of Employee Services from a list of volunteers. The board's decision was "final and binding."

Ms. Renny filed a grievance concerning her discharge and had exhausted the procedure. The board voted five to one to uphold the termination. She then proceeded to file a lawsuit for wrongful discharge. The trial court denied the employer's motion for summary judgment. It permitted the issue of the appropriateness of the plaintiff's termination to then be decided by the jury, which, in turn, found the discharge to be improper and awarded the plaintiff $100,000.00.

On appeal, the four-justice majority upheld the trial court's ruling. The majority found that the ADR established by the employer did not afford the plaintiff "elementary fairness." The plaintiff had not consented to submit her claim to the board. In addition, she objected to the procedures both in her grievance and in her complaint. The majority felt that she was not provided with adequate notice of the identity of the witnesses against her and the specific complaints of the employer. She was not permitted to be present during the hearing, nor offer the testimony of other workers. Based on these facts, the court found that the procedure denied her elementary fairness, i.e., industrial due process. Therefore, the decision of the board was not entitled to preclusive effect. Renny was then permitted to present her evidence to a jury concerning her claim of breach of the employment agreement. Three dissenting judges held that the decision of the grievance board should have been found to be final and binding. They believed the employee's voluntary participation in the ADR precluded her from later challenging the board's decision. For this reason, they found it unnecessary to rule on the merits of the procedure used in the hearing before the grievance board.

Renny casts doubt upon the validity of the Michigan Court of Appeals decision in *Khalifa v. Henry Ford Hospital,*[15] which had issued several weeks earlier. There, a panel of the court split two to one and enforced an ADR similar to the one in *Renny.* The ADR had been unilaterally established by the employer. The court felt that the employee had sufficient opportunity to "air his grievance" before the impartial body of elected fellow employees. In that case, the panel consisted of seven elected nonsupervisory employees, unlike the grievance panel's composition in *Renny.* Similar to *Renny,* however, the plaintiff was not allowed to be present during the entire hearing, given no opportunity to rebut evidence, not permitted cross examination, and not permitted to be represented by counsel.

In *Levin v. City of Ann Arbor,* the Sixth Circuit Court of Appeals held that the plaintiff was not entitled to a "trial de novo" on his *Toussaint* claim where that claim had previously been decided by a "Personnel Board" authorized to review such matters pursuant to the employer's "personnel policies." Relying on the language in *Toussaint* regarding alternative methods of dispute resolution, the court found that the only issues to be reviewed were "(1) whether the [employer] in fact used the procedures which it had contractually promised to use and (2) whether the Board's decision was based upon sub-

15. Khalifa v. Henry Ford Hosp., 156 Mich. App. 485, 401 N.W.2d 884 (1986).

stantial evidence, or, in the alternative, was arbitrary and capricious."[16] Moreover, the court reached this result without any finding as to whether the employee had agreed to such finality. Although the plaintiff challenged the "objectivity" of the process because the employer's own "Director of Personnel" had sat on the Personnel Board, the court of appeals rejected that argument for two reasons: (1) the proofs established that the director of personnel did not actually participate in the deliberations and had no effect on the outcome and (2) there was no evidence that he had "participated either in the investigation of plaintiff's conduct or in the decision to discharge him."[17] With regard to the latter point, the court emphasized that "a decision-maker's mere familiarity with a case does not violate due process. . . ."[18]

In *Vander Toorn v. City of Grand Rapids,* the court of appeals employed a similar analysis but reached a different result on the issue of impartiality. Similar to the *Levin* situation, the plaintiff's discharge had been reviewed by a "Commission" authorized to review such matters pursuant to the grievance procedures set forth in a "staff handbook." Relying on the language in *Toussaint* regarding alternative methods of dispute resolution, the court agreed that

> [a]n employer, in conferring upon an employee the right to be discharged only for cause. might also provide a procedure for resolution of disputes over whether cause to discharge existed, and the decision reached under the procedure might preclude submission to a jury of a wrongful discharge claim and be subject only to limited judicial review. . . ."[19]

Apparently, this would apply even without any agreement from the employee as to finality.

---

16. Levin v. City of Ann Arbor, No. 82-1211, slip op. at 3–4.
17. *Id.;* slip op. at 3.
18. *Id.*
19. Vander Toorn v. City of Grand Rapids, 132 Mich. App. 590, 598, 348 N.W.2d 697, 701 (1984).

Relying on other language in *Toussaint,* however, the court also concluded that this limited scope of review would apply "only where the dispute is resolved by some impartial arbiter."[20] Applying that exception to the facts of the case, the court found that the commission was not impartial, because it had not merely made "an investigation and some preliminary determination" as to the propriety of plaintiff's discharge, "but rather actually participated in the decision to terminate plaintiff's employment, the same decision the propriety of which it later reviewed."[21] Although the *Vander Toorn* opinion is subject to distinction and criticism, it remains the law until overturned by the Michigan Supreme Court.[22] It is important to note that *Khalifa* distinguished *Vander Toorn* by noting that in that case the ADR's adjudicating body only had the power of recommendation, with final decision residing with the employer. The *Renny* decision seems to indicate that that is a distinction without a difference and impliedly endorses the *Vander Toorn* analysis.

A recent decision discussing ADRs is *Dahlman v. Oakland University.*[23] There, the Michigan appellate court upheld a grievance procedure set forth in the employer's handbook as part of the contract of employment and found that because the employee had failed to use the grievance procedure, his contract claim was barred. In addition, the court denied plaintiff's challenge that the grievance panel was biased because it was

20. *Id.* The other language relied on by the court was that language stating that "the promise to terminate employment for cause only would be illusory if the employer were permitted to be the sole judge and final arbiter of the propriety of the discharge." *Id.* Arguably, however, this language was only intended to apply to those situations where the employer had not otherwise conditioned his promise of job security.
21. *Id.* at 601, 348 N.W.2d at 702.
22. *But see* Doster v. Estes, 126 Mich. App. 497, 337 N.W.2d 549 (1983), *appeal denied,* 418 Mich. 913 (1984) (civil service employee must exhaust grievance procedure before pursuing *Toussaint* claim).
23. Dahlman v. Oakland Univ., 172 Mich. App. 502, 432 N.W.2d 304 (1988).

comprised of employees whose future promotions could be affected by their decisions. The court declined "to rule that all grievance committees comprised of employees are inherently defective."[24]

Finality of the Proposed Grievance/Arbitration Procedure as Applied to Contract Claims

Based on the preceding, it appears a carefully drafted ADR procedure would have preclusive effect on a *Toussaint*-type contract claim, provided that it meets the test of "impartiality," and "elementary fairness" set forth in *Renny* and *Vander Toorn.* To further ensure that the procedure is given preclusive effect, however, it is recommended that (1) it contain language stating that it is "final and binding" and (2) the employee sign an acknowledgment to that effect.

Finality as to Noncontract Claims

The use of ADRs and their relation to the legal concepts of exclusivity, exhaustion, and preclusion in resolving employment disputes must be examined from at least three different perspectives: (1) contract claims, (2) tort claims, and (3) statutory claims. The effectiveness of the ADR as an exclusive, exhaustive, or preclusive device will vary depending on whether the employee is asserting one or more of these claims. In general, the ADR as a preventive device will have greater validity and vitality with respect to contract claims than tort claims. In turn, tort claims are more likely to be subject to exclusivity, exhaustion, and preclusive effect by the ADR than statutory claims. Postevent agreements to use an ADR instead of proceeding to a judicial forum for resolution of either contract, tort, or statutory claims appear to have equal chances of suc-

24. *Id.* at 506, 432 N.W.2d at 305–06.

cess if their use is voluntary and knowingly entered into by employees.

General Rules Regarding Finality of Arbitration Awards

Generally speaking, parties can submit any kind of dispute to arbitration, whether arising by statute or common law, and are bound by an award on any such claim submitted.[25] Moreover, while some rights are considered to be inappropriate subjects for "prospective" agreements to arbitrate, that does not necessarily mean that the parties cannot agree to submit those claims to arbitration after the dispute has arisen and with respect to a specific controversy.[26]

Finality of Arbitration Awards as to Discrimination Claims

Applying the preceding principles to the discrimination area, there is no logical reason why an arbitrator's award could not be given preclusive effect as to discrimination claims that are actually submitted and ruled upon. Even if such claims are considered to be inappropriate subjects for a "prospective" agreement to arbitrate, that does not mean that the parties could not agree to submit an existing claim to arbitration. Unfortunately, case law suggests an opposite result.

In *Alexander v. Gardner-Denver,*[27] the Supreme Court held

25. *See* United States v. Eric Elevator Corp., 214 F. Supp. 947, 948 (D. Mass. 1963). *See generally* 8 Callaghan's Michigan Pleading & Practice, *Arbitration & Award* 61.06, 61.47, at 314, 367 (2d ed. 1982); 6 CJS *Arbitration* 11 at 176, 128 at 375 (1975) ("[u]nless prohibited by statute or public policy, practically any known kind of dispute or controversy can be submitted to arbitration").
26. *E.g.,* Cobb v. Lewis, 488 F.2d 41, 47 (5th Cir. 1974). *But see* Overseas Motors, Inc. v. Import Motors Ltd., 375 F. Supp. 499 (E.D. Mich. 1974), *aff'd,* 519 F.2d 119 (6th Cir.), *cert. denied,* 423 U.S. 987 (1975) (claims arising under antitrust laws are not subject to arbitration and no res judicata effect can be given to any such proceeding).
27. Alexander v. Gardner-Denver, 415 U.S. 36 (1974).

that when an employee alleges a violation of a nondiscrimination clause in a collective bargaining agreement and that claim is ruled on by an arbitrator, the arbitrator's decision does not preclude a subsequent lawsuit by the employee to enforce his rights under title VII.[28] In so holding, the Court distinguished plaintiff's contractual right to nondiscrimination under the collective bargaining agreement from his independent statutory right to nondiscrimination under Title VII. "The distinctly separate nature of these contractual and statutory rights," the Court explained, "is not vitiated merely because both were violated as a result of the same factual occurrence."[29]

Later Supreme Court cases extended the rationale of *Gardner-Denver* to claims under the Fair Labor Standards Act[30] and Section 1983 of the Civil Rights Act of 1871.[31] Lower federal courts have also extended the Supreme Court's reasoning to the Age Discrimination in Employment Act (ADEA),[32] to actions under Section 1981 of the 1866 Civil Rights Act,[33] and to purely statutory actions under ERISA.[34]

---

28. *See also,* Clark v. Uniroyal Corp., 119 Mich. App. 820, 824, 327 N.W.2d 372, 374 (1982) (federal precedents are persuasive in determining claims under state discrimination statutes).
29. Alexander v. Gardner-Denver, 415 U.S. at 50.
30. Barrentine v. Arkansas-Best Freight Sys., 450 U.S. 728 (1981) (rights under the FLSA are independent of the labor agreement and are best protected by the courts rather than in arbitration).
31. McDonald v. City of W. Branch, 466 U.S. 284 (1984) (action under 42 U.S.C. 1983 claiming discrimination for exercise of constitutional rights not precluded by an unappealed arbitration award).
32. Nicholson v. CPC Int'l, Inc., 877 F.2d 221 (3d Cir. 1989) (arbitration clause "inherently inconsistent" in a nonunion employee case with the statutory scheme for enforcement of ADEA).
33. Wilmington v. J.I. Case Co., 793 F.2d 909 (8th Cir. 1986) (a § 1981 action protects rights separate and distinct from contractual rights).
34. Gavalik v. Continental Can Co., 812 F.2d 834 (3d Cir. 1987) (an employee with a claim under § 510 of ERISA need not submit the claim to the plan's resolution machinery before seeking relief in the federal court); *cf.*, Hopkins v. City of Midland, 158 Mich. App. 361, 404 N.W.2d 744 (1987), interpreting *Gardner-Denver,* the court held that an arbitra-

The Fourth Circuit Court of Appeals, however, has recently rejected this trend. In *Gilmer v. Interstate/Johnson Lane Corp.,*[35] the court held that a claim by an employee under ADEA *was* arbitrable where the employer and employee had an agreement compelling arbitration of all disputes arising out of his employment or the termination of his employment. It is anticipated that the Supreme Court will soon be resolving this conflict.

Although the *Gardner-Denver* decision is arguably inapplicable in a situation where an employee has actually submitted his statutory claim to an arbitrator and the arbitrator has specifically ruled on that claim, the opinion is not entirely clear on this issue. On one hand, *Gardner-Denver* can be interpreted as being limited to situations where the arbitrator did not rule on the statutory claim. This interpretation is supported by language in the opinion that recognizes that an arbitrator has no "*general* authority to invoke public laws" and ordinarily is "confined to interpretation and application of the collective bargaining agreement."[36] Arguably, if that is the rationale behind the decision, then it would have no application when the parties have given the arbitrator authority to invoke public laws and have not confined his analysis to the interpretation and application of a written employment agreement. This interpretation is further supported by the Supreme Court's recognition in *Gardner-Denver* that "presumably an employee may waive his cause of action under Title VII as part of a voluntary settlement."[37] Logically, if an employee can know-

---

tor has no power over issues not presented for arbitration and that an arbitration decision based on the collective bargaining agreement had no res judicata effect on the employee's subsequent free speech claim.

35. Gilmer v. Interstate/Johnson Lane Corp., 895 F.2d 195 (4th Cir. 1990).
36. Alexander v. Gardner-Denver, 415 U.S. at 53 (emphasis added).
37. *Id.* at 52. *See also* Runyan v. National Cash Register Corp., 787 F.2d 1039 (6th Cir.), *cert. denied,* 479 U.S. 850 (1986) (postdischarge general release knowingly signed for adequate consideration waived ADEA claims).

ingly waive his cause of action under the statute there is no reason why that cause of action, having been voluntarily submitted to arbitration, cannot be preclusively ruled on by the arbitrator.[38]

On the other hand, in a footnote to *Gardner-Denver,* the Court suggested that even "[w]here an arbitral determination gives full consideration to an employee's Title VII rights," the award could, at most, be afforded "great weight" but not preclusive effect.[39] In that same important footnote, the Court went on to suggest that this would be the result, even when "the issue is solely one of fact, specifically addressed by the parties and decided by the arbitrator on the basis of an adequate record."[40] In addition, the Court stated that "Congress intended federal courts to exercise final responsibility for enforcement of Title VII" and that "arbitration procedures . . . make arbitration a comparatively inappropriate forum for the final resolution of rights created by Title VII."[41] The thrust of these statements is that an arbitration award cannot have preclusive effect even if the statutory claim is submitted and decided.[42]

Since *Gardner-Denver* was decided, a number of proposals have been made to circumvent these "finality" problems. One suggestion, made in the union context, is that

> when such claims are asserted, the employer, the union, and the employees, who have been fully advised of their rights, enter

38. *Cf.* Cobb v. Lewis, 488 F.2d at 47 (while antitrust claims are generally inappropriate for arbitration, that does not preclude arbitration of dispute that has already arisen with respect to specific controversy).
39. Alexander v. Gardner-Denver, 415 U.S. at 60 n.21.
40. *Id.*
41. *Id.* at 56.
42. *Cf.* Overseas Motors, Inc. v. Import Motors Ltd., 375 F. Supp. 499 (E.D. Mich. 1974) (antitrust claim is not subject to arbitration, and no preclusive effect can be given to any such proceeding).

> into a settlement agreement providing that, in exchange for the agreement of the employer and the union to arbitrate the discrimination claim, employees waive their right to proceed in other forums.[43]

In this connection, the American Arbitration Association has developed procedures designed specifically to deal with discrimination issues. In those suggested proceedings: (1) the parties voluntarily agree to waive other remedies; (2) the employee is entitled to be represented by an attorney of his choosing; (3) the parties select an arbitrator from a list of impartial arbitrators experienced in employment discrimination matters; (4) the issues involve the *statutory* rights of an employee, not merely his contractual rights; (5) the arbitrator is permitted to conduct discovery, using the Federal Rules of Evidence as a guide; and (6) the arbitrator is authorized to grant any remedy that would be granted in a judicial proceeding. According to leading authorities, however, "[t]his approach remains untested in the courts."[44]

Beginning with *Mitsubishi Motors Corp. v. Soler Chrysler Plymouth,*[45] the Supreme Court has, however, shown a new zest for allowing federal statutory claims to be diverted from the judicial system to alternative means of dispute resolution.[46] None of these cases have been in the employment arena, and none have directly threatened the *Gardner-Denver* line of cases. The refusal to rule automatically, however, that the presence of a statutory claim precludes reliance on arbitration

---

43. B. SCHLEI & P. GROSSMAN, EMPLOYMENT DISCRIMINATION LAW 1086 (2d ed. 1983).
44. *Id. But see* New York v. District Council 37, AFSCME, No. BCD-173-74, slip op. (undated) (requirement that a grievant waive his right to submit discrimination claim to another agency or court in order to pursue grievance under collective bargaining agreement is contrary to public policy and void).
45. Mitsubishi Motors Corp. v. Soler Chrysler Plymouth, 473 U.S. 614 (1985).
46. *See, e.g.,* Shearson/Am. Express v. McMahon, 482 U.S. 220 (1987).

has had its effect in the case law and provides the opportunity for creative argument in the employment field.

Finality of Arbitration Awards as to Public Policy Claims and Other Tort Claims

As to public policy claims and other tort claims, there has been no clear statement by the courts since *Toussaint* regarding whether an arbitration award would be preclusive as to such claims where they are actually submitted and ruled upon by the arbitrator. In one case, however, the Michigan Court of Appeals indicated that a public policy claim is the *kind* of dispute that is subject to arbitration.[47] Presumably, if such a claim is actually submitted to arbitration and ruled upon by the arbitrator, that award would have preclusive effect. By analogy to *Gardner-Denver,* however, it might be argued that any such award would only have persuasive, as opposed to preclusive, effect.[48]

On the other hand, the Michigan Court of Appeals in *Hopkins v. City of Midland*, subsequently held that a collective bargaining employee's statutory claims under the Michigan Whistleblower's Act were not barred by the application of principles of res judicata and collateral estoppel as the result of an underlying arbitration which went against the plaintiff.[49] The court observed that an arbitrator can only bind parties on issues that they have agreed to submit to arbitration. Accordingly, an arbitrator has no power over issues not presented for arbitration. In *Hopkins,* none of the issues submitted to the arbitrator dealt with the alleged "whistleblowing." The court relied on the Supreme Court's reasoning in *Gardner-Denver*

47. Ryoti v. Paine Webber Jackson & Curtis, 142 Mich. App. 805, 371 N.W.2d 454 (1985).
48. *See also* Vander Toorn v. City of Grand Rapids, 132 Mich. App. 590, 601, 348 N.W.2d 697, 702 (1984).
49. Hopkins v. City of Midland, 158 Mich. App. 361, 404 N.W.2d 744 (1987).

and in another Michigan Court of Appeals case, *Tuttle v. Bloomfield Hills School District,*[50] which had held the Whistleblower's Act allows assertion of statutorily guaranteed rights that are not required to be arbitrated. *Hopkins* does, however, leave open the possibility that the parties could agree to arbitrate statutory claims and, if so, the determination could then have preclusive effect.[51]

In other states, there have been a variety of decisions concerning the applicability of arbitration procedures to public policy claims and other related tort claims; but again, these decisions do not provide a clear guide as to whether an arbitrator's ruling on such claims would be given preclusive effect. In one line of cases, it has been held that claims for retaliatory discharge and claims for breach of an implied covenant of good faith and fair dealing are, in essence, claims for unjust discharge and, therefore, are subject to the grievance/arbitration procedure.[52] However, in another line of cases, it has been held that employees who are covered by a collective bargaining agreement cannot *maintain* a tort action for retaliatory discharge, because such a remedy is "unnecessary" when the employee already has the protection of a just cause provision.[53] In still other cases, however, courts have held that claims for retaliatory discharge and other torts are not subject to contrac-

50. Tuttle v. Bloomfield Hills School Dist., 156 Mich. App. 527, 402 N.W.2d 504 (1986), *appeal denied,* 428 Mich. 880 (1987).

51. *Cf.* Polk v. Yellow Freight Sys., Inc., 801 F.2d 190 (6th Cir. 1986) (adverse unemployment compensation decision that plaintiff was discharged for misconduct precluded her *Toussaint* claim under Michigan law but did not preclude claim for retaliatory discharge or intentional infliction of emotional distress).

52. *E.g.,* Bertrand v. Quincy Mkt. Cold Storage, 728 F.2d 568 (1st Cir. 1984) (implied covenant of good faith and fair dealing); Cook v. Caterpillar Tractor Co., 85 Ill. App. 3d 402, 407 N.E.2d 95 (1980) (public policy claim).

53. Smith v. Greyhound Lines, 614 F. Supp. 558 (W.D. Pa. 1984), *aff'd,* 800 F.2d 1139 (1986) (public policy claim); Basak v. Asplundh Tree Expert Co., 122 Ill. App. 3d 240, 460 N.E.2d 1197 (1983) (public policy claim).

tually agreed upon grievance and arbitration procedures, since those claims do not arise out of the contract, but instead arise independently from the contract and are based on reasons of public policy.[54]

Finality of the Proposed Grievance/Arbitration Procedure as Applied to Noncontract Claims

Based on the preceding, it appears there is no logical reason why a determination rendered under an ADR could not be final and binding as to discrimination claims, public policy claims, and other torts, if those claims are *actually submitted* to the arbitrator and are *actually ruled* upon by the arbitrator. Although *Gardner-Denver* and similar cases such as *CPC International* indicate that the arbitrator's ruling would not be given preclusive effect simply because these claims arise from "the same factual occurrence," that does not preclude the possibility that the award would be given preclusive effect if the arbitrator actually rules upon the claim. For instance, if the

54. *See* Hopkins v. City of Midland, 158 Mich. App. at 374–75, 404 N.W.2d at 748–50. *See also* Garibaldi v. Lucky Food Stores, Inc., 726 F.2d 1367 (9th Cir. 1984), *cert. denied,* 471 U.S. 1099 (1985) (public policy claim); Harper v. General Dynamics Corp., 117 LRRM (BNA) 3197 (S.D. Cal. 1984); Messenger v. Volkswagen, 585 F. Supp. 565 (S.D. W. Va. 1984) (public policy claim); Midgett v. Sackett-Chicago, Inc., 105 Ill. 2d 143, 473 N.E.2d 1280 (1984), *cert. denied,* 474 U.S. 909 (1985) (public policy claim); Stocking v. Fred Meyer, Inc., 68 Or. App. 683 P.2d 1021 (Ct. App. 1984) (public policy claim); Brown v. Ellis, 40 Conn. Supp. 165, 484 A.2d 944 (Super. Ct. 1984) (claim for intentional infliction of emotional distress). *See generally* Tameny v. Atlantic-Richfield Co., 27 Cal. 3d 167, 610 P.2d 1330, 164 Cal. Rptr. 839 (1980) (discussing general difference between wrongful discharge theories based on contract and those based on tort). *See also* Jauvtis, *The Impact of Wrongful Discharge Suits on Grievance-Arbitration Procedures in Collective Bargaining Agreements,* 36 LAB. L.J. 307 (1985). In so holding, several of these decisions have relied on the *Gardner-Denver* analysis. *See, e.g.,* Garibaldi v. Lucky Food Stores, Inc., 726 F.2d at 1367, Midgett v. Sackett-Chicago, Inc., 105 Ill. 2d at 143, 151–52, 454 N.E.2d at 1092.

ADR adjudicator actually rules that the discharge was valid under the state fair employment act and was not contrary to public policy, those rulings could have preclusive effect. As stated previously, however, there are cases to the contrary, and the issue remains somewhat in doubt.

To *maximize* the *possibility* that a determination under an ADR would be given preclusive effect as to tort and statutory claims, it is suggested that the general approach recommended by the American Arbitration Association to deal specifically with the discrimination issue be followed. Under that approach: (1) the parties would voluntarily agree in a post-event agreement to waive other remedies for discrimination, public policy, and tort claims; (2) the employee would be entitled to be represented by an attorney of his or her choosing; (3) the parties would select an arbitrator from a list of impartial arbitrators experienced in such matters; (4) the claims to be resolved by the arbitrator would include not only the contract claims, but also the statutory, public policy, and tort claims; (5) the arbitrator would be permitted to conduct limited discovery, using the Federal Rules of Evidence as a guide; and (6) the arbitrator would be authorized to grant any remedy that would be granted in a judicial proceeding.

Exhaustion as a Condition Precedent to Litigation

An inevitable question is whether exhaustion of an ADR would be a condition precedent to any suit for wrongful discharge, including *Toussaint*-type contract claims, as well as statutory and tort claims usually brought in the context of a discharge dispute. This question, of course, is distinguishable from the question of whether an arbitration decision on such claims would be final and binding. Even if an arbitration decision would be exclusive or final and binding on those claims actually submitted to arbitration, that does not necessarily mean that the company could force an employee to submit those claims to arbitration if he or she chose to proceed directly to court. Research indicates exhaustion would be required as to *Toussaint* claims. In addition, it appears that exhaustion would be required as to such claims with or without an actual agreement from the employee, but agreement, as opposed to unilateral implementation, would be preferable and advisable. However, as to tort and statutory claims, it seems that exhaustion could not be required without an actual agreement that meets the common law or statutory test of irrevocability, and even then, such an agreement might be unenforceable as to "future" claims.[55]

General Rules Regarding Exhaustion of Arbitration Remedies

Generally speaking, "[a]rbitration is a matter of contract, and a party cannot be required to submit to arbitration any dispute which he has not so agreed to submit."[56] Moreover, even when there is an agreement to arbitrate, that agreement can be "revoked or repudiated at will by a party any time prior to announcement of the award" unless (1) the "contract language requires arbitration as a condition precedent to bringing suit" or (2) the contract complies with the requirements of the Michigan arbitration statute.[57] Also, there are certain claims that are simply not subject to arbitration, at least when

55. The basic statutory requirement for irrevocability is an agreement "for entry of judgment upon the award by a circuit court." E.E. Tripp Excavating Contractor, Inc. v. Jackson County, 60 Mich. App. 221, 237, 230 N.W.2d 556, 564 (1975).

56. Grosse Pointe Farms Police Ass'n v. MERC, 53 Mich. App. 173, 176, 218 N.W.2d 801, 803 (1974).

57. E.E. Tripp Excavating Contractor, Inc. v. Jackson County, 60 Mich. App. at 235–250, 230 N.W.2d at 563–566 (1975); Revised Judicature Act, MICH. COMP. LAWS ANN. § 600.5001, 600.5011 (West 1968).

the agreement was made in advance of the claim having arisen.[58]

On the other hand, if the statutory or common law requirements for irrevocability have been met and the claim is one that is appropriate for arbitration, an agreement to arbitrate such claim "is enforceable and serves to oust the court from jurisdiction."[59] By statute, such an agreement would be enforceable as to any "existing" controversy between the parties "which might be the subject of a civil action" and also any "controversy thereafter arising between the parties to a contract, with relation thereto."[60] Where the parties have agreed to arbitrate "any controversy or claim arising out of or relating to [an] agreement or the breach thereof," the Michigan Court of Appeals has held that exhaustion is required as to any claim arising from the parties' contractual undertakings even though it "sounds in tort."[61]

---

58. *See generally* Cobb v. Lewis, 488 F.2d at 47 (5th Cir. 1974) (antitrust claim is not appropriate subject of arbitration unless agreement to arbitrate has been made after dispute has arisen with respect to specific controversy); Overseas Motors, Inc. v. Import Motors Ltd., 375 F. Supp. at 523 (E.D. Mich. 1974) (antitrust claim is not subject to arbitration and no res judicata preclusion can be based on any such proceeding).
59. E.E. Tripp Excavating Contractor, Inc. v. Jackson County, 60 Mich. App. at 246, 230 N.W.2d at 568; Revised Judicature Act, MICH. COMP. LAWS ANN. § 600.5011 (West 1968).
60. Revised Judicature Act, MICH. COMP. LAWS ANN. § 600.5001(1)–600.5001(2). *See also* 8 Callaghan's Michigan Pleading & Practice, *Arbitration & Award* § 61.08–61.10, at 318–321 (2d ed. 1982). (*But see supra*, n.2, and accompanying text regarding applicability of arbitration statute.)
61. Stadel v. Granger Bros., 4 Mich. App. 246, 254, 144 N.W. 2d 609, 610–613, (1966); *accord* Tac Travel Am. Corp. v. World Airways, Inc., 443 F. Supp. 825 (S.D.N.Y. 1978) (claim for libel and slander subject to arbitration under contract calling for arbitration of "any dispute between the parties with respect to this agreement").

Exhaustion of Grievance/Arbitration Procedures as to Contract Claims

Applying the foregoing rules, there seems to be little doubt that an employee could agree to submit an existing or future *Toussaint* (contract) claim to ADR, but until *Dahlman v. Oakland University,*[62] there had been no clear decision by the Michigan appellate courts or the federal courts as to whether exhaustion of the arbitration procedure would be required absent an express agreement for arbitration that complies with the traditional common law rules and the statutory rules for irrevocability. Although the *Renny, Khalifa, Vander Toorn,* and *Levin* courts were apparently willing to give finality to a *unilaterally* established grievance/arbitration procedure, each case involved a situation where employees had actually submitted their claims to those procedures and had received determinations on the claims. Thus, neither case involved a true exhaustion question. *Dahlman,* however, involved the failure of a dischargee to use the ADR in the employee handbook, and the court held this barred his contract claim.[63] Similarly, in *Schnelting v. Coors Distributing Co.,*[64] plaintiff sued his former employer alleging, *inter alia,* that he was wrongfully discharged in violation of the just cause provisions of defendant's employee handbook. The company sought dismissal of the claim, arguing that the claim was precluded because plaintiff did not exhaust or even attempt to utilize the procedures provided in the handbook for resolving disputes. The court did not address the fairness of the company's dispute

62. Dahlman v. Oakland Univ., 172 Mich. App. 502 (1988).

63. *See also* Doster v. Estes, 126 Mich. App. 497, 515, 337 N.W.2d 495, 556 (1983) (holding in a public sector case that "[p]laintiffs must first exhaust established grievance procedures before seeking judicial consideration of their claim based upon *Toussaint*").

64. Schnelting v. Coors Distrib. Co., 729 S.W.2d 212 (Mo. Ct. App. 1987).

resolution procedures. Instead, it analogized to the collective bargaining situation, noting that "it has long been the rule in Missouri that the aggrieved employee must exhaust the remedies provided in the agreement before resorting to the court for redress."[65] The court concluded that "[t]his principle is no less applicable where the rights asserted by plaintiff are contained in an employee handbook."[66]

Exhaustion of Alternative Dispute Resolution Procedures as to Statutory Discrimination Claims

As applied to discrimination and other statutory claims, however, it appears unlikely that exhaustion would be required absent an express agreement *(preferably postevent)* to arbitrate, as such claims would arise independently from any promises or assurances contained in the employer's personnel policies.[67] Moreover, even if there is an express agreement to arbitrate discrimination claims, that agreement might be found unenforceable as to "prospective" claims and, therefore, revocable at the will of the employee. The basis for that conclusion is the Supreme Court's holding in *Gardner-Denver,*[68] wherein the Supreme Court specifically stated that "there can be no *prospective* waiver of an employee's rights under Title VII."[69] If there can be no prospective waiver of an employee's

---

65. *Id.* at 215.
66. *Id.*
67. *Cf.* Marlowe v. Fisher Body, 489 F.2d 1057, 1065–1066 (6th Cir. 1973) (Section 1981 and Title VII suit is permissible despite failure to exhaust grievance machinery under collective bargaining agreement); Wilmington v. J.I. Case Co., 793 F.2d 909, 918 (8th Cir. 1986) (federal policy against discrimination in § 1983 outweighs favoring arbitration of labor disputes); Barrentine v. Arkansas-Best Freight Sys., Inc., 450 U.S. 728, 731 (1981) (FLSA claim not deferred to labor agreement's grievance procedure). *See also* Hopkins v. City of Midland, 158 Mich. App. at 361.
68. Alexander v. Gardner-Denver, 415 U.S. at 60 n.21.
69. *Id.* at 51 (emphasis added).

rights under Title VII, it seems to follow that there can be no prospective agreement to arbitrate such claims.

On the other hand, since *Gardner-Denver* involved a collective bargaining situation, its ruling as to prospective waiver might not be applicable in the nonunion context when talking about a waiver by an individual. On this point, it must be noted that the major thrust of that opinion's rationale was that a union cannot prospectively waive the rights of its members under Title VII. In support of that holding, the Court explained that while "a union may waive certain statutory rights related to collective activity," Title VII "stands on plainly different grounds; it concerns not majoritarian process, but an individual's right to employment opportunities."[70] For this reason, the Court's broad language concerning prospective waiver is both factually and conceptually distinguishable from a situation involving an individual who has agreed to present his discrimination claim to an arbitrator as a condition precedent to litigation in the nonunion context. Notwithstanding the general rule, therefore, it is conceivable that an employer and employee could enter into an enforceable agreement to arbitrate discrimination claims and to exhaust those arbitration remedies as a condition precedent to the institution of any proceeding in another forum.[71] Consistent with this view is the Supreme Court's dicta in *Gardner-Denver* that "presumably an employee may waive his cause of action under Title VII as part of a voluntary settlement. . . ."[72] Such a waiver could be effective, of course, only if it is "voluntary and knowing" and, ideally, entered into *after* the "triggering" event.

Notwithstanding *Gardner-Denver,* recent decisions support the view that federal and state statutory claims can be the

70. *Id.*

71. For a model grievance/arbitration procedure incorporating such a clause, *see* Blumrosen, *Exploring Voluntary Arbitration of Individual Employment Disputes,* 16 U. MICH. J.L. REF. 249, 273–275 (1983).

72. *Id.* at 52.

subject of alternative means of dispute resolution.[73] Other cases, while they do not directly attack the general rule, do reflect a trend to not blindly follow the general rule and provide the opportunity to argue that an ADR procedure applies in the employment field. *Mitsubishi Motors Corp. v. Soler Chrysler Plymouth*[74] involved a commercial sales contract dispute and a Sherman Act statutory counterclaim. Arbitration was sought pursuant to the U.S. Arbitration Act. The Supreme Court rejected any presumption against arbitrability for statutory, as opposed to contractual, claims. A two-prong test was developed: (1) Did the parties' agreement to arbitrate cover the statutory claims and (2) if so, could legal limitations "external to the parties' agreement foreclose the arbitration of those claims."[75] The Court emphasized that there is a strong federal interest favoring arbitration and held that a party who has agreed to arbitrate an issue must do so unless Congress has specifically indicated that the statutory rights in issue cannot be waived.[76] A number of courts have required arbitration of state statutory claims.[77]

---

73. *See* Gilmer v. Interstate/Johnson Lane Corp., 895 F.2d 195 (4th Cir. 1990).
74. Mitsubishi Motors Corp. v. Soler Chrysler Plymouth, 473 U.S. 614 (1985).
75. *Id.* at 628.
76. *See also* Shearson/Am. Express v. McMahon, 482 U.S. 220 (1987), applying *Mitsubishi* so as to require SEC and RICO claims to be sent to arbitration.
77. *See, e.g.,* Swensen v. CDI Corp., 670 F. Supp. 1438 (D. Minn. 1987) (court held that a nonunion employee was required to submit claims of sexual discrimination arising under state human rights act to contractually established arbitration); Steck v. Smith Barney, 661 F. Supp. 543 (D.N.J. 1987); Claim of Garcia, 479 N.Y.S.2d 594, 104 A.D. 675 (N.Y. App. 1984) (where an individual attempts to secure unemployment benefits after pursuing his discharge to arbitration, New York courts have held that the arbitration decision is entitled to res judicata or a collateral estoppel effect in the subsequent unemployment proceeding). *See also* Meritor Sav. Bank v. Vinson, 477 U.S. 57 (1986) (Supreme Court indicates that a carefully designed internal dispute procedure may insulate an employer from liability for sexual harassment and possibly other claims that

Exhaustion of Grievance/Arbitration Procedures as to Public Policy Claims and Other Related Tort Claims

As to public policy claims and other tort claims, the exhaustion issue is somewhat less problematic but also largely uncharted. In at least one case decided since *Toussaint,* the Michigan Court of Appeals has specifically held that an employee may agree, prospectively, to submit a public policy claim to arbitration.[78] In *Ryoti v. Paine Webber,* the employee had agreed to submit "any dispute" with his employer to arbitration.[79] Following his discharge, he brought a lawsuit claiming that his discharge was "contrary to public policy."[80] The case was dismissed on the grounds that plaintiff failed to exhaust his arbitration remedy. While recognizing that there is "a cause of action for discharging an employee contrary to public policy," the court reasoned that "this goes to the merits of plaintiff's claim, which should be settled pursuant to the arbitration agreement."[81] Therefore, *Ryoti* clearly recognizes that if there is an agreement to arbitrate and that agreement can be construed as applying to a "public policy" claim, then exhaustion of the arbitration remedy will be a condition precedent to any lawsuit on that claim.[82]

On the other hand, it is not so clear that the same result would occur in the absence of an express *agreement* to arbitrate. Nor is it clear that this result would follow as to other

---

require notice to the employer). *But see* Nicholson v. CPC Int'l, Inc., 877 F.2d 221 (3d Cir. 1989), an important nonunion age case rejecting the argument that exhaustion was required and/or arbitration binding.

78. Ryoti v. Paine Webber Jackson & Curtis, Inc., 142 Mich. App. at 805, 813, 371 N.W.2d at 454, 457.
79. *Id.* at 808, 371 N.W.2d at 455.
80. *Id.*
81. *Id.* at 811, 371 N.W.2d at 456–57.
82. *Accord* Stadel v. Granger Bros., 4 Mich. App. 250, 254, 144 N.W.2d 609, 612–13 (1966) (tort claims case subject to arbitration under clause applicable to "any controversy or claim arising out of or relating to" parties' contract).

statutory or tort claims that do not go to the "merits" of the discharge. As noted earlier, there are varying views as to whether exhaustion of ADR procedures is a condition precedent to such claims.

Exhaustion of the Proposed Grievance/Arbitration Procedure

To maximize the possibility that exhaustion of an ADR procedure is required, not only as to *Toussaint* contract claims, but as to tort and statutory claims, it is recommended an employer do the following: (1) prepare a clear statement that the ADR procedure is applicable to all such claims; (2) develop a "postevent" submission agreement or consent by the employee to submit such claims to arbitration; (3) create a similar agreement or consent by the employee to exhaust such procedures prior to litigation; and (4) draft an agreement or consent by the employee that the award is judicially enforceable.

Evidentiary Use of an Arbitration Award in Later Litigation

Assuming that a determination rendered under an ADR procedure would not be given preclusive effect as to some or all of the possible claims that might be brought by a discharged employee, the next question is whether the results of the arbitration could nonetheless be used as evidence in a subsequent lawsuit. The answer is that case law indicates that the award could be used as evidence, but its weight would depend upon the nature of the arbitration hearing.

In *Alexander v. Gardner-Denver,*[83] the Supreme Court dealt with this specific issue and held that even when an arbitration award cannot be given preclusive effect, it still "may be

83. Alexander v. Gardner-Denver, 415 U.S. at 36.

admitted as evidence and accorded such weight as the court deems appropriate."[84] The Supreme Court and the Sixth Circuit have extended the same principles to employment discrimination claims based on the Civil Rights Acts of 1866 and 1871.[85]

In what has become an often referred to footnote, the Supreme Court in *Gardner-Denver* also provided guidance as to the criteria lower courts should consider in determining the weight to be given arbitral decisions. The Court stated:

> We adopt no standards as to the weight to be accorded an arbitral decision, since this must be determined in the court's discretion with regard to the facts and circumstances of each case. Relevant factors include the existence of provisions in the collective bargaining agreement that conform substantially with Title VII, the degree of procedural fairness in the arbitral forum, adequacy of the record with respect to the issue of discrimination, and the special competence of particular arbitrators. Where an arbitral determination gives full consideration to an employee's Title VII rights, the court may properly accord it great weight. This is especially true where the issue is solely one of fact, specifically addressed by the parties and decided by the arbitrator on the basis of an adequate record. But courts should ever be mindful that Congress, in enacting Title VII, thought it necessary to provide a judicial forum for the ultimate resolution of discriminatory employment claims. It is the duty of courts to assure the full availability of this forum.[86]

Litigation after *Gardner-Denver* clarified to some extent the weight lower courts are prepared to give an arbitrator's finding. Some courts give these determinations "great weight," "considerable weight," or merely "some weight." The Sixth Circuit concluded that: "The court may consider the arbitration decision as *persuasive evidence* that the grounds found by

---

84. *Id.* at 60 (footnote omitted).
85. McDonald v. City of W. Branch, 466 U.S. 284, 292 n.13 (1984); Rogers v. Fisher Body Div., 739 F.2d 1102, 1105 (6th Cir. 1984).
86. Alexander v. Gardner-Denver, 415 U.S. at 60, n.21.

the arbitrator to be just cause for discharge under the collective bargaining agreement are sufficient to amount to just cause."[87]

In *Becton v. Detroit Terminal,* the Sixth Circuit relied on *Gardner-Denver* and rejected the trial court's decision that it was "conclusively bound" by an arbitration decision; however, it then held that the arbitration decision in favor of the employer was not only "persuasive evidence" but was "sufficient to carry the employer's burden of articulating 'some legitimate, nondiscriminatory reason for the employee's rejection.' "[88] This is quite significant, because it automatically shifts the burden back to the employee to prove that the employer's stated reason was a pretext. While *Becton* did not make any mention of it, it is reasonable to assume that courts, in making a determination as to what weight to ascribe to an arbitrator's findings, will apply the standards set forth in *Gardner-Denver.*[89] It should be noted that it is reasonable to believe that the *Gardner-Denver* rationale would apply, not only to discrimination claims, but to other public policy, statutory, and tort claims typically brought in discharge disputes.[90]

Based on this analysis, an ADR adjudication would be useful as evidence in a subsequent lawsuit, even if the award is not given preclusive effect. To maximize the weight afforded to such an award, however, it is important for the employer to promulgate and implement a procedure that, to the greatest extent possible, complies with the criteria listed in *Gardner-Denver* and the dictates of *Renny.*

---

87. Becton v. Detroit Terminal, 687 F.2d 140, 142 (6th Cir. 1982), *cert. denied,* 460 U.S. 1040 (1983) (emphasis added).
88. *Id.*
89. *See also* Darden v. Illinois Bell Tel. Co., 797 F.2d 497 (7th Cir. 1986); Howard v. Holmes, 656 F. Supp. 1144 (S.D.N.Y. 1987).
90. *Cf.* Polk v. Yellow Freight Sys., Inc., 876 F.2d 527 (6th Cir. 1989).

Provision Regarding Admissibility of Arbitrator's Findings in Subsequent Litigation

Another question is whether use of the arbitrator's findings as evidence in a subsequent litigation can be assured by language to that effect in the ADR procedure. For the reasons set forth below, there is some doubt that such a provision would be enforceable in advance of litigation, and it is doubtful that it would be enforceable unless there was a written agreement signed by the employee. In addition, it does not appear that such a provision would be particularly helpful unless the ADR option meets the criteria of *Renny* and *Gardner-Denver,* and is probably unnecessary as long as those criteria are met. Nonetheless, such a provision would be beneficial.

General Rules Regarding Evidentiary Stipulations

Generally speaking, the parties to any *pending* litigation "validly may enter into a stipulation with respect to the evidence."[91] That does not necessarily mean, however, that the parties can enter into such a stipulation in *advance* of litigation. Moreover, under the Michigan Court Rules,

> an agreement or consent between the parties or their attorneys respecting the proceedings in an action, subsequently denied by either party, is not binding unless it was made in open court, or unless evidence of the agreement is in writing, subscribed by the party against whom the agreement is offered or by that party's attorney.[92]

Accordingly, even if a court were willing to honor a *prospective* agreement regarding the admissibility of an arbitrator's award, that agreement would be unenforceable against the

91. 1 Callaghan's Michigan Pleading and Practice, *Stipulations* 20.06 at 744 (2d ed. 1976).
92. MCR 2.507(H).

employee unless it was in writing signed by the employee or his attorney.

Usefulness and Necessity of an Evidentiary Stipulation in the Wrongful Discharge Context

Assuming that the award is admissible by agreement between the parties, that still does not determine the weight to be given that evidence. This is a matter for the court to ultimately decide, and it is unlikely that a judge would abdicate this responsibility, inasmuch as the Supreme Court, in *Gardner-Denver,* left the weight to be given such determinations to the discretion of the court. Accordingly, it is not likely that a judge would blindly accept any such agreement by the parties, and it is equally unlikely that the court would ascribe it any evidentiary value if it failed to meet the criteria set forth in *Gardner-Denver.* On the other hand, if the proceeding does meet the criteria set forth in *Gardner-Denver* and *Renny*'s due process requirements, there is little doubt that the award would be admissible and would be given weight by the court. Therefore, the agreement would be unnecessary. This is not to say, however, that some form of notice to the effect that the findings of the arbitrator may be presented to the court as evidence would not be beneficial. Certainly, it would be consistent with the general tenor of *Gardner-Denver.*

In this regard, it is a good idea to have the grievant or his representative testify on the record (or sign a statement) acknowledging that he has had an opportunity to present his entire case with regard to his statutory claims and all other claims, that the hearing has been fair, that he has been afforded due process. Any prepared notice should incorporate *Gardner-Denver's* criteria. This posthearing statement is often used in Teamster grievance proceedings, and, on occasion, it has been relied on by both the union and the company in subsequent breach of duty of fair representation claims.

ADR Filing Time Limits

The next question concerns the time limits for presenting grievances and taking those grievances to ADR. The most important time limit is that in Step 1, the submission of the Grievance Form, since the employee's failure to meet that time limit cuts off his right to exhaust the remainder of the grievance procedure. Union contracts at this step run anywhere from five days to no limit at all. Most contracts contain an initial time limit of somewhere between five and thirty days. Fifteen calendar days would appear to be about right. Employers should have the employee acknowledge, in writing, at the exit interview, that he has fifteen days to initiate the complaint procedure. Also, employers should include a provision stating that the time limits can be extended by written mutual agreement between the company and the employee. It can, if it wishes, then make an exception to the initial fifteen-day filing period where warranted (e.g., employee illness, unavailability of lawyer, witnesses on vacation, etc.).

In discussing time limitations, it is worth noting that an employer can, through an employment agreement, limit the time within which to bring a lawsuit. See *Perez v. Western-Southern Life Insurance, Co.,*[93] where the court held that a written employment agreement in which an employee agrees not to sue an employer more than six months after termination and waives any statutes of limitations to the contrary bars an action for employment discrimination under the State's Civil Rights Act (which had a three-year statute of limitations), where the suit was commenced two years after discharge. The court also dismissed the breach of employment contract claim, which has a six-year statute of limitations in Michigan.

---

93. Perez v. Western-S. Life Ins. Co., 2 IER Cas. (BNA) 375 (E.D. Mich. 1987).

Alternative Dispute Resolution Expenses: Who Pays What?

The cost of arbitration in a unionized setting has risen dramatically over the last decade. While the per diem cost for an FMCS or AAA arbitrator is not totally unreasonable (in the neighborhood of $300 to $500 per day plus expenses), it is seldom that an arbitration is billed for less than three days. It is also customary to charge a day for hearing even in cases where the actual time spent in hearing testimony runs a couple of hours. In short, a simple arbitration seldom costs less than three days of hearing (or $900 to $1500).

In order to control costs, it is probably desirable to use a permanent panel of umpires, with the umpires agreeing up front to a per diem rate, hourly rate, or fixed fee for each arbitration. It would not be unreasonable to expect most cases to be tried in one day, with a second day devoted to writing an opinion. With the present fee structure of most arbitrators, the arbitrator's cost and his expenses should approximate $650 to $1100. As a related issue, while expedited arbitration might have certain advantages where the number of cases becomes unwieldy, it would be advisable to have a studied written opinion from the arbitrator, both for purposes of persuasiveness as well as any future use to which it might be put in another forum.

Given these cost considerations, and in an effort to eliminate any frivolous invocation of the procedure, employers may wish to require that the employee pay a fee upon the initiation of arbitration. Rather than a filing fee (which in the case of AAA is used for their purposes), the fee should be viewed as an "earnest fee" or "good faith" pledge to proceed with the arbitration. It should not be so low as to encourage everyone to file, nor so high as to make it beyond the reach of affordability for any employee. One possibility is to set the fee at the approximate cost of half of a hearing (perhaps $300 to $500). The fee must be paid either at the time of the initiation of the arbitration or, in any event, no later than the arbitration hearing. This is because an arbitrator will not want to pursue an employee for part of his fee, nor will it be worthwhile for the company to file a collection suit against an employee who refuses to pay. It should be noted that as to indigent employees, however, at least one well-known authority has suggested that the filing fees be waived.[94]

With regard to the total sharing of the cost of arbitration, the employer may want to require the employee-grievant to pay one-half of the arbitrator's costs, and in the event that the employee prevails, the company would pay all of the costs by refunding the initiating fee the employee has paid. The party who orders a transcript should bear its cost and if the other party wants a copy, the cost should be borne equally.

Employee Representation at the Arbitration Hearing

As a general rule, employees should be allowed to have attorneys at the hearing and, while not necessarily so, the failure to afford representation at the hearing may, as *Renny* shows, undermine the validity and finality of the proceeding. This is especially true as pertains to the non-*Toussaint* claims. Moreover, steps should be taken to ensure actual representation at the hearing, if possible. On the other hand, if the proceeding is otherwise fair and regular, it is unlikely that a court would be hesitant in accepting the arbitrator's findings simply because the grievant chose to proceed without counsel, either voluntarily or by necessity. Co-worker representation is also a

---

94. Summers, *Individual Protection Against Unjust Dismissal: Time for a Statute,* 62 VA. L. REV. 481, 524 (1976) [hereinafter Summers].

possibility; if this occurs the co-worker should not suffer a loss of pay as a result of his participation.

General Rules Regarding Representation at Arbitration Hearings

Under the Michigan arbitration statute and court rules incorporated into that statute, "a party has a right to be represented by an *attorney* at a proceeding or hearing [conducted pursuant to the statute and a] waiver of the right before the proceeding is ineffective."[95] (This assumes the applicability of the arbitration statute to this type of case.) The Federal Arbitration Act[96] contains no such requirement; however, an award may be overturned where the rights of any party have been prejudiced.[97] Conceivably, a denial of the right to counsel could constitute such prejudice. At common law, it also appears that "either party has a right to be represented before arbitrators by counsel, and it constitutes misconduct for the arbitrators to permit one party to be represented and assisted by counsel, and to refuse the other party a reasonable opportunity to avail himself of the same assistance."[98]

Effect of Nonrepresentation as Applied to *Toussaint* Claims

Applying these principles to the *Toussaint*-employment contract situation, a compelling argument can be made that if an employee is denied the right to counsel during the grievance/arbitration proceedings, then the procedure is invalid and the determination is not final and binding. *Renny* and

---

95. Revised Judicature Act, MICH. COMP. LAWS ANN. § 600.5021 (West 1975); MCR 3.602(G) (emphasis added).
96. 9 U.S.C. 1, *et seq.*
97. Reichman v. Creative Real Estate Consultants, Inc., 476 F. Supp. 1276 (S.D.N.Y. 1979).
98. 6 CJS *Arbitration* 79 at 295–296 (1975).

Vander Toorn clearly support this view (both courts recognized that certain levels of procedural fairness are necessary before the court would apply a limited scope of review). On the other hand, this does not necessarily mean that the employer and employee could not agree, in advance, that the ADR proceeding will be conducted without the assistance of counsel. While this might preclude enforcement of the arbitration statute, that does not necessarily mean that it would be unenforceable at common law.[99] Moreover, since the *Toussaint* case recognizes that an employer may unilaterally confer upon his employee the right to be discharged only for just cause but is not obligated to make any such promises, it would seem to follow that the employer may unilaterally restrict the procedures under which that right will be enforced. These particular issues, however, have not been tested.

Effect of Nonrepresentation as Applied to Other Claims

If the parties agree to ADR of a *Toussaint* claim without assistance of counsel, this will minimize the preclusive effect of the award as to the non-*Toussaint* claims. In this regard, the Supreme Court, in *Alexander v. Gardner-Denver,*[100] noted that there were several shortcomings in according unlimited deference to arbitration proceedings:

> The record of the arbitration proceedings is not as complete; the usual rules of evidence do not apply; and rights and procedures common to civil trials, such as discovery, compulsory process, cross-examination, and testimony under oath, are often severely limited or unavailable. . . . And as this court has recog-

99. *See generally* E.E. Tripp Excavating Contractor, Inc. v. Jackson County, 60 Mich. App. at 221, 230 N.W.2d at 556 (award that is not enforceable under the statute is still enforceable at common law).
100. Alexander v. Gardner-Denver, 415 U.S. at 36.

> nized, "[a]rbitrators have no obligation to the court to give their reasons for an award."[101]

Therefore, while the participation or availability of counsel is not mentioned in *Gardner-Denver,* it nevertheless must be viewed as the touchstone of the substantive rights that are cited by the Court.

Reviewing courts would obviously look askance at a procedure in which the employer was well represented with labor relations personnel, and perhaps counsel, while the employee was left to fend for himself in this supposedly "neutral setting." For this reason, there is some merit in having an employee represented by an ombudsman, someone from the personnel or human resources department, or perhaps a co-employee. In that event, the company could reciprocate by not having legal counsel present, but could use someone from personnel or human resources to present the case, thereby excluding counsel for both sides and giving the procedure more of a "tell-your-side-of-the-story" flavor than the rather formalistic setting in which most labor-management arbitrations are conducted today.

There are, however, too many significant drawbacks to making the procedure that informal. Initially, an employee's lawyer reviewing such a proceeding after the fact will undoubtedly find ways in which his client's case could have been presented better and in which the employee could have been accorded more due process. After all, the purpose of the procedure is to assist the employee in putting on his best case. If successful, the relief accorded should satisfy him, he will be less likely to seek other remedies, and the system and procedure will gain additional credibility in the eyes of other employees. On the other hand, if he puts on his best case with the assistance of counsel and loses, the employer would have an excel-

101. *Id.* at 57–58 (citations omitted).

lent assessment of the strength of the employee's case and his chances of prevailing in some other forum. The ombudsman approach might have some merit in perhaps a mediation prior to arbitration, but it suffers from the fate that a judge or jury would not likely feel an employee "had his day in court" without a lawyer. Likewise, a co-employee representative suffers from the same fate, but worse, involves other employees, which starts to make what is essentially a private procedure more public. It is also fraught with the risk of generalizing the employee's problems, thus planting the seed for collective action. In this day and age, to preclude the employee from having counsel present, if desired, would undercut a forward-looking and sound employee complaint resolution procedure.

Renny v. Port Huron Hospital[102] is a good example of what happens when "elementary fairness" and due process are not present. There, the lower court denied the defendant's motion for summary judgment because there was a question of fact as to whether the company's grievance procedure was fair. The jury then found the procedure was unfair, that plaintiff was wrongfully discharged, and then awarded her $100,000. Renny argued that the grievance process did not comport with elementary fairness because (1) she could not be represented by counsel, (2) she could not sit through the hearing, (3) she could not bring her own witness or question any witnesses at the hearing, and (4) no record was kept of the meeting. Moreover, key witnesses were not called to provide either a written statement or testify as to the events that led to the discharge. The lower court and jury agreed with plaintiff, and their determination was affirmed by the Appellate and Supreme Courts, which found that in such circumstances, plaintiff was entitled to seek *de novo* judicial review of the merits of her employment claim. *Renny* is important because it describes the type

102. Renny v. Port Huron Hosp., 427 Mich. 415, 348 N.W.2d 327 (1986).

of conduct that will preclude any ADR proceeding from being final and binding.

For these reasons, the ideal situation would be for the grievant to have an attorney of his or her own choice. In theory, counsel would help ensure that there was (1) a high degree of procedural fairness throughout the arbitration and (2) a complete and adequate record with respect to all issues and claims. This, in turn, would serve as a persuasive basis for a court to exercise its discretion and admit the arbitral findings, treat them as "persuasive evidence," and hold that the award satisfies the employer's "articulation" obligation in disparate treatment employment discrimination cases. This reasoning also applies, by analogy to an employee's other possible tort claims, such as claims for retaliatory discharge, negligence, defamation, etc.

If the employee chooses to proceed without counsel or cannot afford counsel, there is little that an employer can do, except to provide legal assistance at company expense. Although this latter alternative has been recommended by at least one authority,[103] it would, of course, be expensive and possibly unnecessary if the criteria in *Renny* and *Gardner-Denver* are met. In the unrepresented case, allowing a co-employee to assist the employee is the next best alternative. In such cases, both the employer and the arbitrator should be mindful to develop a complete and adequate record, as well as to ensure that the grievant be accorded due process throughout the proceeding. The arbitrator should be at liberty to elicit those facts that would assist in making a full record.

---

103. Summers, *supra* note 95, at 524.

Selection of an Arbitrator

There are a number of ways to approach this issue.

An employer could establish a permanent panel of umpires who would hear cases under the ADR's procedures. One suggestion is to use arbitrators that are acceptable in the unionized setting. Those arbitrators usually already have some familiarity with the company and its policies and procedures. Having that background and "feel" for the situation are important and help assure a reasoned arbitral decision. Moreover, management would have some confidence that competent arbitrators are ruling on discharge cases. There might be an additional advantage, since an arbitrator selected in that way would not have any political need to try to keep both sides happy over some period of time, as is often alleged in labor-management arbitrations. If a permanent ADR panel is used, it is desirable to specify that either the procedural rules of the AAA or Federal Mediation and Conciliation, or the company's own rules would apply.

Another alternative in creating a process that is procedurally fair is to have an adjudicative procedure that utilizes employee representatives at either the fact finding or appeal process. A number of enlightened employers have turned to this procedure, and this type of ADR format has been previously approved.[104] For example, an employer might have a five-member board with a nonvoting chairperson in which three of the members are employees chosen by the chairperson out of five nominated by employees. The remaining two are management representatives, three of whom have been nominated by management and two of whom are selected by the chairperson. The result is that every grievance panel starts off with an employee majority. Experience indicates that usu-

104. Khalifa v. Henry Ford Hosp., 156 Mich. App. 485, 401 N.W.2d 884 (1986).

ally management's position is upheld and in the few instances that this has not been the case, it only enhances the fairness and credibility of the procedure.

Limitations on the Arbitrator's Authority

What limits should be placed on an arbitrator's authority and what limits, if any, would affect the validity of the procedure? From a practical standpoint certain limitations are appropriate, but an overly restrictive clause would undermine its usefulness. From a legal standpoint, an overly restrictive arbitration provision would jeopardize its preclusive effect, at least as to the noncontract claims.

Practical Aspects of Restricting the Arbitrator's Authority

From the practical standpoint, the limitations on an arbitrator's authority might include: (1) limitations on his authority to amend the company's personnel policies; (2) limitations on his authority to interfere with the company's management rights; (3) limitations on his authority to determine the appropriate burden and quantum of proof; and (4) limitations on his authority to determine the appropriate relief. Considering these various possible limitations, there should be limitations on the arbitrator's authority to amend an employer's personnel policies and his authority to interfere with the company's exercise of management rights. A clause that would achieve those results might read as follows:

> In reaching a decision, the arbitrator shall interpret, apply and be bound by the employer's handbooks, personnel policies and procedures and by any applicable federal or state law. The arbitrator shall have no authority, however to add to, detract from, change, amend or modify the handbook and personnel policies in any respect. Nor shall the arbitrator have authority

> to consider or decide any matters which are the responsibility of the company in the management and conduct of its business.[105]

As pertains to the burden and quantum of proof in a discharge case, "the burden generally is held to be on the employer to prove guilt of wrongdoing. . . ."[106] Moreover, while the "preponderance of the evidence" rule is used in many cases, some arbitrators require a higher degree of proof "such as clear and convincing" evidence, or "beyond a reasonable doubt," and this is especially true in cases involving an element of moral turpitude or criminal intent.[107] One possible limitation on the arbitrator's authority, therefore, would be to shift the burden of proof or lower the quantum of proof. There appears to be nothing that prevents the parties from contracting as to who has the burden of proof or what standard will apply. Therefore, an ADR procedure could place the burden of proof on the party seeking relief and impose the less stringent "preponderance of evidence" standard.

Beyond these restrictions, any further limitations may undermine the usefulness of an ADR procedure. The more restrictions that are placed on the arbitrator, the greater the chances that the procedure begins to take on a unilateral complexion with less deference being given to the judgment of the outside third party. An arbitrator, upon whom numerous restrictions are placed, may also feel that the procedure is too one-sided or may attempt to bend over backwards to be fair to the employee. For these reasons, substantive restrictions upon the arbitrator's authority and power tend to detract from the neutrality in which the procedure is clothed. More signifi-

---

105. Blumrosen, *Exploring Voluntary Arbitration of Individual Employment Disputes,* 16 U. MICH. J.L. REF. 249, 273 (1983) (model arbitration clause regarding "management flexibility").

106. F. ELKOURI & E. ELKOURI, HOW ARBITRATION WORKS 621 (3d ed. 1973) [hereinafter ELKOURI & ELKOURI].

107. *Id.* at 622–623.

cantly, unduly restricting the arbitrator's authority is at odds with the purposes behind a sound internal ADR procedure (*i.e.,* providing a fair mechanism for all employment claims and having an arbitrator or third party required to take evidence on, consider, and decide all claims).

Legal Aspects of Restricting the Arbitrator's Authority

From a legal standpoint, "the authority of arbitrators to make an award depends upon the arbitration agreement, and they have no authority to make an award outside the contract."[108] Applying that general rule in the contract situation, an arbitrator would have no authority to make any award beyond the limitations agreed to by the employer and the employee. If those limitations are *unilaterally* imposed by the employer, however, their effect is somewhat unclear. On the one hand, it could be argued that since an employer is not obligated to give assurances of job security, he may unilaterally condition any such assurances by establishing a grievance/arbitration procedure and limiting the arbitrator's authority under that procedure. On the other hand, by analogy to *Renny* and *Vander Toorn,* if those limitations undermine the fairness of the award, that might jeopardize its preclusive effect.

In recognition that an agreement to arbitrate might not bar some court actions, some employers have, in the interest of efficiency, sought to preclude arbitration of those actions. In *EEOC v. Board of Governors,*[109] the court addressed a provision in a labor agreement barring arbitration of a grievance if the employee seeks resolution of the matter in another forum. When an employee who was pursuing a grievance filed a charge under the ADEA, the employer terminated the griev-

---

108. 8 Callaghan's Michigan Pleading & Practice, *Arbitration & Award* 61.27 at 348 (2d ed. 1982).
109. Equal Employment Opportunity Comm'n v. Board of Governors, 665 F. Supp. 630 (N.D. Ill. 1987).

ance procedure. The court found the employer's action to constitute retaliation in violation of the ADEA. On the other hand, in *Board of Higher Education v. Professional Staff Congress,*[110] the court held that a provision in a collective bargaining agreement barring arbitration of discrimination grievances, if the employee files a claim related to the grievance before a court or government agency, is valid and bars an employee who files a Title VII action or a state discrimination action from having their claims arbitrated.

With respect to noncontract claims, the risk of undermining the ADR is even greater. As noted in the preceding, the weight to be afforded an arbitrator's decision in subsequent litigation of an employment discrimination case depends on the degree to which the arbitration proceedings comply with the criteria set forth in the *Gardner-Denver* decision. By analogy, those same criteria would apply to other non-*Toussaint* claims, such as other statutory, public policy, and tort claims typically brought in the discharge setting. Limitations on an arbitrator's authority that are contrary to those criteria would adversely affect the validity of the procedure and, in turn, undermine the admissibility and weight of the arbitrator's findings in subsequent litigation. This would include any limitations on the arbitrator's authority to issue relief.[111]

On the other hand, a company might not want an arbitrator to hear certain types of "new frontier" or group issues. There are different types of employment discrimination claims, and some might not lend themselves to the grievance process, e.g., new theories involving protected groups, systematic discrimi-

---

110. Board of Higher Educ. v. Professional Staff Congress, 80 Misc. 2d 297, 362 N.Y.S.2d 985 (Sup. Ct. 1975).

111. *See, e.g.,* Midgett v. Sackett-Chicago, Inc., 105 Ill. 2d 143, 454 N.E.2d 1092 (1984) (in refusing to require exhaustion of contract remedies in action based on public policy, court notes that remedies available to employee in court action are broader than remedies that would be available to him under collective bargaining agreement).

nation, and disparate impact involving class-type policies or practices.

Inclusion of a "Claims" Checklist

Should an ADR grievance form contain a checklist of all possible claims? For a number of reasons, a general checklist approach is appropriate.

As indicated previously, it is important for the parties to submit all possible claims to the ADR and have those claims addressed by the arbitrator in order to maximize the preclusive effect of the procedure. Although some courts have held that an award, under a general submission of all disputes between the parties, is effective to bar matters or differences that were not actually presented to and considered by the arbitrator, "there is considerable difference of opinion" on this issue.[112] At the same time, however, it seems that a detailed checklist of all possible claims might invite employees to conjure up claims that are not really there. With these two competing concerns in mind, is a generalized list of claims advisable? Probably so.

Regarding a grievance form, there should be an acknowledgment that any claim or controversy arising from or relating to the grievant's employment or termination of employment can and will be submitted to the arbitrator, including any claims based on the company's personnel policies and practices, federal law, state law, and local or common law. In addition, the submission form or agreement should ask the employee to list all the reasons why he or she believes the discharge was not legitimate, what it was in violation of (with a general reminder that this would include any claims of unlawful discrimination), and what relief is being sought.

---

112. *See* Hopkins v. City of Midland, 158 Mich. App. at 361. *See also* 6 CJS, *Arbitration* 127 at 374–375 (1975).

Definition of Just Cause

Another question is whether the discharge policy should include a list of offenses or whether it is better to leave just cause undefined. If an employer decides to establish a policy of discharge only for just cause, the general consensus is that there should be a list of offenses that constitute just cause. This list will preclude the arbitrator from imposing a lower standard of conduct than the employer desires.

Under a general promise to discharge only for just cause, without a list of offenses amounting to just cause, the scope of review by jury or arbitrator is wide open. The questions to be decided would include:

1. Did the employee do what the employer said he did?
2. Are the stated reasons for discharge the actual reasons?
3. Does the reason for discharge amount to just cause?
4. Is it a pretext?[113]

In other words, even if the arbitrator were to find that an employee did what the company said he did and determine that those were the actual reasons for the discharge (as opposed to some retaliatory or discriminatory motive), he would still be allowed to second guess the company as to whether this offense, in all the circumstances, was just cause for discharge.

On the other hand, if an employer establishes a policy to discharge only for just cause and then provides a list of offenses that constitute just cause, the inquiry is much narrower. As explained by the Michigan Supreme Court in *Toussaint:*

> An employer who agrees to discharge only for just cause need not lower its standard of performance. It has promised employ-

113. *See* Toussaint v. Blue Cross & Blue Shield, 408 Mich. at 621–623, 292 N.W.2d at 896 (questions for the jury); *accord* EKLOURI & ELKOURI, *supra* note 106, at 621 (questions for the arbitrator).

> ment only so long as the employee does the job required by the employment contract. The employer's standard of job performance can be made part of the employment contract. Breach of the employer's uniformly applied rules is a breach of contract and cause for discharge.[114]

Under such a policy, the only issues to be resolved are:

1. Did the employer actually have a rule or policy?
2. Was the employee discharged for violating that rule or policy?
3. Was the policy uniformly applied?[115]

The adjudicator would not, however, be allowed to second guess the company as to whether this is the type of act or event that justifies termination.[116]

Given these general rules, it makes sense to define just cause. In addition, the procedure should contain a provision limiting the arbitrator's authority to modify the penalty if he finds that the employee committed an offense that has been established by the company as just cause for discharge. This approach still provides an assurance of job security to the employee and still allows an arbitrator to determine the actual reason for the discharge, while at the same time limiting second guessing as to the appropriateness of the penalty in a particular case. The relief section could include a provision for up to two years of front pay in lieu of reinstatement, if that is not an advisable remedy under the circumstances.

---

114. Toussaint v. Blue Cross & Blue Shield, 408 Mich. at 623, 292 N.W.2d at 897.
115. *Id.*
116. *See, e.g.,* Hollowell v. Career Decision, Inc., 100 Mich. App. 561, 568–569, 298 N.W.2d 915, 919–20 (1980) (plaintiff properly discharged for violation of employer's unilaterally imposed standard of job performance); Goerbig v. Dearborn Mach. Prods., Inc., No. 82-16060-CL, slip op. (Muskegon County Cir. Ct. Oct. 4, 1982) (employee properly discharged for violation of rules set forth in same handbook relied on by employee as giving assurance of job security).

General Concluding Observations as to the Merits of the Alternative Dispute Resolution Approach to Unlawful Discharge Claims

ADR is a reasonable approach to dispute management. It reduces an employer's exposure to and liability for wrongful discharge litigation, while at the same time maintaining a positive employee relations climate.

Sample ADR Forms

GRIEVANCE PROCEDURE—GENERAL

PURPOSE: To afford an immediate and fair method for the resolution of disputes that might arise between the company and employees. (For Grievances involving discharge, refer to GRIEVANCE PROCEDURE—DISMISSAL.)

DEFINITIONS: *Days*—As used in this policy statement, shall be working days, except where specifically noted as calendar days.

Grievance—A grievance shall be a complaint or dispute of an employee *(who has completed the ninety-day probationary period)* regarding any condition of employment, or the application, meaning or interpretation of personnel policies or procedures as they affect the work activity of said employee.

POLICY: An employee filing a grievance shall have at every step the right to present witnesses and evidence to support his or her grievance. Decisions may not be made that conflict with existing policy or be precedent setting.

All grievances shall be reduced to writing and submitted to Employee Relations. Upon investigation, if the nature of the complaint is discrimination, appropriate information will be transmitted to the Opportunity Development Center. An employee may seek the assistance of Employee Relations in forming his or her complaint or appeal.

The time limits on the grievant throughout the grievance procedure shall be the grievant's working days. Those limits placed on management shall be the working days of the management representative involved. Through the first three steps of the grievance procedure either party may request an extension of a time limit from Human Resources management, who upon finding sufficient cause, will grant an extension for a specific length of time.

Failure to process a grievance by the grievant within the time limits or agreed upon extensions shall constitute termination of the grievance. The failure of a management representative to meet time limits shall cause the grievance to move on to the next step in the procedure.

FIRST STEP

An employee who has a complaint shall first discuss the matter with his or her supervisor. If the issue cannot be resolved in the initial discussion, the employee shall state the complaint in writing on a Grievance Form (available from Employee Relations). The written grievance must be delivered to the employee's supervisor within fifteen days from the time of the occurrence of the problem. The grievant may be accompanied by an employee of his or her choice or an Employee Relations Representative to the initial discussion and any subsequent meeting held by the immediate supervisor. The supervisor shall reply in writing to the grievance within three days of the day following receipt of the written grievance. If the grievance is resolved at this step, the Employee Relations copy shall be forwarded to Employee Relations.

SECOND STEP

If the supervisor's reply is not acceptable to the employee, he or she may submit written grievance to the Department Head within three days of receipt of the supervisor's reply. The Department Head of his or her designate shall hold a meeting with the grievant within three working days following receipt of such a request. The grievant may have an employee of his or her choice or an Employee Relations Representative present at the meeting.

The Department Head shall reply in writing to the grievance within three working days following the second step meeting. A copy shall be forwarded to the Employee Relations Department.

THIRD STEP

If the Department Head's reply is not acceptable to the employee, said employee may request a hearing before the Assistant Vice President and Director of Human Resources or his or her designate by submitting the grievance to Employee Relations. The request for a hearing shall be made within three days of receipt of the Department Head's reply, and the hearing shall be held within three days following the request.

Hearing participants shall include the grievant, the grievant's immediate supervisor, the Department Head, witnesses for both parties, and appropriate Management and Employee Relations Representatives. The employee may be represented by another company employee. Prior to the third step hearing, both parties must provide names of witnesses who will provide testimony.

The Assistant Vice President and Director of Human Resources or his or her designate shall reply to the grievance within five working days following the third step hearing. (Guidelines on conduct of the third step hearing are available from Employee Relations.)

FOURTH STEP

In the event the grievance remains unsettled after having made full use of the Grievance Procedure in the first three steps, the employee filing the grievance may submit the grievance to a fourth step hearing. The request for the fourth step hearing must be received by Employee Relations within five working days of the receipt of the third step reply.

A three-member hearing panel shall be appointed within five days of receipt of the request for the fourth step hearing. The panel shall be chosen from members of the operating staff or support staff and shall consist of one member selected by the grievant and one member selected by the grievant's Department Head. The Assistant Vice President and Director of Human Resources shall make available a list for selection of a mutually agreed upon hearing chairman.

The hearing panel chairman shall set the time for the hearing, which shall be held as soon as practicable. (Guidelines for conduct of the fourth step hearing are available from Employee Relations.)

The conduct of the hearing should be as follows:

a) The hearing panel chairman may at the beginning of the hearing ask for statements clarifying the issues involved.

b) Exhibits, when offered, may be received in evidence by the hearing panel, and when so received, shall be marked and made part of the record.

c) The grievant or his or her representative, shall then present his or her claim and proofs and his or her witnesses who shall submit to questions or other examination. The department shall then present its claims, which shall include supportive data and any witnesses necessary. The hearing panel may in its discretion vary this procedure but shall afford full and equal opportunity to all parties for presentation of any material or relevant data.

d) The parties shall produce additional evidence as the hearing panel may deem necessary to the understanding and determination of the dispute. The hearing panel shall be the judge of relevance and materiality of the evidence offered. All evidence shall be taken in the presence of the hearing panel and of the parties. No statements, witnesses, or evidence may be presented at this hearing that has not:

   (1) Previously been presented in Steps I–III of the Grievance Procedure *or*

   (2) Been specifically requested by the hearing panel.

The decision of the majority of the hearing panel shall be final. The hearing panel chairman shall specifically inquire of all parties whether they have any further evidence to offer or witnesses to be heard. Upon receiving negative replies, the hearing panel chairman shall declare the hearing closed. The hearing may be reopened by the hearing panel chairman on his or her own motion or upon application of a party for good cause shown at any time before the award is made.

The decision shall be filed in writing by the hearing panel chairman with the Assistant Vice President and Director of Human Resources not later than ten calendar days after the hearing.

Copies of the decision shall be transmitted to the employee, the Department Head, and to Employee Relations.

No decision shall be made that conflicts with the local, state, or federal laws or that is not in compliance with the company's Personnel Policies.

GRIEVANCE PROCEDURE—DISMISSAL

PURPOSE: To provide an equitable and timely method for a final disposition of issues that might arise when an employee is dismissed. (For all other grievances refer to GRIEVANCE PROCEDURE—GENERAL.)

DEFINITIONS: *Days*—As used in this policy statement, shall be working days, except where specifically noted as calendar days.

Grievance—A complaint by a dismissed employee (who has completed the ninety-day probationary period).

POLICY: An employee who has been discharged shall have the right to file a grievance. The grievance shall be filed with the office of the Assistant Vice President and Director of Human Resources or his or her designate. A dismissal conference shall be scheduled, and if the grievant is not satisfied with the conference results, he or she may submit the grievance to outside arbitration.

An employee filing a dismissal grievance shall have the right to produce witnesses and evidence to support his or her grievance.

The parties to the grievance by mutual agreement may extend any or all of the time periods established in this policy.

Failure by the grievant to process a grievance within the time limits, or agreed upon extensions, shall constitute termination of the grievance.

A dismissed employee may have a meeting with an Employee Relations Representative or his or her supervisor within three days following his or her termination. Should the results of the meeting be unsatisfactory to the employee he or she shall reduce the complaint to writing and submit it to Employee Relations within five days following the meeting.

DISMISSAL CONFERENCE

The Assistant Vice President and Director of Human Resources, or his or her designate, shall hold the dismissal conference within seven working days following the submission of the grievance.

Conference participants shall include the grievant, the grievant's immediate supervisor, the department head, other management personnel, witnesses for the employee, and Employee Relations.

At least twenty-four hours prior to the conference the department head shall furnish in writing to the grievant a full statement of the reasons for dismissal.

The Assistant Vice President and Director of Human Resources, or his or her designate, shall reply to the grievance within five working days following the dismissal conference.

ARBITRATION

In the event the grievance remains unsettled after the dismissal conference, the grievant may submit the grievance to arbitration. The request for arbitration must be submitted in writing to Employee Relations within five days following the receipt of the dismissal conference reply. The Assistant Vice President and Director of Human Resources, within seven days following receipt of the request for arbitration shall contact the grievant to arrange a mutually convenient time to meet and select an arbitrator from a permanent panel of arbitrators. No arbitrator shall be in the employ of ____________.

Grievances submitted to arbitration shall be subject to the following terms and conditions:

(1) The arbitrator shall not have authority to subtract from, add to, or otherwise modify ____________ policy, or make decisions that conflict with local, state, or federal laws.

(2) The arbitrator may not award wages the grievant would have earned had he or she not been dismissed.

(3) The fees and expenses of the arbitrator will be borne by ____________. Postponement fees will be borne by the party causing the postponement of the hearing.

(4) Only company employees may represent a grievant in the arbitration proceeding.

(5) An employee who is called as a witness, or who is acting as grievant's representative, shall not suffer loss of pay for the time spent in an arbitration hearing when such hearing is held during the employee's regular work schedule.

(6) Expenses of nonemployee witnesses of the grievant and any other expenses incurred by the grievant must be borne by the grievant.

(7) The arbitration hearing shall be guided by Expedited Labor Arbitration Rules of the American Arbitration Association except where such action would be contrary to this policy.

(8) The arbitrator's decision, when made in accordance with his or her jurisdiction and authority provided in this policy, shall be final and binding on the company and the grievant.

GRIEVANCE FORM

GRIEVANT: ______________ DEPARTMENT ________________

DATE GRIEVANCE SUBMITTED ______________

DATE OF OCCURRENCE THAT PROMPTED GRIEVANCE ________

GRIEVANCE: (Explain in your own words what has occurred)

____

____

____

____

____

____

____

____

____

____

WHAT PERSONNEL POLICY OR POLICIES ARE REFERRED TO ABOVE?

FIRST STEP MEETING: DATE: __________ TIME: __________

REPLY OF SUPERVISOR: ______________________________________

____

____

____

____

____

____

____

(SUPERVISOR) (DATE & TIME)

THIS DECISION (IS) (IS NOT) ACCEPTABLE. ______________

____

(GRIEVANT) (DATE & TIME)

SECOND STEP MEETING: DATE: ______ TIME: ______

REPLY OF DEPARTMENT HEAD: ______________________________

____

____

____
____
____
____

____
(DEPARTMENT HEAD) (DATE & TIME)

THIS DECISION (IS) (IS NOT) ACCEPTABLE. ____________

____
(DEPARTMENT HEAD) (DATE & TIME)
THIRD STEP MEETING: DATE: ________ TIME: ________
REPLY OF ASSISTANT VICE PRESIDENT AND DIRECTOR OF PERSONNEL: ______________________________
____
____
____
____
____
____

____
(ASSISTANT VICE PRESIDENT AND DIRECTOR OF PERSONNEL) (DATE & TIME)

THIS DECISION (IS) (IS NOT) ACCEPTABLE. ____________

____
(GRIEVANT) (DATE & TIME)

DECISION OF HEARING PANEL
FOURTH STEP GRIEVANCE HEARING

Employee's Name:
Date of Hearing:
Appearances:
For the employee:
For the ________________:

The Issue

The Evidence

The Argument

Employee:

____

"XYZ" AND YOUR JOB SECURITY

In most companies, employees are asked to sign statements acknowledging that their employment is "at will" and that they can be fired at any time with or without cause. Here at *XYZ* we have a different philosophy. Our policy is to continue the employment of our employees unless there is just cause for termination or unless there is a legitimate business or economic reason for termination. This policy applies to all nonprobationary, full-time, and regular part-time employees who are not covered by any collective bargaining agreement. The only exception to this policy of job security is for officers of the company. Due to the nature of their employment, officers must serve at the will of the company.

Termination for just cause includes, but is not limited to, termination for unsatisfactory performance, termination for misconduct involving violations of company rules, policies, procedures, or guidelines, or termination for other conduct that is detrimental to or that demonstrates a disregard for customers, coworkers, or company interests.

The company's policy of termination for just cause is subject to the provisions of the Termination Appeal Procedure. This means that if your employment is terminated for cause and you wish to challenge the decision, you must use the Termination Appeal Procedure described in this handbook.

Termination for business or economic reasons includes, but is not limited to, termination resulting from poor economic conditions, technological developments, operational changes, reorganization, subcontracting, use of overtime, elimination or transfer of operations, elimination or transfer of jobs, reductions in hours, or changes in job qualifications. In all such cases, the company will determine what work is available and what employees are needed to do that work.

Decisions to terminate employment for business or economic reasons remain within the sole judgment and discretion of the company because such decisions result from factors relating to the operation of the business and not the performance or conduct of any particular associate. Decisions to terminate employment for business or economic reasons may not be challenged through the Termination Appeal Procedure.

PROBATIONARY PERIOD

Your first months on the job are important ones for both of us. They let you learn about *XYZ* and our way of doing things. In addition, they let us see how well you are fitting in with coworkers and how well you are handling your new job.

You are a probationary employee for the first ninety calendar days of your employment. Probationary employees are employed on an at-will basis and may be discharged at the sole discretion of the company during the probationary period. No one except the Company President can modify this relationship, and he can only do so in a written document signed by him. The probationary period may be extended up to an additional thirty days if circumstances warrant additional evaluation.

YOUR EMPLOYMENT STATUS

Full-Time—Employees who work an average of thirty-two hours or more per week.

Part-Time—Employees who average less than thirty-two hours per week.

Seasonal, Temporary, Call-in—Employees scheduled to work as needed during peak business periods, vacations, and/or other occasions. These employees are paid on an hourly basis and have no prescribed work week.

Staff—Office, supervisory, management, and professional personnel, such as buyers, specialists, heads of departments, and their staff. Hours may vary from forty on up.

Operational Management—Store directors, line and department managers, and distribution center supervisors and management. Hours vary from forty and above.

Active—Employees who are currently working or are available for work.

Inactive—Employees who are currently on leave of absence or layoff.

THE TERMINATION APPEAL PROCEDURE

The Termination Appeal Procedure has been established as a means to resolve all complaints about termination from employment. It is intended to ensure that no employee is terminated from employment without just cause or is terminated for a discriminatory or other unlawful reason. The procedure provides a method by which any nonprobationary full-time or regular part-time employee can have his or her termination from employment reviewed by a neutral person not involved in the decision-making process.

The first step in the appeal procedure is a review by the [*insert designated official*] of the decision to terminate. If your employment is terminated and you believe it was terminated without just cause or for a discriminatory or other unlawful reason, you must submit a written request for review to the [*insert designated official*] within fourteen calendar days of your termination on a form supplied by the company. The form is available from your unit manager or the Human Resources Department. After you submit the request, the [*insert designated official*] or someone from his or her staff will review the circumstances surrounding the termination and might meet with you and other persons to make an independent determination whether there was just cause for termination and whether the termination was otherwise nondiscriminatory and lawful.

The second step in the appeal procedure is arbitration. If you are not satisfied with the decision of the [*insert designated official*], you have the right to have your case heard by an impartial arbitrator. You must request arbitration within twenty-one calendar days of the date the decision of the [*insert designated official*] is mailed to you. The arbitrator will consider all of your claims and has the power to reinstate you to your job, with or without backpay, and to award any relief available in a court of law.

The company will pay the costs of arbitration if you elect to arbitrate your case. Also, you may be represented by an attorney at any step in the appeal procedure. However, your attorney's fees are your responsibility.

The foregoing is only a summary of the Termination Appeal Procedure. A copy of the full procedure is available at any time upon request from your unit manager or from the Human Resources Department. If you have any questions about this procedure or your rights under it, contact the [*insert designated official*].

The Termination Appeal Procedure affords you substantial rights. If you believe that you have a good reason to challenge the decision to terminate your employment, you must use the Termination Appeal Procedure. This procedure is intended to be an exclusive, final, and binding method to resolve all claims arising out of an employee's termination from employment. If you do not use this procedure, you may be precluded from pursuing any legal rights you may have in court or in other forums.

EMPLOYEE PROBLEMS AND COMPLAINTS

Despite the best efforts and good intentions of both employees and their supervisors, circumstances sometimes occur as a result of misunderstandings, differences of opinion, or interpretation of a policy or procedure. Many times these kinds of problems can only be resolved after the facts and circumstances are reviewed by higher levels of management.

Step 1:

Whenever you have a problem or complaint, please discuss it with your immediate supervisor. Your supervisor will investigate the situation, make a determination, and give you an answer as soon as practicable, usually within five working days.

Step 2:

If you are not satisfied with the supervisor's answer or disposition of the matter you should contact the Store Manager or his representative within five working days and request further consideration of the problem. At this point, the employee shall prepare in written form a statement of this problem together with the desired remedy or correction expected of the company and the decision rendered by the employee's supervisor. Personnel will provide you assistance, if desired, in the preparation and typing of the written statement.

Step 3:

If the employee is not satisfied with the decision of the Store Manager, the employee may present within five working days after the receipt of such a decision an appeal to the Human Resources Department. A personnel representative will provide assistance, if desired, in preparing and typing the Notice of Appeal and all documents pertinent to the proceedings and in distributing such notices and documents to the Human Resources Department.

Step 4:

A. Any and all disputes, controversies, or claims not settled in accordance with the foregoing procedures and arising out of or relating to this manual, your employment, or the termination of your employment shall be settled by arbitration before a board of three arbitrators. This provision shall apply to any and all such disputes, controversies, or claims whether asserted against the company and/or against any employee, officer, alleged agent, director, or affiliate of the company with regard to any matter arising out of your employment or the termination of your employment including, but not limited to, any claim relating to the purported validity, interpretation, enforceability, or breach of this manual or any purported employment agreement, and/or any other claim or controversy arising out of the relationship (or the nature of the relationship) or the commencement or termination of that relationship, including, but not limited to, claims for violation of a state or federal statute and/or for breach of covenant, breach of an implied covenant of good faith and fair dealing, wrongful termination, breach of contract, or intentional infliction of emotional distress, defamation, breach of right of privacy, interference with advantageous or contractual relations, conspiracy, or other tort claims of any kind.

One arbitrator shall be selected by the employee, one by the company, and the third by the two persons so selected, all in accordance with the labor arbitration rules of the American Arbitration Association then in effect. In the event that the arbitrator selected by the employee and the arbitrator selected by the company are unable to agree upon a third arbitrator, then the third arbitrator shall be selected from a list of seven provided by the office of the American Arbitration Association nearest to the employee's residence with the parties' striking names in order and the party striking first to be determined by the flip of a coin. Unless otherwise agreed by the parties the arbitrator must be an attorney admitted to practice in the state where the employee was most recently employed. The third, or neutral arbitrator, shall serve as chairman. The arbitration shall be held in a location to be mutually agreed upon by the parties. In the absence of agreement, the chairman shall determine the location.

B. In consideration of the parties' agreement to submit to arbitration all disputes with regard to this agreement and/or with regard to any alleged contract, tort, or any other claim arising out of their conduct, their relationship, and/or the commencement or termination of that relationship, and in further consideration of the anticipated expedition and the minimizing of expense of this arbitration remedy, the arbitration provisions of this agreement shall provide the exclusive remedy, and each party expressly waives any right he, she, or it might have to seek redress in any other forum.

C. Any claim that either party has against the other party that could be submitted for resolution pursuant to this paragraph must be presented in writing by the claiming party to the other within one year of the date the claiming party knew or should have known of the facts giving rise to the claim, except that claims arising out of or related to the termination of employment must be presented by the employee within 180 days of the date of termination. Unless the party against whom any claim is asserted waives the time limits set forth in the preceding, any claim not brought within the time periods specified shall be waived and forever barred.

D. In the event either party contends that the other party's actions are causing injury for which monetary damages would be inadequate, it may seek an injunctive order by submitting to the office of the American Arbitration Association nearest to the employee's residence an affidavit or declaration under penalty of perjury setting forth the facts giving rise to its claim. Said affidavit or declaration shall be served upon the other party personally or by Express Mail, Federal Express, or other comparable service, return receipt requested. If the parties or their designated arbitrators are not able to agree upon a neutral arbitrator within ten days, the American Arbitration Association is authorized to select a neutral arbitrator who shall hold a hearing within ten days of his or her selection. If each party has selected its own arbitrator by the time of the hearing, the hearing shall proceed as a tripartite proceeding. Otherwise the neutral arbitrator selected by the American Arbitration Association shall proceed as the sole arbitrator.

E. In the case of a termination, to the extent it is determined that the relationship created is other than at will, the company shall prevail to the extent permitted by law if a majority of the arbitration board finds that the company had a good faith belief that the employee had committed one or more of the acts or omissions that led to his discipline. The burden of proof shall at all times be upon the party seeking relief.

F. In determining any matter the board of arbitration shall apply all applicable federal, state, and local statutory and common law that is applicable to the dispute.

G. The expenses of the neutral arbitrator and of the transcript of any arbitration proceeding shall be divided equally between you and the company. Each party shall bear the expense of the arbitrator selected by it and of any witnesses it calls.

H. Any decision and award or order of the majority of the arbitrators shall be final and binding between the parties as to all claims that were or could have been raised in connection with the dispute to the full extent permitted by law. In all other cases, the parties agree that the decision of the board of arbitrators shall be a condition precedent to the institution or maintenance of any legal, equitable, administrative, or other formal proceeding by the employee in connection with the dispute, and that the decision and opinion of the board of arbitrators may be presented in any other forum on the merits of the dispute.

I. If any litigation is necessary to enforce the terms of this agreement, or if any legal action, even though prohibited, is brought with regard to this agreement, the prevailing party shall be entitled to reasonable attorney's fees in addition to any other relief to which it may be entitled.

J. In the event that one or more of the provisions contained herein should for any reason be held to be unlawful or unenforceable, such unlawfulness or unenforceability shall not affect any other provision, and the procedures set forth herein shall be construed as if such unenforceable or unlawful provision had not been contained herein.

OFFICE, MANAGEMENT, AND PROFESSIONAL EMPLOYEE TERMINATION APPEAL PROCEDURE

A. Purpose and Scope

In the event an eligible office, management, or professional employee (hereinafter "employee") has a complaint about his or her termination from employment, it will be resolved in accordance with this appeals procedure (hereafter "Termination Appeal Procedure" or "Procedure").

The Termination Appeal Procedure has been established to provide an exclusive, final, and binding method to resolve all claims, controversies, or complaints arising out of or relating to an employee's termination from employment by the company, including any claims or complaints based in whole or in part on federal, state, or local law, whether statutory or common law. For purposes of the Procedure, termination from employment shall mean an involuntary and permanent separation from employment by the company and shall include any actual or constructive dismissal, discharge, firing, or release.

Notwithstanding the preceding, decisions to terminate employment for business or economic reasons may not be challenged through the Termination Appeal Procedure. Decisions to terminate employment for business or economic reasons remain within the sole judgment and discretion of the company because such decisions result from factors relating to the operation of the business and not the performance or conduct of any particular employee. Termination from employment for business or economic reasons includes, but is not limited to, termination resulting from poor economic conditions, technological developments, subcontracting, use of overtime, operational changes, reorganization, elimination or transfer of operations, elimination or transfer of jobs, reductions in hours, or changes in job qualifications.

B. Eligibility

All full-time and regular part-time office, management, and professional employees who have completed ninety calendar days service with the company and who are not covered by a collective bargaining agreement shall have the right to use this Procedure.

C. <u>Steps</u>

Step 1: Internal Review. The first step in the Termination Appeal Procedure is a review by the [*insert designated official*] of the decision to terminate. An employee who has been terminated from employment, and who desires to challenge the termination, must submit a request for review of the termination to the [*insert designated official*] by completing Part 1 of the Termination Appeal Form provided by the company. Part 1 of the Termination Appeal Form must be fully completed and signed, must state every reason why the employee contests the termination, and must specify the relief sought by the employee. The Termination Appeal Form must be delivered to the [*insert designated official*] or must be postmarked within fourteen calendar days of the date of termination. The Termination Appeal Form can be obtained from the employee's unit manager or the Human Resources Department at P.O. Box______, Grand Rapids, Michigan 49______.

The [*insert designated official*], or his or her designee, will investigate the circumstances surrounding the termination and may meet with the employee, if it is deemed necessary, to discuss and/or attempt to resolve the employee's complaint. After investigating, the [*insert designated official*] will answer the employee's complaint on Part 2 of the Termination Appeal Form. The answer will be personally delivered or postmarked no later than thirty calendar days after the receipt of Part 1 of the Termination Appeal Form. If mailed, the answer will be mailed by certified mail, return receipt requested, to the address designated by the employee on the Termination Appeal Form.

Step 2: Arbitration. The second and final step in the Termination Appeal Procedure is arbitration. If the employee is not satisfied with the results of the review of the [*insert designated official*], the employee must elect to arbitrate the termination. The employee must give written notice to the [*insert designated official*] of the employee's election to arbitrate the termination by completing and signing Part 3 of the Termination Appeal Form. Part 3 of the Termination Appeal Form must be delivered to the [*insert designated official*] or must be postmarked no later than twenty-one calendar days after the date the results of the review were personally delivered or mailed to the employee.

If for any reason the employee does not receive a written answer from the [*insert designated official*] within thirty calendar days of the date Part 1 of the Termination Appeal Form was mailed or personally delivered to the [*insert designated official*] by the employee, the relief sought by the employee shall be deemed to have been denied. In that case, if the employee continues to desire to challenge the termination, the employee must give written notice to the [*insert designated official*] of the employee's election to arbitrate the termination. The written notice must be delivered to the [*insert designated official*] or must be postmarked no later than thirty-five days after the date the employee mailed or personally delivered Part 1 of the Termination Appeal Form.

Upon receipt of a timely notice of election to arbitrate, the company and the employee shall submit the case to arbitration in accordance with and subject to the following:

(a) The [*insert designated official*] will promptly deliver or mail a list of names of arbitrators to the employee. The list shall be comprised of the names of the arbitrators on one of the standing panels of arbitrators in use by the company and the collective bargaining representative for bargaining unit employees. The panel used shall be the panel in use for the unit or geographic region where the employee was last employed.

(b) Within fourteen calendar days of the date the list was mailed, the employee or the employee's representative must meet or confer at a mutually convenient place and time with the [*insert designated official*], or his or her designee, to choose an arbitrator from the list. In all cases the arbitrator selected to hear the case shall be an attorney. The arbitrator shall be chosen from the attorneys on the list by alternately striking names, the employee striking first, until only one name remains.

(c) Once an arbitrator has been chosen, the case shall be arbitrated in accordance with the Voluntary Labor Arbitration Rules of the American Arbitration Association, except as herein modified.

D. <u>Standards to be Applied by the Arbitrator</u>

The jurisdiction of the arbitrator shall be limited to complaints protesting termination from employment. The arbitrator shall determine whether the termination was lawful under applicable federal, state, and local statutory and common law and shall determine whether the company had just cause for termination. The company shall prevail to the extent permitted by law if the arbitrator finds the company, based on the nature of the employee's position and responsibilities and the company's lawful stated policies, had a good faith belief that the employee was involved in or committed one or more of the acts or omissions that led to his or her discharge. The burden of proof shall at all times be upon the party seeking relief. The arbitrator must consider and rule on every issue that was specified on the Termination Appeal Form or that was presented at the arbitration hearing and that was not resolved prior to arbitration.

In reaching a decision, the arbitrator shall interpret, apply, and be bound by any applicable company handbooks, rules, policies, and procedures and by any applicable federal, state, or local law. The arbitrator shall have no authority, however, to add to, detract from, change, amend, or modify any law, handbook, rule, policy, or procedure in any respect. Nor shall the arbitrator have authority to consider or decide any matters that are the sole responsibility of the company in the management and conduct of its business.

E. Form of Award

The arbitrator shall submit to the parties a written award signed by the arbitrator. The award shall specify the elements of and basis for any monetary award. The award shall be accompanied by a written opinion signed by the arbitrator that shall include findings of fact and, where appropriate, conclusions of law.

F. Relief

If the arbitrator finds that the employee violated any lawful company rule, policy, or procedure established by the company as just cause for termination, and finds that the employee was terminated for that violation, the employee's termination must be upheld and the arbitrator shall have no power to reduce the termination to some lesser disciplinary action.

If the arbitrator finds that the employee was unlawfully or unjustly terminated, the arbitrator may grant any remedy or relief that a court of competent jurisdiction could grant. However, in no event shall the arbitrator award relief greater than that sought by the employee.

If the arbitrator finds that the employee was unlawfully or unjustly terminated and finds that reinstatement would be appropriate under the circumstances, the arbitrator shall order the company to either offer the employee reinstatement to a position comparable to the one previously held by the employee or, to pay up to two years frontpay in lieu of reinstatement, reduced to present value, in addition to any severance pay to which the employee is entitled.

In any award of backpay, the arbitrator shall deduct any lawful setoffs, including but not limited to setoffs for unemployment compensation benefits, for the employee's interim earnings, for any other sums paid in lieu of employment during the period after discharge, and for any amount attributable to a proven failure by the employee to mitigate the damages.

G. Costs

The arbitrator's fees and expenses shall be borne fully by the company, except that fees incurred as a result of any postponement shall be borne by the party causing the postponement of the hearing.

H. Transcript of Proceedings

Either party may request that a transcript be made of the arbitration proceedings. The party requesting the transcript shall bear the full cost of the transcript, unless the other party also requests a copy of the transcript, in which event the parties shall divide the cost equally.

I. Witnesses

An employee who is called as a witness shall not suffer loss of pay for the time spent in the arbitration hearing when the hearing is held during the employee's regular work schedule. The expenses of any nonemployee witness shall be borne by the party calling the witness.

J. Representation

Either party may be represented by an attorney or other representative at any step in the Termination Appeal Procedure.

K. Attorney Fees

Neither party shall be liable for the payment of expenses or fees charged to the other party by any attorney or other representative who assists the party or participates in any way in the Termination Appeal Procedure, except as may be appropriately awarded under applicable federal, state, or local law.

L. Discovery

The company will supply to the employee a copy of the employee's personnel file upon written request. At least fourteen days prior to the hearing, the parties shall exchange a list of witnesses to be called with a brief summary of the subject matter of each witness's testimony. The arbitrator may authorize further discovery consistent with both the need to provide a full and fair consideration of the relevant and material facts of the case and the need to provide a relatively inexpensive and expeditious method to resolve the parties' dispute.

M. Time Limits

The time limits contained herein may be extended only by the mutual written agreement of the parties. Failure of the employee to meet the time limits, or agreed upon extensions, for filing a request for review, electing arbitration, or meeting to choose an arbitrator shall be deemed to be a binding agreement by the employee to settle all of the employee's claims in accordance with the latest decision of the company and shall constitute a failure to exhaust the Termination Appeal Procedure.

N. Exclusive Remedy, Effect of Arbitration, and Condition Precedent

The Termination Appeal Procedure is intended to be the sole and exclusive remedy and forum for all claims arising out of or relating to an employee's termination from employment and the decision and award of the arbitrator is intended to be final and binding between the parties as to all claims arising out of or relating to an employee's termination from employment that were or could have been raised at any step in the Termination Appeal Procedure. The decision and award of the arbitrator is also intended to be enforceable in any court of competent jurisdiction.

In the event a court of competent jurisdiction should determine that the Termination Appeal Procedure is not the sole and exclusive remedy and forum for some or all of an employee's claims and/or that the decision and award of the arbitrator, if any, is not final and binding between the parties as to some or all of the employee's claims, it is intended that exhaustion of the Termination Appeal Procedure be a condition precedent to the institution or maintenance of any legal, equitable, administrative, or other formal proceeding by an employee for all claims arising out of or relating to the employee's termination from employment.

"*XYZ*" TERMINATION APPEAL—PART 1
PLEASE PRINT

EMPLOYEE'S NAME: __________ TELEPHONE: (__________)
UNIT # ______________________________
ADDRESS:

____

Street City State Zip
POSITION: ______ STATUS (full time or part time): __________

____

DATE OF HIRE: ________ DATE OF TERMINATION: ________

REQUEST FOR REVIEW OF TERMINATION

I hereby request a review of my termination from employment in accordance with the Company's Termination Appeal Procedure. I have read and understood the provisions of that procedure, including the time limits. I understand that in order for the Company to investigate and attempt to resolve my complaint it is necessary for me to fully disclose all of the facts and reasons I believe my termination was unlawful and/or without just cause and to identify all persons with knowledge relevant to my claims. I have fully disclosed below all such facts, reasons, and persons. (Attach additional paper if necessary).

X X X X

1. Do you believe you were terminated without just cause? ______ Yes ______ No

If yes, please explain in detail why you believe your employment was terminated without just cause:

____

____

____

____

2. Do you believe you were discriminated against? ______ Yes ______ No

If yes, please explain in detail why you believe you were discriminated against and state the basis for the alleged discrimination (e.g., race, color, national origin, sex, age, religion, marital status, handicap, height, weight, veteran status, or other):

____

____

____

____

Do you believe you were retaliated against? ______Yes ______No

If yes, please explain why you believe you were retaliated against and identify the activity you believe resulted in retaliation (e.g., filing a claim for workers' disability compensation, making complaints to a federal, state, or local agency, or other activity):

____

____

____

____

SETTLEMENT DESIRED:

____

____

____

____

Employee's Signature: ____________________ Date: _____________

THIS FORM MUST BE FULLY COMPLETED AND MUST BE SENT TO THE [*INSERT DESIGNATED OFFICIAL*] AT P.O. BOX _______, GRAND RAPIDS, MICHIGAN 49______. IT MUST BE RECEIVED OR POSTMARKED NO LATER THAN FOURTEEN DAYS AFTER THE DATE OF TERMINATION. RETAIN A COPY FOR YOUR FILE. THE RESULTS OF THE COMPANY'S REVIEW WILL BE MAILED TO YOU WITHIN THIRTY DAYS AFTER RECEIPT OF PART 1 OF THIS FORM.

TERMINATION APPEAL—PART 2

ASSOCIATE'S NAME:____________ TELEPHONE: (________)
UNIT # ____
ADDRESS:

____

Street	City	State	Zip

RESULTS OF REVIEW

I have reviewed the circumstances surrounding your termination and have found that ____

____

____

____

____

____

____

____

____

____

[*insert designated official's title*] (Date)

If you do not agree with the results of this review, you may request an arbitration hearing by completing Part 3 below.

"XYZ" TERMINATION APPEAL—PART 3
REQUEST FOR ARBITRATION HEARING

I do not agree with the results of the [*insert designated official*] review of my termination. I request that my case be submitted to arbitration in accordance with the company's Termination Appeal Procedure. I agree to accept the decision and award of the arbitrator as final and binding as to all claims relating to my employment relationship with the company that have been or could have been raised at any step in the Termination Appeal Procedure. I understand that all costs associated with the arbitration will be borne by the company except for the cost of any transcripts, legal fees, witness expenses, or hearing postponements on my behalf.

____

(Employee's Signature) (Date)

IN ORDER TO ELECT ARBITRATION, THIS FORM WITH PART 3 COMPLETED MUST BE SENT TO THE HUMAN RESOURCES DEPARTMENT AT P.O. BOX _______, GRAND RAPIDS, MICHIGAN 49______, AND MUST BE RECEIVED OR POSTMARKED NO LATER THAN FOURTEEN DAYS AFTER THE RESULTS OF THE REVIEW WERE PERSONALLY DELIVERED OR MAILED TO YOU. RETAIN A COPY FOR YOUR FILE. UPON RECEIPT OF THIS FORM, THE COMPANY WILL CONTACT YOU TO ARRANGE FOR THE SELECTION OF AN ARBITRATOR.

GRIEVANCE PROCEDURE

I. PURPOSE

The purpose of this grievance procedure is to ensure that all employees are provided due process and treated fairly and consistently in the application and administration of ____________ policies and procedures. It provides the employees of ____________ with a formal procedure for the prompt and equitable resolution of grievances that might arise out of misunderstanding or misapplication of current company policies or procedures. It is intended to be the exclusive remedy for all disputes that are covered.

II. SCOPE

This policy applies to all grievances by factory hourly, factory incentive, office hourly, and salaried nonexempt employees employed by the company at its ____________ locations. It does not apply to grievances by those employees defined as "exempt" by the Fair Labor Standards Act of 1938 as amended.

III. RESPONSIBILITY.

This procedure is to be administered by the employees of ____________ for the employees of ____________ in accordance with the procedure outlined herein.

The immediate supervisor is responsible for the first step in the procedure, the department manager is responsible for the second step, and members of the grievance committee for the third step.

The manager of Human Resources will serve as an advisor and mediator to the grievant, the management representatives, and the grievance committee as they carry out their respective responsibilities.

IV. DEFINITIONS

A. Grievance

A grievance is any dispute as to the meaning or application of company policy contained in the policy and procedure manual or employee handbook. It includes, but is not limited to, any dispute involving discipline, discharge, alleged harassment, or alleged discrimination.

B. Masculine Pronoun.

For ease of reading the masculine pronoun "he" will be used when referring to "he" or "she."

V. STEPS

There are three steps in the grievance procedure. A grievance shall be entered and processed in the following manner:

A. First step.

1. Unless the grievance involves termination of employment, the first step is a meeting between the employee and his immediate department supervisor.

2. The request for a meeting must be made within ten days after the employee knows or has reason to know of the grievance.

3. After discussion of the issue, the supervisor will provide the employee a verbal answer within five working days.

B. Second Step.

1. If the employee is not satisfied with the answer provided by his immediate supervisor, the next step is to put the grievance in writing and present it to the department manager. If the grievance involves termination of employment this will be the first step in the grievance procedure. The written grievance shall be submitted on a standard grievance form. Such forms can be obtained from the employee's immediate supervisor or the Human Resources Department.

2. A grievance to be considered in Step two must be submitted to the department manager within five working days of receipt of the supervisor's first step reply. If the grievance involves termination the grievance must be submitted to the department manager within thirty days after the date of termination.

3. After submission of the forms to the department manager, a meeting will be held with the department manager and the

employee. If practical, this meeting should be scheduled by the department manager within five working days after receipt of the grievance.

4. The employee has the option of taking a fellow employee to the meeting.

5. The manager of Human Resources may be invited to attend the meeting by either the department manager or the grievant. The manager of Human Resources will act as an advisor and a mediator and facilitate the resolution of the problem.

6. In his role as advisor and mediator, the Human Resources Manager may call anyone with knowledge of problem into the meeting.

7. The department manager will provide a written reply to the grievance within ten working days after the Step two meeting.

C. Third step.

1. If the employee is not satisfied with the answer received from the department manager, the next step is to contact the Human Resources Department and request that the grievance be submitted to the grievance committee. This must be done within five days after the employee receives the written reply from the department manager. All forms will be held in sealed envelopes and forwarded to the chairman of the grievance committee.

2. Upon receipt of the grievance the grievance committee will conduct an investigation and hearing in accordance with the procedures set forth in Section VII(E) of this grievance procedure.

3. After such investigation and hearing, the committee will vote on the grievance and will issue a written decision stating the reasons for the decision.

4. Within fourteen working days after the date of the committee's decision, either party may request a reconsideration of the decision. Any such request must be in writing, specifying the reasons for the request. If there is no request for reconsideration the committee's decision will become final and binding.

5. If there is a request for reconsideration the committee may, in its discretion, reopen the matter and hear additional evidence or arguments. Upon reconsideration the committee will either reaffirm, reverse, or modify its original decision, and that decision will become final and binding. There will be no further reconsideration.

D. Time limits.

If the grievant fails to meet any of the time limits specified in this procedure the grievance will be considered abandoned and the grievant will forfeit his right to pursue it further.

VI. AUTHORITY

The grievance committee will have authority to determine whether a written policy or procedure has been violated and grant or deny the grievance on the basis of such determination. The committee may grant relief as may be appropriate to compensate the grievant for any actual losses suffered by him, including reinstatement and back pay. Should the committee determine that back pay is appropriate, the effective date of such back pay shall be no earlier than the date the grievance was submitted in writing to the department manager.

In reviewing individual cases, the committee will be fair to the employee as well as the company by weighing all the facts before arriving at a conclusion. Each grievance will be heard on the merits of the case and not on the personalities involved.

The committee shall have no authority to make new policy, add, detract, or in any way modify existing policies or procedures. Nor does the existence and activity of the committee in any way restrict the right of the company to amend or eliminate current policies or establish new policies and procedures at its discretion.

VII. ORGANIZATION AND OPERATION OF THE GRIEVANCE COMMITTEE

A. Membership

1. The grievance committee will be comprised of seven regular members and two alternates.

2. Representation will be as follows:

a. Factory, hourly, and incentive—five members, one alternate.

b. Office, hourly, and nonexempt salary—two members, one alternate.

B. Elections

1. All members of the grievance committee will be elected by the employees.

2. The grievance committee will establish the rules and procedures for election.

3. Members may not seek re-election to the grievance committee for one year after serving on the committee.

4. The chairman and secretary of the grievance committee will be elected by the committee members annually.

C. Alternates

1. There will be two alternates selected to replace absent committee members.

2. If a committee member is laid off the alternate with the highest vote count will fill the seat on the committee.

3. Alternates may enter into discussions but cannot be assigned to do investigations.

D. Voting

1. Decisions will be made by a majority vote of the committee members who are present.

2. Alternates may not vote unless they are replacing an absent member.

3. The chairman will vote only in the event of a tie.

E. Meetings and Hearings

1. The committee will meet biweekly, provided that there is business to discuss.

2. The chairman of the committee may at any time schedule an emergency meeting if he deems it necessary.

3. When a grievance is received by the committee it will be distributed and reviewed by the committee members.

4. After the committee has reviewed the grievance, the committee will schedule a hearing on the grievance and will invite the grievant and the department manager to attend.

5. The notice of hearing will be in writing and will include the following information:

(1) Time and place of the hearing

(2) Issues to be decided

6. The committee will try to give as much notice as is practical so that both parties will have an opportunity to prepare. If either party needs additional time to prepare, or cannot attend the scheduled hearing for any other reason, an adjournment may be requested.

7. Hearing notices may be delivered by any means, including hand delivery, company mail, or U.S. mail. A record should be kept as to the means of delivery and the date of delivery.

8. At the outset of the hearing the grievant will be advised of his rights. Both parties will then be asked to identify their representatives, witnesses, and written evidence, if any.

9. Both parties will be given the opportunity to present evidence and arguments in their favor. The grievant will present his evidence and arguments first. The department manager will then present his evidence and arguments. The grievant will then have an opportunity to respond.

10. Either party may have a representative at the hearing provided that the representative is an employee of the company.

11. Each party will be given an opportunity to review any written evidence presented by the other party. Each party will also be given the opportunity to hear any witnesses or arguments presented by the other party, provided that there is no objection from any witness. If a witness objects to the presence of any party, that party will be excused from the meeting while the witness is testifying. After the witness has testified, the party who was asked to leave the meeting will be invited back to the meet-

ing, will be advised of what the witness said, and will be given an opportunity to respond.

12. Both parties will be limited to two witnesses, not including the grievant and the department manager. If either party requests an opportunity to present additional witnesses, or it appears to the committee that additional witnesses should be questioned, the committee may request that such witnesses attend the hearing or a subsequent hearing. Both parties will be given notice of any such hearing and will be given an opportunity to hear the testimony of any such witnesses, in accordance with the guidelines stated above.

13. Neither party will be allowed to interrupt the other party while he is presenting his case. Nor will any party be allowed to interrupt a witness while he is testifying. When a party is through presenting his case the other party will be given an opportunity to respond. When a witness is through testifying, each party will be given an opportunity to respond to what the witness said and will be allowed to ask questions, but only through the grievance committee.

14. When both sides have completed their presentations the committee will either make its decision or will table the grievance for further investigation and/or consideration.

15. Between meetings the committee may conduct its own investigation. If any such investigation is done, the committee will report the results of such investigation to the parties and will allow them an opportunity to respond.

16. After the committee has voted on the grievance, the committee will issue a written decision, and will provide a copy of that decision to the parties. The written decision will state that the grievance is granted or denied, will state what corrective action is required, and will state the reasons for the decision. If the grievance is granted the committee will specify the policy or procedure that was violated.

17. In addition to its decision on the grievance, the committee may make recommendations to the Human Resources Department. Those recommendations will be considered by the Human Resources Department but shall not be final and binding on either party.

18. The committee will keep minutes of all meetings and hearings. The minutes will include information as to what grievances were considered, members present, parties present, witnesses present, written evidence presented, and action taken.

19. If there is a request for reconsideration the foregoing procedures will apply. Generally, the committee will not change or modify a prior decision unless a party shows that the decision was clearly wrong or presents new evidence or new arguments that were not previously presented. Any request for reconsideration must be in writing and must state the reasons for the request.

VIII. NOTICE

Copies of this grievance procedure will be distributed to employees and posted in the plant for a reasonable period following its effective date. Copies will also be available through the Human Resources Department.

NOTICE OF HEARING

TO: ______________________________
Grievant

____
Department Manager

RE: Grievance No. _____________________

This is to advise you that a hearing will be held on the above-referenced grievance before the grievance committee. The hearing will take place at ________________. The meeting will take place on _______________, 19____ at ___________ a.m./p.m. The purpose of this hearing is to decide the issues raised by the grievance.

You have a right to be represented at the hearing by a co-employee. You also have the right to present up to two witnesses and any other evidence or arguments in favor of your grievance. You should bring any such witnesses and evidence with you.

The hearing will be conducted in accordance with the grievance procedure. Your rights are more fully spelled out in that procedure. If you would like to review or receive a copy of the procedure prior to the hearing, please contact the Human Resources Department.

Signed: ______________________ Dated: _________________________

This notice should be mailed or delivered to the parties no less than five working days prior to the date of the hearing.

STATEMENT OF RIGHTS

1. I understand that I have the right to have my grievance heard by the grievance committee.

2. I understand that the decision of the grievance committee will be final and binding.

3. I understand that the purpose of the grievance hearing is to decide the issues raised by my grievance.

4. I understand that I have the right to present witnesses, evidence, and arguments in support of my grievance.

5. I understand that I have a right to respond to any witnesses, evidence, or arguments that are offered against my grievance.

6. I understand that I have a right to representation by a co-employee.

7. I understand that the hearing will be conducted in a fair and impartial manner and that the decision will be made in accordance with the procedures set forth in the grievance procedure.

8. I understand that I have a right to review the grievance procedure.

Signed: ______________________ Dated: ______________________
Grievant

MINUTES

Date: ______________________________
Time: ______________________________
Place: _____________________________
Members Present: ____
____
____

1. Grievance # _______________________

Appearances

(1) For the grievant: ____
____
____
____

(2) For the company: _______________________________________
____
____
____

Written evidence presented:

(1) For the grievant: ____
____
____
____

(2) For the company: _______________________________________
____
____
____

Summary: ____
____
____
____

Disposition: ____
____
____
____

GRIEVANCE FORM

This form is to be used for grievances under the grievance procedure. If the grievance does not involve termination of employment, step one must be completed. If the grievance involves termination of employment, proceed directly to Step two.

STEP 1. (To be completed by the employee).

This grievance was first discussed with my immediate supervisor on ____________ ____, 19____.

My supervisor responded to this grievance on ____________ ____, 19____.

STEP 2. (To be completed by employee).

My grievance is as follows. (Please summarize your grievance, providing as much information and detail as possible): ________
____
____
____
____

I believe that the following policy or procedure has been violated. (Please specify the policy in the policy and procedure manual or the employee handbook that you believe was violated): ________
____
____
____
____

The adjustment or action that I am requesting to be made is as follows. (Please state the specific relief you are requesting): __
____
____
____
____

(To be completed by the Department Manager).

I received this grievance on ____________ ____, 19____.

I met with the employee to discuss this grievance on ____________ ____, 19____.

My response to the grievance is as follows: ______________________
____
____
____
____

______________________________ ______________________________
Department Manager Date

STEP 3. (To be completed by the employee).

I received the department manager's response to my grievance on ____________ ____, 19____.

Check one:

_____ The grievance has been resolved to my satisfaction and I do not wish to pursue it further.

_____ I would like to have a hearing before the grievance committee.

______________________________ ______________________________
Grievant Dated

Note to employee: If you wish to have a hearing before the grievance committee you must submit this form to the Human Resources Department no later than five working days after you receive the Department Manager's response to your grievance.

DECISION OF THE GRIEVANCE COMMITTEE

Grievance # ___________

Decision: The grievance is granted. ___
The grievance is denied. ___

Reasons: ____
____
____
____

Corrective action to be taken: ____________________________
____
____
____

Recommendations: ___________________________________
____
____
____

Date of Decision: ___________________________________

_______________________ _______________________

Secretary Chairman

Note to parties: If you disagree with the foregoing decision you have a right to request reconsideration. Any such request must be made in writing within fourteen days after the date of the decision. The request for reconsideration must be in writing and must specify the reasons for the request. Generally, the grievance committee will not change or modify a decision unless one of the parties shows that a clear mistake was made or presents additional evidence or arguments that were not considered by the committee.

Distribution:

Grievant
Department Manager
HRD
Grievance file

EMPLOYEE ACKNOWLEDGMENT

I hereby acknowledge receipt of the Company Handbook and agree that I will immediately become familiar with its contents. I also understand that no employee or representative of the company is authorized to enter into any agreement of employment for any specified period of time or to make any agreement contrary to the provisions of this handbook or any other company policy except by written authorization signed by the President.

I further understand that all disputes of any nature or manner whatsoever, including those that relate in any way to my employment or the termination of my employment, all as more fully described in the handbook, shall be resolved exclusively in accordance with the Employee Problems and Complaints Section of the handbook, which includes binding, neutral arbitration as a final step.

Dated: ____________________ ______________________________

Appendixes

Appendix A

Employment Applications

Appendix A

FORM DISCLAIMERS FOR JOB APPLICATION

Example 1

In consideration of my employment, I agree to conform to the rules and regulations of XYZ Company, and my employment and compensation can be terminated with or without cause and with or without notice at any time at the option of either the Company or myself. I understand that no store manager or representative of XYZ Company other than the president or vice president of the Company has any authority to enter into any agreement for employment for any specified period of time or to make any agreement contrary to the foregoing.

____
[Employee Name]

Example 2

Michigan law requires that we have you read and acknowledge the following:

As an employee of XYZ Company, you have the right to terminate your employment at any time. XYZ Company retains the same right, regardless of any other documents or oral or written statements issued by XYZ Company or its representatives.

____
[Employee Name]

Appendix A

Herein Called The Company

An Equal Opportunity Employer

Application For Employment

Last Name	First Name	Middle Initial	Date

Appendix A

APPLICATION FOR EMPLOYMENT

We Are An Equal Opportunity Employer

This Company supports Federal, State and local laws prohibiting discrimination based on race, sex, color, religion, national origin, ancestry, age, handicap, veteran or marital status. No question on this application is intended to secure information to be used for such purposes.

PERSONAL DATA

Name, Last	First	Middle	Social Security Number
Home Address			Zip Code
Home Telephone Number ( )	Are you under age 18?* ☐ Yes		
Have you ever been employed by the Corporation or its subsidiaries? ☐ Yes ☐ No	If yes give dates, Company and location.		
How were you referred to us?	What type of position are you applying for?		Salary Expectations
☐ Full Time ☐ Permanent ☐ Part Time ☐ Temporary	Geographical Preference		
Are you legally eligible for employment in this country?* ☐ Yes ☐ No			

EDUCATION

Type of School	Name and Address of School	Major Subjects	Did you Graduate?
High School			☐ Yes ☐ No
College or University			☐ Yes ☐ No Degree Receive
Graduate School			☐ Yes ☐ No Degree Receive
Other			☐ Yes ☐ No Degree Receive

Now attending - Please indicate type of school and/or program. ______________________

*Proof of age, eligibility for employment and permanent address will be required after employment.

Appendix A

EMPLOYMENT RECORD Start with your present or last position, include experience in the military service

Employer's Name And Address	May we contact your present employer? ☐ Yes ☐ No	
	DATES EMPLOYED From | To	Position/Title
	SALARY Start | Final	Name and Title of Supervisor
	Duties and Responsibilities	
Telephone Number ( )	Reason for Leaving	
	DATES EMPLOYED From | To	Position/Title
	SALARY Start | Final	Name and Title of Supervisor
	Duties and Responsibilities	
Telephone Number ( )	Reason for Leaving	
	DATES EMPLOYED From | To	Position/Title
	SALARY Start | Final	Name and Title of Supervisor
	Duties and Responsibilities	
Telephone Number ( )	Reason for Leaving	
	DATES EMPLOYED From | To	Position/Title
	SALARY Start | Final	Name and Title of Supervisor
	Duties and Responsibilities	
Telephone Number ( )	Reason for Leaving	

ADDITIONAL INFORMATION Do not supply information which would tend to identify you on the basis of race, sex, national origin, color, age, religion, handicap or marital status.

Please indicate any job related information you believe would be helpful to us.

____

____

Please list all office skills, typing, steno, knowledge of office machines, special qualifications or licenses.

____

____

____

If you were unemployed during any period since leaving school, please explain.

____

____

Appendix A

1. I certify that the statements made in this application are true and correct to the best of my knowledge and that a deliberate falsification will be considered sufficient cause for my dismissal upon discovery thereof. I hereby authorize Company to which I have applied (hereinafter "the Company") to investigate all the statements contained herein. I a authorize the companies, schools, and persons named herein to give any information relevant to my bona fide empl ment qualifications to the Company. I hereby release said companies, schools, and persons and the Company from a and all liability and responsibility arising out of the release or receipt of such information.
2. I understand that an investigative consumer report may be requested by the Company in connection with my employm I further understand that upon reasonable written request, I will be informed whether a consumer report was reques and if requested, the name and address of the consumer reporting agency which furnished the report.
3. Should the position for which I have applied require the issuance of a fidelity bond, I understand that the denial of issua of such a bond for any reason related to my qualifications for employment shall be grounds for termination of my emp ment. I further understand that upon reasonable written request, I may obtain complete and accurate disclosure of reasons for the denial of a fidelity bond.
4. All members of management are dedicated to ensuring that all applicants and employees are treated fairly. Howe understand and agree neither this application nor any other communication by a management representative either wri or oral, made at the time of hire or during the course of employment is intended to create an employment contract f definite duration unless specifically approved in writing by the Corporate Senior Vice President of Human Resources.

If employed, I agree to abide by the company's rules and regulations. Further, I understand that my employment is not f stated period.

Date ______________________ Signed ______________________________
Full Name of Applicant

STATE OF MARYLAND USE ONLY

"UNDER MARYLAND LAW AN EMPLOYER MAY NOT REQUIRE OR DEMAND ANY APPLICANT FOR EMPLOYME OR PROSPECTIVE EMPLOYMENT OR ANY EMPLOYEE TO SUBMIT TO OR TAKE POLYGRAPH, LIE DETECTOR SIMILAR TEST OR EXAMINATION AS A CONDITION OF EMPLOYMENT OR CONTINUED EMPLOYMENT.A EMPLOYER WHO VIOLATES THIS PROVISION IS GUILTY OF A MISDEMEANOR AND SUBJECT TO A FINE NOT TO CEED $100."

Noted ______________________________
Signature of Applicant

THE SUBMISSION OF THIS INFORMATION IS VOLUNTARY

This Company has an Affirmative Action Plan to employ qualified handicapped individuals, qualified disabled Veterans and Veterans of the Vietnam Era.

If you wish to be included in the program please check the appropriate box(es) below.

☐ I am handicapped ☐ I am a disabled Veteran ☐ I am a Veteran of the Vietnam era.

Noted ______________________________
Signature of Applicant

HUMAN RESOURCES DEPARTMENT USE ONLY

Job Title	Job Code	Salary Grade	Annual Salary	Date On Payroll
Department Name/Company		Location (City & State)		Conversion C

APPROVALS

By ______________________________ Title ______________________

By ______________________________ Title ______________________

By ______________________________ Title ______________________
Human Resources

Appendix A

DATE ____________________

LAST NAME ____________ FIRST NAME ____________ MIDDLE INITIAL

STREET ____________ CITY

STATE ____________ ZIP CODE

( ) TELEPHONE NUMBER ____________ SOCIAL SECURITY NO.

IS AN AFFIRMATIVE ACTION EMPLOYER AND IT IS OUR POLICY TO AFFORD EQUAL OPPORTUNITY TO ALL EMPLOYEES AND APPLICANTS. WE COMPLY WITH ALL FEDERAL, STATE AND LOCAL REGULATIONS AS THEY PERTAIN TO AFFIRMATIVE ACTION AND EQUAL EMPLOYMENT OPPORTUNITY.

IR-27-S 4/85

Appendix A

Position Desired ____________ Preferred Salary Range ______ to ______ Date Available ______

What prompted your application to ? *(Please be specific)* ____________

Indicate prior application to if within last 12 months. Date ______ Location ______

Name and relationship of relatives employed by ____________

EDUCATION *(circle highest level completed)*

GRADE SCHOOL	HIGH SCHOOL	COLLEGE	GRADUATE SCHOOL
1 2 3 4 5 6 7 8	1 2 3 4	1 2 3 4	1 2 3 4

EDUCATION OTHER THAN HIGH SCHOOL	LOCATION (CITY & STATE)	COURSE OF STUDY OR MAJOR	FROM MO./YR.	TO MO./YR.	DEGREE OR CERTIFICATE

Other training you have received *(special courses, etc.)* ____________

Special qualifications and skills ____________

Other information or outside experience you wish considered ____________

PERSONAL

Are you under 18? ______ Are you over 70? ______

Are you in the country on a visa which would not permit you to work here? ______

(If you are hired, you may be required to provide proof of age or resident status).

Have you ever been convicted of a criminal offense? ______ If yes, explain: ______

A conviction does not automatically mean you cannot be hired. What you were convicted of and how long ago are important. Give all of the facts so that a decision can be made.

Appendix A

EMPLOYMENT RECORD – *(Start with your present or last job.)*

EMPLOYER	EMPLOYED: FROM MO/YR — TO MO/YR	YOUR RESPONSIBILITIES:
STREET		
CITY — STATE	BASE SALARY (WK/MO/YR)*: FIRST — LAST	
YOUR TITLE		
NAME & TITLE OF SUPERVISOR	OTHER COMPENSATION	
REASON FOR LEAVING	TELEPHONE NO.-IF KNOWN	

MAY WE CONTACT YOUR PRESENT EMPLOYER Yes ☐ No ☐

EMPLOYER	EMPLOYED: FROM MO/YR — TO MO/YR	YOUR RESPONSIBILITIES:
STREET		
CITY — STATE	BASE SALARY (WK/MO/YR)*: FIRST — LAST	
YOUR TITLE		
NAME & TITLE OF SUPERVISOR	OTHER COMPENSATION	
REASON FOR LEAVING	TELEPHONE NO.-IF KNOWN	

EMPLOYER	EMPLOYED: FROM MO/YR — TO MO/YR	YOUR RESPONSIBILITIES:
STREET		
CITY — STATE	BASE SALARY (WK/MO/YR)*: FIRST — LAST	
YOUR TITLE		
NAME & TITLE OF SUPERVISOR	OTHER COMPENSATION	
REASON FOR LEAVING	TELEPHONE NO.-IF KNOWN	

ADDITIONAL EMPLOYMENT

NAME AND ADDRESS OF EMPLOYER	FROM	TO	JOB TITLE	REASON FOR LEAVING

Brief description of U. S. military experience: ______________________________

____

Appendix A

takes affirmative action to employ and advance in employment qualified handicapped individuals and disabled veterans and Vietnam era veterans.

Are you a Vietnam era veteran (from August 5, 1964 through May 7, 1975)? __________ Yes __________ No

Are you a disabled veteran? __________ Yes __________ No

Do you have or have you had a physical or mental disability which you think might prevent you from performing the the job for which you are applying? ☐ Yes ☐ No If "Yes", please explain. *(If your answer is "Yes" be advised that your response will be within the protection of the National Rehabilitation Act of 1973, as amended).*

STATEMENT OF APPLICANT *(PLEASE READ CAREFULLY)*

In applying for employment I want to be fully informed of my previous record and I hereby authorize to investigate my background and to obtain any and all information which may concern me. I hereby release all persons, schools, companies, corporations, credit bureaus and law enforcement agencies from any liability on account of furnishing such information.

I fully understand that: If employed, any misrepresentation of facts on this application is sufficient cause for dismissal; and any offer of employment will be subject to my passing a medical examination* and to satisfactory reference checks. In addition I understand that nothing contained in this employment application, or in the granting of or conducting of an interview, is intended to create an employment contract between and myself either for employment or for the providing of any benefit. No promises regarding employment or duration of employment have been made to me and I understand that no such promises or guarantees are binding upon unless made in writing by the President of the Corporation. If an employment relationship is established, I understand that I have the right to terminate my employment at any time and that retains a similar right, with or without cause.

DATE: ______________ SIGNATURE: ______________________________

(APPLICANT: *DO NOT WRITE BELOW THIS LINE*)

INTERVIEWED BY	DATE	REFERRED TO:	DATE
REFERRED TO	DATE	REFERRED TO:	DATE
REFERRED TO:	DATE	REFERRED TO:	DATE

**Results subject to superseding effects of National Rehabilitation Act of 1973, as amended.*
(Affirmative Action for the Handicapped)

Appendix A

Date

Name LAST FIRST MIDDLE

APPLICATION FOR EMPLOYMENT

IS AN EQUAL OPPORTUNITY EMPLOYER and fully subscribes to the principles of Equal Employment Opportunity. has adopted an Affirmative Action Program to ensure that all applicants and employees are considered for hire, promotion and job status, without regard to race, color, religion, sex, age, national origin, handicap or status as a disabled veteran or veteran of the Vietnam Era.

NOTE: This application will be considered active for 90 days. If you have not been employed within this period and are still interested in employment at please contact the office where you applied and request that your application be reactivated.

Appendix A

Personal Data

Print Name in full ______ (Last) (First) (Middle) Social Security Number ______

Home address ______ (Street) (City) (State) (Zip Code) Telephone ______

Temporary Address ______ (Street) (City) (State) (Zip Code) Telephone ______

If hired, can you furnish proof of age? ☐ YES ☐ NO Licensed to drive car? ☐ Yes ☐ No Is license valid in this State? ☐ Yes ☐ No
(Answer only if position for which you are applying requires driving.)

If hired, can you furnish proof you are legally entitled to work in U.S. ☐ YES ☐ NO

Have you ever been employed by ? ☐ Yes ☐ No If so, when and where last employed? ______ Position ______

Are any of your relatives employed by ? ☐ No ☐ Yes If so, in which unit(s) are they employed? ______

Type of position desired? ______ Date available for work ______ State salary you will consider ______

Are you willing to relocate? ______ What initial location would you prefer? ______

Have you been convicted of a felony involving life or property during the past seven years? ☐ No ☐ Yes

If yes; explain. ______

______

Physical Data

A PHYSICAL OR MENTAL DISABILITY WILL NOT CAUSE REJECTION IF IN MEDICAL OPINION YOU ARE ABLE TO SATISFACTORILY PERFORM IN THE POSITION FOR WHICH YOU ARE BEING CONSIDERED.

Do you have any physical condition which may limit your ability to perform the job applied for? If so, please give details. ______

______

______ Do you have any Service related disability? ☐ YES ☐ NO

To protect the interests of all concerned, applicants for certain job assignments must pass a physical examination before they are hired. Alternative placement of an applicant who does not meet the physical standards of the job for which he/she was originally considered is permitted.

Education

	No. of Years	Name of School	City and State	Course or College Major	Average Grades	Did you Graduate?	Type of Degree
Senior High School							
College							
Graduate Studies							
Other—Give Type							

Military Service

Branch of Service	Service-Related Skills and Experience Applicable to Civilian Employment

Activities

Professional Organizations ______

What are your hobbies or special interests? ______

Experience

Please give a detailed account of your previous experience and training. Specify the type of work done and the type of work you would prefer to do. If more space is needed, continue on a supplementary page.

______

______

Appendix A

RECORD OF EMPLOYMENT AND REFERENCES

LIST BELOW YOUR FOUR MOST RECENT EMPLOYERS, BEGINNING WITH THE CURRENT OR MOST RECENT ONE. IF YOU HAVE HAD LESS THAN FOUR EMPLOYERS, USE THE REMAINING SPACES FOR PERSONAL REFERENCES. IF YOU WERE EMPLOYED UNDER A MAIDEN OR OTHER NAME, PLEASE ENTER THAT NAME IN THE RIGHT HAND MARGIN. IF APPLICABLE, ENTER SERVICE IN THE ARMED FORCES ON THE REVERSE SIDE.

☐ It is not satisfactory to contact my present employer. ☐ It is satisfactory to contact my present employer.

1

NOTE: State reason for and length of inactivity between present application date and last employer.			Nature of Employer's Business	Name of your Supervisor
Name				
Address		Tel. No.		
City	State	Zip Code		

What kind of work did you do?	Starting Date	Starting Pay	Date of Leaving	Pay at Leaving	Why did you leave? Give details
	Month Year	$ ☐ Mo. ☐ Wk. ☐ Hr.	Month Year	$ ☐ Mo. ☐ Wk. ☐ Hr.	

2

NOTE: State reason for and length of inactivity between last employer and second last employer.			Nature of Employer's Business	Name of your Supervisor
Name				
Address		Tel. No.		
City	State	Zip Code		

What kind of work did you do?	Starting Date	Starting Pay	Date of Leaving	Pay at Leaving	Why did you leave? Give details
	Month Year	$ ☐ Mo. ☐ Wk. ☐ Hr.	Month Year	$ ☐ Mo. ☐ Wk. ☐ Hr.	

3

NOTE: State reason for and length of inactivity between second last employer and third last employer.			Nature of Employer's Business	Name of your Supervisor
Name				
Address		Tel. No.		
City	State	Zip Code		

What kind of work did you do?	Starting Date	Starting Pay	Date of Leaving	Pay at Leaving	Why did you leave? Give details
	Month Year	$ ☐ Mo. ☐ Wk. ☐ Hr.	Month Year	$ ☐ Mo. ☐ Wk. ☐ Hr.	

4

NOTE: State reason for and length of inactivity between third last employer and fourth last employer.			Nature of Employer's Business	Name of your Supervisor
Name				
Address		Tel. No.		
City	State	Zip Code		

What kind of work did you do?	Starting Date	Starting Pay	Date of Leaving	Pay at Leaving	Why did you leave? Give details
	Month Year	$ ☐ Mo. ☐ Wk. ☐ Hr.	Month Year	$ ☐ Mo. ☐ Wk. ☐ Hr.	

I certify that the information contained in this application is correct to the best of my knowledge and understand that any misstatement or omission of information is grounds for dismissal in accordance with policy. I authorize the references listed above to give you any and all information concerning my previous employment and any pertinent information they may have, personal or otherwise, and release all parties from all liability for any damage that may result from furnishing same to you. In consideration of my employment, I agree to conform to the rules and regulations of and my employment and compensation can be terminated with or without cause and with or without notice, at any time, at the option of either the Company or myself. I understand that no unit manager or representative of other than the President or Vice-President of the Company, has any authority to enter into any agreement for employment for any specified period of time, or to make any agreement contrary to the foregoing. In some states, the law requires that have my written permission before obtaining consumer reports on me, and I hereby authorize to obtain such reports.

Appendix A

NOT TO BE FILLED OUT BY APPLICANT

Additional Information Resulting from Interview

Signature of Interviewer

Date

Date of Emp.		Job Grade	
Dept. or Div.		Compensation Arrangement	
Job Title		Manager Approving	
Job Title Code		Employe No.	

Tested				(Enter dates as required.)	Mailed	Comple
Physical examination scheduled for				REFERENCE REQUESTS		
Physical examination form completed				CONSUMER REPORT		
				With. Tax (W-4)		
				State With. Tax		
Review Card prepared		Minor's Work Permit		Store/Pers. Rec. Card		
Tickler Card prepared		Proof of Birth		Earnings Rec.		
Timecard prepared		Training Material Given to Employe				

Appendix A

APPLICATION FOR EMPLOYMENT

PLEASE PRINT INFORMATION REQUESTED IN INK.

Date ____________

IS AN EQUAL OPPORTUNITY EMPLOYER and fully subscribes to the principles of Equal Employment Opportunity. has adopted an Affirmative Action Program to ensure that all applicants and employes are considered for hire, promotion and job status, without regard to race, color, religion, sex, national origin, age or handicap.

To protect the interests of all concerned, applicants for certain job assignments must pass a physical examination before they are hired. Alternative placement of an applicant who does not meet the physical standards of the job for which he/she was originally considered is permitted.

NOTE: This application will be considered active for 90 days. If you have not been employed within this period and are still interested in employment at please contact the office where you applied and request that your application be reactivated.

Name ____________ Last First Middle   Social Security Number ____________ (Please present your Social Security Card for review.)

Address ____________ Number Street City State Zip Code

County ____________   Current phone or nearest phone ____________

Previous Address ____________ Number Street City State Zip Code

(Answer only if position for which you are applying requires driving.)

If hired, can you furnish proof of: Age? ☐ Yes ☐ No   U.S. Citizen? ☐ Yes ☐ No   Licensed to drive car? ☐ YES ☐ NO

or Alien legally entitled to work in U.S. ☐ Yes ☐ No   Is license valid in this state? ☐ YES ☐ NO

Have you ever been employed by ? ☐ YES ☐ NO   If so, when and where last employed? ____________ Position ____________

Have you a relative in the employ of in the store or unit to which you are applying? ____________

A PHYSICAL OR MENTAL DISABILITY WILL NOT CAUSE REJECTION IF IN MEDICAL OPINION YOU ARE ABLE TO SATISFACTORILY PERFORM IN THE POSITION FOR WHICH YOU ARE BEING CONSIDERED.

Do you have any physical or mental impairment which may limit your ability to perform the job for which you are applying? ____________

____________ Do you have any Service related disability? ☐ Yes ☐ No

EDUCATION	School Attended	No. of Years	Name of School	City/State	Graduate?	Course or College Major	Average Grades
	Grammar						
	Jr. High						
	Sr. High						
	Other						
	College					Degree	

MILITARY SERVICE	BRANCH OF SERVICE	DATE ENTERED SERVICE	DATE OF DISCHARGE	HIGHEST RANK HELD	SERVICE-RELATED SKILLS AND EXPERIENCE APPLICABLE TO CIVILIAN EMPLOYMENT

What experience or training have you had other than your work experience, military service and education? (Community activities, hobbies, etc.)

I am interested in the type of work I have checked:

Sales ____ Office ____ Mechanical ____ Warehouse ____ Other (Specify) ____________

Or the following specific Job ____________

I am seeking (check only one):

☐ Temporary
☐ Permanent
Employment

If temporary, Indicate dates available ____________.

I am available for (check only one):

☐ Part-Time
☐ Full-Time
Work

If part-time, indicate maximum hours per week ________, and enter hours available in block to the right.

HOURS AVAILABLE FOR WORK	
Sun	To
Mon	To
Tues	To
Wed	To
Thurs	To
Fri	To
Sat	To

Have you been convicted during the past seven years of a serious crime involving a person's life or property?

NO ☐ YES ☐ If yes, explain ____________

10534 Rev. 1-81

(SEE REVERSE SIDE)

REFERENCES

LIST BELOW YOUR FOUR MOST RECENT EMPLOYERS, BEGINNING WITH THE CURRENT OR MOST RECENT ONE. IF YOU HAVE HAD LESS THAN FOUR EMPLOYERS, USE THE REMAINING SPACES FOR PERSONAL REFERENCES. IF YOU WERE EMPLOYED UNDER A MAIDEN OR OTHER NAME, PLEASE ENTER THAT NAME IN THE RIGHT HAND MARGIN. IF APPLICABLE, ENTER SERVICE IN THE ARMED FORCES ON THE REVERSE SIDE.

	NAMES AND ADDRESSES OF FORMER EMPLOYERS, BEGINNING WITH THE CURRENT OR MOST RECENT	Nature of Employer's Business	Name of your Supervisor	What kind of work did you do?	Starting Date	Starting Pay	Date of Leaving	Pay at Leaving	Why did you leave? Give details
	NOTE State reason for and length of inactivity between present application date and last employer								
1	Name Address Tel. No. City State Zip Code				Month Year	Per Week	Month Year	Per Week	
	NOTE State reason for and length of inactivity between last employer and second last employer								
2	Name Address Tel. No. City State Zip Code				Month Year	Per Week	Month Year	Per Week	
	NOTE State reason for and length of inactivity between second last employer and third last employer.								
3	Name Address Tel. No. City State Zip Code				Month Year	Per Week	Month Year	Per Week	
	NOTE State reason for and length of inactivity between third last employer and fourth last employer.								
4	Name Address Tel. No. City State Zip Code				Month Year	Per Week	Month Year	Per Week	

I certify that the information contained in this application is correct to the best of my knowledge and understand that any misstatement or omission of information is grounds for dismissal in accordance with policy. I authorize the references listed above to give you any and all information concerning my previous employment and any pertinent information they may have, personal or otherwise, and release all parties from all liability for any damage that may result from furnishing same to you. In consideration of my employment, I agree to conform to the rules and regulations of , and my employment and compensation can be terminated with or without cause, and with or without notice, at any time, at the option of either the Company or myself. I understand that no unit manager or representative of other than the President or Vice-President of the Company, has any authority to enter into any agreement for employment for any specified period of time, or to make any agreement contrary to the foregoing. In some states, the law requires that have my written permission before obtaining consumer reports on me, and I hereby authorize to obtain such reports.

Applicant's Signature ____________________

NOT TO BE FILLED OUT BY APPLICANT

INTERVIEWER'S COMMENTS			Tested				(Store will enter dates as required.)	Mailed	Completed
	Date of Emp.		Physical examination scheduled for				REFERENCE REQUESTS		
	Dept. or Div.	Regular ☐ Part-Time ☐	Physical examination form completed				CONSUMER REPORT		
	Job Title						With. Tax (W-4)		
	Job Title Code	Job Grade					State With. Tax		
	Compensation Arrangement		Review Card prepared		Minor's Work Permit				
			Timecard prepared		Proof of Birth				
Prospect for	Manager Approving				Training Material Given to Employe				

Have you filed previous Application for Employment with ______ facility? ☐ Yes ☐ No Where ______ When ______

Have you ever worked for ______? ☐ Yes ☐ No Where ______ When ______

Employment depends upon a matching of your physical and mental condition and jobs available. If you have a physical or mental impairment and wish to identify yourself as a handicapped individual or a disabled veteran, please check this block ☐ Do you use drugs not prescribed by a licensed physician or practitioner who is authorized to prescribe drugs? ☐ Yes ☐ No

REFERENCES

List at least two references (do not include relatives or former employers)

NAME	ADDRESS	POSITION	COMPANY OR ORGANIZATION

WORK EXPERIENCE

Use this space to give a brief description of work experience, kind of work desired and reason for kind of work desired. Also, list any activities which are pertinent to the kind of work you are seeking and which would be useful to in assessing your qualifications.

I understand that in the event my application for employment is accepted, the effective date of acceptance and of my employment shall be the time I actually commence work. If I am employed I agree to comply with and be bound by the safety and patent rules and other rules and regulations of the company. I further understand that, if employed, my employment will be subject to the conditions of any applicable probationary period established by labor agreement or company policy. If required, I agree to submit to a prehiring medical examination and periodic medical examinations thereafter. I agree to be photographed and fingerprinted. I agree, if I am presently bound by any agreement with any former employer(s) not to reveal trade secrets or proprietary or other information to other employers, that I will disclose such agreement(s) to representatives before accepting an offer of employment with I authorize investigation of all statements contained in this application and do hereby release any and all persons, companies, or agencies responding to such investigation from any liability for any damage due to releasing information pertaining hereto. I understand that any information that I may have provided herein concerning my status as a handicapped individual will be held confidential, except as may be necessary, if I am employed, to inform my supervisor of necessary accommodations or work restrictions. I further understand that misrepresentation or omission of facts called for on this application is cause for rejection of this application or for subsequent dismissal from employment.

An Equal Opportunity Employer

Signature ______

Applications will be active for 60 days and can be renewed in person or by written request for one additional 60 day period.

Federal Law and Certain State Laws Prohibit Discrimination Because of Age, Race, Color, Religion, Sex, National Origin, Physical or Mental Handicaps.

02.000.0682 REV. 5-78 CAT. #6025.00

APPLICATION FOR EMPLOYMENT

FOR COMPANY USE ONLY

PERSONAL

LAST NAME	FIRST NAME	MIDDLE NAME	SOCIAL SECURITY NO.	BIRTH DATE (Month / Day / Year)	DATE OF APPLICATION	DATE OF RENEWAL (For Company Use Only)

STREET ADDRESS	CITY	STATE	ZIP CODE	TELEPHONE	If not a Citizen, what type of Visa do you hold?	Have you ever been convicted of a felony by a Civil or Military Authority? ☐ Yes ☐ No
Permanent						
Temporary						

WORK PREFERENCE

TYPE OF EMPLOYMENT YOU WANT	KIND OF WORK DESIRED	Indicate preference or restriction regarding work location:	Employment availability:	Date available for work
☐ Permanent ☐ Part-Time ☐ Summer	☐ Production ☐ Maintenance ☐ Technician ☐ Office & Clerical ☐ Other ____		Work shifts? ☐ Yes ☐ No Days of week ☐ All ☐ Other	

List any trades, professional certificates, job licenses and special skills

To be Completed by Applicants for Clerical Positions

Can you type?	W.P.M.	Can you write shorthand?	W.P.M.	Can you keypunch?	S.P.H.
☐ Yes ☐ No		☐ Yes ☐ No		☐ Yes ☐ No	

(LIST MOST RECENT EMPLOYMENT FIRST – INCLUDE FORMER EMPLOYMENT, SELF-EMPLOYMENT AND MILITARY SERVICE)

EMPLOYMENT

NAME OF EMPLOYER (Circle number of any employer whom you do not wish us to contact)	ADDRESS OF EMPLOYER (Include Number, City, State & Zip Code)	DATES From Mo./Year	DATES To Mo./Year	NAME AND TITLE OF IMMEDIATE SUPERVISOR	YOUR JOB TITLE AND RATE OF PAY	REASON FOR LEAVING
1.						
2.						
3.						
4.						
5.						
6.						

If not Graduated from High School, Circle Highest Grade Completed 1 2 3 4 5 6 7 8 9 10 11

EDUCATION

	NAME OF SCHOOL	ADDRESS OF SCHOOL	DATES ATTENDED Mo./Yr. To Mo./Yr.	DATE GRADUATED Month	DATE GRADUATED Year	DEGREE RECEIVED	FIELD OF STUDY	GRADE POINT AVG.	GRADE BASIS
High							1. Major 2. Minor	1. Major 2. Minor	A =
Other							1. 2.	1. 2.	
Other							1. 2.	1. 2.	Lowest Passing =
							1.	1.	

Appendix B

Employment and Placement Policies and Procedures

Appendix B

EMPLOYMENT

I. POLICY

A. New employees will be selected and present employees will be promoted strictly on the basis of the individual's qualifications to meet the needs of the organization. Each Department Head will determine these qualifications, and the Personnel Department will provide the professional guidance needed to see that they are met. The qualifications include ability, attitude, experience, education, character, physical fitness and potential for advancement as they pertain to each position. There shall be no discrimination, either in initial hiring or in subsequent promoting, because of marital status, military obligation, handicap, race, religion, color, national origin, sex or age.

B. The Company believes that its present employees should receive first consideration for any position that becomes available, provided that they have the necessary qualifications. In this way, employees will have the opportunity to progress to more responsible or to more satisfying work.

C. Filling Position Vacancies

1. Position vacancies will be filled in the following sequence:

a. Promotion
b. Job Posting and/or Internal Search
c. New Hire

II. PROMOTION

A supervisor who has a position open may promote or transfer a subordinate directly into that vacancy.

III. <u>JOB POSTING</u>

A. Purpose

The Purpose of the internal posting system is to provide opportunities for the domestic employees who are qualified to bid for available openings. The job posting procedure is a vehicle which serves to fill vacant positions quickly and at low cost. It also supports the Company's commitment to promotion from within.

B. Policy Statement

Any supervisor unable to fill a job opening from within will utilize the intercompany job posting procedure before seeking candidates from outside sources. Employees are to be given primary consideration in filling job openings prior to exerting outside search efforts.

1. Non-Exempt Vacancies

à. All non-exempt vacancies will be posted intercompany, with the exception of those vacancies which can be filled via promotion or transfer.

b. Non-exempt positions will be posted for one week prior to seeking outside candidates.

2. Exempt Vacancies

a. All exempt vacancies level 9 through 13 will be posted intercompany on a regional basis, with the exception of those vacancies which can be filled via promotion or transfer. Positions, level 14 and above, will be covered by our Internal Search policy. (See Section IV)

b. Exempt positions will be posted for two weeks before seeking outside candidates.

C. Procedure

1. No vacancy will be posted without proper written authorization, Salaried Personnel Requisition (Form #48-236). Exempt authorizations will be coordinated by the Corporate Internal Search Department and the non-exempt authorizations by the Personnel Department.

2. All job openings are then edited for posting on the bulletin boards and are listed by company with level designation, job title, reporting relationship and brief job description.

3. Both non-exempt and posted exempt positions will be displayed on company bulletin boards which are strategically located at each affiliate. Posting procedures should be displayed for the employees' review throughout the year.

   a. Non-exempt postings are distributed weekly.

   b. Exempt postings are distributed twice a month.

4. Information pertaining to the job opening may be obtained by calling the Personnel Department at the location at which the vacancy exists.

5. Formal bids should be placed by the employee's immediate supervisor to the Personnel Department which in turn will contact the Personnel Department where the vacancy exists.

6. All related personnel information or data sheets should be forwarded to the Personnel Department wherein the opening exists prior to the arranged interview whenever possible.

7. The two personnel departments will then coordinate the sequence of interviews, i.e. the employee may interview with their respective personnel departments, the searching personnel department and finally the hiring supervisor. It should be noted, however, that only those employees deemed qualified will be referred to the hiring supervisor.

8. At no time should a selection be made until all candidates have been considered. It is the responsibility of the hiring supervisor to notify the personnel department of the decision.

9. Candidates not selected should be informed in writing, within a reasonable amount of time, by either the hiring supervisor or the personnel representative in the searching company and a duplicate letter should be sent to the personnel department which referred the candidate.

IV. INTERNAL SEARCH FOR MANAGERIAL PERSONNEL

A. Policy

It is the policy of   to offer promotional opportunities to qualified employees of the Corporation before seeking outside candidates for those opportunities. The Management Skills Inventory System is designed to assist managers in the implementation of that policy.

B. Procedure

1. General

Any department unable to fill a managerial position (Level 14 and above) with a qualified candidate from within its own ranks, will have the Corporate Internal Search Department make an internal search among the other Companies. Only if such a search fails to produce a qualified candidate will the Company seek candidates outside the Family of Companies to fill the vacancy.

2. Companies Requesting Internal Search

   A Department Head seeking candidates within the Family of Companies will forward a completed Management Search Request (Form #48-227) to the Manager, Corporate Personnel Search. The notification describes the qualifications required of a candidate for the position to be filled. Forms are available in the Personnel Department.

3. Internal Search

   Corporate Internal Search will search the Management Skills Inventory System and related sources for candidates who possess the desired qualifications. A slate of qualified candidates is presented, with corresponding Management Skills profiles, to the requesting manager with a carbon copy to the personnel manager.

4. Selection

   a. The searching Department Head reviews the information referred, selects candidates to be actively considered and requests the Corporate Internal Search office to secure permission to arrange interviews. There should be no direct contact between the searching Department Head and the candidates until this clearance is obtained.

   b. When a selection has been made, the searching Department Head must notify the candidate's present supervisor of the conditions of the offer.

5. Notification of Selection

When an offer has been extended to and accepted by a candidate, the Personnel Department will inform all other individuals who were interviewed. Corporate Internal Search should be kept informed of developments in the process.

6. Dislocation of Management Personnel

Managerial personnel who become displaced due to reductions in force and/or reorganizations should be immediately brought to the attention of Corporate Internal Search in order that qualified individuals may be placed internally wherever possible.

V. <u>TIMING ON TRANSFERS</u>

A. All non-exempt job transfers should be effected in two weeks' time and will be accomplished within a maximum of three weeks' time from the date of actual selection unless other arrangements are made which are mutually acceptable to the areas concerned.

B. All exempt level job transfers should be effected in four weeks' time and will be made within a maximum of six weeks' time from the date of actual selection unless another time span has been mutually agreed upon by the areas concerned.

VI. <u>NEW HIRES</u>

A. New employees will be hired to fill position vacancies once it has been determined that no properly qualified employee can be found within the Company through promotion, job posting or the Corporate Internal Search Department.

B. No job applicant will be discriminated against, in any manner, because of pregnancy.

C. Procedure for New Hires

1. Supervisors will send a Salaried Personnel Requisition, (Form #48-236) to the Personnel Department including a description of the job and the personal skills required.

2. The Personnel Department will use whatever media are necessary to obtain qualified applicants, including its own standby files, college placement bureaus, newspaper advertisements or employment agencies.

3. Applicants will be interviewed first by the Personnel Department.

4. Qualified applicants will be interviewed by the supervisor who has the vacancy and will be informed that a background check of previous employers and academic institutions will be made.

5. The supervisor, assisted by the information obtained from the Personnel Department, will choose the best qualified applicant.

6. The supervisor will notify the Personnel Department of the candidate selected, as well as the specifics of the anticipated offer, and will not communicate with the applicant directly.

7. The Personnel Department will schedule all Pre-Employment Physical Examinations for the candidate selected with the Medical Department. The Medical Department will notify Personnel of the applicant's medical classification together with its recommendation.

8. An offer may be extended by the Personnel Department contingent upon the satisfactory completion of a medical examination conducted to determine whether the potential employee is medically able to perform the functions of the respective position. The potential employee should be informed of this in the offer letter.

9. The Personnel Department will notify the applicant of acceptance after all conditions of employment have been met. It will also notify the accepted applicant that they are required to attend the next regularly scheduled "Benefit Enrollment/Orientation Session".

10. The Personnel Department will notify all rejected applicants of their status in writing.

Appendix B

PERSONNEL POLICY & PROCEDURES

TITLE	POLICY NO.	
EMPLOYMENT & PLACEMENT	E1	
	EFFECTIVE DATE	PAGE
	8/1/80	1 of 3

SCOPE

All employees of

POLICY

It is the policy of   to provide equal opportunity for all people without regard to race, color, creed, national origin, ancestry, sex, age, marital status, religion, or handicap with respect to employment, or in any of the Company's terms or conditions of employment. In addition, physical or mental limitations will not be a factor in the application of Company employment policies or employee practices, except for those situations in which occupational requirements make consideration of such factors necessary.

Recruitment and Placement

Vacant positions will be filled by transfer from within the Company whenever possible. In cases where an affirmative action goal has been established, qualified outside applicants may be considered along with inside candidates.

1. Jobs of 700 Hay points and above.

   a. Employees from all Divisions and Areas of the Company shall be considered on the basis of their qualifications. No vacancies in this category shall be filled from inside or outside the Company until all appropriate sites are contacted by the Corporate Director of Employment and all internally-recommended candidates are fully considered.

   b. If it is determined that there are no well qualified internal candidates, outside recruiting requires the prior concurrence of the Vice President - Human Resources for positions in the 700 - 1090 Hay point range, and concurrence of the Chairman and Chief Executive Officer for positions at 1091 or more Hay points.

   c. Final candidate selection and placement into positions from 700 through 1090 Hay points will be in accordance with Corporate Grants of Authority. Final candidate selection and placement into positions of 1091 or more Hay points requires approval of the Chairman and Chief Executive Officer.

2. Jobs of 450 to 699 Hay points - Candidates from the site having the vacancy will be considered first for these positions. If no well qualified candidates are available at the site, Personnel Relations representatives may review the possibility of candidates at other locations, prior to filling the position from outside the Company.

3. Jobs under 450 Hay points - These positions will normally be filled on the site or from outside the Company.

Minimum Age

The Company will comply with all applicable laws and regulations covering employment.

Authorized Employments

No person shall be employed for a position which has not been duly authorized by the appropriate levels of management, normally defined as the immediate supervisor plus the next higher level of supervision.

G-1180-G

PERSONNEL POLICY & PROCEDURE

POLICY NO.	EFFECTIVE DATE	PAGE	TITLE
E1	8/1/80	2 of 3	EMPLOYMENT & PLACEMENT (Cont'd)

Employment of Relatives

Applicants who are close relatives of employees may be employed and assigned to positions throughout the Company, except that such employees may not be placed in positions in which their supervisor is an employee-relative. Close relatives of officers of the Company are not eligible for employment.

A "close relative" for the purpose of this policy is a relative or relative-in-law of a relationship of nephew (niece) or closer kin. Generally, a "close relative" includes: spouse, child, parent or legal guardian, brother or sister-related by blood, half-blood, or marriage.

Salary Action

Salaries and hourly rates for new or transferred employees shall be established in accordance with the Salary Administration Policy, applicable local wage schedule, or with the wages in effect in the applicable collective bargaining agreement.

Salaries for part-time employees shall be established on a proportionate basis, as described in the Compensation Policy.

Effective Date of Employment

Salaried employees who start work on the first working day of a monthly or semi-monthly payroll period shall be considered employed from the first calendar day of the period. The effective day of employment for unorganized hourly employees shall be the first actual working day. The effective day of employment for organized employees shall be governed by the applicable collective bargaining agreement.

Conditions of Employment

All employees shall be required to execute a standard document which defines the conditions of employment which a new employee agrees to accept when he/she joins
The appropriate Personnel Office shall see that this document is executed in duplicate. One copy of the executed document shall be included in the employee's personnel folder; the second copy is provided to the new employee for future reference.

Physical Examination

Each new employee shall be required to complete successfully a physical examination prior to acceptance by the Company. The Company may request employees to submit to physical examinations from time to time when conditions indicate. Employees may request physical examinations where adequate site medical facilities are available.

Definitions

1. An employment is defined as an action by which an individual not presently employed by the Company is added to the Company's payroll as a regular, part-time, temporary or casual employee.

2. A regular employee is one who is employed on a scheduled basis for a normal work week and who is not classified as part-time, temporary or casual.

3. A part-time employee is one who is employed on a scheduled basis for less than either 20 hours per week or 86.7 hours per month.

PERSONNEL POLICY & PROCEDURES

TITLE	POLICY NO.	
EMPLOYMENT & PLACEMENT (Cont'd)	E1	
	EFFECTIVE DATE	PAGE
	8/1/80	3 of 3

4. A temporary employee is one who is hired for a specific position for a designated length of time which is normally not more than twelve consecutive months in duration and who is committed to leave the Company at the end of that time. Temporary employees who are retained by a Division or Area beyond the twelve month period must thereafter be reclassified as a regular employee.

5. A casual employee is a person who may be called by the Company at any time for employment on a non-scheduled and non-recurring basis, and who becomes an employee of the Company only after reporting for work, and only for the period of time during which he or she is working. The utilization of a casual employee shall normally be limited to not more than 15 consecutive work days and not more than 60 work days in any calendar year. The appropriate Personnel Director or Manager shall approve each person classified as a casual employee, and any exceptions to the above restrictions on work days.

Employment and Placement Procedures

1. All Employment Requisition Forms shall be forwarded to the appropriate Personnel Office prior to the recruitment of the employee. Before forwarding the form, the immediate supervisor shall ascertain that the vacancy is properly authorized and that the position description, job specifications, and job evaluation are current.

2. The immediate supervisor is responsible for preparing and forwarding to the appropriate Personnel Office a Personnel Profile Form to reclassify a temporary employee as a regular employee when the period of employment exceeds the twelve consecutive months as stated in the definition of a temporary employee.

3. Supervisors of employees being considered for promotion into other departments should not refuse to allow an employee to be interviewed without a very strong reason. Such a refusal should be agreed to by at least two levels of supervision, with concurrence by the division Director of Personnel.

4. Sites may elect to use a job opportunity (posting program) to supplement normal screening procedures.

Post-Employment Follow Up

It is in the best interests of the Company and the employee that an early determination be made of an employee's future with the Company. Thus, supervisors should, not later than six months after employment, formally evaluate the new employee's performance. If at that time the supervisor cannot safely state the individual is fully satisfactory, the situation should be discussed with Personnel Relations.

G-1180-G

Appendix C

Performance Appraisals

Appendix C

Headquarters Offices
Non-Exempt Employe Performance Appraisal

Information and Instructions for Completion

I. General Information about the Appraisal Program

A. Purpose and Importance
The purpose of the Headquarters Non-Exempt Performance Appraisal Program is to provide a means for objective evaluation of the competency and effectiveness demonstrated by individual employes in performance of position responsibilities.

The Non-Exempt Performance Appraisal Program is a significant aid in a number of areas of the employment relationship, including: (1) most importantly, employe training and development; (2) compensation decisions; and (3) substantiation and documentation of personnel actions.

B. Types of Performance Appraisals
Performance appraisals are usually of four types:

Probationary-new hire--Normally, two appraisals are conducted within the six-month probationary period. Recommended times are approximately six weeks after employment and at completion of fifth month in position.

Qualifying-after promotion--Two appraisals are conducted for employes advanced within a department or into a department during the first six months in new position. Recommended times are the same as those for new hires.

Regular--Annual review of all employes during established appraisal period.

Other--Special circumstances. May include occasions when performance falls below employe's normal competency or when employe has outstanding achievement in work performance.

C. Performance Appraisal Problems
Behavioral science research and experience show that the following are the most common errors made by appraising supervisors:

Central Tendency--complete all appraisal forms approximately the same for all employes.

Leniency Tendency--say only "good" things about everyone.

Halo Effect--the observer remembers something effective or ineffective about a person's performance and allows this to influence the appraisal of other performance factors.

Errors such as these are counterproductive in terms of employe development and performance improvement, and may result in legal situations where the Corporation cannot substantiate personnel decisions.

D. Appraisal Procedure
The immediate supervisor of the employe whose performance is being reviewed is responsible for filling out the form and for discussing the appraisal with the employe. When the appraisal is completed and the form has been signed by the supervisor and employe, the immediate supervisor should review the appraisal and form with the next-level supervisor within the department, to obtain his/her concurrence and signature. The final review is made by the Personnel Relations Representative, who, after signing the form, will place a copy of the appraisal in the Employe Record Envelope.

Although not the standard procedure, the supervisor may at his/her discretion request the employe to conduct a self-appraisal. Also discretionary is a situation where more than one supervisor (to whom the employe regularly provides assistance) independently evaluates the performance of the employe. In either case, it is the responsibility of the administrative supervisor to prepare and conduct the official performance appraisal.

Appendix C

II. Instructions for Filling Out Appraisal Form

A. Preparation

Prior to beginning the evaluation form, review personnel records of the employe to be sure that you have all the facts about the individual which will contribute to a thorough review. These records include, but are not limited to: Personal History and Service Record or Payroll Personnel Data form, Attendance Record, and previous performance evaluations.

It will also be necessary to review the established Headquarters Position Description for the position occupied by the employe. The Position Description should be particularly helpful in preparation for discussion with the employe of Section I of the appraisal form (Assignment and Duties) and in identifying required knowledge and skills to be noted and evaluated in Section II-A of the form (Position Knowledge and Skills). The functions, work procedures and duties listed on the Position Description may also be helpful in evaluating the other performance factors.

B. Filling out the Appraisal Form

1. **Heading**
   Complete all sections of the heading to furnish complete information about employe and type of review.

2. **Section I - Assignment and Duties**
   Discuss with employe at time of interview, so there is a clear, mutual understanding of the assigned duties and how this position supports departmental objectives. You may wish to show the Position Description to the employe during the interview, but should retain the description in departmental files.

3. **Section II - Effectiveness in Performing Position Responsibilities**
   This section includes five performance factors through which you as supervisor will evaluate employe effectiveness in the position. Consider each factor independently. In the space provided, write in specific representative examples of employe's performance which will help in your evaluation and in the employe's understanding of the rating. Refer to rating key definitions at the bottom of the form and determine level of performance for each factor. Indicate these ratings in right-hand columns of form. **Important**: Evaluations must be objective and based upon observations and results of employe's performance.

4. **Section III - Regularity of Attendance/Punctuality**
   This section requires prior review of employe's Attendance Record (form 4809) and of the reasons for any unusual absence from the office. Consider regularity in attendance and punctuality and what affect, if any, absences or tardiness have on ability to perform effectively in the position.

5. **Section IV - Overall Rating**
   This summary is your judgement of the rating level which most adequately describes employe's overall performance. It should be based upon consideration of the ratings of each of the individual performance factors previously determined.

6. **Section V - Supervisor's Comments**
   As a final step prior to the interview with the employe, enter here any comments or observations which will help clarify the review. Emphasis should be given to factors which contributed to or detracted from employe's overall performance.

7. **Sections VI and VII - Suggestions for Improvement and Action Plan for Improvement and Development**
   These two sections of the form are completed at the close of the performance appraisal interview with the employe, following discussion of the evaluation in Sections I-V. Based on your evaluation and discussion with the employe, offer positive suggestions for improvement of performance and plans for supervisory guidance in improvement and development. This section provides for active participation by the employe to assess strengths and weaknesses, offer suggestions for means of improvement and make his/her own plans for corrective or developmental action. The employe may enter his/her comments on the form if desired.

Appendix C

Headquarters Offices
Non-Exempt Employe Performance Appraisal

ne:			Soc. Sec. No.	Total Employ. Date:
partment:	Position Title:		Position No.:	Position Date:
e of this review:	Date of last review:		Review Period: From: To:	
pe of Review: Check one)	Probationary — (New Hire)	Qualifying — (After Promotion)	Regular	Other — (explain)

Assignment and Duties — Discussion between employe and supervisor of assigned duties, and how this position supports departmental objectives. Review of position description.

Effectiveness in Performing Position Responsibilities (Refer to definitions at bottom of form) PERFORMANCE FACTORS: O — Outstanding E — Excellent S — Satisfactory M — Marginal U — Unsatisfactory	Check One Below O	E	S	M	U
Position Knowledge and Skills — Degree of job knowledge and proficiency in specific, job-related skills as demonstrated by performance. (Refer to Position Description for required knowledge and skills) Specific Examples:					
Quality of Work — How well duties are performed. Degree of accuracy, completeness, neatness. Specific Examples:					
Quantity of Work — Volume of acceptable work performed. How employe meets work schedules. Degree to which new tasks are begun when assigned work has been completed. Specific Examples:					
Working with Others — Cooperation and effectiveness in working with supervisor, associates, and other business contacts. Response to instructions, requests, overtime work. Assistance or instructions provided to others. Specific Examples:					
Work Habits — Planning and organizing of work and finding new and better ways of performing duties. Care of workplace and equipment. Protection of Proprietary information. Observance of safety provisions. Specific Examples:					
Regularity of Attendance/Punctuality — Reliability with respect to attendance and punctuality. (Refer to employe Attendance Record)					

Overall Rating Based on Above:

Outstanding —☐
Accomplishments characterized by exceptionally high quality work, far exceeding normal requirements of position. Performed all tasks assigned and excelled in a substantial number.

Excellent —☐
Accomplishments are clearly above normal requirements. Performed all tasks assigned and excelled in performance of some.

Satisfactory —☐
Accomplishments meet normal requirements of position. Performed substantially all tasks assigned. Some improvement is possible and desirable.

Marginal —☐
Accomplishments meet some of normal requirements of position. Needs improvement in order to achieve normal standards of competency in the position.

Unsatisfactory —☐
Accomplishment is clearly below minimum requirements of position. Many tasks not performed. Improvement in performance is necessary for job retention.

Appendix C

Headquarters Offices
Non-Exempt Employe Performance Appraisal (Page 2)

V. Supervisor's Comments (Enter any remarks to further clarify this review)

VI. Suggestions for Improvement

Supervisor's	Employe's

VII. Action Plan for Improvement and Development

Supervisor's	Employe's

Signatures:

Appraising supervisor____________________ Date
(Name/Title)

Reviewing supervisor____________________ Date
(Name/Title)

Reviewing Personnel
Rels. Representative____________________ Date
(Name/Title)

*Employe

____

*Employe signature indicates only that appraisal has bee reviewed and discussed with employe. Not necessarily a reflection of agreement with evaluation.

Appendix C

Performance Management System
PMS – PA Form (C)

Name ______________________ (EMPLOYE)

Name ______________________ (MANAGER)

Position Title ______________________

Position Title ______________________

Social Security Number ______________________

Division/Location ______________________

Performance Period: From: ____________ To: ____________

PROCEDURE:

1. Employe prepares draft of Sections 1 and 2 and forwards a copy to his/her manager.
2. Manager and employe meet and reach an understanding on Job Elements and Objectives (Sections 1 and 2). PA Form is signed in Section 2 by both parties and a copy is provided to the employe.
3. Manager and employe periodically review progress toward Objectives and document progress in Section 3.
4. Manager and employe meet at end of the appraisal cycle for Final Objectives Review (Section 4) and discussion of overall performance level (Section 5.)
5. PA Form is signed by both parties and is forwarded for signature of next higher level manager (Business Unit option). A copy is given to the employe.

SECTION 1. JOB ELEMENTS – Use this space to list Job Elements, (duties, responsibilities) of your position. Try to keep the list between 4 and 8 Job Elements. Please number your Job Elements.

____

____

____

____

____

____

____

____

____

____

____

____

____

____

FORM 48335A

Appendix C

SECTION 2. PERFORMANCE PLANNING – Use this space to record your Objectives for the appraisal cycle. Review the Job Elements listed in Section 1 and write one or more Objectives for each. Indicate the relationships between Objectives and Job Elements by recording a Job Element number for each Objective. Once Objectives have been written indicate the level of importance (weighting) of each Objective by specifying a percentage which reflects its importance within the context of all objectives established. (Total should not exceed 100).

JOB ELEMENT #	DESCRIPTION OF OBJECTIVES	DUE DATE	LEVEL OF IMPORTANCE (%)
			TOTAL IMPORTANCE =

EMPLOYE'S SIGNATURE DATE

MANAGER'S SIGNATURE DA

Signatures certify both parties discussed and reached an understanding of the meaning of the Job Elements and Objectives listed in Sections 1 and 2.

Appendix C

SECTION 3. PERIODIC OBJECTIVES REVIEW –
Review the status of each Objective and summarize progress by using the following descriptions as well as other appropriate comments to substantiate the summary:
Achieved, Satisfactory Progress, Less Than Satisfactory Progress, or Objective Modified.

SECTION 4. FINAL OBJECTIVES REVIEW –
Review each Objective and indicate Level of Attainment:
Exceeds Objective (4); Met Objective (3); Below Objective (2); Well Below Objective (1). Substantiate levels with appropriate comments and complete mathematical calculations.

PERIODIC REVIEW COMMENTS	REVIEW DATE	LEVEL OF ATTAINMENT	FINAL REVIEW COMMENTS	PRODUCT IMPORTANCE X ATTAINMENT
				TOTAL PRODUCT =

Performance Level = Total Product / Total Importance = ______

Appendix C

SECTION 5. PERFORMANCE SUMMARY

Based on the calculations in Section 4, indicate which of the six levels of performance best reflects the employe's overall performance.

3.7 - 4.0 ☐ Performance consistently exceeds position requirements.

3.2 - 3.6 ☐ Performance meets and often exceeds position requirements.

2.5 - 3.1 ☐ Performance meets position requirements.

2.0 - 2.4 ☐ Performance meets some position requirements.

1.5 - 1.9 ☐ Performance seldom meets position requirements.

1.0 - 1.4 ☐ Performance fails to meet position requirements.

Summary Comments: ______________________________

____

____

____

____

____

____

____

____

Employe's Comments on Performance Evaluation: ______________________________

____

____

____

____

____

____

____

____

Signature does not necessarily signify agreement with the appraisal, but certifies a discussion of the employe's overall performance during this appraisal cycle was held on:

______________________________ ______________________________
MANAGER'S SIGNATURE

______________________________ ______________________________
EMPLOYE'S SIGNATURE NEXT LEVEL MANAGER'S SIGNATURE (OPTIONAL) DATE

Appendix C

EXEMPT PERFORMANCE APPRAISAL

Name ______________________ Division/Dept. ______________________

Title ______________________ Location ______________________

PERIOD COVERED: FROM ______________________ TO ______________________

GENERAL INSTRUCTIONS

This form has been developed to record exempt employee performance (expectations and results) in relation to ongoing position accountabilities and, where applicable, specific short-term objectives.

Parts I through III are used to document performance expectations, and must be completed at the beginning of the appraisal period. These sections are to be completed by the appraiser, or by the employee, subject to the appraiser's approval.

The remainder of the form is to be completed at the conclusion of the appraisal period. Refer to program instructions for further information.

PERFORMANCE LEVEL KEY

5- **Clearly Outstanding**. This rating is reserved for those individuals whose performance is **consistently** far above what is usually expected from an employee at this level. Generally the best performance that can **realistically** be expected.

4- **Exceeds Expectations**. Performance is noticeably better than expected. Results consistently exceed expectations of an employee at this level.

3- **Meets All Expectations**. Results are completely acceptable for an employee at this level. Steady, reliable performance.

2- **Meets Most Expectations**. Results are usually acceptable, although some areas need improvement. With proper training and guidance, employee should be able to meet all expectations in a reasonable timeframe.

1- **Below Standard**. Unsatisfactory results. Immediate and substantial improvement needed to continue employment in current position.

Appendix C

PART IA. GENERAL MANAGEMENT ACCOUNTABILITIES
(Applies to all employees functioning in a managerial or supervisory capacity).

1. Builds an organization and staff capable of effectively carrying out the unit's mission and specific accountabilities.
2. Plans and controls operations.
3. Establishes written operating policy and procedures.
4. Adheres to established department and individual position authority limits and keeps superior fully informed o significant developments, issues, and problems.
5. Contributes to a favorable image for among customers, government officials and th general public.

PART IB. IMPROVEMENT REQUIREMENTS
Indicate areas of required improvement, if applicable.

PART IIA. MAJOR POSITION ACCOUNTABILITIES
List no more than six principal accountabilities from current position description.

PART IIB. IMPROVEMENT REQUIREMENTS
Indicate area(s) of required improvement, if applicable.

PART III. OBJECTIVES
List no more than six specific objectives to be accomplished during the review period. Include measures of quality and/ quantity and timeliness as appropriate.

PART IVA. ACTUAL RESULTS: MANAGEMENT ACCOUNTABILITIES Describe actual results achieved in relation to the ongoing responsibilities listed in Part I, if applicable.	RATING

PART IVB. ACTUAL RESULTS: MAJOR POSITION ACCOUNTABILITIES Describe actual results achieved in relation to position accountabilities listed in Part II.	RATING

PART IVC. ACTUAL RESULTS: OBJECTIVES Describe actual results achieved in relation to the objectives listed in Part III, if applicable.	RATING

PART V. PERFORMANCE SUMMARY

Summarize achievements and indicate where improvement is necessary. Include performance against objectives applicable.

☐ **PART VI. OVERALL PERFORMANCE RATING.** Use the definitions on page 1 to indicate overall performance rating for employee. Take into account the relative importance of each accountability and objective; do not simply average the individual ratings.

PART VII.

APPRAISER'S SIGNATURE ______________________ ________
Date

PART VIII. EMPLOYEE COMMENTS

While I may or may not agree with the comments made in this appraisal, I acknowledge that it has been discussed with me.

______________________ Employee Signature ________ Date

˜ IX. APPRAISER'S S 'PERVISOR

SIGNATURE ______________________ ________
Date

Appendix C

Performance Appraisal
THIS FORM MUST BE ATTACHED TO NEXT SALARY ACTION FORM FOR THE EMPLOYEE.

NAME			POSITION TITLE	GRADE
SECTOR	DEPARTMENT	LOCATION	PRESENT SUPERVISOR TITLE	
DATE OF ENTRY IN CURRENT POSITION			RATING PERIOD FROM TO.	

Part A: Performance Measurement

I) Results meeting or exceeding expectations: ______

II) Results not meeting expectations or which present opportunities for improvement: ______

III) Relative to last performance measurement, performance has (check applicable box):
☐ Improved ☐ Remained Stable ☐ Declined
☐ Not Applicable (employee has changed positions since last review)
(An employee's performance may have improved or declined without changing the numeric rating.)

IV) Overall evaluation of results:
a) Place an X in the area on the scale that best describes the employee's total overall performance.

1.0	1.5	2.0	2.5	3.0	3.5	4.0	4.5	5.0
Outstanding		Exceeded Requirements		Met Requirements		Below Requirements		Unsatisfactory

b) Comments

Form No. C-711
9-84

Part B: Future Career Directions

Check all that apply. (In the event of a disagreement, the supervisor's point of view should be indicated by the check marks and the employee's exceptions should be reflected by reference to the numbered statements in the "comments" space provided.)

(1) ☐ Unless there is a significant improvement in performance, demotion, reassignment or separation is indicated.

(2) ☐ Employee is at or near the job level where the most effective job performance can be expected.

(3) ☐ Employee should remain in present position and gain experience before being considered for a position of increased responsibility.

(4) ☐ Employee appears to be ready for a position of increased responsibility now.

(5) ☐ Supervisor believes employee may have significant potential for advancement.

(6) ☐ In addition to current discipline, employee is interested in (list functional areas and, if applicable, General Management [a broad responsibility embracing several functional areas]):

Comments: ____________________

____

____

____

Part C: Review and Administration

The employee should check the applicable box:

☐ I am in fundamental agreement with the evaluation.

☐ I am in fundamental agreement with the evaluation set forth with the exceptions noted or attached.

☐ I have seen the evaluation and been given an opportunity to comment in writing.

☐ I wish to appeal and participate in a review of the evaluations.

IMMEDIATE SUPERVISOR	EMPLOYEE	DATE
FUNCTIONAL SUPERVISOR		

I have reviewed Parts A through C. Check applicable box:

☐ I have no observations to include as a part of the record.

☐ My observations for the record have been shown to both supervisor and employee and are attached.

REVIEWER'S SUPERVISOR	DATE

☐ Check if C-711A Part D (Performance Analysis) was completed.
☐ Check if C-711A Part E (Development Plan) was completed.

Appendix C

EMPLOYEE SKILLS PROFILE

SSN:

PERS LOC:

NAME:

DIV:

ORG'N:

TITLE:

DEPT:

HAY POINTS:

A. SKILL RATINGS Using the skills definitions contained in the Employee Skills Profile Worksheet, indicate below with an "x" in the appropriate box the employee's current use of each skill.

SKILLS	UNSATISFACTORY	IMPROVEMENT NEEDED	FULLY EFFECTIVE	SUPERIOR SKILL	EXCEPTIONAL	NOT RATED AT THIS TIME
1. Knowledge/Technical Skills						
List Fields of Knowledge and/or Technical Skills →						
2. Written Communications						
3. Oral Communications						
4. Persuasive Skills						
5. Teamwork						
6. Planning/Organizing						
7. Follow-Up and Control						
8. Leadership						
9. Employee Development						
10. Delegation						
11. Analytical Skill						
12. Judgment						
13. Decisiveness						
14. Creativity						
15. Flexibility						
16. Interpersonal Skill						
17. Motivation/Initiative						

B. SUMMARY COMMENTS

Strengths and Potential Contributions

2116.10-S REV 9/82

Appendix C

NAME: DIVISION: SSN:

NEEDS FOR IMPROVEMENT

C. DEVELOPMENT PROGRAMS PREVIOUSLY ATTENDED

PROGRAM NAME	CODE	YEAR	PROGRAM NAME	CODE	YEAR

D. DEVELOPMENT PROGRAMS CURRENTLY RECOMMENDED

	PROGRAM NAME	CODE	LAST RECOMMENDED	CANCEL OPTION		CODE
1.				IF ANY PROGRAM LISTED ON THE LEFT IS NO LONGER APPROPRIATE, CHECK THE CORRESPONDING BOX ON THE RIGHT	1. ☐	
2.					2. ☐	
3.					3. ☐	
4.					4. ☐	
5.					5. ☐	
6.					6. ☐	

E. ADDITIONAL DEVELOPMENT ACTIONS RECOMMENDED (Including coaching and on the job development)

Need	Recommended Action	Action Code
Need	Recommended Action	Action Code
Need	Recommended Action	Action Code

F. SUPERVISORY REVIEW (Date should be the date reviewed with employee)

Date (YR MO DAY)	Supervisor's Last Name Only (Print)	Supervisor's Signature	Review Signature

G. EMPLOYEE COMMENTS

Employee's Signature and Date

NOTE: EMPLOYEE SIGNATURE DOES NOT NECESSARILY INDICATE AGREEMENT.

HUMAN RESOURCES PLANNING AND STAFFI

Appendix C

ME________________ ASSIGNMENT________________ UNIT NO.________

1. JOB DESCRIPTION: PRINCIPAL ACCOUNTABILITIES	Order of Importance	Areas Most in Need of Current Attention (check)

IPLOYE 2. JOB DESCRIPTION: DISCRETION

IPLOYE 3. ACCOMPLISHMENTS AND THINGS LEARNED

What You Accomplished This Past Year

. What You Learned About Managing

4. CAREER DIRECTION

Appendix C

IMMEDIATE SUPERVISOR/DEPARTMENT MANAGER | 5. SUPERVISORY COMMENTS AND REACTIONS

5a. Immediate Supervisor's Comments to Job Description (Accountabilities and Discretion)

5b. Immediate Supervisor's Comments to Accomplishments and Things Learned

5c. Department Manager's Comments to Career Direction

6. REVIEW OF CURRENT PERFORMANCE – EVALUATION

EMPLOYE & IMMEDIATE SUPERVISOR | 7. REVIEW OF CURRENT PERFORMANCE – IMPROVEMENT

Employe's Signature	**Immediate Supervisor's Signature**	**Department Manager's Signature**
Date ____________	**Date** ____________	**Date** ____________

Appendix C

PERFORMANCE APPRAISAL

NAME____________________ DEPARTMENT____________________

POSITION____________________ TIME IN POSITION____________________

REVIEW PERIOD COVERED________________________

Prepared by: Title:

____________________ ____________________

Reviewed by: Title:

____________________ ____________________

Appendix C

Step 1 - RATING OF JOB DUTIES AND RESPONSIBILITIES

List Significant Duties, Responsibilities, and Requirements of the Job. Rate Employee's Ability to Perform these Duties.

A - Technical Knowledge:

B - Analytical Ability and Judgment:

C - Attitude and Personal Characteristics:

D - Other:

Appendix C

POOR

SATISFACTORY

GOOD

OUTSTANDING

Appendix C

Step 2 - PERFORMANCE EVALUATION

A. Identify Employee's Strengths and Weaknesses:

B. Set Goals to Further Utilize the Employee's Strengths and Develop Plans for Improving Deficiencies: [TIMETABLE

Appendix C

Step 3 - EMPLOYEE EVALUATION OF THE COMPANY

Each employee should objectively evaluate the Company -- its practices, procedures, benefits. They should set forth their overall feeling of the Company as a place to work and suggest ways the Company could be improved in the immediate future.

Step 4 - EMPLOYEE'S CAREER ASPIRATIONS

The employee's career goals should be ascertained. Does he or she have promotional aspirations? Based on the employee's performance, potential, motivation, education and attitude the supervisor can assist the employee in reaching his or her goals.

Step 5 - <u>SUMMARY OF OVERALL PERFORMANCE</u>

Overall performance should be evaluated on the basis of the extent to which the employee achieved the performance objectives set up for the review period. Consideration should be given to the way in which the employee carried out his or her job duties, responsibilities and requirements.

Step 6.

Other Comments by Evaluator:____

Comments Of Staff Member Being Evaluated:____________________________

Signatures:

Evaluated Staff Member:____________________________ Date:__________

Evaluator:__________________________________ Date:_________________

Appendix C

Exhibit I

PROCEDURE

The purpose of this procedure is to establish a forum for communication and exchange between the supervisor and the person reporting to the supervisor. The aim of the procedure is to develop mutual understanding and to plan for more effective performance as a result of the understanding.

This review should be a planned, private discussion between the supervisor and the employee. This appraisal is to be conducted at least once every twelve months, and, more frequently, if possible. The procedure to follow is outlined below:

Step 1 - Rating of Job Duties and Responsibilities

a) The supervisor outlines the basic job responsibilities for the position held by the employee and rates the employee's ability to perform the job duties and responsibilities.

b) The employee should be given the sheet "Employee Evaluation of the Company" to complete at least twenty-four (24) hours prior to the interview.

c) An interview should be scheduled with the employee to review the rating of his or her abilities, as well as the comments made by the employee about the Company.

Step 2 - Total Performance Evaluation

Included in the total performance evaluation should be:

1. Identification of the strengths and weaknesses of the employee;

2. Set goals to further utilize the strengths and develop plans for improvement where needed;

3. Specifically set forth the goals with a timetable and checkpoints for review of the goals.

In the event that there is disagreement on the total evaluation or the areas where improvement is needed, the supervisor and the employee should submit separate evaluation analyses.

Step 3 - Employee Evaluation of the Company

The supervisor should review and discuss the evaluation of the Company prepared by the employee.

Step 4 - Review Career Aspirations, if any, of Employee

The supervisor should review career goals and aspirations of the employee as they relate to promotion within the Company.

Step 5 - Summary of Overall Performance

The supervisor should summarize the overall performance of the employee as it relates to the duties and responsibilities of the job.

Step 6 - Overall Comments

Any other comments of the employee or the evaluator should be noted.

After the evaluation form has been completed by the supervisor, the steps outlined below should be followed to complete the evaluation process:

Step 1 - The entire evaluation form including the supervisor's evaluation of the employee's overall performance should be reviewed with the employee for his or her comments.

Step 2 - Submit a copy of the evaluation and recommendations of the employee to the appropriate department head, who will make a recommendation for a percentage wage increase and a year-end bonus.

Step 3 - Retain a copy of the evaluation form in the employee's personnel file.

Appendix C

CHF INDUSTRIES
PERSONNEL PROCEDURE
EMPLOYEE EVALUATIONS

It is important that the performance of all employees be evaluated on a periodic basis. The employee evaluation process is a means by which supervisors can communicate with their employees not only to review the employee's performance, but to identify the employee's aspirations and to determine how the employee feels about the Company. Employee evaluations should be conducted at least once every twelve months and, more frequently, if possible. For new employees, employee evaluations should initially be conducted after thirty days, three months, six months and, thereafter, as a minimum, on an annual basis.

A. JOB DESCRIPTION

Each position within the Company should have a written job description. At the time of the employee's hire, transfer or promotion into a job, the job description should be reviewed with the employee. The employee and his or her immediate supervisor should review all areas of the job description and determine the importance that should be attached to each aspect of the particular job. It is important on an on-going basis to review the job description with longer term employees and to re-evaluate the importance of various aspects of the job with employees who have been on the job for a period of time. In this regard, management should not overlook the value of an on-going dialogue with all employees. Changes in the state of the art, equipment and procedures may make it necessary to modify job descriptions and/or re-evaluate the potential of each employee. If changes are necessary in a job description, the new job description should be forwarded to the personnel department of the Company.

B. PERFORMANCE

The employee's immediate supervisor should review with the employee the employee's performance since the last performance review. All aspects of the employee's performance should be reviewed. The strengths as well as weaknesses should be discussed with the employee. Particular emphasis should be placed on the employee's attitude and motivation. The employee and the supervisor should mutually agree on ways to improve the employee's performance. These objectives should be clearly spelled out in writing on the employee's performance appraisal form with specific time targets for completion. Check points should be established with the employee in order to ascertain whether or not the achievement goals are being accomplished. Periodically, the supervisor should check with the employee on goals established during the performance review. In addition, the employee and the supervisor should ascertain the employee's job related goals, including, if appropriate, the employee's promotional aspirations. If the employee desires promotional advancement, the supervisor should give the employee guidance on requisite training or education in order for the employee to reach his or her goals. If on-the-job training is desired, the supervisor should establish a schedule for such training.

C. EVALUATING THE COMPANY

As part of the employee evaluation, the supervisor should ascertain from the employee "how well is the Company doing by you". In other words, the employee should objectively evaluate the Company, its practices, procedures and benefits. The immediate supervisor should ascertain how the employee feels about the Company and how the employee feels that the Company could be improved in the immediate future. The employee's opinion and evaluation should be set forth in writing on the employee's performance appraisal form.

D. PROCEDURE

After the completion of an employee's probationary period, the employee will be evaluated annually as follows:

1. The initial step in the evaluation process is for the immediate supervisor or department head to outline the basic job responsibilities for the position held by the employee.

2. The immediate supervisor should then rate the employee's strengths and weaknesses in performing his or her basic job responsibilities.

3. At least 24 hours prior to the employee interview, the employee should be given the part of the evaluation in which the employee evaluates the Company. The employee should bring the completed evaluation to the interview.

4. An interview should then be scheduled with the employee to review the evaluation. During such review, the immediate supervisor should review his or her evaluation of the employee as well as point out the employee's strengths or weaknesses.

5. At the end of the interview process, the supervisor should set forth a total performance evaluation. Included in the total performance evaluation should be:

Appendix C

PERSONNEL PROCEDURE
EMPLOYEE EVALUATIONS

a. identification of the strengths and weaknesses of the employee;

b. establishment of goals to improve the deficiencies agreed upon;

c. goals should be specifically set forth with specific timetables and checkpoints for review of the goals;

d. in the event that there is disagreement on the total evaluation of the supervisor and the employee should be permitted to submit a separate evaluation analysis.

6. During the interviewing process the employee's evaluation of the Company should be discussed.

7. The immediate supervisor or department head should also review with the employee, during the interviewing process, the employee's career aspirations, if any, and other goals or aspirations that the employee may have.

8. Once the entire evaluation process is completed, the evaluation form should be completed along with all recommendations and should be finally reviewed with the employee for his or her comment.

9. All employee evaluations and recommendations should be retained in the employee's personnel file. Copies of all evaluations, recommendations and the employee's evaluation of the Company should be submitted to the appropriate department head for review.

10. The employee's evaluation and supervisor's recommendation should be reviewed and considered by the department head when determining an annual wage adjustment and/or bonus for the employee. (See Exhibit I - Evaluation Form).

Appendix D

Termination Checklist

Appendix D

CHECKLIST THAT SHOULD BE FOLLOWED BEFORE TERMINATING AN EMPLOYEE

We urge that the following checklist be reviewed by people in your organization having power to terminate employees. When an employee commits a serious infraction, warranting discharge, he or she can be sent home immediately for the day, or suspended for one, two, or more days and told that he will be informed of the action to be taken. Management can then consider the case without haste.

1. Does management know ALL the facts accurately?

2. Is this employee receiving the same treatment others have received for the same offense?

3. Is the rule which has been violated reasonable?

4. Did the employee know the rule or should he or she reasonably have known it?

5. In this instance, has the rule been applied reasonably?

6. Have preliminary procedures been followed?

7. In cases where appropriate - has the employee been warned, given lesser penalties according to work rules, past practice, in line with current industrial relations practice? This gradual warning and step-up of penalties does not apply to major infractions such as theft or assault when there is absolute proof.

8. Is this employee personally guilty or only guilty by association with another?

9. If a supervisor is pressing the termination, is he or she level-headed, fair and impartial, or inclined to keenly reject

what he or she regards as a challenge to authority?

10. Does the punishment fit the crime?

11. What is the employee's disciplinary record?

12. What is the employee's length of service?

13. Have you spoken to the employee and does he or she have a reasonable excuse for the infraction of the rule?

14. Can the employee's guilt be proved by direct, objective evidence or only by circumstantial evidence or conjecture?

15. Does management have a past record of strict enforcement, generally of the type of cause for discharge that is involved? If not, was there a recent bulletin board notice or meeting warning the employees that management was going to "crack down" on violations of a certain type, etc.?

16. Is the employee's record or management's prior actions documented?

17. Is the proposed termination supported by documentation and investigation?

18. Is the termination fair and equitable? For example:

    Would the employee's termination offend "public policy"?

    a) Terminated for jury duty or exercising political beliefs?

    b) Terminated for refusing to participate in any activity which would constitute a violation of the law?

    c) Terminated to retaliate against employee's reporting any alleged violation (e.g., EEO, OSHA or Workers' Compensation) to authorities?

19. Would termination of the employee prevent the vesting of benefits in the immediate foreseeable future?

    a) Pension or retirement benefits (i.e., within 1 year)?

    b) Bonuses (i.e., within 1 month)?

    c) Stock options (i.e., within 1 month)?

20. If the employee was accused of dishonest or serious misconduct, did a fair and honest investigation support the allegations?

    a) Are any other employees suspects?

    b) Are the witnesses credible?

    c) Action suited to the infraction?

    In addition, such representations may constitute torts for breach of the covenant of good faith and fair dealing, wrongful discharge, negligent misrepresentation and/or fraud.

21. Were any representations other than the employee was terminable-at-will made to the employee? (E.g., was the employee told his job was "secure for life" or "as long as he wanted it" or "as long as the corporation keeps growing")?

    a) Are the representations true?

    b) If the representations were made to the employee about continued employment, were there any conditions to continued employment, such as the employee's satisfactory performance?

    c) Did the employee give up any other employment opportunities based on representations or promises?

    d) Was the employee informed that continued employment was dependent upon the employer's discretion or business needs?

e) Was employee advised that improper conduct or failure to correct actions would result in discharge?

22. Has management explored alternatives to termination, i.e., job transfer, change of supervision, etc.?

Discharges, where at all possible, should be reviewed by a management representative (preferably a member of the Human Resource Department) not associated in a detailed way with the incident.

Appendix D

BASIC CHECKLIST IN REVIEWING DISCHARGE

I. Legal Inquiry (See attached expanded checklist)

A. Have the corporation's disciplinary procedures been followed?

B. Is the employee's improper conduct or failure to respond to corrective suggestions documented?

C. Have any representations, either oral or written, been made to the employee about continued employment?

D. Was the employee participating in or urging concerted activity?

E. Is the employee a member of a "protected group"?

II. General Considerations

A. Does a review of the expanded checklist demonstrate that the termination is supported by FACTS?

1) Fair
2) Accurate
3) Consistent with policies and treatment of others
4) Timely
5) Supported by documentation and investigation

B. What is the effect of the termination upon morale in the department, division, company?

C. Is it the type of termination which might induce non-unit employees to seek out a union?

D. What is the effect of the termination on customer relations or other business-related matters?

E. Is the supervisor or appropriate personnel manager aware that

1) the disciplinary interview should be private and remain confidential?

2) the disciplinary interview should be calm?

3) they should avoid name-calling and unsubstantiated charges of lying, dishonesty, or criminal or immoral behavior?

III. Method of Termination

A. Confidential

B. As humane as possible

Appendix D

YES*	NO*	EXPANDED LEGAL CHECKLIST
		I. Legal Inquiry
		A. Disciplinary Procedures [The emerging law in some states may impose an implied contract between employer and employee to follow disciplinary procedures established by the company. Failure to follow this procedure may constitute a breach of the covenant of good faith and fair dealing or a wrongful termination.]
	x	Were the corporation's procedures and other customary practices followed before the decision was made to terminate the employee?
	x	Has the employee received the requisite verbal warnings?
	x	Written warnings?
	x	Suspension?
	x	Did the employee have fair advance notice of the standards by which his behavior/performance would be judged?
	x	Did the employee have an opportunity to take constructive corrective action?
	x	Did the employee have a chance to give his or her side of the story?

* If the answer is other than the designated, re-evaluate the appropriateness of the discharge and consult your division personnel manager.

YES*	NO*	EXPANDED LEGAL CHECKLIST
		B. Sufficiency of Documentation [the law frequently takes the position that "if it isn't documented in writing, it didn't happen."]
	x	Do the documents demonstrate that the termination is adequately supported by facts?
	x	Is the termination fair and equitable? For example:
	x	Would the employee's termination offend "public policy"?
	x	1) Terminated for exercising a right, i.e., jury duty, political beliefs, etc?
	x	2) Terminated for refusing to participate in any activity which would constitute a violation of the law?
	x	3) Terminated to retaliate against employee's reporting any alleged violation (e.g., EEO, OSHA or Workers' Compensation) to authorities?
	x	Would termination of the employee prevent the vesting of benefits in the immediate foreseeable future?
	x	1) Pension or retirement benefits? (i.e., within 1 year)
	x	2) Bonuses? (i.e., within 1 month)

* If the answer is other than the designated, re-evaluate the appropriateness of the discharge and consult your division personnel manager.

Appendix D

YES*	NO*	EXPANDED LEGAL CHECKLIST
	x	3) Stock options? (i.e., within 1 month)
x		If the employee was accused of dishonesty or serious misconduct, did a fair and honest investigation support the allegations?
	x	1) Are any other employees suspects?
x		2) Are the witnesses credible?
x		3) Action suited to the infraction?
x		Is the employee's conduct sufficient to justify termination at this time?
	x	Are there extenuating circumstances or mitigating factors which justify a lesser penalty?
x		Does the employee's prior disciplinary record support termination?
x		Consistency: Have other employees engaged in similar conduct been terminated?
x		Timely: Are both the documentation and the decision to terminate timely?
x		Is the decision substantiated with facts rather than solely subjective opinion?
x		If the termination is based on results of performance appraisals or evaluations, are they objective and directly related to the job skills?

---

* If the answer is other than the designated, re-evaluate the appropriateness of the discharge and consult your division personnel manager.

YES*	NO*	EXPANDED LEGAL CHECKLIST
x		Is the articulated reason for the discharge the real reason rather than pretext?
	x	Does the employee have a satisfactory or better job appraisal, work commendations, recent promotions, raises or bonuses which negate the articulated reason for discharge?
		C. Representations of Continued Employment [The law in some states may construe an employer's representation to an employee, whether in the form of expressed or implied promise, as giving rise to a perpetual employment contract unless the employer shows "good cause" for terminating the employment relationship. In addition, such representations may constitute a breach of the covenant of good faith and fair dealing, a wrongful termination, negligent misrepresentation and/ or fraud.]
	x	Were any representations other than the employee was terminable-at-will made to the employer? (e.g., Was the employee told his job was "secure for life" or "as long as he wanted it" or "as long as the corporation keeps growing"?)
x		Are the representations true?
x		If the representations were made to the employee about continued employment, were there any

* If the answer is other than the designated, re-evaluate the appropriateness of the discharge and consult your division personnel manager.

YES*	NO*		EXPANDED LEGAL CHECKLIST
			conditions to continued employment, such as the employee's satisfactory performance?
	x		Did the employee give up any other employment opportunities based on representations or promises?
x			Was the employee informed that continued employment was dependent upon the corporation's discretion or business needs?
x			Was employee advised that improper conduct or failure to correct actions would result in discharge?
	x		Has employee worked for the corporation for over 10 years?
		D.	Concerted Activity [Federal law, such as the Labor Management Relations Act and the Occupational Safety and Health Act, and some state laws protect employees from termination or other adverse employment consequences if they are engaged in concerted protected activity.]
	x		Did the employee, for example:
	x		1) Urge safety in the workplace?
	x		2) Urge more breaks, higher wages, or any other benefit for employees in addition to himself?
	x		3) Urge union support?

* If the answer is other than the designated, re-evaluate the appropriateness of the discharge and consult your division personnel manager.

YES*	NO*	EXPANDED LEGAL CHECKLIST
	x	4) "Come to the aid" of another employee who was being criticized?
		E. Protected Groups [Federal and some state laws prohibit discriminatory treatment of "protected groups" and prohibit policies which adversely impact such persons more than non-protected persons. Due to the corporation's federal contractor status, the corporation also has an affirmative action obligation to promote the employment of qualified members of the protected groups.]
	x	Did the employee's protected status adversely affect in any manner whatsoever, the employment decision?
	x	1) Race
	x	2) Sex, for example:
	x	General presumptions of weakness or frailty?
	x	Reproductive concerns?
	x	Childbearing or childrearing concerns?
	x	Unwanted sexual advances or harassment?
	x	3) Marital status, for example:
	x	Presumption that employee won't want to travel or work a shift because married?

* If the answer is other than the designated, re-evaluate the appropriateness of the discharge and consult your division personnel manager.

Appendix D

YES*	NO*	EXPANDED LEGAL CHECKLIST	
	x		Presumption that employee is not "responsible" because not married?
	x		Terminated because of anti-nepotism policy? (If so, is it possible to avoid a supervisorial relationship with relative?)
	x	4)	National origin and ancestry
	x	5)	Religion, for example:
x			Have reasonable efforts been made to accommodate the employee's religion?
	x	6)	Age (over 40), for example:
	x		Generalized presumption that "time is passing him by" or that he is incapable of keeping up with technological innovations?
	x		Generalized presumptions of weakness or frailty?
	x		Attempts to cut direct costs by terminating employees with greater benefits and seniority?
	x	7)	Handicap, for example:
x			Have reasonable efforts been made to accommodate the employee in this job?
	x		Can the employee perform another job with similar pay?

* If the answer is other than the designated, re-evaluate the appropriateness of the discharge and consult your division personnel manager.

YES*	NO*		EXPANDED LEGAL CHECKLIST
	x		8) Veteran Status

II. Legal Actions

Proper procedures by the corporation should help to minimize related actions which a growing number of states are recognizing, such as:

1) breach of employment contract
2) breach of government contract (EEO/OFCCP complaints)
3) employment discrimination
4) tortious breach of the covenant of good faith and fair dealing
5) wrongful discharge
6) negligent or intentional misrepresentations
7) fraud
8) negligent infliction of emotional distress
9) intentional infliction of emotional distress
10) slander, defamation and libel

---

* If the answer is other than the designated, re-evaluate the appropriateness of the discharge and consult your division personnel manager.

Appendix E

Termination Policies and Procedures

Appendix E

ADMINISTRATIVE PROCEDURE

RESPONSIBLE ISSUING DEPT.	SECTION: PERSONNEL AND ORGANIZATION	PROCEDURE NO. 4-28
Corporate Employment	SUBJECT: Termination of Employment Due to Performance for Salaried Employees	PAGE ...... 1 of 3
SUPERSEDES PROC. DATED June 1976		DATES: ISSUED September 1980 EFFECTIVE September 1980

1. GENERAL

The Corporation sets and requires high standards of performance and conduct for all its employees. Members of management and supervision will ensure fair and consistent treatment for all employees.

It is expected that supervisors will devote appropriate effort to retain competent employees who can make a good contribution to the organization. This includes taking corrective measures where necessary to help the employee understand and carry out his/her work responsibilities. All employees are to be given a reasonable opportunity to demonstrate value to the Corporation, including possibly, usefulness elsewhere within the organization. Involuntary termination should only occur as a proper last resort. Should such terminations occur, appropriate counseling and out-placement service will be made available to the terminated person.

Note: In the event of any action by an employee resulting in discharge or termination for cause, the requirement for corrective measures to improve performance is waived. Any such terminations will still require, however, the review as outlined in 3.3 and 3.4.

Also, the following Policy and Procedure is not intended to replace or override any written company/location policy covering "Probationary Employees" which may include "shorter" time periods for demonstrating satisfactory performance.

2. POLICY

*Should employee performance be less than satisfactory and, after proper counselling and a reasonable period of time, established objectives, standards, and/or job requirements are not met, the employee should be terminated. Separation Pay for employees terminated under this policy will be administered in accordance with the Separation Pay Policy (AP 4-5). Exit interviews will be held with all employees leaving the organization and out-placement service will be offered as appropriate (AP 4-29).

ADMINISTRATIVE PROCEDUR

RESPONSIBLE ISSUING DEPT. Corporate Employment	SECTION: PERSONNEL AND ORGANIZATION	PROCEDURE NO......4-2
	SUBJECT: Termination of Employment Due to Performance for Salaried Employees	PAGE ...... 2 of 3
SUPERSEDES PROC. DATED June 1976		DATES: ISSUED September 19
		EFFECTIVE September 19

3. PROCEDURE

3.1 Where performance against previously determined work objectives is less than good, corrective measures should be taken. Counseling to review performance shortcomings, culminating in a general plan of improvement for the employee, should be held. To make sure there is no misunderstanding of the problem or the plan for improvement, this interview should be placed on the corrective action to be taken and the Company's commitment to assisting the employee meet the action plan objectives.

3.2 If, after an appropriate time period (usually not longer than three months) required performance levels have not been attained the employee should again be counseled with the action documented as outlined in 3.1 above. (The Performance/Career Planning Review form may be used to document this action.) Emphasis should be focused on areas needing immediate improvement, the action plan to accomplish this purpose, including the employee's usefulness elsewhere where appropriate, and the consequence if improvement is not forthcoming. Higher levels of supervision and Personnel/Employee Relations should be involved at this stage.

3.3 If, after counseling and reasonable efforts by supervision and/or related staff professionals, performance is still not acceptable, the employee may be terminated. Responsibility for such action is the same as for the annual performance review, plus one level higher of both line and Personnel management.

*3.4 In all cases where the employee is Hay level 9 or above, or is an exempt employee with 10 or more years of service with the Corporation, the proposed termination must be reviewed and approved by the Company President or Corporate Staff Officer involved. Such individuals will be responsible for keeping the Corporate Vice President Employee Affairs informed.

ADMINISTRATIVE PROCEDURE

RESPONSIBLE ISSUING DEPT.	SECTION: PERSONNEL AND ORGANIZATION	PROCEDURE NO. 4-28
Corporate Employment	SUBJECT: Termination of Employment Due to Performance for Salaried Employees	PAGE ...... 3 of 3
SUPERSEDES PROC. DATED		DATES: ISSUED September 1980
June 1976		EFFECTIVE September 1980

3.5 In instances where satisfactory improvement is made, the corrective interview forms maintained in the individual's file should be summarized as part of the employee's normal Performance/Career Planning review along with the current improved performance.

3.6 Employees terminating under this policy shall be processed in accordance with the provisions of the Separation Pay For Salaried Employees (AP 4-5).

Appendix E

PERSONNEL POLICY MANUAL	EFFECT. DATE 6-5-58	PAGE 1 OF 7
	INDEX NO. 220	REVISION NO.

SUBJECT SEPARATIONS	PREPARED BY	AUTHORIZED BY	APPROVED BY
		P.S.K., Jr.	

COVERAGE

All regular salaried employees assigned from or to a permanent plant or office of the Corporation. This policy does not apply to employees in units where a union has been designated as a Collective Bargaining Agent; the terms and conditions of all union agreements shall govern in these cases.

A. DEFINITIONS

For the purposes of this policy, the following definitions and terms shall apply:

1. Lay-Off: a termination from company employment which is involuntary on the part of the employee and due to reasons beyond his control, such as force labor reduction or lack of work.
2. Voluntary Termination: a separation from company employment initiated by action of the employee normally for personal reasons, such as dissatisfaction or better job.
3. Discharge: a permanent separation from company employment caused by conduct or action of the employee which is considered inimical to the best interests of the company.
4. Severance Pay: compensation received at the time of termination of employment in addition to that money which is paid for actual hours worked.
5. Separation Notice: a verbal or written statement of intended action affecting the employment status of an employee issued

Form No. (279)-27-300-9-5?-M

PERSONNEL POLICY MANUAL	EFFECT. DATE 12/1/80	PAGE 2 OF 7
	INDEX NO. 220	REVISION NO. 1

SUBJECT SEPARATIONS	PREPARED BY	AUTHORIZED BY	APPROVED BY

prior to the effective date of termination by either the employer or employee.

6. Regular Employee: employees eligible for all contingent benefits of employment, such as - group insurance, pension coverage, sick leave and vacation.
7. Exempt Employees: employees classified under the Wage and Hour Law as exempt from the forty hour per week overtime provisions.
8. Non-Exempt Employee: employees classified under the Wage and Hour Law as subject to full overtime pay for all hours in excess of forty per week.

B. POLICY

Employees to be laid off shall be terminated in such a way as to serve the best interests of the company and to provide fair and reasonable consideration to all employees. These interests are best served by the maintenance of an experienced, contented working force loyal to the company.

The following criteria in the order listed shall govern when laying off employees:

1. Ability, efficiency, and productive value to the company.
2. Length of service with the company.

All employees to be separated will be considered for transfer and placement in another existing position in the company. Prior service will be given appropriate consideration in the event of rehire dependent on the factors that exist at the time.

Form No. (279)-27-300-9-59-!"

PERSONNEL POLICY MANUAL	EFFECT. DATE 6-5-58	PAGE 3 OF 7
	INDEX NO. 220	REVISION NO.

SUBJECT SEPARATIONS	PREPARED BY	AUTHORIZED BY	APPROVED BY
		P.S.K., Jr.	

C. PROCEDURE

1. General

The following procedure will assist the department head in administering layoffs:

a. Determine the number and classifications of employees to be retained in order to meet present and contemplated future requirements.

b. Reduction in the number of jobs will automatically determine the individuals by group who are to be considered for separation.

c. The exact individuals to be separated will be selected in accordance with policy outlined herein based upon type of work performed and skill possessed.

After the department head has determined the employees no longer required by his department and prior to advising the individuals concerned, the Personnel Department should be consulted. The Personnel Department will determine whether a transfer to some other department can be arranged based on the individual's seniority and other qualifications.

2. Warning Notice

Employees whose conduct or performance is not satisfactory should be advised of their deficiency and given an opportunity to correct the condition prior to being discharged. It is considered good practice to put such warning notice in writing, in which case a copy should be sent to the Personnel Department.

Form No. (279)-27-300-9-58-M

PERSONNEL POLICY MANUAL	EFFECT. DATE 1/3/83(Rev.)	PAGE 4 OF 7
	INDEX NO. 220	REVISION NO. 1

SUBJECT SEPARATIONS	PREPARED BY	AUTHORIZED BY	APPROVED BY

3. Separation Notice

Each employee who is not to be transferred to another department will be notified in writing by the department head or immediate superior of the intention to discontinue his services and the reasons for this action. A properly executed SS-2 form outlining all the circumstances is to be forwarded to the Personnel Department at the same time. Under normal circumstances separation notice shall be given as follows:

A. Layoff

EXEMPT EMPLOYEES

Length of Service	Separation Notice
0 to 1 year	2 weeks
1 yr. less than 3 yrs.	3 weeks
3 yrs. less than 6 yrs.	4 weeks
6 yrs. less than 9 yrs.	5 weeks
9 yrs. less than 12 yrs.	6 weeks
12 yrs. less than 15 yrs.	7 weeks
15 yrs. less than 18 yrs.	8 weeks
18 yrs. less than 20 yrs.	9 weeks
20 yrs. and over	10 weeks

NON-EXEMPT EMPLOYEES

Length of Service	Separation Notice
0 to 1 yrs.	1 week
1 yr. less than 5 yrs.	2 weeks
5 yrs. less than 10 yrs.	3 weeks
10 yrs. less than 15 yrs.	4 weeks
15 yrs. less than 20 yrs.	5 weeks
20 years and over	6 weeks

B. Discharge

If the discharge is due to incompetence, inefficiency or similar, the schedule of separation notice shall be:

Form No. (279)-27-300-9-58-[illegible]

PERSONNEL POLICY MANUAL	EFFECT. DATE 6-5-58	PAGE 5 OF 7
	INDEX NO. 220	REVISION NO.

SUBJECT SEPARATIONS	PREPARED BY	AUTHORIZED BY	APPROVED BY

EXEMPT EMPLOYEES

Length of Service	Separation Notice
0 to 6 mos.	0
6 mos. less than 1 yr.	1 week
1 yr. and over	2 weeks

NON-EXEMPT EMPLOYEES

Length of Service	Separation Notice
0 to 6 mos.	0
6 mos. and over	1 week

Advance separation notice should not be given when discharge is by reason of intolerable conduct.

4. Separation Pay in Lieu of Notice

   a. Separation pay in lieu of notice will not be given unless special conditions justify and prior approval is granted. Not more than one week's pay for separation in lieu of notice for any occasion may be granted and then only when there is no other form of severance compensation. One week's pay under these conditions will be equivalent to two weeks' notice and no employee with less than one year's service may receive such pay.

   b. Allowing time off during the period of notice constitutes severance pay and should be granted in strict conformance with the schedule of severance pay benefits outlined in this policy.

Form No. (279)-27-300-9-58-M

PERSONNEL POLICY MANUAL	EFFECT. DATE 7/1/79	PAGE 6 OF 7
	INDEX NO. 220	REVISION NO. 3

SUBJECT SEPARATIONS	PREPARED BY	AUTHORIZED BY	APPROVED BY

5. Severance

Upon recommendation of the department head, employees laid off involuntarily or retiring who have completed at least one year of service will be eligible for severance as follows:

a. EXEMPT employees - one day of severance for each day of unused sick leave credit up to a maximum of 30 days and one-half day's severance for each additional day of unused sick leave credit up to a maximum additional 15 days. There will be no severance allowance in excess of 45 days.

b. NON-EXEMPT - one-half day of severance for each day of accumulated sick leave credit for the first 30 days of this accumulated credit, and one-quarter day severance for each day of accumulated credit in excess of 30 days up to a maximum severance of 45 days.

c. This severance shall be in the form of a lump-sum payment at the time of retirement or of involuntary layoff.

d. Employees discharged because of breach of discipline, insubordination, incompetence, or similar reasons will receive no separation pay.

e. Exempt employees only, with two or more years of continuous service separated involuntarily who, due to illness or other justified absence, have no accumulated sickness credit

Form No. (279)-27-30C-9-58-M

PERSONNEL POLICY MANUAL	EFFECT. DATE 9/1/79	PAGE 7 OF 7
	INDEX NO. 220	REVISION NO. 2

SUBJECT SEPARATIONS	PREPARED BY	AUTHORIZED BY	APPROVED BY

available may be recommended for severance pay on the basis of five days for two years of service, plus an additional one day for each year of service beyond two years up to a maximum of thirty days' pay.

6. Vacation Benefits

Employees terminated between January 1 and the start of the vacation period shall be compensated for unused vacation earned, in accordance with the vacation policy.

7. Deceased Employees

The foregoing severance pay provisions of this policy are not applicable where employment has been terminated by death. However, in lieu thereof, in such cases, the Company at its discretion may pay an honorarium to the deceased employee's next of kin in an amount not to exceed the amount of severance benefits payable had employment been terminated otherwise. When the honorarium is to be paid to the widow of the deceased employee, payments ordinarily will be made bi-weekly in amounts equal to the deceased employee's bi-weekly salary until the full amount of the honorarium authorized has been paid.

An honorarium is intended to assist the immediate family of a deceased employee, shall not be deemed a legal obligation of the Company to the deceased employee or his estate and, except in unusual circumstances, will not be made in cases where an employee dies leaving no immediate family.

Form No. (279)-27-300-9-53-M

Appendix E

PERSONNEL POLICY & PROCEDURES

TITLE	POLICY NO.	
CLOSURE POLICY	E5	
	EFFECTIVE DATE 11/1/78	PAGE 1 of 4

SCOPE

All employees not covered by a collective bargaining agreement.

DEFINITIONS

An individual's employment with the Company can be terminated in several ways:

1. A dismissal for cause is the termination of employment for a specific action or actions detrimental to the Company or its employees. Such action would include, but not be limited to:

   . Disclosure of proprietary or other confidential information

   . Embezzlement, theft or other misappropriation of Company funds or assets

   . Falsification of records or reports

   . Deliberate or reckless action which causes actual or potential injury or loss to the company or employees of the Company

   . Violation of Company policy or rules

   . Insubordination

   . Illegal acts on Company property or in representing the Company

2. A dismissal for unsatisfactory performance is the termination of employment for failure to perform duties in a satisfactory manner, including, but not limited to, the following:

   . Work output (quantity or quality) not meeting the requirements of the job

   . Work consistently off schedule

   . Failure to meet accepted standards of employment (e.g., excessive or sustained absenteeism or tardiness)

   . Inability to maintain satisfactory relationships with others

3. A separation is the termination of an individual's employment effected by the Company due to the elimination of the individual's duties for reasons such as lack of work, organization changes, or general reduction of force.

4. A resignation is the termination of an individual's employment effected by the individual.

5. A retirement is the termination of an individual's employment effected by the individual and the Company in accordance with the provisions of the retirement plan in which the employee participates.

6. A death of an individual while an employee.

G-1100-G 1163

PERSONNEL POLICY & PROCEDURE

POLICY NO.	EFFECTIVE DATE	PAGE	TITLE
E5	11/1/78	2 of 4	CLOSURE POLICY (Cont'd)

POLICY

1. **Authorization of Dismissals or Separations**

The dismissal or separation of an employee will be in accordance with the following:

a. Normally no employee shall be dismissed or separated without the concurrence of at least one level of supervision above the employee's immediate supervisor.

b. No employee shall be dismissed or separated without the prior concurrence of the local Personnel Director/Manager, who may refer the situation to the Vice President, Personnel Relations.

c. No employee who age plus length of service totals 65 or more shall be terminated without concurrence of the Vice President, Personnel Relations.

2. **Notification to Employee**

The procedure for notifying an employee of a termination effected by the Company will vary with the type of termination.

a. Dismissal for Cause

Dismissal for cause will be immediate and without prior notification.

b. Dismissal for Unsatisfactory Performance or Separation

Dismissal for unsatisfactory performance will be in accordance with the procedure outlined in the Appraisal and Counseling Policy. Employees with one or more years service will be given two weeks advance notice. The Company may, at its option, grant pay in lieu of notification.

3. **Payment**

a. Dismissal

Employees who are dismissed for cause or for unsatisfactory performance shall be paid through the last day they actually work.

b. Separation

Normally, employees who are separated shall be paid through the last day they actually work. In addition, employees who are separated after six months of service shall be paid separation allowance of one-half day's pay for each full month of continuous service. For purposes of separation allowance, the method of computing one day's pay is by dividing the annual salary by 260.

c. Resignation or Retirement

Employees who resign or retire shall be paid through the last day they actually work.

d. Death

The estates of employees who die while on active payroll status (that is, who are not on leave without pay or disability leave) shall be paid the employee's salary which will be extended through the employee's weekly, semi-monthly, or monthly pay period.

4. **Benefit Continuance**

   a. Dismissal, Resignation, Retirement or Death

   Provisions for the continuance of benefit programs or payment of benefits for employees whose employment ceases by virtue of dismissal, resignation, retirement or death are described in the various benefit booklets.

   b. Separation

   In addition to the provisions outlined in benefit booklets, employees who are separated may receive further coverage as described below.

   1. Medical Benefits Plan and Dental Insurance Plan

      Employees may, for a period of up to 30 months, continue their coverage by making monthly or quarterly premium payments in advance.

   2. Group Life Insurance

      Employees may, for a period of up to 30 months, continue their coverage at employee rates by making monthly or quarterly premium payments in advance.

PROCEDURE

1. **Authorization**

   Appropriate authorization as outlined above should be secured prior to informing the employee of closure action.

2. **Placement**

   Regular employees who are to be separated shall be referred to the Personnel Department for possible placement in other positions. Should no suitable position be available, the Personnel Department will counsel employees and provide assistance in preparation for securing employment elsewhere.

3. **Closure Interview**

   When termination is necessary, the line supervisor is responsible for completing and submitting to the site Personnel Director/Manager a Personnel Profile Form (R1250-G). This must be submitted before the closure can be processed by Personnel. The Personnel Department will also conduct a closure interview, handle benefit arrangements and other details.

4. **Final Physical Exam**

   Closure examinations shall be given only to employees who have been exposed to hazardous conditions at work or who have a record of an occupational injury or illness.

5. **Official Company References**

   References which reflect the Company's official opinion shall be cleared and issued by the appropriate Personnel Director/Manager only at the request of a prospective employer and only after a review of the employee's performance, as indicated by his/her personnel record and as reported by his/her former supervisor. Such references shall not be issued directly to employees and letters of reference are not to be addressed to "To Whom It May Concern".

6. **Personal References**

References also may be furnished by other employees, provided that the employee first contacts the appropriate Personnel representative to obtain clearance and guidance. Employees who receive a request for reference information should, as a first step, direct the individual requesting this information to the appropriate Personnel representative (supervisors who have terminated an employee will be advised of the name of the representative).

7. **Exceptions to Policy**

Consideration beyond the provisions of this policy shall be submitted to the appropriate Personnel Director/Manager.

Appendix F

Disciplinary Policies and Procedures

Appendix F

SUPERVISORY TECHNIQUES FOR EMPLOYEE PERFORMANCE SUPPORT (STEPS)

I. OBJECTIVE

One of the basic tenets in the management philosophy is fair, equitable, and consistent treatment of all our employees. These guidelines have been developed to assist supervisors in promoting a better work environment for our employees, by encouraging discussions of employee performance and conduct issues between supervisors and employees. Additionally, they provide a means for developing corrective action, where applicable. In no case shall the guidelines be construed as an employment contract between the employee and the Company.

II. SCOPE

These guidelines apply to non-represented employees in the Corporate Staff Units. Individual cases may require different approaches, though the actions taken should be consistent with the spirit and intent of these guidelines. The manner in which the guidelines are administered is at the discretion of management.

III. RESPONSIBILITIES

It is the responsibility of management to develop and foster a work environment in which each employee has the opportunity to achieve his or her full potential as well as meet Company standards for job performance and professional conduct. It is also management's responsibility to employ sound management practices to ensure fair, equitable, and consistent treatment of employees in connection with addressing employee performance and conduct issues.

The employee is responsible for performing to the fullest extent possible in an acceptable, professional manner. It is also the responsibility of the employee to carry out all reasonable directives set forth by management in a positive and supportive manner.

Employee Relations is responsible for assisting management and employees in the review, counseling, and resolution of employee conduct and performance issues.

IV. MANAGING PERFORMANCE

Informal discussions and performance appraisals are two of several tools supervisors have to provide employees with regular, constructive feedback regarding performance. In cases where an employee requires counseling in order to correct or improve performance or conduct, the guidelines provide the supervisor with a series of steps to clearly communicate the issue(s) with the employee, and to establish a framework for corrective action.

Appendix F

Employee performance and conduct issues should be addressed according to the nature and severity of the problem. Some problems require immediate disciplinary action while others may be addressed through progressive discipline. A discussion of both approaches follows. However, the specific course of action for employee performance and conduct problems may have to be determined on a case-by-case basis.

Corrective Disciplinary Action

The following are examples of employee conduct and performance problems that require corrective action. The examples given below are not intended to be all-inclusive but are listed for illustrative purposes.

- o Failure to meet minimum job performance standards
- o Excessive absenteeism and/or tardiness
- o Abuse of telephone or break privileges

When an unsatisfactory employee performance or conduct problem emerges, corrective action should be initiated as promptly as possible to give the employee an opportunity to address the problem. The following steps, applied progressively, are recommended:

Step 1 *Identify the problem to the employee.*

Step 2 *Counsel the employee (and note for future reference).*

Step 3 *Present a written warning to the employee (and send a copy to the E. R. Representative for inclusion in the employee's personnel file).*

Step 4 *Provide probation counseling and a related letter to the employee (and send a copy for inclusion in the employee's personnel file to the E. R. Representative, who may participate in the counseling session upon request of the supervisor or the employee).*

Step 5 *Recommend the employee's separation (after obtaining approval of second-level management and concurrence of the E. R. Representative).*

In **Steps 2 - 4**, the supervisor should inform the employee of the time period for correcting the performance or conduct problem.

When an employee successfully meets the performance or conduct expectations outlined by management, the supervisor should apprise the employee. A letter regarding the successful results should be prepared by the supervisor and a copy sent to the Employee Relations Representative for inclusion in the employee's personnel file. Any future recurrence of the performance or conduct problem may require resumption of the corrective disciplinary process at whatever step is deemed appropriate by management and Employee Relations.

Step 1 Identification of Performance Deficiencies

A disciplinary process aimed at corrective action should be initiated only after sufficient documentation of the problem exists.

- o Use factual and first-hand information
- o Verify data
- o Differentiate between facts and inferences

Appendix F

Documentation sources may include, but are not limited to, performance ratings, performance criteria as outlined on the review form, records of unsatisfactory work quality or quantity, and a written record of excessive absenteeism and/or tardiness, abuse of telephone or other privileges, etc.

Step 2 Counseling

Counsel the employee regarding the problem, including clearly defining the problem as it affects job performance or conduct. The supervisor should focus on the behavior, rather than the individual. Seek input from the employee on how to address the problem, what actions should be taken, and what time frame should be set for resolution of the problem. The supervisor should document counseling sessions for future discussions and/or reference purposes.

Step 3 Written Warning

A written warning should be issued to an employee when performance or conduct expectations outlined in Step 2 have not been met consistently within the specified time period. The written warning should be reviewed with second-level management and the Employee Relations Representative prior to release to the employee.

Written warnings should define specific performance deficiencies, make references to specific dates on which the employee received prior counseling, outline performance or conduct expectations and a time frame for achieving them, and indicate the consequences which may occur to the employee if the expectations are not consistently met. The written warning should be presented to the employee to read in a counseling session. After discussion, the employee should be asked to acknowledge receipt of the written warning with his/her signature. The employee should also be given a copy of the written warning. After the counseling session, the supervisor should forward a copy of the written warning to the Employee Relations Representative for inclusion in the employee's personnel file.

Step 4 Probation

Probation is appropriate when the employee has not met the conditions of the written warning. A letter should be drafted and reviewed by second-level management and the Employee Relations Representative prior to being presented to the employee in a formal probation counseling session.

The probation letter should include a concise description of the employee's continued failure to meet performance or conduct expectations, the time period (usually 30-90 days) for improvement to at least a satisfactory level, and the possibility of termination should improvement to a satisfactory level not be achieved. The probationary letter should be released to the employee during the counseling session, and the employee should acknowledge receipt of the letter with his/her signature. A copy should also be forwarded to the Employee Relations Representative for inclusion in the employee's personnel file.

It is anticipated that any employee placed on probation will be given the entire length of the probationary period to meet performance expectations. However, if, in management's judgement, the employee is not making significant progress to warrant continuation of the probationary period, management may elect with second-level approval and Employee Relations concurrence to terminate the employee prior to the completion of the stated probationary period.

Step 5 Recommendation for Employee Separation

If the supervisor believes that the employee has failed to meet the conditions outlined in the probation letter, the supervisor should prepare a written recommendation to terminate the employee. The document should be approved by second-level management, and the Employee Relations Representative's concurrence obtained, prior to further action being initiated by the immediate supervisor.

The employee should be informed by the supervisor of the specific reason(s) for termination. Normally, the supervisor should have the Employee Relations Representative or another individual present at the termination meeting. Subsequent to the termination meeting, the supervisor should prepare a memo to file documenting the termination session, sending a copy to the Employee Relations Representative for inclusion in the employee's pesonnel file.

The supervisor should coordinate with the Employee Relations Representative to ensure that the separating employee is properly paid, receives benefits counseling, relinquishes any Company property in his/her possession, and/or arranges to repay to the Company any outstanding debt(s).

Immediate Disciplinary Action

Unfortunately, not all performance or conduct issues lend themselves to the step-by-step approach outlined above. There are times when immediate disciplinary action, including termination, may be warranted on the first occurence of a performance or conduct problem. Examples of such cases, though not all-inclusive, are illustrated by the following:

- Failure to carry out reasonable management directives
- Unauthorized release of confidential Company information
- Misappropriation of Company property
- Falsification of Company records or reports, including expense reports
- Negligence involving the possibility of serious accident or injury to self, other employees, or general public
- Unauthorized possession of weapons or controlled substances
- Assault and/or battery on fellow employees, supervisor, customers, and general public while at work or representing Company

The discharge of an employee is at the sole discretion of the Company

Management, with assistance from Employee Relations, shall investigate each incident and verify all information prior to the discharge of an employee. Employees should be given an opportunity to address any allegations where practical. Under no circumstance should an employee be terminated on the spot. In instances where immediate disciplinary action is required, management may elect to suspend the employee to remove him/her from the workplace until an investigation is completed. The suspension of an employee with or without pay requires the review of second-level management and Employee Relations, even though the review may take place after suspension has occurred. Pay considerations during suspension will be determined by management and Employee Relations upon conclusion of the investigation.

Cases involving drug and/or alcohol possession or abuse, though often necessitating immediate action such as suspension, may also involve additional considerations. Therefore, management should consult with the Employee Relations Representative as early as possible regarding disciplinary action in these cases.

V. RELATED ISSUES

Problem Resolution Policy

A non-represented employee may at any time, including during a period of corrective disciplinary action, register a complaint or disagreement involving the work environment through management, Employee Relations, or the Company's **Employee Problem Resolution Policy For Non-Represented Employees**. An employee who registers a complaint or disagreement in good faith will not be adversely treated as a result of having registered the complaint or disagreement. However, utilization of the Problem Resolution Program does not exempt an employee from an ongoing and/or pending disciplinary action, up to and including termination.

Presence of Co-Workers at Counseling Sessions

Employees have the right to have a co-worker present, if requested, at any counseling session.

Job Applications

An employee on probation is not precluded from applying for any posted job vacancy Questions regarding specific situations should be referred to the Employee Relations Representative.

Performance Review

A performance review which falls during an employee's probationary period should be conducted with the employee at the scheduled time. Consideration should be given to assessing how well the individual's performance meets the requirements for the job during the entire period covered by the performance review.

Merit Salary Action

Merit salary action for an employee on probation should be delayed until the probationary period is completed. Merit consideration, if any, should reflect the entire performance evaluation period, including the probationary period. In cases where salary action is subsequently granted, the merit salary increase should not be paid retroactively for the period during which the employee was on probation.

Demotion

A decision to demote an employee should be handled on a case-by-case basis by management in consultation with the Employee Relations Representative.

VI. DOCUMENTATION

Good documentation not only apprises an employee of his or her performance or conduct deficiencies and the corrective action expected, but also serves as a record of actual corrective action taken and/or achieved. In today's legal climate, the importance of accurate and objective documentation cannot be overemphasized. In many states, the law requires that all documentation maintained on an employee which can impact his or her employment status must be shown to the employee on demand. These provisions also pertain to any files a supervisor may retain on an employee. It is the policy of Company to freely share this information with its employees.

All questions regarding the type and format of documentation should be referred to the Employee Relations Representative.

Appendix F

PERSONNEL POLICY & PROCEDURES

TITLE	POLICY NO.	
PERFORMANCE IMPROVEMENT POLICY	D4	
	EFFECTIVE DATE	PAGE
	5/1/84	1 of 2

A. SCOPE

All employees with at least one year of service, and who are not covered by a collective bargaining agreement.

B. POLICY

It is the policy of the Company to provide counseling, support and development to employees whose performance is marginal or unsatisfactory, in order to assist the employee to meet job requirements and to prevent the need for disciplinary action or termination of such employees from the Company.

C. PHILOSOPHY

The Company is interested in providing each employee with the direction, development and counseling necessary to assure a productive and rewarding career. The Company's Performance Planning and Review Program and Skills Review Program are the primary methods for providing guidance and feedback to employees on their performance and skill development. In cases where employee performance is substandard (i.e., below established expectations) on a sustained basis (i.e., several months), additional counseling and direction may be necessary beyond that provided by the Performance Review and Skills Review Programs. This policy outlines the steps that should be taken to provide this direction and counseling.

Definition of Unsatisfactory Performance

Performance may be unsatisfactory in a number of areas, including but not restricted to:

1. Work output (quality or quantity) is not meeting the requirements of the job.

2. Work is consistently off schedule.

3. The employee is not meeting generally accepted standards of employment (e.g., excessive or sustained absenteeism or tardiness).

4. Inability to maintain satisfactory working relationships with others.

Employees whose performance appears to be unsatisfactory, on a sustained basis, in any of the above categories, should be provided the following steps of counseling:

Step 1

At the first sign of sustained unsatisfactory performance, the manager should:

1. Meet with the employee for a formal discussion of performance.

2. Clarify expectations which are not being met.

3. Discuss specific performance problems.

4. List specific expectations for improvement.

G-1180-G

PERSONNEL POLICY & PROCEDURE

POLICY NO.	EFFECTIVE DATE	PAGE	TITLE
D4	5/1/84	2 of 2	PERFORMANCE IMPROVEMENT POLICY

5. Provide the employee with a dated written summary of the discussion, including a statement discribing the performance problems and a list of specific expectations for improvement.

6. Closely monitor the employee's performance for a period of at least one month following the discussion.

Step 2

If improvement has occurred, the manager should provide feedback to the employee on the improved work performance.

If improvement has not taken place:

1. The employee should be placed on a formal performance improvement plan for a specified duration (typically three or more months). This plan should be documented in writing and signed by the next level of management and the employee. A copy should be sent to the local Personnel Relations office.

2. The manager should again specify improvements which must be made during this time frame and suggest development actions to assist the employee in making the improvements.

3. The manager should specify future disciplinary action to be taken if improvement is not made during the improvement plan period.

4. The manager should monitor performance closely during the improvement plan period. It is also critical that the manager provide frequent guidance and counsel to assist the employee in making the desired improvements.

5. At the end of the improvement plan period, the manager should formally review performance with the employee.

If performance has improved, the employee should be taken off the formal improvement plan and reminded that improved performance is now expected to continue. If performance has not improved or it regresses at a later date, appropriate disciplinary action will be taken. Documentation of unsatisfactory performance will remain in the employee's personnel folder for three years. At the end of three years, the documentation should be destroyed if the employee's performance has been fully satisfactory during the interim period.

The major objective of this policy is to improve marginal or unsatisfactory employee performance and to prevent further deterioration of the employee's work performance. A second important objective is to make certain that when an employee's continued employment is under question, the employee will be provided support, assistance and guidance from the Company's management – before disciplinary action becomes necessary.

D. **EXCEPTIONS TO POLICY**

It is recognized that there may be occasions where it is not in the best interests of either the employee or the Company to continue an employment relationship. In such situations, the use of a formal performance improvement plan may be waived, with the concurrence of both the Division Head and the Vice President, Human Resources. Such exceptions should be rare, and waiver of the performance improvement plan should be considered only in situations where, after careful thought, it is concluded that a period of formal performance counseling will most likely not bring about the changes in performance or work relationships that are necessary.

Appendix F

Job Performance Standards

You and your fellow employees are part of a work team--a team dedicated to providing agents and customers with the best possible service. The hard work and efforts of all our employees have resulted in the success of our organization. Continued growth and success is dependent on a high level of performance by all of us. Fair and equitable job performance standards have been developed to assist in attaining these objectives.

During your first six months of employment, the first six months of your assignment to a new position or after substantial responsibilities have been changed in your current position, your performance will be reviewed by your supervisor. If it is determined that you are unable to perform the required job responsibilities based on knowledge, experience and skill, you will be considered for other available positions within the company.

The job performance of all employees will be reviewed regularly. If you have shown that you are capable of doing your job, but your level of performance becomes unsatisfactory, any problems you are having will be discussed with you and you will be given an opportunity for counseling or assistance from your supervisor. The opportunities to improve performance are provided through a formalized corrective action procedure. If all steps in this procedure fail to improve performance to a satisfactory level, termination will result.

Appendix F

STANDARDS OF JOB PERFORMANCE

Satisfactory job performance by all Employees is the primary means each of us has to impact the retention of agents and customers, attainment of new ones, and the enhancement of individual job security. The dedication and conscientious effort of our Employees has created the success of our organization. The following procedure will be followed when an Employee's Job Performance is unsatisfactory. Each individual Employee is important and the following Standards of Job Performance are designed to assist an Employee in achieving performance that meets expectations.

A. Job Performance Ability - During the first six months of employment, the first six months of an assignment to a new position or after substantial responsibilities have been changed in a current position, the Employee's Job Performance will be reviewed by supervision. If it is determined that the Employee is unable to perform the required job responsibilities based on knowledge, experience and skill, the Employee will be considered for other available positions within the Company.

B. Job Performance/Contents and Results - If an Employee has the ability to perform the assigned duties but the effectiveness or results are considered unsatisfactory, corrective action will be taken. Employees performing within the same job title will be reviewed using the same criteria. The Employee will be given full opportunity to present a position. If appropriate, the following corrective steps will be progressively taken.

1. When a supervisor can document the unsatisfactory performance of an Employee, a meeting will be called to review all the facts with the Employee. If the supervisor determines that corrective action is necessary, a Verbal Warning will be issued to be included in the personnel file for one year. The Employee will be given specific instructions for immediate improvement, counseled and encouraged to succeed.

2. During the next thirty days (the exact timing to be determined based on the repetitive nature of the Employee's responsibilities) the supervisor will review the Employee's Job Performance with the Employee.

   a. If performance improves to an acceptable level, the Employee will be encouraged to continue those efforts so that the Verbal Warning can be removed after one year; failure to maintain satisfactory performance during such year will be cause for a Written Warning.

   b. If the performance remains unsatisfactory, a Written Warning will be issued.

3. If a Written Warning has been issued, a meeting will be held with the Employee, during the next thirty days.

   a. If performance has improved to an acceptable level the Employee and supervisor will meet and the Employee will be encouraged to continue such efforts so that the Written Warning can be removed from the personnel file after one year; failure to maintain satisfactory performance during such year will be cause for a Probationary Period.

   b. If Job Performance remains unsatisfactory, a meeting will be held with the Employee, the supervisor and Human Resources representative to provide all parties with an opportunity to present the facts. Termination will result if satisfactory performance has not been achieved during the Probationary period.

4. An Employee on Probation will be given progress reports and counseling during the Probationary Period (established relative to the repetitive nature of the Employee's responsibilities).

   a. If satisfactory performance has been reached during the Probationary Period, it must continue in order to remove the Probationary letter from the file after one year; failure to do so following a complete discussion of the record at that time will be cause for Termination.

   b. If performance remains unsatisfactory, a meeting will be held with the Employee, the supervisor and Human Resources representative to provide all parties with an opportunity to present the facts. Termination will result if satisfactory performance has not been achieved during the Probationary period.

Appendix F

ADMINISTRATION OF STANDARDS OF JOB PERFORMANCE

INTRODUCTION

The following procedure is to be used to identify and correct unsatisfactory performance of Employees. The procedure requires the use of evenly applied standards, constructive Employee counseling, and substantiating documentation, leading to progressive corrective action if performance fails to meet satisfactory levels.

The corrective procedure involves three basic steps: Verbal Warning, Written Warning, and Probation. Each of these steps are opportunities for the Supervisor to formally and constructively counsel the Employee regarding job performance and to provide specific instructions for improvement.

This procedure is applicable to all levels of Employees. It is to be fairly and consistently applied in keeping with the Corporation's Equal Employment Opportunity Policy. Meeting with the Employee if correction is achieved and encouraging the Employee to continue satisfactory performance is extremely important.

If after following this procedure, corrective action or termination is deemed appropriate but the Employee voluntarily terminates before action can be taken, the file documentation must still be prepared with a copy included in the Employee's personnel file.

Human Resources Assistance

Human Resources has specific responsibilities in the administration of this procedure. These responsibilities are addressed in the following paragraphs. Where Human Resources involvement is provided for in this procedure but not available at the location, a telephone discussion can be held prior to taking any action.

Job Performance/Ability

During the first six months of employment, the first six months of an assignment to a new position or after substantial responsibilities have been changed in a current position, the Employee's Job Performance will be reviewed by supervision. If it is determined that the Employee is unable to perform the required job responsibilities based on knowledge, experience and skill, the Employee will be considered for other available positions within the Company.

The administration of the Job Performance/Ability provisions are simple but must be applied carefully after a meeting is first held between the supervisor, next level of supervision and the Human Resources representative. This is not corrective action, therefore, justification for the determined level of ability must be reasonable and defensible. Its purpose is to rectify the unusual case of poor employee selection for promotion or transfer or a major change in responsibilities which is of benefit to the Corporation's objectives. It will not be used as an easy, quick method to remove a problem Employee who has the ability and or qualifications to satisfactorily perform the assigned job duties; the following progressive corrective action procedure must be used.

Appendix F

Job Performance/Content and Results

If an Employee has the ability to perform the assigned duties but the effectiveness or results are considered unsatisfactory, corrective action will be taken. Employees performing within the same job title will be reviewed using the same criteria. The Employee will be given full opportunity to present a position. If appropriate, the following corrective steps will be progressively taken.

A. Verbal Warning (See Exhibit I)

The Verbal Warning has three objectives:

1. To constructively counsel the Employee regarding satisfactory performance requirements and how these should be achieved.

2. To secure the Employee's understanding to seek to improve job performance within a specific timeframe.

3. To notify the Employee that recent job performance is deficient and that continued unsatisfactory performance will lead to more serious corrective action.

The following guidelines should be observed when verbally warning an Employee about unsatisfactory performance:

1. The meeting should take place in private, free from interruptions.

2. The supervisor should clearly and directly discuss specific deficiencies in job performance, the impact of these deficiencies on the work unit, and what steps need to be taken to improve performance. Give the Employee full opportunity to present a position. If during the discussion with the Employee a personal problem is involved in the reason for an unacceptable record, referral to Special Health Services should be considered. There should be an understanding between the Supervisor and Employee as to what the supervisor's expectations are and what steps are to be taken by the Employee to achieve satisfactory performance and become a fully contributing member of the unit. The supervisor's goal is to get the Employee back on track; individual assistance and direction provided in a positive manner is essential.

3. The supervisor must state that this is a formal Verbal Warning and discuss the consequences of continued unsatisfactory performance.

4. A specific timeframe of no longer than thirty days should be established to review progress, (the exact timing to be determined based on the repetitive nature of the Employees responsibilities). If a timeframe of less than 20 days is contemplated by the supervisor, Human Resources must be contacted for approval prior to meeting with the Employee.

5. The meeting should conclude with agreement from the Employee to improve performance to an acceptable level, with the understanding that failure to do so by the agreed upon date will result in further corrective action.

6. The Verbal Warning must be documented, in the form of a file memorandum, with a copy to the Human Resouces representative and the employee, outlining those facts in items 2 through 5. A copy of the Standards of Job Performance should be given to the Employee.

B. Written Warning (See Exhibit II)

The Written Warning serves to formally notify the Employee in writing that job performance continues to be unsatisfactory, despite a Verbal Warning and that continued unsatisfactory performance will lead to Probation and could ultimately lead to Termination. A review of the case should be made by the Department Manager and Human Resources representative prior to the meeting to confirm the action to be considered. When deemed appropriate, the Special Health Services Coordinator should be called into the meeting or consulted by telephone if a personal problem is involved in the reason for an unacceptable record.

The following guidelines will be followed in issuing the Written Warning to an Employee about unsatisfactory performance:

1. The performance problem is to be reviewed with the Employee no longer than 30 days following the Verbal Warning in a private meeting with full opportunity for the Employee to present a position. Exhibit II, the Notice of Corrective Action, will be issued to the Employee following this review unless information is developed at this meeting that would preclude the necessity of a Written Warning. If performance has not improved to an acceptable level, the Notice of Corrective Action form is to be completed and signed by the Supervisor after all the facts are known. The Employee should sign the form and the Supervisor should so note if the Employee refuses. Copies should be sent to the Human Resources representative and a copy given to the Employee as promptly as possible after corrective action is taken, but in any event, no later than two work days following the meeting.

2. The specifics contained on the form should be brief, but concise. Specifics, such as dates and quantitative measures, should be included. The supervisor should describe the standards against which the Employee's performance is being assessed and specific performance deficiencies. The tone should be factual, avoiding philosophising and allegations concerning the Employee's attitude or other personality characteristics.

3. The Written Warning should state the timeframe within which improved performance to an acceptable level is expected and the consequences of the Employee's failure to do so. In general, this timeframe should be no longer than 30 days. (The exact timing should be determined based on the repetitive nature of the Employee's responsibilities). If a timeframe of less than 20 days is contemplated by the supervisor, Human Resources must be contacted for approval prior to meeting with the Employee. Maintaining satisfactory performance for one year will result in removal of the Written Warning.

C. Final Warning/Probation (See Exhibit III)

The Final Warning/Probation is issued to notify the Employee that Job Performance continues to be unsatisfactory, despite a Verbal and Written Warning. Continued unsatisfactory performance during a Probational Period (of no longer than 30 days) will result in Termination.

Before any Employee is placed on Probation, the Department Manager and the Human Resources representative must review the file documentation regarding the Verbal and Written Warnings and the subsequent performance documentation. When deemed appropriate, the Special Health Services Coordinator should be called into the meeting or consulted by telephone if a personal problem is involved in the reason for an unacceptable record. The Employee's position will be heard in a meeting with the supervisor and the Human Resources representative. The Employee should be excused at the close of the meeting to permit the supervisor and Human Resources representative to have a brief caucus to decide whether to place the Employee on Probation. Following the caucus, the Employee will return to be notified of the Company's decision. The Notice of Disciplinary Action will be completed by the supervisor, and signed by the three parties, and a copy will be given to the Employee as promptly as possible after corrective action is taken, but in any event, no later than two work days following the meeting.

The following guidelines shold be observed in placing an Employee on Probation for performance problems:

1. The Notice of Probation should outline to the Employee the specific areas of deficiency that must be corrected during this Probation. Specific assignments and completion dates will be discussed with the Employee. These assignments should be consistent with the job function.

2. Indicate to the Employee that this Probationary Period has been implemented to help overcome performance deficiencies and to provide encouragement to exercise a conscientious effort to improve to an acceptable level. In addition, the supervisor should outline specific action that will be taken to assist the Employee return to an acceptable level of performance.

3. Advise the Employee that during the Probation Period, the supervisor will hold a private meeting at least twice during the Probationary Period and formally discuss the Employees progress, or lack thereof, in overcoming any job performance deficiencies. Any questions or problems the Employee has regarding any assignments should be brought to the supervisor's attention.

4. At the end of each Probationary Period review, these formal discussions will be recorded on Probation Reports by the Supervisor. (See Exhibits IV & V). The Probation Report should be used to track the Employee's progress to meet the required job standards within the specific timeframe. These reports should be reviewed with the Employee. These reports are to be sent to Human Resources within two work days after the review for inclusion in the Employee's personnel file. As appropriate, documentation (such as work samples) should be attached.

D. Correction During Probation (See Exhibit VI)

Should the Employee's performance improve to an acceptable level during the Probation Period, the Employee should be encouraged to continue such efforts. A follow-up letter should inform the employee that the Letter of Probation will remain in the personnel file for one year and that the recurrence of poor job performance within the timeframe would be cause for immediate termination. During the year that the letter is in the file, if an Employee begins to slip again, the Employee is to be counseled concerning the consequences of unsatisfactory performance.

E. Termination - Poor Performance (See Exhibit VII)

This action is exercised when all efforts have failed to make the individual a productive Employee. Whenever an Employee is terminated for poor performance, his or her personnel file should contain a final performance appraisal, rating the individual as a "1" - unsatisfactory.

If performance has not improved at the end of the Probation Period or is unsatisfactory during the one year Probation letter is active in the personnel file, the supervisor and Human Resources representative should review the entire case with the next level of functional and Human Resources management. If the record supports unsatisfactory performance, the supervisor and Human Resources representative should schedule a meeting with the Employee, without predetermining that Termination will result.

Minutes of the meeting must be taken, summarized in the form of a memorandum and placed in the Employee's personnel file. The manner in which this meeting is conducted is critical. While this meeting should not come as a surprise to the Employee (based on the preceding actions) the Employee must be allowed to fully present a position relative to all of the documented and stated evidence. The Employee should be excused at the close of the meeting to permit the supervisor and Human Resources representative to have a brief caucus to decide whether to terminate the Employee. Following the caucus the Employee will return to be notified of the Company's decision. Every effort should be made to clarify that the actions taken have been fair and unbiased. The Employee should be informed of the decision in writing as soon as possible and if terminated, allowed to gather personal belongings. An example of the administration of the Job Performance Standard is provided in Exhibit VIII. If you have any questions concerning a specific set of circumstance, contact your Human Resources representative as soon as possible.

Appendix F

PERFORMANCE

Appendix F

INTER-OFFICE COMMUNICATION

GEN 119D NY

EXHIBIT I

TO	File	AT	
FROM	Mary Clark, Supervisor	AT	
SUBJECT	Verbal Warning: Jack Doe, Rate and Code Clerk	DATE	February 9, 1981

Yesterday I met with Jack Doe to discuss his declining work performance, which has contributed to a reduction in the quality and quantity produced in this unit.

In our conversation I made him aware of our practice to verbally warn employees whose performance is declining.

In the past two weeks I have had to speak to Mr. Doe about the amount of work that had to be redone, due to serious errors in both rating and coding. As we discussed, if Mr. Doe's work does not improve within the next month (reducing error rate x%) we will have no alternative but to take further corrective action. Further, his performance will have to remain satisfactory for one year in order to avoid corrective action of a Written Warning.

Mr. Doe stated that he did not think his work was any worse than some other employees but he did recognize the errors documented in his prior work. I assured him that all employees are subject to corrective action if unsatisfactory performance is recorded.

I emphasized my sincere hope that Mr. Doe would accept his warning as constructive guidance. He assured me of his cooperation.

Mary Clark
Supervisor

MC:xx

Attachments: Copies of Work

cc: Jack Doe
Human Resources Representative

Printed in U.S.A.

Appendix F

NOTICE OF CORRECTIVE ACTION

COMPANY ____________________ LOCATION Anywhere, USA

Employee Name Jack Doe   Job Title Rate and Code Clerk

Department Rate & Code   Supervisor Mary Clark

Period Covered March 8, 1981 to March 8, 1982

X Written Warning   ___ Final Warning/Probation

I. REASON FOR ACTION

X a. Performance   ___ b. Absenteeism/Lateness   ___ c. Conduct

The employee was verbally warned of the consequences of continued declining work performance on February 9, 1981. This action was the result of continued declining work during the preceding two-week period. During that time several hours worth of work had to be redone because of serious errors in both rating and coding. Our practice is to verbally warn the employee if such behavior persists that it will lead to further corrective action. The employee was informed verbally that if he did not reduce his error rate by x% within one month that further corrective action would be taken. The employee continued to make serious errors. Other departments complain that his errors are slowing them down and causing errors in their work. Average number of errors per week for the last 3 weeks has increased by y%. Copies of work assignments are attached.

II. REQUIRED IMPROVEMENTS

The employee's work must improve so that his error rate is decreased by x% during the next 30 days and remain satisfactory for until March 8, 1982 to avoid probation status, at which time this Written Warning will be removed from the personnel file. Departmental operating procedures, methods of recheck work, and rating and coding mechanics were reviewed and full opportunity was provided for Mr. Doe to ask questions. To assist the Employee, I will review his work to determine the types of errors which are recurring and prepare a checklist for his use.

III. EMPLOYEE COMMENTS

Attachments: (Work Samples)

Mary Clark Supervisor	March 9, 1981 Date
Next Level of Supervision	Date
Human Resources Representative	Date
Employee (Indicates Acknowledgement)	Date

Appendix F

NOTICE OF CORRECTIVE ACTION

COMPANY CIC   LOCATION Anywhere, USA

Employee Name Jack Doe   Job Title Rate and Code Clerk

Department Rate and Code   Supervisor Mary Clark

Period Covered April 6, 1981 to April 6, 1982

___ Written Warning   X Final Warning/Probation

I. REASON FOR ACTION

X a. Performance   ___ b. Absenteeism/Lateness   ___ c. Conduct

Jack Doe received a Verbal Warning about his declining work performance on February 9, 1981. He received a Written Warning on March 9. He was told to reduce his error rate by x%. His error rate continued to be very high. After a Verbal and Written Warning are given and performance does not sufficiently improve, our practice is to issue a Final Warning and put the employee on Probation. The errors are resulting in increased processing time and hindering other employees in the completion of their duties. The seriousness of his job performance record and the possibility of Termination was thoroughly discussed.

II. REQUIRED IMPROVEMENTS

The employee must reduce his error rate by x% during the next 30 day Probation Period and then maintain that level of performance until April 6, 1982 in order to remove the Probationary Letter from his file and avoid termination. The Company's Corrective Action Procedure was reviewed and a discussion was held on the rechecking efforts which should be made to eliminate errors.

III. EMPLOYEE COMMENTS

Attachments: (Work Samples)

Mary Clark Supervisor	April 7, 1981 Date
Next Level of Supervision	Date
Human Resources Representative	Date
Employee (Indicates Acknowledgement)	Date

Appendix F

EMPLOYEE PROBATION REPORT

COMPANY CIC

LOCATION Anywhere, USA

Employee Name Jack D

Job Title Rate and Code Clerk

Department Rate and Code

Supervisor Mary Clark

Biweekly Period of April 7, 1981 to April 21, 1981

I. EVALUATION OF EMPLOYEE PERFORMANCE

X a. Performance ___ b. Absenteeism/Lateness ___ c. Conduct

Jack Doe's work contains many serious errors. His error rate is increasing rather than decreasing. Other Departments are claiming his work is hindering them in performing their jobs. A lack of attention to detail and attention to the work in general is apparent. Concentration on his duties is sporadic. His work load is not greater than other employees and is considered a normal operating level. Further assistance and counseling will be provided.

II. EMPLOYEE COMMENTS

I have the ability to do the job but in order to accomplish the work assigned, I must work faster than I would like. The pressure is too high for getting the work out.

Mary Clark	April 21, 1981
Supervisor	Date
Next Level of Supervision	Date
Human Resources Representative	Date
Employee (Indicates Acknowledgement)	Date

Appendix F

EMPLOYEE PROBATION REPORT

COMPANY ___CIC___ LOCATION ___Anywhere, USA___

Employee Name ___Jack Doe___ Job Title ___Rate and Code Clerk___

Department ___Rate and Code___ Supervisor ___Mary Clark___

Biweekly Period of ___April 21, 1981___ to ___May 5, 1981___

I. EVALUATION OF EMPLOYEE PERFORMANCE

_X_ a. Performance ___ b. Absenteeism/Lateness ___ c. Conduct

Jack Doe's work contains many serious errors. His error rate is increasing rather than decreasing. Other departments are claiming his work is hindering them in performing their jobs. He has made no effort to improve his work methods or to try any of the ideas suggested to improve his performance.

II. EMPLOYEE COMMENTS

I am doing the best I can and I feel it is satisfactory.

Mary Clark	May 5, 1981
Supervisor	Date
Next Level of Supervision	Date
Human Resources Representative	Date
Employee (Indicates Acknowledgement)	Date

Appendix F

INTER-OFFICE COMMUNICATION

GEN 119DNY

SAMPLE LETTER OF REINSTATEMENT TO PRIOR STATUS - EXHIBIT VI

TO	Jack Doe	AT	
FROM	Mary Clark, Supervisor	AT	
SUBJECT	Notice of Reinstatement to Prior Status	DATE	May 5, 1981

During the past 30 days you have been on Probation for poor performance. I am pleased that you have met our requirement that you reduce your error rate by x% during this period.

I must advise you, however, that the Probation Letter will remain in your file for one year and that if your performance should decline again during this time, it would be cause for Termination.

I sincerely hope that you will keep up the good work you demonstrated during the past 30 days. If you have problems please see me immediately so that it can be corrected without affecting your employment. I am confident that your efforts will be successful.

Mary Clark
Supervisor

MC:xx

cc: Human Resources Representative

Printed in U S A

Appendix F

INTER-OFFICE COMMUNICATION

GEN 119D NY

SAMPLE TERMINATION LETTER - EXHIBIT VII

TO Jack Doe

FROM Mary Clark, Supervisor AT

SUBJECT Performance Record DATE May 6, 1981

You were verbally warned about your declining performance on February 9, 1981.

You received a Written Warning on March 8th after continued deficient performance.

You received a Final Warning and were put on Probation on April 6, 1981 and required to reduce your error rate by x% within the next 30 day period.

During Probation your error rate did not improve. Your entire performance record was reviewed with you on May 5th including the background and documentation of your work performance. You have been counseled, instructed, and given opportunities to ask questions and correct your performance without result.

Therefore, following our meeting of today in which you were provided with a full opportunity to present your position, it has been determined that your termination of employment should be effective immediately.

Mary Clark
Supervisor

MC:xx

cc: Next Level of Supervision
Human Resources Representative

Appendix F

EXAMPLE APPLICATION TO AN EMPLOYEE

STEP 1 - Verbal Warning given on January 1, 1982 for poor job performance

Jan. 1, 1982	Jan. 1, 1983
* 30 Day Review	If 30 day review is satisfactory performance must be maintained for the verbal warning to be removed from active file.

STEP 2 - Written Warning given on February 1, 1982 for continued poor performance

Feb. 1, 1982	Feb. 1, 1983
* 30 Day Review	If 30 day review is satisfactory, performance must be maintained for removal of the Written Warning from active file

STEP 3 - Probation status issued on March 1, 1982 for continued poor performance

Mar. 1, 1982	Mar. 1, 1983
* TWO REVIEWS	If the final review is satisfactory, performance must be maintained for removal of Probationary status

STEP 4 - Termination effective April 1, 1982 for continued poor performance.

* (The period of time for review determined by the repetitive nature of the Employee's job responsibilities).

Appendix F

Since lateness can be as disruptive to normal operations as your absence, you should do your best to be on time every day. An unsatisfactory absenteeism record will result in corrective action.

The number of absence occurrences are used to determine whether or not corrective action is necessary. An absence occurrence begins when you are absent from work, paid or non-paid, for one or more hours for reasons other than vacation, holidays, jury duty, paid personal days, bereavement or leaves of absence and continues until you return to work. A late report or early departure—up to 60 minutes from the scheduled starting or quitting time or lunch break—constitutes one half an absence occurrence. If you are late more than 60 minutes from the starting time, you will be recorded as late and charged with one absence occurrence.

If you accumulate five absence occurrences during any 365-day period, your supervisor will hold a counseling discussion to assist you in correcting your record. After seven absence occurrences, you will receive a written warning. You will be placed on probation after the ninth occurrence and terminated after the eleventh occurrence in any 365-day period.

In addition to the counseling discussion, your supervisor will meet with you at each step of the corrective action procedure to review your attendance record and discuss ways of resolving the causes of your absenteeism.

Appendix F

CORRECTIVE ACTION PROCEDURE

ABSENTEEISM

Absences from work for illness or personal reasons are likely to occur during the work history of all Employees. Every absence has an effect on the accomplishments and productivity of an Employee's area of responsibility. The vast majority of all Employees exercise diligent and effective self control of their attendance record and this Absenteeism Control Procedure should have no impact on them.

However, physical or personal problems may accumulate for individual Employees which will significantly reduce their ability to be satisfactorily productive in the performance of their duties. This procedure will be followed when corrective action is necessary to resolve unsatisfactory Employee Absenteeism. It provides for the equitable and uniform application of rules governing absences. The goal of the Corporation is to assist Employees in the control and correction of the causes of unsatisfactory Absenteeism records.

Each Employee is expected to be present at work on all scheduled work days and to report to work on time. Moreover, it is the obligation of each Employee to notify supervision as soon as possible of a late report or absence and to state the reason. Failure to provide timely advance notice shall be treated as a separate violation of Standards of Conduct.

The effective date of this procedure is ____________________. Absenteeism and late reports prior to this date shall not be included in the administration of this procedure.

Definitions:

A. One Absence Occurrence

1. Is a Paid or Unpaid Absence from work for one or more hours (for Employees on flextime one or more hours of core time), continuing until the Employee returns to work.

2. Is not recorded for absences due to vacation, holidays, jury duty, bereavement days, paid personal days and leaves of absence.

3. Includes a period of rehabilitation following an illness or accident approved and documented by a physician or the Medical Department.

B. One Half Absence Occurrence

1. Is a late report - or early departure up to 60 minutes from the scheduled starting or quitting (core) time or lunch break.

Appendix F

Corrective Action Schedule

The Corrective Action Schedule which follows provides for steps to determine the underlying reasons for Absenteeism and to work out effective methods to reduce occurrences. The degree of corrective action is related to the number of Absence Occurrences in any 365 day period, with progressive measures imposed if the record fails to be corrected.

The schedule is simple.

Step 1 If in any 365 day period, an Employee has five Absence Occurrences, supervision will counsel the Employee on methods to improve the record.

Step 2 If further Absence Occurrences continue, a Written Warning will be given after the seventh (7th) occurrence in any 365 day period.

Step 3 The Employee is placed on Probation after the ninth (9th) Absence Occurrence in any 365 day period. The Employee must take corrective actions or Termination will result. In recognition of unforeseen events, a tenth (10th) Absence Occurrence in any 365 day period will be allowed without Termination. The Employee is responsible for conserving and protecting that last occurrence. The eleventh (11th) occurrence in any 365 day period will result in Termination.

SUMMARY OF CORRECTION STEPS

Absence Occurrences in any 365 Day Period	Correction
5	Counseling Session
7	Written Warning
9	Probation - Final Warning
11	Termination

A private discussion with the Employee will be held as soon as possible after the Absence Occurrence, which by schedule calls for corrective action. This will allow the record to be reviewed, problems discussed, and corrective action decided.

Every employee is responsible for being fully aware of this procedure and knowledgeable about how the schedule of corrective action operates. If you have any questions, ask your Supervisor.

Appendix F

ADMINISTRATION OF

CORRECTIVE ACTION PROCEDURE

ABSENTEEISM

The Corrective Action Procedure will be followed when steps are necessary to resolve Employee Absenteeism problems. As "Flextime" is established in more of our facilities late reports or absences should be significantly reduced. This is a formalized plan that establishes specific actions when an attendance record becomes unsatisfactory. The vast majority of Employees are conscientious and this program protects them from the burden of carrying the workload of an excessively absent co-worker. In order to ensure consistent application of this procedure and avoid charges of unfairness against supervisors, all employees are subject to corrective action based on the same schedule of Absence Occurrence. Preferential treatment or overlooking one Employee's record while disciplining another cannot be supported. Paid or non-paid, excused or unexcused criteria is not valid.

If an Employee's attendance record begins to slip, do not postpone a private informal discussion prior to using corrective action. A positive act of concern and caring goes a long way. Often a warning for Absenteeism is an Employee's first experience with corrective procedures and it frequently can be avoided by encouraging an Employee to maintain a record unblemished by a Formal Warning.

The basic principle behind this procedure is correction not punishment or intimidation. It is our objective to keep trained Employees and assist them with solving their problems instead of alienating them into an adversary position with resignation or termination as the result.

As soon as possible but in any event no later than two days after an Absence Occurrence has resulted which activates the corrective action schedule, meet with the Employee privately. Be sure that the Company's position is accurate based on the Human Resources attendance record. If after following this procedure corrective action or termination is deemed appropriate, but the Employee voluntarily terminates before action can be taken, the file documentation must still be prepared with a copy included in the Employee's personnel file.

In order that all Employees are treated fairly, only Absence Occurrences falling after the effective date of the procedure will be considered applicable.

The following are guidelines to be observed when taking the various corrective action steps.

A. Counseling Session

1. After five absence occurrences are recorded in a 365 day period, a meeting should be held within two days with the Employee in an effort to resolve the problems causing Absenteeism. The record should be reviewed as to types and numbers of Absence Occurrences. The Employee must be given a full opportunity to present a position. If during the discussion with the Employee a personal problem is involved in the reason for an unacceptable record, referral to Special Health Services should be considered.

2. Provide the Employee with a copy of the entire Corrective Action Procedure-Absenteeism and review it, informing the Employee that two more occurrences totaling seven (7) within a determined time frame based on any 365 day period will result in a Written Warning.

3. The meeting should end on a positive basis with an understanding reached on what actions will be taken to eliminate future occurrences.

4. The Counseling Session should be documented by memo including the facts and statements outlined in one (1) through three (3) above with copies sent to the Human Resources representative for inclusion in the Employee's personnel file (see Exhibit I) for one year.

B. Written Warning

The Written Warning is to document and formally notify the Employee in writing that the attendance record must be corrected.

1. After an Employee has accumulated seven (7) Absence Occurrences in any 365 day period the record should be reviewed with the next higher level of Supervision and the Human Resources representative prior to meeting with the Employee. When deemed appropriate, the Special Health Services Coordinator should be called into the meeting or consulted by telephone if a personal problem is involved in the reason for an unacceptable record. As soon as possible but in any event no later than two work days after an Absence Occurrence has resulted which activates the corrective action schedule, meet with the Employee privately. Be sure that the Company's position is accurate based on the Human Resources attendance record.

2. During the subsequent meeting with the Employee, the record should be reviewed. The Employee must be given a full opportunity to present a position.

3. As a result of this review, inform the Employee that a formal Written Warning is being issued, that will become part of the employment file for one year.

4. Provide the Employee with a reminder of the corrective action procedure by reviewing it and informing the Employee that two more occurrences totaling nine (9) within any 365 day period will result in Probation.

5. The meeting should end on a positive basis with an understanding reached on what actions will be taken to eliminate future occurrences.

6. The Written Warning should be prepared after the meeting including all the facts and statements outlined in two (2) through five (5) of this section in brief but concise form. (see Exhibit II) The notice should be given to the Employee as promptly as possible after corrective action is taken, but in any event no later than two work days following the meeting. A copy is sent to the Human Resources representative for placement in the Employee's Personnel File.

C. Probation

The Employee is now in jeopardy of losing employment and the extreme seriousness of the situation must be emphasized.

1. Nine (9) Absence Occurrences in any 365 day period must be checked for accuracy. Approval for Probation status must be given by the next higher level of Supervision and Human Resources representative, prior to meeting with the Employee in private. When deemed appropriate, the Special Health Services Coordinator should be called into the meeting or consulted by telephone if a personal problem is involved in the reason for an unacceptable record.

   A meeting is held with the Supervisor, Employee, and Human Resources representative and the record is once again reviewed and the Employee is told that Probation status is effective until less than nine occurrences exist in any 365 day period. This must take place as soon as possible but in any event, no later than two work days after an Absence Occurrence has resulted which activates the corrective action schedule.

2. The Employee should be informed that only one more additional Absence Occurrence in any 365 day period can be recorded without Termination. Therefore, it should be protected and reserved for emergency or essential circumstances.

3. The Probationary Letter should be prepared after the meeting including all the facts and statements outlined in one (1) through four (4) above in brief but concise form. (see Exhibit III). The notice should be given to the Employee as promptly as possible after corrective action is taken but in any event, no later than two work days following the meeting. A copy is sent to the Human Resources representative for placement in the Employee's personnel file for one year.

D. Termination

1. If the eleventh (11th) Occurrence in any 365 day period is recorded the Supervisor, next higher level of Supervision and Human Resources representative should review all of the documentation and the record and submit their joint recommendation to the Regional Human Resources and Regional Management for tentative approval. An employee receiving treatment by Special Health Services shall not be subject to Termination for Absenteeism until released by Special Health Services.

2. A meeting is then held with the Employee to verify and discuss the Employee's Absenteeism record with the Supervisor and the Human Resources representative, with minutes taken of the discussion and placed in the Employee's personnel file.

3. The Letter of Termination should be prepared immediately but carefully checked by the Human Resources representative. (see Exhibit IV). The Employee should be informed of the termination decision and allowed to obtain personal belongings etc.

E. <u>Return to Good Standing</u>

An employee returns to good standing relative to the Corrective Action Procedure for Absenteeism when less than five absence occurrences are recorded in any 365 day period.

Appendix F

INTER-OFFICE COMMUNICATION

GEN 119D NY

EXHIBIT I

TO	File	AT	
FROM	Mary Clark, Supervisor	AT	Quadrant X
SUBJECT	Counseling Session - Absenteeism John Doe, Rate & Code Clerk	DATE	October 12, 1981

Yesterday I met with John Doe to discuss his excessive absenteeism, which has contributed to a reduction in the employee's production and resulted in coverage problems.

In our conversation I made him aware of our practice to counsel employees who are excessively absent and that continued absences will lead to further corrective action, up to and including dismissal. The Corrective Action Procedure was reviewed.

Mr. Doe was absent on five separate occasions: August 5, 1980, September 19, 1980, September 26, October 3, and October 10. As we discussed, if Mr. Doe's record includes seven Absence Occurrences prior to August 5, 1981, we will have no alternative but to issue a Written Warning.

The reason for his absenteeism was discussed. Mr. Doe stated that a case of the flu and other short illnesses resulted in the five occurrences. The employee was counseled to seek professional medical care if illness continues.

I emphasized my sincere hope that Mr. Doe would accept this discussion as constructive guidance. He assured me of his cooperation.

Mary Clark
Supervisor

MC:xx

cc: John Doe
Next Level of Supervision
Human Resources Representative

Printed in U.S.A.

Appendix F

NOTICE OF CORRECTIVE ACTION

COMPANY ____CIC____ ___ LOCATION ____Anywhere, USA____

Employee Name ____Jack Doe____ Job Title ____Rate and Code Clerk____

Department ________________ Supervisor ____Mary Clark____

Period Covered ____August 5, 1980____ to ____less than 7 absences are recorded in any 365 day period____

_X_ Written Warning ___ Final Warning/Probation

I. REASON FOR ACTION

___ a. Performance _X_ b. Absenteeism/Lateness ___ c. Conduct

The employee was counseled on the consequences of continued excessive absenteeism on October 12, 1981. This action was a result of the employee's absence on five separate occasions during the preceding 365 day period. The employee was informed verbally that if he recorded two more occurrences prior to August 5th that corrective action of a Written Warning would be taken. The employee was absent on May 25th and June 1st. The problem sited was continued headaches and nausea.

II. REQUIRED IMPROVEMENTS

The employee must not incur two (2) Absence Occurrences prior to August 5th or further corrective action of probation status will result. The employee has agreed to consult a physician to determine a schedule of treatment to correct his headaches and nausea.

III. EMPLOYEE COMMENTS:

Mary Clark Supervisor	June 2, 1981 Date
________________ Next Level of Supervision	________________ Date
________________ Human Resources Representative	________________ Date
________________ Employee (Indicates Acknowledgement)	________________ Date

Appendix F

NOTICE OF CORRECTIVE ACTION

COMPANY ___CIC___ LOCATION ___Anywhere, USA___

Employee Name ___ack Doe___ Job Title ___Rate and Code Clerk___

Department ________ Supervisor ___Mary Clark___

Period Covered ___August 5, 1981___ to ___less than 9 absences in any 365 day period___

___ Written Warning _X_ Final Warning/Probation

I. REASON FOR ACTION

___ a. Performance _X_ b. Absenteeism/Lateness ___ c. Conduct

John Doe received a counseling about excessive absenteeism on October 12, 1981. He received a Written Warning on June 2. He was informed that two additional Absences Occurrences prior to August 5th (nine in 365 days) would be unacceptable. As a result of his lateness on June 5th and 9th, and a sick day absence on June 29th, this Final Written Warning is issued and he is placed on Probation until August 5th. The employee stated that the lateness was a result of traffic problems and the sick day was for the flu. He was counseled to leave for work earlier to avoid delays resulting in lateness and to recognize that his sick days in combination with other occurrences have resulted in an unsatisfactory record.

II. REQUIRED IMPROVEMENTS

Mr. Doe was informed that he has the responsibility to manage the use of one more Absence Occurrence prior to August 5, 1981. It should be used only when he feels there is no other alternative. The second occurrence prior to August 5, 1981 will result in Termination.

III. EMPLOYEE COMMENTS:

___Mary Clark___ Supervisor ___June 30, 1981___ Date

________ Next Level of Supervision ________ Date

________ Human Resources Representative ________ Date

________ Employee (Indicates Acknowledgement) ________ Date

Appendix F

INTER-OFFICE COMMUNICATION

GEN 1190 NY

SAMPLE TERMINATION LETTER **EXHIBIT IV**

TO	John Doe	AT	
FROM	Mary Clark, Supervisor	AT	
SUBJECT	Absenteeism Record	DATE	July 15, 1981

You were counseled about your excessive absenteeism on October 12, 1981.

You received a Written Warning on June 2nd and were placed on Probation on June 30th and you were notified that two more occurrences prior to August 5th would result in Termination. You have been counseled on the correction of your record and reminded of your responsibilities during the corrective action. Your entire absentee record was reviewed with you today due to your absences on July 6th and July 14th, and it was agreed that eleven (11) Absence Occurrences had been recorded in a 365 day period.

Therefore, following our meeting of today in which you were offered the opportunity to present your position, it has been determined that your Absence Occurrence of July 14, 1981, when considered with your total record, must result in your Termination as of today.

Mary Clark
Supervisor

MC:xx

cc: Next Level of Supervision
Human Resources Representative

Printed in U.S.A

Appendix F

STANDARDS OF CONDUCT

The atmosphere in which you work has an important effect on how you do your job. It is important that your safety and your rights are not jeopardized by anyone with whom you work. With this in mind, certain standards of conduct based on generally accepted behavior and common sense have been established.

Depending on the seriousness of the violation and the circumstances of each individual case, misconduct will result in various degrees of corrective action or termination.

It is impossible to cover every Standard of Conduct for all circumstances. However, there are certain serious major offenses which require immediate probation or termination. The list below is intended to provide you with some examples and is not all inclusive:

- refusal to carry out job responsibilities
- fraudulent statements or actions involving Company records or business activities
- absence from work for three consecutive scheduled workdays without notifying the Company
- misappropriation or theft of Company funds
- possession of a weapon on Company premises
- unauthorized possession, use or sale of alcohol or illegal drugs on Company premises
- disorderly conduct including the use of profane or abusive language
- solicitation during working time or distribution in work areas.
- physical violence or intimidation including racial or sexual harassment.

Appendix F

ADMINISTRATION OF STANDARDS OF CONDUCT

INTRODUCTION

The following procedure is to be used to identify and correct unsatisfactory conduct of Employees. The procedure requires the use of evenly applied Standards, constructive Employee counseling, and substantiating documentation, leading to progressive corrective action, if appropriate. It also provides for immediate termination of Employees whose conduct violation is proven to be too serious for corrective action to be effective. Cause for immediate discharge is to be narrowly viewed; for example, gross misconduct or illegal activity. In all instances, the Human Resources representative must be consulted prior to Termination.

This procedure is applicable to all levels of employees. It is to be fairly and consistently applied, in keeping with the Corporation's Equal Employment Opportunity Policy.

If after following this procedure, corrective action or termination is deemed appropriate but the Employee voluntarily terminates before action can be taken, the file documentation must still be prepared with a copy included in the Employee's personnel file.

Human Resources Assistance

Human Resources has specific responsibilities in the administration of this procedure. These responsibilities are addressed in the following paragraphs. Where Human Resources involvement is provided for in this procedure but not available at the location, a telephonic discussion must be held prior to taking any action.

Investigation

Contact the Human Resources representative immediately upon learning of a Conduct Violation to establish the best method for investigating the facts. Each violation of the Standards of Conduct must be completely investigated prior to any discussion, imposition of corrective action, or termination of an accused Employee.

In more serious cases where there is sufficient evidence to consider termination of the Employee but the investigation will be prolonged due to the circumstances of the case or the possible involvement of other individuals, the Employee should be suspended without pay or benefits until the investigation is completed. The suspension should not be longer than two weeks but in all cases contact Human Resources before taking the action.

All other individuals with knowledge of the facts related to the violation should be interviewed with notes taken of the discussions. If more than one Employee is involved in the violation, special care in defining each Employee's involvement is imperative. Do not consider minor facts unimportant.

Appendix F

All prior corrective actions or terminations of other Employees for the same or like occurrence must be reviewed to determine the practice of correcting the type of violation. Based on:

1) the seriousness of the instant case;

2) the existence of prior conduct violations by the Employee within the last year;

3) the level of corrective action previously given for the violation;

a preliminary determination of the probable level of corrective actions should be made.

If prior incidents of corrective action for Conduct Violations exist within the prior year, at least the next level of correction should be imposed, again based on past practice and the seriousness of the violation. This preliminary decision is not made known to the Employee at this time.

Discussion, Then Decision

After the full investigation and review of prior cases is completed, a meeting should then be held with the Employee. The following persons should be present based upon the probable level of action to be taken. Preliminary determinations to Terminate or place an Employee on Probation must be approved by the next higher level of Departmental and Human Resources Management.

1. Verbal Warning - Supervisor

2. Written Warning - Supervisor

3. Probation - Supervisor, Human Resources Representative

4. Termination - Supervisor, Human Resources Representative

(See Exhibits I, II, III, IV respectively)

The Employee is first offered an opportunity to provide all of the facts of the incident. The results of the Company's investigation is then fully discussed, including the Employee's position relative to those facts. The Supervisor will formally document all of the evidence of all parties before and during the meeting.

If Verbal or Written Warning is considered, a short caucus should be called to contact the Human Resources representative to assure consistent application of the procedure. Following the short caucus the Employee will return to be notified of the Company's decision.

If Termination or Probation is considered after the Employee has provided a position, a short caucus should be called and the next higher level of Departmental and Human Resources Management should be contacted to participate in the final decision. In case of possible Termination, minutes of the meeting must be taken, summarized in the form of a memorandum and placed in the Employee's personnel file. If Termination is deemed appropriate, the Employee should be allowed to gather personal belongings.

The Employee should be notified of Written Warning, Probation or Termination action in writing within two days of the meeting, and the documentation remains in the Employee's personnel file for one year.

Appendix F

CONDUCT

Appendix F

GEN 119DNY

INTER-OFFICE COMMUNICATION

EXHIBIT I

TO	File	AT	
FROM	John Smith	AT	
SUBJECT	Verbal Warning: Ann Jones	DATE	June 9, 1981

On June 9, 1981 a meeting was held with Ann Jones to discuss her absence from work without reporting off on June 8th. The requirement to call in and provide a reason for an absence was reviewed.

The problem her absence caused the department in accomplishing its responsibilities when she provided no notice of absence was reviewed.

Ms. Jones stated that her car broke down and she had to take it to a garage for repair; by the time she remembered to call in it was 10 AM so she decided it was too late to do any good.

Ann was informed that it is her responsibility to notify the Company as soon as possible of her absence. Notification at 10 AM would have been late; however, it should have been provided.

As a result, Ms. Jones was informed that she was to consider this conversation to be a Verbal Warning, that correction of this conduct is required, or further corrective action will result. The notation to her file will be retained for one year.

John Smith
Supervisor

JS:xx

cc: Ann Jones
Next Level of Supervision
Human Resources Representative

EXHIBIT III

NOTICE OF CORRECTIVE ACTION

COMPANY Continental Corporation LOCATION ____________

Employee Name John Doe Job Title ____________

Department ____________ Supervisor John Smith

Period Covered July 17, 1981 to July 17, 1982

___ Written Warning X Final Warning/Probation

I. REASON FOR ACTION

___ a. Performance ___ b. Absenteeism/Lateness X c. Conduct

On July 17th you arrived at work in an unstable condition. You were directed to go to the Medical Facility where it was determined that you were under the influence of alcohol, as verified by the attached statement from Dr. Welby. Employees cannot perform their duties satisfactorily under such conditions.

II. REQUIRED IMPROVEMENTS

It was discovered that you have no medical problems such as alcoholism but due to a personal family problem of a non-recurring nature you used alcohol to excess on July 17th. It was agreed that such conduct was not acceptable or an answer to the problem. The Probation Letter for a Conduct Violation will remain in your file for one year during which this incident will be reviewed if further Conduct Violations occur. In such an event, Termination may result. (An appointment may be made for the Employee to visit Special Health Services; if so document it).

III. EMPLOYEE COMMENTS:

John Smith
Supervisor

July 17, 1981
Date

____
Next Level of Supervision

____
Date

____
Human Resources Representative

____
Date

____
Employee (Indicates Acknowledgement)

____
Date

Appendix F

INTER-OFFICE COMMUNICATION

GEN 1190 NY

TERMINATION LETTER **EXHIBIT IV**

TO	Susan Smith	AT	
FROM	John Doe, Human Resources Officer	AT	
SUBJECT	Termination	DATE	July 8, 1981

Last night as you left the Company Premises you were stopped by the Security Guard because you were carrying a large bag which appeared to be quite heavy. Upon searching the bag a small desk calculator belonging to the Company was found in your possession. You were instructed to report to the Employment Office at 9:00 today to discuss these circumstances.

You stated that you had some work of a personal nature to perform that night and had decided to borrow the calculator and return it today. You stated that you were aware of the Company's requirement that a "Property Pass" signed by your Supervisor was required to remove company property from Continental premises but it was too late in the day to obtain such documentation.

Robert Brown, your Supervisor, stated that at no time did you ask for a "Property Pass," nor were given any verbal permission (which would have been declined without a pass) to remove the equipment. It was further discovered that the calculator in question was not assigned to you but was in another employee's work area who was on extended leave of absence.

Based on all the above the Company has determined that the Standards of Conduct prohibiting theft of Company Property has been violated. This is an extremely severe offense which cannot be tolerated and for which corrective action is inappropriate. Therefore, your employment is terminated immediately.

John Doe
Supervisor

JD:xx

cc: Next Level of Supervision
Human Resources Representative

Appendix G

Severance Policies

Guidelines for Salary and Benefit Continuation 6

The nature of the termination affects salary continuation and benefits.

Salary and Benefit Continuation on Termination of Employment*

Employment with the Company is employment at will. This means that you have the right to terminate your employment at any time and for any reason, and the Company may exercise the same right. However, the nature of the termination affects salary continuation and the benefits set forth on pages 6 and 7 in the following ways.

Voluntary Resignation (including Mandatory Termination at age 70)**

The employee is paid through the last day of work. No payments are made for notice or severance. Employees are encouraged to use all vacation prior to the last day of work.

Death

The employee's estate is paid through the month in which death occurs, plus one additional month in lieu of any other severance pay or notice pay.

Discharge for Cause

The employee is paid through the last day of work and for unused vacation. No payments are made for notice or severance.

All Other Terminations

The employee is paid through the last day worked. A period of salary and benefit continuation is then provided under the Guidelines on page 7. In addition, employees who, at the end of their stated severance period, are within three years of eligibility for full pension at normal retirement (age 65) or for an 80-point pension, will be granted leave with service credit necessary to qualify for the pension. Those within two years of eligibility for a 60-point pension (minimum age 50 and 5 years of credited service) will be granted leave necessary to qualify for this pension. Employees within one year of eligibility for a vested pension will be granted leave necessary to qualify for the vested right to a pension at age 65.

The severance benefits provided under this section for "All Other Terminations" are designed to cushion the effect of loss of employment. In the event of a sale or transfer of a facility or line of business, employees who are offered employment with the successor employer, therefore, are not eligible for notice or severance.

*Those employees who may be entitled to retire following termination of employment should refer to the Corporation Salaried Employee's Pension Plan for an explanation of their rights.

**Age 65 for certain policy-making executives.

7

Severance Pay

Notice Period
Based on management decision in each case, notice pay may be provided in addition to severance — normally two weeks for nonexempt employees and one month for exempt. Then, after vacation, the greater of:

Basic Severance Pay Formula

1 week for each year of service and 1 day for each additional two months of service, up to 30 weeks maximum for nonexempt.

OR

Minimum Severance Pay Formula

	Period at Full Pay*		
Age Plus Service	**Nonexempt**	**Exempt**	**Key Employees (Grade 13 and up)**
Under 55	2 weeks	1 month	2 months
55-59	4 weeks	2 months	4 months
60-64	6 weeks	3 months	6 months
65-69	8 weeks	4 months	8 months
70-74	10 weeks	5 months	10 months
75 and higher	12 weeks	6 months	12 months

*No severance leave will extend beyond age 70 or age 65 for certain policy-making executives. Separate provision is made within this policy for certain senior executives.

Benefits Coverage

Life, AD&D, Dependent Life, Medical and Dental Insurance as well as Long-Term Disability coverage may be continued during the notice period. Life, AD&D, Dependent Life and Medical Insurance may be continued through vacation and severance pay periods at active employee contribution rates but at full cost rates for any leave period which might follow.

Appendix G

Your Rights Under the Law

8

Participation in the salary continuation plan entitles you to certain rights. The Employee Retirement Income Security Act of 1974 (ERISA) guarantees you these rights.

You may:

- Examine all plan documents, without charge, at the plan administrator's office and at other specified locations, such as worksites (including copies of all documents filed by the U.S. Department of Labor, such as detailed annual reports and plan descriptions).
- Obtain copies of all plan documents and other plan information upon written request to the plan administrator. The administrator may make a reasonable charge for the copies.

Besides creating rights for plan participants, ERISA imposes duties upon the people who are responsible for the operation of the employee benefit plan. These people are called "fiduciaries" and have a duty to operate the plan prudently in your interest. No one may fire you or otherwise discriminate against you in any way to prevent you from obtaining your benefits or exercising your rights under ERISA.

If your claim for a benefit is denied in whole or in part, you must receive a written explanation of the reason for the denial. You have the right to have the plan administrator review and reconsider your claim.

Under ERISA, there are steps you can take to enforce the above rights:

- If you request materials from the plan and do not receive them within 30 days, you may file suit in a federal court. In such a case, the court may require the plan administrator to provide the materials and pay you up to $100 a day until you receive the materials, unless the materials were not sent because of reasons beyond the control of the administrator.
- If you have a claim for benefits which is denied or ignored, in whole or in part, you may file suit in a state or federal court.
- If it should happen that plan fiduciaries misuse the plan's money, or if you are discriminated against for asserting your rights, you may seek assistance from the U.S. Department of Labor, or you may file suit in a federal court. The court will decide who should pay court costs and legal fees. If you are successful, the court may order the person you have sued to pay these costs and fees. If you lose, the court may order you to pay these costs and fees.

If you have any questions about this plan, you should contact the plan administrator. If you have any questions about this statement or about your rights under ERISA, contact the nearest area office of the U.S. Labor-Management Services Administration, Department of Labor.

Plan Administration

Administrative information about the salary continuation plan is listed here in case you need to use it.

• **Plan name is as follows:**	The Corporation Salary Continuation Plan for Salaried Employees
• **The plan sponsor is:**	Corporation
• **The plan administrator is:**	
• **The plan is filed with the government under these numbers:**	Employer Identification Number Salary Continuation Plan Number:
• **The agent for legal process is:**	Secretary of the Corporation, Corporation Legal process should be directed to this agent.

This booklet is intended to comply with the Summary Plan Description requirements of the Employee Retirement Income Security Act of 1974 (ERISA).

Appendix G

FOREWORD

This booklet is the summary plan description required by the Employee Retirement Income Security Act of 1974 (ERISA) of the Severance Pay Program for Management Employees. This booklet is applicable to exempt employees in the groups listed on Exhibit A.

The name of the plan under which benefits are provided is the Severance Pay Plan. The Employer identification number assigned by the Internal Revenue Service is and the Plan Number is 505. This is a welfare benefit plan as defined by ERISA.

The plan covers essentially all United States based employees of the Corporation and affiliated domestic companies except for employees in certain groups who have decided not to participate, preferring instead to make other contractual arrangements. Such groups include certain collectively represented workers in the construction, transportation, fence erection, siding and warehousing industries. Upon your written request, the plan administrator will advise you if a particular employer or employee organization is a sponsor of the plan, and if such employer or employee organization is a sponsor of the plan, the address of such employer or employee organization.

As a participant in the plan, you are entitled to certain rights and protections under ERISA. ERISA provides that all plan participants shall be entitled to:

> Examine, without charge, at the plan administrator's office or at the employee benefits office at the plant or office where you work, all plan documents, including copies of all documents filed by the plan with the U. S. Department of Labor, such as detailed annual reports and plan descriptions.
>
> Obtain copies of all plan documents and other plan information upon written request to the plan administrator. The administrator may make a reasonable charge for the copies.
>
> Receive a summary of the plan's annual financial report. The plan administrator is required by law to furnish each participant with a copy of this summary annual report.

In addition to creating rights for plan participants, ERISA imposes duties upon the people who are responsible for the operation of the employee benefit plan. The people who operate your plan, called "fiduciaries" of the plan, have a duty to do so prudently and in the interest of you and other plan participants and beneficiaries. No one, including your employer, or any other person, may fire you or otherwise discriminate against you in any way to prevent you from obtaining a severance allowance or exercising your rights under ERISA.

If your claim for a severance pay is denied in whole or in part you must receive a written explanation of the reason for the denial. You have the right to appeal this denial in accordance with the provisions outlined in this summary plan description.

Under ERISA, there are steps you can take to enforce the above rights. For instance, if you request materials from the plan and do not receive them within 30 days, you may file suit in a federal court. In such a case, the court may require the plan administrator to provide the materials and pay you up to $100 a day until you receive the materials, unless the materials were not sent because of reasons beyond the control of the administrator. If you have a claim for benefits which is denied or ignored, in whole or in part, you may file suit in a state or federal court. If it should happen that plan fiduciaries misuse the plan's money, or if you are discriminated against for asserting your rights, you may seek assistance from the U. S. Department of Labor, or you may file suit in a federal court. The court will decide who should pay court costs and legal fees. If you are successful, the court may order the person you have sued to pay these costs and fees. If you lose, the court may order you to pay these costs and fees; for example, if it finds your claim is frivolous. If you have any questions about your plan, you should contact the plan administrator. If you have any questions about this statement or about your rights under ERISA, you should contact the nearest Area Office of the U. S. Labor-Management Services Administration, Department of Labor.

Fund (a non-profit Pennsylvania membership corporation), , is the plan administrator, trustee and agent for service of legal process under the plan. The telephone number for the plan administrator is

The benefits described herein are provided without cost to you. Such benefits and the cost of administering the plan are paid by the . Records of the plan are kept on a calendar-year basis.

Appendix G

SEVERANCE PAY PROGRAM FOR MANAGEMENT EMPLOYEES
As Amended August 1, 1983

I. Coverage

1.0 The Corporation Severance Pay Program for Management Employees ("Program") covers all exempt employees in the groups listed in Exhibit A ("covered employees").

1.1 As used herein, participant means any covered employee who has completed at least three years of continuous service as of his last day of active employment.

1.2 As used herein, continuous service means continuous service as calculated under the Non-Contributory Pension Rules applicable to the affected participant, excluding any continuous service preceding the last date of hire.

1.3 As used herein, "Company" means a company listed on Exhibit A as having employees covered by this Program.

II. Eligibility

2.0 A participant shall be eligible for a severance pay calculated in accordance with Section 5.0 only if

(a) his active employment is terminated as a direct result of

(i) a permanent management force reduction occasioned by a shutdown or abandonment of a facility, department or subdivision of a department or a reorganization of organization structure or forces, or

(ii) a relocation of the facility or organization, or

(b) his continuous service is broken by reason of two years of absence due to layoff during which period he was eligible for benefits under the Corporation Layoff Unemployment Benefit Program for Management Employees, or

(c) his continuous service is not broken but he has been on layoff during which period he was eligible for benefits under the Corporation Layoff Unemployment Benefit Program for Management Employees and his return to active employment is declared unlikely by the Company

and he is not otherwise ineligible under Sections 2.1 through 2.3 or Section 2.5.

2.1 A participant shall be ineligible for severance pay if such participant (i) resigns or (ii) is discharged for cause. Determination of whether a discharge is for cause or not for cause shall be at the sole discretion of his Company.

2.2 A participant otherwise eligible for severance pay shall not be eligible for severance pay if he is eligible for immediate pension under the Non-Contributory Pension Rules applicable to him.

2.3 A participant otherwise eligible for severance pay shall not be eligible for severance pay if he receives a reasonable offer of employment from a Company made on or before his last day of active employment in the case of a participant covered by 2.0(a), or on or before his last day of continuous service in the case of a participant covered by 2.0(b), or on or before the date eligibility for Layoff Unemployment Benefits ceases in case of a participant covered by 2.0(c).

2.4 A job offered by a Company shall constitute a reasonable offer of employment if:

(a) The participant is physically qualified to perform the job.

(b) The participant has the ability and skills required to perform the job or has the ability to absorb such training for the job as is necessary to enable the participant to perform the job satisfactorily.

(c) The job is not a temporary job or a job known to be of limited duration.

(d) The rate of pay (including any incentive pay provided pursuant to a collective bargaining agreement if the job offered is in a represented bargaining unit) for the job offered is at least 90% of the participant's base rate of pay as of the last day worked on his previous position.

(e) The job offered is not covered by the maximum hours provision of the Fair Labor Standards Act, except that a job covered by the maximum hours provision of the Fair Labor Standards Act may be offered if established local practices or contractual provisions permit reemployment on a job covered by a collective bargaining agreement or if the job offered is comparable to the job the participant had immediately prior to employment on the job held as of the last day worked.

(f) The overall benefits package (i.e., pension, life insurance, health and medical, thrift, vacations, etc.) for the job offered is generally equivalent to the overall benefits package on his previous position, except that this paragraph (f) shall not apply in the event that there is an increase in the participant's rate of pay (including any out-of-line make-up pay or any incentive pay provided pursuant to a collective bargaining agreement if the job offered is in a represented bargaining unit) which equals or exceeds the difference between the value of the overall benefits package applicable to the participant's previous position and the value of such package applicable to the participant's new position.

2.5 A participant otherwise eligible for severance pay shall not be eligible for severance pay if his termination of employment with his Company is caused by a sale of assets or stock to another business entity and he receives a job offer from such purchasing business entity which would constitute a reasonable offer of employment if such offer had been made by a Company.

III. Layoff of Covered Employees

3.0 A covered employee who would be otherwise eligible for severance pay except for the fact that he has not completed three years of continuous service as of his last day of active employment shall be placed on layoff status.

3.1 A participant who is eligible for severance pay under Section 2.0(a) of the Program may, as of his last day of active employment, elect to waive severance pay and be placed on layoff status. Such an election shall be irrevocable.

3.2 A participant who is eligible for severance pay under Section 2.0(c) of the Program may, as of his last day of eligibility for payments under the Corporation Layoff Unemployment Benefit Program for Management Employees, elect to waive severance pay and be placed on layoff status. Such election shall be irrevocable.

3.3 A participant who elects to receive severance pay pursuant to Section 3.1 shall be terminated as of his last day of active employment with his continuous service being broken on that day.

3.4 A participant who elects to receive severance pay pursuant to Section 3.2 shall be terminated as of his last day of eligibility for payments under the Corporation Layoff Unemployment Benefit Program for Management Employees with his continuous service being broken on that day.

3.5 Each participant eligible to elect between receipt of severance pay and placement on layoff shall make such election on a form provided by the Company. If a participant does not make such an election on the proper form, he shall be deemed to have waived severance pay and elected layoff.

3.6 A participant who is not eligible for severance pay solely because of Section 2.2 of the Program shall, if he does not elect to retire, be placed on layoff status as of his last day of active employment and continued on such status until the earlier of the date on which he retires or the date on which he incurs a break in continuous service.

IV. Disability Status of Covered Employees

4.0 A covered employee who is absent due to disability at the time active employment would have terminated shall not at that time be laid off or be paid severance pay.

4.1 Such covered employee who becomes qualified for permanent incapacity pension or any other immediate pension under the Non-Contributory Pension Rules applicable to him shall be retired on such pension, provided that (i) retirement shall not be required before five full calendar months from the end of the month in which absence due to disability began and (ii) if qualified only for a sole option early retirement pension, election may be made to continue on disability absence if qualified for another type of early retirement pension prior to the date continuous service would break as a result of such absence.

4.2 A covered employee who becomes physically able to return to active employment before continuous service breaks by reason of absence due to disability or retirement, pursuant to Section 4.1, shall:

(a) be laid off for the remainder of a two-year period commencing with the date disability absence began if the employee has less than three years of continuous service on the date active employment would have terminated;

(b) be retired on pension if then qualified for an immediate pension under the Non-Contributory Pension Rules, applicable to him provided that, if then qualified only for a sole option early retirement pension, election may be made to be laid off if qualified for another type of early retirement pension prior to the date continuous service would break.

4.3 If a covered employee does not qualify for immediate pension under the

Non-Contributory Pension Rules applicable to him on the date physically able to return to active employment, he shall elect either to be laid off for the remainder of a two-year period commencing with the date disability absence began or to receive severance pay. If severance pay is elected, (i) the date on which the covered employee became physically able to return to active employment shall be considered the date active employment terminated (except that the amount of severance pay shall be calculated only on the basis of continuous service up to the date on which active employment would have been terminated had the covered employee not been absent due to disability) and (ii) the severance pay otherwise payable shall be reduced by 50% of the amount of base salary paid as salary continuance for the period after the date on which active employment would have been terminated if the covered employee had not been absent due to disability.

4.4 If a covered employee is unable to return to active employment before continuous service breaks by reason of a two-year absence because of disability, this section shall not be applicable.

V. Payment of Severance Pay

5.0 A participant who elects to receive severance pay shall receive an amount calculated on the basis of one-half month's current base salary for each full year of continuous service. Such amount of severance pay will be adjusted under Section 4.3 or 5.2 if applicable.

5.1 (a) A participant covered by 2.0(a) or (c) who elects to receive severance pay will receive such severance pay in one installment within 60 days of the date the participant makes such election.

(b) A participant covered by 2.0(b) will receive severance pay in one installment within 60 days of the date he incurs a break in continuous service.

5.2 The amount of severance pay otherwise payable under this Program shall be reduced by the amount of any discharge, liquidation, dismissal or severance pay or payment of similar kind which is payable under another plan or policy of any Company, in respect to which any Company shall have directly or indirectly contributed, or by reason of any law.

5.3 A participant who is eligible for severance pay pursuant to Section 2.0(b) or (c) shall receive severance pay calculated on the basis of one-half month's base salary as of the last day worked for each full year of continuous service. Such amount of severance pay will be reduced as provided under Section 4.3 or 5.2, if applicable, and shall be further reduced by the total amount of payments made to the participant pursuant to the

Corporation Layoff Unemployment Benefit Program for Management Employees during the period of layoff immediately preceding the break in continuous service. Such severance pay will be paid in one installment within 60 days of the date the participant incurs a break in continuous service.

VI. Claims and Appeals

6.0 A participant who believes that he is entitled to receive severance pay under this Program must file a claim for such severance pay within ninety (90) days of his last day of active employment. Such a claim should be filed with the employee benefits office of the plant or office where the participant last worked.

6.1 If a participant's claim for benefits under this Program is denied or if he believes that the amount of the benefits which he receives is incorrect, he shall within sixty (60) days of the date the Company notifies him of such denial or the date on which he receives the benefits which he believes were paid in an improper amount, write to the Vice President-Administration,

(the Pension Fund),

furnishing all information supporting his position. His appeal will be reviewed by the Vice President-Administration and a reply will be made within sixty (60) days of the date the appeal is received.

6.2 The decision of the Vice President-Administration, with regard to the dispute, shall be final and conclusive except insofar as a participant, within 60 days after notification of the Vice President's decision, submits a written demand for arbitration. A dispute so appealed shall be submitted to an arbitrator selected by the Chairman of the Board of Arbitration, , unless the participant requests that the dispute be submitted to another arbitrator. In such event, the participant and the Pension Fund shall mutually agree upon an arbitrator to hear such dispute with the costs shared equally by the Pension Fund and the claimant. The arbitrator shall have authority only to decide the question pursuant to the provisions of the Program, but shall not have authority in any way to alter, add to or subtract from any of such provisions. The decision of the arbitrator shall be binding on the employer, the Pension Fund and the participant.

The appeals procedure established by this Section shall be the sole, exclusive and mandatory procedure for resolving any dispute described in this Section.

VII. Other Provisions

7.0 Each participant actively at work will be given at least 30 days' notice of termination of employment; provided, however, that an employee who, following the giving of such notice, is placed on vacation status shall, for the purpose of this Program, be considered to be actively at work until the termination of such vacation. This 30-day notice does not apply to a participant who was eligible for the Layoff Unemployment Benefit Program for Management Employees or who quits or is discharged.

7.1 The Corporation may at any time, and from time to time, by action of its Board of Directors, modify or amend, in whole or in part, or terminate any or all of the provisions of this Program.

Appendix G

EXHIBIT A

Employees covered by the Corporation Severance Pay Program for Management Employees as amended August 1, 1983, are all exempt employees (other than employees who are initially employed for a specific period of time and who are employed on project assignments) of the companies listed below except as otherwise indicated:

except -

(a)

(b)

(c)

(d)

Appendix H

Separation Agreements and General Releases

Appendix H

SEPARATION AGREEMENT AND GENERAL RELEASE

THIS SEPARATION AGREEMENT AND GENERAL RELEASE is made and entered into by and between (hereinafter referred to as "Employee") and (hereinafter referred to as the "Company").

W I T N E S S E T H:

WHEREAS, Employee was employed by the Company from July 1, 1979 to October 25, 1984; and

WHEREAS, Employee's active services for the Company will terminate on October 25, 1984; and

WHEREAS, Employee and the Company desire to settle fully and finally all differences between them, including, but in no way limited to, any differences that might arise out of Employee's employment with the Company, and the termination thereof;

NOW, THEREFORE, in consideration of the premises and mutual promises herein contained, it is agreed as follows:

FIRST: This Separation Agreement and General Release shall not in any way be construed as an admission by the Company that it has acted wrongfully with respect to the Employee or any other person, or that the Employee has any rights whatsoever against the Company, and the Company specifically disclaims any liability to or wrongful acts against Employee or any other person, on the part of itself, its employees or its agents.

SECOND: Employee represents, understands and agrees that his active employment with the Company will terminate on October 25, 1984.

THIRD: Employee represents that except for the charge filed with the New Jersey Division on Civil Rights, Charge he has not filed any complaints or charges or lawsuits alleging age discrimination against the Company with any governmental agency or any court, and that he will not do so at any time hereafter; provided, however, this shall not limit Employee from filing a lawsuit for the sole purpose of enforcing Employee's rights under the Separation Agreement and General Release. The Employee shall withdraw the above age discrimination charge with prejudice. Said withdrawal is attached hereto and made a part hereof. Employee shall also sign the Standard Settlement Form of the New Jersey Civil Rights Division.

FOURTH: The Company will continue Employee's regular current gross salary of $5,791.68 per month less legal deductions for a period of six months, terminating on April 25, 1985.

Any monies owed to the Company by Employee may be deducted from the amounts payable pursuant to this paragraph. The Company will continue Employee's coverage under the present Company medical program until the earlier of the following dates:

a. April 25, 1985; or

b. when employee first obtains a position with another employer.

It is a specific condition of this Agreement that Employee notify the Company immediately in the event Employee obtains other employment prior to April 25, 1985. The payments called for in this paragraph shall be in lieu of and discharge of any obligations of the Company to Employee for compensation or any other expectations of remuneration or benefit on the part of Employee.

Employee will receive an Executive Incentive Compensation Bonus for 1984 in accordance with the requirements of said bonus plan. Payment will be made in or about February 1985. In addition, the employee will receive six weeks of earned and banked vacation. Should the payments set forth in this paragraph amount to less than three months gross salary, the Company shall pay Employee the difference between said payments and three months' gross salary.

During the period of salary continuation, Employee shall be allowed to utilize an office assigned by the Company at reasonable times and intervals and use a secretary to do reasonable typing and taking of message for the Employee for the sole purpose of searching for employment. This shall cease on April 25, 1985.

Employee will receive a letter of reference from the Division stating, among other things, that he held the position of Vice President of Accounts. Said reference is attached hereto and made a part hereof.

FIFTH: Employee understands and agrees that effective October 25, 1984, he was and is no longer authorized to incur any expenses or obligations or liabilities on behalf of the Company.

SIXTH: Employee understands and agrees that under the Company's Group Life Insurance Program, he will be covered through April 25, 1985, and that he must contact the life insurance company within thirty days of April 25, 1985 if he desires to have an individual policy issued.

SEVENTH: Employee has returned or will immediately return to the Company all Company Information and related reports, maps, files, memoranda, and records; credit cards, cardkey passes; door and file keys; computer access codes; software; and other physical or personal property which Employee received or prepared or helped prepare in connection with his employment; and Employee has not retained and will not retain any copies, duplicates, reproductions, or excerpts thereof. The term "Company Information" as used in this Agreement means (a) confidential information including without limitation information received from third parties under confidential conditions; and (b) other technical, business, or financial information, the use or disclosure of which might reasonably be construed to be contrary to the interest of the Company.

EIGHTH: Employee agrees that in the course of his employment with the Company, he has acquired Company Information as defined in the Seventh paragraph above. Employee understands and agrees that such Company Information has been disclosed to Employee in confidence and for Company use only. Employee understands and agrees that he (i) will keep such Company Information confidential at all times during and after his employment with the Company, (ii) will not disclose or communicate Company Information to any third party, and (iii) will not make use of Company Information on Employee's own behalf, or on behalf of any third party. When Company Information becomes generally available to the public other than by Employee's acts or omissions, it is no longer subject to the restrictions in this paragraph Eight. However, Company Information shall not be deemed to come under this exception merely because it is embraced by more general information which is or becomes generally available to the public. The undertakings set forth in this paragraph shall survive the termination of this Agreement or other arrangements contained in this Agreement.

NINTH: Moreover, the provisions of this Agreement are severable, and if any part of it is found to be unenforceable, the other paragraphs shall remain fully valid and enforceable. This Agreement shall survive the termination of any arrangements contained herein.

TENTH: Employee represents and agrees that he will keep the terms, amount and fact of this Separation Agreement and General Release completely confidential, and that he will not hereafter disclose any information concerning this Separation Agreement and General Release to anyone except his immediate family; provided, they agree to keep said information confidential and not disclose it to others.

ELEVENTH: Employee represents and agrees that he fully understands his right to discuss all aspects of this Separation Agreement and General Release with his private attorney, that he has availed himself of this right, that he has carefully read and fully understands all of the provisions of this Separation Agreement and General Release, and that he is voluntarily entering into this Separation Agreement and General Release.

TWELFTH: As a material inducement to the Company to enter into this Separation Agreement and General Release, Employee hereby irrevocably and unconditionally releases, acquits and forever discharges the Company and each of the Company's owners, stockholders, predecessors, successors, assigns, agents, directors, officers, employees, representatives, attorneys, divisions, subsidiaries, affiliates (and agents, directors, officers, employees, representatives and attorneys of such parent companies, divisions, subsidiaries and affiliates), and all persons acting by, through, under or in concert with any of them (collectively, "Releasees"), or any of them, from any and all charges, complaints, claims, liabilities, obligations, promises, agreements, controversies, damages, actions, causes of action, suits, rights, demands, costs, losses, debts and expenses (including attorneys' fees and costs actually incurred) of any nature whatsoever, known or unknown, suspected or unsuspected, including, but not limited to, rights under federal, state or local laws prohibiting age or other forms of discrimination, claims growing out of his employment and termination or any other legal restrictions on the Company's right to terminate its employees ("Claim" or "Claims"), which Employee now has, owns or holds, or claims to have, own or hold, or which Employee at any time heretofore had, owned or held, or claimed to have, own or hold, or which Employee at any time hereinafter may have, own or hold, or claim to have, own or hold against each or any of the Releasees.

THIRTEENTH: As a material inducement to Employee to enter into this Separation Agreement and General Release, the Company hereby irrevocably and unconditionally releases, acquits and forever discharges Employee and each of the Employee's heirs, successors, assigns, agents, representatives, attorneys and all persons acting by, through, under or in concert with him (collectively "Employee Releasees"), or any of them, from any and all charges, complaints, claims, liabilities, obligations, promises, agreements, controversies, damages, actions, causes of action, suits, rights, demands, costs, losses, debts and expenses (including attorneys' fees and costs actually incurred) of any nature whatsoever, known or unknown, suspected or unsuspected, claims growing out of Employee's employment and termination which the Company now has, owns or holds, or claims to have, own or hold, or which the Company at any time heretofore had, owned or held, or claimed to have, own or hold, or which the Company at any time hereinafter may have, own or hold, or claim to have, own or hold against each or any of the Releasees.

FOURTEENTH: As a further material inducement to the Company to enter into this Separation Agreement and General Release, Employee hereby agrees to indemnify and hold each and all of the Releasees harmless from and against any and all loss, costs, damages, or expenses, including, without limitation, attorneys' fees incurred by Releasees, or any of them, that may be incurred by reason of any representation made herein by Employee which was false, and known by Employee to be false when made.

FIFTEENTH: Employee represents and acknowledges that in executing this Separation Agreement and General Release he does not rely and has not relied upon any representation or statement not set forth herein made by any of the Releasees or by any of the Releasees' agents, representatives, or attorneys with regard to the subject matter, basis or effect of this Separation Agreement and General Release or otherwise.

This Separation Agreement and General Release sets forth the entire agreement between the parties hereto, and fully supersedes any and all prior agreements or understandings between the parties hereto pertaining to the subject matter hereof.

Appendix H

PLEASE READ CAREFULLY. THIS RELEASE HAS BEEN REVIEWED AND DISCUSSED WITH EMPLOYEE'S ATTORNEY,

Executed at ______________________, this ______ day of ____________________, 19__

____

Executed at ____________________, this _____ day of __________________, 19__.

____

Appendix H

SEPARATION AGREEMENT AND GENERAL RELEASE

1. I, , for and in consideration of the obligations of set forth in paragraph 2 herein, and intending to be legally bound, do hereby permanently and irrevocably sever my employment with , by voluntarily resigning and retiring and do also hereby REMISE, RELEASE AND FOREVER DISCHARGE , its officers, directors, employees and agents, its predecessors, successors and assigns, of and from all manner of actions and causes of action, suits, debts, claims and demands whatsoever in law or in equity, which I ever had, now have, or hereafter may have, or which my heirs, executors or administrators hereafter may have by reason of any matter, cause or thing whatsoever, and particularly any claims concerning or relating in any way to my employment relationship or the termination of my employment relationship with including, but not limited to, any claims which have been asserted, could have been asserted, or could be asserted now or in the future against , including any claims arising under the New Jersey Law Against Discrimination Title 10:5-1 et seq., and/or any and all other federal, state or local laws or ordinances and any common law claims now or hereafter recognized.

2. In full consideration of my signing this Agreement, will, upon the termination of my employment:

a.

b.

c.

3. I further agree and covenant that neither I, nor any person, organization or other entity, on my behalf, will file, charge, claim, sue or cause or permit to be filed, charged or claimed, any action for legal or equitable relief (including damages, injunctive, declaratory, monetary relief or other) involving any matter occurring at any time or related in any way whatsoever to my employment relationship or the termination of my employment relationship with or involving any continuing effects of any acts or practices which may have arisen or occurred during my employment relationship or the termination of my employment relationship with

4. I agree and acknowledge that this Agreement between and me is not and shall not be construed

to be an admission of any violation of any federal, state or local statute, ordinance or regulation or of any duty owed by to me and that my resignation and retirement and the execution of this Agreement are voluntary acts to provide an amicable conclusion to my employment relationship with

5. I hereby certify that I have read all of the terms of this Agreement and that I have had an opportunity to discuss it with individuals of my own choice who are not associated with . I understand the terms of this Agreement, including the fact that I have permanently and irrevocably severed my employment relationship with and that this Agreement RELEASES AND FOREVER DISCHARGES from any legal action arising out of my employment relationship and the termination of my employment relationship by . I sign this Agreement of my own free will in exchange for the consideration to be given to me, which I acknowledge is adequate and satisfactory. Neither , nor its agents, representatives or employees have made any representations to me concerning the terms or effects of this Agreement other than those contained herein.

IN WITNESS WHEREOF, and intending to be legally bound hereby, I , and have executed the foregoing Agreement this day of , 198 in

WITNESS;

__________________________ __________________________ (SEAL)
Employee

WITNESS;

__________________________ By: __________________________
Title: __________________________

Appendix H

SEPARATION AGREEMENT AND GENERAL RELEASE

THIS SEPARATION AGREEMENT AND GENERAL RELEASE is made and entered into by and between JOSEPH A. EMPLOYEE (hereinafter referred to as "Employee") and ______________________ (hereinafter referred to as the "Company").

WITNESSETH:

WHEREAS, Employee was employed by the Company from ______________ to ______________; and

WHEREAS, Employee's active services for the Company will terminate on ______________; and

WHEREAS, Employee and the Company desire to settle fully and finally all differences between them, including, but in no way limited to, any differences that might arise out of Employee's employment with the Company, and the termination thereof;

NOW, THEREFORE, in consideration of the premises and mutual promises herein contained, it is agreed as follows:

FIRST: This Separation Agreement and General Release shall not in any way be construed as an admission by the Company that it has acted wrongfully with respect to the Employee or any other person, or that the Employee has any rights whatsoever against the Company, and the Company specifically disclaims any liability to or wrongful acts against Employee or any other person, on the part of itself, its employees or its agents.

SECOND: Employee represents, understands and agrees that his active employment with the Company will terminate on ____________, that he will not be reemployed by the Company, and that he will not apply for or otherwise seek employment with the Company at any time.

THIRD: Employee represents that he has not filed any complaints or charges or lawsuits against the Company with any governmental agency or any court, and that he will not do so at any time hereafter; provided, however, this shall not limit Employee from filing a lawsuit for the sole purpose of enforcing Employee's rights under this Separation Agreement and General Release.

FOURTH: [Insert in this paragraph what the Company will provide as a termination package for Employee. Depending on the package you are willing to offer, it might read something like the following:

The Company will continue Employee's regular current gross salary of $________ per month less legal deductions for a period of ________ month less legal deductions for a period of _____ months, terminating on ________________.

If Employee has found alternate employment prior to said date, at Employee's request, the Company will pay the unpaid portion of said continued gross salary in a lump sum, less legal deductions. Any monies owed to the Company by Employee may be deducted from the amounts payable pursuant to this paragraph. The Company will continue Employee's coverage under the present Company medical program until the earlier of the following dates:

a. __________________________; or

b. when employee first obtains a position with another employer.

It is a specific condition of this Agreement that Employee notify the Company immediately in the event Employee obtains other employment prior to ________________. The payments called for in this paragraph shall be in lieu of and discharge of any obligations of the Company to Employee for compensation, unused accrued vacation, or any other expectations of remuneration or benefit on the part of Employee.

FIFTH: Employee understands and agrees that effective ____________________, he was and is no longer authorized to incur any expenses or obligations or liabilities on behalf of the Company.

SIXTH: Employee understands and agrees that under the Company's Group Life Insurance Program, he will be covered through ____________________, and that he must contact the life insurance company within __________ days if he desires to have an individual policy issued.

SEVENTH: Employee has returned or will immediately return to the Company all Company Information and related reports, maps, files, memoranda, and records; credit cards, cardkey passes; door and file keys; computer access codes; software; and other physical or personal property which Employee received or prepared or helped prepare in connection with his/her employment; and Employee has not retained and will not retain any copies, duplicates, reproductions, or excerpts thereof. The term "Company Information" as used in this Agreement means (a) confidential information including without limitation information received from third parties under confidential conditions; and (b) other technical, business, or financial information, the use or disclosure of which might reasonably be construed to be contrary to the interest of Company.

EIGHTH: Employee agrees that in the course of his/her employment with the Company, he/she has acquired Company Information as defined in the Seventh paragraph above. Employee understands and agrees that such Company Information has been disclosed to Employee in confidence and for Company use only. Employee understands and agrees that he/she (i) will keep such Company Information confidential at all times during and after his/her employment with the Company, (ii) will not disclose or communicate Company Information to any third party, and (iii) will not make use of Company Information on Employee's own behalf, or on behalf of any third party. In view of the nature of Employee's employment and the nature of Company Information which Employee has received during the course of his/her employment, Employee agrees that any unauthorized disclosure to third parties of Company Information or other violation, or threatened violation, of this Agreement would cause irreparable damage to the trade secret status of Company Information and to Company, and that, therefore, the Company shall be entitled to an injunction prohibiting Employee from any such disclosure, attempted disclosure, violation, or threatened violation. When Company Information becomes generally available to the public other than by Employee's acts or omissions, it is no longer subject to the restrictions in this paragraph Eight. However, Company Information shall not be deemed to come under this exception merely because it is embraced by more general information which is or becomes generally available to the public. The undertakings set forth in this paragraph shall survive the termination of this Agreement or other arrangements contained in this Agreement.

NINTH: It is agreed that the benefits contained in this Separation Agreement and General Release which flow to Employee from the Company are subject to termination, reduction or cancellation in the event that Employee takes any action or engages in any conduct deemed by the Company to be in violation of this Agreement.

TENTH: Moreover, the provisions of this Agreement are severable, and if any part of it is found to be enforceable, the other paragraphs shall remain fully valid and enforceable. This Agreement shall survive the termination of any arrangements contained herein.

ELEVENTH: Employee represents and agrees that he will keep the terms, amount and fact of this Separation Agreement and General Release completely confidential, and that he will not hereafter disclose any information concerning this Separation Agreement and General Release to anyone except his immediate family; provided, they agree to keep said information confidential and not disclose it to others.

TWELFTH: Employee represents and agrees that he fully understands his right to discuss all aspects of this Separation Agreement and General Release with his private attorney, that to the extent, if any, that he desired, he has availed himself of this right, that he has carefully read and fully understands all of the provisions of this Separation Agreement and General Release, and that he is voluntarily entering into this Separation Agreement and General Release.

THIRTEENTH: As a material inducement to the Company to enter into this Separation Agreement and General Release, Employee hereby irrevocably and unconditionally releases, acquits and forever discharges the Company and each of the Company's owners, stockholders, predecessors, successors, assigns, agents, directors, officers, employees, representatives, attorneys, divisions, subsidiaries, affiliates (and agents, directors, officers, employees, representatives and attorneys of such parent companies, divisions, subsidiaries and affiliates), and all persons acting by, through, under or in concert with any of them (collectively "Releasees"), or any of them, from any and all charges, complaints, claims, liabilities, obligations, promises, agreements, controversies, damages, actions, causes of action, suits, rights, demands, costs, losses, debts and expenses (including attorneys' fees and costs actually incurred) of any nature whatsoever, known or unknown, suspected or unsuspected, including, but not limited to, rights under federal, state or local laws prohibiting age or other forms of discrimination, claims growing out of any legal restrictions on the Company's right to terminate its employees ("Claim" or "Claims"), which Employee now has, owns or holds, or claims to have, own or hold, or which Employee at any time heretofore had, owned or held, or claimed to have, own or hold, or which Employee at any time hereinafter may have, own or hold, or claim to have, own or hold against each or any of the Releasees.

FOURTEENTH: Employee expressly waives and relinquishes all rights and benefits afforded by Section 1542 of the Civil Code of the State of California, and does so understanding and acknowledging the significance of such specific waiver of Section 1542. Section 1542 of the Civil Code of the State of California states as follows:

> "A general release does not extend to claims which the creditor does not know or suspect to exist in his favor at the time of executing the release, which if known by him must have materially affected his settlement with the debtor."

Thus, notwithstanding the provisions of Section 1542, and for the purpose of implementing a full and complete release and discharge of the Releasees, Employee expressly acknowledges that this Separation Agreement and General Release is intended to include in its effect, without limitation, all Claims which Employee does not know or suspect to exist in his favor at the time of execution hereof, and that this Separation Agreement and General Release contemplates the extinguishment of any such Claim or Claims.

FIFTEENTH: As a further material inducement to the Company to enter into this Separation Agreement and General Release, Employee hereby agrees to indemnify and hold each and all of the Releasees harmless from and against any and all loss, costs, damages, or expenses, including, without limitation, attorneys' fees incurred by Releasees, or any of them, arising out of any breach of this Separation Agreement and General Release by Employee or the fact that any representation made herein by Employee was false when made.

SIXTEENTH: Employee represents and acknowledges that in executing this Separation Agreement and General Release he does not rely and has not relied upon any representation or statement not set forth herein made by any of the Releasees or by any of the Releasees' agents, representatives, or attorneys with regard to the subject matter, basis or effect of this Separation Agreement and General Release or otherwise.

This Separation Agreement and General Release sets forth the entire agreement between the parties hereto, and fully supersedes any and all prior agreements or understandings between the parties hereto pertaining to the subject matter hereof.

PLEASE READ CAREFULLY. THIS SEPARATION AGREEMENT AND GENERAL RELEASE INCLUDES A RELEASE OF ALL KNOWN AND UNKNOWN CLAIMS.

Executed at ____________________, California, this _____ day of ______________, 19___.

____
Joseph A. Employee

Executed at ______________________, California, this _____ day of ____________________, 19___.

COMPANY

____

Appendix H

FORM A: Individual Release

VOLUNTARY SEPARATION AGREEMENT AND GENERAL RELEASE

This Agreement entered into this _____ day of ____________ by and between ____________________ (herein referred to as "Employee"), and XYZ Company and all related companies (herein collectively referred to as the "Company").

WHEREAS, Employee has been employed by the Company and has voluntarily decided to terminate employment; and

WHEREAS, the parties wish to set forth the conditions which shall apply to Employee in connection with the termination of Employee's employment by the Company;

NOW, THEREFORE, Employee and the Company do hereby agree by the execution of this document to the following terms and conditions:

1. Employee's final day on the Company's active payroll will be ___________. By ____________, 1990, Employee will receive a lump sum payment of $__________, less normal statutory and employee benefit deductions. Employee shall have the option to continue the current Company medical, life and dental insurance coverage until _____________ as if he or she were an active employee. Further, Employee will receive all vacation pay accrued and unused as of ______________, less normal statutory and employee benefit deductions, on or about __________________.

2. By virtue of the execution of this Separation Agreement, Employee voluntarily terminates active employment effective _________________. Further, Employee agrees that should he or she become employed by the Company or any related company subsequent to the execution of this Separation Agreement, all monies paid pursuant to this Separation Agreement shall be immediately recoverable by the Company.

3. Employee acknowledges that during the course of employment with the Company he or she has had access to and received information which the Company considers and has treated as confidential. Therefore, Employee agrees that he or she will not directly or indirectly disclose any confidential records, data, formulae, specifications and/or

other trade secrets owned by the Company to any person or use any such information, except pursuant to court order or as a result of valid government order. All records, files, drawings, data, documents, models, equipment and the like relating to the businesses of the Company and any related company or operation which Employee has used, prepared or come in contact with during his or her employment by the Company, shall be and remain the sole property of the Company and shall not be removed from the premises of the Company without its written consent.

4. All payments provided under this Separation Agreement are in lieu of any severance payments or any other payments provided pursuant to any Company employee benefit plans, except the Company Retirement Plan or other benefits Employee has vested in prior to ____________. It is understood that except for the benefits provided in the Separation Agreement, and the benefits Employee was vested in prior to ____________, Employee specifically waives any and all rights to any other payments or benefits from the Company.

5. Employee, for him or herself, his or her family, representatives, successors and assigns, except for the undertakings provided for herein, covenants to forever refrain from instituting, maintaining, pressing, collecting or in any way aiding and proceeding upon, and releases and forever discharges the Company and its representatives, successors, assigns, subsidiaries, affiliates, directors, officers, employees, attorneys, agents, and trustees or administrators under any Company plans, from any and all claims, demands, debts, damages, injuries, actions or rights of action or any nature whatsoever, whether known or unknown, which Employee had, now has or may have against the Company, its successors, assigns, subsidiaries, affiliates, directors, officers, employees, attorneys, agents, trustees or administrators under any Company plans, from the beginning of Employee's employment to and including the date of this Separation Agreement, on account of, or arising out of any matter related to Employee's employment with the Company or termination of employment with the Company.

6. Employee agrees and acknowledges that the consideration received by him or her for this Separation

-2-

Agreement in support of all of the provisions contained herein and for the execution thereof is greater than benefits normally given to similarly situated employees of the Company and shall constitute full payment, satisfaction, discharge, compromise and release of and from all matters for which the other party have mutually released it herein.

7. Employee acknowledges that he or she has read each and every paragraph of this Separation Agreement and that he or she understands his/her respective rights and obligations and has been advised that he or she can consult an attorney of his or her choice. Further, Employee acknowledges that he or she has had at least twenty-one (21) days to consider and review this Separation Agreement and has the opportunity to revoke this Separation Agreement within seven (7) days of its execution. Should Employee revoke this Separation Agreement, all monies and benefits provided herein shall cease and benefits provided to Employee under this Separation Agreement prior to such revocation shall be recoverable by the Company.

8. Employee declares that he or she understands the terms and contents of this Separation Agreement and freely, voluntarily and without coercion enters into this Separation Agreement. Further, Employee agrees and acknowledges that the waiver or release by him or her of rights he or she may have to receive monetary damages under Title VII of the Civil Rights Act of 1964, as amended, the Employee Retirement Income Security Act of, the Age Discrimination in Employment Act of 1967 and/or any other local, state or federal law, is knowing and voluntary and that it shall be a breach of this Separation Agreement to institute any action or to recover any damages which would be in conflict with or contrary to the acknowledgment. In the event of such breach, all monies paid pursuant to this Separation Agreement shall be immediately recoverable by the Company.

9. This Separation Agreement contains the entire agreement of the parties pertaining to the subject matter contained in it and supersedes and is in lieu of any and all other employment arrangements, statements or promises, written or oral, between Employee and the Company.

10. This Separation Agreement cannot be amended, modified, or supplemented in any respect except by

-3-

written agreement entered into by the parties hereto.

IN WITNESS WHEREOF, the Company by its duly authorized representative and Employee have executed this Separation Agreement.

Employee: Witness:

By:________________________ ________________________

THE COMPANY

____
Name (Print)

________________________ ________________________
Address (Print)

Appendix H

FORM B: Group Plan Releases

VOLUNTARY SEPARATION AGREEMENT AND GENERAL RELEASE

This Agreement entered into this ___ day of __________ by and between __________________ (herein referred to as "Employee"), and the XYZ Company and all related companies (herein collectively referred to as the "Company").

WHEREAS, Employee has been employed by the Company and has voluntarily decided to terminate employment; and

WHEREAS, the parties wish to set forth the conditions which shall apply to Employee in connection with the termination of Employee's employment by the Company;

NOW THEREFORE, Employee and the Company do hereby agree by the execution of this document to the following terms and conditions:

1. Employee's final day on the Company's active payroll will be ____________. By __________ _________ ____, 1990, Employee will receive a lump sum payment of $___________, less normal statutory and employee benefit deductions. Employee shall have the option to continue the current Company medical, life and dental insurance coverage until ______________ as if he or she were an active employee. Further, Employee will receive all vacation pay accrued and unused as of _______________, less normal statutory and employee benefit deductions, on or about ____________.

2. By virtue of the execution of this Separation Agreement, Employee voluntarily terminates active employment effective __________________. Further, Employee agrees that should he or she become employed by the Company or any related company subsequent to the execution of this Separation Agreement, all monies paid pursuant to this Separation Agreement shall be immediately recoverable by the Company.

3. Employee acknowledges that during the course of employment with the Company he or she has had access to and received information which the Company considers and has treated as confidential. Therefore, Employee agrees that he or she will not directly or indirectly disclose any confidential records, data, formulae, specifications and/or

other trade secrets owned by the Company to any person or use any such information, except pursuant to court order or as a result of valid government order. All records, files, drawings, data, documents, models, equipment and the like relating to the businesses of the Company and any related company or operation which Employee has used, prepared or come in contact with during his or her employment by the Company, shall be and remain the sole property of the Company and shall not be removed from the premises of the Company without its written consent.

4. All payments provided under this Separation Agreement are in lieu of any severance payments or any other payments provided pursuant to any Company employee benefit plans, except the Company Retirement Plan or other benefits Employee has vested in prior to ____________. It is understood that except for the benefits provided in the Separation Agreement, and the benefits Employee was vested in prior to ____________, Employee specifically waives any and all rights to any other payments or benefits from the Company.

5. Employee, for him or herself, his or her family, representatives, successors and assigns, except for the undertakings provided for herein, covenants to forever refrain from instituting, maintaining, pressing, collecting or in any way aiding and proceeding upon, and releases and forever discharges the Company and its representatives, successors, assigns, subsidiaries, affiliates, directors, officers, employees, attorneys, agents, and trustees or administrators under any Company plans, from any and all claims, demands, debts, damages, injuries, actions or rights of action or any nature whatsoever, whether known or unknown, which Employee had, now has or may have against the Company, its successors, assigns, subsidiaries, affiliates, directors, officers, employees, attorneys, agents, trustees or administrators under any Company plans, from the beginning of Employee's employment to and including the date of this Separation Agreement, on account of, or arising out of any matter related to Employee's employment with the Company or termination of employment with the Company.

6. Employee agrees and acknowledges that the consideration received by him or her for this Separation

-2-

Agreement in support of all of the provisions contained herein and for the execution thereof is greater than benefits normally given to similarly situated employees of the Company and shall constitute full payment, satisfaction, discharge, compromise and release of and from all matters for which the other party have mutually released it herein.

7. Employee acknowledges that he or she has read each and every paragraph of this Separation Agreement and that Employee understands his or her respective rights and obligations and has been advised that he or she can consult an attorney of his or her choice. Further, Employee acknowledges that he or she has had at least forty-five (45) days to consider and review this Separation Agreement and has the opportunity to revoke this Separation Agreement within seven (7) days of its execution. Should Employee revoke this Separation Agreement, all monies and benefits provided herein shall cease and benefits provided to Employee under this Separation Agreement prior to such revocation shall be recoverable by the Company. Finally, Employee acknowledges that he or she has been given information as to the group of individuals eligible to receive the benefits specified herein, any eligibility factors for such benefits, time limits to obtain such benefits, and job titles and ages of all individuals eligible for such benefits as well as such information for such individuals in the same job classification or organizational unit who are not eligible for such benefits.

8. Employee declares that he or she understands the terms and contents of this Separation Agreement and freely, voluntarily and without coercion enters into this Separation Agreement. Further, Employee agrees and acknowledges that the waiver or release by him or her of rights he or she may have to receive monetary damages under Title VII of the Civil Rights Act of 1964, as amended, the Employee Retirement Income Security Act of, the Age Discrimination in Employment Act of 1967 and/or any other local, state or federal law, is knowing and voluntary and that it shall be a breach of this Separation Agreement to institute any action or to recover any damages which would be in conflict with or contrary to the acknowledgment. In the event of such breach, all monies paid pursuant to this Separation Agreement shall be immediately recoverable by the Company.

-3-

9. This Separation Agreement contains the entire agreement of the parties pertaining to the subject matter contained in it and supersedes and is in lieu of any and all other employment arrangements, statements or promises, written or oral, between Employee and the Company.

10. This Separation Agreement cannot be amended, modified, or supplemented in any respect except by written agreement entered into by the parties hereto.

IN WITNESS WHEREOF, the Company by its duly authorized representative and Employee have executed this Separation Agreement.

Employee:	Witness:
By:________________________	________________________
THE COMPANY	________________________ Name (Print)
________________________	________________________ Address (Print)

Appendix I

Sample Employee Handbook

Appendix I

XYZ, INC.
GENERAL EMPLOYEE HANDBOOK
(FOR ALL EMPLOYERS)

XYZ, INC.

805 Third Avenue
New York, New York 10022
(212) 702-5853
FAX: (212) 702-5941

Appendix I

XYZ, INC.

GENERAL EMPLOYEE HANDBOOK

(FOR ALL EMPLOYEES)

Welcome to XYZ. We are delighted to have you join our company and hope that this shall be the beginning of a mutually satisfying relationship. Because this Employee Handbook is intended to acquaint you with our personnel policies, regulations and benefits, please read it through carefully, and if you have any questions, contact your supervisor. However, in reviewing this Employee Handbook please note that this Employee Handbook is not intended to establish contractual rights between you and XYZ. Rather, it is only intended to be a general outline of our policies. This Employee Handbook may be changed at any time by the Company, but may only be amended by a written document signed by an officer of XYZ. Finally, when specific benefit plans conflict with this Employee Handbook, the benefit plan document will prevail.

EMPLOYMENT

XYZ is an equal opportunity employer. We offer employment opportunity based on job qualifications, regardless of race, color, national origin, sex, age, religion or physical handicap. However, all employees upon hire shall be required to comply with the verification requirements of the Immigration and Control Act of 1986.

Appendix I

ARTICLE 1. EMPLOYEE STATUS

Except where provided in writing, all employees of XYZ are employed at-will, may be terminated with or without cause or notice and are not guaranteed employment for any length of time.

1.0. Probationary Employees.

A. A newly hired employee shall be on a temporary, trial basis, for the first three (3) months of employment.

1. This trial period is intended to provide the probationary employee with an opportunity to demonstrate his or her job skills and ability to work with others.

2. Since this trial period is a learning and orientation experience for both the probationary employee and XYZ, the probationary employee is expected to work closely with his or her supervisor and is encouraged to ask any questions regarding his or work for XYZ.

B. During this trial period the probationary employee is not a regular employee of XYZ.

1. Upon satisfactory completion of this trial period, the probationary employee shall become a regular employee of XYZ.

2. The Company reserves the right to

terminate a probationary employee prior to the completion of the trial period.

1.1. Temporary Employees.

A. Any employee who is hired as a temporary employee shall be one who is hired for either:

1. Full-time work for a period of less than twelve (12) months, or

2. Part-time work of less than six (6) hours per day on the average.

1.2. Regular Employees.

A. Any employee who is not a probationary employee or a temporary employee shall be a regular employee of XYZ.

B. Except for an employee hired on the basis of a written employment contract, a regular employee shall be deemed to have been hired for an indefinite term until he or she resigns or is terminated, but in no way shall "indefinite term" be interpreted as an implied promise on the part of XYZ to employ a regular employee for a certain minimum period of time. Regular employees shall be employed at-will and subject to termination with or without cause.

1.3. Length of Service. "Length of service," "years of service," and terms of similar import, shall mean the period of time an employee has been employed by XYZ as a full-time employee. Length of service shall be terminated by resignation, discharge, layoff for more than ninety (90) days or failure to return from an approved leave of absence. An employee's length of service shall not be interrupted when an employee is reemployed within ninety (90) days after layoff or reemployed after an approved leave of absence in accordance with the Company's reinstatement policy. In the event of a leave of absence the loss, retention, or accumulation of service, shall be determined when the leave of absence is granted.

ARTICLE 2. WORK SCHEDULE

2.0. Workday. Unless otherwise designated, the normal workday for all employees, except temporary employees, shall be eight (8) hours of work over a twenty-four (24) hour period commencing at 9:00 a.m. The workday shall be interrupted by rest and meal periods.

2.1. Workweek. Unless otherwise designated, the normal workweek for all employees, except temporary employees, shall be a Monday to Friday, five (5) workdays or forty (40) hours of work.

ARTICLE 3. PAY

3.0. Exempt Employees. All exempt employees shall be paid on a bi-weekly salary basis.

3.1. Non-Exempt Employees. All other employees, unless expressly designated as an exempt employee, shall be paid on an hourly pay basis.

3.2. Payment by Check. All non-exempt employees shall be paid by check on a bi-weekly basis.

A. The pay check shall represent pay for work performed during the prior pay period.

B. XYZ is required by law to make deductions from an employee's pay for such items as Federal and State income taxes and Social Security taxes. Also, if XYZ offers group plans, such as medical and life insurance, and employees request to participate, payments for such plans may be deducted from an employee's pay.

3.3. Overtime.

A. Depending upon the nature of their work, some employees are exempt from the overtime pay provisions of the law. Those employees who are non-exempt shall be paid overtime pay, based on his or her base hourly wages or salary at the time the overtime is worked.

B. Unless otherwise required by applicable law, overtime pay shall be one and one-half (1½) times the employee's normal hourly rate of pay for time worked in excess of either of the following:

1. Eight (8) hours of work in a normal workday; or

2. Forty (40) hours of work in a normal workweek.

C. Break time, lunch time, vacation, holiday, sick and other non-working paid time will not be counted as "hours of work" for overtime purposes. There shall be no pyramiding of overtime, i.e., overtime on overtime hours.

D. No employee shall work overtime unless first authorized by his or her supervisor, and no overtime pay shall be paid to employees for unauthorized overtime.

E. Because of the nature of XYZ's business, XYZ may not be able to have all employees observe the usual office-type hours, weekends or holidays. Therefore, designated employees may be expected to regularly work during holidays, weekends or non-office hours, and there shall be no premium pay for such work. For those employees who must observe religious holidays, the Company shall try to accommodate such needs by switching days-off with others. The Company shall also try to rotate work schedules, where possible, so that no one employee shall have to work an excessive number of weekends or holidays.

ARTICLE 4. PERFORMANCE EVALUATIONS

All full-time Employees will be evaluated at the conclusion of their probationary period to determine whether they are offered regular employment by XYZ. Once a non-exempt employee becomes a regular employee, they will then be evaluated after three months, six months and twelve months from their initial date of employment. Thereafter, regular employees will be evaluated on their anniversary date, or on the anniversary date of any promotion or transfer, whichever is later. Exempt regular employees will be evaluated on their anniversary date, or the anniversary date of any promotion or transfer, whichever is later. Wage or compensation increases will be determined on the employee's anniversary date, or on the anniversary date of any promotion or transfer, whichever is later. Wage or compensation increases may be deferred based on performance or the financial condition of XYZ.

ARTICLE 5. VACATION

All regular employees shall be entitled to take their accrued vacation time off with pay as follows:

5.0. Accrual. For a certain number of full workweeks actually worked, regular employees shall be entitled to take paid vacation time off.

A. For a regular employee with less than one (1) year of employment with XYZ as of January 1 in each calendar year [equivalent to completing less than forty-eight (48) cumulative workweeks within a twelve (12) months period], one (1) vacation day shall accrue for each ten (10) cumulative workweeks fully and actually worked in the prior calendar year up to a maximum of five (5) vacation days.

B. For a regular employee, who as of January 1 in each calendar year, is employed by XYZ for two (2) years but less than four (4) years [equivalent to completing more than forty-eight (48) but less than one hundred forty (140) cumulative workweeks within a three (3) year period], such employee shall accrue vacation at a rate of one (1) vacation day for each five (5) cumulative workweeks fully and actually worked in the prior calendar year up to a maximum of ten (10) vacation days.

C. For a regular employee, who as of January 1 in each calendar year, is employed by XYZ for four (4) years but less than six (6) years [equivalent to completing more than one hundred forty (140) but less than two hundred thirty (230) cumulative workweeks within a five (5) year period], such employee shall accrue vacation at a rate of one (1) vacation day for each fifteen (15) workweeks fully and actually worked in the prior calendar year up to a maximum of fifteen (15) vacation days.

D. For a regular employee, who as of January 1 is employed by XYZ for five (5) years or more [equivalent to completing two hundred thirty (230) cumulative workweeks], such employee shall accrue vacation at a rate of two (2) vacation days for each five (5) workweeks fully and actually worked in the prior calendar year up to a maximum of twenty (20) vacation days.

E. In calculating accrued vacation time, only work performed at the standard rate of pay shall be utilized. Work performed at an overtime rate of pay shall not be counted toward vacation accrual, nor shall bonus or any other incentive pay be included in the calculations.

F. Compensation for vacation time will be at the employee's rate of pay at the time the vacation is taken or paid.

5.1. <u>Conditions</u>. Vacation shall begin to accrue as of the first day of regular employment with XYZ but vacation time off may only be taken as follows:

A. Each regular employee shall be entitled to take his or her accrued vacation time only after six (6) months of employment [equivalent to completing twenty-four (24) cumulative workweeks] with XYZ.

B. Each regular employee shall be entitled to take his or her accrued vacation time no more frequently than twice during any one (1) calendar year.

C. If the vacation time is to be split and taken twice during one (1) calendar year, only the vacation time that has been accrued during one-half (½) of the preceding calendar year may be taken, and if the vacation is to be taken once during one (1) calendar year, the vacation time that has been accrued during the entire preceding calendar year may taken.

D. No unaccrued vacation time may be taken in advance.

E. Within two (2) weeks of termination from employment, a regular employee shall be entitled to all unused and accrued vacation time as of the employee's date of termination.

5.2. Carry-Over. Unless the business requirements of XYZ result in a regular employee's being unable to take his or her accrued vacation time off during the calendar year (in which case his or her unused vacation time may be taken during the following calendar year), no employee may carry over his or her unused vacation time into the next calendar year. Any voluntarily unused vacation time shall be compensated by payment in lieu of time off at the end of each calendar year.

5.3. Scheduling.

A. In order to facilitate the smooth operations of the business of XYZ, each employee wishing to take a vacation on specific days is encouraged to request his or her supervisor's approval as early as possible.

B. Vacation scheduling requests shall be considered on a first-come first-serve basis and shall be subject to the business requirements of XYZ.

5.4. Non-Regular Employees. No probationary or temporary employees shall be entitled to paid vacation time off. However, subject to the same provisions that apply to the regular employees, all non-regular employees shall be entitled to take unpaid vacation time off. For those non-regular employees who subsequently become regular employees without any interruption of employment, the accumulated workweeks actually and fully worked during the same calendar year shall be retroactively counted toward the vacation time to be accrued.

ARTICLE 6. LEAVES AND HOLIDAYS

6.0. Leaves of Absence. All non-emergency leaves of absence must be requested by the employee and authorized by his or her supervisor prior to the commencement of the leave, and all emergency leaves of absence must be requested and authorized as promptly as possible; otherwise, an employee shall be deemed absent without leave. All leaves of absence are non-cumulative beyond the calendar year. There shall be no payment in lieu of any unused paid leave of absence time.

A. Jury Duty. All regular employees shall be entitled to take a leave of absence for jury duty (including service as a witness in a case to which he or she is not a party or personally affected by the outcome). Regular employees shall be paid their regular weekly salary for up to a maximum of two (2) weeks while serving on jury duty. During any paid leave of absence for jury duty, the employee will remit to the company any compensation received for jury duty.

B. Military Service. All regular employees shall be entitled to take an unpaid leave of absence for active military service with any branch of the United States Military.

C. Military Reserve. All employees shall be entitled to take an unpaid leave of absence for military reserve duty.

D. Bereavement Leave.

1. All employees shall be entitled to take a paid leave of absence for a maximum of up to five (5) workdays for attendance at a funeral or critical illness of a member of the employee's immediate family.

2. Immediate family shall mean the employee's (i) spouse, (ii) children, (iii) parents, (iv) brothers and sisters, (v) parents-in-law, or (vi) any other more remote relative that lives with the employee.

E. Sick Leave.

1. All employees shall be entitled to take an unpaid leave of absence for reason of illness.

2. All regular employees shall be entitled to take up to four (4) workdays of paid sick leave per calendar year. Paid sick leave may not be taken in less than one-half (½) day segments.

3. Sick leave may be taken in either full-day or half-day segments. Employees who call in

sick and later that day report for work, one (1) hour or more beyond their normal starting time, will be charged for one-half (½) day of sick time. Further, employees who leave work ill after working at least half of their work day will be charged for one-half (½) day of sick time.

4. For any absence caused by illness of more than three (3) consecutive workdays, the employee must bring his or her physician's verification of illness in writing; otherwise, the absence shall be deemed unauthorized. Further, the Company may require a physician's verification for repeated absences caused by illness.

5. Paid sick leave shall not accumulate from year to year and shall have no monetary value at termination.

F. Maternity Leave. All regular employees shall be entitled to an unpaid leave of absence for her pregnancy or his spouse's pregnancy for up to ninety (90) days or such time as his or her physician deems necessary medically.

G. Discretionary Leave. All regular employees shall be entitled to one (1) unpaid discretionary leave of absence of up to five (5) workdays per calendar year.

H. Unless otherwise provided or required by law, with the exception of medical leaves of absence, including maternity, any leave of absence in excess of thirty (30) workdays may result in the employee's being deemed to be laid-off for the purpose of rehiring or return to work. Employees on any medical leave of absence, including maternity, shall be reinstated to their prior position upon the conclusion of their leave provided:

1. The employee indicates in writing prior to the commencement of the leave or immediately upon the commencement of the leave, a desire to return to work upon the completion of the medical leave of absence.

2. The position has not been eliminated.

3. Business conditions do not require hiring a permanent replacement.

4. The employee would not have been laid off if employed during the leave.

5. The employee returns to work within ninety (90) days of the commencement of the leave of absence.

If employees on any medical leave of absence are not reinstated to their prior position, such employees shall be deemed to be laid-off as of the date the leave of absence terminates for the purpose of rehiring or return to work.

I. There shall be no break in service for

benefit or layoff purposes for leaves of absence of ninety (90) days or less.

6.1. Holiday.

A. XYZ observes the following national holidays:

1. New Year's Day,
2. Martin Luther King Day,
3. Presidents Day,
4. Memorial Day,
5. Independence Day,
6. Labor Day,
7. Thanksgiving Day,
8. Day after Thanksgiving Day,
9. Christmas Day.

B. Only regular employees shall be paid for the national holidays that are observed on their regular workday or during their vacation. Employees on leave of absence shall receive holiday pay only for all holidays occurring within the first thirty (30) days of such leave of absence. Temporary employees shall not be paid for such holidays unless they actually work on such days. Probationary non-exempt employees shall receive holiday pay for all holidays during their trial period only upon successfully completing their trial period.

C. Should a holiday fall on a regular non-exempt employee's regularly scheduled workday and the employee be required to work, such regular employee shall be paid time and one-half (1½) for all hours worked on that day.

ARTICLE 7. MEDICAL INSURANCE

All regular employees shall be entitled to participate in whatever group insurance policy that XYZ may elect to make available in general for its regular employees.

7.0. The medical insurance premiums for each eligible employee, who desires such coverage, shall be paid by XYZ.

7.1. Any deductible portion of such coverage shall be paid by the employee.

7.2. The additional medical insurance premiums (and deductibles) for any eligible dependent of an employee, who desires such coverage, shall be paid by the employee.

7.3. Each newly eligible employee should be aware that such insurance application process can often take up to two (2) months or more before the policy will become effective.

ARTICLE 8. ABSENTEEISM/TARDINESS

8.0. One of the most disruptive acts on the part of any employee is that of absenteeism or tardiness. As such, absenteeism and tardiness must be subject to appropriate, progressive discipline, applied in a consistent manner. If absences equal or exceed the following standards, discipline as indicated should result:

1. An employee exceeding six (6) incidents of unauthorized absence or tardiness in any twelve-month period will receive a verbal warning regarding same. Documentation of the verbal warning will be placed in the employee's personnel file. In the event that the employee's absence was due to illness authorized by a physician's note, no action should be taken.

2. Should an employee be absent or tardy on a seventh occasion after an oral warning, the employee shall receive a written warning detailing the absences or tardiness. Copies of the written warning will be placed in the employee's personnel file.

3. A one-day suspension will follow the occasion of an eighth incident of tardiness or absence within the same twelve-month period.

4. A three-day suspension shall follow on the occasion of a ninth incident of tardiness or absence within the same twelve-month period.

5. If, following a three-day suspension for tardiness or absenteeism, an employee should again

be absent or tardy, the employee will subject to termination.

8.1. The number of incidents of tardiness or absenteeism shall be viewed on a twelve-month basis with incidents of tardiness or absenteeism being removed after twelve months.

8.2. In addition, employees may be subject to discipline, equal to or more severe than indicated herein, for related incidents, such as absenteeism occasioned with holidays and vacation, failure to call in indicating that they will be late and/or absent, excessive excusable lateness and/or absences or similar conduct.

ARTICLE 9. CODE OF BUSINESS ETHICS

The Company's reputation for honesty and integrity is the sum of the personal reputations of our employees. To protect this reputation and to assure uniformity in standards of conduct, XYZ has established the following code of ethics. The code basically reaffirms and clarifies our basic policy concerning conflicts of interests. This statement, obviously, does not cover all situations. Therefore, whenever there are any doubts as to the propriety of a particular situation, please discuss it with the chief operating officer of the Company before engaging in such conduct. Essentially, the following conduct is prohibited:

A. An employee may not act on behalf of XYZ in any transaction involving persons or organizations with whom he or she or his or her family has any significant connection or financial interest. In any closely held enterprise, even a modest financial interest held by an employee or a member of the employee's family, may be viewed as significant.

B. No employee may accept personal fees or commissions from any transactions on behalf of XYZ.

C. Employees are prohibited from accepting bribes, kickbacks, remuneration or any other type of consideration given by any organization in order to attract business or for any other reason. Should an employee be in a position to engage suppliers for XYZ, all such transactions and/or contracts must be engaged in without any hint of favoritism.

D. Employees are prohibited from violating any state or federal statute or violating any procedures issued by XYZ, including accounting and reporting procedures.

ARTICLE 10. SEXUAL HARASSMENT POLICY

The Federal Equal Employment Opportunity Commission guidelines concerning discrimination on the basis of sex declare that sexual harassment of employees is in violation of Title VII of the Civil Rights Act of 1964. These guidelines state:

"Unwelcome sexual advances, requests of sexual favors, and other verbal or physical conduct of a sexual nature constitute sexual harassment when (1) submission to such conduct is made either explicitly or implicitly as term or condition of an individual's employment, or (2) submission to or rejection of such conduct by an individual is used as the basis for employment decisions affecting such individual, or (3) such conduct has the purpose or effect of substantially interfering with an individual's work performance or creating an intimidating, hostile or offensive working environment."

XYZ has never tolerated sexual harassment and adopts the EEOC guidelines on this subject. Therefore, any person who is found to have engaged in acts of sexual harassment will be disciplined appropriately. This Company's commitment to a sexual harassment-free environment requires supervisory personnel to use their best efforts to eliminate sexual harassment of co-workers by employees under their supervision. Any incident of sexual harassment should be immediately reported to the Personnel office and will be investigated promptly. Appropriate discipline, which may include termination, will be imposed upon employees found to have engaged in such conduct.

ARTICLE 11. <u>WORK RULES</u>

11.0. <u>Timecards</u>.

A. All non-exempt employees who are requested to keep timecards shall do so conscientiously and punctually.

B. Each non-exempt employee must punch or enter his or her own timecard only and shall not punch or fill out another employee's time card under any circumstance. Punching or entering another's timecard may subject both employees (one punching or entering for someone else and one requesting someone else to punch or enter his or hers) to dismissal.

C. Timecards must also be signed-in and signed-out. If any employee forgets to sign-in or sign-out his or her timecard, the employee shall immediately notify his or her supervisor. Unsigned timecards cannot be accepted without authorization from the supervisor.

D. Timecards shall reflect all times worked. Overtime shall only be worked without <u>prior</u> approval of the supervisor in charge.

E. Falsification of timecards shall be deemed dishonesty and shall be cause for immediate termination.

11.1. Other work rules as may be posted from time to time by XYZ must be followed by all employees.

ARTICLE 12. <u>RESIGNATION AND TERMINATION</u>

12.0. <u>Resignation</u>.

A. Any employee may resign at will, but XYZ requests that he or she shall:

1. Notify XYZ in writing of his or her intent to resign and the effective date of resignation, and

2. Whenever possible his or her notice shall be at least equal to his or her pay period.

B. Whenever an employee desires to resign, XYZ may choose to either:

1. Allow the employee to continue to work until the effective date of resignation, or

2. Request that the employee cease work immediately and pay the employee until the effective date of resignation or to end of the employee's normal pay period, whichever is less, or

3. Any acceptable combination of above.

12.1. Termination.

A. Lay-off. Whenever the business of XYZ can no longer employ all of its current employees or for any other valid reason, employees may be laid-off as follows:

1. For each position to be eliminated or to be cut back, the most newly-hired employee in that position shall be laid-off first, provided the employees retained are, in the opinion of XYZ, qualified to do the available work. Temporary employees shall be laid-off before probationary employees, and probationary employees shall be laid-off before regular employees.

2. If there are two (2) or more employees hired at the same time, the temporary and probationary employees and those with the least number of actual

work hours or workweeks shall be laid-off first, provided the employees retained are, in the opinion of XYZ, qualified to do the available work.

3. Whenever the business of XYZ recovers and requires additional employees, the laid-off employees shall be given priority. One (1) notice of rehiring shall be mailed to the laid-off employee's last known address. If no answer is received in one (1) week, another laid-off employee or person shall be hired and the first employee shall lose all recall rights. If any employee is on lay-off status for ninety (90) days from the date of the lay-off, the lay-off shall become permanent and the employee shall have no recall rights.

4. Whenever possible, any employee to be laid-off shall be given a written notice at least equal to his or her pay period.

5. XYZ shall have no obligation to seek alternative employment for individuals whose positions are eliminated.

B. Termination. Any employee may be terminated by XYZ as follows:

1. Any employee may be terminated for various reasons, including but not limited to the following:

a. Willfully or repeatedly violating or disregarding the established rules of XYZ.

b. Dishonesty.

c. Insubordination.

d. Incompetence - inability to learn or perform the assigned work.

e. Serious misconduct.

f. Uncooperativeness - unwillingness or inability to work with co-workers and supervisors.

g. Any other reason deemed appropriate by management.

2. Employees who are terminated shall not receive any severance pay; such employees shall only receive his or her pay for work actually performed prior to termination and for any accrued and unused vacation time.

3. Whenever possible a written termination notice at least equal to one pay period shall be given. However, for termination not involving serious misconduct, insubordination or dishonesty, if the termination is to become effective immediately, a termination pay equal to one normal pay period amount shall be given instead of the advance notice.

4. For termination involving serious misconduct, insubordination or dishonesty, the termination may be without advance notice or termination pay.

ARTICLE 13. WARNING AND HEARINGS

13.0. Warnings. Depending upon the circumstances, breach of work rules, misconduct or any other matter that has come to the attention of XYZ, a warning to the employee in question may be warranted. Such warning is intended to make the employee aware of the seriousness of the problem and of the immediate need for correction on his or her part. If the problem persists, the employee may be subject to dismissal. XYZ may disregard issuing a warning in appropriate circumstances.

13.1. Hearings. For any serious grievance, including warnings, an employee shall be entitled to and encouraged to freely discuss the matter with his or her supervisor. If the matter cannot be resolved through such a discussion, the employee should make a written request to XYZ management for a hearing. Such hearing shall be given as promptly as possible.

ARTICLE 14. MISCELLANEOUS

14.0. Safety. It is the policy of XYZ to provide and maintain safe and healthful working conditions and to promote operating practices that will safeguard employees and result in the efficient operation of business. For this purpose we expect all employees to be safety-conscious and to assist us in correcting workplace conditions that may be potential problems. Any unsafe or unsanitary condition or any injury on our premises must be reported immediately to the supervisor in charge. Employees engaging in unsafe or unsanitary conduct may be subject to disciplinary action, up to and including discharge.

14.1. Confidentiality. It is of utmost importance that the confidential nature of records, documents, and information about XYZ, its employees or its customers and clients be maintained by every employee employed by XYZ. Therefore, the disclosure of information about XYZ, its employees, or its customers and clients the dissemination of such information, dissemination of documents and records by employees employed by XYZ, without the approval of an officer of XYZ, will subject an employee to immediate termination. This prohibition includes the disclosure of information to any outside source including members of the media.

14.2. Equipment. Each employee using company property or equipment has a responsibility to employ full care in its use and in safeguarding it from theft or vandalism.

14.3. Employment Records. All employment records are maintained by the personnel office. Employees should inform the personnel office of any changes in name, address, telephone number, dependents, and the person to notify in case of an emergency. Upon request, employees may review their personnel files.

14.4. Solicitation. No solicitation (including collection of funds, securing of pledges or subscriptions, or similar activities) is permitted by any employee during work time. No distribution of literature is permitted in working areas. No solicitation will be permitted by any non-employee on Company property. Exceptions to this rule may be granted by an officer of XYZ in writing.

14.5. Verification of Absence. If it is necessary to be absent from work for any reason, the Company should be notified as soon as the reason for the absence arises, but no later than at least one hour after the employee's scheduled starting time as to the reason for and the anticipated duration of the absence. Should the reasons for the absence continue beyond the original anticipated date, the employee should keep the Company informed as to his/her expected return date. Failure to give such notice will result in the forfeiture of any compensation due for such absence. Employees must present a doctor's note when returning to work upon being absent for two days or more, absent for illness before or after a holiday, or upon request. Employees who are absent for three consecutive workdays without notice shall be terminated.

14.6. Smoking Policy. Since XYZ is concerned about the health of its employees, the following policy will be in effect:

A. Smoking will be permitted in individual enclosed offices at the option of the occupant;

B. Smoking will be permitted in a designated area. This will be the only designated smoking area in the office. This area will be posted and may change from time to time at the discretion of the Company;

C. If in a work area of two or more employees or in a conference room a reasonable accommodation between smokers and non-smokers cannot be reached, then the rights of the non-smoker shall take precedence at all times and smoking will be prohibited;

D. Smoking will not be permitted in any common use area - hallways, lobbies, reception areas, restrooms, elevators, stairways, and duplicating areas unless otherwise designated by the Company as in Item 2 above; and

E. "No Smoking" signs will alert the public to our smoking restrictions in areas where there is public access.

14.7. Housekeeping. Each employee is expected to contribute to good housekeeping by keeping their work area neat and clean. By doing so the possibility of accidents and damage to equipment is minimized. Further, professional appearance of one's self and work area is important.

14.8. Telephone. Employees are requested to discourage personal incoming phone calls, except for emergencies. Outgoing personal calls should be reasonably limited.

14.9. Visitors. Visits from outside guests or family members should be limited to necessary situations, be of limited duration, and during normal office hours. During other hours (nights and weekends especially) it is requested that there be no guests and/or non-staff members in the office.

14.10. Security. Employees are expected to be security-conscious about the employees' and the Company's belongings. The possible loss of personal property can be substantially reduced by simply not bringing unnecessary items of value to the office. However, should employees bring personal valuables to the office, the employee is responsible for safeguarding them.

14.11. Changes. This Employment Handbook is not an employment agreement. It may changed by XYZ, from time to time, with or without prior notice, unless otherwise set forth elsewhere herein. Any change that may be made shall be either posted or a copy given to each employee. This Employee Handbook may not be amended by any oral statements made by any employee of XYZ.

Tables of Authorities

(References are to pages and footnotes.)

Cases

A

B

C

D

E

F

G

H

M

N

S

T

U

State Legislation

Indiana Code

Kentucky Revised Statutes Annotated

Louisiana Revised Statutes Annotated

Maine Revised Statutes Annotated

Annotated Code of Maryland

General Laws of the Commonwealth of Massachusetts

Massachusetts General Laws Annotated

Michigan Compiled Laws

Code of Federal Regulations

Restatement (Second) of Judgments

Restatement (Second) of Torts

United States Code

Index

A

B

C

L

M

N

O

P

R